UNEQUAL RELATIONS

AN INTRODUCTION TO RACE, ETHNIC, AND ABORIGINAL DYNAMICS IN CANADA

Seventh Edition

AUGIE FLERAS
University of Waterloo

Toronto

Vice-President, Editorial Director: Gary Bennett
Editor-in-Chief: Michelle Sartor
Editor, Humanities and Social Sciences: Joel Gladstone
Marketing Manager: Lisa Gillis
Supervising Developmental Editor: Madhu Ranadive
Developmental Editor: Cheryl Finch
Project Manager: Lesley Deugo
Manufacturing Coordinator: Susan Johnson
Production Editor: Purnima Narayanan (MPS Limited, a Macmillan Company)
Copy Editor: Claudia Forgas
Proofreader: Barbara Kamienski
Compositor: MPS Limited, a Macmillan Company
Art Director: Julia Hall
Cover Designer: Miguel Acevedo
Cover Image: Getty Images / D-BASE

10 9 8 7 6 5 4 3 [WC]

Library and Archives Canada Cataloguing in Publication
Fleras, Augie, 1947–
    Unequal relations : an introduction to race, ethnic, and Aboriginal dynamics in Canada / Augie Fleras. — 7th ed.
Includes bibliographical references and index.
ISBN 978-0-13-231060-4

    1. Canada—Race relations—Textbooks. 2. Canada—Ethnic relations—Textbooks. 3. Multiculturalism—Canada—Textbooks.
I. Title.

FC104.F55 2011   305.800971   C2011-902553-1

ISBN 978-0-13-231060-4

Acknowledgements

Thanks to everyone who has been involved in this edition, and previous editions, of *Power and Resistance*. To all the contributors (several who have joined us for this, the 5th edition and to those who revised chapters), our thanks: your insights, your patience, your hard work have made the process of doing a multi-authored book a pleasure and made this, we think, a great book. To everyone involved in the production of the book — Beverley Rach for overseeing production, Eileen Young for copy editing, John van der Woude for the new cover design, Brenda Conroy for designing the book, Debbie Mathers for pre-production — thank you. Finally, our gratitude to all the people, individuals and groups, who continue the struggle for social justice in Canada; your dedication is inspiring.

Wayne Antony
Les Samuelson

About the Authors

WAYNE ANTONY is a founding member of Canadian Centre for Policy Alternatives-Manitoba (CCPA-MB) and has been on its board of directors since its inception. He also taught sociology at the University of Winnipeg from 1980 to 2000. Wayne is the co-author of three CCPA-MB reports on the state of public services in Manitoba and co-editor of two other books (both with Dave Broad): *Citizens or Consumers? Social Policy in a Market Society* and *Capitalism Rebooted: Work and Welfare in the New Economy*.

JESSICA ANTONY received her master's degree in Media Studies at Concordia University. She lives in Winnipeg, working as a publishing editor and copy editor, and is a writing instructor at the University of Winnipeg.

PAT ARMSTRONG is Professor of Sociology and Women's Studies at York University and holds a CHSRF/CHIR Chair in Health Services with a focus on gender. A former Chair of Sociology and of Women and Health Care Reform, she has published on a wide variety of issues related to health care, women's work, theory, and social policy.

WENDY CHAN is Professor of Sociology in the Department of Sociology and Anthropology at Simon Fraser University. Her research interests are in the areas of racism and immigration enforcement, the criminalization of poverty, racialization and the criminal justice system, race, crime, and mental health, violence against women, and gender issues in the legal system. She is the author of four books, including *Criminalizing Race, Criminalizing Poverty* and *Women, Madness and the Law*.

DEBRA DAVIDSON is Associate Professor of Environmental Sociology at the University of Alberta, and Director of the University of Alberta Environmental Research and Studies Centre. Her research and teaching are in natural resource politics, the social dimensions of climate change, and environmental risk. She has written for *Society and Natural Resources* and *Canadian Journal of Sociology,* among others, and is the co-editor of *Consuming Sustainability: Critical Social Analyses of Ecological Change*.

MIKE GISMONDI is Professor of Sociology and Global Studies at Athabasca University. His research and teaching are in critical development studies, the social dimensions of sustainability, and the social economy. He is co-author (with Joan Sherman and Mary Richardson) of *Winning Back the Words: Confronting Experts in an Environmental Public Hearing* and co-editor (with Josee Johnson and James Goodman) of *Nature's Revenge: Reclaiming Sustainability in an Age of Ecological Exhaustion*.

NORMAND LANDRY teaches at Téluq (UQAM). Before coming to Téluq, he was affiliated with McGill@McGill unit for critical communications research (McGill University) and the Communication Policy Research Laboratory (LRPC) at Université de Montréal. His current work focuses on social movement theory, law and democratic communications.

SALLY MILLER has worked for almost twenty years in the alternative food, agriculture and co-op sectors, as a manager, consultant, organizer and researcher. She has an MA and PhD in Anthropology (Cornell University) and a master's degree in Environmental Studies (York University). She has taught anthropology, writing, and environmental sociology at Cornell University and York University, and designed and implemented curriculum, workshops, and materials for non-profits and co-ops in the U.S. and in Canada. She helped to found the Fourth Pig Worker Co-op and the West End Food Co-op, a non-profit, multi-stakeholder co-op dedicated to creating a food hub in Toronto's west end.

DAVID MCNALLY is Professor of Political Science at York University. He is a long-time activist in global justice and socialist movements and the author of six books, including *Another World Is Possible, Global Slump: The Economics and Politics of Crisis and Resistance,* and *Monsters of the Market.*

MARIANNE PARSONS has been teaching at several universities in Nova Scotia for the past seventeen years as a contract faculty in Sociology and Women's and Gender Studies. Issues surrounding gender and embodiment are a central focus of her teaching, as well as her public sociology (which includes talks and workshops that include the politics of fat phobia as a key component). Her research interests explore the relationship between fat phobia, gender, and sexuality.

Mi'kmaq Elder **DR. DANIEL N. PAUL**, C.M., O.N.S., is a powerful and passionate advocate for social justice and the eradication of racial discrimination. He is an outspoken champion for First Nations peoples and all other disadvantaged members of society. Through his newspaper columns and his book, *First Nations History — We Were Not the Savages — Third Edition*, he has widely publicized the proud heritage and histories of the Mi'kmaq and other First Nations.

TRACEY PETER is Associate Professor of Sociology at the University of Manitoba. Her research and publication interests include mental health and well-being, trauma and violence, suicide prevention, social inequality and marginalization, youth, and research methods/statistics. She is co-investigator on the first National Climate Survey on Homophobia and Transphobia in Canadian Schools. She is also a co-investigator for a follow-up study of Canadian teachers' responses to issues pertaining to sexual and gender diversity.

CLAIRE POLSTER is Associate Professor of Sociology and Social Studies at the University of Regina. Her research focuses on the transformation of Canadian higher education. She has published widely on higher education issues including government policy, the commodification of academic research, the erosion of university autonomy, democracy and collegialism, and the corporatization of Canada's universities. She is also co-editor of *Callings Cards: The University We Have Had, Now Have, and Could Have* and co-founder of the University of Regina's Faculty of Arts Community Research Unit.

LES SAMUELSON is Associate Professor of Sociology at the University of Saskatchewan. His current research, in conjunction with a Nepali co-researcher and grass-roots Nepali agencies, focuses on the 2006 Post-Civil war peace accord in Kathmandu and, in conjunction with Aboriginal bands, on crime prevention and social development for central Saskatchewan on-reserve youth.

LESLIE REGAN SHADE is Associate Professor at the Department of Communication at Concordia University. Her research and teaching examines the social and policy aspects of information and communication technologies, with a focus on gender and youth.

JIM SILVER is Professor and Director of the University of Winnipeg's Urban and Inner-City Studies program. He is one of the founding members of the Canadian Centre for Policy Alternatives-Manitoba, and writes frequently about inner-city and poverty issues. Recent books include *Good Places to Live: Poverty and Public Housing in Canada* and *In Their Own Voices: Building Urban Aboriginal Communities.*

CATHERINE TAYLOR is Professor in the Faculty of Education and the Department of Rhetoric, Writing, and Communications at the University of Winnipeg. Her recent work on research ethics, LGBTQ well-being and LGBTQ -inclusive education, and confrontations between LGBTQ and heteronormative discourses, has been published widely in scholarly books and in journals. She has been Principal Investigator in partnership with Egale Canada for "The First National Climate Survey of Homophobia and Transphobia in Canadian Schools," and is now Principal Investigator for a follow-up study of Canadian teachers' perceptions and experiences of sexual and gender diversity education.

1

Social Problems and Social Power

Wayne Antony and Les Samuelson

YOU SHOULD KNOW THIS

- Alberta's tar sands extraction process uses an amount of natural gas every day that would heat 3.2 million Canadian homes; by the end of 2012 the natural gas used would heat all of Canada's homes. The process also uses between 230 and 530 million cubic feet of water annually, an amount similar to that used by all the residents of Toronto.
- One in 3, or 33 percent, low-income children had at least one parent who worked full-time throughout the year in 2008, and still lived in poverty. Poverty costs Canada $72-84 billion — for Ontarians this means between $2,299 and $2,895 every year, and for British Columbians, this equates to over $2,100 each year; it costs Canada's health care system $7.6 billion per year.
- In Canada in 2007, 83 percent of victims of spousal assault were female, and in 96 percent of family-related sexual assaults male family members were identified as the accused. Girls are four times more likely to be physically and/or sexually assault by a family member than boys.
- Refugees make up 0.23 percent of Canada's population. Deportations rose by over 45 percent between 2002 and 2007, from 8,683 to 12,636. All the countries with average annual incomes of $10,000+ host a mere 9 percent of the world's refugees.
- As a result of recent corporate tax cuts, Canadian banks will have an estimated $40 billion in excess cash by the end of 2012, which is equivalent to the sum of all federal and provincial deficits projected for 2012–13. Canadian banks have enjoyed an average 23 percent profit during 2000–2010.
- In 2008, close to 100 First Nation communities were on drinking water advisories. One community, Neskantaga, has been on boil water advisory for 13 years. In a 2007 survey more than one-third of people living on reserves believe their water is still unsafe to drink. The U.N. recommends 50 litres of water per person each day, but First Nation communities in Northern Manitoba average around just 10 litres per day.

Sources: CCPA 2010a, 2010b; CWP n.d.; Moller 2011; Polaris Institute 2008; Sanger 2011; Statistics Canada 2009.

THIS BOOK IS ABOUT THINKING ABOUT SOCIAL ISSUES... thinking about the pollution of our air, water, and soil, about the poverty that is increasingly widespread and seemingly impervious to all efforts to eradicate it, about the truly horrible experiences of violence between men and women, about the difficulties faced by immigrants and refugees in Canada, about the effects of the global economic crisis, about the legacy of colonialism in Canada. It is about trying to figure out the conflicts, troubles, and dilemmas that confront us as Canadians.

In a simple but absolutely crucial sense, how we think about social problems depends on how we approach thinking about social life in general. At the risk of oversimplification, we can say that there are two basic approaches to getting below the surface of our social lives. There is what we will call the "traditional" way — some would call it individualistic or perhaps "neoliberal"— and there is what we will call the "critical" way. (In chapter 1

> How we think about social problems depends on how we approach thinking about social life in general.

Murray Knuttila describes the social and political theories that make up these two approaches in much more detail: traditional (structural functionalism and pluralism) and critical (Marxism, neo-Marxism, and feminism.)

One way of explaining these different ways of knowing about social life is to go back to a classic statement on the nature and value of the "sociological imagination," made over fifty years ago. In 1959 C. Wright Mills distinguished between "private troubles" and "public issues." Using the gendered language that was typical in his day, Mills wrote:

> Troubles occur within the character of the individual and within the range of his immediate relations with others; they have to do with his self and with those limited areas of social life of which he is directly and personally aware. Issues have to do with matters that transcend these local environments of the individual and the range of his inner life. They have to do with the organization of many such milieux into the institutions of [a] historical society as a whole, with the ways in which various milieux overlap and interpenetrate to form the larger structure of social and historical life. (Mills 1959: 8)

For some analysts, again at the risk of a little oversimplification, social problems are mainly about private troubles; for others, social problems involve public issues.

The Traditional Approach — Individuals and Freedom

For the traditional approach, society is essentially a bundle of private troubles. In his distinction between troubles and issues, Mills was pointing to a profound bias in North American thinking: the tendency to see society in individual terms. In this way of thinking, the understanding or explanation of how society works really comes down to the *choices* that individual people make. As human beings, we decide what we will eat, where we will live, what work we will do, how we will treat others, whether we will go to university or community college, what music we will listen to, who or if we will marry, and so on. Almost always, it is assumed, we choose to do what is best for us. If we need to, we may decide to co-operate with others to achieve some of our goals. These choices are, and should be, constrained, but only within very wide boundaries. We cannot act in ways that threaten others — their lives, their freedom, their rights. For instance, we cannot take our neighbour's new car just because driving around in it will make us feel good or because we need a car.

These constraints on freedom, the traditional approach argues, tend to have two bases: obvious and natural boundaries, and choices on which everyone, or at least a majority of people, agrees. We know, without there being laws against it, that we cannot take someone else's car just because it may be good for us. We also agree with laws that protect our property and our lives. But, say the traditionalists, and especially the neoliberals among them, the legal constraints on freedom must be kept to a minimum.

This is a perspective that is also preoccupied with the problem of social order — that is, the social imperative for individuals and the parts of a social system to be working together. Achieving this working together, this social "equilibrium," the traditionalists argue, comes from a "set of widely shared and accepted beliefs and values" that "serve as a kind of moral cement, binding and bonding… a social system together" (Knuttila, chapter

> Constraints on freedom, the traditional approach argues, have two bases: obvious and natural boundaries, and choices on which everyone agrees.

2). In other words, there is an assumption that a consensus or agreement exists among the members of society that freedom is paramount, individual merit and responsibility are important, and family values, hard work, respecting others' property are what society and life are all about. More than that, traditionalists contend that the social system does generally fit together and function effectively; that it is generally, and must be, in a long-term state of equilibrium. For some traditional social analysts, the democratic capitalism that currently dominates and characterizes the societies of the developed industrial world epitomizes such a free and prosperous social world (see Klein 2007: ch. 2).

Social theorists who call themselves pluralists share the emphasis on freedom (see chapter 2 for details about pluralism). Pluralists argue that capitalist, liberal democracies are free because there are no groups that dominate society, at least not for long periods of time. These societies have a free press, and most people have access to the information that they need in order to know what is going on. Everyone is free to vote and to try to influence social and political processes. Everyone is free to pursue any form of education and work, and the lifestyle accompanying them, that they desire. Without these kinds of individual freedoms such a society would break down. Pluralists agree that there are powerful people and groups in a society, but that power is always restricted and tempered by the power held by other individuals and groups.

In its most radical form, this traditional, individualistic approach can lead to the claim — made by Margaret Thatcher, prime minister of Britain from 1979 to 1990 — that there is no society, only individuals. This sense of radical individualism underlies the neoliberal revolution, of which Thatcher was the political architect in England. Neoliberalism, a term used mostly in political economy, proclaims the efficiency and effectiveness of the competitive, free market. In a broad political sense, neoliberalism rests on a holy trinity: eliminating the public sector, liberating corporations from government regulation, and bare-bones social spending (Klein 2007: 17). To use the words of Debra Davidson and Mike Gismondi (chapter 12), in neoliberal ideology "it would be imprudent to intervene, because markets are most efficient when left to their own devices. The state's responsibility is not to control [economic and social] development but to ensure that market forces prevail unfettered; to manage the impacts of development, and explicitly not its pace." In strictly economic terms, this means that it is the state's responsibility to ensure the conditions of profitability for private corporations, the economic equivalent of individuals. In more general social terms, neoliberals see society as made up of freely interacting individuals who are responsible for the choices they make. If there is even such a thing as the common good, it is produced when these freely interacting individuals are not restricted in the pursuit of their own best interests. For neoliberals, most restrictions on individual freedom, especially in the form of government regulation, are counterproductive to a prosperous and harmonious society.

The Critical Approach — Social Structures and Power

In this book we approach social issues in a different way. We look at society through a critical lens. Keeping in mind Mills's distinction between public issues and private troubles, this approach begins with the observation that to understand our lives we need to examine the institutions — the social structure — of our community and society. As Mills (1959: 10–11) argues, what we experience in various and specific social settings is often caused by social structures. As such, "to understand the changes of many personal milieux we are required to look beyond them…. To be aware of the idea of social structure and to use it with sensibility is to be capable of tracing [the] linkages among a great variety of milieux. To be able to do that is to possess the sociological imagination."

In other words, to fully understand our lives and the society in which we live involves adopting a structural or institutional — not an individualistic — framework.

One way of getting at what this means is to return to the idea of the individual choices that we can and do make. If we think, even for just a minute, about how our choices — clothes, food, jobs, partners, education — play out in everyday life, one of the first things we recognize is that some people have a wider range of choices than others. For instance, some people have the privilege to choose whether they go to university. Others can choose which university they will go to (regardless of whether it is close to home or far away). But many others do not have these choices available to them; the option of attending university is not even on their radar screen. Instead, they have to work to support themselves and others close to them. That is, not everyone is free to make any choice — there are inequalities between individuals.

> If we think, even for just a minute, about how our choices — clothes, food, jobs, partners, education — play out in everyday life, one of the first things we recognize is that some people have a wider range of choices than others.

For critical thinkers, a key feature of our social structure, and the second main component of a critical approach, is social inequality. Inequalities are not just about individual lifestyle choices. It is true that some people may want bigger cars, the latest clothing fashions, to dine at the most expensive restaurants, or to live in luxurious houses, while others may not want any of these things. The point, however, is that the existence of social inequality means a narrowing of life choices for many people — not just in what they may want but also in what they can do and become. That is, inequality is actually about *power differences*, not merely lifestyle differences.

Power resides in social relationships, and it can take many forms. Power can be exercised by virtually anyone, almost anywhere. A CEO tells the executive committee that they must devise plans to increase profits by 20 percent over the next four fiscal quarters. A software development supervisor forces a programmer, who insists on wearing a Rage Against the Machine T-shirt, to work night shifts or irregular overtime or on weekends. The big kid in Grade Six forces a smaller kid to give up a place in the cafeteria queue. In other words, there are many possible bases of power, especially when it comes to one individual pitted against another.

But even in these examples the people acting are not just individuals. That is, power is not randomly distributed; it has a social basis and social patterns. Power, in the social sense, involves the ways in which people in particular social

> Power, in the social sense, involves the ways in which people in particular social groups can force people in other social groups to act in certain ways.

groups can force people in other social groups to act in certain ways, narrowing their choices in life. These powerful social groups tend to coalesce around race, gender, class, and sexuality:

- white people expropriating land from Indigenous people, labelled "Indian" people by Canadian legislation, who then find that their social and economic activities cannot conform to their own views of who they want to be and what kind of direction they want to pursue as individuals and as nations (see Daniel Paul, chapter 7);
- men using their physical strength and capacity for violence to control women, while the surrounding culture encourages such behaviour and the society as a whole turns a blind eye, providing many women with little choice but to cope with the fallout (see Ruth Mann, chapter 3);
- banks and investment corporations making billions of dollars after convincing governments to let them to take on more and more risky debts, then having middle and working class people pay through multi-trillion dollar government bailouts when these gambles collapsed (see David McNally, chapter 6).
- heterosexual people, for so many years, deciding that their sexual choices are "normal," thus complicating and denigrating the lives of and experiences of LGBQT people (see Tracey Peter and Catherine Taylor, chapter 4).

Power can also be enacted through the state or government. For example, Les Samuelson (chapter 16) shows that what the state legislates as criminal offences in Canada are not always the most harmful or dangerous behaviours. For example, most of us, at one time or another, will have money unwillingly taken from us by corporations, through everything from misleading advertising to predatory pricing to violations of labour standards regulations. But most of these harmful business activities are not defined and treated as criminal theft, while taking money unwillingly from a convenience store owner certainly is. Big business has enough power to ensure that the state will protect its need to maximize profits.

Relations of power also occur in other contexts. As Marianne Parsons (chapter 9) points out, even how we relate to our bodies is connected to social power. People come in all sizes and shapes, some bigger than others. Yet, particular sizes and shapes are demonized. Unlike other times and places, ideal body image in our contemporary society is defined by the domination of the billion dollar fashion industry (which is controlled mainly by white men in big corporations). The fashion industry has become fat-phobic, and with devastating consequences — especially for women. Similarly, Sally Miller (chapter 11) tells us about how the ways in which we think about food reflect the desire of agri-business to control food production and distribution. As she points out, we tend to see food mainly in terms of supply and demand, as commodities to be bought and sold — agri-business spends much time and resources making sure we do see it this way. But taking the culture and compassion out of food — that is, turning food into nothing more than commodities — and denying that adequate, safe, nutritious food is a human right not only ensures that large numbers of people will go hungry because they are "unwilling to pay" the going prices, it also increases the profits and control of food by multinational corporations.

Knowing that our society is characterized by inequality does not mean that we can be certain of how power will operate. For example, Murray Knuttila (chapter 2) sets out a critical theory of how the state acts on behalf of the interests of powerful (class, gender, racialized) groups. But as Knuttila argues, while we know that such powerful interests dominate society, we cannot specify ahead of time the mechanisms through which power is exercised; we can only do this theoretically or abstractly. An understanding of how power actually operates can come only through careful historical research, by uncovering the ways in which the powerful try to protect their interests — sometimes through the state and sometimes elsewhere, all too often successfully, but sometimes not.

So, as you can see, there are some basic disagreements about the nature of society and how it is organized and operates. These disagreements find their way into thinking about social issues — especially, but not only, their causes. In general, thinking about social issues involves trying to understand not only what comes to be seen as a social problem but also how to resolve those problems, both of which are connected to what we think causes social problems.

Defining Our Problems

In thinking about social issues, we have to first consider what behaviours and conditions (in sociological terms, which groups of people) are social problems. Without getting into a long discussion of how to "define social problems" (which many social problems textbooks do), it is sufficient to say that social problems are behaviours and conditions that *both* (objectively) harm a significant group of people *and* behaviours and conditions that are (subjectively) defined as harmful to a significant group of people. Both elements are part of identifying what is a social problem. Nelson and Fleras (1995: 1–9), for example, say defining social problems involves considering conditions that both threaten, and are defined as threatening, by a significant segment of the population. Loseke (1999: 5–13) says that social problems involve both the actual harm caused by behaviours and conditions and what people worry about. These definitions, which are representative, are useful and accurate (see Eitzen, Zinn and Smith 2011: ch. 1 for a more recent but similar discussion). But beyond agreement at this very general level, what we think of as a social problem is not so simple; our conceptions of social problems are tied up with how we see society being organized.

> Social problems are behaviours and conditions that *both* (objectively) harm a significant group of people *and* behaviours and conditions that are (subjectively) defined as harmful.

Conditions That Harm — Objective Element of Social Problems

- In 2008, 13.9 percent of Canadians lived below Statistics Canada's low-income cut-off, and in March 2009, 794,738 Canadians used food banks, double the number in 1989 (chapter 5).
- In 2008–09, governments spent more than $20 trillion to bail out banks and financial institutions, one and a half times more than the entire annual output of the U.S., which must be paid back by taxpayers (chapter 6).
- Between 1998 and 2008, eight out of ten police-reported intimate partner victims were female, as were 79 percent of spousal homicide victims and 98 percent of victims of forcible confinement and sexual assault perpetrated by an intimate partner (chapter 3).
- Tar sands production emits roughly three times the volume of greenhouse gases per barrel than conventional oil; this currently represents 5 percent of Canada's emissions at 30 megatonnes, but is projected to increase to 300 megatonnes by 2050. These emissions create a threat of unprecedented environmental and social catastrophe (chapter 12).
- In a national survey, over 70 percent of LGBQT high school students report being subject to homophobic comments all the time, leading to their isolation, social disengagement, and even suicide (chapter 4).

These facts all indicate serious problems that invade the lives of many people. There is no doubt that particular social conditions and behaviours that cause suffering to a significant set of people are problems, both for those people and for society. Equally, there is no doubt that such conditions are objectively real, and we can articulate and observe those conditions, even though it may be difficult to define just when a social condition becomes a social problem — what level of harm needs to be done and to how many people before we define it this way. Yet, in many ways, all that this part of the definition tells us is that we can and must articulate who is being harmed in order to call something a social problem.

All too often, though, traditional social analyses accept as self-evident the problematic nature of some set of social conditions. In this view, there are behaviours that clearly, objectively, and obviously disrupt the functioning of society as-it-exists. For example, of late we are constantly being told that violence is a serious problem in our society. From many sources we are relentlessly warned about the dangerousness of certain parts of the cities we live in. There can be no doubt that violence is harmful and disruptive to anyone who encounters it. Yet, as Les Samuelson (chapter 16) and Ruth Mann (chapter 3) show us, we are much more likely to encounter violence at work or at the hands of people we know intimately (mainly males) than in those "certain parts of the city." This is not to make light of or dismiss the harmful violence that may exist in "certain parts of the city," particularly for the people who live there. But even that violence is most likely to occur between people

> Traditional social analyses accept as self-evident... that there are behaviours that clearly, objectively, obviously disrupt the functioning of society as-it-exists.

who are known to each other. In these terms, the nature of the problem of violence is not self-evident, even though violence is harmful.

To take another example: Like many revolutionary technologies before it, the Internet is often self-evidently taken to be a sign of social progress (in fact, there tends to be a generalized sense that all technological change is progress). There is no doubt that the Internet has made life more interesting, easier, and richer for many people; indeed, the instant communication it facilitates about other parts of the world is a positive feature. Yet, as Leslie Shade and Normand Landry (chapter 13) point out in their examination of the new social media, technological design can hide vested interests: corporations who own the social media sell private information to marketers, governments use Internet devices to keep close watch on all citizens. In these and other ways, the new social media can actually be a social problem.

Thus, we do have to ask about and determine the objective contours of the conditions we define as social problems. But social conditions are actually about people's needs, so — to think this through critically and as the above examples illustrate — we have also to ask about whose needs are being met by the existing social set-up. And, on the other side of that coin, we have to ask about whose needs might be better met by disrupting the functioning of society as-it-exists. That is, taking some social condition as self-evidently problematic ignores who is raising the question. Some social actors — academics, bureaucrats, politicians, business people — are positioned so that our society as-it-exists functions well for them. As such, they often characterize social conditions from their standpoint and in their interests. This difference of standpoint at times manifests itself in disputes about the facts. For example, there is a long-standing dispute over how many people are poor in Canada. Jim Silver (chapter 5: appendix) outlines the two main ways of measuring poverty, one of which is championed by the Fraser Institute, a think-tank that draws its support from corporations and wealthy people. According to their way of defining and measuring it, there is very little real poverty in Canada. From their point of view, most of the people who are defined as poor in Canada have food, shelter, and access to education and health care, unlike the poor in the so-called undeveloped world, who are destitute. Such a characterization is clearly in the interests of the groups who support the Fraser Institute.

> We have to ask about whose needs are being met by the existing social set-up. And... about whose needs might be better met by disrupting the functioning of society as-it-exists.

In a related context, there is a world food crisis, given the large numbers of starving and hungry people around the world, the magnitude of which is not disputed. Yet, this hunger becomes a particular kind of problem depending on how it is framed and from whose standpoint it is viewed. Sally Miller (chapter 11) tells us that the Food and Agriculture Organization of the United Nations knows, and tells the world through its reports, that there is actually about 1 ½ times the food needed to feed everyone in the world. Yet, the food crisis is mostly presented as one in which more food production is necessary. The real problem, according to Sally Miller's analysis, is the dysfunctional ways food is distributed by a system largely controlled by multinational agri-business and governments in developed countries. Such a framing serves the needs of these powerful interests rather than the needs of the starving people in the world. She gives the example of Haiti, which went from providing almost all its staple food, rice, to becoming an importer of rice, mainly from the U.S. Thus, how we think and talk about a particular social condition is important to defining a social problem.

The Stories That Are Told — The Subjective Element of Social Problems

Many traditional analysts do take the step beyond seeing a social situation as self-evidently, or objectively, a problem. They go on to argue that social conditions become problems or issues when "some value cherished by publics is felt to be threatened" (Mills 1959: 8). That is, it is not "just the facts" and social harm that lead a social condition to be defined as a social problem. A condition or behaviour can become a social problem if it threatens an important social value or if it is perceived by the public as being such a threat (see Nelson and Fleras 1995: 8; Loseke 1999: 5, 8–9). Values are certainly not irrelevant in building an understanding of why some behaviours or conditions are deemed to be social problems. In this regard, both traditional and critical social analysts would agree that values (and percep-tions) are an important part of the social problem process. There is, however, a tendency among traditional analysts to define problems as arising from a violation of an assumed value consensus within society. When we conceptualize and study social issues, we must ask and be clear about the cherished values that are being threatened. It is on this issue — what values and whose values — that traditional and critical analysts part company.

The case of immigration into Canada is very much about values. Wendy Chan (chapter 8) tells us that it is the feelings of insecurity that makes immigration a problem for many Canadians. It is true that there has been a significant increase in the level of immigration to Canada in the past two to three decades. Yet, the people who see immigration as a problem tend to call for strict regulations and law enforcement to deal with the maladaptation of im-migrants (in terms of their work skills and economic needs, and their cultural norms) and with the criminals and terrorists who enter Canada as refugees. For them, it is not just too many immigrants, but not enough "good" immigrants, that threaten the safety, prosperity, and harmony of Canada. But, as Chan demonstrates, it is difficult to establish that there is lax enforcement of immigration law, or that immigrants are actually an economic drain. Lurking behind the transformation of Canadian immigration law and enforcement and the idea that immigration is a problem is racism. When we drill down into the actual practices of immigration policy and enforcement, the matter of "good" immigrants is not really about skills and adaptation. The new immigrants — who in recent decades have come mainly from Asia and Africa — actually threaten to upset a decades-old policy aimed at "keeping Canada white." Thus, in analyzing social problems we need not only to clearly identify the values that are at risk, but also, more importantly, to ask about whose values are at risk.

We also cannot assume that public perceptions are freely formed. Some analysts within the traditional framework do suggest that "a problem exists when an influential group defines a social condition as threatening to its values" (Sullivan and Thompson, 1988: 3). Janet Mosher (2008) refers to the ability of "claims makers" to convince the rest of us that some condition or group is a problem and to define the problem in ways that suit their interests.

She investigates how so-called welfare fraud is treated, in legislation, enforcement, and public discourse, as a crime, while tax evasion (which robs society of much more money) is not treated as a crime. As Debra Davidson and Mike Gismondi (chapter 12) put it regarding the issue of environmental sustainability, "political power defines who has an opportunity to influence environmental governance, and which issues get attention ... elites seek to contain public concerns and dominate the meaning and practice of sustainability in Canada." In general, these powerful elites tend to define environmental issues as in conflict with economic needs; that acting aggressively to alter environmental degradation will cause economic harm. Neighbourhood, environmental, and other groups, with access to fewer resources, face difficult struggles in challenging how environmental concerns are defined by governments, corporations, and their expert scientists.

The people who have access to the means of public debate and discourse can dominate the public agenda not only by defining what will be seen as social problems but also by framing *how* certain issues or conditions will be seen as problems.

> The people who have access to the means of public... discourse can dominate the public agenda not only by defining what... but also by framing *how* certain issues or conditions will be seen as problems.

Powerful and socially privileged groups tend to have more access to the means of public discourse. Corporations and the wealthy people who own and control the mass media do not force all of us to think in particular ways, but they have more influence than others regarding what social issues will get into the public domain, and they are more likely than not to frame these issues in ways that support the status quo. A good example is the conflict over the Alberta tar sands. Debra Davidson and Mike Gismondi (chapter 12) show that, while Alberta's state and corporate elites do not deny that the tar sands do have environmental consequences, they have worked hard to reframe sustainability. These two groups of social elites have, for example, presented the tar sands "initially as clean energy, and now as 'ethical oil.'" Moreover, "in a spectacular reframing feat, environmental costs would be borne were we to *stop* development, since tar sands development generates revenues that support environmental sustainability."

Corporations and the wealthy also have privileged access to think-tanks and policy networks. Organizations such as the Canadian Council of Chief Executives and policy research institutes such as the Fraser Institute and Conference Board of Canada were organized precisely to produce statistics and analyses that shape the social-issues and public-policy agendas in Canada. These organizations have multi-million-dollar budgets financed by donations from corporations and wealthy Canadians (most of whom are also male and white) (Brownlee 2005: ch. 4, 5).

Closer to home, Claire Polster (chapter 15) shows that through funding university research, corporations are having a huge impact on the kinds of work being done and on how the results of that work are used. As she says, this skews "the general scientific research agenda towards industry needs and interests." Thus, "the research needs of other social groups (particularly those who cannot afford to sponsor academic research) are neglected in favour of the needs of paying clients," and there is an "incentive to pursue lucrative research questions and areas, which are not always the most scientifically valuable or socially useful ones."

For critical analysts, then, the focus is on social power and not merely social values and perceptions. The whole of Mills's *The Sociological Imagination* is taken up with examining the tendencies in sociology that led to what he terms the "cultural and political abdication" of classical (or traditional) social analysis. He castigates value-oriented theories and analyses (like those of his influential contemporary, Talcott Parsons) that are obsessed with the concept of the normative order — that norms and values are the most important element of social analysis. In the normative view, institutional structures are transformed into a sort of "moral sphere," making it "quite difficult even to raise several of the most important problems of any analysis of social structure" (Mills 1959: 36). Such an approach, says Mills, absolves the analyst from any concern with power and political relations, thereby legitimating the existing structures and social arrangements that produce major inequalities in our society. Without putting norms and values into the context of social inequality, such a view turns the values, views, and experiences of society's dominant groups into society's values, views, and experiences. To update and modify an old phrase: "What is good for Microsoft, is good for society."

Resolving Our Problems — Changing Individuals?

The other key aspect in thinking about social issues is trying to figure out how to resolve them. Thinking about resolving social problems is really thinking about what causes them. Even more obvious than the link between our understanding of society and what gets defined as a social problem is the connection between that understanding and the kinds of solutions proposed to resolve social problems.

Given its general social outlook, not surprisingly, the traditional approach tends to see the problems of a community or society in individual, pathological terms. In other words, these analyses usually see social problems as emanating from the personal inadequacies of individuals, from their "private troubles." These personal inadequacies are, in turn, often seen as deriving from inappropriate socialization and dysfunctional behaviour choices. For example, the predominant view of violence between men and women — the so-called "gender symmetry" perspective (see chapter 3) — is just such an individualistic approach. In this view, women, it is argued, are just as violent as the men with whom they have intimate relationships. Research using the Conflict Tactics Scale finds that women use violence as much as men. In an important sense, this violence is between two people; it is not particularly relevant that either one of them is a man or woman. Given this individualistic frame, it is not really surprising, says Ruth Mann, that the federal government has been generally degendering public policy (also see Brodie and Bakker 2008). In the case of female-male violence, she shows that there is an ongoing "invisibilization" of violence against women supported by the federal government which "has reoriented its sponsored funding and Internet disseminated resources away from a focus on women's victimization towards a broad degendered concern with violence against intimates."

In recent years the traditional focus on individualism has taken a new twist. Much traditional analysis — neoliberal in this new form — calls for using the competitive market

> The traditional approach tends to see the problems of a community or society in individual, pathological terms as emanating from the personal inadequacies of individuals.

as a model in all our social undertakings. In this view, the market or business way of doing things, as opposed to a collective approach, is seen as the solution for our economic woes and for a host of other social and political problems — not just in deregulating our economy but also in applying business principles to schooling, cultural production, assistance to the destitute, prisons, environmental protection, and so on. In a nutshell, the market is seen as being based on and promoting the individual freedom that will pave the way to a prosperous and harmonious society. In health care and education, for example, this push has taken the form of privatization — the variety of ways of shifting authority, ownership, or ideology for producing and/or delivering public services from state-controlled to private, market-oriented organizations and frameworks (see Antony et al. 2007). Privatization can involve selling public resources to for-profit corporations, but also occurs when management of public social programs is turned over to corporations, and when public institutions, whose goals are far broader than profit making, are managed through corporate models.

Pat Armstrong (chapter 14) documents the multiple ways in which our health-care system is being privatized, as the means of fixing its problems and the problem of adequate health care. Even though the "crisis" in health care is not always clearly defined, making health care more like just another commodity in the market — privatizing it — is the goal of many "reformers." "Privatization by stealth" has taken many forms: the trend towards shifting the burden of payment to individuals; opening health-service delivery to for-profit providers; moving care from public institutions to community-based organizations and private households; transferring care work from public-sector health-care workers to unpaid caregivers; and adopting the management strategies of private-sector businesses, applying market rules to health-service delivery, and treating health care as a market good.

Claire Polster (chapter 15) gives us a detailed examination of the privatization of university education in Canada. In response to a number of educational issues, governments and universities are treating education increasingly as a private responsibility oriented more and more to private, individual goals. This privatization is taking place through a wide range of processes and transformations. Advertising on campuses and exclusive contracts for food and beverages are growing every year. Corporations are becoming much more involved by providing university research facilities and grants. And as universities adopt a business model of operation, collegiality and participatory governance are disappearing.

What both the health-care and education examples show is that privatization — far from resolving problems of health/health care and education — has all kinds of negative consequences. Put simply, these examples of the individual, market solutions do not solve our health and education problems because they do not address the abiding inequalities that are at the root of our social problems.

Resolving Our Problems — Resistance and Social Change

The authors of this book use a different approach, one that sees social inequality as underlying the problems we face. Social harm, and thus social problems, arise from excesses of private power and are exacerbated when public resources are shifted to the control of elites such that benefits go to the privileged (Barlow 2005: 142). Seen in this way, the search for solutions takes a different tack. "Critical perspectives ask not only whether individual people have maintained their responsibility to the community, but also whether the community has maintained its responsibility to individuals. The approach does not focus on individual flaws; rather, it questions societal structures... inequality and disenfranchisement, abuse and victimization, classism, racism, and sexism" (Brooks 2002: 47).

> The [critical] approach does not focus on individual flaws; rather, it questions societal structures... inequality and disenfranchisement, abuse and victimization, classism, racism, and sexism.

In a sense, for critical observers, social problems are partly the result of choices — the choices of powerful groups in society. As Daniel Paul (chapter 7) shows, in the case of First Nations peoples, it is not their failure to assimilate into Canadian society that explains their various dire circumstances, but rather centuries-old white supremacy. As he says, almost from the very beginning, it has been the policy of white governments to eliminate First Nations peoples through various subtle and not so subtle means. From the scalping proclamations of the mid-1700s to the starvation practices of the early 1800s to the *Indian Act* of 1876 (which made it an offence for an Indian agent not to try to dispose of reserve land, for example) through to the implementation of residential schools, the goal, however disguised, has always been genocide. Duncan Campbell Scott, Indian Commissioner in 1920, put it clearly: "I want to get rid of the Indian problem.... Our objective is to continue until there is not a single Indian in Canada that has not been absorbed into the body politic and there is no Indian question."

Similarly, but in a different context, David McNally (chapter 6) demonstrates that the current economic crisis is the result of the actions and choices of multinational banks and investors along with their allies in government. After the truly massive bailouts of 2009, governments had to figure out who would pay for them. David McNally says: "Not surprisingly, they all came up with the same answer: working people and the poor shall foot the bill, by way of lower wages, higher unemployment and huge cuts to the social services on which all but the rich rely. With this declaration, they inaugurated an 'age of austerity.'" A columnist with the *Times* of London put it starkly:, "The rich have come through the recession with flying colours.... The rest of the country is going to have to face spending cuts, but it has little effect on the rich because they don't consume public services."

Thus, for a critical approach to social problems, solutions lie in resistance and social change action — in working to overturn the basic social inequalities of our unjust social structure. What we also see when we look carefully is that Canadians do act to resist inequality, and we do this in a variety of ways. We do it as individuals and as collectivities; we do it through the state and in non-state organizations. We do not always do it intentionally, and some resistance may be more symbolic than material. But the logic of inequality forces us to reject and try to change fundamental elements of our society.

> Solutions lie in resistance and social change action — in working to overturn the basic social inequalities of our unjust social structure.

Individually, we engage in a myriad of day-to-day, small activities that are part of the long-term process of changing society. For instance, we buy what we need (as opposed to what we are told we want) from local producers and worker co-operatives; we refuse to be silent around racial slurs; and we show our children that men must be involved in caring for them and cleaning our houses. In this vein, Jessica Antony (chapter 10) shows us that women, as individuals, do not necessarily consume the commodification agenda of capitalism. It has been profitable for a burgeoning tattooing industry to distance itself from the "deviants" associated with tattoos in the past, thereby stripping permanent body art of any meaning other than as a new form of fashion. What she found in talking to tattooed women is that while many do not see their tattoos as "political," neither do they see them as being akin to wearing fashionable clothing. Tattoos have meaning — from spiritual to familial to feminist — because people want and need meaning in what they do. They do resist the tendency in capitalism to make consumption the only meaningful activity and to promote the idea that everything should be about consumption.

We also join with others in resisting inequality and pursuing social change. The most obvious of these collective actions are the social movements that have already changed our world — the movements we are familiar with, including feminist organizations, labour unions, anti-racist groups, gay and lesbian rights organizations, and environmentalists. In his chapter, David McNally documents the breadth, strength, and social basis of the worldwide resistance to forcing working people and the poor to bear the brunt of paying for the excesses of international financial corporations — to suffering through an "age of austerity" to pay for the decades of casino capitalism. As he says, "an impressive wave of working class resistance was unleashed. In response to factory closings and layoffs, workers staged plant occupations in Chicago, in several cities in Ontario, in Ireland, Scotland, and beyond; in France they coupled "bossnappings" to their factory occupations; and in France, Spain, Greece, and beyond they waged general strikes. The occupation of the Wisconsin legislature, initiated by students, blossomed when labour unions joined the protest. The society-changing demonstrations in the Middle East, triggered by the mass unemployment, poverty, and rising food prices resulting from the global financial crisis, were huge collective undertakings.

Sometimes the distinction between individual and collective resistance can be blurred. Leslie Shade and Normand Landry (chapter 13) show us that "botnets" and "swarming" are, in an important sense, individual actions; they are not the typical kind of collective action of street protests and demonstrations that are organized and carried out in a face-to-face manner. Nonetheless, they do bring people together in a cooperative action. The success of "Operation Payback, meant to launch a global 'cyberwar' against censorship… was unique because it relied on… the keen cooperation of those who are usually the unwilling accomplices of hackers and pirates." As is the case with much resistance, activist use of the social media subverts the purposes and prescribed uses of technology that is owned by economically and politically powerful groups.

Despite the demands and desires of some neoliberals that government disappear from the social scene, it is clear that we cannot live in a society without some form of state. It is through the state, albeit a more participatory and democratic one, that we can make the kinds of collective decisions we must make if we are to live together and realize our collective responsibility to each other. Government is a key part of our social lives. Thus it is no surprise that collective resistance can and does also take place through the state. Tracey Peter and Catherine Taylor (chapter 4) discuss some of the ways that homophobia can be overturned in schools, and in society generally. While they recognize the limits of a declaration like the *Charter of Rights and Freedoms* in producing a discrimination-free society, for example, and do see the important place of Gay Student Alliances for creating safe spaces for LGBQT students, they are optimistic that lobbying governments can have positive social change results. They tell us that schools have become safer for LGBQT students where school divisions have mandated a "whole-system approach" to include gender and sexual minority content in policies, programs, and curriculum.

Still, collective action against inequality does not necessarily take place through the state, nor does it have to. At the very least, given the scale of state activities, these institutions can be insensitive to the needs of some people and, in some cases, oppressive. Jim Silver (chapter 5) shows that poverty in Canada has become seemingly intractable, in large part because almost every approach that has tackled economic conditions in recent years has been market-oriented, and too often state-centred. He argues that along with some necessary changes in government social- and labour-market policies, a key strategy for anti-poverty action will be found within poor communities themselves. In particular, he says, it will be found through community-based economic development, which will plug the many holes through which wealth produced in poor communities "leaks out" to corporations and other groups. Just as importantly, social enterprises that are developed and run locally can provide the skills development and self-confidence necessary for dispossessed people to pull themselves out of poverty.

Power and Resistance

The title and focus of this book, then, are power and resistance. The chapters emphasize that — depending on class, race, gender, and sexual orientation — people face inequalities of treatment and life chances. Emphasizing power means first of all recognizing that some groups have privileged access to the resources that make life viable in our society. More importantly, a critical emphasis means revealing how those groups act to maintain and enhance their privilege, thereby creating problems for other groups of people. These inequalities — inherent in an unjust social structure — are the social problems in Canadian society. Our focus is not just on documenting existing conditions but also on ways of generating emancipatory resistance and change.

Glossary of Key Terms

Inequality: Inequality refers to the more or less narrow life choices and life chances for individuals and groups of people. It refers not just to what people have; it is not just differences in lifestyle, but also what they can do and what they can become.

Objective element of social problems: This is the basis in reality for whether a social condition or behaviour pattern is a problem or not. This basis involves identifying who is harmed and who benefits, and in what ways, from a social condition or behaviour pattern.

Power: Power is the ability to set limits on the behavioural choices for ourselves and for others. Power is clearly in play when individuals and groups act in ways that achieve their desires, needs, and interests against those of others. Power has many bases and faces, from the schoolyard bully to influence over public discourse.

Private troubles: Private troubles occur within the character of the individual and within the range of immediate relations with others; they have to do with the self and with those limited areas of social life of which we are directly and personally aware.

Public issues: Public issues have to do with matters that transcend the local environments of the individual and the range of inner life. They have to do with the organization of many such milieux into the institutions of a historical society, with the ways in which various milieux overlap and interpenetrate to form the larger structure of social and historical life.

Resistance: Resistance comes in acting to change the basic social inequalities of society. Resistance can be an individual act and can occur in collectivities; it happens through the state and in non-state organizations. It is not always intentional, and some resistance is more symbolic than material. But the logic of inequality forces us to reject and try to change fundamental elements of our society.

Structure: Social and political structures are the patterns of behavioural relationships between groups of people in society. They include how men and women, racialized people, young and old, wealthy and poor, governments and citizens, relate to one another.

Subjective element of social problems: In regard to social issues, this is often called public perception. What people perceive as real will guide their actions and their understanding of society. This aspect of social problems refers to what people think are the consequences — who is harmed and who benefits — of a social condition or pattern of behaviour.

Questions for Discussion

1. Take an issue in the neighbourhood or city you live in, or the university you go to. What are the "facts" about it? Where do you get information about those facts? Who provides that information? Is there a debate about the facts? What individuals, groups, and organizations represent the various elements of the issue and its debate? What resources do they have to make their case known to other people and groups? To government?

2. Does a focus on structure and inequality mean that individuals bear no responsibility for social problems and their solutions?

3. How are the following private troubles? How are they public issues? Youth gangs. Urban sprawl. Voter turnout in elections.

4. For the issue you thought about in question 1, think about possible solutions. What government policies are involved? What changes might help? What community organizations and resources are there to help resolve the issue? What new community resources could be developed?

Websites of Interest

Canadian Centre for Policy Alternatives <policyalternatives.ca>
Canadian Dimension <canadiandimension.mb.ca>
Council of Canadians <canadians.org>
Democracy Now! <democracynow.org>
Herizons <herizons.ca>
New Internationalist <newint.org>
Rabble — News for the Rest of Us <rabble.ca>
This Magazine <thismagazine.ca>
Briarpatch <briarpatchmagazine.com>

References

Antony, Wayne, Errol Black, Sid Frankel, Dick Henley, Pete Hudson, Wendy Land, Dennis Lewycky, Emily Ternette, and Russ Tychonick. 2007. *The State of Public Services in Manitoba*. Winnipeg: CPPA-Manitoba.

Barlow, Maude. 2005. *Too Close for Comfort: Canada's Future Within Fortress North America*. Toronto: McClelland and Stewart.

Brodie, Janine, and Isabella Bakker. 2008. *Where Are the Women? Gender Equity, Budgets, and Canadian Public Policy*. Ottawa: Canadian Centre for Policy Alternatives.

Brooks, Carolyn. 2002. "New Directions in Critical Criminology." In Bernard Schissel and Carolyn Brooks (eds.), *Marginality and Condemnation: An Introduction to Critical Criminology*. Winnipeg and Black Point, NS: Fernwood Publishing.

Brownlee, Jamie. 2005. *Ruling Canada: Corporate Cohesion and Democracy*. Winnipeg and Black Point, NS: Fernwood Publishing.

CCPA (Canadian Centre for Policy Alternatives). 2010a. "Tar Sands Index." *CCPA Monitor* 17, 1 (May).
____. 2010b. "Deportations Index." *CCPA Monitor* 17, 3 (July/August).

CWP (Canada Without Poverty). n.d. "Just the Facts." At <cwp-csp.ca/poverty/just-the-facts>.

Eitzen, D.S., M. Zinn, and K. Smith. 2011. *Social Problems*. 12th edition. New York: Pearson.

Klein, Naomi. 2007. *The Shock Doctrine: The Rise of Disaster Capitalism*. Toronto: Knopf Canada

Loseke, D. 1999. *Thinking About Social Problems*. New York: Aldine de Gruyter.

Mills, C. Wright. 1959. *The Sociological Imagination*. New York: Oxford University Press.

Moller, Melanie. 2011. "Water Crisis on Reserves, Students Say." At <charlatan.ca/content/water-crisis-reserves-students-say>.

Mosher, Janet. 2008. "Welfare Fraudsters and Tax Evaders: The State's Selective Invocation of Criminality." In C. Brooks and B. Schissel (eds.), *Marginality and Condemnation*, second edition. Winnipeg and Black Point, NS: Fernwood Publishing.

Nelson, E., and A. Fleras. 1995. *Canadian Social Problems*. Englewood Cliffs, NJ: Prentice Hall.

Polaris Institute. 2008. *Boiling Point*. At <polarisinstitute.org/boiling_point_0>.

Raphael, D. 2009. "Poverty, Human Development, and Health in Canada: Research, Practice and Advocacy." *Canadian Journal of Nursing Research* 41, 2.

Sanger, T. 2011. "Canada's Undertaxed Banks, not Workers, Should Pay Crisis Costs." *CCPA Monitor* 18, 1 (May).

Sullivan, T., and K. Thompson. 1988. *Introduction to Social Problems*. New York: Macmillan.

2

The State and Social Issues
Theoretical Considerations

Murray Knutilla

YOU SHOULD KNOW THIS

- In 1916 Saskatchewan, Manitoba, and Alberta granted women the right to vote, but it was not until 1920 that women could vote in federal elections. Aboriginal persons could not vote until 1960.
- The first elected government in Canada, Sir John A. Macdonald's Conservatives, was forced to resign after it was disclosed that Sir Hugh Allan and interests associated with the proposed Canadian Pacific Railway Company had made donations to the Conservatives in return for favours in the granting of the contract to build the transcontinental railroad.
- The *Canadian Charter of Rights and Freedoms* came into force on April 17, 1982. An example of its potential role came on September 9, 1999, when the Supreme Court overturned two lower court rulings against secondary picketing and leafleting as violations of workers' constitutional rights.
- On March 31, 2006, 1,809 individuals in Ottawa were registered to lobby on behalf of 276 corporations, an increase of 847 percent in one year. At the same time the number of individuals registered to lobby for organizations increased from 266 to 2,306, or 767 percent.
- Federal government revenue sources for 2004/05: personal income tax — $89.8 billion (over 45 percent of total revenue); GST — $29.8 billion (15 percent); corporate income tax — $30 billion (15 percent); other taxes — $16.7 billion (8 1/2 percent); employment insurance premiums — $17.3 billion (8.7 percent).
- In 2005, bank employees working for the Royal Bank of Canada generated a profit of $56,439 per employee, while those at the Bank of Montreal generated $71,037.

Sources: Office of the Registrar of Lobbyists 2006; Canada, Department of Finance 2006a; *Globe and Mail Report on Business* 2006 (July/August): 120.

THE STUDY OF SOCIAL ISSUES RAISES A NUMBER of important questions, ranging from how we define social issues to what causes them and how individuals and social institutions respond to them. Here our focus is on the state's relationship to social issues. Specifically, this means looking at some of the theoretical frameworks that have been used to analyze the role of the state in capitalist society. If we are to explain specific state policies as they relate to various social issues, we must begin with a general understanding of how the state or polity fits into the larger structures of society.

The emphasis here tends to be on a macro or a structural approach, which means that social problems are examined and explained in terms of structural and social relations and processes. Because the state in Western capitalist societies is generally understood as the institution that is primarily concerned with the organization of political and social power and the exercise of authority in the interests of social stability and order, an adequate understanding of social problems requires an analysis of the role of the state.

> The state is primarily concerned with the social organization of political, or broadly speaking, social power and the exercise of authority. It follows that an adequate understanding of most social problems requires an analysis of the role of the state.

There is no agreement on the best way of theoretically understanding the state in advanced capitalist or liberal-democratic society. Two major perspectives on the state dominate: structural functionalism and Marxism. However, there are other recent approaches.

Structural Functionalism: The Beginnings

Throughout the modern era social scientists in general have been concerned about the "problem of social order"; for some sociologists, however, this problem has been a major preoccupation.

For Emile Durkheim, the French thinker recognized as one of the founding figures in sociology, social order was a central issue. He was preoccupied with the basis of social order and how it is possible in complex modern societies. Durkheim lived during a period of rapid industrialization and came to believe that when a society industrialized, its members became more heterogeneous, differentiated, unlike each other. In his book, *The Division of Labour in Society*, he argues that industrialization brings with it greater specialization of the tasks, jobs, and functions performed by both individuals and institutions (Durkheim 1964). Durkheim believed that in pre-industrial society it was easier to establish a common set of beliefs, morals, and values that would hold society together, because people tended to share a way of life and thus beliefs, values, and morals. The emergence of a division of labour, with its attendant specialization and even fragmentation, undermines the shared experiences and concerns that facilitated the "natural" sharing of a belief system. Modern industrial society thus faces the problem of establishing a new system of beliefs and values that can serve as the basis of social order. Durkheim argues that, fortunately, some of the very characteristics of modern industrial society provide a solution to the problem of order. He maintains that, as society develops and evolves, a new moral code emphasizing the interdependence of individuals and institutions also develops. As a result people come to realize that while they do different jobs, they are all part of a larger whole and all contribute to the survival of society. In the case of the political system, the state becomes responsible for making decisions on behalf of everyone in society, and it plays a role in maintaining social order by assisting in the dissemination of values, beliefs and morals.

In acting on behalf of society as a whole, Durkheim points to the role of corporate and occupational groups both within society as a whole and within the polity. As the division of labour develops, occupational and corporate groups become more important in terms of organizing and co-ordinating the multitude of roles in society. These different kinds of groups eventually become important conduits between individuals and the polity; they take information and concerns from the population to those in government and relay information on actions and policies back from the government to the members of society (Durkheim 1933: 27–28).

Durkheim's work is important for a number of reasons. He first became known to many North American political sociologists through the writings of Talcott Parsons, one of the founders of North American structural functionalism who had a significant impact on how the polity and state have come to be understood in this century.

Twentieth-Century Functionalism

Structural functionalism is an understanding of society developed by thinkers such as Emile Durkheim, Talcott Parsons, Robert Merton, Melvin Tumin, and Daniel Rossides. Although the theoretical ideas of modern functionalists are complicated and sophisticated, they still share a set of basic premises and assumptions about human society.

First, this perspective suggests that human society must be understood as a system. Like all systems, human society faces basic problems that must be solved if it is to survive. Functionalists tend to employ an organic analogy to assist understanding. The analogy draws out certain features of the social system by comparing it to a living biological system such as the human body. We begin the analogy by noting that if a human body is to survive, certain basic needs must be met and certain basic problems must be solved. Employing this same logic, structural functionalists argue that there are certain basic individual and species needs that must be satisfied if a human society is to survive. For example, the future of every human society depends on the development of arrangements to facilitate producing and distributing the material goods and services necessary for biological survival. In addition, some arrangements must be established to look after spiritual needs, enhancing and transmitting culture, biological reproduction and childcare, education, and social decision making.

Society is a complex unity composed of many different parts of subsystems. The functionalist approach thus explains the various parts of a social system in terms of what those parts do for the total system or, put slightly differently, in terms of their functions. An organ's functions in a biological system is to perform certain tasks or jobs for the whole system. A social institution similarly functions to solve or satisfy one or more of society's basic problems or needs.

An additional key issue in structural functionalist thought is the question of social order. The social system is composed of many complex components or parts, all presumably working in unison to solve the system's problems: just how this system is held together has been an issue for social and political philosophers for centuries. Following Durkheim, structural functionalists argue that social systems tend to be stable and orderly as long as they possess a set of widely shared and accepted beliefs and values. Such belief and value systems serve as a kind of moral cement, binding and bonding the various components of a social system together. Normally, then, a social system tends to be stable. As long as each of the institutions is functioning normally and there is an accepted value system bonding the various elements together, the system exists in a condition of equilibrium and order.

In terms of political arrangements, Parsons, for example, maintains that the polity functions to make decisions for the entire social system and is responsible for maintaining order in the larger social system. He argues that despite the existence of different groups and interests in society it is possible to develop a political system that operates to establish goals, policies, and priorities for the entire society. After World War II, much of the thinking and theorizing about the state took place within a theoretical tradition, closely linked to Parsons, known as pluralism.

Pluralism

Asking how a society composed of different individuals, groups, and interests develops goals, priorities, and social policies that enjoy widespread support, Parsons touched on a question long at the forefront of North American, and indeed all Western, political thought.

Among these thinkers was Charles Merriam. In his book, *Political Power*, Merriam explicitly addresses the polity in terms of power. For Merriam (1964: 32) the polity, government, and political power all have to do with the development of a decision-making process that mediates and stabilizes relations in a society divided into classes, groups and factions.

American pluralists assume that the United States represents a social system that has successfully addressed the key issue: it is a society divided into many classes, groups and factions, that has established a system of political decision making that is open and democratic, and capable of performing its essential functions.

Robert Dahl's (1967, 1972) work is a classic statement of the pluralist approach. According to Dahl, a complex industrial society is inevitably divided into different kinds of groups, classes, and factions based on a multitude of religious, class, occupational, regional, ethnic, and sexual differences. When understood in this context, the function of government and the entire social political decision-making process becomes a practice of mediation and arbitration among and between these interests and factions.

Dahl makes a case for what he refers to as "polyarchy." A polyarchy is a complex system which, though controlled by elites, typically involves institutional guarantees both protecting citizens from the exercise of arbitrary power and protecting basic human rights by employing broadly accepted procedures defining legal powers, rights, and privileges for both the government and citizens. Although the rights of citizens are enshrined, there is also general acceptance of the right of governments to use violence to protect the national interest. Polyarchies are typically predicated on constitutional frameworks that support legal and accepted modes of conduct determining and specifying the actual conduct of government or the selection of state officials (Dahl 1972: 40–43).

Pluralists argue that Western democracies — with the U.S. system being typical — are sets of structures and processes that fulfill the best possibilities for democratic political activity in an advanced industrial society. For them, the electoral system with its one-person, one-vote is a great "leveller." Regardless of an individual's income, prestige in society, or authority in a particular institution, on election day every person is equal. The fact that everyone is entitled to vote once and only once means, formally at least, that all citizens potentially have the same power and opportunity to make an impact on the political process.

The political process is not, however, just about elections. Individuals, groups, and classes have other opportunities to influence government policies and actions. Since liberal-democratic systems are open societies with a free press, citizens have access to information about what the government is doing. When the government is about to decide on an issue, the individuals or groups interested in that issue will know about it and have the opportunity to present their case to the government. Lobbying is available to all, even if the participants did not support the particular party or individual who was victorious in the electoral process. Thus, all members of society have the opportunity to influence the government through that process.

In a complex society, lobbying is also important and complex, and many individuals come to realize that they can be more effective if they are organized. Rather than working solely as individuals, students, farmers, teachers, and businesses have united and formed formal groups to press their interests with the government. Thus today governments will typically find themselves under pressure from many organized pressure or interest groups, each pushing the interests of its members. Democracy now may not be as direct as it was when individuals pressed their own cases, but, even in his day, Durkheim held that the intervention of organized groups would still facilitate democratic decision making.

Based on this sort of analysis of Western democracies, pluralists argue that political power is dispersed across a multitude of centres that compete through the electoral and lobbying processes to influence government. That there is a plurality of centres of power in the long run means that no one of those centres is able to dominate. The government must be willing to attempt to accommodate all of the various interests, or else it runs the risk of becoming viewed as being corrupt and tied to one centre of power. If this happens the government will face certain electoral defeat once it becomes apparent to all the various interests that they have become excluded from the political process. Assuming that the various excluded interests comprise the majority, they will be in a position to develop a coalition and remove the offending government from power.

The liberal-democratic polity, thus, facilitates social decision making in the complex and divided society. The polity is the site of mediation and "trade-offs" as the government seeks to establish policies and priorities that it sees as representing the interests of the majority (Dahl 1967: 24). No centre of power is dominant or able to consistently get its way, at least over the long haul. "You win some, you lose some" truly characterizes how different interest groups fare in the political process.

It follows that a pluralist approach tends to view the functioning of the state in liberal-democratic societies as basically democratic. In its actions, decisions, and policies the state tends to reflect the broader public or national interests; it tends to act in a manner beneficial to society as a whole. Since one of the state's main functions is the maintenance of social order and harmony, the emergence of social problems tends to produce some manner of state intervention. The precise nature of the state's actions will vary depending on the nature of the problems.

Given the logic of structural functionalism, those adopting this position will see some social problems as "normative" — those problems are the result of some breakdown or dysfunction in the society's overall system of values and norms. Under such circumstances the state is expected to actively attempt to re-establish a normative consensus or establish some new normative orientation. We might, for instance, envision a situation in which racist or sexist beliefs and ideas lead to social problems. A structural functionalist might view such problems as being rooted in the society's values and norms and would therefore advocate state actions geared towards changing those values and norms, through educational programs and efforts to re-educate and resocialize individuals, thus establishing norms more suited to social harmony, order, integration, and stability.

Other social problems might be explained in terms of individual pathologies. For a functionalist, appropriate state actions might range from the provision of policing services to discourage the "acting out" of individual pathologies, to the provision of penal, correctional, and rehabilitative services, as well as medical facilities where appropriate. All of these actions are designed to "safeguard" the public and preserve social order by discouraging or preventing behaviour harmful to the general public, as well as by punishing, assisting, and rehabilitating those committing actions or undertaking activities that disrupt society or cause social problems.

A functionalist might also be inclined to seek the causes of certain other social problems in the "dysfunction" of important institutions. The concept of dysfunction has been an integral part of functionalist thought. The possibility always exists that a complex institution may not adequately perform its socially necessary functions. If this occurs it is possible that other institutions, or even the entire social structure, may be affected. If the impact of such dysfunction is serious enough to threaten the entire social system, then state intervention might be necessary. Again, by way of a general example, we might envision a situation in which more and more women enter the labour force and, as a result, the traditional nuclear family begins to change in such a way that some of its traditional functions are no longer performed. An orthodox functionalist might view such a situation as a case of family dysfunction and argue that the government should intervene, perhaps, as some progressive functionalists would suggest, by providing greater funding for daycare centres to fill the void caused by women no longer being available to perform child-care duties in the home, or by taking action to encourage women to return to their more traditional familial roles.

In general this sociological perspective views the structures of liberal-democratic society as sound. Structural functionalists understand that, for a variety of reasons, social problems do emerge. But, they say, there are structures, particularly the polity, in place to deal with such circumstances.

Some pluralists suggest that the political process may not be quite this smooth. Charles Lindblom (1977), for example, notes that the concentration of economic power in capitalist society has significant implications for political processes. Social and political stability within capitalist systems requires a smooth, functioning economy; therefore it is important that the state does everything in its power to see that certain economic conditions prevail. On this basis, Lindblom, and many others, shows that businesses occupy a "privileged position." The enormous resources controlled by the corporate sector can give it overwhelming advantages in the competition to influence the government — a situation quite contrary to pluralist analysis.

> Some thinkers... of a pluralist approach suggest that the political process may not be quite this smooth.... Charles Lindblom notes that the concentration of economic power in capitalist society has significant implications for political processes.

The critical questions raised by the privileged political position of corporations indicate the need for an alternative framework. Over the past fifty years a different framework has been emerging. This alternative framework follows from the theoretical insights of Karl Marx.

Marxism

Whereas structural functionalists might use an organic analogy to explain their general view of human society, Marxist analysis proceeds from a different set of basic assumptions — also known as materialism.

For Marx the key defining characteristic of humans is that we are the only life form that *produces* the goods and services necessary to satisfy our basic material needs. Human beings do not merely rely or depend on what is found in nature for material and physical survival. Human beings alone engage in a process of material production that is active, social, and intentional, and that relies on the cumulative development and use of knowledge, skills, and technology.

Marx's approach to human material production can be crudely, though effectively, summarized: before humans can engage in any social and political activity they must ensure that their basic material needs are met. That is, they must provide themselves with food, clothing, and shelter. Further, the nature of our productive activity is of central importance in understanding our overall mode or manner of living. Marx further argues that the mode of material production gives a society its general shape and character.

Marx also argues that two aspects define a particular mode of material production: 1) the "social relations of production" (the structure of ownership, control, and use of society's productive resources); and 2) the "forces of production" (technology, knowledge, skills, or tools that aid material production). Examining the social relations of production and the forces of production helps us to understand the larger patterns of social organization. The organization of the polity, the educational system, the family, culture in its broadest meaning, and indeed the entire social structure will be fundamentally influenced by the mode of material production.

Marx engaged in a lengthy and systematic examination of the capitalist mode of production. One of his many conclusions is that capitalist society is divided into classes. For Marx, classes are primarily determined by relationships to the forces of production, which means that class position is determined by whether a group owns the forces of production — known as "productive property" — and purchases the labour power of others, or whether a group does not own productive property and is thus forced to sell the capacity to work to the owners of productive property. Although Marx recognizes that there is another class, whose members own some productive property and neither buy nor sell labour power, he is mainly concerned with the relationship between those who own society's major productive resources and those who sell labour power, namely the capitalist and the working classes.

In addition, Marx concludes that the owners of productive property "exploit" those who have to sell their labour power. That is, as owners of the forces of production, the capitalist class determines what gets produced, how and where it is produced, and controls the surplus between the costs of production and the sale of goods and services — the profits. By doing so, they are exploiting the labour of the working class that goes into producing goods and services. Because one class exploits the other, the two major classes exist in a relationship of conflict and contradictory interests. Further, the class that owns the society's productive resources and capacities possesses economic power. That economic power can be and is translated into other types of power, particularly, political power. For Marx, then, capitalist society is characterized by fundamental, structural inequalities of wealth and power.

The Marxist approach presents a radically different perspective on the treatment of social problems. Flowing out of these systemic or structural relations is the poverty, differential educational levels, unequal access to health care and housing, unemployment and other social and economic problems that characterize advanced capitalist society. In Marxian theory, class is at the centre of a critical analysis of society and the root of most social problems.

In addition, the concept of "contradiction" is also key to Marxian analysis. A Marxian analysis of social problems links those problems to the inherent contradictions found in capitalist society. Those contradictions include the workings of the economy, which give rise to the recurring economic crises that characterize capitalist societies. Whether it is the tendency for wealth and power to become concentrated and centralized, the process of economic internationalization with its associated transfers of capital and economic dislocations, or the tendency for rates of unemployment to grow and investment to stagnate, the implications for society as a whole, especially for the exploited classes, can be devastating.

A Marxian analysis of capitalist society would conclude that certain kinds of social problems are "normal." Contrary to structural functionalist assumptions, social conflict, change, and instability are the norm, not the exception. To the extent that one of the essential functions of the state is to provide the basis of social stability and order, the state will become an ever more important part of the social structure. In an odd way, there is a similarity to functionalism on this issue, although Marxists would argue that the main beneficiaries of the state's actions are the members of the dominant capitalist class and not all members of society.

> To the extent that one of the essential functions of the state is to provide the basis of social stability and order, the state will become an ever more important part of the social structure... although Marxists would argue that the main beneficiaries of the state's actions are the members of the ruling class and not all members of society.

The State in Capitalist Society

Although there is no systematic and well-developed conception of the state in Marx's original works, for most of his life the issue of political power occupied him at both a practical and a theoretical level. In *The German Ideology* ([1845] 1970: 80) Marx and Engels argued that the state had to be understood within the context of capitalist economic structures which are predicated on class relations: thus, the state is a part of the process of class domination of society generally: "The State is the form in which the individuals of a ruling class assert their common interests."

Marx and Engels developed a series of further statements on the nature of the state in capitalist society. They sometimes see the state in quite simplistic terms, as in their claim that "the executive of the modern state is but a committee for managing the common affairs of the whole [capitalist class]" (Marx and Engels 1952: 44). In other works they present more complex pictures of the state (Marx 1972a, 1972b). But a constant theme is the that the state is a central part of the process of class domination.

Following Marx's death, some of his ideas were reinterpreted and restated by Engels, Lenin, and others. The Russian Revolution of 1917 became an important worldwide development and resulted in the emergence of what Russell Jacoby (1971: 121) calls a "bolshevized" Marx. Some critics argue that Marxism was turned into a rigid and simplistic caricature of Marx's thinking in the form of "Soviet-style Marxism" (Marcuse 1961). During the 1960s an interest in Marx re-emerged in the West, and a large number of thinkers began to re-examine Marx. These thinkers — loosely referred to as neo-Marxists — undertook to clarify a Marxian perspective, including the role of the state in capitalist society.

Neo-Marxist Perspectives: Structuralism and Instrumentalism

Neo-Marxist approaches to the role of the state in capitalist society must be considered in the context of the domination of the pluralist approach and the failure of Marx and Soviet-style "Marxism" to develop an adequate theory. It is not surprising, then, that the development of a systematic critique of pluralism and the articulation of a more adequate Marxian approach to the state in capitalist society were among the first projects undertaken by neo-Marxists in the late 1960s and early 1970s.

> The development of neo-Marxist approaches to the role of the state in capitalist society must be considered in the context of the domination of the pluralist approach and the failure of Marx and Soviet-style "Marxism" to develop an adequate theory.

Instrumental Marxism

Among the first systematic neo-Marxist treatments of the state was Ralph Miliband's *The State in Capitalist Society*. One of Miliband's explicit purposes was to show the inadequacies of the pluralist model (Miliband 1973: 6). He first of all points out that a key feature of capitalist society is its class structure, with one class overwhelmingly holding and controlling economic power. Furthermore, the development of large-scale corporations and the continuing concentration and centralization of economic power have made the capitalist class even more powerful — indeed, so powerful that it controls political power and should thus be understood as forming a "ruling elite."

To illustrate capitalist class control of the operation of the state, Miliband breaks the state down into its various components: the elected government, the bureaucracy and administrative apparatus, and the military. He shows that the primary decision-making positions in the major branches of the state are controlled by either representatives of the capitalist class or people sympathetic to the interests of the capitalist class. By "sympathetic" he is referring to how those in command positions in the state generally share lifestyles, networks, and value systems with the capitalist class. These connections result in a tendency for the state to act in the interests of the capitalist class, with most of its actions geared towards facilitating the overall operation of the capitalist system. Miliband rejects arguments about the state being a neutral mediator seeking to establish social policies and priorities for "the nation" in "the national interests." He argues that notions such as the "national interests" are too often really just ideological manipulations of public opinion designed to provide a façade of legitimation for class domination.

Structural Marxism

The French neo-Marxist Nicos Poulantzas also produced a study of the state in capitalist society. In *Political Power and Social Classes*, Poulantzas sought to provide a different type of theoretical approach based on the insights of Marx. For Poulantzas the main task at hand for neo-Marxists was not to criticize pluralism, but rather to provide an alternative theoretical approach.

Poulantzas argued that it is a mistake to simply examine the personnel and personal connections between the capitalist class and the state. What really matters is the role and function of the state in the capitalist mode of production, not the particular individuals who staff the state. Since the central characteristic of the capitalist mode of production is its division into classes with fundamentally conflicting interests, concerns, and unequal structural positions, some means of alleviating class conflict must be developed if this system is to survive. According to Poulantzas the state is the institution that functions to stabilize the whole system: "The state is precisely the factor of cohesion of a social formation and the factor of reproduction of the conditions of production of a system" (Poulantzas 1972: 246).

Poulantzas' theory is a form of Marxian functionalism; that is, a study of the state in terms of its functions. Yet, his approach fundamentally differs from North American structural functionalists and pluralists and is captured in the question "In whose interests are social functions performed?" For the structural functionalists the state performs its functions of stabilizing the economy and class conflicts, mediating, and facilitating equilibrium for the entire society, while for Poulantzas, the state functions in the long-term interests of the capitalist class. The capitalist class has the most to gain from the smooth, conflict-free operation of the system. In large part the state is forced to do this because the capitalist class, not the state, controls the economy. An important aspect of this position is the notion that the state can perform these functions only if it has a considerable degree of autonomy from the capitalist class.

In the end, there are not fundamental differences between instrumental and structural Marxism. Poulantzas understood the state largely in terms of the functions it performed for the capitalist class. Miliband also argued that the state in capitalist society performs four essential functions: 1) maintaining law and order; 2) establishing and maintaining value consensus; 3) facilitating economic stability; and 4) advancing a nation's interests in the international arena (Miliband 1977: 90). The essence of the argument is that, in acting to preserve the total system, the state is also acting in the interests of the class that benefits most from the maintenance of the status quo.

Thus, two elements of a neo-Marxist approach developed. One is commonly referred to as *structuralism* because it directs our attention to an understanding of the structures, role, and functions of the state by examining the overall structures, dynamic, and logic of the capitalist mode of production.

The other Marxist strand looks to more direct connections between the capitalist class and the state. Called *instrumentalism*, it explains how the state operates in the interest of the capitalist class by looking at state personnel: the personal, lifestyle, interactive, and ideological similarities between the capitalist class and those in charge of the state.

Alternative Directions in Neo-Marxist Theory

Among the difficulties with many of the neo-Marxists theories of the state was an inability to facilitate empirical explanation and research. Within the structuralist tradition, the state is assumed to operate in the interests of the capitalist class, and this assumption turned out to be the explanation for the state's role. The instrumentalist approach has difficulty explaining those instances when there are no immediate or direct connections between the state and the capitalist class; yet it maintains that the state tends to operate so as to serve the long-term interests of capital. Several scholars (see Block 1977, Skocpol 1980, Szymanski 1978) argue for an alternative approach. Szymanski's approach is illustrative.

In *The Capitalist State and the Politics of Class* (1978) Szymanski offers a critique of the existing approaches while recognizing some of their strengths. He maintains that it is necessary to recognize that in liberal-democratic society the capitalist class does not absolutely control the state — many elected politicians and state bureaucrats come from classes other than the capitalist class. However, the state does tend to act in their interests. Nor, is the state purely controlled by the structural economic power of the capitalist class — the state does enact policies that are economically important to the working class, such as the social safety net. He offers instead an analysis based on the idea that in liberal-democratic society the various classes, groups, and individuals can influence the operation, policies, actions, and decisions of the state through direct and indirect linkages or mechanisms of power.

There are three essential, direct mechanisms of power. First, as the instrumentalists argue, the operation of the state can be directly influenced by having members of the capitalist class in the operational and command positions, that is, running the state. Second, the state can be influenced through the lobbying process. Third, the state can be influenced through the policy-formation process. Because governments and state agencies often rely on advice to make decisions, establishing organizations to offer that advice can be a mode of influencing the state.

In addition there are several indirect linkages between the capitalist class and the state (Szymanski 1978: 24–25). These include the use of ideological power and economic power, and the funding of the electoral processes.

Given that the state and governments operate within a larger ideological environment, it is possible to influence the state by influencing that environment, particularly through the process of public opinion. If the capitalist class can convince the majority of the people that they all share the same interests, then the public as a whole will resist any state actions that run counter to the interests of the capitalist class. As a result, the state's ability to act will be limited or constrained. Ruling classes always attempt to present their interests as the "national interest" or as the "public good," thereby ideologically constraining the actions of the state. Since the capitalist class tends to own and control the major mechanisms of public information and debate — the mass media, think-tanks, and the like — they have the means to develop an ideological consensus.

In terms of economic power, we know that the state and governments are dependent on the existence of a healthy and stable economy. The class that controls economic decision making and planning is in a position to exert major influence on the state because, in the event that the state acts against their interests, they can decide not to invest or to withdraw investment or transfer investments elsewhere. All those types of actions will have a negative impact on employment, prosperity, and indeed the entire social and political systems. The actions and policies of the state are often constrained by the need to maintain "business confidence."

Turning to how the political process is funded, it is important to note, in its simplest terms, the common sense wisdom that "he who is pays the piper, calls the tune." At the political level this means that groups or individuals able to fund political parties and candidates can influence the policies and actions of governments when those parties are in power.

Szymanski (1978) attempts to offer an approach to the state in capitalist society that provides a way of explaining why and how, in specific instances, the state acts in the manner that it does, but he is also concerned about avoiding simplistic instrumentalist or abstract structuralist explanations. He argues that the overwhelming economic power of the capitalist class means that it is most capable of using the various mechanisms of power. In a liberal democracy those mechanisms of power are available to everyone, but because the class structure means that economic resources are unequally allocated, in reality it is the capitalist class that has the overwhelming advantage in influencing the state. There is no doubt in Szymanski's mind that the state in capitalist society operates in the interests of the capitalist class, but the process is complex and contradictory.

Regulation Theory

In other words, the state, like other social phenomena, is indeterminate and contested. Some of the most interesting recent thinking about the state involves an approach commonly referred to as "regulation theory." A central assumption of regulation theory is that the social and economic structures of capitalist society are unstable and incapable of maintaining themselves in the long term without significant transformations and interventions. The theorists argue that regulatory mechanisms form the basis of the transformations and interventions that make it possible for the capitalist system and its concomitant institutional structures and arrangements to survive. As Bob Jessop states, "They all focus on the changing social forms and mechanisms in and through which the capital relation is reproduced despite its inherent economic contradictions and emergent conflictual properties" (1990: 309). Regulation theorists tend to examine both the economic and non-economic processes and structural conditions that allow various forms of capitalism — called "accumulation regimes" — to exist and function despite inherent contradictions and class conflicts. They further assume that no abstract, necessary, or typical systems of regulation work in all or even most capitalist systems. The modes of regulation that characterize a particular society or nation are the outcome of historically specific social, economic, and political conditions (Jessop 1990: 309).

The state is able to provide the required modes or systems of regulatory mechanisms because it is "neither an ideal collective capitalist whose functions are determined... by the imperatives of economic production nor is it a simple parallelogram of pluralist forces" (Jessop 1990: 315). The process of establishing the necessary regulatory system to facilitate capitalism is complex. As Jessop (1990: 315) indicates:

> Securing the conditions for capital accumulation or managing an unstable equilibrium of compromise involves not only a complex array of institutions and policies but also a continuing struggle to build consensus and back it with coercion…. The state itself can be seen as a complex ensemble of institutions, networks, procedures, modes of calculation and norms as well as their associated pattern of strategic conduct.

According to Jessop the overall approach that emerges out of the regulationist perspective offers a useful antidote to the simplistic or economic reductionism arguments, conventional functionalist positions, and approaches that exaggerate the separateness of the state from the political processes that surround economic processes.

In *Power Resource Theory and the Welfare State* Julia O'Connor and Gregg Olsen (1998: 5–6) are such regulationists. They introduce power resource theory as an alternative approach: "Power resources theory emerged… in an attempt to redress some of the problems with existing mainstream and radical accounts of the welfare state" (1998: 6). O'Connor and Olsen explain that in this approach, power is neither widely dispersed nor simply concentrated. They note, rather, that "the balance of power between [the working class and the capitalist class] was fluid, and therefore variable" and that "while [capitalists]… always have the upper hand within a capitalist framework, [the working class] had the potential to access political resources which could increase its power, and thereby allow it to implement social reform and alter distributional inequities to a significant degree." In other words, while capitalists can and do dominate political processes and decisions, other classes have the ability — even if they have less capacity — to organize to press for their (political) interests. The most obvious example is the relative success of the labour movement, over the past 150 years, in lobbying for and obtaining better working condition, health and safety and unionization laws and regulation in Canada. Similarly, in countries where unions are strong, as in Sweden, laws and programs have been put into place that make the lives of working class people much better.

In the same book Walter Korpi (1998: vii) argues that power must be conceptualized as a resource that shifts over time, and that it cannot be readily understood through the study of immediately observable behaviours. As he says: "The power resources approach therefore focuses not only on the direct, but also the indirect consequences of power, indirect consequences mediated through various alternative strategies and actions available to the holders of power resources." According to Korpi, the exercise and distribution of power occur within a variety of institutions such as the market, the polity, and the family. Power relations are dynamic and subject to change, so that the precise configuration and operation of institutions will also change. Like regulation theory, power resource theory draws our attention to the need for historical and empirical research providing insights into the actual mechanisms and modes of exercising power.

Is the Nation-State Still Relevant?

Recently, in the wake of economic globalization, the question of the state's continued relevancy has become central. For example, Thomas Courchene (1996: 45) states: "The Canada that we have come to know and love no longer exists! There is no viable status quo! We have to remake our nation and society in the light of irreversible external forces of globalization and of the knowledge/ information revolution."

Neoconservative and neoliberal politicians, along with elements of the mass media, have also popularized the notion that we are in a global era in which nation-states are impelled to act in a certain direction by the constraints and strictures of a global market. Linda Weiss (1997: 4) summarizes the message of these spokespersons of inevitable and unfettered globalization: "According to this logic, states are now virtually powerless to make real policy choices; transnational markets and footloose corporations have so narrowly constrained policy options that more and more states are being forced to adopt similar fiscal, economic and social policy regimes."

Gary Teeple (2000: 74) sounds a warning about the potential political implications of globalization: "For the state the consequences of economic globalization are above all those of erosion of its functions and redefinition at the international level." He continues:

> Without fear of exaggeration, it can be said that the national state has lost and continues to lose much of its sovereignty, although the degrees of independence vary with the degree of remaining integrity to national economic and military formations. It is not so much that a political state cannot act independently because of the erosion or usurpation of its powers, but that its raison d'être — the existence of a nationally defined capitalist class — has been waning. Taking its place has been the rise of an international capitalist class with global interests. (Teeple 2000: 75)

David Korten's *When Corporations Rule the World* (1995: 54) puts the matter even more starkly: "Corporations have emerged as the dominant governance institutions on the planet." For Korten (1995: 66), the relationship between economic resources and democracy is clear: "In the market, one dollar is one vote, and you get as many votes as you have dollars. No dollar, no vote." Korten (1995: 140) summarizes: "The greater the political power of the corporations and those aligned with them, the less the political power of the people, and the less meaningful democracy becomes."

We find ourselves in an interesting situation: some critics claim that the state has lost virtually all its power, some argue that it is losing power, and others maintain that it is erroneous to place too much emphasis on the new globalization and the apparent attendant loss of national state power. William Tabb warns that it is defeatist for workers to accept that the power of global capitalists is supreme (Tabb 1997: 21). Ellen Meiksins Wood argues that although capitalism is changing, the nation-state remains essential to its continued functioning, arguing, "Capital now needs the state more than ever to sustain maximum profitability in a global market" (Meiksins Wood 1998: 42). Judy Fudge and Harry Glasbeek (1997: 220) make a similar point: "We observe that despite repeated assertions about nation-states being outmoded political units, the very roles that governments of nation-states are asked to play on behalf of the forces that favour the development of a differently structured capitalism — a globalized one — make them a pertinent."

Others argue that we must continue to pay attention to the state. Boyer (1996: 108) points out the limitations of the free market in providing many of the goods required by the majority of the population and concludes: "The state remains the most powerful institution to channel and tame the power of the markets." Janine Brodie (1996b) argues that the state has not lost its relevance and power but, rather, states have adopted radically different policies. Her argument meshes well with Claus Offe, who points out that the state deregulation accompanying globalization is itself a form of state intervention. As Offe (1996: 75) reminds us, "A politics of deregulation, no less than one of regulation, has a character of massive state 'intervention.' For both cases involve a decisive change in the situations and market opportunities brought about by public policy."

> Some critics claim that the state has lost virtually all its power, some argue that it is losing power, and others maintain that it is erroneous to place too much emphasis on the new globalization and the apparent attendant loss of national state power.

B. Mitchell Evans, Stephen McBride, and John Shields (1998) have also argued that it is a mistake to underestimate the continued importance of the nation-state in the global era. To claim that the nation-state is irrelevant or has lost most of its power serves "to mask the active role the state has played in establishing the governance mechanisms and the new state form congruent with [globalization]" (Evans, McBride, and Shields 1998: 18). An obvious example in Canada is the North American Free Trade Agreement. This international treaty has removed many Canadian laws and regulations that maintained national control of our economy giving multinational (mainly U.S.) corporations much more control. Without the state this treaty would not have been enacted and could not be enforced.

David Held added a systematic and thoughtful theoretical treatise on globalization, *Democracy and the Global Order*. Although he maintains that we need to think about new models of global governance, he notes that the nation-state has not become totally irrelevant. "If the global system is marked by significant change, this is perhaps best conceived less as an end of the era of the nation-state and more as a challenge to the era of 'hegemonic states' — a challenge which is as yet far from complete" (Held 1995: 95). Held undertakes the task of examining the consequences and implications of the rise of international and intra-state entities for democratic theory and the state. Here Held is referring to global institutions, such as the World Trade Organization, the International Monetary Fund and the World Bank, all of which have over-ruled laws and regulations in particular nations.

He suggests that we have no choice but to think our way through and around the existence of global structures and relations of power. Such centres and relations of power now exist; it is just that we do not theorize them, control them, understand them, or even realize they exist (Held 1995: 138–39). Held encourages us to begin to think more systematically about how citizens in every part of the world can understand the complex and multidimensional relations of power that characterize the contemporary era. Given that there are many international agencies, institutions, and regulatory regimes that operate to maintain and facilitate the operations of the global market place, but that are outside the control of any nation state, how do citizens of the world start to think about exercising democratic control over these entities? He suggest we start to think about global, or to use his term, cosmopolitan, models of democracy that extend the democratic ethos to these entities and not just to our local or national governance processes.

Moving Beyond Class Politics: Feminism and the State

Thus far we have examined two major analytical approaches to the study of the polity in capitalist society. In the case of the pluralist and structural functionalist approaches, the polity is seen as part of a social decision-making process in which there are no dominant forces, interests, or players who consistently get their way, at least in the long run. According to the various Marxian positions, the state in capitalist society is "connected" to the capitalist class instrumentally, structurally, or through mechanisms of power, and as a result the state tends to function in the interests of that class. As a result of its ability to influence the state, the capitalist class is truly a ruling class, having both economic and political power.

Still, it has been argued that none of these positions is adequate as a basis for understanding the complexities of the role of the state in advanced capitalist society and the state's role in the emergence and unfolding of social issues.

The most important and systematic critique of the analytical and explanatory capacities of the older theoretical approaches has come from scholars and activists associated with various schools of feminist thought. Feminist theoreticians have posed new questions concerning the nature and role of the state, especially as it relates to sex and gender relations, and have found the existing approaches wanting in two related, but different, aspects. First,

> Feminist theoreticians... have shown that the state plays a central role in the subordination of women and the domination of men. This has in turn led to... demands that the existing theoretical frameworks be radically rethought.

convincing arguments, supported by overwhelming evidence, have shown that the state plays a central role in the subordination of women and the domination of men — that is, patriarchy. This evidence has in turn led to the second important development, namely, demands that the existing theoretical frameworks be radically rethought to account for the role of the state in maintaining the dominant patriarchal and heterosexual relations that characterize Western society.

An early work pointing out the state's important role in sex and gender relations is that of Mary McIntosh (1978). McIntosh argues that the state is involved in the oppression of women through its support of the household system, which in capitalist society is intimately linked to the creation of the conditions necessary for the continuing accumulation of wealth and capital. She maintains that the household is the site of the production and reproduction of the essential commodity in the capitalist mode of production, namely labour power. Further, she argues that the state plays a central role in the maintenance of the specific household form, the patriarchal family, in which women produce and reproduce labour power. Thus, in performing one of its main functions of maintaining the conditions necessary for the continuation of the system, the state oppresses women through various measures that serve to maintain the patriarchal family.

Numerous feminist writers have elaborated on these themes. Michèle Barrett (1980) presents a more elaborate account of the oppression of women in which she cautions against explaining the persistence of patterns of male dominance and the patriarchal family solely in terms of economic factors; she argues that we need to consider the role of ideology as well. Varda Burstyn (1985) questions the value of a Marxian concept of class for addressing sex and gender oppression. Indeed, she argues that we need to develop the concept of "gender class" to understand that the oppression of women is not just a matter of women in capitalist society itself, but also part of a larger transhistorical pattern. Burstyn suggests that the state has played a central role in both economic-class domination and gender-class domination because its structures have been dominated by men.

Jane Ursel (1986) develops a somewhat different argument. She advocates an analytical approach, recognizing the importance of both material production and biological reproduction in determining the shape of human society. Ursel argues that the concept of capitalism, understood in Marxian analysis, is useful for understanding the nature of material production in Western society, while the concept of patriarchy is most appropriate for an analysis of reproduction. She notes that the state has played a central role in material production and biological reproduction, serving the interests of those who benefit from the class-based relations of production in capitalist society and the sexual oppression of patriarchal society.

The relationship between the state and sex and gender relations is complex. Norene Pupo examines the rise and role of what we might term "family-related" legislation in Canada, noting its contradictory nature. She writes:

> Through its vast system of laws, regulations, and the institutional structure of the welfare state, the state shapes both personal and social lives. Historically women have both welcomed and resisted the encroachment of the state in the family home. The state at once is regarded as a source of protection and justice and as the basis of inequality. Such contradictions are inherent in a state under capitalism. (Pupo 1988: 229)

She notes that while the actions and policies of the state may appear to be liberating, in the long run they work to reproduce patriarchal relations. An example might be the unintended consequences of some forms of state support paid to women that reinforce the notion that women are essentially consumers who look after the immediate needs of their families.

Jenson and Stroick (1992) provide a similar analysis. Drawing on the experiences of women in France and England, they conclude that it is not possible to make generalized theoretical statements; however, they note: "Beginning with the logic of the capitalist state's location in any conjuncture, and mapping the articulation of power relations such as those of class and gender in the politics of any social formation, it is possible to understand the ways in which the state contributes to the oppression of women" (Jenson and Stroick 1992: 229). They then make a very important point: that within the system there is also "space for resistance" (Jenson and Stroick 1992: 229). The notion that people who are oppressed have opportunities to resist is central.

Similarly, the argument that there are opportunities to use the contradictions in the system in a positive way is developed by Pat and Hugh Armstrong. They (Armstrong and Armstrong 1990: 214) note: "More and more feminists have come to realize that the state is not simply an instrument of class or male rule: that it can indeed work for the benefit of at least some women." They go on to reiterate the idea that the state remains a complex and contradictory phenomenon.

Catharine MacKinnon (1989) focuses on the negative impact that many state actions have for women. MacKinnon (1989: 169) notes: "The state, through law, institutionalizes male power over women through institutionalizing the male point of view in law. Its first state act is to see women from the standpoint of male dominance; its next act is to treat them that way." She concludes: "However autonomous of class the liberal state may appear, it is not autonomous of sex. Male power is systemic. Coercive, legitimized and epistemic, it is the regime" (MacKinnon 1989: 170).

We have barely scratched the surface, but it is crystal clear that there is plenty of evidence illustrating the role of the state in sex and gender oppression. The task of theorizing and understanding the integral connection of sex and gender relations to the polity and the state means that we must break with existing approaches. Such a task is not easy, as Mary O'Brien (1981: 5, 62) notes when she warns against the persistence of, and problems associated with, "malestream" thought and its attendant tendency to reductionism.

These concerns about gender and the state were typically developed during an era when political structures and policies in most Western societies could have been described as liberal-democratic welfare, or otherwise called Keynesian. These political systems and policies involve the provision of a limited set of social policies that provided minimal standards for health care, public education, and workplace regulation, among other things.

Since the 1980s these policies and the state infrastructure to support them have been under incessant attack from the neoliberal right. As a result even the minimal levels of support for vital public services, including health and education, have been steadily eroded. As North America moves more and more to a new order — one that Janine Brodie (1996b) refers to as being driven by "market-based, self-reliant and privatizing ideals" — the position of women and many others who suffer the most egregious forms of oppression in a class-based patriarchal system deteriorates even further. Others (see Brodie 1996a) explore the negative impact of the transformation of the liberal-democratic welfare state into a neoliberal, market-oriented state, which has as its main concern global competition and not the welfare or rights of its citizens.

Carole Pateman provides a key critique of the inherent logic of most political theorizing. Pateman argues that the basic concepts of all Western political discourse and theory are founded on a set of assumptions and arguments that are patriarchal and thus exclusionary for women. In *The Disorder of Women*, Pateman (1989) examines the theory of the polity, showing that the core language, concepts, and discourse assume political actors are men. While she agrees that much Western political theory and thinking about the state are predicated on patriarchal thought, Chantal Mouffe (1997) argues that others err in assuming there is something essentially different about women that provides them with an alternate and presumably more democratic and humane conception of citizenship. Mouffe (1997: 82) explains:

> My own view is quite different. I want to argue that the limitations of the modern conception of citizenship should be remedied, not by making sexual difference politically relevant to its definition, but by constructing a new conception of citizenship where sexual difference would become effectively irrelevant. This, of course, requires a conception of the social agent... as the articulation of an ensemble of subject positions, corresponding to the multiplicity of social relations in which it is inscribed.

Mouffe's last comment means that we need to understand women as complex beings with their sex being only one of many possible markers of their various and complex social positions and statuses. Rather than allocating priority to an individual's sex, as is often the case with women, we should be prepared to indicate that an individual is, say, a union president, a teacher, a social worker, a mechanic, or whatever, and that this individual is from Manitoba and, oh yes, she is a woman. This would be different from the conventional discourse in which we tend to say "a woman president,"" a woman mechanic," etc.

In recent years feminist theory, like every other stream of social theory, has been criticized for adopting overly simplistic approaches to complex social phenomena. Both "postmodernists" and "third wave feminists" have been critical of feminist theory. Leslie Heywood and Jennifer Drake's *Third Wave Agenda* (1997) acknowledges that they are building on the foundation of earlier feminisms, but their intellectual and political project has a distinctly different focus. The new agenda demands a recognition and an incorporation of multiple social, economic, and political voices of women. Patricia Madoo Lengermann and Jill Niebrugge-Brantley (1998: 332–33) explain:

> Third-wave feminism's focal concern is with differences among women.... Third-wave feminism looks critically at the tendency of work done in the 1960s and 1970s to use a generalized, monolithic concept of "woman"... and focuses instead on the factual and theoretical implications of differences among women... [such as] class, race, ethnicity, age, and affectional preference.

Third wave feminists call for an explicit acknowledgement of women's varied lived experiences. Nelson and Robinson (2002: 96) note that "inclusive feminism" is critical of the apparent search by earlier feminists "for the essential experience of generic 'woman.'" Patricia Elliot and Nancy Mandell (1995: 24) refer to the new approach as "postmodern feminism" — emphasizing the need to include the voices and perspectives of "women of color and women from developing countries," as well as "lesbian, disabled and working-class women." Nelson and Robinson (2002: 98) note that postmodern feminists maintain that there is not "a single or even a limited plurality of causes for women's oppression." Indeed Lengermann and Niebrugge-Brantley identify an additional characteristic of third wave feminism: its tendency to maintain that not all suffering is equal. They quote Lourdes Arguelles's argument that there is a "calculus of pain" that is "determined by the intersection of one's individual life of global location, class, race, ethnicity, age, affectional preference, and other dimensions of stratification" (Lengermann and Niebrugge-Brantley 1998: 334). Put simply, the feminism of the 1960s emerged out of the experiences of mainly white, middle/professional class women and reflected their critique of patriarchal capitalism and their needs. Various feminists and streams of feminism argued that social analysis needed to be, ironically, more inclusive and diverse so as to be able to address the multiple forms of oppression confronted, for example, daily by working-class women of colour living in substandard housing in an urban ghetto.

Third wave feminism is only beginning to develop an approach to the study of the polity. Yet, all feminists remind us that political power in patriarchal society will remain complex and contested by multiple voices; however, like most social institutions, the actions, policies and regulations generated by the state will be tainted by the underlying power dynamics of patriarchy. For the student of social problems, the core questions is — can we best understand the patriarchal tendencies of liberal democratic states by employing the insights of liberal feminism or do we require the deeper insights offered by the prisms of Marxian and socialist feminism? Perhaps we need to move beyond analytical capacities of all second wave feminism and embrace the complexities of the modern world by acknowledging the limits of all traditional systematic theory, and engaging with Third Wave feminism's insistence that we pay attention to the nuances and subtleties of the everyday oppression of all women in patriarchy.

The Task for Critical Thinking

So much dramatic change has happened in the world of politics and state structures since the 1990s that at times we are left wondering if past theories of the state have any relevance in an era of market hegemony, global capitalism, U.S. international domination, a so-called war on terror, and virtually countless regional, national, and international conflicts. One response to this intense realignment of forces has been the argument that we have entered a new historical epoch or era characterized by fragmentation, instability, indeterminacy, conflicting and alternate definitions of reality, and even reconsiderations of the very notion of reality (Harvey 1989).

So much has happened in the world of politics and state structures over the past decade and a half that, at times, we are left wondering if the ideas outlined above have any relevance in an era of market hegemony, global capitalism, American international domination, so-called wars on terror, and virtually countless regional, national, and international conflicts.

For those who see the current era as marking the transition from what has been called modernity to a fragmented postmodern era , the theories, arguments, and narratives set forth above are not just irrelevant — they are also dangerous because they provide a false picture of reality as being subject to systematic and coherent analysis, understanding, and perhaps improvement. We need not lapse into such political pessimism and paralysis because whether we understand it or not, and whether it is getting more complicated or not, our lives and the society in which we live still have a material and substantial reality. Further, it remains the task of critical thinkers not only to figure out what is happening in that reality but also to reflect on that reality by using a prism informed by a commitment to social justice. Neil Postman describes what happens when we lack an appropriate theoretical framework for understanding our world:

> It may be said here that when people do not have a satisfactory narrative to generate a sense of purpose or continuity, a kind of psychic disorientation takes hold followed by a frantic search for something to believe in or, probably worse, a resigned conclusion that there is nothing to find. The devil-believers reclaim a fragment of the great narrative of Genesis. The alien-believers ask for deliverance from green-grey creatures whose physics has overcome the speed of light. The deconstructionists keep confusion at bay by writing books in which they tell us that there is nothing to write books about. (Postman 1999: 10)

Although there is no doubt that capitalism and the world it creates have and are changing, the task of the critical thinker remains essentially the same — analyzing and understanding our social, economic, and political world. In *The Condition of Postmodernism*, David Harvey (1989: 12) argues that the seeming chaotic, fragmented, and transitory dimensions of our lives today do not in themselves mean that we have passed into a new postmodern era because capitalism has always been dynamic and changing. Harvey argues that what has changed is the nature of the social and political regulation of capitalism, not the fundamentals of capitalism (1989: 121–23).

In the historical era from the end of the Second World War to the early 1970s, a particular form of capitalism was dominant. This was an era of mass production and mass consumption of consumer goods under the growing international leadership of the United States. Although the twentieth century was punctuated by the national and international horrors of two world wars, the Great Depression, and revolutions in Russia and China, it was an era that saw the emergence of the welfare state as part of an overarching political and class compromise (called "corporatist") in most Western industrial nations. That compromise involved a set of social and political structures through which business/corporations, the labour movement, and the state regulated economic, social, and political affairs more or less to everyone's agreement and benefit. In this post–Second World War social contract, it was accepted that unions would exist and would struggle to improve pay and working conditions. The state would provide a social safety net and use its resources to direct investment and economic activity (especially economic development aid for selected regions and industries) for the benefit of both capitalists and the working class. Business would be free to make most of the nation's economic decisions within these broad constraints. In particular, in key industrial sectors (autos, rubber, steel, for example) owners and managers were given a free hand to introduce technological change and other labour-saving innovations; and workers, through their unions, would get wage increases in line with productivity gains plus inflation. This overall system came to be called "Fordism."

According to Harvey there were, however, contradictions arising from the fact that capitalism, as a class-based system based on the necessity of continual economic growth, is prone to instability. As a result the Fordist accumulation regime began to face a number of interrelated crises. Particularly after World War II, there were growing rivalries within and between capitalist nations, as Japan and Western Europe were rebuilt with new and more efficient technologies. In addition, capitalists, especially big business, found themselves with large amounts of cash and increasingly fewer investment opportunities. Harvey, among others, argues that ongoing investment in profitable ventures is a necessary precondition for sustained economic activity in the capitalist system. Added to these problems were the advancing globalization of business and growing state fiscal deficits.

What emerged after the early 1970s was a new system or mode of economic organization called "flexible accumulation" (see Harvey 1989: ch. 11). According to Harvey, the world was becoming smaller in part because of advances in telecommunications and transportation: this marked the end to Fordism, which was largely centred on particular nation-states. In this new economy significant attention was paid to local markets and smaller-scale production. So-called "flexible" work patterns emerged, characterized by workers frequently changing jobs and moving to different industries and different places over a lifetime. In addition consumption and cultural patterns shifted, becoming more diverse with international foods and other commodities, such as clothing, readily available to western consumers with an attendant shift away from traditional western or northern industrial domination. Flexible accumulation also brought new roles and dynamics to the functions and operation of the nation-state.

Bob Jessop (2003) has systematically addressed the implications of flexible accumulation for the state. He concentrates on the transformation of the Keynesian welfare nation-state into what he calls the "Schumpeterian workfare state" (a term based on the work of Joseph Schumpeter, a contemporary of economist John Maynard Keynes and a critic of Keynes's political and economic ideas). Jessop (2003: 4) summarizes the essential feature of the Keynesian welfare state regime as based on maintaining high levels of consumption, a substantial social welfare, and political support within the confines of national economies such as Canada. He also sees the 1970s as marking the emergence of a series of crises for the Keynesian welfare state system. These crises included growing government deficits, international competition among capitalist economies, increasing regional disparities, and the growing internationalization of capital. In response to these upheavals many governments began to implement a series of neoliberal, pro-market public policies (2003: 5–6), making widespread and deep cuts to a range of social programs, including Medicare, school support, day-care programs, and international aid. All these were designed to reduce government spending and regulation while making the market more dominant in every aspect of our lives.

Whereas Harvey suggested that Fordism had become transformed into the system of flexible accumulation that benefits business competition in a global economy, Jessop sees the Keynesian welfare state system as being transformed into a post-Fordist polity. In other words, a new kind of state more "suited" to flexible global business needs and practices emerged. The key feature of this new political system is a nation-state that loses its central position; many state functions are taken over by non-government or private organizations, and corporations becomes fully internationalized. The end result of this process of "denationalization, destatization and internationalization" (2003: 6) is the movement to the Schumpeterian workfare state (sws):

> The distinctive features of the Schumpeterian workfare state are: a concern to promote innovation and structural competitiveness in the field of economic policy; and a concern to promote flexibility and competitiveness in the field of social policy. Naturally the sws will also express other concerns and perform many other functions typical of capitalist states but it is the combination of these twin concerns, together with their implications for the overall functioning of the state which differentiate it from other capitalist [states]. (Jessop 1993: 10–11)

In the Canadian context the promotion of what Jessop refers to as innovation and structural competitiveness can be seen in a range of government programs and policies, from the direct funding of research in universities to the proliferation of offices devoted to the immediate commercial application of knowledge. State spending on biotechnology, highway infrastructure, and education are all about competitive advantage. Indeed, the Canadian government now maintains a website called "Invest In Canada," which offers a number of reasons as to why investors should consider moving their funds into this country. These include: "Smart Workforce; Leading Economy; Strong Fiscal Policy; NAFTA Advantage; Cost Competitive; Sophisticated Infrastructure; A Great Place to Live; Incentives and Taxes." Absent are references to decent welfare rates and programs aimed at social justice and equity.

A key question remains regarding the extent to which these new approaches to state actions did make the state irrelevant in the face of the social issues plaguing society. Although Jessop argues that some state activities are delegated to the non-government, local, or private realm (ranging across activities as diverse as the use of private police and security companies for neighbourhood patrols to food banks and private donations to foundations providing capital funds to hospitals and schools) and other activities to international agencies (such as the use of private security forces in war zones, the regulation of food quality by international trade agreements, and the prohibitions against expanding the social safety net contained in agreements such as NAFTA), he sees a continuing role for the nation-state. The major role left, according to Jessop (2003: 12), is one already identified by many state theorists: namely the generic function of establishing and maintaining social order, consensus, and cohesion.

As was the case with the Keynesian welfare state, there are, and will be, many variations of the Schumpeterian workfare state found in various nations. These states share a commitment to facilitating capitalist economic interests through policies that assist corporations through investment subsidies for the private sector; continued de-regulation; and efforts to eliminate much, if not all, support for publicly funded health care, education, and other social services. They are opposed to supporting policies associated with the so-called welfare state (policies that assist and enrich the lives of working class people through educational subsidies, Medicare, social assistance, subsidized childcare, and so on).

Perhaps most interesting was the return to active state interventions that the 2008–09 economic collapse brought about. As the housing crisis and the stock market collapse threatened the entire economic order (discussed elsewhere in this volume), western democratic states rushed in with various bailout packages for a variety of sectors of the economy, from the banks and insurance industries to the automotive companies. Although the full impact of these measures is still to be determined, they did result in significant increases to debts and deficits in virtually every western polity — deficits and debts that we will most likely be addressing for the next decade or more. It would seem that the prevalence of neoliberal thinking means that these deficits and debts will be addressed through cuts in government spending and services, and not tax increases, thus giving rise to another decade or more of instability in terms of the provision of social services.

So, how do we understand the role and function of the liberal democratic state in the second decade of the twenty-first century? As the Conservative Government elected in Canada in 2011 goes about "slaying the deficit" and the British Government presses on with a full-scale assault on the remnants of the welfare state, and the U.S. deficit spins ever more out of control, how can all citizens gain a sense that they can have an impact on social policy? The frustrations of many citizens, particularly the youth, seems apparent in the routine protest and violence that accompanies meeting of world leaders and the increasing withdrawal from participation in electoral activity as measure by voter turn-out. The challenge facing all democratic polities is counter-balancing the growing global and domestic inequalities with political structures and processes that allow meaningful participation of all citizens. We face no easy task here, but one that is facilitated by beginning to understand some of the social problems we need to confront.

Politics and Power

How, you might ask, does this litany of theories, arguments, and ideas prepare us to fully understand the various issues addressed throughout this book? What does any of this have to do with welfare systems, poverty, education, health, the media, crime, sexuality, violence against women, and the complexities of racism? Although the various theories of the state and its role differ in many respects, they tend to agree that social issues are political in both the broad and narrow senses of the word. In the broad meaning of political, these issues have to do with power and human relations. In a narrow sense they are political in that they are issues often debated, discussed, and acted upon within political institutions of the state. How you analyze and understand the relationship between the activities of human social agents and the structures and dynamics of the institutions comprising the polity is therefore central to an understanding of these various issues. As you prepare to engage with the various issues taken up in this book, you can begin by asking yourself some fundamental questions about how you understand the workings of power at different levels of individuals, collectivities, and major institutions of the state in capitalist society.

Glossary of Key Terms

Feminism: A complex term used to describe a diverse set of beliefs, political practices, social practices, social movements, and sociological theories predicated on a set of underlying assumptions and principles that recognize the historical subordination and oppression of women. Feminists not only are committed to explaining this phenomenon, but also seek alternative non-oppressive modes of social organization.

Fordism: An economic and political system in which the state would provide a social safety net and use its resources to direct investment and economic activity. But business would make most of the economic decisions, especially in key industrial sectors where they were given a free hand to introduce technological change and other labour-saving innovations. Workers, through their unions, would get wage increases in line with productivity gains plus inflation.

Instrumentalist Marxism: A particular neo-Marxist view, this approach places emphasis on personal and personnel connections between representatives of the capitalist class and the state. Instrumentalists maintain that the capitalist class is able to control and direct the activities of the state because the people operating the state either come directly from the capitalist class or share the values, ideologies, and objectives of the capitalist class.

Liberal feminism: A stream of feminist thought that primarily locates women's inequalities in the dysfunction of the existing social institutions. Liberal feminists argue that sexist ideas and beliefs are a central cause of women's inequalities and that these conditions can be altered through the introduction of non-sexist ideas, values, and norms and intensive resocialization without any major or radical change to the basic institutional orders.

Mechanisms of power: An element of an approach to the state that stresses the need to understand that there is a number of different means that can be employed to influence the state in capitalist society. A liberal-democratic system includes both direct (personnel and personal connections, lobbying, and impacting policy formation) and indirect (using economic power, ideological power, and political funding) mechanisms of power. All classes and individuals are able to use these mechanisms of power; however, the class with overwhelming economic power is better able to exercise them.

Pluralism: Pluralists recognize that individuals will differ in terms of their income, social status, or authority, but liberal-democratic systems prevent these from becoming entrenched social inequalities. Pluralists maintain that democratic electoral systems, an open process of decision making, and group lobbying ensure a democratic decision-making process because all groups and interests in society have a more or less equal opportunity to influence the government through electoral and lobbying activities.

Socialist feminism: A political approach that tends to understand the situation of women in capitalist society in terms of two forms of oppression. Women are part of the historical and overall system of class exploitation of capitalist society; and women are oppressed by the structures and dynamics of patriarchy. Rather than merely arguing that the capitalist relations of class domination and exploitation are at the root of women's oppression, socialist feminists advocate the need to confront and change all forms of patriarchal social organization.

State system/polity: All of the institutions, organizations, and agencies connected with the political processes in societies with formally organized political institutions make up the state system, or polity. In Western liberal democracies the state system or polity includes the formally elected apparatus of government, the appointed officials, the state bureaucracy, the judiciary, police, and military, and national and international agencies.

Structural functionalism: An approach to social analysis that employs an organic analogy. Each component of society is assumed to have certain basic needs that must be met if society is to survive. Each social institution performs a specialized function that contributes to the maintenance of the overall system. Among the functions of the polity are the establishment of social goals, priorities, and objectives and the maintenance of social order.

Structuralist Marxism: A version of neo-Marxist theory that draws on functionalist logic. The state's major role is seen as attempting to prevent the conflicts and contradictions from destroying the capitalist system. It is the needs and logic of the system that determine the role and function of the state and not the connections that state personnel have to the capitalist class.

Third wave feminism: A stream that emphasizes the necessity of recognizing the complexities of women's situations and experiences by rejecting any simple notion of women as a homogeneous category or group. Third wave feminists draw attention to issues of class, race, ethnicity, age, geographic location, national identity, and a host of other differences and divisions that combine to oppress women. Thus, there cannot be a singular, totalizing, or universal feminist theory.

Questions for Discussion

1. Why might the polity or the state system be considered a "special institution"? What is unique about the decisions made in this institution?

2. What are the core tenets of the pluralist understanding of political power? Do these assumptions stand up to critical scrutiny given the inequality of incomes that typically characterize market society?

3. Is the state another dimension of domination in patriarchal domination? Explain your answer.

4. What are the essential differences between a power resource approach and an approach using the notion of mechanisms of power? Are the two compatible? Explain.

5. Can the state or the polity be understood without first understanding sex/gender power relations?

6. Compare and contrast how two different theories or approaches to understanding the state would explain the decline of the welfare state over the past three decades.

Websites of Interest

Social Theory/Popular Culture

Marxists Internet Archive <marxists.org>

Sociology Online

Government, Law and Politics <eserver.org/govt/theory.html>

References

Armstrong, Pat, and Hugh Armstrong. 1990. *Theorizing Women's Work*. Toronto: Garamond Press.

Barrett, Michèle. 1980. *Women's Oppression Today: Problems in Marxist Feminist Analysis*. London: Verso.

Block, Fred. 1977. "The Ruling Class Does Not Rule." *Socialist Register* May–June.

Boyer, Robert. 1996. "State and Market: A New Engagement for the Twenty-First Century." In Robert Boyer and Daniel Drache (eds.), *States against Markets: The Limits of Globalization*. London: Routledge.

Boyer, Robert, and Daniel Drache (eds.). 1996. *States against Markets: The Limits of Globalization*. London: Routledge.

Brodie, Janine (ed.). 1996a. *Women and Canadian Public Policy*. Toronto: Harcourt Brace.

____. 1996b. "New State Forms, New Political Spaces." In Robert Boyer and Daniel Drache (eds.), *States against Markets: The Limits of Globalization*. London: Routledge.

Burstyn, Varda. 1985. "Masculine Domination and the State." In *Women, Class, Family and the State*. Toronto: Garamond.

Courchene, Thomas J. 1996. "Globalization, Free Trade and the Canadian Political Economy." In Raymond-M. Hebert (ed.), *Re(Defining) Canada: A Prospective Look at our Country in the 21st Century*. Winnipeg: Presses Universitaires de Saint-Boniface.

Dahl, Robert. 1967. *Pluralist Democracy in the United States*. Chicago: Rand.

____. 1972. *Democracy in the United States*. Chicago: Rand.

Domhoff, G. William. 1967. *Who Rules America?* Englewood Cliffs, NJ: Prentice-Hall.

Durkheim, Emile. 1933. *The Rules of Sociological Method*. New York: Free Press.

____. 1964. *The Division of Labor in Society*. New York: The Free Press.

Elliot, Patricia, and Nancy Mandell. 1995. "Feminist Theories." In Nancy Mandell (ed.), *Feminist Issues*. Scarborough, Ontario: Prentice-Hall.

Evans, Mitchell B., Stephen McBride, and John Shields. 1998. "National Governance Versus Globalization: Canadian Democracy in Question." *Socialist Studies Bulletin* 54, October–December.

Fudge, Judy, and Harry Glasbeek. 1997. "A Challenge to the Inevitability of Globalization: The Logic of Repositioning the State as the Terrain of Contest." In Jay Drydyk and Peter Penz (eds.), *Global Justice, Global Democracy*. Winnipeg/Halifax: Society for Socialist Studies/Fernwood Publishing.

Harvey, D. 1989. *The Condition of Postmodernity*. Cambridge, MA: Blackwell.

Held, David. 1995. *Democracy and the Global Order: From the Modern State to Cosmopolitan Governance*. Cambridge: Polity Press.

Heywood, Leslie, and Jennifer Drake. 1997. *Third Wave Agenda: Being Feminist, Doing Feminism.* Minneapolis: University of Minnesota Press.

Jacoby, Russell. 1971. "Towards a Critique of Automatic Marxism: The Politics of Philosophy from Lukacs to the Frankfurt School." *Telos* 10 (Winter).

Jenson, Jane, and Sharon M. Stroick. 1992. "Gender and Reproduction, or Babies and the State." In M. Patricia Connelly and Pat Armstrong (eds.), *Feminism in Action.* Toronto: Canadian Scholars Press.

Jessop, Bob. 1990. *State Theory: Putting the Capitalist State in its Place.* University Park, PA: Pennsylvania State University Press.

____. 1993. "Towards a Schumpeterian Workfare State? Preliminary Remarks on Post-Fordist Political." *Studies in Political Economy* 40.

____. 2001 "Capitalism, the Regulation Approach, and Critical Realism." Department of Sociology, Lancaster University, Lancaster LA1 4YN. <comp.lancs.ac.uk/sociology/papers/Jessop-Capitalism-Regulation-Realism.pdf>.

____. 2003 "Narrating the Future of the National Economy and the National State? Remarks on Remapping Regulation and Reinventing Governance." Department of Sociology, Lancaster University, Lancaster LA1 4YN. <comp.lancs.ac.uk/sociology/papers/Jessop-Narrating-the-Future.pdf>.

Korpi, Walter. 1998. "The Iceberg of Power Below the Surface: A Preface to Power Resource Theory." In Julia O'Connor and Greg Olsen (eds.), *Power Resource Theory and the Welfare State.* Toronto: University of Toronto Press.

Korten, David C. 1995. *When Corporations Rule the World.* San Francisco: Berrett-Koehler Publications and Kumarian Press.

Lengermann, Patricia Madoo, and Jill Niebrugge-Brantley 1988. "Contemporary Feminist Theory." In George Ritzer (ed.), *Sociological Theory.* New York: Alfred A. Knopf.

Lindblom, Charles E. 1977. *Politics and Markets.* New York: Basic Books.

MacKinnon, C. 1989. *Toward a Feminist Theory of the State.* Cambridge, MA: Harvard University Press.

Marcuse, Herbert. 1961. *Soviet Marxism.* New York: Vintage.

Marx, Karl. 1972a [1850]. *The Class Struggles in France.* Moscow: International.

____. 1972b [1852]. "The Eighteenth Brumaire of Louis Bonaparte." In Robert Tucker (ed.), *The Marx–Engels Reader.* New York: Norton.

Marx, Karl, and Frederick Engels. 1952 [1848]. *Manifesto of the Communist Party.* New York: International.

____. 1970 [1845]. *The German Ideology.* New York: International.

McIntosh, Mary. 1978. "The State and the Oppression of Women." In Annette Kuhn and Anne Marie Wolpe (eds.), *Feminism and Materialism: Women and Modes of Production.* London: Routledge and Kegan Paul.

Merriam, Charles E. 1964. *Political Power.* New York: Free Press.

Miliband, Ralph. 1973. *The State in Capitalist Society.* London: Quartet.

____. 1977. *Marxism and Politics.* Oxford: Oxford University Press.

Mouffe, Chantal. 1997. *The Return of the Political.* London: Verso.

Nelson, Adie, and Barrie Robinson. 2002. *Gender in Canada.* Second edition. Toronto: Prentice-Hall.

O'Brien, Mary. 1981. *The Politics of Reproduction.* London: Routledge and Kegan Paul.

O'Connor, Julia, and Greg Olsen. 1998. "Understanding the Welfare State: Power Resource Theory and Its Critics." In Julia O'Connor and Greg Olsen (eds.), *Power Resource Theory and the Welfare State: A Critical Approach.* Toronto: University of Toronto Press.

Offe, Claus. 1996. *Modernity and the State, East, West*. Cambridge, MA: MIT Press.

Pateman, Carole. 1989. *The Disorder of Women*. Stanford, CA: Stanford University Press.

Postman, Neil. 1999. *Building a Bridge to the 18th Century*. New York: Alfred Knopf.

Poulantzas, Nicos. 1972. "The Problem of the Capitalist State." In Robin Blackburn (ed.), *Ideology in Social Science*. Glasgow: Fontana Collins.

Pupo, Norene. 1988. "Preserving Patriarchy: Women, the Family and the State." In Nancy Mandell and Ann Duffy (eds.), *Reconstructing the Canadian Family: Feminist Perspectives*. Toronto: Butterworths.

Skocpol, Theda. 1980. "Political Responses to the Capitalist Crisis: Neo-Marxist Theories of the State and the New Deal." *Politics and Society* 10, 2.

Szymanski, Albert. 1978. *The Capitalist State and the Politics of Class*. Cambridge: Winthrop.

Tabb, William. 1997 "Globalization Is *An* Issue, the Power of Capital Is *The* Issue" *Monthly Review* June.

Teeple, Gary. 1995. *Globalization and the Decline of Social Reform*. New Jersey and Toronto: Humanities Press and Garamond Press.

____. 2000. *Globalization and the Decline of Social Reform into the Twenty First Century*, first edition. Toronto: Garamond Press.

Ursel. J. 1986. "The State and the Maintenance of Patriarchy: A Case Study of Family, Labour and Welfare Legislation in Canada." In J. Dickinson and B. Russell (eds.), *Family, Economy and State*. Toronto: Garamond Press.

Weiss, Linda. 1997. "Globalization and the Myth of the Powerless State." *New Left Review* 225, September–October.

Wood, Ellen Meiksins. 1998. "Class Compacts, the Welfare State, and Epochal Shifts." *Monthly Review* 49, 8 (January).

3

Invisibilizing Violence Against Women

Ruth M. Mann

"YOU SHOULD KNOW THIS"

- Canada's Family Violence Initiative (fvi) was established in 1988 with the aim of bringing together federal, provincial-territorial, and community-based agencies to forge understandings and develop resources to address violence and abuse in intimate relationships.
- While self-report surveys identify women and men as roughly equally likely to sustain some form of intimate partner victimization, women are three to six times more likely to report severe and chronic victimization, injury, and fear for their lives.
- Between 1998 to 2008, eight out of ten police-reported intimate partner victims were female, as were 79 percent of spousal homicide victims and 98 percent of victims of forcible confinement and sexual assault perpetrated by an intimate partner.
- fvi factsheets on various aspects of family violence increasingly use gender-neutral language that invisibilizes the gendered risks and consequences of intimate partner violence.
- In March 2011 the fvi dismantled its online Library Reference Collection of almost 12,000 family violence resources, disappearing the body of research and analyses produced by participating fvi agencies since 1988.

Sources: Government of Canada 2010; Brennan 2011; Dauvergne 2009; Mahony 2010; Department of Justice Canada, 2009; Royal Canadian Mounted Police 2007; National Clearinghouse on Family Violence (NCFV) email to author, 25 March 2011.

INTIMATE VIOLENCE AGAINST WOMEN CONTINUES to be a serious problem in Canada. Yet the public and public policy discourse has shifted away from violence against women and gender inequality towards one that nominally prioritizes family, children, and, most recently, elders. As part of this shift, women's issues are being displaced, or as Jane Jenson describes it, "folded in" (2008b: 139), with other policy concerns, resulting in an "invisibilization" (Dobrowolsky 2008) of women's systemically structured vulnerability to abuse and the problem of gender inequality that is at the root of this problem. Or, as Janine Brodie and Isabella Bakker (2008) phrase it, women's issues are being delegitimized, dismantled, and disappeared from Canadian public policy. This is particularly apparent in the federal Family Violence Initiative (FVI), a multi-agency co-ordinating and funding authority established in 1988 to reduce and eliminate violence against women and other aspects of abuse in relationships of intimacy and trust. Since 2006, the FVI has reoriented its sponsored funding and Internet-disseminated resources away from a focus on women's victimization towards a broad degendered concern with violence against intimates. At the same time, it has significantly restricted the resources and the mandate of what has been a key FVI partner, Status of Women Canada (DeKeseredy and Dragiewicz 2007).

This chapter situates recent changes in the focus of FVI activities in relation to the problem of violence against women and in relation to broader changes in Canadian society and Canadian public policy. Drawing on Jane Jenson (2008a: 235–36), it situates the diminishing visibility of violence against women in relation to a broad and fundamental shift in Canada's "citizenship regime," a construct that captures ways the Canadian state allocates responsibilities among state, market, and community sectors, defines rights and duties, affords citizens access to policy arenas and selects voices for inclusion and exclusion in policy considerations.

The Family Violence Initiative

The FVI was launched by the Progressive Conservative government of Brian Mulroney in 1988 with an initial $40 million time-limited investment directed towards the establishment of 200 shelters for abused women and the development of a long-term prevention strategy. From 1997 forward, the Government of Canada has provided an annual budget of $7 million, which is currently distributed among eight of fifteen partnering agencies. These eight agencies channel project funding to an array of governmental and civil society partners that participate in efforts to advance FVI aims at provincial-territorial and local levels. In addition, all fifteen agencies are expected to direct funds from their general operating budgets to FVI activities, and all serve on the FVI steering committee, which "monitors and co-ordinates networking and information sharing" across the fifteen agencies along with a representative of the Privy Council (which serves the prime minister and Cabinet) (Government of Canada 2010: 5).

The mandate of the FVI is to promote public awareness of the risk factors of family violence and the need for public involvement, to strengthen the ability of the criminal justice, health, and housing systems to respond and support data collection, and to research and evaluate efforts to identify effective interventions (Government of Canada 2002, 2004, 2010). Table 3.1 summarizes the FVI activities that are relevant to this mandate. As this table indicates, Public Health Agency of Canada is currently the lead and most heavily funded partner agency, having replaced Health Canada as the lead agency in 2005. As the lead agency, Public Health Agency of Canada hosts the National Clearinghouse on Family Violence (NCFV), which currently operates as a set of webpages that post selected resources on various aspects of the family violence problem. In addition, the Department of Justice hosts a dedicated FVI webpage with links to research reports and other resources. Of the remaining thirteen partner departments, two provide links to one or both of these FVI identified resource lists and nine post their own family-violence-relevant publications or provide links to other FVI partner department resources (see Table 3.1).

Official Evidence on Violence Against Women in Canada

FVI partner Statistics Canada has played a key role in developing and analyzing knowledge on the prevalence and nature of violence against women and other aspects of family violence in Canada. The most recent ten of Statistics Canada's heretofore annual *Profile on Family Violence in Canada* reports (hereafter *Profile* or *Profiles*) are among the twenty-seven resources posted on the NCFV webpage (Resources > Family Violence [general]). Holly Johnson's (2006) assessment of statistical trends on violence against women, published by Statistics Canada

Table 3.1: FVI Partner Departments (Funding as per 2010 Performance Report, April 2004 to March 2008)

	FVI funded $	FVI cited	Link to FVI and/ or partner depart.	Posts/ links FVI resources	Search FVI	Search FV	Search VAW	Search gender equality
Canada Mortgage and Housing Corporation (CMHC)	1,900,000	—	INAC	—	9	143	6	—
Citizenship and Immigration Canada (CIC)	new 2010	6 links buried	DJC-FVI	links to resources	—	29	8	8
Correctional Services of Canada (CSC)	—	2 links logical	DJC-FVI PHAC- NCFV HC RCMP	posts/ links to resources	29	271	47	8
Department of Canadian Heritage (DCH)	460,000	3 links buried	SWC INAC	links to resources	16	117	62	24
Department of Justice Canada (DJC)	1,450,000	FVI host	FVI homepage	posts/ links to resources	344	2.474	252	78
Department of National Defence (ND)	—	—	—	—	—	—	—	—
Health Canada (HC) (*lead role 1988-2004*)	—	3 links logical	PHAC- NCFV	posts/ links to resources	11	48	24	7
Human Resources and Skills Development Canada (HR)	—	—	—	—	3	95	10	134 (not FV relevant)
Indian andNorthern Affairs Canada (INAC)	—	3 links buried	cmhc	—	12	148	11	24
Public Health Agency of Canada (PHAC)	2,140,000	NCFV host	FVI homepage	posts resources	76	312	143	32
Public Safety Canada (PSC)	—	—	—	posts/ links to resources	3	74	8	—
Royal Canadian Mounted Police (RCMP)	450,000	3 links buried	FVI homepage DJC-FVI	posts/ links to resources	1	28	10	5
Service Canada (SC)	—	—	—	—	5	4	5	2
Statistics Canada (StatsCan)	350,000	—	—	posts resources	8	103	45	24
Status of Women Canada (SWC)	250,000	3 links buried	PHAC- NCFV StatsCan	links to resources	5	84	443	88

and commissioned by Status of Women, is located under "Additional resources > Women > Reports and Articles." All thirteen *Profiles* (1998-2009, 2011) and Johnson's (2006) violence against women report are also posted on the Statistics Canada website itself, as are past and current *Juristat* reports relevant to family or intimate violence. Finally, Edward's (forthcoming) assessment of gender and elder abuse, using Statistics Canada data, is listed on the NCFV "What's New" webpage, and is provided on request by NCFV personnel.

Criminalized Violence

As in other national jurisdictions, Canadian crime reports identify men as both the primary perpetrators and the primary victims of assaults and homicides (Kong and AuCoin 2008). Focusing on perpetration, from 1997 to 2007, men represented approximately 80 percent of all persons accused of violent offences and women represented a very small, indeed "negligible" (Kong and AuCoin 2008: 4), proportion of persons accused of the most serious violent offences, namely homicide, attempted murder, and sexual assault.

In the case of intimate partner violence, a subcategory of police-reported violence, women and girls are the primary victims while men and boys remain the primary perpetrators. From 1998 to 2008, more than eight out of ten police-reported victims of physical assault perpetrated by an intimate partner were female, as were 98 percent of intimate partner victims of forcible confinement and sexual assault, 79 percent of victims of spousal homicide, and comparable proportions of victims of attempted homicide at the hands of a spouse or dating partner (83 percent and 71 percent respectively) (Dauvergne 2009; Mahony 2010; Taylor-Butts and Porter, 2011; see also Kong, Johnson, Beattie and Cardillo 2003). In the case of criminal harassment or stalking, 90 percent of spousal related perpetrators were male (Bressan 2008:13). Even in same-sex relationships, violence that comes to the attention of the police is overwhelmingly more likely to be male-perpetrated. In 2008, 10 percent of male intimate partner victims compared to 1 percent of female intimate partner victims were victims of a same-sex spouse or dating partner (Mahony 2010: 12).

The 2011 *Profile* does not provide a breakdown of perpetrators by gender for family-related violence and homicide against children — a probable consequence of decreased funding for analysis allocated to Statistics Canada (Ditchburn 2010). Instead, much like the updated NCFV and Department of Justice factsheets and overviews, the latest *Profile* contrasts perpetration by "parents," "siblings," and "extended family" with perpetration by non-family members, and ignores in particular how perpetration varies by gender (Sinha 2011a; Taylor-Butts and Porter 2011). This is a notable change from the 2009 Profile, which documents that in 2007 men accounted for 96 percent of all police-reported family-related sexual assaults against children and 71 percent of all family-related physical assaults against children (Nemr 2009; Ogrodni 2009). The 2009 Profile also reports that from 1997 to 2007, fathers accounted for 54 percent and mothers 32 percent of all family members accused of murdering an infant or child, and men represented an overwhelming majority of other family-related homicide perpetrators (Ogrodnik 2009: 51).

Family-related violence against seniors, the rarest variety of intimate violence (Ogrodnik 2009), is likewise overwhelmingly male perpetrated at nearly 80 percent (Edwards, forthcoming: 17). Unfortunately, as in the case of family-related violence against children, the most recent *Profile* neglects to provide a gender breakdown of perpetration of physical or sexual violence or harassment against seniors (Sinha 2011b). Focusing therefore on homicides, between 1999 and 2009, more than three of every four (77 percent) of female seniors killed by a family member were killed by either a husband or an adult son, while 72 percent of male seniors were killed by an adult son. In the extremely rare phenomenon of spousal homicides involving seniors, female seniors were eight times more likely to be killed by a spouse than were male seniors (41 percent of family-related homicides against female seniors versus 5 percent of family-related homicides against male seniors) (Taylor-Butts and Porter 2011: 37), a gender ratio that is twice as large as for spousal homicides overall (Dauvergne and Turner 2010).

Self-Reported Violence — The General Social Survey

Every five years Statistics Canada measures self-reported experiences of victimization through the General Social Survey (GSS), which, since 1999, has included victimization at the hands of a current or previous married or common-law spouse (Brennan 2011). Findings on spousal violence are generated through a special module that uses a modified version of Murray Straus's Conflict Tactics Scale (CTS) in conjunction with other measures that were developed for the groundbreaking Violence Against Women (VAW) survey in 1993 (Johnson and Sacco 1995). In addition to CTS measures of physical violence, which range from pushes and shoves to assaults with knives and guns and sexual assaults, the spousal victimization module assesses what previous Profiles termed "controlling and emotionally abusive" behaviours (Bunge and Levette 1998; Bunge 2000) or alternately tactics of "power and control" (Mihorean 2005). These range from verbal putdowns, name calling, and jealous efforts to limit contacts with friends and family, to threats to harm someone close to the victim, destructions of property, and financial abuse — acts identified as "emotional and financial abuse" in the latest *Profile* (Brennan 2011). Finally, the spousal victimization module assesses consequences that range from injuries and fear to seeking help from friends, family, medical services, community services, and police authorities.

Three GSS findings are important in highlighting the invisibilization process. First, in both victimization data and crime reports, women are overwhelmingly the victims of intimate or family-related criminal harassment and stalking (AuCoin 2005; Bressan 2008). Notably, while analysis of intimate partner stalking perpetration by gender is not yet available from the 2009 GSS, a majority of women who reported intimate stalking or other criminal harassment in the 2004 GSS also reported having experienced physical violence at the hands of a current spouse or ex-spouse over the previous five years (Ogrodnik 2006: 22).

Second, in all three cycles women and men have reported roughly equivalent prevalence rates for experiencing at least one CTS-measured act of spousal violence over the previous five years. In 2009, this was reported by 6.4 percent of female and 6 percent of male GSS respondents respectively. As in previous cycles, however, the most chronic and severe patterns of spousal violence, the most physically and emotionally injurious spousal violence, and spousal violence most associated with fear and efforts to involve police and other formal helping agents was much more likely to be reported by women. As noted above, the most recent Profile does not address how "power and control" is evidenced in GSS findings. Nevertheless, as in previous cycles, forms of emotional abuse that result in the denigration and terrorizing of a current or previous spouse are overwhelmingly male-perpetrated (Brennan 2011, see Chart 1.5: 14). Moreover, as in previous cycles, female victims report dramatically higher rates of injury, fear and help seeking — at ratios ranging from three women to one man to six women to one man, depending on the measure (Brennan 2011: 10–12). Finally, as in previous cycles, respondents who describe spousal violence as having "little effect" remain overwhelmingly male.

Third, while female versus male distributions in victimization and offending have remained more or less stable, the overall prevalence of spousal violence victimization has declined significantly since the 1993 VAW survey, in which 12 percent of female spouses reported one or more acts of violence at the hands of a current or ex-spouse over the previous five years (Brennan 2011; Holly Johnson 2006). By 1999, and in each of the two subsequent GSS cycles, women were reporting progressively lower victimization rates, as have men since 1999. This decline in self-reported victimization is consistent with declines in intimate partner homicides and family-related violence generally — spousal homicides are at a thirty-year low (Ogrodnik 2009). This in turn is consistent with declines in the prevalence and severity of crime and homicide generally (Dauvergne and Turner 2010).

Intersecting Vulnerabilities

Police reports and victimization data confirm that both female gender and same-sex orientation are risk markers for victimization. Sex and gender are not, however, the sole indicators of risk or vulnerability. Police and self-report data show that young people, Aboriginal people and disabled people, including in particular people struggling with drug and alcohol abuse, are also consistently overrepresented as victims of physical and sexual violence, stalking and other criminal harassment at the hands of an intimate partner (AuCoin 2005; Brennan 2011; Bressan 2008; Perreault and Brennan 2010). Importantly, youth, Aboriginal status and substance abuse problems also characterize offender populations — both intimate violence offender populations and offender populations overall (Brzozowski, Taylor-Butts, and Johnson 2006; Mahony 2010). That is, while there are multiple dimensions of vulnerability in intimate partner violence, gender intersects with other risks to produce heightened vulnerabilities for females (H. Johnson 2006). Put simply, while young, Aboriginal, and disabled people in general are more often the victims of violence, it is young, Aboriginal, and disabled women who are most likely to be the victims of intimate partner violence. Only in the case of same-sex intimate partner violence are males more likely than females to be victims, and, with the exception of the statistically very rare case of infanticide, perpetrated almost equally by mothers and fathers (51 percent and 47 percent respectively), in no facet or variety of the larger family violence problem are females equally or more likely to be perpetrators (Ogrodnik 2009: 51).

> Young, Aboriginal, and disabled women are most likely to be the victims of intimate partner violence.

Status of Women and the Evidence

Canada's successes in reducing the prevalence of intimate homicide and the severity of intimate violence is in part attributable to the influence of Status of Women within the FVI prior to 2006. Though never officially feminist, this 1976-founded "women's policy machinery" (Weldon 2002: 149) enabled feminist and feminist-sympathetic individuals and groups across the country to network and strategize to enhance supports for women, conduct research, inform the public, and pressure federal and provincial governments on violence against women and other issues relevant to women's struggle for social, economic, and political equality (see also Mann 2008; Morrow, Hankivsky, and Varcoe 2004; Rankin and Vickers 2001; Shaw and Andrew 2005; Teghtsoonian and Chappell 2008; Walker 1990).

In 2005, the year after FVI leadership was transferred from Health Canada to Public Health Agency of Canada (Government of Canada 2010), Status of Women's extensive collection of research and analysis was folded into Library and Archives Canada, which posts some publications but increasingly refers clients to institutional libraries that house listed but no longer archived texts on a host of policy concerns. However, during the first phase of this research many Status of Women publications were posted on the NCFV Library References Collection. Included were a number of frequently cited and also frequently critiqued reports that unapologetically focus on violence against women and link physical and sexual battering of women to historically constituted structures of gender inequality (e.g., Canadian Panel on Violence Against Women 1993).

Recent Status of Women-produced and -commissioned reports note that abuse takes multiple forms and that multiple risks intersect to foster victimization and offending (e.g., F-P-T Ministries Responsible for the Status of Women

> In recent Status of Women reports, the focus on violence against women and gender inequality is moderated by comments that abuse takes multiple forms and that multiple risks intersect to foster victimization and offending.

2002). This observation draws upon an emergent feminist intersectionality perspective that is displacing earlier versions of violence-against-women analyses in the work of many scholars (see M. Johnson 1995; Mann 2003, 2007; Tutty 1999). Similar to the feminist multifactor ecological model described by Dragiewicz (2011: 83), feminist intersectionality is shaped by theoretical developments and, importantly, by the voices of Aboriginal and other racalized women who testify to the multiple injustices that fuel violence both against women and by women in marginalized communities (e.g., Burgess-Proctor 2006; DeKeseredy and Dragiewicz 2007; Jenson 2008b; MacQuarrie 2005; Nixon and Humphreys 2010; Mann 2007, 2008; Perilla, Frndak and Lillard 2003; Rankin and Vickers 2001; Swan and Snow 2006; Tutty 2006; Weldon 2002).

Intersectionality makes an important contribution to discourse and theory on violence against women and family violence generally. It fosters awareness of the heightened vulnerability of racially and economically marginalized women and men to abuse, including the abuse inherent in a predominantly criminal-justice-focused response to family violence (Minaker and Snider 2006). Unfortunately, the intersectionality construct has been co-opted in recent FVI discourse. This is evidenced in the endorsement of intersectionality on the Status of Women website, which focuses on "issues" and "factors" rather than the systemically anchored structures of inequality which feminist discourse identifies as key to the struggle to eliminate violence against women, on the one hand, and promote equality for women, on the other. The Status of Women website continues to espouse these two goals (SWC homepage, as modified 2011-03-04). However, consistent with the Harper government's imposed "no advocacy" mandate, Status of Women's endorsement of intersectionality directs attention not to impediments to equality but rather to a need to address "issues" and "factors," not "in isolation," but rather in how these come together in the lives of "diverse" categories of women:

> The issues that affect women are as diverse as the circumstances in which they live and can seldom be viewed in isolation. For this reason, Status of Women Canada promotes an awareness of the combined impact, or intersectionality, of a variety of factors in women's lives such as age, place of residence, economic status, level of education, immigration status, and whether they are Aboriginal, among other factors. (SWC "Who We Are" webpage, as modified 2011-03-04)

Anti-Feminist Backlash — The Ascendance of Gender Symmetry

In October 2006, the Harper government officially removed research and advocacy from the Status of Women mandate and closed twelve of the sixteen federal-provincial-territorial offices — offices through which a host of civil society groups had networked to build supports and knowledge on women's issues since the establishment of Status of Women more than three decades ago (Ditchburn 2006; see also DeKeseredy and Dragiewicz 2007). Canadian Heritage Minister Bev Oda, under whose authority Status of Women then operated, justified this effective dismantling and silencing of Status of Women as an end to the practice of separating women from men:

> In October 2006, the Harper government officially removed research and advocacy from the Status of Women mandate and closed twelve of the sixteen federal-provincial-territorial offices.

> We don't need to separate the men from the women in this country…. This government as a whole is responsible to develop policies and programs that address the needs of both men and women. (cited in Canadian Press 2006)

Minister Oda's justification for the Harper government's effective dismantling of Status of Women reflects the ascendant influence of anti-feminist "men's rights" lobbying. This lobbying is documented in press reports on the Harper government's decision to change the funding and mandate of Status of Women, and in scholarship on challenges to feminist-influenced domestic violence policy on both sides of the Canadian and U.S. border (DeKeseredy 1999, 2009; DeKeseredy and Dragiewicz 2007; Dragiewicz 2008, 2010; Girard 2009; Mann 2003, 2005, 2007, 2008; Minaker and Snider 2006). This backlash draws upon a "gender symmetry" analysis and argument that is based almost exclusively on survey evidence generated through various versions of the CTS. In what Straus (2010) estimates are now over 200 studies, CTS-based research indicates that women and men are roughly equally likely to perpetrate one or more act of violence against an intimate partner over a twelve month, five year or lifetime reporting period. As in Canada's GSS, CTS-measured violence ranges from throwing things, shoves, pushes and slaps, to kicking, choking and beating up, to assaults with knives and guns and sexual assaults. As feminist critics have long observed (see review in Mann 2007), CTS-based findings are generated by practices which include, for example, coding a single punch or kick by a female as "severe" violence, and a push that results in a woman falling down the stairs as "minor," while sexual abuse, social isolation, stalking, financial control, and other features of battering lay outside the analysis. While women and men both clearly express or perpetrate acts of violence against intimate partners, these cannot, especially from the perspective of social policy, be conflated. The truly terrorizing battering by males, captured in studies of women's shelter clients and other clinical populations is qualitatively different from the characteristically minor physical explosions of male and female partners captured in social surveys.

However, with increasing insistence, gender symmetry advocates contend that, regardless of the greater rates of physical and emotional injury sustained by women compared to men, CTS-based evidence "proves" that in intimate contexts men are equally or "more" victimized than women. Some gender symmetry advocates even argue that men and women are equally "battered," or in contemporary language "terrorized" and "controlled" (Dutton 2006; Dutton and Nicholls 2005; Dutton and Corvo 2006; Laroche 2005, 2008; Lupri 2004; Straus 2006, 2007, 2009, 2010). Gender symmetry advocates contend, moreover, that feminist-inspired claims that women are the primary victims of abuse are founded in an ideologically rooted denial and suppression of evidence, particularly evidence that psychopathological issues are the principal cause of intimate violence for women and men alike. They further contend that feminism is responsible for a pervasive anti-male bias that allegedly pervades social and criminal justice policy and front-line intervention. Finally, they contend that research confirming gender symmetry is concealed, distorted, and suppressed as a consequence of the influence of feminism — a claim that coincides with the assertion that more than 200 publications "prove" gender symmetry (Straus 2009: 552, 2010: 332).

> Gender symmetry advocates argue that men and women are equally "battered," or in contemporary language "terrorized" and "controlled" [and] that research confirming gender symmetry is concealed, distorted, and suppressed as a consequence of the influence of feminism.

The invisibilization of violence against women in FVI discourse and action that is the primary focus of this chapter must be situated in relation to the increasing vehemence and prominence of this gender symmetry perspective. As documented in the work of Ruth Mann (2005, 2008), April Girard (2009) and others, this perspective has made its way into Canadian policy deliberations at provincial and federal levels, as has also occurred in the United States and other jurisdictions (see for example, Dragiewicz 2008, 2010, 2011). Across these policy forums progressive politicians and representatives of civil society groups concerned with women's equality and freedom from violence have lobbied to maintain a central focus on the problem of violence against women, while conserva-tive politicians and anti-feminist advocates for men have advanced claims that this focus constitutes bias against men. Increasingly, this "men are equally victims" stance is supplanting a focus on women's victimization, as is dem-onstrated in the resources on intimate violence featured on the websites of partnering agencies within the FVI.

> Increasingly, this "men are equally victims" stance is supplanting a focus on women's victimization, evidenced in the resources on intimate violence featured on the websites of partnering agencies within the FVI.

National Clearinghouse on Family Violence — Disseminating Knowledge

Public Health Agency of Canada (PHA) hosts the National Clearinghouse on Family Violence (NCFV), as noted earlier in this chapter. As described on its home webpage, the NCFV is a "one-stop source for information on violence and abuse within the family" that operates on behalf of the fifteen partner departments within the FVI. Its mandate is to collect, develop and disseminate resources on prevention, protection and treatment with the aim of "encouraging Canadian communities to become involved in reducing the occurrence of family violence" (NCFV, About Us). Prior to March 2011 the NCFV housed an online Library Reference Collection of almost 12,000 family violence resources published or commissioned by the NCFV itself, or deemed worthy of inclusion in the NCFV collection (Government of Canada 2010: 24). In March 2011, the NCFV dismantled this collection. Curiously, while some previously housed resources are available through the Library and Archives Canada collection, to which Status of Women Canada refers web visitors, the NCFV website does not inform the public of this resource. Rather, it provides links to webpages that provided a small number of selected resources.[1]

FVI factsheets and overviews of various aspects of family violence produced and commissioned by the Department of Justice, the Royal Canadian Mounted Police (RCMP), and the NCFV itself reflect a reframing of the intimate violence problem that draws on both a co-opted intersectionality perspective and gender symmetry arguments. The result is a discourse that effectively writes women out by folding gender in with other aspects of vulnerability and inequality (Brodie and Bakker 2008; Dobrowolsky 2008; Jenson 2008b).

> National Clearinghouse on Family Violence (NCFV) posted factsheets and overviews reflect a reframing of the intimate violence problem that draws on both a co-opted intersectionality perspective and gender symmetry arguments.

This writing-out and folding-in of women and gender is explicit in an overview of fam-ily violence posted both on the Department of Justice FVI website and on the PHA-NCFV website. As Jenson (2008b) would predict, this text does not exclude women or gender; rather it situates gendered vulnerability to victimization in the context of what is "clear" when analysis moves beyond competing arguments on the salience of social structures and individual pathologies. This is that "regardless of gender" a number of identifiable categories of individuals may be vulnerable to being abused, while "webs of intersecting inequalities" may foster vulnerability. In the list of "people" who may be vulnerable, women come third, or fourth, depending on whether children and youth are counted as one or two categories of people:

Some experts believe that family violence is linked to power imbalances in relation-ships and inequities in our society…. Other experts focus on the socio-psychological characteristics of the individuals involved …. Regardless of the diversity in perspec-tive, it is clear that … people from every walk of life — regardless of gender… may be vulnerable to being abused.

The most vulnerable groups in our society are Aboriginal people, children and youth, women, individuals with low socio-economic status, people with disabilities, visible minorities, immigrants and refugees, gays and lesbians and individuals liv-ing in rural and remote communities. For people in these vulnerable groups, being victimized and abused are linked to the web of intersecting inequalities… that may contribute to abuse. (DJC 2009: 12)

NCFV "Resources" — Women and Men

The NCFV disseminates selected materials on six key aspects of intimate abuse. These six "Resources" webpages contain seemingly unorganized lists of articles, reports, analyses, over-views, factsheets, pamphlets and posters on "Abuse of Older Adults" (12 resources), "Abuse and Neglect of Children" (28 resources), "Child Sexual abuse" (15 resources), "Intimate Partner Abuse Against Women" (20 resources), "Intimate Partner Abuse Against Men" (3 resources), and "Family Violence (generally)" (27 resources). During the first phase of the research for this chapter, three reports were posted under each heading, "Intimate Partner Abuse Against Women" and "Intimate Partner Abuse Against Men" — a rhetorical strategy that indicates an NCFV commitment to frame violence against women and men as equal concerns. When the webpage was updated in March 2011, however, seventeen additional resources were added to the "Intimate Partner Abuse Against Women" set, while the other five resource sets remained unchanged.

The three reports under "Intimate Partner Abuse Against Women" posted in 2009 and remaining at the top of the 2011 update do not engage with the gender symmetry debate. Nor do these three reports explicitly cite intersectionality. Rather each addresses a specific vulnerable population, namely Aboriginal women (NCFV 2008), lesbian women (Chesley, MacAulay and Ristock 1998), and immigrant women (DJC 2006). This focus on special populations is also evident in the seventeen resources added in the March 2011 update. What is noteworthy, however, is that the 2011 update includes a number of texts produced by FVI partner departments or commissioned by the NCFV that ignore women's heightened vulnerability to victimization and/or cite research that challenges or purports to refute it. These texts include pamphlets on dating violence, stalking, and spousal abuse produced by the RCMP (RCMP 2007a, 2007b, 2007c). All of these use gender neutral terms when referring to perpetrators, such as "a partner," "an individual," and "his/her" or "him/her." While the spousal abuse pamphlet acknowledges women's heightened vulnerability to severe violence, it emphasizes that "men are also victims." The pamphlets on dating violence and stalking, in contrast, neglect entirely to address how victimization or perpetration vary by gender.

A NCFV commissioned report on dating violence (Kelly 2006) goes even further in erasing women's disproportionate vulnerability to intimate violence. In addition to citing Straus (2004) and other research that purports to "prove" gender symmetry, it addresses "tests" of Michael Johnson's argument that there are multiple types of intimate partner violence and that the prevalence and consequences of female versus male victimization and perpetration vary according to type, by framing Johnson's argument as empirically challenged and as salient to only the rarest variety or type of intimate violence, so-called "intimate terrorism" (Kelly 2006: 2–3, see also footnote #10). Prominent in their absence are Statistics Canada's reports on dating violence (Mahony 2010), forcible confinement (Dauvergne 2009), and stalking (Perreault and Brennan 2010) — to access these one must go to the Statistics Canada website. Also prominent for their absence are the *Profiles,* where these and other facets of intimate partner abuse are addressed. For the *Profiles,* one must go to either Statistics Canada or to the NCFV webpage "Resources > "Family Violence (general)."

This elision of women is equally evident in the three "Resources" posted on the "Intimate Partner Abuse Against Men" webpage in 2009, which remain unchanged after the 2011 update. These resources consist of a *Directory of Services for Abused Men in Canada* (Government of Canada 2008), a NCFV commissioned report on abuse in gay male relationships (Kirkland 2004), and, most significantly, a NCFV commissioned report on *Intimate Partner Abuse Against Men* (Lupri and Grandin 2004) that uses 1999 GSS findings and other CTS-based research to advance a strong, yet muted, gender symmetry argument (see discussion on an alleged Health Canada enforced muting of this argument in Lupri 2004). Prominent for its absence is Leslie Tutty's (1999) earlier report on *Husband Abuse,* the first NCFV commissioned publication to address intimate abuse against men, denounced by Lupri (2004) and other anti-feminists as biased (see Mann 2008). Tutty reviews findings and arguments advanced in research and lobbying that challenge the prioritization of violence against women in policy initiatives, and concludes that while clearly men may also be abused, assertions by "some Canadian scholars that research is proving men are equally victims" is unsupported, but that more research is needed (23). Currently, this pre-2009 posted text is only available through institutional libraries — listed by Library and Archives Canada. It has, therefore, effectively disappeared from the FVI landscape.

NCFV "Additional Resources"

Focusing on intimate partner abuse against women and men, the "Additional Resources">"Women" webpage posts thirty-eight documents identified as "Research and Reports." Among these documents is Holly Johnson's (2006) analysis of violence against women as evidenced in GSS data. In contrast, the "Additional Resources" > "Men" webpage posts two research reports in English, plus a French version of one of these, authored by Denis Laroche (2005, 2008). The Laroche reports use the same GSS data to document the extent and nature of male victimization.

Holly Johnson's (2006) report frames inequality as a root or principal source of women's vulnerability to spousal and other forms of intimate abuse, but she does not frame this as a polemic. She does, however, preface her analysis of GSS and other indicators of the prevalence and nature of intimate partner abuse with a justification for the gender-specific focus on violence against women. This justification speaks to an emergent de-legitimation of gender in research and policy on intimate abuse in Canada:

> Generic programs meant to address violence against all Canadians risk failing to adequately address women's experiences of violence. Gender-specific data can pinpoint those areas where the need for support services is different for women and men…. Data that are made available by gender demonstrate the specific risk areas for men and women and highlight the need for targeted programs to address violence for each gender…. To achieve true equality, actions must be taken that adjust for the differences in experiences and situations between women and men, and among women, and that correct the systemic nature of inequality. (H. Johnson 2006: 8)

Holly Johnson's (2006) analysis does not address whether and how intimate violence is or is not symmetrical. Nor does she address debates on whether and how motivations differ by gender. Rather, she reports on the ways GSS measures of serious violence, stalking and control fit with other measures, particularly measures of fear, cited forty-nine times (e.g., pp. 13, 27, 30, 32–34). More importantly, in an implicit nod to a feminist version of the intersectionality perspective, Holly Johnson links violence against women to other dimensions of diversity that she argues foster heightened vulnerability for women and men who are "outside the dominant culture" — and calls for action to "correct the systemic nature of inequality":

> Barriers to equality are rooted in long-standing attitudes and traditions not only about women, but also about race, age, sexual orientation, disability, colour, etc. In particular, the life situations of women outside the dominant culture… are quite different from the mainstream. For them, the path to equality has been, and continues to be, even more difficult…. To achieve true equality, actions must be taken that adjust for the differences in experiences and situations between women and men, and among women, and that correct the systemic nature of inequality. (H. Johnson 2006: 8)

Holly Johnson's (2006: 13) main conclusion is that while both the prevalence and severity of intimate violence against women has declined significantly since the 1993 VAW survey, women continue to be the principal victims of the most severe forms of spousal assault, spousal homicide, sexual assault, and stalking, and that the concentration of these most serious forms of intimate violence among marginalized women must be addressed.

In contrast, Denis Laroche (2008) uses GSS data to "reveal" the context and consequences of intimate abuse against men. Using variations of the word "reveal" over sixty times, his major goal is not to document prevalence, consequences, or correlates, but rather to refute the argument that self-report data confirm women are the predominant victims of intimate terrorism and that control is the key motivation for and dynamic of this predominantly male-driven variety of intimate violence. Specifically, Laroche challenges Michael Johnson and Janel

Leone's (2005: 334) "very conservative test" of what they clearly frame as "hypotheses" on how four theoretically distinct varieties of intimate violence vary by gender and how these fit with tactics of power and control assessed in the 2004 GSS:

1) common couple or situational violence: intimate partner violence marked by a single or occasional — rarely physically consequential — push, shove, slap or other act of violence perpetrated in the context of anger and frustration, hypothesised to be more or less equally male- or female-perpetrated;
2) intimate terrorism: intimate partner violence marked by the systemic and instrumental use of violence and associated threats and abuse aimed at or resulting in denigration, control and fear, hypothesised to be primarily male-perpetrated;
3) resistance violence: intimate partner violence marked by violence perpetrated in defence of self or a child in the face of intimate terrorism, hypothesised to be primarily female-perpetrated; and
4) mutual violent control: intimate partner violence marked by violent and controlling acts perpetrated by both partners in a struggle for dominance.

Consistent with other critiques of Michael Johnson's work (e.g., Dutton 2006; Dutton and Corvo 2006; Dutton and Nicholls 2005; Fergusson, Horwood and Ridder 2005a, 2005b; Kelly 2006; Straus 2006), Laroche (2008: 66) contrasts Johnson and Leone's "argument" that intimate terrorism is driven by male control with what he frames as the methodologically and conceptually more validated body of evidence on psychopathology and intimate violence. He concludes that while "gender asymmetry" (Laroche 2008: 102) is unquestionably in evidence for the most severe patterns of intimate violence, especially with respect to consequences, policy needs to attend to "diverse types of psychopathology and personality disorder" rather than gender (Laroche 2008: 103). This is to say, rather than research on "control" and the "patriarchal ideology" (Laroche 2008: 73) alleged to be at its root, policy needs to address the mental health issues that fuel intimate violence regardless of the gender of perpetrators.

> These observations [on psychopathology and personality disorder] empirically contradict Johnson's assertion… that domestic violence is not the result of individual pathology or a mental health problem. (Laroche 2008: 103)

It is important to note that Michael Johnson does not advance the "assertion" that mental health problems are irrelevant to intimate abuse. To the contrary, he directs considerable attention to mental health outcomes of intimate partner victimization. Moreover, from 1995 forward, Michael Johnson has acknowledged that the causes of intimate abuse are multiple, as have other feminist researchers from the mid 1990s forward. What he does emphatically argue, based on Canada's GSS and other feminist influenced research, is that the most serious variety of intimate partner violence is gender-specific, that gendered power and control tactics are at the heart of this truly terrorizing variety of intimate violence, and that social and criminal justice policies need to continue to prioritize reducing the prevalence of violence against women and providing victimized women and their children with protection and support (M. Johnson 2005, 2006; Johnson and Ferraro 2000; Johnson and Leone 2005).

Policy and Governance

The analysis of the FVI advanced in this chapter draws upon theorizing on governance and citizenship as outlined in the works of Mitchell Dean and Jane Jenson. Mitchel Dean (2007) focuses on the importance of politics and therefore the state in late modern democracies. He posits a new authoritarian brand of politics that can be and is mobilized to undo progressive achievements. This is accomplished, Dean argues, through the folding of neoconservative mentalities and values into state agendas — a process that proponents legitimize as essential to safeguard economic, security, and cultural interests. The result is enhanced exclusion and punishment of an expanding contingent of individuals and groups identified as outside the confines of what the state is willing to recognize as responsible, self-supporting, and self-regulating citizenship. Jane Jenson (1997, 2008a, 2008b) outlines mechanisms at play in this process — in particular mechanisms involved in shifts in how responsibilities are allocated and how evidence and the voices making claims on evidence are heard in the development and reform of policy.

Changes in the governance of the FVI described in the three performance reports are consistent with Dean's and Jenson's analyses. Each of the three reports describes the FVI as a collaborative horizontal management strategy aimed at reducing the prevalence of violence and abuse in "relationships of kinship, intimacy, dependency and trust" (Government of Canada, 2002, 2004, 2010). Formally instituted in 1997, the original intent of horizontal management was "to ensure a shared federal perspective, foster collaboration, create partnerships and provide opportunities for joint action" (Government of Canada 2002: ii). By 2004 horizontal management had become an "evolving management approach" that aimed to "ensure a shared federal perspective," "prevent duplication," and "offer opportunities for joint action and partnership" (2004: 2), a rhetorical shift that reflects the ascendant influence of neoliberal or market mentalities under the Liberal governments of Jean Chrétien and Paul Martin. Under the Harper Conservatives, horizontal management was again reconstituted. As described in the 2010 report, horizontal management had become a strategy to "ensure a strategic focus and guard against overlap and duplication of effort," ensure "partners continue to focus on addressing the issues and often unique circumstances of specific sub-populations affected by violence," and, as "a key focus," refine "initiative-level performance measurement, reporting and evaluation activity" (2010: 32). Facilitated by the introduction of the Privy Council as a member on the FVI steering committee in 2007 (Government of Canada 2010: 5), horizontal management was reconfigured to situate politics at the head of FVI action. Rhetorically and practically, collaboration between state and civil society actors disappears, except in the delivery of services deemed by the government to not involve advocacy (Canadian Press 2006; DeKeseredy and Dragiewicz 2007; Ditchburn 2006, 2010).

One effect of these changes has been the elision of violence against women from FVI discourse. This action was well underway in 2009, evidenced in the texts selected by the

PHA for posting on NCFV "Resources" and "Additional Resources" webpages. The 2011 updates took this elision of violence against women further. In addition to adding texts to the webpages dedicated to the intimate abuse of women that explicitly challenge arguments that women are the principal victims of intimate partner abuse, the NCFV dismantled their archive that documents this. Importantly, the 2010 performance report boasts that between 2004 and 2008 the NCFV distributed "over 475,000 publications across the country and abroad" (Government of Canada 2010: 24). Rather than formally fold this "immediate expected result" (Government of Canada 2010: 24) of FVI activities into the Library and Archives Canada collection, the Public Health Agency of Canada is opting to treat this rich body of research and analysis as though it never existed. The message seems clear: prior to the election that resulted in Prime Minister Harper winning a "stable, secure Conservative majority" (2011 campaign rhetoric), the government had decided that this "Canadiana collection" (NCFV email to author March 28, 2011) is no longer useful to the purpose of governing family violence, in Canada or internationally.

> The 2011 updates [of NCFV webpages and resources] took this elision of violence against women further. In addition to adding texts to the webpages dedicated to the intimate abuse of women that explicitly challenge arguments that women are the principal victims of intimate partner abuse, the NCFV dismantled their archive that documents this.

Prior to the coming into power of the Harper government, gender symmetry arguments had already entered into FVI discourse (e.g., Lupri and Grandin 2004; Tutty 1999). This accelerated subsequent to changes to the mandate and funding of Status of Women in 2006, which was followed by the addition of the Privy Council to the FVI steering committee. Under the surveillance of the prime minister and Cabinet, partner departments began updating factsheets and overviews to reflect a degendered discourse that ignores or challenges research produced and analyzed by key FVI expert Statistics Canada. At the same time, Statistics Canada began removing gender from among the factors routinely addressed in analyses of child and elder abuse (Sinha 2011a, 2011b; Taylor-Butts and Porter 2011), reducing the extent and depth of gendered analyses of GSS data on spousal violence, and in particular muting discussions on the salience of controlling behaviours as evidenced in measures of emotional and financial abuse (Brennan 2011). Gender analysis is left, therefore, to special reports such as Holly Johnson's soon outdated (2006) analyses of trends in violence against women since 1993, the NCFV-ignored report on dating violence (Mahony 2010), and a 2010 NCFV "What's New" report, produced but still forthcoming, on gender and elder abuse (Edwards forthcoming).

The major voice lost in these developments is that of Status of Women. For decades Status of Women provided moral leadership in a citizenship regime committed to advancing equality and justice for women, and for all oppressed people. However, the feminist intersectionality perspective that Status of Women reports and website commentary endorse has been co-opted, as Jenson (2008b) notes is occurring across jurisdictions.

> The major voice lost in these developments is that of Status of Women, [which] for decades provided moral leadership in a citizenship regime committed to advancing equality and justice for women, and for all oppressed people.

Under the Harper Conservatives, however, women's heightened vulnerability to intimate abuse is not simply folded in with other concerns, it is effectively invisibilized (Dobrowolsky 2008). This erasure of violence against women draws on a self-proclaimed "scientific" body of research and analyses that refuses to consider evidence on the salience of gender to abuse (e.g., Dutton and Corvo 2006; Straus 2006). Misrepresenting and denigrating research that focuses on how motivations and consequences of intimate violence vary by sex, gender symmetry analysts increasingly choose to prioritize psychopathological responses to situations and experiences identified as too "rare" (Kelly 2006) to serve as a primary focus for family violence policy. They interpret these rare psychopathological responses, moreover, as a refutation of research and policy associated with the "ideology" (e.g., Dutton and Corvo 2006; Laroche 2008; Straus 2006) or indeed the "groupthink" (Dutton and Nicholls 2005) that purportedly underpins research into the salience of gender and other systemically anchored inequalities.

Politics Trumps Evidence

Over the past several decades, feminists have endeavoured to "marshal the evidence" (Nixon and Humphries, 2010) to better account for the ways multiple and intersecting structures, processes, and factors foster women's heightened vulnerability to intimate violence. Status of Women and Statistics Canada have been co-participants in these efforts, exemplified in Holly Johnson's (2006) analysis of GSS data on violence against women. As Jenson (2008a) emphasizes, however, and as recent shifts in FVI discourse demonstrate, it is politics that mediates both what counts as evidence and whether evidence is considered in policy processes (see also Dobrowolsky 2008; Brodie and Bakker 2008). As a Statistics Canada spokesperson stated to the press in relation to the recent elimination of Canada's long-form census and other socially significant surveys, evidence and its analysis are being removed from the domain of state action in the Harper government's "new world order" (Ditchburn 2010). Violence against women is one casualty among many in this development.

Those of us who recognize gender and other inequalities as important evidence-based policy concerns will seek to retain and reinstate not only research and analysis but also supports aimed at what remains the principal family violence problem — male-perpetrated violence against women. Those who see this evidence, analysis, and associated supports as divisive, ideological, and biased will instead welcome the changes to the FVI. Those who see truth in both perspectives will look for something more, or something else. In a democracy, it is a responsibility of citizenship to evaluate policy and the interests that shape what counts as evidence in various policy domains — in the media, in scholarly articles, and, not least, in policy arenas where individuals and groups give testimony on pending legislation and policy, as described in various publications cited in this chapter (e.g., Dragiewicz 2011; Mann 2005, 2008; Girard 2009). Looking to the future, it is incumbent upon us to choose, in Jenson's

> Those of us who recognize gender and other inequalities as important evidence-based policy concerns will seek to retain and reinstate not only research and analysis but also supports aimed at what remains the principal family violence problem — male-perpetrated violence against women.

(1997: 644) words, "what kind of citizens we wish to be" in the "interesting times" that lie ahead for Canada and the world.

Changes in the way the FVI is led, implemented, and monitored, a concurrent delegitimizing and curtailment of research and advocacy, and a resulting invisibilization of violence against women participate in shifts in governance that are determining the kind of society that Canada is and will be. These developments participate in and signal a fundamental shift in how responsibilities among state, market, and community domains are allocated, in how rights and duties are defined, in how citizens are afforded access to legislative and policy arenas, and in how voices are selected for inclusion and exclusion (Jenson, 2008a). In this "new world order" major exclusions are violence against women, gender equality, power and control, feminism, Status of Women, Canada's national storehouse of information on family violence — the NCFV — and predictably, sooner rather than later, the Family Violence Initiative itself.

Glossary of Key Terms

Citizenship regime: A theoretical construct that draws attention to shifts in the ways states allocate responsibilities across sectors, define rights and duties, afford citizens access to legislative and other policy arenas, and select voices for inclusion and exclusion in policy considerations.

Conflict Tactics Scale: Developed by Murray Straus, the CTS is a questionnaire-based survey that measures intimate violence in terms of actions ranging from pushing, shoving, and slaps to beatings and assaults with weapons, perpetrated by and against intimate partners in the course of "spats and fights" that occur "no matter how well a couple gets along." CTS-based research consistently finds that, while women suffer greater injury, women and men perpetrate and instigate violence at equivalent rates.

Family Violence Initiative (FVI): The multi-partner co-ordinating agency established by the Government of Canada in the 1980s to reduce and eliminate violence and abuse in relationships of kinship, dependency, and trust.

Feminism: A social movement that, from the nineteenth century to the present, advocates for full social, legal, political, and all other rights and opportunities of women equal to those of men, including rights to bodily integrity and autonomy.

Gender equality: The goal of ensuring that women and men enjoy equal status, equal rights, and equal opportunities and that this is realized across all levels of family/intimate, educational, occupational, and political life.

Gender symmetry: The contention that men are equally or more victimized than women in relationships marked by intimate partner violence, notwithstanding the greater rates of physical and emotional injury sustained by women compared to men.

General Social Survey: Undertaken by Statistics Canada, the General Social Survey gathers data on social trends in Canadian families. It collects information on conjugal and parental history, family origins, children's home leaving, and fertility intentions as well as work history and other socioeconomic characteristics. Since 1999, it has included victimization at the hands of a current or previous married or common-law spouse.

Intersectionality: A feminist theoretical development shaped by the voices of Aboriginal and other racalized women who testify to the ways multiple injustices associated with gender, race, and class come together to fuel violence both against women and by women in marginalized communities.

Intimate partner violence: Emotional, financial, physical, and sexual violence and abuse perpetrated against a spouse or dating partner in an opposite-sex or same-sex relationship.

Intimate terrorism: Emotional, financial, physical, and sexual violence and abuse aimed at or resulting in control of, or dominance over, a spouse or dating partner; intimate partner violence entailing severe psychological and/or physical injury and fear.

Men's rights: An anti-feminist "backlash" social movement that advocates on behalf of men and fathers with the aim of reasserting male privilege and power in the face of alleged anti-male bias, framed as equal rights for men or justice for men.

Research and advocacy: Activity aimed at developing knowledge and convincing legislative bodies to act on this knowledge to achieve desired social goals, for example, the goal of eliminating violence against women.

Status of Women Canada (swc): The women's policy machinery established by the Government of Canada in the 1970s to monitor and advance women's struggle for full equality in all areas of social life.

Violence against women: Emotional, financial, physical, and sexual violence and abuse perpetrated against women by men in private and public contexts, aimed at or resulting in male dominance across family/intimate, social, economic, and political domains.

Questions for Discussion

1. How does the progressive invisibilization of female victimization in FVI discourses fit with evidence on intimate violence summarized in Statistics Canada reports?

2. Can the disproportionate victimization of women be made fully visible without invisibilizing male victims? How?

3. Does the dismantling of the NCFV Reference Library Collection matter? To whom?

Websites of Interest

Family Violence Initiative <phac-aspc.gc.ca/ncfv-cnivf/initiative-eng.php>

National Clearinghouse on Family Violence <phac-aspc.gc.ca/ncfv-cnivf/index-eng.php>

Department of Justice, Family Violence Initiative <justice.gc.ca/eng/pi/fv-vf/index.html>

Statistics Canada, Family Violence Profile <statcan.gc.ca/bsolc/olc-cel/olc-cel?catno=85-224-X&chropg=1&lang=eng>

Status of Women Canada <swc-cfc.gc.ca/index-eng.html>

Library and Archives Canada <collectionscanada.gc.ca/lac-bac/search-recherche/arch.php?Language=eng>

Note

1. The NCFV archive was "taken down" in late March 2011 (NCFV email to author, 25 March 2011).

References

AuCoin, K. 2005. "Stalking — Criminal Harassment." In K. AuCoin (ed.), *Family Violence in Canada: A Statistical Profile 2005*. Ottawa: Canadian Centre for Justice Statistics.

Brennan, S. 2011. "Self-Reported Spousal Violence, 2009." *Family Violence in Canada: A Statistical Profile*. Ottawa: Statistics Canada.

Bressan, A. 2008. "Spousal Violence in Canada's Provinces and Territories." *Family Violence in Canada: A Statistical Profile 2008*. Ottawa: Statistics Canada.

Brodie J., and I. Bakker. 2008. *Where Are the Women? Gender Equity, Budgets and Canadian Public Policy*. Ottawa: Canadian Centre for Policy Alternatives.

Brzozowski, J.A., A. Taylor-Butts, and S. Johnson. 2006. "Victimization and Offending among the Aboriginal Population in Canada." *Juristat* 26, 3.

Bunge, V.P. 2000. "Spousal Violence." In V.P. Bunge and D. Locke (eds.), *Family Violence in Canada: A Statistical Profile 2000*. Ottawa: Statistics Canada.

Bunge, V.P., and A. Levett. 1998. "Spousal Violence." In *Family Violence in Canada: A Statistical Profile 1998*. Ottawa: Statistics Canada.

Burgess-Proctor, A. 2006. "Intersections of Race, Class, Gender, and Crime: Future Directions for Feminist Criminology." *Feminist Criminology* 1.

Canadian Panel on Violence Against Women. 1993. *Changing the Landscape: Ending the Violence-Achieving Equality*. First edition. Ottawa: Minister of Supply and Services Canada.

Canadian Press. 2006. "Tories Shutting Status of Women Offices." *CBC News Online*, November 30.

Chesley, L., D. MacAulay, and J. Ristock, J. 1998. *Abuse in Lesbian Relationships: Information and Resources*. Public Health Agency of Canada, Catalogue Cat. H72-21/153-1998. <phac-aspc.gc.ca/ncfv-cnivf/pdfs/fem-lesbianabuse.pdf>.

Dauvergne, M. 2009. "Trends in Police-Reported Serious Assault." *Jurista* 29, 4.

Dauvergne, M., and J. Turner. 2010. "Police-Reported Crime Statistics in Canada, 2009." *Juristat* 30, 2.

Dean, M. 2007. *Governing Societies: Political Perspectives on Domestic and International Rule*. New York: McGraw Hill.

DeKeseredy, W.S. 1999. "Tactics of the Antifeminist Backlash against Canadian National Woman Abuse Surveys." *Violence Against Women* 5.

____. 2009. "Canadian Crime Control in the New Millennium: The Influence of Neo-Conservative US Policies and Practices." *Police Practice and Research* 10.

DeKeseredy, W.S., and M. Dragiewicz. 2007. "Understanding the Complexities of Feminist

Perspectives on Woman Abuse: A Commentary on Donald G. Dutton's *Rethinking Domestic Violence." Violence Against Women* 13: 874–84.

Department of Justice Canada. 2006. *Abuse Is Wrong in Any Language.* Ottawa: Department of Justice Canada. <justice.gc.ca/eng/pi/fv-vf/pub/abus/abus_lang/fe-fa/eng-ang.pdf>.

____. 2009. *Family Violence: Department of Justice Canada Overview Paper.* <justice.gc.ca/eng/fv-vf/facts-info/fv-vf/fv-vf.pdf>.

Ditchburn, J. 2006. "Social Conservatives Press Harper Government to Axe Status of Women Canada." *Canadian Press,* August 25. Online.

____. 2010. "Tories Scrap Mandatory Long-Form Census." *Globe and Mail,* June 19. Online.

Dobrowolsky, A. 2008. "Interrogating 'Invisibilization' and 'Instrumentalization': Women and Current Citizenship Trends in Canada." *Citizenship Studies* 12.

Dragiewicz, M. 2008. "Patriarchy Reasserted: Fathers' Rights and Anti-VAWA Activism." *Feminist Criminology* 3.

____. 2010. "A Left Realist Approach to Antifeminist Fathers' Rights Groups." *Crime, Law and Social Chage* 54.

____. 2011. *Equality With a Vengence: Men's Rights Groups, Battered Women, and Antifeminist Backlash.* Boston: Northeastern University Press

Dutton, D.G. 2006. "A Briefer Reply to Johnson: Re-Affirming the Necessity of a Gender-Neutral Approach to Custody Evaluations." *Journal of Child Custody: Research, Issues and Practices* 3.

Dutton, D.G., and K. Corvo. 2006. "Transforming a Flawed Policy: A Call to Revive Psychology and Science in Domestic Violence Research and Practice." *Aggression and Violent Behavior* 11.

Dutton, D.G., and T.L. Nicholls. 2005. "The Gender Paradigm in Domestic Violence Research and Theory: Part 1 — The Conflict of Theory and Data." *Aggression and Violent Behavior* 10.

Edwards, P. Forthcoming. *Elder Abuse in Canada: A Gender-Based Analysis.* Ottawa, ON: Public Health Agency of Canada.

Federal/Provincial/Territorial Ministries Responsible for the Status of Women. 2002. *Assessing Violence Against Women: A Statistical Profile.* Status of Women Canada. At 'orphaned' SWC website <swc-cfc.gc.ca/pubs/0662331664/200212_0662331664_e.pdf>.

Fergusson, D.M., L.J. Horwood, and E.M. Ridder. 2005. "Rejoinder." *Journal of Marriage and Family* 67.

____. 2005. "Partner Violence and Mental Health Outcomes in a New Zealand Birth Cohort." *Journal of Marriage and the Family* 67.

Girard, A.L. 2009. "Backlash or Equality? The Influence of Men's and Women's Rights Discourses on Domestic Violence Legislation in Ontario." *Violence Against Women* 15.

Government of Canada. 2002. *The Family Violence Initiative: Year Five Report 2002.* <phac-aspc.gc.ca/ncfv-cnivf/pdfs/fv-fiveyear-report_e.pdf>.

____. 2004. *The Family Violence Initiative Performance Report 2002–2003 and 2003–2004.* <phac-aspc.gc.ca/ncfv-cnivf/pdfs/fv-2004-FVI-eng.pdf>.

____. 2008. *Directory of Services for Abused Men in Canada.* National Clearinghouse on Family Violence, Catelogue # HP20-8/2008. <phac-aspc.gc.ca/ncfv-cnivf/pdfs/male-dir-services-progs_e.pdf>.

____. 2010. *Family Violence Intiative Performance Report for April 2004 to March 2008.* <phac-aspc.gc.ca/ncfv-cnivf/pdfs/fvi-perf-rprt-eng.pdf>.

Jenson, J. 1997. "Fated to Live in Interesting Times: Canada's Changing Citizenship Regimes." *Canadian Journal of Political Science* 30: 627.

____. 2008a. "Getting to Sewers and Sanitation: Doing Public Health within Nineteenth-Century Britain's Citizenship Regimes." *Politics and Society* 36.

____. 2008b. "Writing Women Out, Folding Gender In: The European Union 'Modernises' Social Policy." *Social Politics* 15.

Johnson, H. 2006. *Measuring Violence Against Women: Statistical Trends 2006*. Statistics Canada. <dsp-psd.pwgsc.gc.ca/Collection/Statcan/85-570-X/85-570-XIE2006001.pdf>.

Johnson, H., and V.F. Sacco. 1995. "Researching Violence Against Women: Statistics Canada's National Survey." *Canadian Journal of Criminology. Special Issue: Focus on the Violence Against Women Survey* 37.

Johnson, M.P. 1995. "Patriarchal Terrorism and Common Couple Violence: Two Forms of Violence Against Women." *Journal of Marriage and the Family* 57.

____. 2005. "Domestic Violence: It's Not About Gender. Or Is It?" *Journal of Marriage and the Family* 67.

____. 2006. "Conflict and Control: Gender Symmetry and Asymmetry in Domestic Violence." *Violence Against Women* 12.

Johnson, M.P., and K.J. Ferraro. 2000. "Research on Domestic Violence in the 1990s: Making Distinctions." *Journal of Marriage and the Family* 62.

Johnson, M.P., and J.M. Leone. 2005. "The Differential Effects of Intimate Terrorism and Situational Couple Violence: Findings From the National Violence Against Women Survey." *Journal of Family Issues* 26.

Kelly, K.D. 2006. *Violence in Dating Relatoinships*. National Clearinghouse on Family Violence. <phac-aspc.gc.ca/ncfv-cnivf/pdfs/fem-2006-dat_e.pdf>.

Kirkland, K. 2004. *Abuse in Gay Male Relationships: A Discussion Paper*. National Clearinghouse on Family Violence. <vawnet.org/advanced-search/summary.php?doc_id=938&find_type=web_desc_GC>.

Kong, R., and K. AuCoin. 2008. "Female Offenders in Canada." *Juristat* 28, 1.

Kong, R., H. Johnson, S. Beattie, and A. Cardillo. 2003. "Sexual Offences in Canada." *Juristat* 23.

Laroche, D. 2005. *Aspects of the Context and Consequences of Domestic Violence-Situational Couple Violence and Intimate Terrorism in Canada in 1999*. Institut de la statistique du Québec. <stat.gouv.qc.ca/publications/conditions/pdf/AspectViolen_an.pdf>.

____. 2008. *Context and Consequences of Domestic Violence Against Men and Women in Canada in 2004*. Institut de la statistique du Québec. <stat.gouv.qc.ca/publications/conditions/pdf2008/ViolenceH_F2004_an.pdf>.

Lupri, E. 2004. "Institutional Resistance to Acknowledging Intimate Male Abuse, Revised." Counter-Roundtable Conference on Domestic Violence Calgary, Alberta, Canada, May 7. <fact.on.ca/Info/dom/lupri05.htm>.

Lupri, E., and E. Grandin. 2004. *Intimate Partner Abuse Against Men*. National Clearinghouse on Family Violence, Catelogue # H72-21/190-2004E. <phac-aspc.gc.ca/ncfv-cnivf/pdfs/fv-intime_e.pdf>.

MacQuarrie, B. 2005. *Voices from the Front Lines*. The Middlesex County Coordinating Committee to End Woman Abuse and the London Coordinating Committee to End Woman Abuse. <crvawc.ca/documents/VoicesfromfrontlinesFinalReport.pdf>.

Mahony, T.H. 2010. "Police-Reported Dating Violence in Canada, 2008." *Juristat* 30, 2.

Mann, R.M. 2003. "Violence Against Women or Family Violence: The 'Problem' of Female Perpetration in Domestic Violence." In L. Samuelson and W. Antony (eds.), *Power and Resistance: Critical Thinking About Canadian Social Issues*. Third edition. Halifax, NS: Fernwood.

____. 2005. "Fathers' Rights, Feminism, and Canadian Divorce Law Reform, 1998–2003." *Studies in Law Politics and Society* 35.

____. 2007. "Intimate Violence in Canada: Policy, Politics, and Research on Gender and Perpetration/Victimization." In W. Antony and L. Samuelson (eds.), *Power and Resistance*. Fourth edition. Halifax: Fernwood Publishing.

____. 2008. "Men's Rights and Feminist Advocacy in Canadian Domestic Violence Policy Arenas: Contexts, Dynamics and Outcomes of Anti-Feminist Backlash." *Feminist Criminology* 3.

Mihorean, K. 2005. "Trends in Self-Reported Spousal Violence." *Family Violence in Canada: A Statistical Profile 2005*. Statistics Canada.

Minaker, J.C., and L. Snider. 2006. "Husband Abuse: Equality with a Vengence." *Canadian Journal of Criminology and Criminal Justice* 48.

Morrow, M., O. Hankivsky, and C. Varcoe. 2004. "Women and Violence: The Effects of Dismantling the Welfare State." *Critical Social Policy* 24.

National Clearinghouse on Family Violence. 2008. *Aboriginal Women and Family Violence*. Public Health Agency of Canada. <phac-aspc.gc.ca/ncfv-cnivf/pdfs/fem-abor_e.pdf>.

Nemr, R. 2009. "Fact Sheet — Police-Reported Family Violence Against Children and Youth." *Family Violence in Canada: A Statistical Profile*. Ottawa: Statistics Canada.

Nixon, J., and C. Humphreys. 2010. "Marshalling the Evidence: Using Intersectionality in the Domestic Violence Frame." *Social Politics* 17.

Ogrodnik, L. 2006. "Spousal Violence and Repeat Police Contact." In L. Ogrodnik (ed.), *Family Violence in Canada: A Statistical Profile 2006*. Statistics Canada.

____. 2009. "Fact Sheet — Family Homicides." In *Family Violence in Canada: A Statistical Profile*. Statistics Canada.

Perilla, J.L., K. Frndak, and D. Lillard. 2003. "A Working Analysis of Women's Use of Violence in the Context of Learning, Opportunity and Choice." *Violence Against Women* 9.

Perreault, S., and S. Brennan. 2010. "Criminal Victimization in Canada, 2009." *Juristat* 30, 2.

Rankin, L.P., and J. Vickers. 2001. *Women's Movements and State Feminism: Integrating Diversity into Public Policy*. Ottawa: Status of Women Canada. <rwmc.uoguelph.ca/cms/documents/88/Rankin_1-68.pdf>.

Royal Canadian Mounted Police. 2007a. *Dating Violence — Say No*. National Clearinghouse on Family Violence. <phac-aspc.gc.ca/ncfv-cnivf/publications/rcmp-grc/fem-crimedatvio-eng.php>.

____. 2007b. *Criminal Harassment: Stalking — It's NOT Love*. National Clearinghouse on Family Violence. <phac-aspc.gc.ca/ncfv-cnivf/publications/rcmp-grc/fem-crimeharas-eng.php>.

____. 2007c. *Spousal and Partner Abuse — It Can Be Stopped*. National Clearinghouse on Family Violence. <rcmp-grc.gc.ca/cp-pc/spouse-epouse-abu-eng.htm>.

Shaw, M., and C. Andrew. 2005. "Engendering Crime Prevention: International Developments and the Canadian Experience." *Canadian Journal of Criminology and Criminal Justice* 47.

Sinha, M. 2011. "Police-Reported Family Violence Against Seniors, 2009." *Family Violence in Canada: A Statistical Profile*. Statistics Canada.

____. 2011. "Police-Reported Family Violence Against Children and Youth, 2009." *Family Violence in Canada: A Statistical Profile*. Statistics Canada.

Straus, M.A. 1999. "The Controversey Over Domestic Volence by Women: A Methodological, Theoretical, and Sociology of Science Analysis." In X.B.Arriaga and S. Oskamp (eds.), *Violence in Intimate Relationships*. Thousand Oaks, CA: Sage.

____. 2004. "Prevalence of Violence against Dating Partners by Male and Female University Students Worldwide." *Violence Against Women* 10.

____. 2006. "Future Research on Gender Symmetry in Physical Assaults on Partners." *Violence Against Women* 12.

____. 2007. "Processes Explaining the Concealment and Distortion of Evidence on Gender Symmetry in Partner Violence." *European Journal on Criminal Policy and Research* 13.

____. 2009. "Why the Overwhelming Evidence on Partner Physical Violence by Women Has Not

Been Perceived and Is Often Denied." *Journal of Aggression* 18.

____. 2010. "Thirty Years of Denying the Evidence on Gender Symmetry in Partner Violence: Implications for Prevention and Treatment." *Partner Abuse* 1.

Swan, S.C., and D.L. Snow. 2006. "The Development of a Theory of Women's Use of Violence in Intimate Relationships." *Violence Against Women* 12.

Taylor-Butts, A., and L. Porter. 2011. "Family-Related Homicides, 2000 to 2009." *Family Violence in Canada: A Statistical Profile.* Ottawa: Statistics Canada.

Teghtsoonian, K., and L. Chappell. 2008. "The Rise and Decline of Women's Policy Machinery in British Columbia and New South Wales: A Cautionary Tale." *International Political Science Review* 29.

Tutty, L. 1999. *Husband Abuse: An Overview of Research and Perspectives.* National Clearinghouse on Family Violence. <phac-aspc.gc.ca/ncfv-cnivf/familyviolence/pdfs/husbandenglish.pdf>.

____. 2006. *Effective Practices in Sheltering Women: Leaving Violence in Intimate Relationships, Phase II Report 2006.* Toronto: YWCA Canada. <ywca.ca/public_eng/advocacy/Shelter/YWCA_ShelterReport_EN.pdf>.

Walker, G.A. 1990. *Family Violence and the Women's Movement.* First edition. Toronto: University of Toronto Press.

Weldon, S.L. 2002. *Protest, Policy, and the Problem of Violence Against Women: A Cross-National Comparison.* Pittsburgh: University of Pittsburgh Press.

4

"Homophobia High"

Sexual and Gender Minority Youth in Canadian Schools

Tracey Peter and Catherine Taylor

YOU SHOULD KNOW THIS

LGBTQ Rights in Canada Timeline
- 1967 - Justice Minister Pierre Elliott Trudeau declares, "There's no place for the state in the bedrooms of the nation."
- 1969 - Consensual sex between two adults of the same sex over the age of twenty-one is decriminalized.
- 1977 - Quebec prohibits discrimination on basis of sexual orientation.
- 1992 - Justice Minister Kim Campbell ends ban on gay and lesbian people in the armed forces.
- 1995 - Supreme Court rules that "sexual orientation" should be read into the list of prohibited grounds of discrimination in the *Charter of Rights and Freedoms*.
- 1996 - Sexual orientation is added to the *Canadian Human Rights Act*.
- 1999 - Supreme Court rules in favour of same sex couples' adoption rights.
- 2005 - Canada legalizes same-sex marriage.
- 2009 - Ontario Ministry of Education requires school districts to implement policies and programming to support LGBTQ-inclusive education.
- 2011 - Transgender rights bill passed by House of Commons and sent to Senate.

IN THE YEARS SINCE IT WAS PROCLAIMED IN 1982, the *Charter of Rights and Freedoms* has come to function as Canada's chief nation-building document in the crucial sense of providing a mechanism for disenfranchised citizens to seek protection from discrimination in the forms of racism, sexism, and other systems of oppression "in and before the law." Because of the Charter, lesbian, gay, and bisexual (LGB) people have been able to use the court system to overturn provincial and federal laws that discriminated against them in areas such as property, hospital visitation, marriage, and adoption rights. Because of this progress on the juridical front, it is often said that discrimination against "gay" people is a thing of the past. (Legislation that would also protect transgender people from discrimination on the grounds of gender identity or gender expression has been approved by the House of Commons and, as of this writing, is before the Senate.) The Charter has been opposed all along by socially conservative groups, who regard it as left-wing social engineering: those same groups still denounce the inclusion of sexual and gender minority people in Charter protections, since they see this as caving in to the "homosexualist agenda." Nevertheless, while activists and social theorists alike are well aware that discrimination persists in the Charter era, and that legal equality does not necessarily translate into social justice or social equality, the Charter has tremendous symbolic value in legitimizing marginalized people, a value that goes beyond its admittedly limited spheres of legal application. Indeed, the symbolic value of the Charter has been so broadly endorsed in Canada that it is now a cornerstone of social studies curricula in which school children and youth across the land learn that Canada has a proud tradition of upholding minority rights and celebrating diversity.

Yet there is still a "disconnect" between official Canadian human rights discourse and the lived experience of sexual and gender minority people, who continue to suffer from discrimination in various spheres of everyday life, both public and private. For example, even the innocuous everyday practice (for heterosexual couples) of holding hands with one's partner is still unsafe for sexual minority couples in the vast majority of public places in Canada, and identifiably transgender people remain at high risk of harassment and assault in the simple act of entering a public washroom. Sexual- and gender-minority Canadians encounter discrimination and disrespect in their families (being evicted, not being allowed to be alone with family children, partners not being welcome at family gatherings); in their religion (being shunned, expelled, required to be celibate); in employment (being denied an interview or advancement within an organization for reasons ostensibly unrelated to sexual or gender identity); and in housing (being denied rental accommodation, being ostracized or harassed by hostile neighbours). They may encounter hostility from homophobic and transphobic restaurant staff, sales clerks, and health care providers who express their disapproval of LGBTQ people in ways ranging from the subtle (being less respectful than with other clients) to the blatant (flat refusal of service).

Admittedly, this grim picture is not universally true of life for all Canadians, nor in all places in Canada. Although most LGBTQ Canadians are resigned to enduring the daily indignity involved in not demonstrating public affection for their partners, many live relatively openly, in stark contrast to the almost unbroken practice of self-concealment in the "closet" of a few decades ago. This is especially true of middle- or professional-class Canadians living in major urban centres who seem conventionally gendered (masculine male or feminine female), are not members of socially conservative groups or faith traditions, are not members of racialized groups — and are not under twenty-one years of age.

In fact, most Canadian youth spend much of their lives in a world seemingly untouched by the legal and social advances of recent decades: the world of school culture. The disconnect between human rights discourse (i.e., legal equality) and lived experience (i.e., social equality) is demonstrated acutely in the high levels of both symbolic violence and direct harassment of all kinds that sexual- and gender-minority youth reported in the "First National Climate Survey on Homophobia in Canadian High Schools."[1] We draw on the findings of this study throughout this chapter. While distinct in ways suggested here (the relatively isolated school culture), the experiences of high school students illustrate, at least in part, the contours of experience for all LBGTQ people in Canada.

What Does LGBTQ Stand For?

LGBTQ is an acronym for "Lesbian, Gay, Bisexual, Trans, Two-Spirit, Queer and Questioning" people and is an umbrella term for all sexual minority (lesbian, gay, bisexual) and gender minority (transgender and transsexual) people. Gender minority ("trans people") includes transgender people, whose gender expression and sense of self do not match mainstream gender conventions for their birth sex, and transsexual people, who seek sex reassignment surgery in order to bring their bodies into alignment with their sense of gender. "T" also stands for "Two Spirit," which is an identity term used by many First Nations LGBTQ people. Some LGBTQ people identify as "queer," often to signify their opposition to what can be seen as an apartheid-like system of sexual and gender categories that oppresses anyone outside the mainstream. "Q" also stands for "Questioning" since high school-aged youth in particular are often just figuring out their own sexual and gender identities. They may feel same-sex attractions, for example, but wonder if they can be heterosexual, or they may think they are gay but realize eventually that they are transgender.

What Is Homophobia?

"Homophobia" denotes a broad spectrum of social-climate indicators of hostility to LGBTQ people, ranging from casual use of pejorative language to aggressive personal attacks. Although a problematic term in some ways, it is a much clearer term than alternatives, such as "heterosexism" and "heteronormativity," since it keeps the focus on active hostility to LGBTQ people rather than broadening the focus to include subtler forms of discrimination (an issue that is also worthy of study and critique). We use the term here not to invoke an individualistic concept denoting an irrational fear of homosexuals, but instead to refer to a sociological concept with an established history of denoting hostility to LGBTQ people. This hostility is the logical and often intended product of social institutions (such as school systems) that are implicated in creating and re-creating relations of inequality (see, for example, Pharr 1988; Murray 2009).

What Is Transphobia?

"Transphobia" refers to discrimination against individuals based on their expressions of gender or gender identity. Many trans people also experience homophobia, when their gender identity is incorrectly associated with homosexuality. The experiences of LGB people (who experience attractions to people of their own sex, and who may or may not be conventional in their gender identity and gender expression) should not be confused with those of trans people (whose gender identity or gender expression does not match societal conventions of their birth sex, and who may or may not experience same-sex attractions).

Where's the Canadian Evidence?

Many advocates and allies have attempted to bring up the issue of homophobia and transphobia in Canada. However, in schools, for example, they have typically been told that generic safe schools policies are sufficient to protect all students; or that homophobic and transphobic bullying is quite rare; or even that it is relatively harmless (e.g., "Kids don't really mean 'homosexual' when they say, 'that's so gay'"). When asked for empirical proof that specific attention to sexual and gender minority bullying is needed, advocates and allies have offered statistics from large scale U.S. (Kosciw, Diaz, and Greytak 2008) and British

(Hunt and Jensen 2007) studies as evidence that LGBTQ youth are more likely to be exposed to symbolic violence and to be directly victimized, as compared to heterosexual youth. For instance, 86.2 percent of LGBTQ students in the 2007 U.S. Climate Survey reported experiencing homophobic harassment, while 66.5 percent indicated that they were harassed because of their gender expression (Kosciw, Diaz, and Greytak 2008).

Despite the breadth of empirical data, these advocates and allies are still often told that "the situation is not as bad in Canada" or are asked, "Where are the Canadian data?" A B.C. study, *Not Yet Equal*, conducted by Elizabeth Saewyc and her colleagues (2007), found that homophobia and transphobia are widespread. For example, the provincial survey found that 61 percent of gay students and 66 percent of lesbian students between grades 7 and 12 reported having been verbally harassed, compared to 29 percent and 37 percent of heterosexual boys and girls, respectively (Saewyc, et al. 2007). Nevertheless, although we can assume that the experiences of students in other parts of Canada would be similar to those in B.C., the United States, and the United Kingdom, we also understand that adults may only see the tip of the iceberg of school culture, that there are differences across provinces as well as countries, and that it is reasonable for Canadian educators to want Canadian evidence on which to base their responses. The study we undertook clearly illustrates the problems and impact of homophobia and transphobia across Canadian schools.

Poststructuralism

It is crucial to social change movements to examine discourse and the language practices because they powerfully structure our sense of self and our social relations. This is the subject of poststructural analysis. Poststructuralists critically question the status of "common sense" and challenge mainstream assumptions (for example, that all teenagers are heterosexual). Put another way, poststructuralist theory offers a way to critically examine how social patterns become constituted, reproduced, and contested — all of which are necessary tools for resistance to oppression and change (Ristock 2002; Weedon 1997).

Within the context of homophobia and transphobia in Canada, poststructuralism is especially useful because it offers a reflexive approach whereby dominant discourses of heteronormativity can be critically analyzed, in order to understand how life experiences are influenced by various social constructions. Heteronormativity is short for "normative sexuality," which refers to the way in which social institutions (especially familial, educational, religious, and legal) overtly or covertly work to reinforce heterosexual standards (Weiss 2001). Included within these dominant standards is the belief that all individuals fall into one of two distinct gender categories: male or female; that sexual attraction is only "normal" when it occurs between two people of opposite genders; and that each gender has certain natural or essential roles and behaviours to which all individuals should conform, depending on which sex they are born into. Those who critique heteronormative discourse argue that it stigmatizes alternative sexualities, or ways of "doing gender," that do not conform to mainstream notions of heterosexuality or masculinity/femininity. Thus, critically investigating heteronormativity enables an exploration of the ways in which homophobia and transphobia become constituted through the power of discourse and language, and how that power can be resisted.

Discourse

The study of discourse primarily stems from Michel Foucault's (1979, 1980, 1981) work. Foucault argued that, as humans, we are in a constant state of incarceration — imprisoned by the practices (including language practices) of modern social systems and institutions, which he calls "discourses." Foucault promoted the study of discourses (instead of focusing strictly on structural inequalities like capitalism and patriarchy) in order to analyze how "regimes of truth" are socially constructed or produced, and attain the status of common sense that structures our lives. Drawing on Foucault's work, Janice Ristock (2002) maintains that critically analyzing discourses is useful because assumptions of what is normative are maintained through categories that include some (i.e., those who are heterosexual) and exclude others (i.e., LGBTQ people). Discourse analysis, then, can describe how who we think we are and how we act are created through an interplay of power and knowledge. As such, we can explore how the social constructions of gender (i.e., masculinity and femininity) and heterosexuality form dominant discourses, which create truth claims and normalize the way all people should act and behave. Thus, dominant discourses provide a working language to which all should conform (as what Foucault called "docile bodies"), thus becoming themselves the "bearers of discourse" by thinking and acting as though they really are what discourse requires them to be.

In Foucault's (1979) analysis, the social regulation of human behaviour through dominant discourses is labelled as "normalized judgement." Normalized judgement refers to a desire to produce conformity through the creation of a homogenous group whereby everyone is encouraged to adopt the same behaviour and enforce it in others. There is, however, an individualizing effect because each person is measured against the dominant discursive norm. This is achieved by measuring an individual against an essential criterion (or ideal type) of appropriate behaviour and then assessing how much of a gap exists between this individual and the desired norm. For LGBTQ people, the outcome of such restrictive boundaries is both the effective regulation of their sexuality through heteronormativity, as well as their own participation in enforcing heteronormativity through sexuality-and-gender policing.

> For high school students, the outcome of such restrictive boundaries is both the effective regulation of their sexuality through heteronormativity and their own participation in enforcing heteronormativity through sexuality-and-gender policing.

The significance of normative discourses can be seen is we examine how social rules are often followed because of the threat of stigma on those who disregard or violate them. For instance, in order to secure normative ideals of heterosexuality or femininity/masculinity, there needs to be individuals who "fall" outside these socially constructed expectations. This is one of the ways that particular gender identity and sexuality are normalized.

Normalizing Gender

Feminist writers, such as Judith Butler (1987, 1990, 1993, 1996) and Denise Riley (1988), question approaches that dichotomize Man and Woman. They argue that the binaries of man/woman, or heterosexual/homosexual reflect universal, static, and ahistorical assumptions where some individuals, women and homosexuals, are oppressively relegated to the subordinate end of the dichotomy. Such dualisms deal strictly with difference and opposition. The problem with the rigid dichotomy within gender is that it depends on a false binary split of femininity and masculinity as opposites that are strictly attached to female and male bodies, respectively. Only through deconstructing such social constructions can the regulative and normative formations of gender identity be exposed.

Especially in the case of gender identity, feminist theory has contested the presumed fundamental assumptions of masculinity and femininity because, like heterosexism, they prohibit the possibility of alternative accounts and experiences. Linda Alcoff (1988), for instance, acknowledges that gender is not a pre-discursive entity. In other words, gender does not exist prior to the ways we think and talk about it. Rather, it is a construction that is logically formalized through a matrix of practices and customs that most people consent to perform. Likewise, for Butler (1990), identity does not precede the performance of one's gender ("doing gender"), which is constituted through the convergence of multiple discourses (those of family, religion, media, and so on) in our lives, where we repeat, perform, and act out our sex. "Doing gender," then, encompasses how males and females "perform" various roles in society. In this regard, if gender is performative rather than a natural function of birth sex, why should all young people be expected to "perform" the feminine female or the masculine male?

Within a performative framework, the ideals inherent in dominant discourses of masculinity and femininity are not suitable to all males and females; as a result, some people learn that they have a range of possibilities. Although it could be argued that most people are more or less comfortable with playing their parts as laid out in heteronormative discourse, it is nevertheless possible to both resist and reproduce norms of masculinity and femininity: such a process creates alternatives or resistant identities and allows for subcultural variations of gender roles or identities.

Normalizing Heterosexuality

In the *History of Sexuality,* Foucault (1981) explores the "truth effects" of sex rather than its "origins." This is a crucial distinction, as the study of "truth effects" is much more interested in the consequences of beliefs being accepted as true than in whether they do in fact correspond to some objective reality. Because sexuality, as we experience it, is so powerfully structured by discourse, it cannot be specifically located or contained within an individual's body; nor is it a natural phenomenon. Rather, sexuality is formed within and informed by social forces. Sexuality, then, is something that is culturally constructed, sustained, and reproduced, through a collection of socially proscribed norms. That does not mean that without discourse there would be no sexual desire (or death, or sunrises); it means, rather, that our experience of sexuality is inseparable from the discourses about sexuality in which our lives are lived, and that the feeling of "naturalness" is itself a product of discourse.

Foucault explains the inseparability of sexuality from discourse by arguing that the Victorian era (mid to late nineteenth century) saw a "proliferation of discourse" around sex in which sexual relations needed to be strictly regulated in order to produce and reproduce docile bodies that served the interests of the new industrial economy and social order.

> Same-sex attractions continue to be stigmatized as deviant, while heterosexuality continues to be maintained in part through the spectacle of the social penalties for failing to conform, which range from fairly trivial to brutal.

Sexuality was no longer seen as the property of just a body. Instead, it became the quintessential representation of self, which influenced the way people talked about sex. This "deployment of sexuality" operated through normalizing techniques, which created — via social discourse — "compulsory heterosexuality" (Rich 1980), which continues to be socially regulated.

As mentioned earlier, even today, years after the repeal of most discriminatory laws against lesbian, gay, and bisexual people, heteronormative categories resonate in various communities, including many high schools. Implicit in heterosexual assumptions are normalcy and naturalness, which thereby construct all other sexualities as abnormal and unnatural. Same-sex attractions continue to be stigmatized as deviant, and heterosexuality continues to be maintained in part through the social penalties for failing to conform, which range from fairly trivial to brutal. Heterosexuality, then, becomes regulated and is regarded as not just the normalized, but the *normal*, form of sexuality.

Power/Knowledge/Resistance

Also central to a poststructuralist framework are power, knowledge, and resistance. Specifically, Foucault (1979, 1980) maintains that a conventional model of power focuses on the repressive state apparatus of law enforcement, overlooking the complex and multi-faceted existence of domination via the knowledge-producing institutions of society — institutions such as religion, psychiatry, and education, which produce knowledge that comes to be accepted as the truth in our society. Foucault (1980) contends that power and knowledge are so implicated in each other that the two are inseparable; hence his use of the term *"pouvoir/savoir"* or "power/knowledge." This is a concept of knowledge seen as having powerful effects on people — a very different idea from the truism that (acquiring) knowledge results in one having power. However, Foucault was not interested in the exercise of juridical power through incarceration or corporal punishment, where there is little or no possibility of resistance, but rather in the kinds of power that are exercised throughout our social relations and that exist without use of brute force. For him, therefore, "where there is power, there is resistance" (1979: 95). Resistance is like power in that it has no life outside the relationship in which it is occurring. Power and resistance are like two sides of a single coin; as a result, only the specifics of power and resistance can be examined in particular contexts, and thus not its generalities. Finally, resistance manifests itself in multiple ways, because it is not a homogeneous, fixed phenomenon.

Such theorizing enables the examination of situations where someone, for example, may feel powerless in one instance (e.g., students among teachers and school administrators) but powerful in another (e.g., the same students participating in homophobic and transphobic bullying). The interrelatedness of power and powerlessness also allows us to conceptualize how people can be in a privileged and an oppressed situation at the same time.

LGBTQ and heterosexual people alike are bound to the dominant sexual discourses that locate them in very different positions in the social-sexual hierarchy — one that subordinates non-heterosexuals. Nevertheless, it is possible to disrupt this control of sexuality and people by engaging in counter-discourses, such as LGBTQ rights, that challenge what is accepted as "real" or "natural." This allows space for "agency," or living out alternatives, where individuals do not behave like docile bodies; they thereby jeopardize the "naturalness" of everyday sexual knowledge and custom, exposing it as a set of oppressive fictions, and thus open up spaces for others to act in ways that dominant discourses otherwise foreclose.

Language

Knowledge is embedded in language, which does not always reflect "reality." Instead, language reproduces a world that is constantly in transition and is never definitive. Language, then, organizes experience. Yet, language is not an expression of unique individuality. Rather, there is an enormous social influence in the construction of an individual's subjectivity. However, that process is neither fixed nor stable. We can conceive of language as a system of "signs." Embedded in each sign is a "signifier" (a sound, text, or image) and a "signified" (the meaning of the signifier). For instance, there is nothing inherent to the term "faggot": rather the meaning of faggot is produced in relation to other signifiers of sexuality, such as "straight," to which meaning is attached, and vice versa (Weedon 1997: 23). Language, then, is a powerful tool of oppressive discourses, particularly for gender and sexuality because it classifies and orders experiences by signifying what is normal (heterosexuality) and, conversely, what is not (homosexuality).

The best way to understand the effects of language is to analyze the discourse systems in which it is used. For example, language like "that's so gay" is pretty much an everyday occurrence, that both draws on and reinforces homophobic and transphobic discourses. When such language is used, normalized discourses of femininity and masculinity as well as compulsory heterosexuality are reinforced because statements like "that's so gay" are usually used as analogous to "that's so stupid," and in so doing reinforce heterosexuality as "not stupid."

These processes of discourse and language play out in everyday life, enforcing heteronormativity, but also producing the counter-discourses of diverse sexuality. Examining the discourses around gender and sexuality show that the "promise" of the Charter has been far from achieved when it comes to gender and sexuality.

Experiences of LGBTQ Youth

To give empirical substance to the general and theoretical discussions above, we discuss the results of a major study of homophobia among students and young people in Canada. We think the case of homophobia in high schools illustrates these general processes of heteronormativity and resistance to it in Canadian society.

A Questionnaire and Its Participants

Our questionnaire,[2] which was hosted on its own website, asked participants a series of questions on their school climate in the past year, with a particular focus on experiences of hostile climate, targeted harassment, impacts, and interventions.[3] In total, 3607 individuals answered the questionnaire. Their social characteristics are broad, representing much of Canada:

- Nearly three-quarters (71 percent) identified as Straight/Heterosexual. A quarter (26 percent) identified as LGB or Q, and 3 percent as Trans.
- Participants were distributed among the regions of Canada (except Quebec): 25 percent were from British Columbia, 24 percent from the Prairie provinces (Alberta, Saskatchewan, and Manitoba), 30 percent from Ontario, 15 percent from the Atlantic provinces (New Brunswick, Nova Scotia, Prince Edward Island, and Newfoundland), and 6 percent from the North (Northwest Territories, Yukon, Nunavut, and Labrador).
- Participants approximately represented the ethnic diversity of Canada, with 66 percent identifying as White/Caucasian, 19 percent as Asian, 6 percent as Aboriginal, 6 percent as mixed ethnicity, and 3 percent as "other."
- Almost half (46 percent) indicated that they lived in a small city or suburban setting, followed by 43 percent from urban areas, and 11 percent from rural environments, First Nation Reserves, or Armed Forces Bases.
- The average age of respondents was 17.4 years with a median age of 17 years.

The Hostile Discourse within Canadian Schools

It appears that, despite any popular conceptions to the contrary, Canadian schools, like Canadian society generally, are an extremely hostile place for LGBTQ students. There is a good deal of symbolic violence in schools and elsewhere — LGBTQ people hear lots of homophobic comments, either directed at them or just voiced generally, all the time. Seventy percent of our students, for example, reported hearing expressions like "that's so gay" every day in school, and only 2 percent commented that they never heard such remarks in school. In addition, almost half (47 percent) of the students reported hearing remarks such as "faggot," "queer," "lezbo," or "dyke" daily in school, while only 6 percent commented that they never heard such remarks in school.

> 70 percent of all participants reported hearing expressions like "that's so gay" every day in school, and only 2 percent of respondents commented that they never heard such remarks in school.

Not surprisingly, those who belong to the LGBTQ groups are more likely to recall the use of the hostile language. For instance, 81 percent of transgender identified students and 76 percent of LGBQ respondents recalled hearing the expression, "that's so gay," daily in school, compared to 68 percent of non-LGBTQ participants,[4,5] In terms of expressions like "faggot," "queer," "lezbo," or "dyke," over half of transgender (54 percent) and LGBQ (53 percent) participants reported hearing such remarks daily, compared to 45 percent of non-LGBTQ students.[6]

Even though the signifier "that's so gay" does not directly mean "homosexual," its signified message implies that something is stupid or worthless. As one student wrote:

> The expression "that's so gay" is extremely commonly used but I've found that, more often than not, people don't use it as a way to verbally bash gay people, just simply as a synonym for "stupid" or "weird" and don't actually have the anti-gay beliefs behind the phrase.

For LGBTQ students, that means hearing a word that goes to the core of their identity used as a synonym for stupid or loser:

Sometimes, people don't even realize what they're saying (that's so gay!). A lot of people don't care, even if they do offend others. Sometimes it is done on purpose to offend. Sometimes people "joke" about it ("Shut up faggot"). Then they laugh and say they were just joking, even though it could have been offensive anyway. Overall, people are becoming more and more negative towards people's sexual nature. Sometimes it is referred to as a joke, but anyone who is LGBTQ could be deeply offended by "joking."

Fun Fact: I've counted myself hearing "that's so gay" and other homophobic terms up to around fifteen times per class. That's up to sixty times a day and usually (depending on the teacher and other students around of course) the language never gets dealt with unless I say something to try and stop it. I have never been a victim of homophobia, but I hear comments like "that's so gay" every single day at my school. Who wants to come out to that negativity?

As in all contexts, language is relational and is a powerful tool of oppression because it structures experience by signifying what is normal and what is not. Since the majority of students in the majority of schools across Canada regularly are subjected to hearing "that's so gay" in their school, the implicit message is that homosexuality is stupid and worthless and that heterosexuality, conversely, is cool and valuable. Such homophobic language practices reinforce heteronormative discourse in which LGBTQ identities are not recognized as acceptable or natural.

Negative gender-related or transphobic comments are very common in our society, as common as homophobic comments. For instance, men and boys who display feminine qualities are often chastised for acting like a woman/girl. Schools clearly illustrate this kind of discursive oppression. "Don't be a girl" is a common phrase directed at boys in high schools. Sexual and gender minority students were somewhat more likely to report hearing transphobic language. More specifically, 79.1 percent of transgender and 69.4 percent of LGBQ students indicated that they frequently (i.e., daily) or sometimes (i.e., weekly) heard comments about boys not acting "masculine" enough, compared to 59.4 percent of non-LGBTQ participants.[7] Similarly, 62.2 percent of transgender and 53 percent of LGBQ respondents reported hearing comments about girls not acting "feminine" enough on a daily or weekly basis, compared to 42.2 percent of non-LGBTQ students.[8] Similarly, the U.S. Gay, Lesbian, Straight Education Network (GLSEN) survey found that 82 percent of transgender students heard remarks about boys not acting "masculine" enough sometimes, often, or frequently, while 77 percent of their transgender participants indicated hearing comments about girls not acting "feminine" enough (Kosciw, Diaz and Greytak 2008). It is not surprising that trans students reported hearing transphobic comments the most frequently, given that they would be the most aware about violations of heteronormativity, as well as dominant discourse that works to uphold the normative structure of gender identity in schools. In addition to trans students being more acutely aware, it is also more likely that such remarks are deliberately made in their presence.

Consequences of Violating Dominant Discourse

There are significant consequences for individuals, whether LGBTQ or heterosexual, who violate the heteronormative rules of dominant sexuality and gender discourse. The contours and variations of these negative consequences are well illustrated by life in high schools. For students, this process occurred in three contexts: in regards to unsafe spaces; more directed forms of violence (i.e., verbal and physical harassment as well as other forms of victimization); and in the impact of such violations.

Unsafe Spaces

There are a variety of spaces in everyday life that are not safe for LGBTQ people; spaces that heterosexual people take for granted as non-threatening — some highly visible and public, some more hidden from view — ranging from restaurants to workplace hallways to elevators and stairwells. We gave students a list of places involved in everyday life at school (i.e., hallways, the cafeteria, classrooms, the library, stairwells/under stairs, the gymnasium, physical education change rooms, the school grounds, washrooms, school buses, and spaces occupied while travelling to and from school) and asked them to identify any that they thought would be unsafe for LGBTQ students. Overall, we found that 52.5 percent of all students identified at least one area at school that was unsafe for LGBTQ individuals. Not surprisingly, there was a positive relationship between sexual orientation/gender identity and how unsafe high school seems for LGBTQ students, with the students most stigmatized in heteronormative discourse being most likely to see school as unsafe for LGBTQ students. For example, 79 percent of transgender and 70 percent of LGBQ participants acknowledged as least one area of their school as being unsafe for LGBTQ students, compared to 47 percent of non-LGBTQ respondents.[9] Moreover, compared to non-LGBTQ students, LGBTQ youth were significantly more likely to see the physical education change room (48.8 versus 30.1 percent), washrooms (43.1 versus 27.8 percent), and hallways (42.5 versus 25.1 percent) as unsafe,[10] which is consistent with the GLSEN study (Kosciw, Diaz, and Greytak 2008). It is interesting to note that two of these spaces are private areas (physical education change rooms and washrooms), while the third (hallways) is a public place. However, these three spaces are largely unsupervised places, which makes them easy sites for student-to-student harassment.

The prevalence of homophobic harassment was highlighted by several students:

> During phys. ed. in grade 9, we could hear the guys in the boys' change rooms making fun of the other boys who weren't as "manly" as they would say, or as muscular as they were. They would call them pansies, fags, butt pirates, queers, anything homophobic... you name it, they most likely called them it.

> I was forced to drop my phys-ed class when my peers decided to not let me in the change rooms. I was forced to skip my wood shop class due to peers threatening me with equipment.

> I've been spit on by students and called a faggot, and each time I was in the hallways and there were like three teachers watching and they didn't do anything.

> I was threatened by a group of eight girls who cornered me in the washroom and demanded that I "shut my mouth, or they will shut it for me."

As is evident in these narratives, prejudice is more likely to occur in some places than others, depending on factors such as opportunity, exposure, presence of potential witnesses, and the type of activity associated with the place (i.e., showering and contact sports).

Directed Violence

The safety of a space is largely determined by the likelihood, or the perception of the likelihood, of encountering some kind of violence. LGBTQ people find many "normally" safe places to be ones in which they often encounter violent behaviour — verbal and physical — directed at them by others. This represents another more direct way that heteronormativity is enforced. In our study, for example, we asked students whether they had been harassed in various ways during the last twelve months. Just over 60 percent (60.2) of transgender students, 46 percent of LGBQ and 8 percent of heterosexual students reported having had rumours or lies spread about their sexual orientation or their perceived sexual orientation at school.[11] Almost two-thirds of transgender (64.4 percent), 49.5 percent of LGBQ, and 8 percent of heterosexual youth were verbally harassed about their sexual orientation or perceived sexual orientation at school.[12] In addition, 74.2 percent of transgender, 55.2 percent of LGBQ, and 25.5 percent of heterosexual identified respondents reported being the targets of verbal harassment because of their gender expression.[13] Tragically, 37.1 percent of transgender, 21.3 percent of LGBQ, and 10.4 percent of heterosexual students indicated that they had been physically harassed or assaulted due to their gender expression, while 25 percent of LGBQ and 20.4 percent of transgender reported they were physically bullied due to their sexual orientation.[14]

These statistics, indicating the high level of directed violence experienced by sexual and gender minority students, take on a more human quality in the narratives of our students:

> I got beat up in grade 10 for dating a girl. The people who jumped us got suspended, but we did also. It wasn't fair, I never asked to get beat up and I surely didn't deserve getting suspended because I got beat up.

> My friend and I both got sent to the hospital — and he's straight, but was just trying to help me. I feel bad that he got hurt, and we don't talk anymore 'cuz afterwards he had to leave the school as well for being labelled a fag for being known as my friend.

> [I don't tell people I'm transgender] because I am worried what most people will think or say to me — I already get teased enough and I don't want to lose friends for being trans.

> It isn't safe. I learned that the hard way at other schools. I had to transfer out of the public school system and my parents now pay tons of cash per year to keep me in a secluded school — and at this new place I don't risk my parents' investment by outing myself.

> I can see why other people wouldn't want to come out here. It's because, quite simply, it's not a safe move. People here are VERY homophobic; to the point of violence/hate mail.

Clearly, there is a high level of victimization (as well as the depression, anxiety, and fear associated with it) endured by LGBTQ students in Canadian schools. It is also important to point out that anywhere between 8 percent and 25 percent of heterosexual-identified students reported experiencing directed violence due to their gender expression or perceived sexual orientation. In a school of 1000 students, where up to 90 percent are heterosexual, this translates to approximately ninety straight youth who are physically harassed or assaulted because they don't live up to the dominant discourses of gender within a school culture (i.e., girls who are not feminine enough or boys who are not masculine enough).

LGBTQ people experience many forms of physical violence up to, and including, murder. This is actually a form of oppression that goes beyond discursive — it is brute force, even if not done by the state. In schools, this brute force most often takes the form of bullying because of one's sexual orientation and shows clearly that gender makes a significant difference to the quality of the lives of sexual minority students. Interestingly, we found that female LGBQ students were more likely to be verbally and physically harassed, compared to male LGBQ participants (59.1 versus 43.3 percent, respectively for verbal harassment and 25.4 versus 17.0 percent for physical assault).[15] In this regard, female LGBQ levels were similar to those of transgender students for most of the directed violence indicators (for example, 59.1 versus 63 percent for verbal harassment). It is sometimes perceived that the school climate (and the climate elsewhere in society) is less targeted at lesbians than at gay males, because society in general is more tolerant of lesbians — being a lesbian or a bisexual female can even be trendy. The lives of our study participants refute these popular conceptions of life for sexual minority girls and women.

> In a school of 1000 students, where up to 90 percent are heterosexual, this translates to approximately ninety straight youth who are physically harassed or assaulted.

Impacts

Not surprisingly, these levels of violence and abuse have dire consequences for LGBTQ people. Harassment, violence, and verbal abuse can only add to the stress levels of the lives of LGBTQ people. They feel emotionally distressed, as well as alienated from the communities they live in. These stresses can lead to serious health consequences and are often causes of suicidal feelings and suicide. Our students illustrate these general trends quite starkly. In terms of emotional distress, we found that 78 percent of transgender and 62.8 percent of LGBQ students felt unsafe at school, compared to 15.2 percent of heterosexual identified participants.[16] Moreover, 57.5 percent of transgender and 55.7 percent of LGBQ respondents indicated that sometimes they felt depressed about school, compared to 28.2 percent of straight students.[17] Two students indicate just how hard it is to be a sexual minority (or to be perceived as one) in Canadian schools:

> Public school is probably one of the worst places to be different. I can't speak from experience, but homosexuals must have it so incredibly hard. To go into school each day knowing that people in those hallways would tear you apart....

> The vice-principal of my school used to be my guidance counsellor. I went to her because I was extremely depressed and wanted to commit suicide. She then found it necessary to point out that she goes to church every Sunday, and that all these things had nothing to do with me wanting to commit suicide.

We also asked students whether or not they ever skipped school because they felt unsafe either at school or on the way to school. Results show that 30.2 percent of sexual and gender minority students, compared to 11 percent of non-LGBTQ respondents, reported skipping because they felt unsafe at school or on the way to school.[18] Transgender participants were even more likely to miss school because they felt unsafe (43.5 versus 28.9 percent for LGBQ respondents).[19] They were also more likely to have skipped more than ten days because they felt unsafe at school (14.6 percent, compared to 4.8 percent of LGBQ and 1.2 percent of non-LGBTQ).[20] Our results are similar to GLSEN reports where 46 percent of transgender students skipped school due to feeling unsafe, and 13 percent indicated that they skipped more than five days (Greytak, Kosciw, and Diaz 2009).

These impacts are important, not only because of what they reveal about the degree of fear sexual and gender minority students experience on a regular basis, but also because of the potential impact missing classes can have on the academic achievement for these students. In short, the experiences of these students do seem to suggest that being on the outside of heteronormative discourse in a school setting where sexuality and gender norms are strictly regulated makes it much harder for LGBTQ students to like being at school.

Another negative impact of homophobic and transphobic bullying is that students feel less attached to their school communities. For instance, almost half of the LGBTQ participants (44.3 percent) strongly agreed (15.8 percent) or somewhat agreed (another 28.5 percent) that "It is hard for me to feel accepted at my school," compared to fewer than one in six non-LGBTQ students (3.5 percent strongly and 11.9 percent somewhat[21]). Transgender students were also more likely to disagree with positive comments assessing school attachment. For example, 55 percent of transgender respondents disagreed with the statement, "I feel like a real part of my school," compared to 41.4 percent of LGBQ students and 24.5 percent of non-LGBTQ participants.[22]

Although we did not ask students directly about suicidal thinking and/or behaviour, studies have suggested that there is a link between bullying and suicide, and that there is a disproportionately high rate of suicidal behaviour among LGBTQ students (O'Donnell et al. 2004; Remafedi et al. 1998; Robin et al. 2002; Russell 2003; Russell and Joyner 2001; Udry and Chantala 2002; Wichstrom and Hegna 2003) — as there is among LBGTQ people generally. Several students talked about the link between homophobia and suicidal behaviour:

> I was bullied so bad in grade 10 that I attempted suicide. I dropped out of school after that, after being pressured by my counsellor and principal to stay in the school, because they were afraid of increasing the drop-out rate.

> Bullies, I already get bullied enough and I self-harm and always think about suicide. I don't need any more things to deal with at school. If I came out about being bisexual, the bullying [would] increase!

> One of our classmates committed suicide — a gay male, who "came out" in a suicide note left for students. These events were not processed appropriately by school officials.

Higher incidences in suicidal behaviour might be expected, given the amount of bullying and other homophobic and transphobic experiences sexual and gender minority students face. However, there is some suggestion that school attachment — the feeling that one belongs in the school community — is a crucial issue in this regard because of its connection to lower rates of suicidal behaviour in the general school population and among LGBTQ students (O'Donnell et al. 2004). School attachment has also been linked to academic performance for LGBTQ students, especially for boys (Pearson, Muller, and Wilkinson 2007).

Conflicting Discourses: Human Rights versus Hallway Pedagogy

> Most of the gay community in my school are bullied. We all stick together, but that doesn't always help. Many gays are depressed because of this, and teachers and adults need to help and stand up for our community. We are not aliens, we're people, and we have rights.

Time spend in high school is very tumultuous for most students, but, as this student suggests, for sexual and gender minority students it represents not only a hostile experience, but one that occurs in a deeply contradictory discourse context. On the one hand, schools promise safety and respect for all students. For example, students learn in social studies that Canada defends everyone's human rights and celebrates diversity/multiculturalism. On the other hand, however, they witness the disrespect of LGBTQ students every day, and they often see their teachers look the other way. The combined pedagogical effect of these conflicting discourses is the message that "the *Charter of Rights and Freedoms* applies to everyone but gay people — if it applied to them, our teachers would be saying something about all the abuse they take." It is no different for LGBTQ people in general — we live in a society that constantly proclaims the great freedoms we all enjoy. Our participation in the war in Afghanistan is defended everywhere as bringing freedoms, such as those expressed in the Charter, to people on the other side of the world. Yet, the promises of life, liberty, freedom made in the Charter conflict with the lived experiences of LGBTQ people.

> The combined pedagogical effect of these conflicting discourses is the message that "the *Charter of Rights and Freedoms* applies to everyone but gay people — if it applied to them, our teachers would be saying something about all the abuse they take."

Some school systems have begun to implement interventions that are designed to send the message that LGBTQ people are indeed entitled to the same rights as everyone else and that LGBTQ students are fully welcome in the school community. These interventions, such as Gay Straight Alliance Clubs (GSAs), LGBTQ-inclusive curriculum, and anti-homophobia policies, can be thought of as counter-discourse and resistant strategies. In order to assess the impact of these strategies, we specifically asked students to comment on their knowledge of, and their experiences with, anti-homophobia policies as well as GSAs.

GSAs

Gay-Straight Alliances (GSAs) are official student clubs with LGBTQ and heterosexual student membership and typically one or two teachers who serve as faculty advisors. The purpose of GSAs is to provide a much-needed safe space in which LGBTQ students and allies can work together on making their schools more welcoming for sexual and gender minority students. As one questioning student commented:

At this point I'm not really comfortable talking to other people about it, when I don't even know what's going on myself. I think if I did come out eventually it would be okay, because I'm a fairly private person and probably only my friends would know about it. I'm also a member of our school's GSA so I know I would have somewhere safe to be if it came to that.

In general, as well, it seems it is the case that students from schools with GSAs were much more likely to agree that their school communities were supportive of LGBTQ people, compared to participants from schools without GSAS (53.1 versus 26.4 percent[23]). LGBTQ students in schools with GSAs were much more likely to be open with some or all of their peers about their sexual orientation or gender identity (81.5 versus 67.5 percent) and were somewhat more likely to see their school climate as becoming less homophobic (75 versus 65.2 percent).[24]

Institutional Responses

One of the main findings of the U.S. Climate Survey (Kosciw, Diaz, and Greytak 2008) was that sexual and gender minority students in schools with comprehensive safe-school poli-cies that clearly address homophobia report lower levels of harassment, fewer homophobic comments, more staff intervention when such comments are made and more willingness to report harassment and assault to staff members. Moreover, the U.S. survey also found that generic safe-school policies that do not include specific measures on homophobia are ineffective in improving the school climate for LGBTQ students. As was done in the U.S. survey, we asked Canadian students whether their schools had anti-homophobia policies or procedures and analyzed their responses in the context of what those participants were reporting about their lives at school. Asking students about policy, of course, does not tell us whether schools actually have policies, only whether students think that they do. It is likely that some students were wrong about their schools or school divisions not having policies. However, when students are reporting either that anti-homophobia policies do not exist when in fact they do or that they do not even know whether their schools or school boards have such policies, this suggests that schools need to make further efforts to publicize their policies among their student bodies: a procedure for reporting homophobic incidents that youth do not know about is not effective.

Several students who did go to schools without anti-homophobia policies indicated that overall the climate was not supportive of sexual and gender minority issues:

If my school had breached the topic of homosexuality in the classroom and had teachers who were not afraid to discuss it, my school would have been a much better place. I feel that the students in my school had the ability to accept gay people but were never given a reason to question their stance that gay people were bad and immoral.

My school has absolutely no support (no awareness) of the LGBTQ community within and around it. The biggest fear for myself is the unknown, not knowing how people will accept someone who is LGBTQ.

Nobody is stepping up to the plate (especially adults/teachers) to stop it. It's really pretty depressing that this piece of society is not being respected.

I've never seen the issue discussed in any class or assembly (despite our school having at least two anti-racism assemblies a year) nor does the school apparently have any policies on queer issues. If they do have policies, they obviously don't enforce them, as students make anti-queer slurs all the time, in front of teachers, and nothing is said to the students.

Sexual and gender minority students who reported that their schools had anti-homophobia policies were significantly more likely to feel that their school community was supportive of LGBTQ individuals (58.4 versus 25.3 percent); to report homophobic incidents to teachers or other staff (58.1 versus 33.6 percent); to comment that teachers or other staff intervened more effectively (71.4 versus 31.2 percent); and to feel more attached to their school (for instance, 76.5 percent of students who went to schools with anti-homophobia policies agreed with the comment, "I feel like a real part of my school," compared to 61.6 percent of participants who did not go to such schools).[25]

LGBTQ participants who reported that their schools had anti-homophobia policies were much less likely to have had lies and rumours spread about them at school (45.3 versus 61 percent); to feel unsafe at school (61.4 versus 75.8 percent); to feel very depressed about their school (50.7 versus 68.7 percent); and to have been physically harassed (20 versus 32.9 percent) because of their sexual orientation.[26]

While the presence of a specific anti-homophobia policy does not eradicate homophobic bullying, nor does it completely transform school culture, it does make a substantial difference. Some interventions are more effective in some ways than others. For example, we found that LGBTQ students who had been exposed to even a little LGBTQ-inclusive curriculum (perhaps one teacher explaining the history of Pride Day, or the significance of Pink Triangle day in connection with the Nazi era) were more likely to feel attached to their school, but no less likely to have been verbally or physically harassed. The microphysics of power at work in particular contexts call for different strategies of resistance and different forms of counter-discourse. GSAs might be better received in a big city school with a fine-arts program than in a religious school in a remote area of Northern Canada. However, this did not always hold true: throughout the life of the Climate Survey project, we were surprised to find expressions of solidarity and support for LGBTQ rights from educators in places where we had anticipated a solid wall of heteronormative discourse. We concluded that, if school officials are to effectively address problems in school climate, they need to know what kinds of institutional responses are appropriate and effective in their particular schools and school districts.

The Bad News and the Good News

As the experiences of the students show, the bad news is that both homophobia and transphobia are widespread in Canadian schools. One could argue that this is similar to the myth that social equality based on sexual orientation and gender identity has been achieved in the larger society. The good news, however, is that in schools where even small efforts have been made, students report better climates. For instance, the presence of GSAs as well as institutional policies denouncing homophobia have made significant improvements in those schools.

The substantial improvements in school culture associated with even modest interventions such as minor curricular inclusion suggest that even though the problem of homophobia and transphobia may be widespread in Canadian schools, it is perhaps not very deeply rooted. In this regard, much like the "legal equality" guaranteed through official legislation as well as the Charter, institutional legislation within schools does provide students with some safety.

And yet, there is even better news. Fifty-eight percent of heterosexual-identified students, or roughly 1400 of the 2400 straight students, reported that they too found it upsetting to hear homophobic remarks. There are many reasons why so many heterosexual students would be upset by homophobic bigotry. For some of these students, they are perceived to be LGBTQ themselves and targeted accordingly. Statistically, if there are upwards of ten times as many heterosexual students as LGBTQ students (assuming that roughly one in ten students identify as LGBTQ), and some of them are homophobically harassed because they are seen as queer, in raw numbers this translates to a larger number of straight students than LGBTQ students who are bullied in this manner. Other students are upset by homophobia because they have an LGBTQ parent or sibling, or they are friends with an LGBTQ peer. Still other students are simply kind and feel empathy for their peers who are being grossly mistreated. And then there are those who are ashamed of themselves for participating in it, or for remaining silent when it was going on. Finally, some simply find the presence of homophobia depressing to the human spirit and are disheartened to be a part of a school community that continually abuses people who have done nothing to deserve it. This 58 percent suggests

> We found that 58 percent of heterosexual identified students, roughly 1400 of the 2400 straight students who filled out our survey, reported that they too found it upsetting to hear homophobic remarks.

that there is a great deal of untapped solidarity out there and that the majority of students would welcome some help from the adult world in shifting their school culture towards a social justice approach.

If so many students are upset by such degradation, why do so few intervene when homophobic comments are made or they witness homophobic/transphobic harassment and abuse? Many of these students are afraid to act because they are well aware that challenging homophobic discourse puts them in danger of being perceived as LGBTQ and becoming the targets of name-calling and violence. For them, the costs of speaking up outweigh the benefits.

High school is a time in the human life course when fitting in is one of the most important elements of well-being and survival. Teenagers fall into line with using language like "that's so gay" or "you faggot" without fully understanding the painful bite of these words for LGBTQ people, who are well aware of their lowly positions in heteronormative discourse. Students using such language may not like these phrases, but the thought of leaving the "group" and finding themselves in the uninhabitable zone of schoolyard discourse is also inconceivable. This is not to suggest that students are blind followers with no agency or ability to engage in transformative social change on issues pertaining to social justice or human rights; indeed, in some schools, students have led the way on this and other social justice issues, lobbying the school administration to implement GSAs, organizing LGBTQ-inclusive events, participating in LGBTQ Pride marches, and speaking up in class to critique homophobia or address the absence of LGBTQ content. It is simply to remind us that young people learn life lessons not only when adults demonstrate apparent hypocrisy, but when they demonstrate the courage of their convictions as well.

The silence of teachers not only helps to validate homophobia and transphobia, it helps to ensure the recirculation of fear by teaching young people that they are on their own on this issue and that adults will not help them. Sadly, some school authorities and some parents tacitly approve of homophobia as an efficient strategy for enforcing compulsory heterosexuality. Unfortunately, some parents are so terrified of their kids turning out gay that they would rather see them unhappy than see them unheterosexual. Yet, if all teachers, administrators, and school boards started to speak respectfully of LGBTQ people (literally and through specific interventions both at the school and district levels), the silent majority of students — the 58 percent of heterosexual students and the approximately 10 percent of students who are LGBTQ

> Sadly, some school authorities and some parents tacitly approve of homophobia as an efficient strategy for enforcing compulsory heterosexuality.

— would have more reason for courage. Young people may learn new ways to say "that's stupid," and they may come to understand that most of their peers are not homophobic either. Homophobia, or rather anti-homophobic behaviour, could go in a new direction altogether, and the 58 percent of young people who quietly wish for something better would have a solid group of allies, backed by numerous human rights legislations, that could alter the discourse systems of students across Canada.

Social Change

If sexual and gender minority students are experiencing disproportionate amounts of bullying and the majority of heterosexual students are distressed by this, where do we go from here to change the homophobic and transphobic landscape across Canadian schools, and in Canada generally? There is a clear disconnect between Canada's official human rights discourse, endorsed broadly in society and specifically in classrooms, and the homophobic discourse of Canadian high schools. On one hand, public opinion polls consistently show that the majority of Canadians believe that homophobia is wrong; they support gay marriage; and they believe that being gay, lesbian, or bisexual is simply what one is — like being Jewish, Aboriginal, or female — not a moral issue or lifestyle choice that can be turned on and off (see, for example, Ipsos-Reid 2004). Yet, on the other hand, Canadian school systems, and other social institutions, remain frozen in time, often fearful of backlash from extreme-right-

> The majority of Canadians believe that homophobia is wrong; they support gay marriage; and they believe that being gay, lesbian, or bisexual is simply what one is — like being Jewish, Aboriginal or female — not a moral issue or lifestyle choice that can be turned on and off.

wing Christian organizations that tirelessly work to deride LGBTQ people as sinful and dangerous to society (see, for example, Canada Family Action Coalition — <familyaction.org>). The end result is that schools are too often failing the children and youth they are sworn to protect and respect, and as a result too many LGBTQ students are going through school being abused and disrespected.

What needs to change? School system officials at all levels of the education system from ministries of education to school principals need to mandate the development of LGBTQ-inclusive interventions in the form of thoroughly implemented policy and resource development. Some provinces are embracing such change, most notably Ontario, through their Equity and Inclusive Education Strategy, implemented in 2009. More specifically, they are taking a "whole-system approach" (similar to the Winnipeg School Division's whole-staff approach) and are mandating the inclusion of gender and sexual minority content throughout the education system, within a four-year time frame for the development and implementation of appropriate policy, program, and curriculum.

School system policies cannot in themselves produce respectful school climates for LGBTQ students, any more than declaring the *Charter of Rights and Freedoms* can suddenly produced a discrimination-free society across Canada. However, what human rights policies and laws can do, apart from their general symbolic value of conferring institutional legitimacy on marginalized groups, is support the efforts of people working at the forefront of change. Classroom teachers are expected to do the heavy lifting where changing school culture is concerned: if they are to fulfill their professional obligations to practise truly inclusive education, they need policies that require their principals to support them if complaints are made. Similarly, principals need to know that school district directors will support them, and directors need to know that education ministers will support them. A positive start would be a strong mandate from ministries of education to integrate sexual and gender diversity into classroom teaching, complete with curriculum resources and professional development opportunities, just as ethnic diversity is now integrated into the curriculum. Without such a high level of government commitment, both the fear of repercussions and the lack of training and resources will continue to prevent school districts as well as teachers and administrators from finding the courage to implement the interventions required to disrupt the homophobic and transphobic discourses that dominate Canadian school cultures.

A number of factors converge to make high schools a particularly hostile environment for LGBTQ people: the coincidence with adolescents' fascination with sexuality; the existence of a generalized culture of bullying and exclusion; fear of the repercussions for opposing homophobia and transphobia among students, teachers, and administrators; and, as we have argued in this chapter, the disconnect between a heartily endorsed official discourse promising respect for all and a widespread unofficial discourse that disrespects LGBTQ people. All of these combine to create the heightened levels of abuse signalled as specific to school life in 2010s "It gets better" campaign, in which thousands of adults across North America made YouTube videos with the message to LGBTQ youth, "Hang on; endure high school; don't consider suicide; life gets better once you get out of that environment."

But high school students did not invent the system of homophobia, and high schools are not the only places where homophobia and transphobia persist in Canadian society. In coming years, we will see continued arguments against human rights for LGBTQ people by members of radically conservative communities who claim religious authority for their positions. On the legal front, the clash of LGBTQ Charter rights and Charter rights to freedom of religious "conscience" will be seen in areas including the right of Justices of the Peace to refuse to marry a same-sex couple; the right of psychologists to refuse to provide treatment that supports LGBTQ identity; and the right of religious schools and other organizations to refuse to employ LGBTQ people. On the social front, we can expect continued harassment of LGBTQ couples and indeed of any person who falls outside the binary system of conventionally gendered heterosexuality that remains dominant in our society. To this end, official policies denouncing homophobia and transphobia will not eradicate such discrimination in Canadian schools — much like the Charter does not necessarily translate into social (as compared to legal) equality for LGBTQ individuals — but it is a good place to start; after all, a waterfall begins with a single drop— and look what becomes of that.

Glossary of Key Terms

Bisexual: A person who is attracted physically and emotionally to both males and females.

Gay: A person who is physically and emotionally attracted to someone of the same sex. Gay can include both males and females, or refer to males only.

Gender expression: The way a person publicly shows their gender identity through clothing, speech, body language, wearing of make-up and/or accessories, and other forms of displaying masculinity or femininity.

Gender identity: A person's internal sense or feeling of being male or female. Gender expression relates to how a person presents their sense of gender to the larger society. Gender identity and gender expression are often closely linked with the term transgender.

Gender minority: A transgender or transsexual person.

Lesbian: A female who is attracted physically and emotionally to other females.

Perceived sexual orientation: When someone wrongly assumes that you are lesbian, gay, or bisexual without knowing what your true sexual orientation really is (heterosexual).

Queer: Historically, a negative term for homosexuality, but more recently reclaimed by the LGBT movement to refer to itself. Increasingly, the word "queer" is popularly used by LGBT youth as a positive way to refer to themselves.

Questioning: A person who is in the process of figuring out their sexual orientation or gender identity.

Sexual minority: Persons who thinks of themselves as other than completely heterosexual.

Sexual identity/orientation: A person's deep-seated feelings of emotional and sexual attraction to another person. This may be with people of the same gender (lesbian or gay), the other gender (heterosexual/straight) or either gender (bisexual).

Straight/Heterosexual: A person who is sexually and emotionally attracted to someone of the "opposite" sex.

Transgender: A person whose gender identity, outward appearance, expression, and/or anatomy does not fit into conventional expectations of male or female. Often used as an umbrella term to represent a wide range of nonconforming gender identities and behaviours.

Transsexual: A person who experiences intense personal and emotional discomfort with their assigned birth gender. Some transsexuals may undergo treatments (i.e., sex reassignment surgery and/or hormone therapy) to physically alter their body and gender expression to correspond with what they feel their true gender is.

Two Spirit: Some Aboriginal people identify themselves as two spirit rather than as lesbian, gay, bisexual, or transgender. Historically, in many Aboriginal cultures two-spirited persons were respected leaders and medicine people. Two-spirited persons were often accorded special status based upon their unique abilities to understand both male and female perspectives.

Questions for Discussion

1. Thinking back to when you were in high school, would you agree that there was a disconnect (i.e., contradictory experience) between human rights discourse and the discourse of your school environment (i.e., high levels of homophobia and transphobia)? How widespread were homophobic and transphobic language and harassment in your school?

2. Why do you think narratives like "that's so gay" are used so frequently in high school and among young people?

3. In your high school, was there a GSA club? Were there specific anti-homophobic policies and procedures for reporting incidents of abuse and harassment? If yes, do you think it made your school community a more welcoming environment? If no, do you think your school community would have benefited from being a more accepting place for LGBTQ youth?

4. Discuss the aggressive gender policing that youth participate in with reference to Foucault's concept of docile bodies and the constitutive effects of dominant discourse. What practices are involved in gender policing? What might happen if students stopped acting as agents of heteronormative discourse in school culture?

5. Some people prefer "queer" to "LGBT" because it signifies a rejection of the heteronormative system of sexuality and gender categories. If that system has always oppressed sexual and gender minority people, why would some still prefer the identity terms "lesbian," "gay," "bisexual," "trans," and "two spirit" over the term "queer"? Account for this using some of the discourse concepts discussed in this chapter. What difference might it make if LGBTQ people and their allies stopped referring to themselves as LGBTQ or "straight," and instead started using "queer" this way?

6. It is often said that homophobia is a "natural" response to "unnatural" sexual practices and gender expression. However, now that dominant discourses such as those emanating

from health care, law, and the media have become more LGBTQ-inclusive, polls show that far fewer Canadians are homophobic. This suggests that homophobia is not natural, but discursively constructed. If homophobia is not natural, and seems to be on the decline, why might some discourse communities be so adamantly opposed to LGBTQ-inclusive education? In other words, who benefits from the maintenance of homophobia and transphobia? What is all this discrimination for? In your answer, think about how the "deployment of alliance" might function to serve the interests of dominant culture by maintaining socially conservative family and economic arrangements.

Websites of Interest

Egale (Equality for Gays and Lesbians Everywhere) Canada <egale.ca>

Institute for Sexual Minority Studies and Services (ISMSS) <ismss.ualberta.ca>

Gay, Lesbian, Straight Education Network (GLSEN) <glsen.org>

McCreary Centre Society <mcs.bc.ca>

MyGSA.ca <MyGSA.ca>

Stonewall <stonewall.org/uk>

Notes

1. The research in this chapter is based on a large-scale study of over 3700 youth, which was conducted in partnership with Egale Canada with major funding from the Egale Canada Human Rights Trust and additional funding from a University of Winnipeg Social Sciences and Humanities Research Council (SSHRC) grant and from a grant awarded to the research team SVR by the Institute of Gender and Health (IGH), Canadian Institutes of Health Research (see Taylor, Paquin, and Peter 2011, in press; Taylor and Peter 2011, in press; Taylor, Peter, and Paquin 2011; Taylor, Peter, et al. 2011a, 2011b).

2. Two methods were used to reach participants. First we compiled a list of every organization in the country known to have LGBTQ youth group components or clients and provided them with information about the survey. In addition, a link to the survey was posted on the Egale Canada website and Facebook site in order to encourage participation from individuals who may not be associated with any LGBTQ youth groups. Some participants learned of the survey through mainstream and LGBTQ media coverage. Others were informed of the survey by educators, whose boards had approved the survey, but had not implemented it in their schools. Finally, although not specifically asked of respondents, a number of participants certainly heard about the survey through a friend or acquaintance. The second method was based on formal research applications to a random selection of forty school districts proportionally distributed across the regions and population densities of Canada to conduct the survey during class time. In the end, twenty school districts representing all regions of Canada except Quebec approved the study (A parallel study was conducted at the same time by Line Chamberland, Université du Quebec à Montréal.).

3. The questionnaire was drafted in consultation with members of the Education Committee of Egale Canada. The questionnaire was finalized after pre-testing for age-appropriate vocabulary, clarity/unambiguity, neutrality, relevance, and completeness by administering it to members of an LGBTQ youth group. Finally, an Ethics Protocol was approved by the Senate Committee on Ethics in Human Research and Scholarship at the University of Winnipeg.

4. Cross-tabulations with chi-square (X^2) estimations, independent samples t-tests, and analyses of

variance (ANOVAs) were conducted, depending on the classification or "level of measurement" of the variables/questions (i.e., whether they are dichotomous, ordered, or continuous). Effect sizes were calculated for all chi-square (used Cramer's V). Content analyses of qualitative data were conducted to identify patterns and counter-patterns in the responses of different subgroups of participants.

5. $X^2(6, N=3340) = 30, p<.001$, Cramer's V=.07.
6. $X^2(6, N=3338) = 18.9, p=.004$, Cramer's V=.05.
7. $X^2(6, N=3335) = 58.6, p<.001$, Cramer's V=.09.
8. $X^2(6, N=3323) = 81.8, p<.001$, Cramer's V=.11.
9. $X^2(2, N=3369) = 164.5, p<.001$, Cramer's V=.22.
10. P.E. change room $(X^2(1, N=3369) = 105.8, p<.001$, Cramer's V=.18), washrooms $(X^2(1, N=3369) = 74, p<.001$, Cramer's V=.15), and hallways $(X^2(1, N=3369) = 99.2, p<.001$, Cramer's V=.17).
11. $X^2(2, N=3275) = 679, p<.001$, Cramer's V=.46.
12. $X^2(2, N=3267) = 767.5, p<.001$, Cramer's V=.49.
13. $X^2(2, N=3273) = 307.7, p<.001$, Cramer's V=.31.
14. Gender expression $(X^2(2, N=3257) = 102.1, p<.001$, Cramer's V=.18) and sexual orientation $(X^2(2, N=3262) = 109.2, p<.001$, Cramer's V=.18).
15. Verbal harassment $(X^2(2, N=928) = 26.7, p<.001$, Cramer's V=.17) and physical assault $(X^2(2, N=928) = 9.6 p=.008$, Cramer's V=.10).
16. $X^2(2, N=3369) = 808.8, p<.001$, Cramer's V=.49.
17. $X^2(2, N=3369) = 222.9, p<.001$, Cramer's V=.26.
18. $X^2(1, N=3254) = 179, p<.001$, Cramer's V=.19.
19. $X^2(2, N=3254) = 191, p<.001$, Cramer's V=.24.
20. $X^2(8, N=3283) = 241, p<.001$, Cramer's V=.19.
21. $X^2(6, N=3271) = 381, p<.001$, Cramer's V=.34.
22. $X^2(6, N=3288) = 130, p<.001$, Cramer's V=.14.
23. $X^2(2, N=2370) = 168.6, p<.001$, Cramer's V=.27.
24. Open about sexual orientation or gender identity $(X^2(1, N=698) = 16.7, p<.001$, Cramer's V=.15) and school climate becoming less homophobic $(X^2(1, N=751) = 8.1, p=.005$, Cramer's V=.10).
25. School community supportive of LGBTQ individuals $(X^2(2, N=1171) = 135.9, p<.001$, Cramer's V=.34), report homophobic incidents to teachers $(X^2(1, N=529) = 28.7, p<.001$, Cramer's V=.23), comment that teachers intervened more effectively $(X^2(1, N=738) = 112.9, p<.001$, Cramer's V=.39), and feel like a real part of school $(X^2(1, N=1169) = 26.7, p<.001$, Cramer's V=.15).
26. Lies and rumours spread about them at school $(X^2(1, N=414) = 9.2, p=.002$, Cramer's V=.15), feel unsafe at school $(X^2(1, N=421) = 9.4, p=.002$, Cramer's V=.15), feel very depressed about school $(X^2(1, N=414) = 12.6, p<.001$, Cramer's V=.18), and physically harassed $(X^2(1, N=417) = 7.5, p=.006$, Cramer's V=.13).

References

Alcoff, L. 1988. "Cultural Feminism versus Post-Structuralism: The Identity Crisis in Feminist Theory." SIGNS: *Journal of Women in Culture and Society* 13, 3.

Butler, J. 1987. "Variations on Sex and Gender: Beauvoir, Wittig, and Foucault." In S. Benhabib and D. Cornell (eds.), *Feminism as Critique.* Minneapolis: University of Minnesota Press.

____. 1990. *Gender Trouble: Feminism and the Subversion of Identity.* New York: Routledge.

____. 1993. *Bodies that Matter: On the Discursive Limits of "Sex."* New York: Routledge.

____. 1996. "Sexual Inversions." In S. Hekman (ed.), *Feminist Interpretations of Michel Foucault.* University Park: Pennsylvania State University Press.

Foucault, M. 1979. *Discipline and Punish: The Birth of the Prison.* Translated by A. Sheridan. New York: Vintage Books.

____. 1980. *Power/Knowledge: Selected Interviews and Other Writings.* Translated by C. Gordon. New York: Pantheon Books.

____. 1981. *The History of Sexuality: An Introduction.* Translated by R. Hurley. Harmondsworth: Penguin.

Greytak, E.A., J.G. Kosciw, and E.M. Diaz. 2009. *Harsh Realities: The Experiences of Transgender Youth in Our Nation's Schools.* New York: GLSEN. <glsen.org>.

Hunt, R., and J. Jensen. 2007. "The School Report: The Experiences of Young Gay People in Britain's Schools." London: Stonewall. <stonewall.org.uk/education_for_all/ research/1790.asp>.

Ipsos-Reid. 2004. *Canadians and Same Sex Marriage as the Supreme Court of Canada Makes Its Ruling: 71% Support Concept, 27% Don't.* <ipsos-na.com>.

Kosciw, J.G., and E.M. Diaz. 2006. *The 2005 National School Climate Survey: The Experiences of Lesbian, Gay, Bisexual and Transgender Youth in Our Nation's Schools.* New York: GLSEN. <glsen.org>.

____. 2008. *Involved, Invisible, Ignored: The Experiences of Lesbian, Gay, Bisexual and Transgender Parents and Their Children in Our Nation's K–12 Schools.* New York: GLSEN. <glsen.org>.

Kosciw, J.G., E.M. Diaz, and E.A. Greytak, 2008. *The 2007 National School Climate Survey: The Experiences of Lesbian, Gay, Bisexual and Transgender Youth in Our Nation's Schools.* New York: GLSEN. <glsen.org>.

Kosciw, J.G., E.A. Greytak, E.M. Diaz, and M.J. Bartkiewicz. 2010. *The 2009 National School Climate Survey: The Experiences of Lesbian, Gay, Bisexual and Transgender Youth in Our Nation's Schools.* New York: GLSEN. <glsen.org>.

Murray, D. (ed.). 2009. *Homophobias: Lust and Loathing Across Time and Space.* Durham: Duke University Press.

O'Donnell, L., C. O'Donnell, D.M. Wardlaw, and A. Stueve. 2004. "Risk and Resiliency Factors Influencing Suicidality Among Urban African-American and Latino Youth." *American Journal of Community Psychology* 33, 1/2.

Pearson, J., C. Muller, and L. Wilkinson. 2007. "Adolescent Same-Sex Attraction and Academic Outcomes: The Role of School Attachment and Engagement." *Social Problems* 54, 4.

Pharr, S. 1988. *Homophobia: A Weapon of Sexism.* Inverness: Chardon Press.

Remafedi, G., S. French, M. Story, M. Resnick, and R. Blum. 1998. "The Relationship Between Suicide Risk and Sexual Orientation: Results of a Population-Based Study." *American Journal of Public Health* 88, 1.

Rich, A. 1980. "Compulsory Heterosexuality and Lesbian Existence." SIGNS: *Journal of Women in Culture and Society* 5, 4.

Riley, D. 1988. *"Am I That Name?" Feminism and the Category of 'Women' in History.* Minneapolis: University of Minnesota Press.

Ristock, J.L. 2002. *No More Secrets: Violence in Lesbian Relationships*. New York: Routledge.

Robin, L., N. Brener, N. Emberley, S. Donahue, T. Hack, and C. Goodenow. 2002. "Association between Health-Risk Behaviors and Gender of Sexual Partner in Representative Samples of Vermont and Massachusetts High School Students." *Archives of Pediatric and Adolescent Medicine* 156.

Russell, S.T. 2003. "Sexual Minority Youth and Suicide Risk." *American Behavioral Scientist* 46, 9.

Russell, S.T., and K. Joyner. 2001. "Adolescent Sexual Orientation and Suicide Risk: Evidence from a National Study." *American Journal of Public Health* 91, 8.

Saewyc, E., C. Poon, N. Wang, Y. Homma, A. Smith, and the McCreary Centre Society. 2007. *Not Yet Equal: The Health of Lesbian, Gay, and Bisexual Youth in BC*. Vancouver: McCreary Centre Society. <mcs.bc.ca/pdf/not_yet_equal_web.pdf>.

Sedgwick, E.K. 1985. *Between Men: English Literature and Male Homosocial Desire*. New York: Columbia University Press.

____ 1990. *Epistemology of the Closet*. Berkeley: University of California Press.

Taylor, C., S. Paquin, and T. Peter. 2011 (in press). "Homophobia Research as Discourse Intervention: Ecological Factors in the Success of the First National Climate Survey on Homophobia in Canadian Schools." In L. Sokal and K. McCluskey (eds.), *Community Connections: Reaching out of the Ivory Tower*. Ulm, Germany: International Centre for Innovation in Education.

Taylor, C., and T. Peter. 2011 (in press). "'We Are Not Aliens, We're People, and We Have Rights': Canadian Human Rights Discourse and High School Climate for LGBTQ Students." *Canadian Review of Sociology*.

____. 2011 (in press). "Left Behind: Sexual and Gender Minority Students in Canadian High Schools in the New Millennium." In T. Morrison, M. Morrison, D.T. McDermott, and M.A. Carrigan (eds.), *Sexual Minority Research in the New Millennium*. Hauppauge, NY: Nova Science.

Taylor, C., and T. Peter, with T.L. McMinn, K. Schachter, S. Beldom, A. Ferry, Z. Gross, and S. Paquin. 2011a. "Every Class in Every School: Final Report on the First National Climate Survey on Homophobia, Biophobia, and Transphobia in Canadian Schools." Toronto: Egale Canada.

____. 2011b. "Every Class in Every School: Final Report on the First National Climate Survey on Homophobia, Biophobia, and Transphobia in Canadian Schools." Executive Summary. Toronto: Egale Canada.

Taylor, C., T. Peter, and S. Paquin. 2011. "'School Is Not a Safe Place for Anyone like Me': The First National Climate Survey on Homophobia in Canadian Schools." In W. Craig, D. Pepler, and J. Cummings (eds.), *Creating a World Without Bullying*. PREVNet Series, Volume 3. Ottawa: PREVNet.

Udry, J., and K. Chantala. 2002. "Risk Assessment of Adolescents with Same-Sex Relationships." *Journal of Adolescent Health* 31, 1.

Weedon, C. 1997. *Feminist Practice and Poststructuralist Theory*. Second edition. Cambridge: Blackwell.

Weiss, J.T. 2001. "The Gender Caste System: Identity, Privacy, and Heteronormativity." *Law and Sexuality* 10.

Wichstrom, L., and K. Hegna. 2003. "Sexual Orientation and Suicide Attempt: A Longitudinal Study of General Norwegian Adolescent Population." *Journal of Abnormal Psychology* 112, 1.

5

Persistent Poverty in Canada
Causes, Consequences, Solutions

Jim Silver

YOU SHOULD KNOW THIS

- Although declining, the child poverty rate of 14.2 percent in 2008 is only slightly lower than the 1989 rate of 15.1 percent, the year the House of Commons passed a unanimous resolution to end child poverty by the year 2000.
- A 2005 UNICEF study found that out of 26 high-income Organisation for Economic Co-operation and Development (OECD) countries, Canada's child poverty rate ranked 17th worst. Canada's rank was 14.9 percent, compared to Denmark at 2.4 percent, Finland at 2.8 percent, and Norway at 3.4 percent.
- By 2001, the poverty rate was approximately 40 percent for Aboriginal children, more than double the rate for all children.
- In 1976 the richest 10 percent of Canadian families with children under 18 years of age earned 31 times what the poorest 10 percent earned. By 2004 that gap had almost tripled to 82 times.
- The 100 most highly paid Canadian CEOs earned an average of $9.1 million each in 2005. This was 240 times what the average Canadian worker was paid.
- In March 2009, 794,738 people in Canada used food banks — more than the population of large cities such as Winnipeg, Hamilton, or Quebec City, and more than double the 378,000 who had used food banks in 1989.
- Government spending in Canada as a share of GDP has dropped below the average of the G7 industrial economies, and now ranks ahead of only Japan and the United States.
- For government expenditures on social programs, Canada now ranks 24th out of 30 OECD countries.
- Using international poverty measurements Canada ranks 19th of 30 industrialized nations for poverty among adults, 21st for families with children, and 20th for children.

Sources: Statistics Canada 2010a; Thompson 2005; Campaign 2000 2005; Yalnizyan 2007; Canadian Association of Food Banks 2009; Canada, Department of Finance 2005; Mikkonen and Raphael 2010; Raphael 2009.

POVERTY RATES IN CANADA HAVE REMAINED persistently high since 1980. In 1980, 15.9 percent of the population had incomes below the Statistics Canada low-income cut-off.[1] The rate peaked in 1996 at 19.9 percent — one in every five Canadians — and then declined to 13.6 percent by 2008 (see Table 5.1). The poverty rate can be expected to climb again, back to the rate of 1980 or perhaps even higher, because of the severe economic crisis of 2007–2008 — poverty rates tend to move in lockstep with the ups and downs of the economy.

Canada's record in combating poverty is not impressive. Dennis Raphael (2009: 8) shows that if we use a common international measurement — poverty incomes being those that are 50 percent below a country's median income — the results show "Canada perform-

Table 5.1: Persons in Low Income Trends, 1976-2008

Year	Number of persons in low income (millions)	Persons in low income, percentage of total population (%)
1980	3836	15.9
1984	4706	18.7
1988	3949	15
1992	5062	18.3
1996	5770	19.9
2000	4919	16.4
2004	4923	15.8
2008	4426	13.6

Source: Statistics Canada 2010a.

ing very poorly in terms of poverty ranking: 19th of 30 industrialized nations for adults, 21st for families with children, and 20th for children."

The lower rates of poverty elsewhere suggest that Canada's high rates are not inevitable: they could be lowered if Canadian governments made different policy decisions. Canadian governments put relatively little effort into reducing poverty.

> The lower rates of poverty in other industrialized countries suggest that Canada's high rates are not inevitable: they could be lowered if Canadian governments made different policy decisions.

People at Risk of Poverty

In Canada, particular groups of people are more likely than others to be poor. One important determinant is family type: single-parent mothers and unattached individuals are more likely to be poor than are couples. In 2008, 20.9 percent of single mothers had incomes below the poverty line. Unattached individuals experienced poverty rates ranging from about 12 percent to just over 36 percent, depending upon the sex and age of the individuals. Rates for elderly married couples, by contrast, were less than 1 percent, while the average for two-parent families with children was 6 percent (see Figure 5.1).

Gender and age are also determinants. Women are more likely than men to be poor. Since 1980, poverty rates for women have consistently been one-quarter higher than poverty rates for men. In all age categories except ages forty-five to fifty-four, where the rates are equal, the incidence of poverty is higher for women than for men, and the spread by gender is especially wide for older (sixty-five plus years) and younger (eighteen to thirty-four years) women (NCW 2004: 107–10).

Young people, both women and men, have a relatively high incidence of poverty. For all family types, those under the age of twenty-five years have a much higher incidence of poverty than do those twenty-five years and over (NCW 2004: 44).

Figure 5.1 Poverty Rate by Family Type, 2008

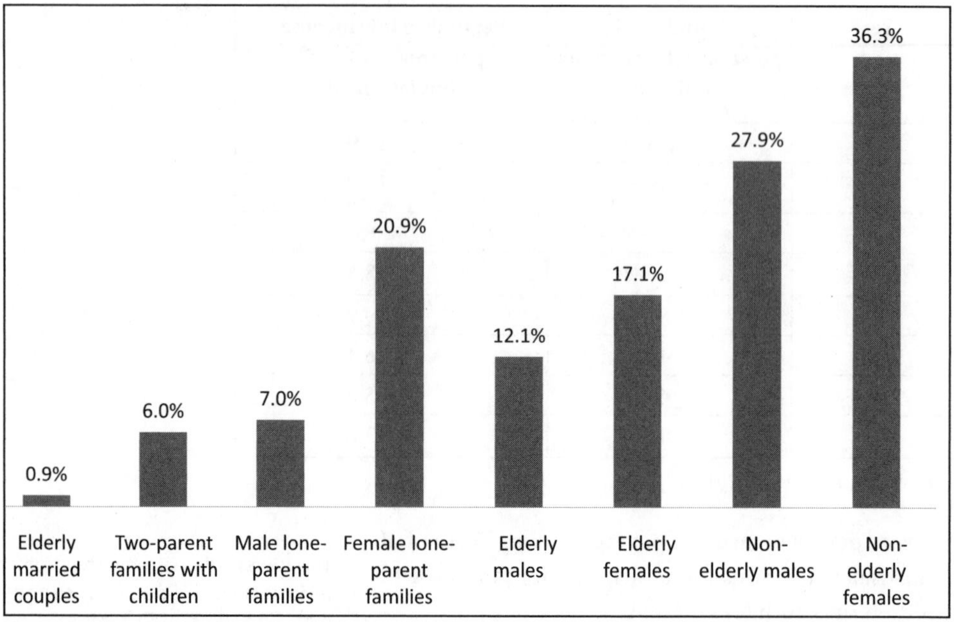

Source: Statistics Canada 2010b, table 202-0804.

The incidence of poverty also correlates with the number and age of children. The greater the number and the younger the age of children in a family, whether in a two-parent or single-parent family, the greater the likelihood of poverty.

Members of racialized groups — people (other than Aboriginal peoples) who are non-Caucasian in race or non-white in colour (Galabuzi 2001: 7) — have a much greater chance of being poor. In 1996 the incidence of poverty for members of racialized groups was double that for the Canadian population at large (Galabuzi 2006: 183, 186). A more recent study using 2006 Census Canada data for families with children under eighteen years in Ontario found that the poverty rate for racialized Ontarians was three times that of non-racialized families, and that racialized women earn just over half — 53.4 percent — of what non-racialized men earn (Block 2010: 10, 7).

For Aboriginal peoples, rates of poverty are even higher. For example, according to 1996 Census Canada data almost two-thirds — 64.7 percent — of Aboriginal households in Winnipeg had incomes below the poverty line (Lezubski et al. 2000: 39). In 2001 this number had declined to 54.7 percent — still over half of Aboriginal households in the city as a whole — while 71.3 percent of Aboriginal households in Winnipeg's inner city had incomes below the poverty line (Statistics Canada, customized data, Social Planning Council of Winnipeg). For Canada as a whole the median income for Aboriginal people was 30 percent lower than for the rest of Canadians, and, although that gap had narrowed since 1996, the rate at which Aboriginal people were catching up was such that "it would take 63 years for the gap to be erased" (Wilson and Macdonald 2010: 8).

Food bank usage reflects the high levels of poverty and its continued growth. In March 2009, 794,738 people in Canada used food banks — more than the population of large cities such as Hamilton or Quebec City, and more than double the 378,000 who had used food banks twenty years earlier, in March 1989. The number of people using food banks increased by 18 percent from March 2008 to March 2009, the largest-ever single-year increase, and approximately 40 percent of users were under the age of eighteen years (Canadian Association of Food Banks 2009). At the beginning of the 1980s there was no such thing as a food bank in Canada. It speaks volumes about the persistence of poverty that in a country as rich as Canada, we now take the existence of food banks for granted.

Poverty and the Labour Market

The relationship of poverty to family type is based in large part on varying positions in the labour market. Not surprisingly, two-parent families and couples without children have the lowest incidence of poverty, mainly because they tend to have a second wage-earner in the family — an option not available, by definition, to unattached individuals. Single-parent families have high rates of poverty, largely because of the much greater likelihood that they will have no wage-earners. A single parent with children under seven years of age is more likely to be poor because of the obvious difficulty of going out to work in the paid labour force when the children are not yet in school.

A person's relationship to the paid labour force is the most important determinant of poverty, and Canada's "precarious labour market" — the increasingly large number of jobs that are part-time, non-union, low-waged, and have neither benefits nor security — has been "the main cause of persistent poverty" (Battle 1996: 1). As the Ecumenical Coalition for Economic Justice (1996: 9) put it: "Unemployment is the single most reliable predictor of poverty for those aged 18 to 65." In other words, employment is a poverty fighter. But not just any employment. "A *good* job is the best insurance against poverty for Canadians under the age of 65" (NCW 1996: 37, emphasis added). The level of poverty depends as

> Growing numbers of jobs are either part-time or low-wage positions, or both; even though people are working, their earnings may be so low that they are still below the poverty line.

well on the number of weeks worked. Generally speaking, the more weeks of work that a family puts in, the less likely its members are to be poor (see Figure 5.2). This is another factor in the persistence of poverty: the number of weeks worked by working poor families has declined dramatically since the 1970s. For those with earned incomes in the lowest 10 percent of working families, the average number of weeks worked per year fell by almost half by the mid-1990s, from 43.3 to 23.5 (Yalnizyan 1998: 41, 46).

The majority of heads of poor families, 60 percent, were in the paid labour force. In 1998 less than one-half — 40 percent — of heads of all poor families under sixty-five years of age had no employment, while 34 percent worked part-time and 26 percent — just over one in four — worked full-time. For unattached individuals under sixty-five years of age the situation was similar: 52 percent of those who were poor in 1998 were among the working poor. Growing numbers of jobs are either part-time or low-wage positions, or both; even though

Figure 5.2 Poverty Rate by Weeks Worked, Families <65, 2007

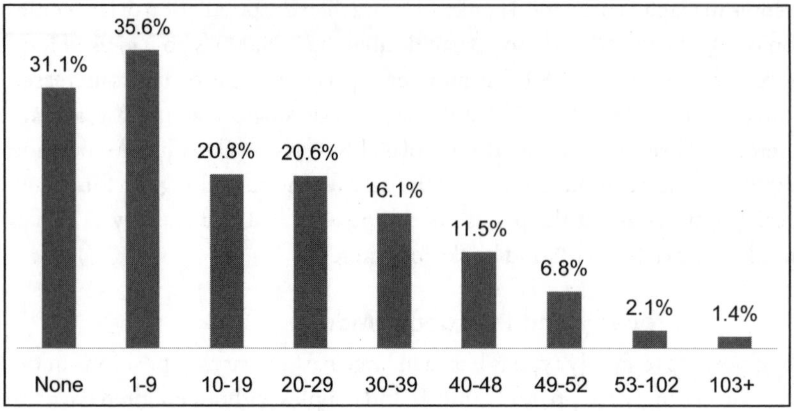

Source: National Council of Welfare 2008a.

people are working, their earnings may be so low that they are still below the poverty line. The majority of the poor, then, are, in fact, the working poor.

Part-Time and Low-Wage Jobs

The growth of part-time jobs is an important factor in explaining persistently high rates of poverty. The proportion of jobs that are part-time grew steadily from under 5 percent in the 1950s to over 17 percent and higher in the mid-late 1990s, and was still at 17.5 percent in 2009 (see Table 5.2).

As economist Jim Stanford (1996: 132–33) has observed: "Fully one-half of the new jobs created in Canada during the 1980s were non-standard: that is, jobs that were not full-time, were not year round, or involved working for more than a single employer." By 2009 part-time jobs were making up more than one in six job opportunities (see Table 5.2), compared to one in ten in the mid-1970s (Yalnizyan 1998: 26). In clerical, sales, and service occupations, six of every ten workers are part-time, a fact contributing to the relatively high proportion of people in those occupations who have incomes below the poverty line (Statistics Canada 2009a).

Part-time workers are usually paid lower wages than full-time workers. In 1995, 43 percent of part-time workers earned less than $7.50 per hour; fewer than 10 percent of full-time workers earned less than $7.50 per hour. While 60 to 70 percent of full-time workers had access to benefits packages — pensions, medical/dental, paid sick leave — fewer than 20 percent of part-time workers had such benefits. Members of racialized groups, especially women, are overrepresented in part-time, low-wage jobs — a major factor in their higher incidence of poverty (Galabuzi 2006: xii, 125).

Taking a part-time job is often a matter of choice; but still the percentage of part-time workers who wanted but could not find full-time jobs tripled between 1975 and 1994, from 11 to 35 percent (Schellenberg 1997: 39). In 2005 just over one-quarter (25.6 percent) of those working part-time did so because they were unable to find full-time work (Statistics

Table 5.2: Growth in Part-Time Work as a Percentage of Total Employment, 1976–2009

Year	Total labour force (millions)	Part-time workers (millions)	Part-time employed as percentage of total number employed (%)
1980	11,879	1,569	13.2%
1984	12,748	1,892	14.8%
1988	13,779	2,136	15.5%
1992	14,336	2,360	16.5%
1996	14,854	2,560	17.2%
2000	15,847	2,671	16.9%
2004	17,182	2,949	17.2%
2008	18,245	3,149	17.3%
2009	18,369	3,220	17.5%

Source: Statistics Canada 2010b, table 2.1-1.

Canada 2006). The result is a "polarization of the work force — with one group of workers receiving good wages, benefits and job security, and another group, including most part-time workers, receiving poor wages, no benefits and little security" (Schellenberg 1997: 2).

Another factor in poverty's persistence is the growth of self-employment. The downsizing of corporations and cutbacks in government employees, plus high rates of unemployment more generally, have made self-employment not just an option but often a necessity for more people. From 1980 to 2009 the number of self-employed Canadians almost doubled, from 1.4 million to 2.7 million; their share of the total numbers employed grew from 11.5 percent to 14.7 percent (see Table 5.3). On average, self-employed workers earn less than paid employees (Stanford 1999: 132; Delage 2002: 20).

Low wages are an important cause of persistent poverty in Canada. In the twenty-year period from 1976 to 1995, the annual earnings of a full-year, full-time worker employed at the minimum wage declined by 25 to 30 percent in almost every Canadian province (Battle 1999: 4; see also Black and Shaw 2000). In the past decade the national average minimum wage has increased, so that by 2010 it was almost back to the level it had reached in 1976, as expressed in 2010 dollars (Battle 2011: 2). Battle (2011: 44) attributes this recent gain to the "growth of provincial and territorial poverty reduction strategies ... [which have] focused attention on the importance of minimum wages," but he cautions that "history shows that

Table 5.3: Self-Employment, 1976–2009

Year	Total labour force	Self-employed workers	Self-employment as % of total labour force
1980	11,879	1,364	11.5
1984	12,748	1,570	12.3
1988	13,779	1,774	12.9
1992	14,336	1,928	13.4
1996	14,854	2,172	14.6
2000	15,847	2,374	15.0
2004	17,182	2,453	14.3
2008	18,245	2,630	14.4
2009	18,369	2,702	14.7

Source: Statistics Canada, 2010b Table 2.1-1.

what goes up can later go down when it comes to minimum wages."

Low wages appear to be of particular importance for young people. As Yalnizyan (1998: 24) has observed:

> People under 35 years of age are evidently worth less than workers of the same age before the recession of 1981–82. But it is the young men whose hourly rates of pay have been most sharply and consistently eroded over the past 15 years. Virtually every data source, from Census to special surveys, documents this same trend. Study after study shows that we are devaluing our young.

This combination — the rise in part-time jobs and self-employment, and a drop in the real value of minimum (and near-minimum) wages — directly relates to the anomaly that occurred in the mid-1990s: the break in the long-term correlation between rates of poverty and of unemployment. Historically, when unemployment has declined, the rate of poverty has declined; when unemployment has risen, the rate of poverty has risen. This is the general pattern. However, this pattern was temporarily broken in the mid-1990s: unemployment declined starting in 1993, while poverty rates rose significantly to 19.9 percent in 1996. In 1997 the traditional pattern resumed: both unemployment and poverty rates declined to 2008, although poverty rates continued to be very high (see Table 5.4).

> The rise in part-time jobs and self-employment and a drop in the real value of minimum wages directly relate to the anomaly that occurred in the mid-1990s: the break in the long-term correlation between rates of poverty and of unemployment.

It is likely that the "anomaly" from 1993 to 1996, when unemployment declined but poverty rates did not, occurred because so many of the jobs in which people were employed

Table 5.4: Unemployment and Poverty Rates, 1976–2008

Year	Unemployment rate (%)	Poverty Rate (%)
1980	7.5	15.9
1984	11.3	18.7
1988	7.8	15
1992	11.2	18.3
1996	9.6	19.9
2000	6.8	16.4
2004	7.2	15.8
2008	6.1	13.6
2009	8.3	

Sources: Statistics Canada 2010b, table 2.1-4; Statistics Canada 2010a.

were "contingent" jobs — part-time, non-union, low-wages, no benefits, no security. To the extent that this is the case, "official" unemployment rates can be misleading. People may be employed, but in jobs that do not lift them above the poverty line. "Official" unemployment rates do not, for example, indicate what percentage of part-time workers want but cannot find full-time employment — that is, how many people are underemployed. Statistics Canada does gather such information, and when the unemployed and "discouraged" workers — those who have given up actively looking for work — are included, the real unemployment rate is much higher than the official rate: from 1993 to 2001 the real unemployment rate — which includes people who have given up actively searching for work and part-time workers who want full-time jobs — was 18.9 percent, more than double the 8.7 percent official rate (Silver et al. 2004: 8).

Child Poverty

A particularly troubling aspect of Canada's persistently high poverty rate is the growth of child poverty. Canada's child poverty is so high that we rank twentieth of thirty industrialized nations in the incidence of child poverty, with rates three times as high as those in most Nordic countries (Raphael 2009: 8). In 1980 just over a million children under eighteen years of age were living in poverty. By 1988 the number and proportion of children living in poverty had declined slightly. But in the 1990s child poverty grew dramatically. By 1996 the number of children under eighteen living in poverty had grown to 1,618,000, an increase of more than half a million children since 1980, and the poverty rate had grown to 23 percent (see Table 5.5). In the mid-1990s the poverty rate for children was higher than the overall poverty rate, and for Aboriginal children was higher still. By 2001 the poverty rate was about 40 percent for Aboriginal children, more than double the rate for all children (Campaign 2000 2005).

Table 5.5: Poverty Trends, Children under 18 Years of Age, 1976–2008

Year	Numbe of persons <18 in low-income (millions)	Number of persons <18 (millions)	Low-income rate (%)
1980	1,107	6,833	16.2
1984	1,382	6,525	21.1
1988	1,042	6,594	15.8
1992	1,371	6,889	19.9
1996	1,618	7,034	23
2000	1,264	6,945	18.2
2004	1,218	6,804	17.9
2008	950	6,690	14.2

Source: Statistics Canada 2010a.

The notion of "child poverty" is misleading. As the National Council of Welfare (1996: 13) quite rightly observed: "Children are poor because their parents are poor." The issue is poor families. Growing up in a poor family can severely harm a child's life chances. Researchers David P. Ross and Paul Roberts examined the correlation between family income and twenty-seven indicators of child development: a child's family, community, behaviour, health, cultural and recreational participation, and education. They found that for each of these aspects of development, children living in low-income families were "at a greater risk of experiencing negative outcomes and poor living conditions than those in higher-income families. It is also evident from these data that child outcomes and living conditions improve gradually as family incomes rise" (Ross and Roberts 1999: 3).

Some of these correlations are striking. For example, delayed vocabulary development occurs four times more frequently among children from low-income families than among children from high-income families; and "about one in six teens from low-income families is neither employed nor in school, compared to only one teen in twenty-five from middle- and high-income families." The result is what Ross and Roberts call "poverty of opportunity." Children who grow up in poor families are, on average, less likely to do well in life than are children who grow up in non-poor families (Ross and Roberts 1999: 8, 25, 34, 36).

Campaign 2000, which describes itself as "a national movement to build awareness and support for the 1989 all-party House of Commons resolution 'to seek to achieve the goal of eliminating poverty among Canadian children by the year 2000,'" describes child poverty's lasting effects: "child poverty is associated with poor health and hygiene, a lack of a nutritious diet, absenteeism from school and low scholastic achievement, behavioural and mental problems, low housing standards, and in later years, few employment opportunities and a persistently low economic status" (CCSD 1994: 1). In its 1975 study titled *Poor Kids*, the National Council of Welfare (1975: 1) made much the same argument:

Figure 5.3 Poverty Rates by Family Type, 2007

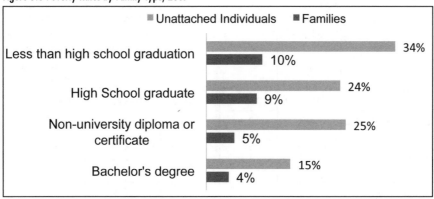

Source: *National Council of Welfare 2008b.*

> To be born poor is to face a lesser likelihood that you will finish high school, lesser still that you will attend university. To be born poor is to face a greater likelihood that you will be judged a delinquent in adolescence and, if so, a greater likelihood that you will be sent to a "correctional institution." To be born poor is to have the deck stacked against you at birth, to find life an uphill struggle ever after.

The relationship between poverty and educational attainment is a crucial factor in the reproduction of poverty. The lower the level of educational attainment, the higher is the risk of poverty, and this applies for all family types (see Table 5.6). A vicious cycle is created: poor children are less likely to do well in school; those who do less well in school are more likely to experience poverty as adults; their children, in turn, will probably do less well in school, and thus poverty is reproduced.

We know also that poverty has particularly adverse effects on health. There is now a vast body of literature, both international (Wilkinson and Pickett 2009; who 2008) and Canadian (Fernandez et al. 2010; Raphael 2008) on what are called the "social determinants of health." If we ask, "Why are some groups of people healthier than others?" the answer has far less to do with biomedical factors, or lifestyle factors (whether one smokes or is overweight or fails to exercise), than with *social* determinants. It is our living conditions — quality of housing, employment status, and especially poverty — that are particularly important factors in shaping health outcomes. Those who are poor are much more likely to suffer poor health (Brownell et al. 2010; Raphael 2007).

We know too that poverty is about much more than a shortage of money, as important as that is in a money-based economy. The effects of poverty — and racism and colonization — are often internalized by those who are poor, resulting in a loss of self-confidence and an erosion of self-esteem, and in some cases even a sense of hopelessness about the future, a sense of being trapped (Silver 2010). This too produces adverse health and educational outcomes and contributes to the persistence of poverty in Canada.

This is particularly the case for the spatially concentrated and racialized poverty now so

Table 5.6: Economic Performance Indicators

	Golden Age (%)	Recessionary Period (%)		Resumption of Growth (%)	Period Reflecting 2007–2008 Economic Crisis (%)
	1950–80	1981–97	1990–97	1998–2006	2007–2009
Average annual growth real GDP	4.7	2.4	1.8	3.6	0.1
Average annual growth real GDP per capita	2.8	1.1	0.5	10.2	-2.8
Average annual growth total employment	2.6	1.4	0.8	0.4	-0.6
Average unemployment	5.4	9.8	10	7.3	6.8
Change in government spending (% of GDP)	16.3	1.1	-2.5	-9.5	2.9
	1950–80	1981–96	1997–2003	2004–09	
Annual federal deficit (% of GDP)	0	4.2	0.9	3.6	
Closing federal debt (% of GDP)	23	73	53	34	

Sources: Canada 2010; Statistics Canada 2010b, table 1.3-2; Statistics Canada 2009a; Statistics Canada 2010b, table 2.1-4; Statistics Canada 2010c; World Bank 2009a, 2009 b.

common in large urban centres (Silver 2011). The effects of this kind of particularly complex and persistent poverty has recently been described by the use of two metaphors:

> One is the notion of a complex web — a web of poverty, racism, drugs, gangs, violence. The other is the notion of a cycle — people caught in a cycle of inter-related problems. Both suggest the idea of people who are trapped, immobilized, unable to escape, destined to struggle with forces against which they cannot win, from which they cannot extricate themselves. The result is despair, resignation, anger, hopelessness, which then reinforce the cycle, and wrap them tighter in the web. (CCPA-MB 2005: 24)

The Economy

The high levels of poverty throughout the 1980s and into the mid-1990s were associated with the relatively weak economy during that period. As measured by almost any indicator, the Canadian economy — like virtually all economies in the industrialized world — was much weaker in the 1980s and first half of the 1990s than it had been during the long, post-war economic boom. The average annual rate of growth in both Gross Domestic Product (GDP) and employment from 1950 to 1980 was about double the rate from 1981 to 1997 and about triple the rate from 1990 to 1997. In 1998 to 2006, the rate of growth in GDP returned to levels almost as high as those from 1950 to 1980, but the rate dropped again in the 2007–2009 period to its lowest level, largely attributable to the financial crisis of 2007–2008 (see Table 5.6). Unemployment rates from 1981 to 1997 were almost double the rates from 1950 to 1980, and remained half again as high from 1998 to 2006. This relative economic stagnation was reflected in the emergence of annual deficits and a buildup of accumulated debt from 1981 to 1997, a problem that has returned subsequent to the severe economic crisis of 2007–2008.

Why did the Canadian economy experience such a decline in the twenty-five years or so to the late 1990s? The character of the global economy is a partial explanation. The prevailing capitalist system has certain intrinsic features, chief among which is the constant, competitive drive of individual business firms to earn profits. This relentless drive for ever more profits has certain inevitable results. One of them is a constant revolutionizing of the means of production, leading to rapid technological change, as firms relentlessly innovate in attempts to find ways of producing goods and services less expensively and thus gain an advantage over their competitors. Another is the constant drive to expand, which results in both ever-larger firms and geographic expansion, as transnational corporations scour the globe in search of lower wages, bigger markets, and cheaper raw materials in order to maximize their profits.

While economic activity has become much more global in the past quarter-century, globalization is not a new phenomenon. Rather, it is an accentuation of the drive to expand that is intrinsic to capitalism. In the past few decades, trade between nations and investment across national borders has increased dramatically. Companies do not confine their production to their home nations. They set up production facilities anywhere in the world, locating wherever they are most likely to maximize profits: "as transnational entities, corporations can play one nation off against another by moving to where the concessions and incentives are greatest, the relative labour costs lowest … and environmental and employment standards the most limited" (Teeple 2000: 91). This trend has been accelerated by international trade agreements, such as the Canada-U.S. Free Trade Agreement and the North American Free Trade Agreement, which significantly reduce the capacity of elected governments to regulate, to place limits on, the profit-seeking activities of transnational corporations (TNCs). They free these corporations from many of the "obstacles" — what most of us would look upon as benefits, such as environmental regulations and labour standards — formerly imposed by governments. The changes increase the freedom of TNCs to search the globe for the most profitable production sites, making it more likely that the corporations will set up shop wherever they can maximize their profits. This is especially the case for heavily unionized, relatively high-wage, mass-production industries. According to Teeple (2000: 67): "The effects of this emerging global labour market began to become visible from the early 1970s on with a general downward pressure on wages in the industrial world."

In the face of the intensified competition created by globalization, companies have sought not only to reduce wage levels, but also to create what the corporate sector calls more "flexible" workforces. Corporations have sought to move away from the relatively fixed and permanent high-wage regime characteristic of the mass-production industries of the 1950s and 1960s — sometimes called "Fordism," after the mass-production, relatively high-wage system introduced early in the century by Henry Ford — to a more flexible labour force, increasingly characterized by the use of part-time, lower-waged, and non-unionized work. The resultant increase in part-time work and decrease in wages at the lower end of the income scale have been significant factors in creating persistently high levels of poverty.

The increased degree of globalization, and the problems that the phenomenon creates for many working people, have been facilitated by the particularly rapid technological change associated with the microelectronics revolution and the use of computers. By the mid-1970s computers were beginning to be widely employed in industry, with dramatic results. Not only has their use facilitated the increased globalization of economic activity, including an acceleration of the ease and rapidity by which investments can be moved around the globe, but their use in industry — in both factories and offices — has resulted in massive job losses. The loss of jobs has exerted downward pressure on wage levels at the lower end of the wage scale, and it has contributed to the growth of (generally low-paid) self-employment. Most of the jobs open to relatively unskilled school-leavers in the 1950s and 1960s — jobs that could support a family — have now disappeared. These jobs have relocated elsewhere or been eliminated by technology, only to be replaced by low-wage and often part-time work in the service sector. The labour market has increasingly become bifurcated, with a gap between very well-paid jobs, and contingent jobs that are poorly paid and insecure. This is an important factor in the growing gap between rich and poor in Canada.

> Most of the jobs open to relatively unskilled school-leavers in the 1950s and 1960s, jobs that could support a family, have relocated elsewhere or been eliminated by technology, replaced by low-wage and often part-time work.

The Growing Gap

The economic decline of the 1980s and most of the 1990s was replaced in the late 1990s by a resumption of economic growth to about 2007. Yet this recent decade of economic growth was characterized by a dramatically widening gap between the richest Canadians and the rest of us. Armine Yalnizyan (2007) examined the before- and after-tax earnings of Canadian families with children eighteen years and younger. She found that in 1976 the richest 10 percent earned 31 times what the poorest 10 percent earned; by 2004 that gap had almost tripled to 82 times. During that period the bottom half of Canadians saw their real earnings decline — despite the healthy economy — while the earnings of the richest 10 percent grew by 30 percent. The 100 most highly paid Canadian CEOs "saw a 262% increase in compensation, pocketing an average of $9.1 million in 2005" (Yalnizyan 2007: 28). In 1998 they had earned 106 times what the average Canadian worker earned; in 2005 they earned a remarkable 240 times the income of the average Canadian worker.

Even greater inequality prevails in the U.S. (McNally 2009: 38). Yalnizyan (2007: 3-4) concluded that:

> Only the richest 20% are experiencing gains from Canada's economic growth, and most of those gains are concentrated in the top 10%. The share of income going to the bottom 80% of Canadian families is smaller today than it was a generation ago, in both earnings and after-tax terms.

In short, the resumption of strong economic growth in the late 1990s did not produce growth in the earnings of most Canadians; almost all of that growth accrued to the benefit of the richest Canadians.

The same trend has occurred in Quebec (Couturier and Schepper 2010) and Manitoba (Fernandez and Hudson 2010), although in both of these cases the gap has not widened as much as in Canada as a whole, primarily because provincial governments in those provinces were more interventionist than the federal government. As will be seen, government spending is especially important for those at the bottom of the income scale.

What is striking is that this widening of the earnings gap, with declines at the bottom of the scale and stagnation for the majority of Canadians, has happened not during an economic downturn, as might be expected, but during what was an economic boom. Writing in 2007, before the economic crisis of 2007–2008, Yalnizyan (2007: 9, 15) said: "In Canada, this is the best of economic times. Over the past decade, Canada's economy has consistently been firing on all cylinders," and yet "the gap between rich and poor families has risen in recent years at a rate not previously recorded … at a time when the gap should be shrinking, not growing."

The Economic Crisis of 2007–2008

Then came the especially dramatic economic crisis of 2007–2008. For a variety of reasons the global economy has in recent decades become increasingly financialized — that is, financial markets and institutions have come to play an increasingly important role in global capitalism, relative to previous times and relative also to the production of goods and services. An example of financialization was the case of subprime mortgages, although it is important to note that subprime mortgages have been simply the most visible symptom of a deeper and more complex phenomenon (see, for example: McNally 2011; Panitch and Gindin 2009; Foster and Magdoff 2009). Mortgages for low-income homeowners in the U.S. had been packaged and sold to corporate investors in the form of complex financial products — a case of the commodification (that is, turning something into a commodity, to be bought and sold for profit) of a basic human need, namely housing. Major banks and other financial institutions throughout the world purchased these financial products, and, when the investments went sour, some of the world's largest financial institutions collapsed, with a powerful ripple effect throughout the global economy. Banks and other financial and non-financial institutions were bailed out by the U.S. government at an immense cost, measured in *trillions* of dollars (McNally 2009: 33, 43; also see McNally, chapter 6 of this book), in order to prevent a slide into another Great Depression like that of the 1930s. Governments throughout the world,

Canada included, each pumped billions of dollars in stimulus spending into their economies in order to generate a return to economic growth. The consequences of this economic crisis are far from over, and those consequences are almost certain to include a growth in poverty, but a complete collapse has been prevented by the injection into the economy of staggering sums of public money.

The result of the dramatic increase in government spending to bail out a floundering capitalist economy, together with the sharp decline in tax revenues because of the economic downturn, has been a return to very high government deficits. The legitimate fear now is that neoliberal governments will eliminate those deficits just as they eliminated the deficits of the 1980s and 1990s — by making (still more) dramatic cuts to social spending, with especially adverse effects on those at the bottom of the income scale.

Social Policy

The high poverty levels of the 1980s and 1990s were made worse by the dismantling during that period of the many social policy mechanisms put in place during the post-Second World War boom as a means of protecting individuals from the hazards of the inevitable ups and downs of the capitalist economy. Overall government spending — particularly government spending on social programs — was dramatically reduced during the 1980s and 1990s. Canada now ranks twenty-fourth out of thirty Organisation for Economic Co-operation and Development (OECD) nations on expenditures on social programs (Mikkonen and Raphael 2010: 35). Unemployment insurance was restructured to the disadvantage of unemployed workers and the social safety net was significantly weakened.

> Overall government spending — particularly government spending on social programs — was dramatically reduced during the 1980s and 1990s. Canada now ranks twenty-fourth out of thirty Organisation for Economic Co-operation and Development (OECD) nations on expenditures on social programs.

These and other changes in social policy were directly related to the dramatic changes in the economy. The social policy initiatives from the 1950s to the early 1970s were funded out of the proceeds of the long postwar economic boom. Sustained economic growth and relatively low levels of unemployment generated the government revenue, the "fiscal dividend," needed to pay for new social programs. With the end of the postwar boom in the early 1970s and its replacement with a long period of relative economic stagnation, the fiscal dividend disappeared, and was replaced by government deficits and the buildup of accumulated debt (see Table 5.6).

Most governments responded to the problem by cutting social spending, which had, in certain minds at least, become too effective in reducing the fear and anxiety that forces workers to pull back on their wage demands and accept jobs of lesser quality. The various elements of the welfare state had provided at least a semblance of security, however limited. To some degree the much-lauded safety net removed the fear of unemployment and poverty that made people anxious to work at whatever wages and under whatever conditions were on offer. As early as 1975 advocates of unfettered free enterprise were expressing concerns about the perceived consequences of the redistributive character of the welfare state in advanced capitalist economies. As the 1975 Trilateral Commission put it, Western states had too much democracy — an "excess" of democracy — and the solution was to attack "big government" (Crozier et al. 1975). If profitability was to be fully restored, the relative security created by the welfare state had to be eroded, especially because, as time went by, an increasingly competitive global economy and global labour market were making strong demands for the creation of a more "flexible" labour force.

In Canada, federal program spending as a share of GDP began to decline after 1975. By 1995, even before Finance Minister Paul Martin had announced massive spending cuts in that year's federal budget, "Government in Canada was already smaller as a share of our economy than it had been two decades earlier" (Stanford 1998: 31). Federal program spending in the 1996/97 fiscal year was 13 percent of GDP, the lowest level as a share of the Canadian economy since 1950/51 (Yalnizyan 1998: 64); it continued to decline, to 11.6 percent of GDP for the fiscal year 2003/04 (Canada 2005).

Cuts were made to federal programs that transfer funds to the provinces for health, education, and social assistance. In 1996 Established Programs Financing (EPF) (by which federal funds were transferred to the provinces for health and post-secondary education) and the Canada Assistance Program (CAP) (the cost-shared, federal-provincial program under which welfare and social assistance services were financed) were rolled into a new program, the Canadian Health and Social Transfer (CHST). In its first two years of operation (1996/97 and 1997/98) the CHST transferred to the provinces for health, post-secondary education, and social assistance an amount $7 billion less than what would have been the case under the previous arrangements (Pulkingham and Ternowetsky 1999: 93; Yalnizyan 1998: 56).

In addition, under the CHST the standards that had existed under the CAP were eliminated. Certain forms of assistance were "no longer mandated by legislation or directly supported by cost-shared transfers" (Pulkingham and Ternowetsky 1999: 94). Previously, under CAP, in order to receive federal funds for social assistance the provinces were required to ensure that all people judged to be in need received funding; that benefit levels met basic needs; that an appeal procedure existed, enabling people to challenge welfare decisions; and that no work requirement was imposed as a condition of receiving social assistance. The removal of these standards, critics warned, would almost certainly lead to reduced levels of social assistance: the CHST "opens the way for jurisdictions to provide little or no assistance to those in need" (CCSD 1996).

Indeed, that is precisely what happened in the years after 1995. One by one the provinces of British Columbia, Alberta, Manitoba, Ontario, Quebec, Nova Scotia, Prince Edward Island, and Newfoundland cut back their benefit rates and/or shelter allowances and altered the rules of eligibility to programs of assistance (Yalnizyan 1998: 57). The Ontario government cut welfare rates by 21.6 percent in 1995. Several provinces introduced provincial workfare programs (MacKinnon 2000). Social assistance recipients experienced a greater degree of financial insecurity and became subject to a variety of forces that

> One by one the provinces of British Columbia, Alberta, Manitoba, Ontario, Quebec, Nova Scotia, Prince Edward Island, and Newfoundland cut back their benefit rates and/or shelter allowances and altered the rules of eligibility to programs of assistance.

pushed them into the paid labour force, usually at the low-wage end of the job market.

Changes to Unemployment Insurance (UI) had the same effect. In 1989/90 the federal government effectively privatized UI. As the result of Bill C-21 the government withdrew from its previous role as financial contributor to this crucial program, leaving its financing completely in the hands of employees and employers. There followed a series of changes to UI in the early to mid-1990s, each making the provision of UI more restrictive: stricter qualifying requirements and reductions in the level and duration of benefits, for example (Pulkingham and Ternowetsky 1999: 86). These trends were intensified with the introduction in 1996 of Bill C-12, creating the new, renamed Employment Insurance (EI) system. The more restrictive provisions applying to EI served to accelerate the downward trend in the proportion of unemployed Canadians receiving benefits. While 74 percent of unemployed Canadians received UI benefits in 1990, only 39 percent of unemployed Canadians received EI benefits in 2001 (Canadian Labour Congress 2003).

Over the past decade and a half these changes to EI served to make employment still more precarious, with the result that wage demands were reduced. This is no accident, since the purpose, according to Stanford (1996: 144), is to "harmonize Canada's labour market outcomes with those of our trading partners (especially the U.S.)." The goal of the reforms — "to enhance the international competitiveness of Canada's economy on a low-wage basis" — was to be achieved by "deliberately increasing the economic insecurity facing Canadian workers, hence moderating their wage demands and disciplining their behaviour in the workplace." When unemployment is high and social benefits for those not employed are weak, the fear and insecurity created by the risk of job loss reduce the willingness of workers to fight for higher wages. The fear and insecurity created by higher levels of unemployment and reduced social benefits are therefore seen by the proponents and primary beneficiaries of the capitalist economy to be functional.

> The social policy changes were, at least in part, an attempt to create a more flexible, competitive labour force in Canada in response to the increased global competitiveness arising from economic changes. But from start to finish those economic changes and cuts to and changes in social policy have together resulted in the country's persistently high poverty levels.

The cuts in social spending and redesign of programs were the result of conscious government policy. The social policy changes were, at least in part, an attempt to create a more flexible, competitive labour force in Canada in response to the increased global competitiveness arising from economic changes. But from start to finish those economic changes and cuts to and changes in social policy have together resulted in the country's persistently high poverty levels.

Solutions to Poverty

Persistently high levels of poverty are not inevitable. Nations are fully capable of achieving greater degrees of equality and lower levels of poverty. We know with certainty that this is the case because, as shown above, so many other advanced industrialized nations have poverty rates lower, and in some cases much lower, than Canada's. What can be done to reduce Canada's persistently high levels of poverty?

Any serious anti-poverty strategy will have to include a dramatic increase in public invest-ment — exactly the opposite of what neoliberal governments believe in doing. The creation of more good jobs and the construction of a set of economic and social policies that are con-sciously and deliberately aimed at producing benefits and opportunities for those who are poor, as opposed to policies that are consciously intended to benefit those who are rich, will have to be at the heart of an effective anti-poverty strategy. Many good jobs could be created as part of the process of responding to the now exceptionally serious global environmental crisis: the retrofitting of buildings to make them more energy efficient; the production of fully functional public transit systems in Canadian cities; the production of low-income and energy-efficient housing as part of a desperately needed national housing strategy, for example.

Additional measures would include higher minimum wages, together with legislation to make it easier for those who choose to do so to form unions. An expansion of the benefits of trade unionism to the retail and service sectors, for example, would help to push up wage levels at the lower end of the income scale and thus address the problems of the working poor (Black and Silver 2006: Chapter 6). We have evidence that unions contribute to im-proved health and well-being in a wide variety of ways (Black and Silver 2010). Mikkonen and Raphael (2010: 54) observe that "there is strong evidence that an essential aspect of improving the quality of the social determinants of health is making it easier for Canadians to unionize their workplace."

We also need public investment to increase the availability and accessibility of child-care facilities, which would create significantly improved opportunities for young parents, especially young women. There is strong evidence that public investment in early childhood education produces a financial return far beyond the initial investment. We need investment in education more generally, given strong evidence that levels of educational attainment cor-relate with success in finding jobs and with lifetime earnings. We need a much more serious approach to the development of a range of anti-racism initiatives; the evidence is clear that poverty in Canada has increasingly been racialized (Galabuzi 2006).

Taking such a proactive approach implies a more activist and interventionist state, and a state that would govern, to the maximum extent possible, in the interests of those at the lower end of the income scale. This implies the promotion of a greater degree of equality. The prevailing ideology in Canada over the past thirty years has been the opposite. Governments have, for the most part, governed in the interests of the most well-to-do, by reducing or eliminating state inter-vention on behalf of those at the lower end of the income scale. As a result, over the past thirty years government policies have disproportionately benefited a minority of Canadians at the upper end of the income scale, and the results can be seen in both the growing gap between the rich and the rest of us, and the persistently high levels of poverty.

This will not change in the absence of effective political action that emphatically demands government

> Such a proactive approach implies a more activist and interventionist state, and a state that would govern, to the maximum extent possible, in the interests of those at the lower end of the income scale. The prevailing ideology in Canada over the past thirty years has been the opposite. Governments have, for the most part, governed in the interests of the most well-to-do.

policies that benefit the majority of Canadians, including those who are poor. At the moment there are few signs that we will soon see the emergence of this kind of socially and economically progressive political action. However, there are reasons to believe that such a campaign, if properly constructed, could find resonance among the broad Canadian population.

Canadians' Attitudes about Poverty

At the moment, most Canadians believe that poverty simply cannot be solved, that the problem is too overwhelming (the ideas in this section are drawn largely from Hennessey 2010). Most Canadians see themselves as "middle class," and they are worried about their own economic circumstances — and quite rightly, given "the growing gap" described above. Canadians are concerned about their growing levels of personal indebtedness and fear that the "intergenerational bargain" — the deeply held assumption, and hope, that their children and grandchildren will do as well as they did, or better — is slipping away. They see the poor as the "Other," and are inclined to place the blame for poverty on poor people themselves — a "blame-the-victim" approach that has a long history in North America (Swanson 2001; Katz 1989). All of this makes the development of an effective anti-poverty strategy particularly difficult.

Yet at the same time Canadians see themselves as being, and have aspirations to be, a caring society. They want leadership from their prime ministers and premiers in the development of specific plans to create opportunities for people who are poor. "In an Environics poll taken in the fall of 2008, 90 percent of Canadians said they wanted the federal government to take leadership in reducing poverty. In virtually equal numbers (89 percent), they called for the Prime Minister and the Premiers to set targets and timelines to achieve this objective" (Broadbent 2010: 8). This widely felt desire could be the basis upon which to build an effective anti-poverty strategy.

Such a strategy would include public investment in alternative educational and job creation initiatives. Over the past thirty years, in exceptionally difficult times, many such initiatives have been developed at the grassroots level in low-income communities, and we have evidence that they work (Silver 2009). In the case of Winnipeg, to take just one of many such examples, the Urban Circle Training Centre has been in existence for a quarter century. It offers the mature grade 12 certificate, plus several job-specific educational programs. Students are Aboriginal adults, almost all of whose lives have been made difficult by the myriad adverse effects of poverty, racism, and colonization (Hart 2010; Silver 2006). Yet the graduation rate at Urban Circle is 90 percent, and 85 percent end up in jobs or post-secondary education. Eleanor Thompson (2010) has conservatively estimated that Urban Circle has saved Manitobans approximately $51 million in the past twenty-five years, in reduced public payments for social assistance, employment insurance, health care and justice system costs, and increased tax revenues as the result of the graduates being employed. This is completely consistent with the literature on the social determinants of health, discussed above, which demonstrates the exceptionally high costs associated with poverty. In short, public investment in anti-poverty solutions that work is not only ethically appropriate; it is also economically advantageous — not only to those who are poor but to almost all of us.

Based on the many cases with similar achievements to the Urban Circle, I firmly believe the following: there are job creation and educational strategies developed at a grassroots level with the direct involvement of poor people themselves that have very high success rates; significant economic benefits would follow from greater public investment in such initiatives; and there are very large costs associated with the neoliberal-inspired refusal to make such productive public investments.

At the moment, what prevents public investment in such measures is the absence of organized political pressure — from trade unions and social movements and citizens in general — that *demands* such a rational, ethical, and economically beneficial approach to public policy. Those currently exercising political power will continue to promote the neoliberal strategies of disinvestment at the lower end of the income scale until they are forced to do otherwise. It is in the interests of the vast majority of Canadians, including, but not only, the large numbers who are poor, to force them to do otherwise.

> Those currently exercising political power will continue to promote the neoliberal strategies of disinvestment at the lower end of the income scale until they are forced to do otherwise. It is in the interests of the vast majority of Canadians, including, but not only, the large numbers who are poor, to force them to do otherwise.

Glossary of Key Terms

Commodification: Turning something into a commodity, to be bought and sold for profit. Housing is a good example. Housing is a basic human need, and as a matter of human rights decent quality housing ought to be available to all Canadians. This is not the case, because in our system housing is commodified — it is bought and sold for profit, like any other commodity — and there are no profits to be made in producing low-income rental housing, however great the need.

Discouraged workers: Those who have given up looking for work. They are not counted when unemployment rates are calculated, with the result that unemployment rates appear lower than they would if discouraged workers were counted. If they were, the "real" unemployment rate would be higher than the official rate.

Financialization: The fact that financial markets and institutions have come to play an increasingly important role in global capitalism, relative to previous times and relative also to the production of goods and services.

The Growing Gap: The fact that in the past fifteen years or so, only the top 20 percent, and especially the top 10 percent of Canadians have benefited from what was, until 2007–2008, a strong economy; the share of income going to the bottom 80 percent of Canadians has been declining. The gap between the rich and the rest of us has been growing.

Neoliberalism: The form of governance that seeks to reduce the role of the state and increase the role of the market. The means of doing so include de-regulation; privatization; cuts in taxes, in order to reduce the resources available to the state for public purposes and to leave more money in the hands of individuals for private purposes; and cuts in public spending.

Own-account self-employment: When a self-employed person works on their own and has no employees.

Precarious labour market/Contingent jobs: The increasingly large numbers of jobs that are part-time and low-wage, and have no benefits, no security, and no union protections. Such jobs are sometimes called "contingent" jobs.

The social determinants of health: Our health is shaped much more by our living conditions — quality of housing, access to food — than it is shaped by biomedical determinants such as medicines and hospitals and forms of surgery, or our lifestyles, such as the extent to which we exercise or smoke. Poverty, in particular, makes people sick.

Workfare: A program in which government forces people on social assistance to work in order to qualify for social assistance benefits. It is rooted in the assumption — many believe a false assumption — that people are not working because they do not have the incentive to work, and therefore must be forced.

Working poor: People who are employed, but whose employment earnings generate incomes that are below the LICO, or low-income cut-off measure.

Questions for Discussion

1. Discuss the relationship between poverty and family type. How are changes in the structure of the family over the past thirty years related to poverty? What kinds of solutions to poverty could be designed in response to changes in family type?

2. What relationship does poverty have to jobs? How are changes in the structure of the labour market over the past thirty years related to poverty? What kinds of solutions to poverty could be designed in response to changes in the labour market?

3. How are changes to Canada's social welfare system over the past thirty years related to poverty? What kinds of solutions to poverty could be designed in response to changes in the social welfare system?

4. What benefits would follow from a program of massive public investment in jobs and educational opportunities in Canada?

5. Consider the debate about poverty lines in Canada. Do you think the LICO is a useful measure of poverty? Do you think a market-basket approach would be better? Why?

6. Why are poverty levels so high in Canada compared to many European countries? Why have governments failed to institute policies that are known to reduce poverty levels? What might be done to encourage governments to introduce such policies?

Websites of Interest

Canada Without Poverty

Campaign 2000

Canadian Association of Food Banks .

Canadian Centre for Policy Alternatives <policyalternatives.ca>

Caledon Institute of Social Policy

Make Poverty History

National Council of Welfare

PovNet

Notes

I am especially grateful to Matthew Rogers for his assistance in preparing the tables and figures and for much additional assistance in revising this chapter, and to Wayne Antony, Shauna MacKinnon, Tara Rudy, Todd Scarth, and Lisa Shaw for contributions to earlier versions.

1.   Statistics Canada's low-income cut-offs (LICO) are used to determine poverty rates. See the appendix to this chapter, "The Debate about Poverty Lines."

References

Battle, Ken. 1996. *Precarious Labour Market Fuels Rising Poverty*. Ottawa: Caledon Institute.

____. 1999. *Poverty Eases Slightly*. Ottawa: Caledon Institute.

____. 2011. *Restoring Minimum Wages in Canada*. Ottawa: Caledon Institute.

Black, Errol, and Lisa Shaw. 2000. "The Case for a Strong Minimum Wage Policy." In Jim Silver (ed.), *Solutions That Work: Fighting Poverty in Winnipeg*. Halifax and Winnipeg: Fernwood Publishing and Canadian Centre for Policy Alternatives-Manitoba.

Black, Errol, and Jim Silver. 2008. *Building a Better World: An Introduction to Trade Unionism in Canada*. Second edition. Halifax: Fernwood Publishing.

____. 2010. "The Union Makes Us Strong — and Keeps Us Healthy." In Lynne Fernandez, Shauna MacKinnon and Jim Silver (eds.), *The Social Determinants of Health in Manitoba*. Winnipeg: Canadian Centre for Policy Alternatives-Manitoba.

Block, Sheila. 2010. *Ontario's Growing Gap: The Role of Gender and Race*. Ottawa: Canadian Centre for Policy Alternatives.

Broadbent, Ed. 2010. *The Rise and Fall of Economic and Social Rights: What Next?* Ottawa: Canadian Centre for Policy Alternatives.

Brownell, Marni, Randy Fransoo and Patricia Martens. 2010. "Social Determinants of Health and the Distribution of Health Outcomes in Manitoba." In Lynne Fernandez, Shauna MacKinnon and Jim Silver (eds.), *The Social Determinants of Health in Manitoba*. Winnipeg: Canadian Centre for Policy Alternatives-Manitoba.

Campaign 2000. 2005. *Decision Time for Canada: Let's Make Poverty History, 2005 Report Card on Child Poverty in Canada*. Toronto: Campaign 2000.

Canada. 2010. *Public Accounts of Canada 2010: Summary Report and Financial Statements*. Ottawa: Minister of Public Works and Government Services Canada.

Canada. Department of Finance. 2005. *The Budget Plan 2005* (Catalogue # F1-23/2005-3E). Ottawa. Department of Finance.

Canadian Association of Food Banks. 2009. *Hunger Count 2009*. Toronto.

Canadian Labour Congress. 2003. *Falling Unemployment Insurance Protection for Canada's Unemployed.* Ottawa: Canadian Labour Congress.

CCPA-MB (Canadian Centre for Policy Alternatives-Manitoba). 2005. *The Promise of Investment in Community-Led Renewal. The State of the Inner City Report 2005.* Part Two: A View from the Neighbourhoods. Winnipeg: CCPA-MB.

CCSD (Canadian Council on Social Development). 1994. *Countdown '94: Campaign 2000 Child Poverty Indicator Report.* Ottawa: CCSD.

Couturier, Eve-Lyne, and Bertrand Schepper. 2010. *Who Is Getting Richer, Who Is Getting Poorer: Quebec 1976–2006.* Ottawa and Montreal: Canadian Centre for Policy Alternatives and Institut de Recherche et d'Informations Socio-Economiques.

Crozier, M., S.P. Huntingdon, and J. Watanuki. 1975. *The Crisis of Democracy. Report on the Governability of Democracies to the Trilateral Commission.* New York: New York University Press.

Delage, Benoit. 2002. *Results from the Survey of Self-Employment in Canada.* Ottawa: Human Resources and Development Canada.

Ecumenical Coalition for Economic Justice. 1996. *Promises to Keep, Miles to Go: An Examination of Canada's Record in the International Year of the Eradication of Poverty.* Toronto: Ecumenical Coalition for Economic Justice.

Fernandez, Lynne, and Ian Hudson. 2010. "Income Inequality in Manitoba." In Lynne Fernandez, Shauna MacKinnon, and Jim Silver (eds.), *The Social Determinants of Health in Manitoba.* Winnipeg: Canadian Centre for Policy Alternatives-Manitoba.

Fernandez, Lynne, Shauna MacKinnon, and Jim Silver (eds.). 2010. *The Social Determinants of Health in Manitoba.* Winnipeg: Canadian Centre for Policy Alternatives-Manitoba.

Foster, John Bellamy, and Fred Magdoff. 2009. *The Great Financial Crisis.* New York: Monthly Review Press.

Galabuzi, Grace-Edward. 2001. *Canada's Creeping Economic Apartheid: The Economic Segregation and Social Marginalization of Racialized Groups.* Toronto: Centre for Social Justice.

____. 2006. *Canada's Economic Apartheid: The Social Exclusion of Racialized Groups in the New Century.* Toronto: Canadian Scholars' Press.

Hart, Michael. 2010. "Colonization, Social Exclusion and Indigenous Health." In Lynne Fernandez, Shauna MacKinnon, and Jim Silver (eds.), *The Social Determinants of Health in Manitoba.* Winnipeg: Canadian Centre for Policy Alternatives-Manitoba.

Hennessey, Trish. 2010. *The Great Communications Challenge: The Growing Gap.* Presentation to ad hoc anti-poverty group in Winnipeg, July 20.

Katz, Michael. 1989. *The Undeserving Poor: From the War on Poverty to the War on Welfare.* New York: Pantheon Books.

Lezubski, Darren, Jim Silver, and Errol Black. 2000. "High and Rising: The Growth of Poverty in Winnipeg's Inner City." In Jim Silver (ed.), *Solutions that Work: Fighting Poverty in Winnipeg.* Halifax and Winnipeg: Fernwood Publishing and Canadian Centre for Policy Alternatives-Manitoba.

MacKinnon, Shauna. 2000. "Workfare in Manitoba." In Jim Silver (ed.), *Solutions that Work: Fighting Poverty in Winnipeg.* Halifax and Winnipeg: Fernwood Publishing and Canadian Centre for Policy Alternatives-Manitoba.

McNally, David. 2009. "Inequality, the Profit System and Global Crisis." In Julie Guard and Wayne Antony (eds.), *Bankruptcies and Bailouts.* Halifax: Fernwood Publishing.

____. 2011. *Global Slump: The Economics and Politics of Crisis and Resistance.* Halifax: Fernwood.

Mikkonen, Juha, and Dennis Raphael. 2010. *Social Determinants of Health: The Canadian Facts.*

Toronto: York University School of Health Policy and Management. <thecanadianfacts.org/>.

NCW (National Council of Welfare). 1975. *Poor Kids: A Report by the National Council of Welfare on Children in Poverty in Canada*. Ottawa: National Council of Welfare.

____. 1996. *Poverty Profile 1995*. Ottawa: National Council of Welfare.

____. 2004. *Poverty Profile 2001*. Ottawa: National Council of Welfare.

____. 2006. *Poverty Profile 2002 and 2003*. Ottawa: National Council of Welfare.

____. 2008a. Custom Tabulation of Statistics Canada, Survey of Labour and Income Dynamics. Calculations by National Council of Welfare. Ottawa: National Council of Welfare.

____. 2008b. *Poverty Profile 2007: Bulletin No. 2 — Poverty Trends by Family Type, 1976–2007*. Ottawa: National Council of Welfare.

Panitch, Leo, and Sam Gindin. 2009. "The Current Crisis: A Socialist Perspective." *Studies in Political Economy* 83, Spring.

Pulkingham, Jane, and Gordon Ternowetsky. 1999. "Neoliberalism and Retrenchment: Employment, Universality, Safety Net Provisions and a Collapsing Canadian Welfare State." In Dave Broad and Wayne Antony (eds.), *Citizens or Consumers? Social Policy in a Market Society*. Halifax: Fernwood Publishing.

Raphael, Dennis. 2007. *Poverty and Public Policy in Canada: Implications for Health and Quality of Life*. Toronto: Canadian Scholars' Press.

____. 2008. *Social Determinants of Health: Canadian Perspectives*. Second edition. Toronto: Canadian Scholars' Press.

____. 2009. "Poverty, Human Development, and Health in Canada: Research, Practice and Advocacy." *Canadian Journal of Nursing Research* 41, 2.

Ross, David, and Paul Roberts. 1999. *Income and Child Well-Being: A New Perspective on the Poverty Debate*. Ottawa: Canadian Council on Social Development.

Sarlo, Christopher. 1996. *Poverty in Canada*. Second edition. Vancouver: Fraser Institute.

Schellenberg, Grant. 1997. *The Changing Nature of Part-Time Work*. Ottawa: Canadian Council on Social Development.

Schellenberg, Grant, and David Ross. 1997. *Left Poor by the Market: A Look at Family Poverty and Earnings*. Ottawa: Canadian Council on Social Development.

Silver, Jim. 2006. *In Their Own Voices: Building Urban Aboriginal Communities*. Halifax: Fernwood Publishing.

____. 2009. "Complex Poverty and Home-Grown Solutions in Two Prairie Cities." In Sharon McKay, Don Fuchs, and Ivan Brown (eds.), *Passion for Action in Child and Family Services: Voices from the Prairies*. Regina: Canadian Plains Research Centre.

____. 2010. "Spatially Concentrated Racialized Poverty as a Social Determinant of Health: The Case of Winnipeg's Inner City." In Lynne Fernandez, Shauna MacKinnon and Jim Silver (eds.), *The Social Determinants of Health in Manitoba*. Winnipeg: Canadian Centre for Policy Alternatives-Manitoba.

____. 2011. *Good Places to Live: Poverty and Public Housing in Canada*. Halifax and Winnipeg: Fernwood Publishing.

Silver, Jim, and Owen Toews. 2009. "Combating Poverty in Winnipeg's Inner City: Thirty Years of Hard-Earned Lessons." *Canadian Journal of Urban Research* 18, 1 (Summer).

Silver, Susan, Sue Wilson, and John Shields. 2004. "Job Restructuring and Worker Displacement: Does Gender Matter?" *Canadian Women's Studies* 23, 3/4

Social Planning Council of Winnipeg and Winnipeg Harvest. 1997. *Acceptable Living Level*. Winnipeg: Social Planning Council of Winnipeg.

Stanford, Jim. 1996. "Discipline, Insecurity and Productivity: The Economics Behind Labour Market

'Productivity.'" In Jane Pulkingham and Gordon Ternowetsky (eds.), *Remaking Canadian Social Policy: Social Security in the Late 1990s*. Halifax: Fernwood Publishing.

____. 1998. "The Rise and Fall of Deficit-Mania: Public Sector Finances and the Attack on Social Canada." In Wayne Antony and Les Samuelson (eds.), *Power and Resistance: Critical Thinking about Canadian Social Issues*. Second edition. Halifax: Fernwood Publishing.

____. 1999. *Paper Boom: Why Real Prosperity Requires a New Approach to Canada's Economy*. Ottawa and Toronto: Canadian Centre for Policy Alternatives and Lorimer.

Statistics Canada. 2006. *Reasons for Part-Time Work by Sex and Age Group*. (Catalogue No. 89fo133xie). Ottawa: Statistics Canada.

____. 2009a. *Labour Force Historical Review 2009* (Table 002). Catalogue No. 71F0004XVB.

____. 2009b. *Persons in Low Income, by Economic Family Type*, CANSIM table 202-0804.

____. 2010a. *Income in Canada 2008* (Tables 202-0802 and 202-0804). Catalogue No. 75-202-X.

____. 2010b. *Canadian Economic Observer: Historical Statistical Supplement*. Catalogue No. 11-210-X.

____. 2010c. *Labour Force Survey Estimates*. CANSIM table: 282-0087.

Swanson, Jean. 2001. *Poor-Bashing: The Politics of Exclusion*. Toronto: Between the Lines.

Teeple, Gary. 2000. *Globalization and the Decline of Social Reform into the Twenty-First Century*. First edition. Toronto: Garamond Press.

Thompson, Eleanor. 2005. *Child Poverty in Rich Countries 2005*. Report Card No. 6. Florence, Italy: Innocenti Research Centre.

____. 2010. "Calculations of the Benefits of Winnipeg's Urban Circle Training Centre." Document in author's possession.

WHO (World Health Organization). 2008. *Closing the Gap in a Generation: Health Equity Through Action on the Social Determinants of Health*. Geneva: World Health Organization.

Wilkinson, Richard, and Kate Pickett. 2009. *The Spirit Level: Why More Equal Societies Almost Always Do Better*. London: Penguin Books.

Wilson, Daniel, and David Macdonald. 2010. *The Income Gap Between Aboriginal Peoples and the Rest of Canada*. Ottawa: Canadian Centre for Policy Alternatives.

Wolfson, M., and J. Evans. 1989. *Statistics Canada's Low-Income Cutoffs: Methodological Concerns and Possibilities*. Ottawa: Statistics Canada.

World Bank National Accounts Data. 2009. *World Development Indicators*, GDP.

____. 2009. *World Development Indicators*, GDP *Growth Annual Percentage*.

____. 2009. *World Development Indicators*, GDP *Per Capita*.

Yalnizyan, Armine. 1998. *The Growing Gap: A Report on Growing Inequality Between Rich and Poor in Canada*. Toronto: Centre for Social Justice.

____. 2007. *The Rich and the Rest of Us: The Changing Face of Canada's Growing Gap*. Toronto: Canadian Centre for Policy Alternatives.

Appendix: The Debate about Poverty Lines

The most commonly used measurement of poverty is the Statistics Canada low-income cut-off (LICO), which is used as a poverty line by most social policy groups in Canada. However, Statistics Canada itself does not see the LICO as a poverty line, and objections — including from the Fraser Institute (Sarlo 1996) — have been expressed regarding this "relative" approach to poverty. Some argue that an alternative measurement based on the market costs of a "basket" of goods and services deemed to be "essential" would be a more accurate measurement of poverty.

The LICO

The LICO is a relative approach to poverty that uses Statistics Canada family expenditures data to determine what proportion of its total income the average Canadian household spends on food, clothing, and shelter. Any household whose expenditures on these necessities is 20 percentage points or more higher than the average household has, by definition, an income below the LICO. The reasoning is that any household spending so much of its income on these three essentials has too little left for such other necessary expenditures such as transport, personal care, household supplies, recreation, health, and insurance.

The Statistics Canada researchers have established thirty-five separate LICOs in Canada. These are the result of dividing the population into seven different household types, based on the size of household, and establishing five different types of geographic area, based on the size of the community in which people live. Thus a family of four in a large centre like Vancouver would have a different LICO than a single person in Corner Brook, who in turn would have a different LICO than a single-parent with two children in Kingston.

Those who object to the LICO as a poverty line advance several arguments. One is that choosing to establish a LICO at 20 percentage points above what the average household spends on food, clothing, and shelter is arbitrary. But all poverty lines, including those based on absolute measures, are arbitrary, as shown below. More importantly, those opposed to the LICO as a poverty line argue that it is a relative, and not an absolute, measure. They argue that it measures not poverty, but income inequality, because it is based on a given family's expenditures relative to an average Canadian figure. A more meaningful measurement, these critics argue, would be to determine the cost of the basic necessities of life for any Canadian household. The cost of a "basket" of such necessities then becomes the poverty line; those with incomes below that amount are below the poverty line. This is the argument advanced by Christopher Sarlo (1996), whose work is associated with the Fraser Institute. This absolute approach, though, raises as many problems as it solves.

The Fraser Institute Approach

The main problem with the absolute approach is the difficulty of determining what should be included in the basket of necessities and what should be excluded. Beyond agreement about food, clothing, and shelter, we can legitimately differ about what constitutes "necessities." The determination of what those necessities are becomes, at least in part, arbitrary. Sarlo defines basic necessities narrowly. He argues, for example, that the cost of health services and products not covered by Medicare and the cost of newspapers are not to be included in a basket of basic necessities. He calls those items "social comforts" or "social amenities" (Sarlo 1996: xvii, 28, 46). Basic necessities by his definition include only the physical necessities of life: "People are poor if they cannot afford all basic physical necessities — items the absence of which is likely to compromise long term physical well-being" (Sarlo 1996: 196). By this definition far fewer Canadians live in poverty than is the case when, for example, the LICO is used. Sarlo has argued, "Poverty, as it has been traditionally understood, has been virtually eliminated. It is simply not a major problem in Canada" (Sarlo 1996: 2). Existing government programs, he claims, are sufficient to lift all Canadians above his poverty line, and so governments need not spend anything more to combat poverty. This conclusion is consistent with the ideological orientation of the Fraser Institute, an organization strongly in favour of reduced government expenditures.

A strong case can be made that the Sarlo approach is too narrow and that the basic necessities of life in Canada include more than simply what is needed to avoid compromising long-term physical well-being. For example, why would health and dental costs that are excluded by Medicare not be included in a "basket" of necessities? What about school supplies and school outings for children? Reasonable people may disagree about exactly what items to include in a market basket of necessities, but most would conclude that for a healthy and reasonably equitable society the basket should not be as small as the one Sarlo advocates.

An innovative experiment in Winnipeg in 1997 provided that larger viewpoint. The Social Planning Council of Winnipeg and Winnipeg Harvest recruited seven low-income Winnipeggers to determine what should be included in a basket of goods and services that would provide an acceptable living level — what they called "a reasonable but not extravagant expectation of living costs." Using a hypothetical family of three that included a single mother who neither smoked nor owned a car, plus a girl under six and a boy of fifteen years, they concluded that the cost of a basket of goods and services necessary to produce an acceptable living level required an annual income of $26,945.60 — a figure very close to the LICO of $27,672 (Social Planning Council of Winnipeg and Winnipeg Harvest 1997: iii). As the National Council of Welfare (1998/99: 37) put it: "That led them to the view that the market basket and statistical approaches validate each other and make both approaches more credible."

The Statistics Canada LICO has certain advantages. Although it is, in part, arbitrary, so is the basic necessities approach, because someone must determine what is a basic necessity and what is not. Furthermore, although the LICO is a relative as opposed to an absolute measurement, poverty itself is a phenomenon having much to do with a particular person's relative position in society. Consider school supplies and money for school outings. In Canada today most children live in families that can afford school supplies and money for school outings; the child whose family cannot afford these is socially excluded from the "normal" activities of our society. In other words, poverty has a social and psychological component as well as simply a physical component. Sarlo can say, "I am not at all offended by inequality. I have no problem with large variations of income and wealth. I do not regard it as unjust or unfair that Wayne Gretzky earns one hundred times as much as most men his age" (Sarlo 1996:

3). But most Canadians find it both unjust and unfair that some families cannot purchase school supplies or pay for school outings while others earn six-figure incomes. In a society of material affluence, there is more to poverty than simply the absence of the material means to meet bare physical needs.

Whatever its limitations as a measurement of poverty, the Statistics Canada LICO is a useful measurement for research purposes. It enables us to determine, for instance, that poverty is higher in Winnipeg than in most other Canadian centres, and that it is higher in Winnipeg's inner city than in Winnipeg as a whole. It enables us to determine that poverty in Canada has been persistently high in recent decades, and that certain categories of people — those in particular family arrangements and those with a particular relationship to the labour market — are more likely than others to be poor. These useful research findings are made possible by the use of the Statistics Canada LICO; and they are confirmed by innovative approaches such as the Social Planning Council/Winnipeg Harvest market-basket study, which established acceptable living levels roughly equivalent to the Statistics Canada LICO. Sarlo's claim that poverty "is simply not a major problem" in Canada has a hollow ring, and it throws into doubt the merits of his alternative approach to the measurement of poverty.

6

Power, Resistance, and the Global Economic Crisis

David McNally

YOU SHOULD KNOW THIS

- Governments spent over $20 trillion — an amount equivalent to one and a half times the U.S. gross domestic product — to bail out the world's banks and kick-start the economy in 2008–9.
- In 2007, less than half the grain produced in the world was used to feed people. The bulk went to producing bio-fuels or animal feed while millions starved.
- In Canada the poorest half of the population owns merely 3 percent of all wealth, while the richest 10 percent holds 58 percent — making an individual in the top 10 percent more than 100 times wealthier than the average person in the bottom half.
- In the late 1970s a Canadian CEO made twenty-five times what their average worker earned; just twenty-five years later they earned 250 times as much.

Sources: Alessandri and Haldane 2009; Pittman and Ivry 2009; Cowan 2009; Reuters 2009; *New Internationalist* 2008; Osberg 2008; McQuaig 2010.

THE GLOBAL ECONOMIC CRISIS OF 2008–09 REPRESENTS a dividing line, after which our world can never be the same. With that crisis, we entered a new period of economic and social turbulence that is redrawing the political landscape. Mainstream politicians and corporate media work overtime to deny this reality, of course, uttering constant reassurances that economic growth and recovery are now the order of the day and that global capitalism has returned to business as usual. But the more intelligent liberal economists understand that something dramatic happened over the last few years.

Take the following comment, for instance, from a former research director at the International Monetary Fund, writing with one of his colleagues: "The global financial crisis of the late 2000s," they state, "stands as the most serious global financial crisis since the Great Depression. The crisis has been a transformative moment in global economic history whose ultimate resolution will likely reshape politics and economics for at least a generation" (Reinhart and Rogoff 2009: 208). This clearly captures the magnitude of what has happened. However, it is not a question as to whether the global economic crisis *will* reshape world politics; as I show below, it is already reshaping politics and economics for the next generation. But before turning to that question, let us take stock of the enormity of the crisis itself.[1]

Dimensions of the Crisis

According to his memoir of those tumultuous months, U.S. Treasury Secretary Hank Paulson confided to his wife on September 14, 2008, "I am really scared" (Paulson 2010: 215). Small wonder: that day the century-old Lehman Brothers investment bank was disintegrating, sending shockwaves through global credit markets. Lehman officially collapsed the next day, followed twenty-four hours later by AIG, the world's largest insurance company. Before the month was out Washington Mutual would melt down, registering the biggest bank failure in U.S. history. Then America's fourth largest bank, Wachovia, went on life support. A wave of European bank collapses rapidly followed.

By this point, it was not just Hank Paulson who was traumatized. Governments, corporate CEOs, and media pundits were in full panic mode. Alan Greenspan, former chair of the U.S. Federal Reserve Bank, informed a Congressional committee that he was in a state of "shocked disbelief" over the failure of markets to self-regulate (Greenspan 2008). The rich and power-ful men (and a handful of women) who dominate our planet seemed to have been rendered powerless in the face of an economic tsunami. By the fall of 2008 the global financial system was in full-fledged meltdown. Not only did all five Wall Street investment banks collapse; stock markets plummeted, losing $35 trillion in a matter of months. Global trade plunged, and worldwide credit seized up as financial institutions refused to lend for fear that borrow-ers would not survive. With shaken commentators invoking memories of the 1930s, two U.S. investment bankers openly compared the situation with the Great Depression (Farrell 2008; *Globe and Mail* 2008). Looking back a year or so later, Canada's Finance Minister Jim Flaherty remarked that the world economy had hov-ered on the edge of "catastrophe" (cited in Perkins 2009).

> The rich and powerful men (and a handful of women) who dominate our planet seemed to have been rendered powerless in the face of an economic tsunami.

And while it had started on Wall Street, the catastro-phe seemed to be frighteningly contagious. From Ireland to Spain, Britain, Germany, Iceland, and beyond, banks were falling like dominoes. Furthermore, although the epicentre was in the financial sector, major manufacturing corporations went bust too, as General Motors and Chrysler did before being bailed out by governments in the U.S. and Canada. With factories and service providers shutting down and cutting back, millions of people lost their jobs, and many of them their homes. Homelessness and hunger soared; by the World Bank's estimates, an additional 64 million people were driven into poverty in 2010 alone.

Through its first year or so, the crisis tracked the contours of Great Depression of the 1930s. The collapse of world industrial production, global trade, and stock market values was as severe as in 1929–30, sometimes more so (Eichengreen and O'Rourke 2009, 2010). For the first time in seventy years the unthinkable seemed thinkable again: that world capitalism might have entered a crisis with no clear end in sight. So destabilizing was the capitalist crisis of confidence that in March 2009 the *Financial Times*, the most venerable business paper in the English-speaking world, ran a series on "The Future of Capitalism," as if that were now an issue. Introducing the series, its editors declared, "The credit crunch has destroyed faith in the free market ideology that has dominated Western economic thinking for a decade. But what can — and should — replace it?" The next day the paper's editors opined that "The world of the past three decades is gone." One of its columnists quoted a Merrill Lynch banker who fretted, "Our world is broken — and I honestly don't know what is going to replace it" (Tett 2009).

By the final months of 2009, however, the bank meltdown was receding. Led by the U.S. Federal Reserve, central banks had poured trillions of dollars into financial institutions in the largest co-ordinated bailout in history. In concert with their treasuries and finance departments, they also rescued collapsing auto companies and pumped further trillions in stimulus money into their economies. All told, governments in the world's largest economies anteed up over $20 trillion — an amount equivalent to one and a half times the U.S. gross domestic product — via a massive intervention without historical precedent.[2]

But having bailed out the international financial system, governments then turned to the question of who shall pay for these extraordinary rescue packages. Not surprisingly, they all came up with the same answer: working people and the poor shall foot the bill, by way of lower wages, higher unemployment, and huge cuts to the social services on which all but the rich rely. With this declaration, they inaugurated an "age of austerity," which will be with us for many years to come. We shall return to this theme below. Before that, however, it is vital to address the question of what it is that creates such profound crises of the capitalist economy.

The Instability of a Profit-Driven System

Today we largely take for granted the idea that we use money to purchase all the basic things of life. Our morning coffee, the bread and rice we consume, the clothes we wear, the housing in which we live are all procured through market exchange. Yet, contrary to the image most of us have, this has not been the norm throughout human history. For most of our history people made the basic goods of life — food, clothing, shelter, furniture — on the land on which they resided. To be sure, they might visit markets for the occasional purchase of specific things. But weeks, even months, might go by in which people did not enter into market exchange.

Because most people in non-capitalist societies possessed land — both their own plots and the common lands which could be used by all — they could produce almost everything they consumed. They grew crops and raised livestock. They made their own clothes, furniture, candles and soap. They gathered firewood, herbs, and berries from the forests. They fished and drew water from the lakes, ponds, rivers, and streams, which they shared. They collected wood, straw, rocks, and mud to build their dwellings. In all these ways, they had direct access to the means of life. This is not to say that life was easy; nor is it to say they were free from exploitation — in fact, they generally had to pay rent and taxes to landlords and the state. But possession of land (as either owners or tenants) meant that, outside periods of drought or warfare, most people could count on having food and shelter.

Capitalism ended all that by privatizing land. Through economic pressures (huge rent increases) and use of force, peasants were driven from their farms, and their common lands were privatized. No longer able to produce for themselves, people had no option but to enter market exchange — transactions between buyers and sellers — in order to make ends meet. For the vast majority, this meant seeking a (capitalist) buyer for their labour so that they might earn wages with which to purchase the goods necessary to survival (McNally 2006: 89–96). As a result, displaced peasants were frequently forced to migrate, often to towns and cities, in search of work for a wage. In the countryside, meanwhile, land was concentrated into great farms worked by landless labourers who produced a "cash crop" sold by capitalists on the market; while factory towns emerged employing masses of dispossessed labour. In many parts of the world today, perhaps most dramatically in China at the moment, we can see similar processes at work, as millions of peasants are dispossessed of land and compelled to migrate to urban areas in search of work (McNally 2006: 96–109).

With the rise of capitalism, people thus become market dependent (Wood 2002). Human survival was no longer based on working the land, but on buying and selling in the market. The market thus became an ever-present part of people's daily lives, rather than something they might attend from time to time, as it was for people

> With the rise of capitalism, human survival was no longer based on working the land, but on buying and selling in the market.

in peasant-based societies. Capitalism allows us no other way of living but to purchase the goods of life on the market. And you can purchase these only if you can sell something that provides the cash with which to buy goods. Unless you are independently wealthy, this means selling your ability to work, your labour (McNally 1993).

But what drives such a market economy? What is the point of producing goods for exchange on the market rather than for your own use? Why should business owners make investments that bring huge amounts of grain, cell phones, cars, steel, and DVDs to the market?

A blunt statement by a former CEO of U.S. Steel Corporation offers an important clue to the mystery of a capitalist economy. Explaining why his company was closing mills and laying off thousands, he remarked, "U.S. Steel is in business to make profits, not to make steel" (cited in Bensman and Lynch 1988). Rarely is it put with greater clarity: under capitalism, use is irrelevant; profit is king. Capitalist enterprises have no particular attachment to what they turn out, be it flat-rolled steel, loaves of bread, or pairs of blue jeans. They produce these things if, and only if, they think they can make a profit in doing so. When they invest in a bakery, the real goal is not to produce bread; when they buy a garment factory, the objective is not to turn out jeans; and when they build a steel mill the purpose is not to turn out steel. Bread, jeans, steel, and everything else are for them merely means to an end: profit.

Put differently, bread, steel, water, houses, blue jeans, books, computers, and cars count for capitalist firms only as potential sums of money. The specific human needs they satisfy are ultimately irrelevant to the drive to accumulate wealth. They will invest in producing bombs or bread, cigarettes or vitamins — it doesn't matter which — as long as it will generate wealth. We can see this logic at work in the case of one of the most vital necessities of life: food.

> They will invest in producing bombs or bread, cigarettes or vitamins — it doesn't matter which — as long as it will generate wealth.

In 2007, less than half the grain produced in the world was used to feed people. The global grain harvest that year was 2.1 billion tons. But just one billion of that went to human consumption. The rest went to producing bio-fuels or animal feed (*New Internationalist* 2008). So, while a billion people teetered on the brink of starvation, most of the world's grain was diverted away from them — because that was the more profitable thing to do. This single example graphically illustrates how survival for millions can literally turn on the dictates of the market. It also illustrates how the logic of capitalism — production for profit — can directly clash with the logic of human survival. For the vast majority of people it makes human sense that the corn being grown will be used for food, rather than as fuel for trucks or for heating factories. But what makes human sense is not what drives a capitalist economy.

That is why our world economic system displays the staggering capacity to both produce the wealth necessary to feed, clothe, shelter, and educate everyone while simultaneously denying billions access to those goods. In the most extreme and scandalous situations, we witness the obscenity of people starving amidst mountains of food. The example of the "free market famine" in Niger in 2005 illustrates the point. As a British journalist explained at the time,

> In Tahou market, there is no sign that hard times are at hand. Instead, there are piles of red onions, bundles of glistening spinach, and pumpkins sliced into orange shards. There are plastic bags of rice, pasta and manioc flour....
>
> Starving infants are wrapped in gold foil to keep them warm. There is the sound of children wailing or coughing....
>
> This is the strange reality of Niger's hunger crisis. There is plenty of food, but children are starving because their parents can't afford it. (Vasagar 2005)

It is important to understand that this drive for profit is not a mere personal obsession of individual investors. Rather than a psychological quirk, there is a systemic basis to such behaviour. Capitalists, after all, inhabit a competitive environment. Each owner of a bakery, every investor in a garment factory, is competing with many others. Each is trying to bring to market a product of roughly equal quality at less cost. That is the only way to be sure of sales and profits. And this means that profits must regularly be ploughed back into the company in order to buy new technologies that render the firm more efficient, capable of producing the same good more quickly and cheaply. But these investments are not possible without making profits; they can only be paid for if the company earns more than it spends. As a result, the imperative to minimize costs and maximize profits is imposed on every capitalist by pressures of competition. And this is why capitalism is an economy characterized by frenetic growth — at least until a crisis comes, which itself will have been caused by the very process of feverish growth, as we shall see.

Over-Accumulation and Economic Crises

Since the company that stands still is the one that loses the competitive race, each and every firm is driven to expand incessantly. And this constant drive to expand is at the very heart of economic crises of the sort the world has experienced in recent years. For, as every capitalist firm invests in order to lower costs, boost sales, and increase profits, they all build new production facilities — factories, offices, mines, mills, hotels, and shopping centres — at a manic pace, all the while retooling their factories, mines, and offices with new equipment and technologies. This produces an economic boom in the early stages. Then, when things start to falter, companies borrow to keep financing more investment, while pressing governments to lower interest rates so that consumers can keep borrowing and buying too.

But a point comes at which there are simply too many factories and too much equipment producing the same good, be it bread, jeans, or cars, and too many service companies opening restaurants or selling trips to the Caribbean. Some of these companies become entirely unprofitable. But, as long as they can, they stay in business desperately hoping to generate revenues that will keep them afloat. This is the point at which capital has over-accumulated — more capacity to produce goods and services has been built than can be utilized profitably — and profit rates start to decline.

A crisis in the capitalist economy thus has three inter-related features. The first is "over-accumulation": more means of producing wealth (factories, machines, and so on) have been accumulated than can be profitably used. The second is "overproduction": more goods and services have been created than can be profitably sold. Finally, there is declining profitability: having over-accumulated (which also means over-investing in machines relative to workers), companies find themselves earning less for every dollar invested (McNally 2011b).

To get a sense of the extent of over-accumulation that has accompanied the crisis of 2008 onward, consider China, the most dynamic centre of global accumulation over the past twenty years. In the steel industry, where China had an excess capacity of between 100 and 200 million tons in late 2008, there were another 58 million tons of new capacity under construction by early 2010. At the World Economic Forum that year, the deputy director of the People's Bank of China acknowledged that the country's excess capacity in steel equals 200 million tons, slightly more than the total output of the twenty-seven economies of the European Union in 2008 (McNally 2011c: 7). And a manic building boom encouraged by a massive government stimulus program has only made all this worse. As one commentator put it, a "forest" of empty office buildings, shopping malls, and housing developments now dominates China's urban geography (Mackinnon 2010).

Once corporations are hit by an over-accumulation and profitability crisis, they desperately start slashing costs in order to stay afloat. They lay off workers, close factories, and shelve investment plans. But logical as this is for the individual firm, it only makes the crisis worse by lowering demand for goods and services, which in turn leads to further layoffs and plant closings, and so on, in a vicious downward cycle. Then all of this begins to hit banks, since many of their (effectively broke) corporate and (un- or under-employed) personal borrowers are no longer able to repay loans. If the crisis is severe, bank failures can then follow in quick order. And the cumulative effect of all this is an economic recession, sometimes a very deep one.

In some circumstances, economic crises will actually begin in the banking sector and then spread to the wider economy. Indeed, that is the pattern of the global slump that erupted in 2008–9. One of the reasons for that is the enormous increase in social inequality that has occurred since the 1970s.

Inequality and Financial Instability

It is fascinating to observe that both the Great Depression of the 1930s and the so-called "Great Recession" of 2008–09 were preceded by dramatic increases in social inequality. Put simply, the rich got fabulously richer, while the poor got persistently poorer. And this seems to have fed into the instability of the financial system, as we shall see.

> Both the Great Depression of the 1930s and the so-called "Great Recession" of 2008–09 were preceded by dramatic increases in social inequality.

Growing social inequality from the 1970s was driven by the co-ordinated effort of corporations and governments to break or weaken unions and roll back wages in the wake of an emerging crisis of capitalism (Brenner 2006). In some cases, unions were brutally crushed, as was the air traffic controllers union in the U.S., or massively defeated, like the miners unions in Bolivia and Britain. In other cases, labour leaders, like the president of the Canadian Union of Postal Workers, were jailed for defying new anti-union laws. In all these ways, union militancy was curbed. At the same time, corporations were closing unprofitable plants, introducing new labour-saving technologies to speed up work, and relocating to low-wage regions — from the southern U.S. to Mexico, or East Asia. All of this drove unemployment rates up and wages down. At the same time, social services, from health care to welfare, were cut, driving more people below the poverty line. And in the countries of the global south a debt crisis was used to impose "structural adjustment" programs that privatized public firms, from airlines to telephone companies, fired public employees, like nurses and teachers, and eliminated subsidies on necessities of life, such as food and fuel. The combined effect of these developments was a process of neoliberal wage compression which, in lowering wages, increased social inequality.

In the course of reducing the living standards of working-class people, these strategies spectacularly concentrated wealth at the top of the economic ladder. According to detailed studies for the United States, between 1973 and 2002, average real incomes for the bottom 90 percent of Americans fell by 9 percent. Incomes for the top 1 percent rose by 101 percent, while those for the top 0.1 percent soared by 227 percent. Recent updates to these remarkable data show that between 2002 and 2007 fully two-thirds of all new wealth created in the U.S. went to the richest 1 percent of the society (Atkinson, Picketty and Saez 2010). And a recent study done by researchers at the International Monetary Fund suggests that the poorest Americans have seen their real earnings chopped by 25 percent since the late 1960s (OECD 2008; Kumhof and Ranciere 2010: 6). Similar trends are at work in Canada, where incomes for the top 5 percent rose by nearly 44 percent between 1992 and 2004, while those of the top 0.01 percent rocketed 142 percent higher (Osberg 2008: 11). It is important to remember, furthermore, that income data do not capture the full picture of inequality. We get a more accurate view when we examine the ownership of corporate wealth. After all, income measurements look at the annual wage or salary that someone earns, while data on wealth track the total value of the assets people own — real estate, stocks, bonds, and so on. Using this lens, we again observe staggering growth of inequality. In Canada the poorest half of the population owns merely 3 percent of all wealth, while the richest 10 percent holds 58 percent — making an individual in the top 10 percent more than 100 times wealthier than the average person in the bottom half. And that degree of inequality has been steadily rising since the late 1970s (Osberg 2008: 24). In the United States, meanwhile, the richest 1 percent of Americans owned 38.7 percent of corporate wealth in 1991 and their share soared to 57.5 percent by 2003 (Johnston 2006). Similar trends are evident at the global level. According to the Boston Consulting Group, since the year 2000 the assets of the wealthiest 16.5 percent of global households (with at least $100,000 to invest) have soared by 64 percent, to $84.5 trillion. The bulk of that wealth resides in the portfolios of millionaire households. Although they comprise just 0.7 percent of the households on the planet, these millionaire families now hold over a third of the world's wealth (Boston Consulting Group 2007).

This explosion in social inequality can be usefully considered from two other angles. Viewed in relation to the average incomes, we see that whereas the richest 1 percent in the U.S. earned 100 times the national average income in 1970, today they earn 560 times the average. The disparity between the pay of chief executive offic-ers (CEOs) of U.S. corporations and the income·of their

> Whereas the average Canadian CEO made 25 times what their average worker earned in the late 1970s, a mere quarter-century later years later they earned 250 times as much.

average employees is equally instructive. In 1980 CEOs earned about forty-two times more than their employees. By 2000, they were pulling in 525 times as much (United for a Fair Economy 2008). And while executive pay is not quite as obscene in Canada, here too the wealth disparity is rocketing. Whereas the average Canadian CEO made twenty-five times what their average worker earned in the late 1970s, a mere quarter-century later years later they earned 250 times as much (McQuaig 2010).

As noted above, there are two periods in North American history during which income distribution became most unequal: the 1920s and the years 2005–8 — with the rich taking about half of total income in both periods. Interestingly, both of these were periods of fever-ish financial speculation that led to overinflated prices for real estate and stocks and then to financial meltdowns — the stock market and banking crashes of 1929–32, and the banking and financial crisis of 2007–9. Moreover, they were also periods of enormous increases in the debt loads carried by ordinary wage-earners. What is the link here? Why is it that, as the rich grab a larger and larger share of total income and the poor become more indebted, conditions are created for a financial meltdown?

These questions take us back to our starting point. Recall that the purpose of wealth for capitalists is not to produce goods for consumption, but to generate profits with which to invest in order to accumulate even greater wealth. And over the last thirty years or so, financial assets — paper titles to wealth such as stocks, bonds and a whole host of esoteric instruments — have often provided the highest rates of return. This process is frequently described as "financialization," a trend that has seen the share of total U.S. profits going to the financial sector double, relative to the share claimed by non-financial firms in manufacturing, mining, agro-business, and so on (Leonhardt 2008; Krippner 2005).

While this process was at work during the neoliberal period, it accelerated after 1997, when a severe crisis hit the economies of East Asia, and then further in the aftermath of the U.S. recession of 2000–1, when the dotcom bubble burst (McNally 2011c: 57–60; 101–02). In response, the U.S. Federal Reserve Bank repeatedly cut interest rates in hopes that making it cheaper to borrow money would encourage consumers to take out loans for cars, appli-ances, and houses, and would similarly induce businesses to borrow for new investments.

But with interest rates low, the wealthy, along with large institutional investors (like pen-sion and hedge funds), sought out more profitable places to park their money. And getting a piece of the ever-growing debt machine seemed to offer the most lucrative returns. In essence, finance is the business of lending money — for a price, measured by the interest rate on a loan. And this business of lending money and profiting on the interest payments made by debtors, be they governments, corporations, or working class consumers, had become the biggest growth industry around. Moreover, with working-class people's incomes squeezed, they were increasingly turning to debt markets to make ends meet. During the period during which Alan Greenspan was head of the Federal Reserve Bank (1987–2002), the central bank of the United States, private and public debt in the U.S. quadrupled, from slightly more than $10 trillion to $43 trillion (Phillips 2008). The structure of social inequality was thus fuelling a new debt economy in which the rich invested in the loans taken out by the poor.[3]

Such investments had become much easier thanks to a process known as "securitization," which refers to turning a loan into a "security" that can be purchased, just like a company's stock. With the rich and institutional investors clambering for more and more profitable IOUs to buy, ever more dubious debt — mortgages, credit card and car loans, commercial paper issued by corporations — was packaged together and given obscure names, like collateralized debt obligations (CDOs) and mortgage backed securities (MBSS), meant to make them sound low-risk. While all kinds of loans could be and were securitized, the largest market for financial securities was in mortgages. So, one financial institution after another devised ever more misleading ways of getting poor people to take out mortgages, while others created ever more obscure ways of packaging up these loans for sale (McNally 2011c: 102–07; Guttman 2009). Initially, hedge funds and other "shadow banks" dominated the market for these products; but traditional banks quickly moved into more aggressive and speculative short-term strategies in order to retain and attract business (Prins 2004: Ch. 1).

Consequently, competition to sell financial "products" (other people's debts) was intensifying. And this in turn contributed to both overproduction — a proliferation of more and more such financial "commodities" — and declining rates of profit on these products. As *Financial Times* columnist Gillian Tett noted, with more and more banks and investment funds getting into the market for these financial products, "the profits to be made on each deal declined" (Tett 2009a: 126). Taking the case of hedge funds — basically large non-bank investment firms — annual profits fell from around 18 percent in the 1990s to 7 percent or less between 2000 and 2006, when the first major cracks in the global financial system appeared (Ferguson 2008: 330; Collett 2011; *Economist* 2008). And this only induced further waves of speculative buying and selling of ever-riskier financial products, making the whole system more vulnerable to a meltdown.

What all this indicates is that the problems endemic to the capitalist economy — overaccumulation, overproduction and declining profit rates — were at play in the financial sector too, especially in a period of increasing social inequality, growing indebtedness of working people, and financialization. By the mid-2000s, it was only a question of time before the financial bubbles burst. And when they did we entered a new period of global slump.

Global Resistance in the Age of Austerity

As we have seen, the extraordinary bank bailout and stimulus programs of 2008–10 arrested the wave of bank collapses. But it did so at an enormous cost: roughly $20 trillion in bailout and stimulus spending. Sooner or later, the bill for rescuing global capitalism had to be paid. And in 2010 it became clear that the world's rulers had decided how that should be done: by way of an "age of austerity" — an era of huge cuts to pensions, education budgets, social welfare programs, and public sector wages and jobs. With this declaration, the ruling class decreed that working people and the poor will pay the cost of the global bank bailout. These payments may well last a generation — producing higher rates of poverty, more disease and ill health, ever more undersupplied schools, and greater hardship in old age. Consider the following. In response to financial market reactions to its debt, Latvia has fired one third of all teachers and slashed pensions by 70 percent. Ireland has chopped wages of government employees by 22 percent. The state of California has eliminated health insurance for 900,000 poor children. As I write these lines, the state of Michigan has ordered Detroit's public education officials to close half the city's schools (Granholm 2011). While austerity measures have not yet hit Canada as hard as many other countries, they are well underway. Already, the Ontario government has eliminated its "special diet" program designed to increase social assistance support for people with medical conditions, and the government of British Columbia, after binging on an Olympic extravaganza, has slashed a similar nutritional supplement program for low-income people. Meanwhile, the majority Conservative federal government elected in 2011 plans billions in cuts that will eliminate 40,000 public service jobs and slash spending on culture and the environment (Delacourt 2011). And this is just the beginning. Commentators are predicting a "decade of austerity," ten years or more of huge cuts to public sector jobs and to the social services on which poor and working class people rely (Guha 2009).

> Commentators are predicting a "decade of austerity," ten years or more of huge cuts to public sector jobs and to the social services on which poor and working class people rely.

For the majority of people, then, the crisis has not ended. The bad bank debt that triggered the meltdown in 2008 was simply shifted on to governments. Private debt became public debt. Rather than truly ending, the economic crisis of 2008-9 simply changed form; it mutated.

But that mutation shifted the crisis from banks to working class people. As a result, observes a columnist with the *Times* of London, "The rich have come through the recession with flying colours…. The rest of the country is going to have to face spending cuts, but it has little effect on the rich because they don't consume public services" (Beresford 2010). Despite huge job loss and enormously elevated rates of unemployment, especially for the young, profits are rising, bank bonuses are in style again, and luxury items are being bought with abandon.

This, of course, is merely a reminder of a basic theme that runs across this book: that in modern society who wins and who loses, who profits and who suffers depends on the power of different social groups and classes. So, when one U.S. economist observes that we have today "a statistical recovery and a human recession," we need to add, as one California teacher put it to me, that there is a statistical recovery exactly because there is a human recession.[4] Put simply, profits have improved (the "statistical recovery") largely because working class people have paid for them, through layoffs, wage cuts, reduced work hours, and the decimation of social services.

There is nothing inevitable about poor and working people being the losers in such struggles, however. Indeed, at the moment there is good reason to think that we might be entering an era of a "Great Resistance" to the age of austerity (McNally 2011c: Ch. 6).

From the moment the crisis hit, an impressive wave of working class resistance was unleashed. In response to factory closings and layoffs, workers staged plant occupations in Chicago, in several cities in Ontario, in Ireland, Scotland, and beyond; in France they coupled "bossnappings" to their factory occupations; and in France, Spain, Greece, and beyond they waged general strikes.

Yet, for all of the determination exhibited in the struggles waged in the global north during the early months of the crisis, working class people were unable to substantially reverse the corporate agenda of bank bailouts, plant closures, and mass layoffs. Even strikes and mass mobilizations of hundreds of thousands, and occasionally more than a million, in Greece, France, and Ireland, could not turn the tide. But then the focus of resistance turned to the global south, particularly North Africa, and things changed dramatically.

While the global north was the initial epicentre of the crisis, it was inevitable that the slump would wreak havoc on economies of the global south, whether via crises in export-based industries, like textiles in Egypt and Bangladesh, or sharp declines in national income as remittances from migrants in the north fell off (Hanieh 2009). As those effects took hold, forms of insurrectionary mass resistance burst out in parts of the south.

The earliest outburst of popular insurgency occurred in Guadeloupe and Martinique in early 2009, just as the global crisis was nearing its worst point.[5] Unemployment and poverty rates are twice as high on these Caribbean islands as on the French mainland, with youth unemployment well over 50 percent. Equally significant, Guadeloupe and Martinique represent textbook cases of racialized, neo-colonial capitalism. The local ruling classes, descendants of French slave-owners, are almost entirely white, while the working class is of African or mixed descent.

The battle started on January 20, 2009, when a coalition of fifty unions and social movement groups, known as "Stand Up Against Exploitation" (Liyannaj Kont Pwofitasyon, or LKP in the local dialect) initiated a strike for a 200 euro ($260 U.S. dollars) per month raise for the lowest paid workers. Under the leadership of the General Union of Workers of Guadeloupe, strikers shut down banks, schools, government offices, gas stations, hotels, the main shipping terminal, and the airport. Ten days into the strike, 60,000 people demonstrated in the streets of Pointe-à-Pitre — a mobilization of 15 percent of the island's population. Then the movement spread to the neighbouring island of Martinique, where 25,000 people (out of a population of 400,000) took to the streets with similar demands.

As the movements grew and street battles flared, the French government caved in, agreeing on March 4, 2009, to raise salaries for the lowest paid by 200 euros, a 40 percent increase, along with modest improvements of 3 to 6 percent for better paid workers. As celebrating protesters marched through the streets, they learned that the government had also agreed to lower water rates, hire more teachers, aid farmers and fishers, fund jobs and training for unemployed youth, freeze rents, and ban evictions. While the workers of Guadeloupe and Martinique did not bring about all the political transformations they sought, their militancy, creativity, and determination achieved tremendous things, proving that one can make major gains in the face of a deep recession.

But no struggle in the global south has more fired the popular imagination than the popular insurgency in Tunisia. The Tunisian uprising emerged around the interconnected demands for "Bread and Freedom," a sentiment that quickly resonated, inspiring upheavals in Jordan, Algeria, Egypt, Yemen, northern Sudan, and beyond. Mainstream commentators typically saw these struggles as specific to the Arab world — and there are certainly features distinctive to a number of Arab regimes at work here. But serious analysis indicates their integral links to the effects of the global slump, particularly in terms of the intersection of mass unemployment, poverty, and rising food prices.[6]

After all, neoliberal structural adjustment has been a driving factor in all these respects. Trade liberalization and privatization have produced widespread job loss, while the creation of low-wage export-processing regions, like the qualifying industrial zones (QIZs) in Egypt, has intensified the poverty of workers. Fully 40 percent of Egypt's population now lives on $2 a day or less. But workers have been organizing and fighting back; indeed the QIZs have been rocked by strikes in recent years. This is the volatile context in which rising food prices helped trigger large-scale revolt.

Rising food prices are themselves directly connected to neoliberalism and the global slump. Liberalization of world trade, intense competition from the heavily subsidized agro-industries in the North, and removal of subsidies for poor farmers in the South have all conspired to drive millions of peasant-farmers off the land from India to Mexico and beyond. Furthermore, national indebtedness causes governments to pressure farmers to grow export crops (like cotton or coffee) rather than foodstuffs. As a result, fewer countries today are capable of feeding themselves — all of which creates conditions for rising prices and profits for global agro-business.

Soaring prices for food provoked a wave of food riots throughout 2008. After a brief pause — in part due to slumping demand for food as layoffs and unemployment swept the U.S. and Europe in the early stages of the crisis — food prices started to rise again in 2010. By early 2011, the United Nation's food price index reached an all-time high. As a result, food is now more expensive than ever, aggravating economic hardship across the global south and throwing fuel on the fire of popular resentment. By early 2011, even the World Bank president was warning that rising food costs had driven an additional 44 million people into extreme poverty and pushed the number of chronically hungry people on the planet above one billion (Blas 2011).

> Food is now more expensive than ever, aggravating economic hardship across the global south and throwing fuel on the fire of popular resentment.

This food crisis is directly linked to new flows of "hot money" generated by the world-wide bank bailouts and economic stimulus programs. With trillions pumped into the banking system and interest rates pushed down to record lows, investors and speculators have leapt at the opportunity to borrow on the cheap to purchase commodities (and currencies) that look set to appreciate. Add into the equation two further factors — the increasing use of arable land for the production of bio-fuels rather than food, and speculative gambles that a poor Russian harvest or floods in Australia will damage food supplies and further drive up prices — and we have all the ingredients for huge price spikes. Wagering on exactly this, investment bankers and managers of pension and hedge funds have funnelled over $200 billion into bets on food since the financial crisis first broke, driving up prices in a frenzy of speculation.

All of this made "food riots" inevitable. But it did not determine that these would develop into insurgent political uprisings against governments of the sort we have seen in Tunisia and Egypt. That required robust grassroots networks (independent unions, social movements, student groups) capable of providing organizing hubs of resistance and of fusing together immediate economic grievances with political demands for democracy. In Tunisia, a critical role was played by labour unions. The General Union of Tunisian Workers (GUTW/UGTT), quiescent for years and with its leaders initially hesitant to join the struggle, became a key hub of resistance thanks to pressure by rank-and-file members who had spearheaded independent workers' protests in recent years. Spurred into action and radicalized by events, the labour movement began organizing rallies and launched a general strike, proving itself, as one commentator put it, "to be a serious political force with currently unmatched organizing capacity and national reach" (*Democracy Digest* 2011; see also Temlali 2011). Alongside strikes, activists of the GUTW have organized sit-ins and a "Caravan of Liberation," in efforts to sweep away all political officials linked to the regime of former dictator Zine el-Abidine Ben Ali. Nevertheless, there remain conservative as well as radical forces contending for the leadership of the GUTW: the outcomes of those struggles will have a huge impact on how far forward the liberation movement in Tunisia can go.

The Tunisian Intifada sparked waves of mass actions for Bread and Freedom throughout North Africa and the Middle East. Without a doubt, the most significant of these is the uprising in Egypt. It is not only that Egypt has an enormous geopolitical importance, affecting as it does the whole of international politics. It is also that the Egyptian Revolution was characterized by inspiring examples of people's power and working class organizing. As philosopher Peter Hallward wrote in the days prior to the removal of former president Hosni Mubarak from office, "with each new confrontation, the protestors have realised, and demonstrated, that they are more powerful than their oppressors.... Again and again, elated protestors have marvelled at the sudden discovery of their own power" (Hallward 2011).

Such shifts do not happen at the level of consciousness alone; they are inextricably connected to a revolution in the relations of everyday life — by way of the birth of popular power. So, when violently attacked, as they were on February 2, 2011, by undercover police and goons of the ruling party, wielding guns, knives, Molotov cocktails and more, the insurgents held their ground and fought back, holding Tahrir Square in downtown Cairo. In the process, they extended their grassroots self-organization. As reporters for the *Washington Post* noted, the activists in Tahrir Square created popular prisons to hold undercover security forces they had detained, and they opened people's clinics to care for the wounded (Fadel, Englund, and Wilgoren 2011). In the same spirit, the movement formed People's Protection forces, staffed by both women and men, to provide safety and security in neighbourhoods and in the mass marches and assemblies.

Alongside these forms of popular self-organization there emerged new practices of radical democracy. In Tahrir Square, the nerve centre of the Revolution, the crowd engaged in direct decision making, sometimes in its hundreds of thousands. Organized into smaller groups, people discussed and debated, and then sent elected delegates to consultations about the movement's demands. As one journalist explained, "delegates from these mini-gatherings then come together to discuss the prevailing mood, before potential demands are read out over the square's makeshift speaker system. The adoption of each proposal is based on the proportion of boos or cheers it receives from the crowd at large" (Shenker 2011). Prior to Mubarak's removal from office, the people truly felt they had "created a liberated republic within the heart of Egypt," in the words of one demonstrator (quoted in Hallward 2011).

Here too, we need to appreciate that years of courageous struggle by Egypt's workers were decisive in creating the conditions for the popular uprising. Social movements generally had been on the move recently in Egypt. The years 2002–03 saw important stirrings of political protest in solidarity with the Palestinian Intifada and in opposition to the U.S. invasion of Iraq. Shortly after this, the Kefaya (Enough) movement organized for democratic reform and the feminist group, Shayfenkom (We Are Watching You) came out in defence of women's rights.

But by 2004 it was strike action, sit-ins, and demonstrations by workers that comprised the most determined and persistent oppositional activity — most of it illegal under laws that denied workers the right to form independent unions. Over the past six years or so, more than two million workers engaged in thousands of direct actions. Most importantly, they regularly won significant concessions on wages and working conditions. The result was a growing confidence among workers — so much so that genuinely independent unions began to emerge in a society where the official unions were nothing but extensions of the state.

In 2006–07 mass working class protest erupted in the Nile Delta, spearheaded by the militant action of 50,000 workers in textiles and the cement and poultry industries. This was followed by strikes of train drivers, journalists, truckers, miners, and engineers. Then 2007–08 saw another labour explosion, with riots at the state-owned weaving factory in Al-Mahla Al-Kobra. The youth-based April 6th Movement emerged at this point in support of workers' strikes.

During the January–February 2011 Revolution, workers' struggles again surged to the fore. In the course of a few days during the week of February 7, tens of thousands stormed into action. Thousands of railway workers struck, blockading railway lines in the process. Six thousand workers at the Suez Canal Authority walked off the job, staging sit-ins at Suez and two other cities. In Mahalla, 1,500 workers at Abul Sebae Textiles walked out and blockaded the highway. At the Kafr al-Zayyat hospital hundreds of nurses staged a sit-in and were joined by hundreds of other hospital employees. Across Egypt, thousands of others — bus workers in Cairo, employees at Telecom Egypt, journalists at a number of newspapers, workers at pharmaceutical plants and steel mills, faculty members at Cairo University — joined the strike wave. Everywhere, these workers demanded improved wages, the firing of ruthless managers, back pay, better working conditions, and independent unions. And over and over again, they also called for the resignation of President Mubarak (McNally 2011a). In the face of this rising of the Egyptian working class, Mubarak's days were numbered. He resigned mere days into the strike wave.

While the great uprisings of Tunisia and Egypt resonated across the region — Yemen, Bahrain, Algeria, Libya, and beyond — it was especially significant to see the chord they struck among union activists, students, and others in the United States.

Global Resistance Emerges in North America

In February 2011, Madison, Wisconsin became centre-stage for the conflict between the neoliberal austerity agenda and progressive forces resisting it. On one side stood Wisconsin Governor Scott Walker, proposing a nine percent cut to state spending, attacks on workers' pensions, depriving tens of thousands of medicare, and elimination of most collective bargaining rights for state employees. On the other side converged students, teachers, parents, firefighters, and thousands of ordinary citizens determined to stop the attacks on public services and the workers who deliver them. And everywhere, the inspiration from Egypt was on display.

As thousands occupied the legislative building in Madison, where people rallied, sang, and spent the night, and as thousands more marched and demonstrated in the streets, signs proclaimed, "Welcome to Wiscairo" and "From Egypt to Wisconsin: We Rise Up" (Benjamin 2011; Sernatinger 2011; Sustar 2011). The struggle in Wisconsin soon inspired labour and social justice activists in many parts of the U.S., helping to swell numbers at rallies in Ohio, Indiana, Michigan, New Jersey, and beyond (BBC 2011; Brown and La Botz 2011.) And while anti-austerity protests are yet to rise to these heights in Canada, the spring and early summer of 2011 saw significant strikes at Canada Post and Air Canada and bubbling anti-cuts movements in many cities. These are almost certainly early indicators that, as the cutback axe falls more heavily in the years ahead, such protests will escalate.

Challenging Capitalism

At the time of writing, it was not yet clear to what degree "a new American labor movement has begun," as one astute commentator surmised (La Botz 2011 and 2011a). What is clear, however, is that, in the context of the global slump and the age of austerity, sharp class lines have been drawn. Every U.S. governor proposing to cut Medicare, public school funding, and pensions as well as curtail union rights is also pushing through multi-billion dollar tax cuts for corporations and the rich. We thus see, in all these confrontations, the basic logic of capitalism at work: that wealth is produced not to satisfy human needs — for food, education, health care, housing, security in old age — but to engender corporate profit. But we also see a counter-logic at work here: the logic of a resistance pointing toward a society that puts people before profit, one that makes human well-being and the eradication of poverty its priority.

From the people in the streets of Cairo or Tunis demanding "Bread and Freedom" to those in Athens, Paris, or Madison refusing to accept the gutting of social services we can discern an emerging movement toward anti-capitalism.[7] For in challenging the logic of markets and profits, these movements effectively insist that there is no good reason that a global society with the capacity to feed, clothe, shelter, educate, and care for everyone on the planet should tolerate massive poverty and hardship. Equally, there is no good reason our society should have to undergo debilitating economic crises. To change that — to end global hunger and poverty and to eliminate devastating crises — would require establishing a form of social and economic life based on production for need, not production for profit. This would mean a system based on democratic planning, worker self-management, and global solidarity (McNally 2006: Ch. 5). That may seem a remote possibility at the moment. But mounting hardship wrought by the global slump and the age of austerity are provoking powerful movements of mass resistance across our planet. In their struggles lies a profound search for a better world.

> From the people in the streets of Cairo or Tunis demanding "Bread and Freedom" to those in Athens, Paris, or Madison refusing to accept the gutting of social services we can discern an emerging movement toward anti-capitalism.

Glossary of Key Terms

Austerity: This term refers to the commitment by governments to restrain and reduce spending on social programs. Since the bank bailouts of 2008–9 it has often been used to describe the arrival of a new "age of austerity."

Capital: In everyday language and mainstream economics, this refers to the assets accumulated by banks and non-financial corporations in order to make profits. Factories, offices, mines, agri-businesses, investment funds, and so on are business assets of this sort. It was Karl Marx's innovation to insist that capital is not just a stock of things (like business assets) but also a social relation between owners of such assets ("capitalists") and wage-earners who sell their ability to work.

Financialization: The process through which relations among people become ever more embedded in financial transactions, in buying and selling. The result is greater dependence on markets and money for everything from food and water to housing, health care, education and pensions. In some usages, the term also refers to increasing reliance of the capitalist economy on credit; in others it denotes the growing share of wealth and profits going to banks and other financial institutions.

Globalization: This term typically refers to the international spread of manufacturing corporations and banks since the 1960s, often promoted by the World Bank and International Monetary Fund. It is also associated with neoliberalism (see next entry below) since the latter advocates the global spread of capitalist markets. In response, social justice movements have often called for the globalization of resistance.

Neoliberalism: The policies, practices, and ideas associated with the sharp turn to market regulation of society since the 1970s. Because glorification of the market was first preached by the liberalism of the eighteenth and nineteenth centuries, the recent version is commonly referred to as a new or neo liberalism. Neoliberalism preaches hostility to socialism, trade unions, and social welfare programs, all of which are alleged to "interfere" with the market. According to critics, the effects of neoliberalism have included increased poverty and social inequality, indebtedness for countries of the global south, and heightened policing and militarism.

Over-accumulation: The process by which capitalist enterprises accumulate more productive capacity — factories, machines, offices, mines, shopping malls, buildings, and so on — than they can profitably utilize. This is caused by intense competition to boost the productiveness of their companies by investing in new plants and technologies, which results in overcapacity.

Questions for Discussion

1. What similarities and differences does the economic crisis of 2008–09 have with the Great Depression of the 1930s?

2. What are the sources of economic instability in a capitalist economy?

3. What is the Age of Austerity and what are its causes?

4. How have some resistance movements been able to effect significant changes in their societies? Provide some examples.

Websites of Interest

Canadian Centre for Policy Alternatives
Ontario Coalition Against Poverty <ocap.ca>
Focus on the Global South
Left Business Observer
Blogs by David McNally <davidmcnally.org>

Notes

1. What follows draws closely on the much more detailed analysis developed in McNally 2011c.
2. The Bank of England tagged the rescue cost for the financial system in the U.S., United Kingdom, and Eurozone at about $14 trillion (Alessandri and Haldane 2009). But even that figure underestimates the full scale of the bailout, which has been more accurately placed at nearly $12 trillion for the U.S. alone once all forms of financial sector support are tallied, including the rescue of the auto sector (Pittman and Ivry 2009). I have then factored in global fiscal stimulus plans — of nearly $1 trillion in the U.S., almost $600 billion in China, over $200 billion in Japan, alongside nearly $500 billion between Russia, France, Canada, Australia, South Africa, Italy, Britain, and Argentina (Cowan 2009; Reuters 2009), and then added in the $1 trillion emergency fund created by the European Union in April/May 2010 to halt the spread of the Greek crisis to other parts of Europe. This combined global anti-crisis intervention appears to be in excess of $20 trillion,

an amount equal to almost one and a half times U.S. GDP. I recognize that not all of these funds will necessarily be spent in the end, and small amounts have been repaid. Nonetheless, this figure does give us some sense of the extraordinary scale of the intervention.

3. Another crucial factor was at work in all this — the accumulation of enormous reserves in the hands of China and other countries with huge trade surpluses, much of which was poured into financial investments in the U.S. It is not possible to explore this phenomenon in any detail here.

4. This astute observation was made by Los Angeles socialist and teacher activist, Sarah Knopp, in discussion during my presentation, "The Mutating Crisis of Global Capitalism," at the Socialism 2010 conference in Chicago, June 20, 2010.

5. In what follows, my account draws upon McNally 2011c: 161–63, and the sources cited there.

6. It is important to realize that at the same time major protests over food and fuel prices were rocking Bolivia and hitting parts of India.

7. Of course, it is in the nature of mass movements that people often act before they fully think through the social and political logic of their commitments. It is the task of organized political currents to assist the process of political self-clarification that such movements need.

References

Alessandri, Piergiorgio, and Andrew G. Haldane. 2009. *Banking on the State*. London: Bank of England, November.

Atkinson, Tony, Thomas Picketty, and Emmanuel Saez. 2010. "Top Incomes in the Long Run of History." *Journal of Economic Literature* 49, 1.

BBC (British Broadcasting Corporation). 2011. "US Union Protests: Demonstrations Move beyond Wisconsin." February 22. <bbc.co.uk/news/world-us-canada-12541294>.

Benjamin, Medea. 2011. "From Cairo to Madison: Solidarity and Hope Are Alive." *Huffington Post*, February 21.

Bensman, David, and Roberta Lynch. 1988. *Rusted Dreams: Hard Times in a Steel Community*. Berkeley: University of California Press.

Beresford, Philip. 2010. "The Sunday Times Rich List 2010: Rising from the Rubble." *The Sunday Times*, April 25.

Blas, Javier. 2011. "Chronic Hunger to Affect 1bn People." *Financial Times*, February 15.

Boston Consulting Group. 2007. *Global Wealth 2007*.

Brenner, Robert. 2006. *The Economics of Global Turbulence*. London: Verso.

Brown, Jenny, and Dan La Botz. 2011. "Wisconsin Spirit Sweeps across the Midwest." *Labor Notes*, February 23. <labornotes.org/2011/02/wisconsin-spirit-sweeps-across-midwest>.

Collett, John. 2011. "There's No Hiding behind the Hedge." *Sydney Morning Herald*, February 19.

Cowan, Tonia. 2009. "Fiscal Stimulus Plans of Select G20 Countries in Billions ($U.S.)." *Globe and Mail*, April 2.

Delacourt, Susan, 2011. "Ottawa's Summer of Layoffs." *Toronto Star*, July 7.

Democracy Digest. 2011. "Tunisian Unions Eclipsing Parties as Democratizing Force?" January 24.

Doane, Deborah. 2011. "The Threat of Rising Food Prices." *New Statesman*, January 11.

Economist. 2008. "Hedge Funds in Trouble." October 23.

Eichengreen, Barry, and Kevin H. O'Rourke. 2009 and 2010. "A Tale of Two Depressions." *Vox*, June 4, 2009, updated March 8, 2010. <voxeu.org/index.php?q=taxonomy/term/1619>.

Fadel, Leila, Will Englund, and Debbi Wilgoren. 2011. "5 Shot in 2nd Day of Bloody Clashes; Amid Outcry Egyptian PM Apologizes." *Washington Post*, February 3.

Farrell, Greg. 2008. "Merrill Chief Sees Severe Global Slowdown." *Financial Times*, November 11.

Ferguson, Niall. 2008. *The Ascent of Money: A Financial History of the World.* New York: Penguin Press.

Financial Times. "The Future of Capitalism." March 8.

Globe and Mail. 2008. "Doom and Gloom Rule on Wall Street." November 13.

Granholm, Jennifer. 2011. "Detroit Schools Closing: Michigan Officials Order Robert Bobb to Shut Half the City's Schools." *Huffington Post,* February 21.

Greenspan, Alan. 2008. "Testimony to the House Committee on Oversight and Government Reform." October 23. <oversight/hoU.S.e.gov/documents/20081023100438.pdf>.

Guha, Krishna. 2009. "Ten Years of Cuts and Tax Rises Lie Ahead IMF Says." *Financial Times,* November.

Guttman, Robert. 2009. "Asset Bubbles, Debt Deflation, and Global Imbalances." *International Journal of Political Economy* 38, 2: 45–68.

Hallward, Peter. 2011. "Egypt's Popular Revolution Will Change the World." *Guardian,* February 9.

Hanieh, Adam. 2009. "Hierarchies of a Global Market: The South and the Economic Crisis." *Studies in Political Economy* 83: 63–84.

Johnston, David Cay. 2004. *Perfectly Legal: The Covert Campaign to Rig Our Tax System to the Benefit of the Super Rich — and Cheat Everybody Else.* New York: Portfolio Books.

____. 2006. "Corporate Wealth Share Rises for Top-Income Americans." *New York Times,* January 29.

Krippner, Greta R. 2005. "The Financialization of the American Economy." *Socio-Economic Review* 3.

Kumhof, Michael, and Romain Rancière. 2010. *Inequality, Leverage and Crisis.* Washington: International Monetary Fund Working Paper, November.

La Botz, Dan. 2011. "A New American Labor Movement Has Begun." *The Bullet,* February 21. <socialistproject.ca/bullet/466.php>.

____. 2011a. "The New American Workers' Movement and the Confrontation to Come." *New Politics,* February 26. <newpolitics.mayfirst.org/node/432>.

Leonhardt, David. 2008. "Bubblenomics." *New York Times,* September 21.

Mackinnon, Mark. 2010. "The Garlic Barometer: Inflation Threatens to Slow China's Racing Economy." *Globe and Mail,* May 11.

McNally, David. 1993. *Against the Market: Political Economy, Market Socialism and the Marxist Critique.* London: Verso.

____. 2006. *Another World Is Possible: Globalization and Anti-Capitalism.* Winnipeg and London: Arbeiter Ring Publishing and Merlin Press.

____. 2011a. "Mubarak's Folly: The Rising of Egypt's Workers." February 11. <davidmcnally.org/?p=354>.

____. 2011b. "Economic Crisis." In Marcello Musto (ed.), *The Marx Revival.* New York: Palgrave MacMillan.

____. 2011c. *Global Slump: The Economics and Politics of Crisis and Resistance.* Oakland: PM Press.

McQuaig, Linda. 2010. "The Growth of Extreme Inequality in Canada." *Rabble.ca,* December 28.

New Internationalist. 2008. "Food Crisis: The Facts." December.

OECD (Organisation for Economic Co-operation and Development). 2008. *Growing Unequal? Income Distribution and Poverty in OECD Countries.* Paris, October.

Osberg, Lars. 2008. *A Quarter Century of Economic Inequality in Canada: 1981–2006.* Toronto: Canadian Centre for Policy Alternatives.

Paulson, Jr., Henry M. 2010. *On the Brink: Inside the Race to Stop the Collapse of the Global Financial System.* New York: Business Plus.

Perkins, Tara. 2009. "Weak Growth Delays Attack on Deficit." *Globe and Mail,* November 21.

Kevin Phillips. 2008. "The Destructive Rise of Big Finance." *Huffington Post,* April 4.

Pittman, Mark, and Bob Ivry. 2009. "Financial Rescue Package Approaches GDP as U.S. Pledges

$12.8 Trillion." *Bloomberg*, March 31. <bloomberg.com/apps/news?pid=newsarchive&sid=a rmOzfkwtCA4>.

Prins, Nomi. 2004. *Other People's Money: The Corporate Mugging of America*. New York: New Press.

Reinhart, Carmen M., and Kenneth S. Rogoff. 2009. *This Time Is Different: Eight Centuries of Financial Folly*. Princeton: Princeton University Press.

Reuters. 2009. "Keeping the Stimulus Tap Open." December 9.

Sernatinger, Andrew. 2011. "Battle of Wisconsin." In multiple parts, including <solidarity-us.org/current/node/3193>.

Shenker, Jack. 2011. "Cairo's Biggest Protest Yet Demands Mubarak's Immediate Departure." *Guardian*, February 5.

Sustar, Lee. 2011. "The Battle for the Capitol." *Socialist Worker*, March 1. <socialistworker.org/2011/03/01/battle-for-the-capitol>.

Temlali, Yassin. 2011. "Pourquoi l'UGTT a joué un role aussi important dans l'intifafda tunisienne." *Maghreb Emergent*, January 25. <maghrebemergent.com/actualite/maghrebine/1976-pourquoi-le-syndicat-a-joue-un-role-aussi-important-dans-lintifada-tunisienne.html>.

Tett, Gillian. 2009. "Lost Through Destructive Creation." *Financial Times*, March 9.

____. 2009a. *Fool's Gold*. New York: Free Press.

United for a Fair Economy. 2008. *Executive Excess 2008*. <faireconomy.org/issues/ceo_pay>.

Vasagar, Jeevan. 2005. "The Hungry Reality of Free-Market Niger." *Guardian*, August 2.

Winship, Michael. 2011. "Attacks on Unions Barking Up the Wrong Money Tree." *Truthout*, February 25. <truth-out.org/attacks-unions-barking-up-wrong-money-tree68063>.

Wood, Ellen Meiksins. 2002. *The Origin of Capitalism: A Longer View*. London: Verso.

7

"We Were Not the Savages"
Indian Residential Schools

Daniel Paul

YOU SHOULD KNOW THIS

- The last Indian residential school in Canada, the White Calf Collegiate, closed in 1996.
- The foundations of Indian residential schools were *The Act to Encourage the Gradual Civilization of Indian Tribes in this Province, and to Amend the Laws Relating to Indians* (commonly known as the *Gradual Civilization Act)* of 1857 and the *Gradual Enfranchisement Act* of 1869.
- Egerton Ryerson's study of native education, done for the assistant superintendent general of Indian Affairs, was the model for future Indian residential schools. He recommends domestic education and religious instruction as the best education for the Indians.
- Most residential schools operated on a half-day system, in which students spent half the day in the classroom and the other at work. The theory was that students would learn skills to allow them to earn a living as adults, but the reality was that work had more to do with running the schools inexpensively.
- The exact number of residential schools is not known. Religious orders operated such schools before 1867, but it was not until the 1880s that residential schools became the model for Aboriginal education. The Indian Residential School Settlement Agreement has identified 139 residential schools. This excludes residential schools that were run by religious orders or provincial governments.

Sources: CBC News 2008b; Canadian Encyclopedia n.d.; TRC n.d.

SYSTEMIC RACISM IS STILL A HEAVY UNWARRANTED BURDEN upon the backs of the Indigenous Peoples of Canada and the United States of America. It is the product of American Indians being dehumanized by demonizing European colonial and, consequently, Euro-American and Euro-Canadian propaganda, which has, until recent times, depicted us to be the offspring of bloodthirsty barbarian savages. That the lies had malicious intent is witnessed by the fact that throughout the ages Caucasians have used every communication means that were at hand to communicate to future generations of Caucasians the fictitious picture of the barbarian savages. Born in 1938, I have seen movies and read books designed and written with the intent to continue to imprint the demonizing colonial propaganda in the mindset of future generations.

After considering many alternatives, I've concluded that the only way that this fiction can ever be rooted out of the subconscious of Non-American Indians is by education. Such a goal will not be easy to achieve, simply because it will be necessary for Anglo-American and Anglo-Canadian societies to determine who actually were the "savages" when their ancestors invaded the Americas, and who is responsible for the consequent

> Systemic racism is still a heavy unwarranted burden upon the backs of the Indigenous Peoples of Canada and the United States of America.

colonizing of the lands that their ancestors seized by force from free and sovereign Nations. This chapter is a short overview of some of the horrors that befell my People as a result of the demonizing colonial propaganda and practices, which were the basis for the creation by federal governments of such items as Indian residential schools, which were designed to realize tribal extinction and, therefore, genocide.

The following statement by Rev. Martin Luther King Jr., in reference to the racial demeaning of the Indigenous people of the United States of America by the country's Caucasian government, is equally applicable to Canada: "Our nation was born in genocide when it embraced the doctrine that the original American, the Indian, was an inferior race" (King 1964). In fact, when one does an honest comparison of which country treated its Indigenous Peoples in the most barbaric manner, the conclusion would be a tie.

King's statement neatly describes the warped Euro-White supremacist mentality that propelled the colonial British, and later Canadian, effort, which lasted for centuries, to get the "Indian out of the Indian" and to assimilate the Indigenous People into extinction. It is without question this warped mindset that begot the horrors that First Nations Peoples have suffered since the English invasion of North America began. Speeches by an American president and a Canadian superintendent of Indian Affairs, offer proof that the White supremacist mentality previously described prevailed over the centuries.

U.S. President Martin Van Buren's words, uttered in 1837, unequivocally articulate the predominant White supremacist mentality that the Indigenous peoples of the Americas have had to contend with since Columbus landed in 1492.

> No state can achieve proper culture, civilization, and progress … as long as Indians are permitted to remain. (Wright 1993: 218)

Federal Indian Commissioner Dr. Duncan Campbell Scott in 1920, when supporting assimilation legislation, echoed Van Burin's thoughts:

> I want to get rid of the Indian problem. I do not think as a matter of fact, that the country ought to continuously protect a class of people who are able to stand alone…. Our objective is to continue until there is not a single Indian in Canada that has not been absorbed into the body politic and there is no Indian question, and no Indian Department, that is the whole object of this Bill."

> Our objective is to continue until there is not a single Indian in Canada that has not been absorbed into the body politic and there is no Indian question.

The Mi'kmaq Experience

A short historical overview of the development of the Indian-Anglo/Euro relationship, will help to better understand the Caucasian mentality that would eventually lead Caucasian governments to establish Indian residential schools throughout Canada and the United States. For this exercise I'll use the Mi'kmaq experience. However, it should be kept in mind that the abuses by Anglo society described here can be applied to all First Nations in varying degrees across Canada.

Mi'kmaq students attending French colonial schools in the early 1600s, especially those residing in Acadian homes at Port Royal, Acadia (Nova Scotia), were in all likelihood among the first, if not the first, Indigenous children to attend European educational institutions in what is now Canada. I've concluded from reading about this, and from the later behaviour of the French colonials, who developed a working relationship with the Mi'kmaq, that this effort by the French was more focused on trying to help the Mi'kmaq acquire the skills needed to survive and prosper in a new monetary economy, where greed was, and still is, the motivator, than on trying to get the "Indian out of the Indian."

However, after the English assumed control of Mi'kmaq territory in 1713, via the *Treaty of Utrecht*, without the knowledge and consent of the Mi'kmaq, the intent of the new colonizers was the complete opposite of the French approach — destruction of the culture by all means possible. To achieve their insidious goal of eventual extermination, the new "owners" of the land resorted to every means possible, including what today would be termed crimes against humanity, or genocide.

The *Convention on the Prevention and Punishment of the Crime of Genocide*, adopted by the United Nations on December 9, 1948 (United Nations 1948), defines genocide:

> Genocide means any of the following acts committed with intent to destroy, in whole or in part, a national, ethnical, racial or religious group, as such:
> (A) Killing members of the group;
> (B) Causing serious bodily or mental harm to members of the group;
> (C) Deliberately inflicting on the group conditions of life calculated to bring about its physical destruction in whole or in part;
> (D) Imposing measures intended to prevent births within the group;
> (E) Forcefully transferring children of the group to another group."

Canada has violated all provisions.

The First Ethnic Cleansing

The effort to cleanse the Province of Nova Scotia (which at that time included what is today New Brunswick) of its original inhabitants by barbarous means was first used by the White supremacist colonial English with great success in eliminating Indigenous populations in what is now identified as New England. This was undertaken in the mid-1700s, when British military colonial government officials issued proclamations stipulating the monetary rewards that they would pay to bounty hunters for the harvesting of the scalps of Mi'kmaq men, women and children. The first proclamation, at the request of Nova Scotia colonial Governor Paul Mascarene, was issued by Governor William Shirley of the Mass Bay Colony, November 2, 1744 (Lincoln 1912); the second by Nova Scotia colonial Governor Edward Cornwallis, October 2, 1749 (Council Minutes 1747); and the third by Nova Scotia colonial Governor Charles Lawrence, May 14, 1756 (Governor Charles Lawrence 1756).

After failing to realize its goal of eliminating the Mi'kmaq by direct genocidal means, the British began concluding Peace and Friendship treaties with the Mi'kmaq Districts. They were made pursuant to the terms of the Treaty of 1725, which was ratified by Mi'kmaq Districts at Annapolis Royal in 1726 — one in 1752 and the rest during the 1760s. Several were signed at a Burying of the Hatchet ceremony at the Governor's Farm in Halifax on June 25, 1761. At the ceremony the Mi'kmaq were promised that they would henceforth be treated to English justice. As Colonial Governor Jonathan Belcher said that day,

> As this Mighty King can chastise and punish, so he has the power to protect you and all His Subjects against the rage and cruelties of the Oppressor.... Your traffic will be weighed and settled in the scale of honesty, and secured by severe punishment against any attempts to change the just balance of that scale.... In this faith I again greet you with this hand of friendship, as a sign of putting you in full possession of English protection and liberty. (Governor's Farm 1761)

Thus began a more genteel era of ethnic cleansing. The Mi'kmaq were to live in a state of malnutrition and starvation for the next century. Virginia Miller (1982) vividly describes the unspeakable misery the Mi'kmaq were suffering during this period:

> The lack of game animals and trade items also meant that the Micmac (sic) had no way of making or otherwise obtaining clothing. This meant that in the middle of a cold Nova Scotia winter, they were at the double disadvantage of having neither food nor clothing, and this took its toll as well. Reports of Indians naked or "miserably clad" in "filthy rags," and whole families owning only one blanket among them "as they lay in sleep in turns" in the middle of winter abounded. As in the case of food, the legislature authorized distribution of small amounts of cloth, a few yards at a time, but this, too, was certainly inadequate to the needs of the Indians. The situation was so desperate that one settler reported that: "I have seen them in so much distress that those of large families were obliged, while a part of them put on all the clothing they have to beg around the settlement, the rest sat naked in the wigwams....
>
> By 1827, reports of the Micmac situation drew comment from the Lieutenant Governor who said in a message to the Legislature that "the distresses of these poor people are much greater than is commonly supposed, and there is reason to believe that unless something is done, they must altogether perish." Nothing was done, and petitions continued to come in. An 1831 petition from Rawdon stated that the Indians there were desperate, there being no animals to hunt for food, and only about ten ragged blankets altogether among an encampment of fifty people. An 1834 petition stated that the Micmac camped near Windsor were: "Unable to maintain themselves through hunting... many of them are at this instant almost naked and are compelled to sit down in their open and exposed camps without anything to cover or shelter them from the severity of the season," and added that if relief did not appear soon, "they must inevitably perish"....
>
> The situation not only continued, but worsened if that is possible, as in 1846

the natives at Digby were reported dying "for want of food and sustenance." In 1851 it was the Micmac in Cape Breton again, this time alleged to be in a state of "famine." In 1855 the Micmac of New Glasgow "were ready to drop from hunger," while in 1856 in nearby Pictou, the Indians were "actually starving, and crying for food." There can be no doubting an Indian Superintendent's 1861 assessment of all the Indians in Nova Scotia and Cape Breton as "destitute and miserable"....

But of course Micmac people were dying from causes other than simple starvation and exposure during this time. The malnutrition and cold they suffered, the excessive consumption of alcohol by some Micmac, all contributed to lower the Indians' resistance to diseases, and in the historical records and reports after 1800, we see evidence of much disease among them. (Miller 1982: 4)

Judging from the historical records, the principal cause of this decline was disease; as one Indian Superintendent put it, "numbers are swept off annually by complaints unknown to them in their original state." The second most important cause was outright genocide perpetrated by the British, and the third major cause was starvation, once again brought on by the British presence (Miller 1982: 13).

Indian Misery Made Public

Reports of the situation must have reached the government in London because, in a letter to the colonial governor dated August 22, 1838, British Colonial Secretary Lord Glenelg asked for an accounting:

I have to request, that you will, at your early convenience, furnish me with a report on the state of any of the Aboriginal Inhabitants who may still exist in the Province under your Government, showing their numbers and present condition, increase or decrease, which has, during the last few years, occurred among them, their moral state, and any efforts which have been made for their Civilization.

The proportion settled on the land and cultivating it, and the numbers who still adhere to the habits of Savage life, the amount, if any, of property belonging to them, and the effect of any local Statutes which may have been passed for their Government. I would request you add to this report any other information which you may consider important, and more especially to favour me with any suggestions as to the measures which would be best calculated to ameliorate the condition of these people. (Journal of Assembly Papers 1838)

On January 25, 1841, Mi'kmaq Grand Chief Pemmeenauweet wrote a letter to Queen Victoria, begging mercy for his people:

I cannot cross the Great Lake to talk to you, for my Canoe is too small, and I am old and weak. I cannot look upon you, for my eyes do not see so far. You cannot hear my voice across the Great Waters. I therefore send this Waumpum and Paper talk to tell the Queen I am in trouble. My people are in trouble.

I have seen upwards of a thousand Moons. When I was young I had plenty, now I am old, poor and sickly too. My people are poor. No Hunting Grounds, No Beaver, No Otter, No Nothing. Indians poor, poor forever, No Store, No Chest, No Clothes. All these woods once ours. Our Fathers possessed them all. Now we cannot cut a Tree to warm our Wigwam in Winter unless the White Man please.

The Micmacs now receive no presents but one small blanket for a whole family. The Governor is a good man, but he cannot help us now, we look to you the Queen. The White Waumpum tell that we hope in you. Pity your poor Indians in Nova Scotia! (Chief Porminout 1841)

Resulting from this, on March 19, 1842, an act entitled *An Act to Provide for the Instruction and Permanent Settlement of the Indians* was passed by the General Assembly of Nova Scotia:

WHEREAS, it is proper to provide for the Education and Civilization of the Aboriginal Inhabitants of this Province, and for the preservation and productive application for their use of the Lands in different parts of this Province, set aside as Indian Reservations: ...

(I) BE IT ENACTED, by the lieutenant governor, council and assembly, that it shall, and may be lawful for the Governor to appoint ... a fit and proper person to be Commissioner for Indian Affairs, who, upon entering on the Office, shall give security for the faithful performance of its duties, to the satisfaction of the Governor, and Her Majesty's Executive Council ...

(III) AND BE IT ENACTED, that it shall be the duty of the said Commissioner for the time being, to take the supervision and management of all Lands that now are, or may hereafter be, set apart as Indian Reservations, or for the use of the Indians, to ascertain and define their boundaries, to discover and report to the Governor all cases of intrusion, and of the transfer or sale of the said Lands, or of their use or possession by the Indians; and generally, to protect the said Lands from encroachment and alienation, and preserve them for the use of the Indians.

(IV) AND BE IT ENACTED, that in cases where there have been, or hereafter may be, erected or made valuable buildings, or improvements on such Lands, it shall be in the power of the Governor, by and with the advice of Her Majesty's Executive Council, to make Agreements with the persons who shall have made the same, or those claiming under them, either by way of satisfaction and compensation for the value of the lands so improved, with so much adjacent Land as may be necessary, or by way of rent or allowance for the use of such Lands, for such term of years, and under such considerations, as may be expressed in the Agreements, and all such Agreements shall insure by way of sale or demise, as may be therein expressed, and shall convey a legal Title to the Parties accordingly; and all monies received in compensation or satisfaction as aforesaid, shall be laid out, either in the purchase of other Lands for the use of the Indians, or in some other manner, for their permanent benefit ....

(V) AND BE IT ENACTED, that in all cases of intrusion, encroachment, or unauthorized settlement, or improvement upon any such Lands as aforesaid, it shall be lawful to proceed by information, in the name of Her Majesty, before Her Majesty's Supreme Court of Halifax, or in the County where the Lands may lie, notwithstanding the legal Title by grant or otherwise, may not be vested in Her Majesty.

(VI) AND BE IT ENACTED, that it shall be the duty of such Commissioner, under such Instructions, to put himself in communication with the Chiefs of the Different Tribes of the Micmac Race throughout the Province, to explain to them the wishes of the Government, and to invite them to cooperate in the permanent settlement and instruction of their people.

That it shall be his duty, subject to such instructions aforesaid, to parcel out to each head of family a portion of the Reservations, with such limited power of alienation to Indians only as the said Instructions may, from time to time, authorize; and also, to aid them in the purchase of Implements and Stock. With such moderate assistance from the Fund placed at his disposal, as they may seem... by their Industry and Sobriety to deserve, to aid in the erection of a dwelling for each Chief, a School House and a place of Worship, and generally, to take such measures as, in his discretion... carry out the Objects of this Act.

(VII) AND BE IT ENACTED, that such Commissioner shall have power to make arrangements with the Trustees, or Teachers of any Schools, or Academies throughout the Province, for the Board and Tuition of such number of Indian Children as may be desirous of acquiring Education; and... the expenses shall be paid out of the funds placed at his disposal.

(VIII) AND BE IT ENACTED, that in order to form a permanent Fund, applicable to the purposes of this Act, the Commissioner shall be authorized to raise subscription, to apply for Contributions from Charitable Institutions, either in this Province, or elsewhere, and to draw from the Treasury, by Warrant from the Governor... such sum or sums of money, as may, from time to time, be granted by the Legislature for that purpose.

(IX) AND BE IT ENACTED, that the said Commissioner shall, at the close of every year, furnish the Governor, to be laid before the two Branches of the Legislature, a detailed report of his proceedings, and an account of his receipts and expenditures, together with the names of each Chief, for the time being the number of Heads of Families Settled, and Children Educated, and generally, such other information as may enable the Governor and the Legislature to judge of the value and correctness of his proceedings. (Statutes of Nova Scotia 1842)

Assimilation/Genocide Continued

Indicative of their "humanity," fully 129 years after they had taken over the province, the British had finally made provision to educate the Mi'kmaq. However, it was done with the intention of speeding up assimilation, not preserving the Nation.

Joseph Howe, a renowned Nova Scotia and Canadian statesman, was appointed first commissioner for Indian Affairs by Governor Lucius Bentinck Cary. If it had not been for the intercession of this great statesman, the Mi'kmaq of Nova Scotia would probably have passed into extinction. In his first report, of January 25, 1843, in a compelling diplomatic manner, Howe strongly condemned the government for permitting the poverty among the Mi'kmaq to exist. The following are a few excerpts from his report (Joseph Howe 1843):

> At this rate (of decline) the whole Race would be extinct in forty years, and half a Century hence the very existence of the Tribe would be as a dream.

At this rate (of decline) the whole Race would be extinct in forty years, and half a Century hence the very existence of the Tribe would be as a dream and a tradition to our Grandchildren, who would find it difficult to imagine the features or dwelling of a Micmac, as we do to realize those of an Ancient Breton.... Assuming the statistics of 1838 as a basis of a calculation, and deducting 10 percent, your Lordship will perceive that there must be at least 1,300 Souls still in this Province, appealing to the sympathies of every honourable mind by the contrast of their misfortunes with our prosperity, their fading numbers with our numerical advancement, their ignorance and destitution with the wealth and civilization which surrounds and presses upon them from every side....

For many weeks in the Spring my dwelling was besieged, at all hours, by Indians, who had been taught to believe that unbounded wealth was at my disposal, and that they were to be fed and clothed hereafter at the expense of the Government. Had I yielded to the clamorous demands and even reproaches of these Visitors, the sum voted would barely have sufficed to supply the wants of the Halifax Indians alone for a single month....

For many years past, the Legislature has granted £100 per annum for the use of the Indians, which has usually been laid out in Great Coats and Blankets, to be distributed in various parts of the Province.

His report continued on the uselessness of reserve lands:

The present condition and capabilities of such of these Lands as I have been enabled to visit may be gathered from the journal which accompanies this report. It is to be regretted that so little judgement has been exercised in the selection of them; the same quantity, if reserved in spots where the soil was good, on navigable streams, or in places where fish were abundant, and game within reach, would now be a valuable resource.

Equally appalling were the educational provisions:

Having secured the aid of the Rev. Mr. Geary, to whose kind cooperation I am much indebted, a Sunday School was opened for the instruction of the Indians in the Chapel at Dartmouth, and, for several weeks, the attendance was very good, and our pupils of both sexes, and all ages, making fair progress; but as Mr. Geary was often necessarily absent, visiting different portions of a widely extended Mission, it was found impossible to ensure that certainty and regularity which were essential to the success of the design, and the Sunday School was subsequently abandoned ...

Should the Legislature make a further Grant, and your Excellency honour me by employing me in this work of humanity for another season, I propose to visit Cumberland, and the Eastern Counties, including Cape Breton; and shall endeavour to place within the reach of my successor such information as will enable him to conduct the business chiefly by correspondence, with the aid of an occasional tour of inspection, every third or fourth year.

In concluding this Report, I have again to solicit your Excellency's favourable consideration of the difficulties of the task. Difficulties scarcely to be overcome in a single year by the sedulous devotion of one person's entire time. I have been able to give to such preliminary measures as seemed requisite for their ultimate mastery, only the leisure hours which could be borrowed from other and various duties, both of public and private nature ....

I trust, however, that should your Excellency not be satisfied with the results of these first experiments, the blame may be laid upon the Commissioner, rather than be charged upon the capacity, or urged against the claims of a people, for whose many good qualities a more extended intercourse has only increased my respect, and who have, if not by Treaty, at least by all the ties of humanity, a claim upon the Government of the Country, which nothing but their entire extinction, or their elevation to a more permanent, and happy position in the scale of Society, can ever entirely discharge.

The Mi'kmaq population is reported by some historians to have stopped declining between 1843 and 1847, when, in their estimation, the numbers slowly began to increase. They report that at Confederation the population was about 1,600. However, from my research on Mi'kmaq family trees for Indian registration purposes, I can say that this increase was not a result of births. It came mostly from Mi'kmaq moving to Nova Scotia from New Brunswick, Prince Edward Island, other parts of Canada, and the U.S. Without this influx the population would have decreased during the period. My view is supported by Commissioner of Indian Affairs Abraham Gesner, a knowledgeable man who was sympathetic towards the Mi'kmaq and who based his assessment of their numbers on his history of close contact with them. In an 1847 report, he said:

> Unless the progress of their annihilation is soon arrested, the time is close at hand, when ... the last of their race, to use their own idea, "will sleep with the bones of their fathers." Unless the vices and diseases of civilization are speedily arrested, the Indians ... will soon be as the Red Men of Newfoundland, or other Tribes of the West, whose existence is forever blotted out from the face of the Earth. (Abraham Gesner 1847)

Commissioner Gesner identified the causes of the decline in population as follows:

> It might be supposed that after their wars ... and encounters with the whites had terminated, the Aborigines would multiply, yet experience has proved exactly the reverse .... Exposed to the inclemency of the weather, and destitute of the proper diet and treatment required for contagious diseases, numbers are swept off annually by complaint unknown to them in their state ....
>
> From the clearing and occupation of the forests, the wild domain of the moose and caribou has been narrowed. Being hunted by the dogs of the back settlers, these animals have become scarce — thus the Indian has been deprived of his principal subsistence, as well as the warm furs that in olden times lined his wigwam. Indigenous roots once highly prized for food have been destroyed by domestic animals .... These united causes have operated fearfully, and have reduced the whole tribe to the extreme of misery and wretchedness ....
>
> Almost the whole Micmac population are now vagrants, who wander from place to place, and door to door, seeking alms. The aged and infirm are supplied with written briefs upon which they place much reliance. They are clad in filthy rags. Necessity often compels them to consume putrid and unwholesome food. The offal of the slaughter-house is their portion. Their camps or wigwams are seldom comfortable, and in winter, at places where they are not permitted to cut wood, they suffer from the cold. The sufferings of the sick and infirm surpass description, and from the lack of a humble degree of accommodation, almost every case of disease proves fatal ....
>
> During my inquiries into the actual state of these people in June last, I found four orphan children who were unable to rise for the want of food — whole families were subsisting upon wild roots and eels, and the withered features of others told too plainly to be misunderstood that they had nearly approached starvation. (Mitcham 1995: 59–61)

Canada Is Born

The Mi'kmaq continued to live in starvation conditions under British colonial rule until 1867, at which time Canada was created by the *British North America Act*. Section 91-24 of the *Act* mandated that the federal government had responsibility for Indians and Indian lands. Under their new rulers, Canadian First Nations People went from near starvation to a malnourished existence, which was almost as deadly, since subsistence diets and insufficient medical care ensured that diseases would continue to take a large toll.

But the creation of a new Canadian state did not change the Euro-Indian relationship. In effect, up to the enactment of the *Indian Act* in 1876, the pre-Confederation situation continued unabated. The new federal government assumed its constitutional trust responsibilities for "Indians" and "Indian lands" with little enthusiasm. What little it did muster had a White supremacist bent, for they adopted the same policy the English had chosen "to solve the Indian problem forever" — extinction by assimilation. The government delayed for more than a year before appointing an Indian agent for Nova Scotia. Then, by appointing a man who had already proven to be less than supportive of the Mi'kmaq cause, it demonstrated a completely uncaring attitude regarding its responsibilities to the Mi'kmaq:

> Department of Secretary of State, Ottawa, September 28, 1868
>
> Mr. Samuel Fairbanks:
>
> I have the honour to inform you that, by an Order in Council... you have been appointed... Agent for Indian Affairs in the province of Nova Scotia, with an allowance of ten per cent on all moneys collected by you in that capacity.... Patents for Lands will be prepared on your transmitting descriptions of the lands sold and paid for; and... will be forwarded to you for delivery to the purchasers.
>
> I have the Honour to be, Sir, Your Obedient Servant,
> Hector L. Langevin, Secretary of State. (Langevin to Fairbanks 1868)

> The government intended, by agreeing to pay Fairbanks a commission of 10 percent on all the revenues he could raise by leasing or selling Indian Reserve lands... to protect Mi'kmaq lands by alienating them from Mi'kmaq use as fast as possible.

Langevin made it plain in his memo that the government intended, by agreeing to pay Fairbanks a commission of 10 percent on all the revenues he could raise by leasing or selling Indian Reserve lands in Nova Scotia, to manage its constitutional responsibility to protect Mi'kmaq lands by alienating them from Mi'kmaq use as fast as possible. This was the beginning of a pattern of dereliction of legal duty by the federal government that still continues to a certain extent today.

Canadian governments continued to get away with such blatant neglect of duty over the ensuing decades because, like the English, they denied to First Nations peoples even the most basic of civil and human rights. We were designated "wards of the crown" and as such were paternalistically treated as "non-citizens" and forced by the authorities, who shackled us with legislated and unwritten apartheid restrictions, to live in a very confined and regulated "non-person" world.

Afflicted by a poverty caused by denial of human rights and enforced by exclusion, the Mi'kmaq population, which had been approximately 1,400 to 1,500 at Confederation, remained almost stationary until the late 1940s. The main cause was malnutrition, which kept disease resistance drastically low, causing susceptibility to the ravages of tuberculosis, typhoid, and other foreign diseases. The population had increased to only two thousand by 1950.

The Indian Act

If one needs more hard evidence to cement the view that the new country displayed careless indifference towards the management of its Indian and Indian land constitutional trust responsibilities, this fact should provide it: it took the government almost a decade to enact the legislation it needed to manage Indian affairs.

In 1876, Parliament finally devised, then legislated the legal code needed to manage its constitutional obligations. However, in direct contradiction of its trust obligations, the government included sections in the *Indian Act* that were not in the best interests of the people they were constitutionally bound to protect. Sections 138 and 86 are excellent examples of the federal government's dereliction of duty.

Section 138 made it illegal for an Indian Agent not to make every effort to sell off Indian Reserve lands:

> Every Agent who knowingly and falsely informs, or causes to be informed, any person applying to him to purchase any land within his division and agency, that the same has already been purchased, or who refuses to permit the person so applying to purchase the same according to existing regulations, shall be liable therefore to the person so applying, in the sum of five dollars for each acre of land which the person so applying offered to purchase, recoverable by action of debt in any court of competent jurisdiction.

This section, because it clearly dictates that the sale of Reserve land to interested Caucasian parties take precedence over First Nations' interests, would have made Indian Affairs a difficult place for a person of conscience to work. Such a person would have recognized that it was not in the best interests of the First Nations to sell off their remaining lands and thus to do so would be unethical. Quit or subvert personal ethics would have been the choice.

Section 86, the 1876 enfranchisement section:

> Whenever any Indian man, or unmarried woman, of the full age of twenty-one years obtains the consent of the Band of which he or she is a member to become enfranchised, and whenever such Indian has been assigned by the Band a suitable allotment of land for that purpose, the local Agent shall report such action of the Band and the name of the applicant to the Superintendent General.
>
> Whereupon the said Superintendent General, if satisfied that the proposed allotment of land is equitable, shall authorize some competent person to report whether the applicant is an Indian, who from the degree of civilization to which he or she has attained, and the character for integrity, morality and sobriety which he or she bears, appears to be qualified to become a proprietor of land in fee simple; and upon the favourable report of such person, the Superintendent General may grant such Indian a location ticket as a probationary Indian for the land allotted to him or her by the Band.
>
> (1) Any Indian who may be admitted to the degree of Doctor of Medicine, or to any other degree by any University of Learning, or who may be admitted in any Province of the Dominion to practice law, either as an Advocate or as a Barrister, or Counsellor, or Solicitor, or Attorney, or to be a Notary Public, or who may enter Holy Orders, or who may be licensed by any denomination of Christians as a Minister of the Gospel, shall ipso facto become and be enfranchised under this Act.

The New Solution — Residential Schools

In all probability, it was shortly after the Act was enacted that bureaucrats and politicians began to ponder ways and means to solve Canada's "Indian problem" forever — they settled on debriefing and brainwashing First Nations children as the optimum solution:

> In the 19th century, the Canadian government believed it was responsible for educating and caring for the country's Aboriginal people. It thought their best chance for success was to learn English and adopt Christianity and Canadian customs. Ideally, they would pass their adopted lifestyle on to their children, and native traditions would diminish, or be completely abolished in a few generations. (CBC News 2008a)

However, one should not be lulled into believing that Indian residential and Indian day schools were the only means that the government utilized in trying to solve the "Indian problem." For instance, the malnutrition diets and insufficient medical care it provided permitted diseases to run their deadly courses among First Nations people until the late 1940s; as well, many children were seized from their parents and adopted out to people in foreign countries, where many were physically and sexually abused. Schools were only a part of the genocidal strategy.

> Shortly after the [Indian] Act was enacted... bureaucrats and politicians began to ponder ways and means to solve Canada's "Indian problem" forever — they settled on debriefing and brainwashing First Nations children as the optimum solution.

The first Canadian Indian residential schools were established in the late 1800s. The Shubenacadie Indian Residential School in Nova Scotia was opened in 1930. All the schools, including Indian day schools, were operated by religious denominations. All of the physical and sexual abuses that occurred in these schools cannot be chronicled in this small space; suffice it to say that the abuses were was horrific. The following incidents capture the general nature of those schools.

Starting in 1935, two of my late brothers, John and Robert, were incarcerated in the Shubenacadie Indian Residential School for two years. When a small Indian day school on Shubenacadie Indian Reserve opened in 1937, they were permitted to attend it. However, the stories they told us of the abuse they saw, and suffered, such as children being horsewhipped and forced to eat their own vomit, were terrifying, so much so that if we weren't behaving my Mom would say, "Behave, or I'll put you in the residential school." That threat got good behaviour from us!

One distinguished former resident, Elsie Basque (née Charles), born in May 1916, has memories of her experiences in the Shubenacadie Residential School that are far from fond. Elsie remembers "papa" as being her most important childhood influence. His advice that "to be somebody, one needs a good education" is still fondly recalled. In tune with his belief, Joe enrolled her in the old one-room school in Hectanooga where she completed grade 7. Then her life was drastically changed by the information contained in an article her father read in a 1929 edition of the *Halifax Chronicle*, which touted the new horizons being opened up for the Mi'kmaq by the opening of the residential school. Believing the school was a golden opportunity to secure his daughter's education, Joe enrolled her.

This is Elsie's assessment of the two years she spent there:

> I've always regarded these years as time wasted.... I was in the 8th grade when I arrived at the school in February 1930 and in the 8th grade when I left in 1932. What had I learned in those 28 months? How to darn a sock, sew a straight seam on the sewing machine, and how to scrub clothes on a washboard. Educationally, how to parse and analyze a sentence.

> Volumes have been written about the school. Its total disastrous effect upon the Mi'kmaq/Maliseet Nations will never be known. Generations later, the scars remain. It was not an education institution as we define education. Older children, boys and girls, were taken out of the classroom to do chores — milk cows, clean the barn, plant and harvest, etc. The girls were ordered to launder clothes, make uniforms, scrub the floors and so on. (personal correspondence and Paul 1995)

After this disappointment, Elsie returned to Clare and enrolled at Meteghan's Sacred Heart Academy, where she graduated with a high school diploma in 1936. She then entered classes at the Provincial Normal College (teacher's college) in Truro and was awarded a teacher's certificate in 1937. Thus she became the first licensed

> What had I learned in those 28 months? How to darn a sock, sew a straight seam on the sewing machine, and how to scrub clothes on a washboard.

Mi'kmaq teacher in Nova Scotia. Notably, she was well treated at the college by peers and administration. The students elected her class president and she describes her time there as a "fun year." She graduated with honours (also see Paul 1995).

In 1936 a fifteen-year-old girl from the nearby Shubenacadie Indian Reserve refused to return to the school and gave the following statement to the agent and the Royal Canadian Mounted Police:

> I have been going to Indian school for the past five years.... Before my holidays this year I was employed in kitchen for eleven weeks.... In the eleven weeks... I spent a total of two weeks in school. The Sister has beaten me many times over the head and pulled my hair and struck me on the back of neck with a ruler and at times grabbed ahold of me and beat me on the back with her fists.

> I have also been ordered to stand on the outside of the windows with a rope around my waist to clean windows on the fourth floor with a little girl holding the rope. When I told the Sister I was afraid to go out the window she scolded me and made me clean the window and threatened to beat me if I did not do it. This is being done to other children.

> After we get a beating we are asked what we got the beating for and if we tell them we do not know we get another beating. The Sisters always tell us not to tell our parents about getting a beating. (Millward 1992)

"Centralization"

In the early 1940s the federal Crown hatched a plan to speed up Mi'kmaq and Maliseet assimilation, christened "centralization." The intent was to round up all the Indians in the Maritimes and move them to four Indian reserves. The designated reserves in Nova Scotia were Eskasoni and Shubenacadie. The Nova Scotia government was most enthusiastic about it and gave full support. Premier A.S. MacMillan penned the following memo to the federal minister of Mines and Resources, the department that had responsibility for Indian Affairs:

> Dear Mr. Grerar:
>
> I have your letter with regard to the Indian Reserves in this Province and note carefully all that you have to say. This is entirely a new departure and no doubt will meet with some opposition from the Indians themselves — this, due to the fact that a number of these reservations are located near towns, for instance Shubenacadie, Truro, etc. and being near of course the Indians have the habit of spending their time loafing around the towns. However, I think if an agreement could be reached that the idea is a practical one and there are plenty of vacant lands where they can be placed in this Province.
>
> I shall be glad to meet your representative when he comes, and go into the matter with him and shall also put him in touch with the proper persons in our Lands and Forests Department as well as with our Farm Loan Board which is also an operating body. Possibly when he comes to Halifax he had better see me before discussing this matter with others. (DIAND 1938–1952)

That centralization and racism were synonymous was amply demonstrated throughout the founding and implementation of the plan. Without a doubt the prime factor in choosing Eskasoni and Shubenacadie was the desire to accommodate the Caucasian population's wish to move the "Indian problem" out of sight and out of mind. J. Ralph Kirk, Member of Parliament for Antigonish-Guysborough, affirms this in a memo he wrote on November 15, 1944, to the Director of Indian Affairs, Mr. Hoey:

> Would you be good enough to advise me as to whether or not the Department of Indian Affairs intends to take any move in the near future respecting the transfer of all Indians in Nova Scotia to one or two central places of habitation?
>
> I have had inquires from some of my constituents, expressing the hope that the Indians living in the neighbourhood of Bayfield, N.S. would be moved away from there soon, and this leads me to inquire as to the present status of the Department's plans in this connection.
>
> Your early reply re the matter will be much appreciated. (DIAND 1938–1952)

Responding to Mr. Kirk's inquiries, the acting director of the Department's welfare program penned a letter dated January 6, 1945, which included this gem:

It was felt that we would also improve the amenities of the White communities which are not improved by the immediate presence of isolated groups of Indians. (DIAND 1938–1952)

To assure that Whites could improve the "amenities" of their communities by having Indians removed from close proximity, the government included this section in the *Indian Act*:

Removal of Indians

46. (1) In the case of an Indian reserve which adjoins or is situated wholly or partly within an incorporated town or city having a population of not less than eight thousand … the Governor in Council may, upon the recommendation of the Superintendent General, refer to the judge of the Exchequer Court of Canada for inquiry and report the question as to whether it is expedient, having regard to the interest of the public and of the Indians of the band for whose use the reserve is held, that the Indians should be removed from the reserve or any part of it ….

If the judge finds that it is expedient that the band of Indians should be removed from the reserve or any part of it, he shall proceed, before making his report, to ascertain the amounts of compensation, if any, which should be paid respectively to individual Indians of the band for the special loss or damages which they will sustain in respect of the buildings or improvements to which they are entitled upon the lands of the reserve for which they are located ….

The judge shall transmit his findings, with the evidence and a report of the proceedings, to the Governor in Council, who shall lay a full report of the proceedings … before Parliament … and upon such findings being approved by resolution of Parliament the Governor in Council may thereupon give effect to the said findings and cause the reserve, or any part thereof from which it is found expedient to remove the Indians, to be sold or leased by public auction after three months advertisement in the public press, upon the best terms which in the opinion of the Governor in Council, may be obtained therefore.

The proceeds of the sale or lease, after deducting the usual percentage for management fund, shall be applied in compensating individual Indians for their buildings or improvements as found by the judge, in purchasing a new reserve for the Indians removed, in transferring the said Indians with their effects thereto, in erecting buildings upon the new reserve, and in providing the Indians with such other assistance as the Superintendent General may consider advisable ….

For the purpose of selecting [a] new reserve to be acquired for the Indians … the Superintendent General shall have all the powers conferred upon the Minister by the *Expropriation Act*. (Exchequer Court 1911)

Shortly after the turn of the century the provision was used in Nova Scotia. The victims were the Mi'kmaq residing near Kings Road in Sydney. Whites residing close to the area went to court and used the provision to force the Band members to move to a new reserve, called Membertou. To add insult to injury, the Mi'kmaq had to pay for their own removal.

During the implementation of "centralization," the Shubenacadie Indian Residential School was used as a tool to force families to move to the four designated Indian Reserves in New Brunswick and Nova Scotia. Many children were seized by the Department and placed in the school, with the proviso that if the parents moved to one of the designated Indian Reserves the children would be returned to their care.

It would be remiss not to mention that while "centralization" was being implemented, new Indian day schools were built on the four designated Indian reserves. As with the residential schools, they were staffed by a religious order. Because the band members were Roman Catholic, priests and nuns were retained. In most cases the principal was a priest and the teachers nuns. These schools had the same mandate as residential schools, the assimilation of children. Both Mi'kmaq culture and language were strictly banned from the premises. A child caught talking Mi'kmaq on school grounds was severely punished.

> Doctors withheld specialized dental care, such as professional cleaning and treatment of decay, for Aboriginal children living in eight residential schools.

In 1948 the United Nations adopted the Universal Declaration of Human Rights, a document that would eventually prod Canada into treating its two most persecuted minorities, African Canadians and First Nations People, more humanely. However, rest assured: it did not stop the effort to solve the "Indian problem" through the extinction of First Nations by assimilation; in fact the sick pursuit proceeded with gusto. Even medical experimentation was tried. The following example, reminiscent of Nazi procedures, makes one wonder whether this is a description of modern Canada or a throwback to the Dark Ages:

> Natives denied dental care. Federal government doctors withheld specialized dental care, such as professional cleaning and treatment of decay, for Aboriginal children living in eight residential schools in the 1940s and 1950s to see what the effect would be on their health. The director of the study, Dr. L.B. Pett, said last week that students' teeth and gums were in terrible condition to begin with, and that delaying treatment did not create more decay, but helped keep the study's results accurate. (*Maclean's Magazine*, May 8, 2000)

Such views about experiments using people deemed "inferior" as guinea pigs were expressed by another majority group, the Nazis. As might be expected from a systemically racist society, to my knowledge, not one word of condemnation has been uttered about this revelation from any level of government or human rights commission in Canada, and no effort to prosecute has ever been made.

Today, thankfully, all Indian residential and Indian day schools are closed, but their nightmare legacy of implanting in First Nations children the notion that they are the offspring of inferior races of people lives on. This emphasizes the urgent need to include in school curricula the truth about First Nations cultures, which is completely opposite to the demonizing, dehumanizing propaganda invented by European colonials.

First Nations Resistance

However, while awaiting such an enlightened development, our people are picking up the pieces and are fighting back. In the 1980s, led by such human rights activists as Nora Bernard, the groundwork was established to collect research that would eventually lead to a class action suit against the Federal Crown by former inmates of Indian residential schools. They won. A court-approved Settlement Agreement was implemented on September 19, 2007. It was negotiated by representatives from various First Nations organizations, church entities, legal representatives for former students, and the Government of Canada.

Although the agreement was helpful to many of the surviving First Nations Peoples that were incarcerated in residential schools, in my opinion it is deeply flawed. The reason for this is quite simple: it excluded and denied justice to those, such as my brothers John and Robert, who had suffered abuse in the Shubenacadie school, and had passed away before the settlement was implemented. It also failed to address the issue of Indian day schools, which were almost as bad as the residential schools. When you have a settlement that gives a token of justice for some, but not for all, is it really justice? I dare say it isn't.

As far as the so-called Truth and Reconciliation Commission of Canada is concerned I expect that it will accomplish what the 1993 Royal Commission on Aboriginal Affairs accomplished, which was next to nothing, except for its use by the federal government as a propaganda tool. As the executive director of the Confederacy of Mainland Mi'kmaq in 1993 when the Royal Commission was first announced, I initially had great expectations for a good output from it. I thought it would be crossing the country as a body seeking out the truth about the mistreatment of First Nations people, questioning witnesses under oath, such as former Indian Affairs ministers, deputy ministers, director generals, health and welfare officials, etc., about such things as scalp proclamations, past malnutrition diets, poor housing, neglectful medical care, and so on, and, most important, educating the Canadian public with the truth about First Nations cultures.

In plain English, I was looking forward to results similar to those that the Nova Scotia Marshall Royal Commission produced, which laid bare to the public the monumental shortcomings of the Nova Scotia justice system and its terrible mistreatment of racial minorities, especially Black and Mi'kmaq. Its recommendations were so effective that Nova Scotians saw the complete overhaul of the province's antiquated justice system. However, after I had a good look at its terms of reference, and saw individual members of the Commission crisscrossing the country with no public hearings held by the body, nor any authority to compel witnesses to testify under oath, I gave it up as a lost cause and a gross waste of fifty million dollars. My expectations for the Truth and Reconciliation Commission, after reviewing its terms of reference, are much the same.

This statement is not meant to be a negative reflection upon the good names and reputations of the honourable men and women who have served, and are serving, on these commissions. Rather, it is meant to be a negative reflection upon government intentions, which are not geared toward removing colo-

> Government intentions are not geared toward removing colonial demonizing.

nial demonization from the mindset of Canada's population and replacing it with the truth, but more toward being able to tell First Nations people, "Hey, we're doing something."

To erase, once and for all, the negative effects of colonial propaganda upon First Nations, this country needs a full-fledged Royal Commission crisscrossing the country as a body, with the widest terms of reference, and the ability to call people to testify under oath before it, in order to discover and lay bare the complete truth about Canada's past mistreatment of registered Indians. Although federal authorities would like to continue with the hoax that Indian residential schools were the only means the Canadian state used to try to destroy First Nations, it should be revealed that the schools were only a small part of the overall effort. Medical experimentation; the past inhumane lack of proper diets, medical treatment, education and proper housing; centralization; Indian day schools; scalp proclamations; the gross racism by which the people have consistently been degraded — all horrors, barring none, should be on the table for examination. When this happens, and only then, will justice have finally arrived for the abuses suffered, at the hands of British and Canadian governments, by our peoples over the ages.

The English were the only oppressor that the Mi'kmaq ever knew. So when Colonial Governor Jonathan Belcher uttered the following words in 1761, "As this Mighty King can chastise and punish, so he has the power to protect you and all His Subjects against the rage and cruelties of the Oppressor," the Mi'kmaq in attendance must have wondered how the English were going to protect them from the English. As history relates, the "Mighty King" and his successors did not in fact protect the Mi'kmaq and all other Canadian First Nations from their oppressor, the English!

Glossary of Key Terms

Assimilation: The set of social policies, practices, and institutions designed to eliminate the culture and social practices of subjugated (that is, Indigenous) peoples. In the Canadian context, assimilation has meant to get the "Indian out of the Indian."

British North America Act Section 91-24: Mandated that the federal government had responsibility for Indians and Indian lands.

Genocide: Policies and programs, behaviours designed to realize national, ethnical, racial, or religious group extinction. Genocide takes many forms, from killing members of the group to deliberately inflicting conditions of life that will bring about its physical destruction to imposing measures intended to prevent births or forcefully transferring children from the group.

Indian Act (1876): This act defines the responsibilities and authority of the Department of Indian and Northern Affairs to govern the lives of registered Indians in Canada. For example, Section 138 made it illegal for an Indian agent not to make every effort to sell off Indian reserve lands. The act also disenfranchised any registered Indian woman who married a non-Indigenous man, and any registered Indian who acquired a university degree.

Residential schools: These schools were government funded but run by Christian churches. Registered Indian children were forced into these schools to learn English and adopt Christianity and Canadian customs, ostensibly deemed their best chances for success. Realistically though, they were intended to transfer a White lifestyle onto Indian children and foster their assimilation. The intent was to see that native traditions were diminished, or completely abolished, in a few generations. Schools were both fully residential or day schools: in residential schools Indian children were in classrooms for a half-day and worked at chores to maintain the schools for the other half-day.

Systemic racism: Institutions and social practices, rather than individual attitudes and behaviours, that discriminate against non-White peoples; for example, the *Indian Act* in Canada, which controls and subjugates the behaviour of registered Indians.

Truth and Reconciliation Commission of Canada (TRC): The TRC has a mandate to learn about what happened in the residential schools and to inform all Canadians about this. The Commission set as one of its goals to guide and inspire First Nations, Inuit, and Métis peoples and Canadians in a process of establishing the truth and promoting healing, toward reconciliation and renewed relationships based on mutual understanding and respect. The TRC is mandated to undertake a historical recording and public recording of the residential schools through gathering statements from former students and their families, and hosting national and community events, and public education and commemoration.

White supremacy: Ideas and social practices that assume and institutionalize the idea that the society and promotion of White (Caucasian) people are not just different from, but are superior to, those of people of colour.

Questions for Discussion

1. What kinds of social, individual, and family effects follow from forced attendance at residential schools? How long would they last?

2. How is racism harmful to the oppressors in a racist relationship/society?

3. In what ways are White supremacy hidden from view?

4. How are residential schools a form of genocide?

5. Is it possible to reconcile the legacy of the colonial past in Canada, including the legacy of residential schools?

Websites of Interest

Truth and Reconciliation Commission of Canada <trc.ca>
First Nations History, Paintings and Photos <danielnpaul.com/Images.html>
Turtle Island <turlteisland.org>
Aboriginal Multi-Media Society <ammsa.com>

References

Secondary Sources

Canadian Encyclopedia. n.d. "Residential Schools." <thecanadianencyclopedia.com/index.cfm?Pg Nm=TCE&Params=A1ARTA0011547>.

CBC News. 2008a. "A History of Residential Schools in Canada." <cbc.ca/news/canada/ story/2008/05/16/f-faqs-residential-schools.html>.

____. 2008b. "A Timeline of Residential Schools, the Truth and Reconciliation Commission." <cbc. ca/news/canada/story/2008/05/16/f-timeline-residential-schools.html>.

King, Martin Luther, Jr. 1964. *Why We Can't Wait*. New York: Signet Books.

Lincoln, Charles Henry. 1912. *Correspondence of Governor Shirley*. New York: MacMillan.

Miller, Virginia. 1982. "The Decline of the Nova Scotia Micmac Population, 1600–1850." *Culture* 3. (Also in Public Archives of Nova Scotia, VF Volume 280, # 7).

Millward, Marilyn. 1992. "Clean Behind the Ears? Micmac Parents, Micmac Children, and the Shubenacadie Residential School." *New Maritimes* March/April.

Mithcam, Allison. 1995. *The Best of Abraham Gesner*. Hantsport, NS: Lancelot Press.

Paul, Daniel. 1995. "Elsie Basque: Micmac Pioneer." *Halifax Chronicle-Herald*, October 6.

Truth and Reconciliation Commission of Canada. n.d. "Residential School Locations." <trc.ca/ websites/trcinstitution/index.php?p=12>.

United Nations. 1948. "Convention on the Prevention and Punishment of the Crime of Genocide." Adopted by Resolution 260 (III) A of the United Nations General Assembly on 9 December 1948. <hrweb.org/legal/genocide.html>.

Wright, Ronald. 1993. *Stolen Continents*. Toronto: Penguin Books.

Public Archives

Chief Benjamin Porminout to Queen Victoria. January 25, 1841. Public Archives of Nova Scotia, CP 217/179/406, microfilm.

Council Minutes authorizing scalping proclamation. October 1, 1747. Provincial Archives of Nova Scotia, RG1, Volume 186, pp. 22–23, microfilm 15287.

Department of Indian and Northern Affairs (DIAND). 1938–1952. Centralization correspondence, Eskasoni and Shubenacadie Indian Agencies. Public Archives of Canada.

Exchequer Court. 1911. *Indian Act*, Section 46. *Inquiry and Report of the Exchequer Court as the Removal of Indians*. Chapter 14.

Gesner, Abraham. 1847. *Report by [Nova Scotia] Commissioner of Indian Affairs*. Public Archives of Nova Scotia, RG1, Volumes 431 and 432, Number 43.

Governor Charles Lawrence, scalping proclamation. 1756. Public Archives of N. S., RG1, Vol. 187, no. 117.

Governor's Farm. "Burying the Hatchet Ceremony. June 25, 1761. Halifax. Public Archives of Nova Scotia, RG1, Volume 165, pp. 162–65.

Hector Langevin to Samuel Fairbanks. 1868, September 28. Department of Indian and Northern Affairs Archives, Ottawa.

Journal of Assembly Papers (Nova Scotia). 1838. Letter from Lord Glenelg, August 22. Appendix 80, page 154.

Joseph Howe. 1843. Indian Commissioner's Report, January 25. *Journal of Assembly Papers*, Appendix 1, pg. 3. Public Archives of Nova Scotia.

Statues of Nova Scotia. *An Act to Provide to the Instruction and Permanent Settlement of Indians*. March 9, 1842.

8

Keeping Canada White
Immigration Enforcement in Canada

Wendy Chan

YOU SHOULD KNOW THIS

- In 2009, a total of 252,179 immigrants were admitted to Canada as permanent residents.
- In 2009 and 2008 the top source countries for immigrants to Canada were China, Philippines, India, the United States, and Pakistan. In 2009, of 252,179 immigrants, 56,326 came from China and the Philippines.
- In 2009, there were 11,589 refugee claims in Canada. Along with the 11,007 claims in 2008, these are the lowest numbers of claims since 1986.
- Under the *Immigration and Refugee Protection Act*, detention reviews for refugee protection claimants are held in-camera. This process recognizes the need to protect the confidentiality of the claimant.
- The *IRPA* permits the arrest and detention of people in Canada who are unco-operative and fail to establish their identities, provided that they are not permanent residents or protected persons. In 2008–2009, 14,362 individuals were detained by Canadian Border Services Agency (CBSA) for immigration reasons. In the same year, 13,249 individuals were removed from Canada.
- At the end of 2008, Canada received 10 percent, or 36,900, of all asylum claims globally. The top six countries of origin making asylum claims in Canada are Mexico, Haiti, Colombia, United States, China, and Sri Lanka.

Sources: Citizenship and Immigration Canada 2010b; Canadian Council for Refugees listserve, January, 2006; *IRPA* 2002; Global Detention Project 2009; CBSA 2010.

IN THE FALL OF 2010, THE MINISTER FOR IMMIGRATION, Jason Kenney, and the Minister for Public Safety, Vic Toews, announced in a press release new legislation aimed at preventing the irregular entry of individuals into Canada. The aim, they said, is to send a clear message to smugglers that they are not welcomed in Canada. As Minister Toews states, "through this legislation, we are cracking down on human smugglers, protecting the safety and security of our communities, and helping to ensure the integrity of Canada's generous immigration system" (CIC 2010a). In the months leading up to this news announcement, close to 500 Tamil refugee claimants had arrived on the west coast of Canada aboard the MV *Sun Sea* (*Vancouver Province* 2010). Their arrival fuelled a public surge of anger that so many people would be allowed, once again, to bypass the normal channels of refugee processing and "jump the queue" (*Toronto Star* 2010a). The voices of those defending the need for Canada to be open-minded about refugees, to avoid making racist remarks about the Tamils, was largely lost in the debate. Instead, the government tabled Bill C-49, *Preventing Human Smugglers from Abusing Canada's Immigration System Act*, in an effort to "crack down" on human smuggling into Canada.

During this period of heightened anxiety about the arrival of the Tamils, newspapers in Canada were also reporting on the continued need for more immigrants to come to Canada in order to address the forthcoming labour shortages due to the anticipated retirement of the boomer generation (*Toronto Star* 2010b). Critics argued that the economic consequences of failing to act would result in slower economic development and growth for Canada. Yet the process of determining how to select the "best" immigrants continued to fuel debate and controversy. Canada wants to attract "good" immigrants while also ensuring that "undesirable" immigrants are not allowed in.

What are we to think about Canada's approach to immigration enforcement? Is it too harsh and racist, as many immigrants argue? Or is it not harsh enough because it permits immigrants and refugees who arrive through irregular channels to enter into Canada?

Many immigration scholars agree that successive reforms to immigration policies in Canada have resulted in increasingly harsh and punitive measures, particularly as related to the enforcement provisions of the *Immigration Act*. Both the language used and the substantive changes contained in various amendments construct negative images of immigrants as "abusers" of Canada's "generous" immigration system, as "bogus" refugee claimants, and as "criminals" who "cheat" their way into Canada. The latest immigration Act, the *Immigration and Refugee Protection Act* (IRPA), exemplifies the criminalizing and retributive tone that is now commonplace in immigration policy making. The convergence of criminal justice strategies with concerns regarding immigration control found in the IRPA, the most comprehensive set of amendments since the introduction of the *Immigration Act* in 1975, marks an important direction in Canadian immigration policy making.

Yet immigration critics continue to argue that not enough is being done to ensure that the best immigrants are allowed entry while potential immigrants who pose a threat are screened out. Critics also argue that the rules must be the same for everyone, and therefore undocumented immigrants should not be given "special" treatment. A letter to the editor published in the *Toronto Star* (2006b) is typical:

> Our illegal immigrants have paraded through the streets of Toronto demanding their rights, which obviously includes the right to ignore our laws and just do as they please. This is a criminal act and should be viewed as one. Demanding your rights does not include ignoring the law of any country, including this one. Therefore, I believe immediate expulsion is in order in spite of all the overzealous lawyers who have in the past encouraged disregard for these laws.

Ironically, after being elected in early 2006, Stephen Harper's minority Conservative government — many of whose members were once among Canada's harshest immigration critics — recognized that these issues are more complex and difficult than newspapers would suggest.

Untangling the myths and controversies around immigration enforcement requires a critical examination of enforcement provisions in the IRPA. Taking a critical approach involves asking how immigration laws and policies acknowledge issues of gender, race, and class differences in the development, interpretation, and application of the country's approaches. The allegations of an effort to keep Canada "white" by excluding immigrants of colour call for a close consideration of how well (or not) immigrants of colour fare under the current immigration Act. As we shall see, the trend towards criminalizing and demonizing immigrants is nothing new, and race and racism have played an important role in organizing racial identities and enforcing a specific racial reality in Canada. Then too, the enforcement provisions of the *Immigration and Refugee Protection Act* seek to address public concerns over "problem" immigrants, which means that it is important to consider the rationale for these provisions, as well as the responses and criticisms to them. Is there an adequate balance between enforcement and protection for immigrants? The *IPRA* appears to mark racialized immigrants as criminals and outsiders, with enforcement provisions driven by the need to scapegoat and punish immigrants for a range of fears and insecurities, an approach legitimized by racist ideologies and practices. Immigrants of colour pay the price for Canadians' need to be reassured that their established way of life will not be lost and that immigrants are not "taking over" their country. The result is that many immigrants will continue to be marginalized and excluded as full participants in Canadian society.

Canadian Immigration Policy: Recent Years

Canada, like many Western democratic countries, experienced a continued decline in births after the 1960s, combined with a relatively low level of immigration. The implications of this demographic raised concerns about whether there would be enough people to keep the country afloat. In the 1980s Brian Mulroney's Progressive Conservative government sought to address these problems, and boost the economy, by increasing levels of immigration, targeting both young people, particularly those of child-bearing age, and skilled immigrant workers. In particular, the Business Immigration Program added a new category of immigrants, investors, to boost the number of educated and skilled immigrants entering Canada (Li 2003: 27). The result was a significant increase in immigration levels during the late 1980s and early 1990s. Between 1980 and 2000, immigration accounted for almost half of the country's population growth, with over 3.7 million immigrants admitted (Li 2003: 32). In comparison, between 1955 and 1970 Canada had admitted just over 1.6 million immigrants, accounting for 30 percent of total population growth.

The composition of immigrants was also shifting. Whereas in the post-World War II period immigrants came mainly from Britain and continental Europe (87 percent of immigrants from 1946 to 1955), by the 1980s and 1990s Asia and the Pacific region had become the key source continent for immigrants (53.8 percent from 1970 to 2000). By 1998–2000 the top four source countries were China, India, Pakistan, and the Philippines (CIC 2001a: 8). Much of this shift can be attributed to alterations in immigration policies in the 1960s. The changes allowed Canada to abandon national origin as a selection criterion, and admit immigrants from all over the world. The implementation of the point system in 1967[1] and, subsequently, the *Immigration Act of 1976* removed the explicit racial and ethnic discrimination found in previous policies, with the effect that many more immigrants from non-European countries were now being admitted into Canada (Li 2003: 33).

Throughout the 1980s and 1990s, the public debate about immigration was also heating up. The increasing numbers of non-white immigrants had not gone unnoticed and had contributed to a backlash that promoted views that Canada could not absorb all this "diversity" (Li 2001) and that the "quality" of immigrants was threatening to destroy the nation (Thobani 2000). While immigration was on the increase, so too were unemployment rates. Public-opinion polls highlighted immigration as a hot-button issue — primarily, many pollsters believed, because the public associated high unemployment rates with too much immigration (Palmer 1996; Economic Council of Canada 1991). Opinion polls recorded between 1988 and 1993 found that 30–45 percent of the Canadian population believed the country had too many immigrants, and indicated that hostility towards immigrants was on the rise (Palmer 1996). The polls expressed fears and anxieties about immigrants not assimilating sufficiently and creating social problems. Clearly, the issue of immigration had become highly charged, with pro-immigration and anti-immigration sentiments being strongly asserted in all types of public forums.

The issue, however, was not so black and white. While immigration was increasing, only certain types of immigrants were gaining access to Canada. The gender, class, and race dynamics of the immigration system were not lost on many critics of the recent reforms. Although the point system appeared to be neutral in terms of how it evaluated potential immigrants, the resources provided to immigration offices abroad were having an impact on who actually got their applications processed in a timely manner. The United States, Britain, and Western Europe had reasonably adequate immigration services, but in non-traditional source areas, such as Africa and parts of South Asia, immigration services were few and far between, resulting in administrative delays and long waiting periods. As well, the professional qualifications of potential immigrants from countries in the Northern Hemisphere were given greater weight than the qualifications of immigrants trained in the South (CCR 2000: 12). Wealthier applicants were also given preferential treatment in that they were not assessed on all criteria of the points system if they met the criteria of the investors program.[2] These hidden biases resulted in continued racial and ethnic as well as class-based discrimination by favouring potential immigrants from countries more similar to Canada than not.

> Although the point system appeared to be neutral in terms of how it evaluated potential immigrants, it was the resources provided to immigration offices abroad that had an impact on who actually got their applications processed in a timely manner.

Gender biases also played a role, particularly in the types of categories that immigrants slotted themselves into when they applied for entry into Canada. Typically, men are the primary or main applicant, and women are in the category of dependent spouse. Although many women who come to Canada are skilled, they may not have had access to a traditional education, which is recognized through the point system and which in turn makes it difficult for them to succeed as the main applicant. Abu-Laban and Gabriel (2002: 49) also point out that how skills are constructed relies on a sexual division of labour. Women's work, both paid and unpaid — for example, cleaning, caring, cooking — is devalued in the point system because it is classified as unskilled or semi-skilled, and offers few if any points. Furthermore, patriarchal attitudes continue to cast women into the role of being dependent on men, and Canadian immigration policies and practices rely on these assumptions in the processing of applications. The net effect is that potential female immigrants have the best chances of entering into Canada by assuming the role of dependent spouse regardless of whether they fit that category or not. For women who do not have male applicants to support their immigration applications, the chances of successfully immigrating are greatly diminished. The only category in which women's applications have been largely successful is when they are able to enter Canada through the Live-In Caregivers Program (LCP). This program allows women to migrate to Canada and work as a live-in caregiver, after which they can apply for permanent residence status once they have completed two years or 3900 hours of work within four years of their arrival.[3] Yet the relationship of these women to Canada is still precarious, because upon entering Canada they are not given landed status, but a temporary permit only. They have to satisfy the contractual agreement with their employers before they become eligible for landed status and possibly citizenship.[4]

The worry over illegal immigration to Canada and the high numbers of refugee applications further intensified the debate about the effectiveness of Canada's immigration system. Although the problem of "illegal" entry is an accepted problem in any immigration system, a number of high-profile cases of immigrants and refugees (for example, Tamil boat people) seeking entry led the public to conclude that Canada's immigration system was no longer effective and that more reform was necessary. What the public wasn't aware of, however, was that most "illegal" immigrants were not in fact cases of people seeking entry, but of people whose visas had expired and who had not yet left the country. Furthermore, governments have never, historically, regarded the problem of "illegal" entry into Canada to be a major immigration issue. Indeed, over the years a number of amnesty programs had been implemented to regularize immigrants who lacked proper documentation (Robinson 1983). If a "crisis" situation did exist, it was more likely the result of the media and political opportunists creating a crisis in the public imagination, allowing it to run unchecked, resulting in uninformed speculation about Canada's immigration system.

Controlling Immigration and Immigrants

A key element of many Western countries' immigration programs includes determining who is denied access. In Canada the perceived need to control the flow of immigrants resulted in a marked resurgence of strictures in Canadian policy in the 1980s, a trend that peaked in the 1990s and coincided with the politicization of immigration. Beginning with the *Immigration Act of 1975*, numerous reforms and amendments led to more strict and exclusionary requirements. Search and seizure provisions were expanded, and refugee claimants were photographed and fingerprinted upon arrival. Fines and penalties were increased for transportation companies that brought in individuals who lacked appropriate documentation (Kelley and Trebilcock 1998).

Various explanations have been offered for why these changes occurred. Many authors cite the breakdown in Canada's refugee system combined with the rise in requests for asylum as a major contributing factor (Creese 1992; Matas 1989). The backlog of applications, the cumbersome administrative process, and allegations that the refugee system was being abused

> These conditions paved the way for independent immigrants (typically male, business class) to be viewed as more desirable than dependent immigrants (typically women and children, family class).

challenged the legitimacy of the system. Other explanations included the lack of consensus amongst the political parties over what is an acceptable level of immigration, along with the belief that immigrants applying to Canada should be more self-reliant. These conditions paved the way for independent immigrants (typically male, business class) to be viewed as more desirable than dependent immigrants (typically women and children, family class). Racist beliefs — to the effect that different racial and ethnic backgrounds of immigrants were eroding Canadian values and traditions — shaped the contours of the debates around these issues (Frideres 1996).

In 1987 the federal government introduced two major policy reforms, Bill C-55 and Bill C-84, in response to unanticipated high levels of refugee claims, which were placing a major strain on the immigration system. The *Refugee Reform Act* (Bill C-55) created the Immigration and Refugee Board of Canada (previously the Immigration Appeal Board) and restructured the refugee determination process to respond to the problem of unfounded refugee claims. Refugees were now required to undergo a screening hearing to determine the credibility of their claims. The *Refugee Deterrents and Detention Act* (Bill C-84) gave immigration officers and agents more power to detain and remove refugee arrivals, particularly those considered criminals or a security threat (Kelley and Trebilcock 1998: 386). Both of these reforms led to heated debates, with many critics arguing that the changes proposed were not well-thought-out pieces of legislation but, rather, a reactionary and knee-jerk response to an alleged refugee "crisis" that had been created by the media (Creese 1992: 140–41). Due to these intense debates, the implementation of these bills did not occur until January 1989. Interestingly, the procedure of screening refugees at the beginning of the refugee determination process was eventually eliminated when it was discovered that 95 percent of refugee claims were legitimate (Garcia y Griego 1994: 128). In other words, the speculation that many refugees were "bogus" was unwarranted; the process of forcing refugees to undergo a screening was eventually removed in 1992.

Attempts to curtail and control immigration continued into the 1990s, when two more pieces of legislation were introduced to address security concerns and the growing belief that illegal immigrants rather than legitimate refugees were infiltrating Canada's borders. Introduced in June 1992, Bill C-86 proposed primarily restrictive revisions to the refugee determination system. The restrictions included fingerprinting refugee claimants, harsher detention provisions, making refugee hearings open to the public, and requiring Convention Refugees[5] applying for landing in Canada to have a passport, valid travel document, or "other satisfactory identity document" (CCR 2000). In addition, individuals with criminal or terrorist links would no longer be admissible. In July 1995 the government introduced Bill C-44, better known as the "Just Desserts" bill because it was enacted in response to the killing of a Toronto police officer by a landed immigrant with a long criminal record. Sergio Marchi, the immigration minister, reminded Canadians that immigration is a privilege and not a right, and proposed changes that would "go a long way to stopping the tyranny of a minority criminal element" (Marchi 1995). Bill C-44 made it easier to remove from Canada permanent residents who were deemed by the minister to be a "danger to the public." This would be done by restricting their ability to appeal their deportation orders or submit a refugee claim. The bill included additional measures to address fraud and multiple refugee claims.

Like the earlier reforms, these two bills were equally divisive and resulted in intense public and political debates. The most controversial change implemented was the discretionary power given to the immigration minister to deport a permanent resident. Widespread academic and public discussions ensued, with legal scholars arguing that returning discretionary power to the minister was "a throwback to a less enlightened era" (Haigh and Smith 1998: 291), and advocates for a fairer immigration policy arguing that the new provisions were racist and would have the result of increasing the criminalization of non-European individuals in Canada (Hassan-Gordon 1996; Noorani and Wright 1995). Yet some critics believed that Bill C-44 had not gone far enough in tightening up the system against false claimants and criminals. The Reform Party argued that a "criminal is a criminal" and that it was not sufficient to define "serious criminality" as offences carrying a ten-year sentence or longer (Kelley and Trebilcock 1998: 434). That party's position highlights how, despite the lack of research demonstrating any links between immigrants and high crime rates, public fear about crime, based only on several high-profile cases, could be easily manipulated to argue for tighter immigration controls.

These debates highlight how immigration had, by the mid-1990s, become a hot-button issue for politicians and policy makers as the Canadian public became more involved in shaping Canada's immigration system. Teitelbaum and Winter (1998: 188) attribute this change to the presence of the Reform Party, and that party's calls in the 1993 election for an abandonment of the policy of multiculturalism and significant reductions in Canada's annual immigration levels. The right-wing populist movement in Canada, as elsewhere, often used immigration and immigrants as easy targets in placing blame for the economic troubles of the time:

> The Fraser Institute report says newcomers pay about half as much in income taxes as other Canadians but absorb nearly the same value of government services, costing taxpayers roughly $6,051 per immigrant and amounting to a total annual cost of somewhere between $16.3-billion and $23.6-billion.
>
> "It's in the interest of Canada to examine what causes this and to fix it," said Herbert Grubel, co-author of the report Immigration and the Canadian Welfare State. "We need a better selection process.... We're not here, as a country, to do charity for the rest of the world." (*National Post* 2011)

Such views coincided neatly with the shift to neoliberal approaches in public-policy development — approaches that fostered a belief in how the more vulnerable sectors of society, such as single mothers and immigrants, were to blame for the lack of jobs or high crime rate (Abu-Laban 1998: 194). Good immigrants, it was understood,

The right-wing populist movement in Canada, as elsewhere, recognized that immigration and immigrants were easy targets in placing blame for the economic decline of the time.

were those who could look after themselves and their families. With this came the "common-sense" view that strong immigration controls were a necessary component of any effective immigration system. The harsh government reforms of the 1980s and 1990s delivered the message that security and enforcement were now key priorities in immigration policy making.

The Immigration and Refugee Protection Act 2002

Crepeau and Nakache (2006: 4) note that while immigration controls emerged years before 9/11, those attacks gave authorities more incentive to radically overhaul policies and make them harsher towards unwanted migrants. Canada, like many other states affected by aspects of globalization, transformed immigration from an economic and population policy issue into a security issue. The introduction of the *Immigration and Refugee Protection Act* (IRPA) in 2002 thus marks an important shift in Canadian immigration policy making. As the Standing Committee on Citizenship and Immigration (2001b) affirmed, "The *Immigration and Refugee Protection Act* represents a significant step in addressing current security concerns. Even though drafted before September 11th, the legislation was clearly created with the threat of terrorism in mind." The Canadian government's response in deterring these activities and individuals is to impose tighter sanctions and increase levels of scrutiny and authority for immigration officers.

According to Citizenship and Immigration Canada (CIC), the IRPA is intended to serve a number of different immigration goals, such as attracting skilled workers, protecting refugees, allowing family reunification, and deterring traffickers. The aim, according to the Liberal government of the time, was to accomplish these goals by simplifying the legislation and striking the necessary balance between efficiency, fairness, and security. CIC asserts that there is a need to "simplify," "strengthen," "modernize," and "streamline" the immigration system. A key priority in this set of policy reforms was to close "the back door to criminals and others who would abuse Canada's openness and generosity." This would be achieved by including in the Act the necessary provisions to "better ensure serious criminals and individuals who are threats to public safety are kept out of Canada, and, if they have entered the country, that they are removed as quickly as possible" (CIC 2001b).

The IRPA did have a significant impact on controlling immigration to Canada. While some immigrant and refugee groups applauded the changes to the family reunification and sponsorship requirements, immigrant supporting organizations pointed to growing concerns and trepidation about an Act that was overly reactive and too obsessed with security issues. As the Maytree Foundation[6] (2001: 3) stated, IRPA "is much more about who cannot come to Canada and how they will be removed, than it is about who we will welcome, who we will protect, and how we will do that." Many organizations expressed an uneasiness that racialized immigrants would suffer the consequences of immigration officers' concerns about the need to maintain border security. Moreover, women refugees and immigrants would be likely to shoulder the burden of the many changes that encompassed racist and sexist practices.

> As the Maytree Foundation stated, IRPA "is much more about who cannot come to Canada and how they will be removed, than it is about who we will welcome, who we will protect, and how we will do that."

Targeting Traffickers and Smugglers

Within the IRPA, the crime of human smuggling and trafficking involves several types of activities. It is an offence to organize, induce, aid, or abet immigrants to Canada who do not have the necessary travel documents (s. 117). The trafficking of persons through abduction, fraud, deception, the use or threat of force or coercion (s. 118), and leaving a person or persons at sea for the purposes of helping them come to Canada (s. 119) are also offences subject to criminal penalties. The difference between trafficking and human smuggling rests in the distinction between coerced and consensual irregular migrants. People who are trafficked (usually into forced labour or prostitution) are assumed not to have given their consent and are considered "victims," whereas migrants who are smuggled are considered to have willingly engaged in the enterprise (Bhabha 2005).

The penalty for organizing the smuggling of less than ten people is a maximum of ten years imprisonment or a $500,000 fine, or both, for the first offence, or a maximum of fourteen years imprisonment or a $1 million fine, or both, for subsequent offences. When ten persons or more are involved, the penalty is a maximum of life imprisonment or a $1 million fine, or both. Trafficking persons or leaving them at sea carries a maximum penalty of life imprisonment, a fine of $1 million, or both (s. 120). Aggravating factors (s. 121) such as the occurrence of harm or death during the offence or the association of the offence with a criminal organization will be considered in determining the penalty imposed.

The Canadian Council for Refugees (CCR) argues that attempting to deter the activities of human smuggling and trafficking can have the unintended consequence of criminalizing family members who help refugees escape from their home countries (given that the law does not distinguish between smugglers for profit and others who are just trying to help). While the claimants can escape prosecution if they are found to be refugees (s. 133), their family members are not equally protected because they can be denied an asylum hearing or lose permanent residence without the possibility of an appeal (Crepeau and Jimenez 2004). Nor are individuals who apply for asylum in good faith, but are rejected, adequately protected. Given the lack of differentiation, both categories of individuals — those who engage in human smuggling for profit and those who are motivated by humanitarian concerns — will suffer the same penalties.

Moreover, while these provisions are intended to bring Canadian immigration policy in line with international protocols such as the *U.N. Convention against Transnational Organized Crime*, and thus have included strong enforcement measures to curtail and deter human smuggling and trafficking in persons, the bill has no provisions for protection of those being smuggled or trafficked, even though Canada is a signatory to the *U.N. Convention on the Status of Refugees*. It would seem that while Canada has sought to meet some of its international obligations, in other agreements that Canada has undertaken it has yet to fully realize compliance. As the CCR points out, "The migrant protocol states that the criminalization measures are not to apply to people who are smuggled into a country, whereas Bill C-11 [now the IRPA] gives an exemption only to those recognized as refugees." As a result, protection from prosecution is limited only to those who can make a successful refugee claim.

With the introduction of Bill C-49, *Preventing Human Smugglers from Abusing Canada's Immigration System Act,* refugee advocacy groups and immigration lawyers believe that making a refugee claim in Canada will now be more difficult than ever before. They argue that the measures contained in Bill C-49 will do little to target smugglers, and is more likely to exacerbate the suffering of asylum-seekers. Some of the key concerns about the Bill include detaining refugees, including children, for a year without the possibility of an independent review; denying refugee claimants access to an appeal process; denying some refugees the right to apply for permanent residency in Canada for five years and thus delaying their reunification with family members; and denying refugee claimants freedom of movement because they will not be able to travel outside of Canada until they are permanent residents (CCR 2010a). The CCR also point out that the immigration minister has sole discretion to determine whether or not the arrival of a group of persons into Canada is irregular or not (CCR 2010b). Those deemed irregular will be subjected to all kinds of special rules. They argue this effectively creates two classes of refugees, with those designated irregular, based on model of arrival, treated worse than the other group (CCR 2010b).

To date, over eighty organizations have called on MPs to defeat the second reading of Bill C-49. They argue that the Bill punishes refugees and does little to target smugglers (*Toronto Star* 2010c). Furthermore, they claim that key elements of the Bill are simply unlawful insofar as they contravene the *Charter of Rights and Freedoms* and Canada's international human rights obligations (*Star Phoenix* 2010). Jack Costello, speaking on behalf of the Jesuit Refugee and Migrant Service of Canada sums up the objections to Bill C-49:

> Just as Bill C-49 fails to maintain Canada's legal commitments nationally and internationally, it fails abysmally at supporting the dignity and worth of every person, in this case refugee claimants in desperate straits. This bill is not Canadian. It is not a voice for encouraging greater care and compassion among Canadians for their suffering sisters and brothers. On what basis, then, has the government cobbled together this harsh, unjust and totally unhelpful proposal? (CCR 2010b)

Most immigration experts do not believe that the government's efforts to curtail the arrival of irregular refugees will have much of an impact. Morrison and Crosland (2001) argue that the deterrent effect of such grossly exaggerated penalties is doubtful, since entry into the "Western fortress" necessitates that irregular migrants and refugees use some kind of help to enter Western countries for any reason.

Interdiction and Detention

Attempts to prevent and deter irregular migrants from entering Canada have resulted in a number of measures that were initiated or retooled in the IRPA either to stop migrants from setting foot in Canada or to swiftly remove them. Interdiction measures include the Smart Border Agreement between Canada and the United States. In that agreement Canada increased the number of countries for which it requires visas to be held by foreign nationals to enter the country (DFAIT 2004). Coupled with this are penalties (up to $3,200 per traveller) against airlines, railways, and shipping companies that fail in advance to check their passengers for adequate documentation (IRPA s. 148[1][a] and s. 279[1]). Finally, immigration officers are also stationed at various countries of origin or of transit with the aim of stopping migrants before they reach Canada (DFAIT 2004).

With the IRPA, immigration detention and the power to detain have been fortified. Sections 55 and 56 of the new Act state that someone can be detained if there are reasonable grounds to believe that the person would be inadmissible to Canada, a danger to the public, or unlikely to appear for future proceedings. Enhanced powers have also been given to immigration officers at ports of entry to detain people on the basis of administrative convenience, suspicion of inadmissibility on the grounds of security or human rights violations, and failure to establish identity for any immigration procedure under the Act. Immigration officers also have wider discretion to arrest and detain a foreign national but not a protected person without a warrant, even in cases where they are not being removed (s. 55[2]). The length of detention is not specified for any of these grounds although periodic reviews are mandatory. Thus, someone who fails to provide adequate identification can be detained for the same length of time as can a person who is considered a danger to the public (s. 58[1]). Children can be detained, but only as a measure of last resort (s. 60). If Bill C-49 is passed, the detention of refugees will have a dramatic impact as refugees may be detained for a year without the possibility of a review.

A report by the Canadian Border Services Agency (CBSA) on the Detention and Removal Program in Canada notes that considerable variation exists across the country in detention practices within the first forty-eight-hour period (CBSA 2010). While detainees in the Atlantic, Prairie, and Pacific regions are released early, those in Central Canada are detained for longer periods. Similarly, the practice of detaining children and individuals with mental health issues also varies across the country (CBSA 2010). The report recommends a number of changes to improve services as well as reduce the cost of detention by exploring alternatives for low-risk detainees (CBSA 2010).

Many concerns have been raised about the nature of the detention provisions and the manner in which they are or will be executed. The fear amongst most immigrant and refugee organizations is that conferring greater powers to individual immigration officers will result in racial profiling and that a high proportion of racialized migrants will end up being detained (CCR 2001; Getting Landed Project 2002). Other worries include the broad arbitrary use of power by immigration officers, the possibility of long-term detention of migrants who fail to establish their identities, the criminalization of trafficked or smuggled migrants who will be detained for the purpose of deterring human traffickers, and the use of detention on the basis of group status rather than on the particular circumstances of the person involved.

The United Nations High Commission for Refugees (UNHCR) states that it opposes any detention policy that is fashioned to deter asylum seekers or to discourage them from pursuing their refugee claims. Moreover, it cautions against establishing a policy that detains migrants on the basis of being "unlikely to appear" at an immigration hearing because of their "*mode of arrival*" to Canada, because many refugees are forced to use smugglers in order to reach safety (UNHCR 2001: 29). Finally, it argues that the act of detaining a person for failing to establish their identity, which includes making determinations about the person's level of co-operation with authorities, calls for a recognition of the difference between a willful intention to deceive and the inability to provide documentation (UNHCR 2001: 30). The UNHCR joins the voices of others (CCR 2001; Maytree Foundation 2001) who also recommend that the government needs to establish clear guidelines and criteria as to what constitutes a refusal to co-operate.

The drift towards the use of preventative detention to deal with migrants perpetuates the mistaken and prejudiced perceptions that those being detained are a threat to public safety and are behaving illegally rather than being people who actually need safety from danger (CCR 2010b). Indeed, the culture of criminalization within the present immigration system points to disturbing trends. Unlike convicted offenders, migrants can face indefinite lengths of detention as they wait for the arrival of their identity documents, and they can be detained on the basis of suspicion or convenience. Statistics published since the implementation of the IRPA note that the use of detention has increased, both in the number of non-citizens held and the length of time people have been detained. For example, in 2004–2005, there were 10,774 individuals detained. By 2008-2009, the number had increased one-third to 14,362 (CBSA 2010).

> Statistics published since the implementation of the *IRPA* note that the use of detention has increased, both in the number of non-citizens held and the length of time people have been detained. For example, in 2004–2005, there were 10,774 individuals detained. By 2008–2009, the number had increased one-third to 14,362.

Somewhat ironically, the increased federal spending in this area has resulted in detention being used not for people who are considered threats to security, but instead to detain migrants who arrive irregularly or without adequate documentation (CBSA 2010).

Loss of Appeal Rights

The elimination of immigration appeals in Canada, particularly in cases where "serious criminality" is involved, is a measure that many other countries have not implemented to the same extent. Section 64 of the new Act states that individuals found to be inadmissible on considerations of security, violating human rights, serious criminality, or organized criminality, or individuals convicted of a crime and given a term of imprisonment of two years or more may not be allowed to appeal to the Immigration Appeal Division. Although judicial review remains available, applicants who lose their right to appeal can apply to the federal courts but only with leave from the court and only if there is a purely legal issue that needs to be dealt with. Therefore, if a factual mistake is made, or if all the evidence was not reasonably considered by the original decision maker (even if that person reached the wrong conclusion), the federal court will not intervene. The effect of this change is to disallow any of the discretion formerly exercised in determining whether an individual should or should not be removed based on the circumstances of their case. While these changes may make the system more efficient, they do so at the cost of diminishing the rights of immigrants. As one commentator notes, such an approach illustrates a move towards a "mechanical application of the rules," which is the antithesis of the just administration of the law (Dent 2002: 762).

The introduction of the Act also included provisions for the establishment of a Refugee

Appeal Division, where refugee determinations could be reviewed. However, the number of Immigration and Refugee Board members was reduced from a panel of two to one to balance the right to an appeal for refugees (Crepeau and Nakache 2006: 15). In 2010, the Refugee Appeal Division was finally established, almost eight years after the implementation of *IRPA*. The provisions for the Refugee Appeal Division were part of the reforms found in the *Balanced Refugee Reform Act*. However, also contained in this Act were less welcoming reforms such as the denial of appeal to refugee claimants arriving from "safe countries of origin" (CCR 2010c). The problem with this criterion is that it is unclear what constitutes a "safe" country, and activists argue that refugee determination should never be based on a blanket judgment such as country of origin. Instead, each case is unique and requires an individual assessment in order to achieve a fair outcome (CCR 2010c). Although the government argued that designating some claims as "safe" will help to streamline the refugee determination process, critics fear that many claimants may fall through the cracks if they do not have access to a full hearing. Further attempts to restrict refugee rights continues with Bill C-49, where tighter restrictions to the appeal process is being proposed to exclude some refugees from appealing a negative decision based on their mode of arrival. When refugees and immigrants do have the right to an appeal, their access to the process is made all the more difficult because of reduced funding in legal aid. Depending on which province the appeal takes place in, some appellants may never see the inside of a hearing room because some provinces do not have any funding available to migrants.

Protecting Immigrants' Rights

Many critics of the *IRPA* note the erosion of immigrant rights in the legislation. The emphasis on security and terrorism has clearly overshadowed migrants' rights and the need for a more balanced approach. Kent Roach (2005) observes that governments have taken advantage of concerns around security to reconfigure immigration law to bypass the human rights of migrants. He states, "Immigration law has been attractive to the authorities because it allows procedural shortcuts and a degree of secrecy that would not be tolerated under even an expanded criminal law" (Roach 2005: 2).

Critics argue that the *IRPA* has a detrimental effect on racialized individuals, groups, and communities. For example, the attempts by government to combat human smuggling and trafficking should not occur at the expense of further victimization of the migrants smuggled or trafficked. The National Association of Women and the Law (NAWL) and the United Nations High Commission for Refugees (UNHCR) assert that by failing to include adequate protection for trafficked or smuggled migrants, the Canadian government is reneging on its responsibility to international protocols. The UNHCR notes that many reasons exist as to why migrants resort to smugglers and traffickers. While many migrants are people searching for better economic opportunities, many others are refugees whose only option for escape is with the smugglers or traffickers. NAWL believes that this new category of immigration enforcement will result in smugglers and traffickers charging migrants higher prices to escape. For women and children, who are less likely to have the financial resources to pay, the possibilities of fleeing persecution, conflict, and human rights abuses will become even more remote unless they are willing to pay the costs in the form of enforced prostitution and sexual violations (NAWL 2001). It has been strongly recommended that the Canadian government provide protection to migrants by granting them immigration relief, access to permanent residency, or the opportunity to submit applications to stay on humanitarian and compassionate grounds (see briefs by NAWL 2001; CCR 2001; and UNHCR 2001). Affording migrants the necessary protection would help to alleviate their vulnerability to the smugglers or traffickers.

Racialized women migrants in particular will experience the impact of the IRPA in harsh and uncompromising terms because they are typically more vulnerable to the effects of migration. For example, a third of all women who immigrate to Canada do so through the family class category, which means that they are sponsored by a Canadian citizen or permanent resident who agrees to ensure that their essential needs are met so that the sponsored person will not resort to social assistance (NAWL 2001). In its brief to the Standing Committee on Citizenship and Immigration, NAWL (2001) recommended that family reunification be recognized as a fundamental human right, and, specifically, that people who are being reunited with their families in Canada be given the right to obtain permanent residence in Canada in order to avoid the development of exploitative or abusive relationships. In its review of the first several years of the IRPA, NAWL points out that neither this recommendation nor any of the others it submitted has been implemented, although cursory attention to the issue of gender in immigration has been paid. It notes, "Almost four years after the adoption of the new legislation, the only tangible result of any gender based analysis of the legislative commitment to gender based analysis of the Act is the sex-disaggregated data in the Annual Report 2005" (NAWL 2006).

> Racialized women migrants in particular will experience the impact of the new Act in harsh and uncompromising terms because they are typically more vulnerable to the effects of migration.

The decrepit state of detention centres in Canada and the now increased potential for long-term detention of migrants add to the growing list of concerns that detainees' civil liberties will be violated, particularly when the majority of the detainees are racialized migrants. Indeed, many organizations believe that the heightened powers of detention are a racist and reactionary response to the arrival of boatloads of Chinese and Tamil migrants to the shores of British Columbia — primarily economic migrants seeking a new life in Canada.[7] That their arrival resulted in their immediate detention without much public outcry highlights how racism, through the practice of racial profiling, was used to gain legitimacy for the government's practices. The assumption was that if one boatload of migrants were "bogus" refugee claimants, then all migrants would be as well, which justified the government's "tough"[8] stance on "illegal" immigrants (CBC Online 1999a, 1999b, CCR 2010a). Not surprisingly, issues of due process and other human rights abuses surfaced in a United Nations Human Rights Commission report over the treatment of the Chinese (Canadian Press, April 12, 2001; CBC Online 1999c), and again with the Tamil migrants (Amnesty International 2010). The U.N. investigator said that Canada "needed to avoid criminalizing the victims." Her report pointed to the poor psychological state of some of the Chinese women who were detained, and how mistreatment by penitentiary guards had led one woman to attempt suicide. In her report, the U.N. investigator reminded Canadian authorities that the migrants had been doubly victimized because they were also the victims of the traffickers. Similarly, Amnesty International has expressed concern that, with Bill C-49, the rights of refugees and migrants are violated "solely on the basis of how they have travelled to Canada and how many others have travelled with them" (2010). Like others, they remind Canada that this is in direct contravention to various U.N. covenants binding on Canada.

For many activists and scholars involved in debating and discussing the IRPA, the government's recognition of the importance of human rights does indeed appear to be either non-existent or timid at best. Crepeau and Nakache (2006) argue that governments need to recognize that the principle of territorial sovereignty is not incompatible with protecting individual rights and freedoms. One way of recognizing this principle is to clearly identify and justify all security exceptions to the recognition of human rights that are normally conferred by the state to migrants (Crepeau and Nakache 2006: 25). The extent to which Canada and other Western nations will give priority to human rights while pursuing an immigration agenda focused on security and control remains to be seen. Catharine Davergne (2004: 613) observes: *desirable immigrants over human rights?*

> The proliferation of human rights norms over the last half century has not markedly increased rights entitlements at the moment of border crossing, nor has it significantly increased access to human rights for those with no legal status, those "illegals" beyond the reach of the law but at the centre of present rhetoric.

As a result, the approach taken continues to reinforce the unequal distribution of rights on the basis of birthplace, and it leaves those who are unprotected vulnerable and open to intimidation and exploitation.

Race and Nation
National Fears and Immigrant Scapegoating

As the successor to the 1975 *Immigration Act*, the IRPA represents a different era of immigration policy making. The 1975 Act was born out of a perceived need for "race-neutral" categories of eligibility and non-discriminatory treatment of immigrants and is considered to be liberal in its approach.[9] The IRPA emerged out of the continuing racialization[10] of immigration, whereby immigrants of colour have come to be viewed not only as threats to the social, cultural, and linguistic order of the nation, but also as threats to the security of the nation. Martin Rudner (2002: 24), for example, blames Canada's immigration policy for the presence of "large, identifiable homeland communities from societies in conflict," communities that presumably became an attractive arena for fostering international terrorist networks. These anti-immigrant sentiments are not new and were present in various forms during previous immigration debates. However, in recent times they occupy a greater role in framing immigration debates as a result of the negative representation of immigrants of colour by the media in Canada and the realignment of immigration policy making towards a conservative agenda (Abu-Laban 1998; Teitelbaum and Winter 1998).

It would seem that public concerns and anxiety about immigrants and national security are linked to "perceived immigrant desirability and legitimacy," as Buchignani and Indra (1999: 416) remark, rather than to any real threat to Canada's borders or sovereignty. Garcia y Griego (1994: 120) concurs, stating, "Canada has never lost control over its borders, but it has, on more than one occasion, lost control over its own admission process." This state of affairs has been made possible through the belief that it is the "outsider," the migrant or foreign national, that poses the greatest threat, and that this threat can only be contained by retaining a tighter control over the criteria for determining who can immigrate to Canada. This view is evident in statements made by Public Safety and Emergency Preparedness Canada (2004), which notes that "many of the real and direct threats to Canada originate from far beyond our borders."

The implication is that problems are imported into the country via immigrants, and that only through the adoption of a security-driven, regulatory agenda will those problems be contained. Indeed, the flurry of immigration reforms post-9/11 is perhaps more a reflection of the government of the time demonstrating that it had matters under control than it is a proportionate response to security issues. What this allows for, as Maggie Ibrahim (2005: 169) points out, is the legitimization of new racist fears. Instead of focusing on how to support immigrants who are at risk, a security-driven approach emphasizes the need to protect citizens because the incorporation of immigrants will result in an unstable host state (Ibrahim 2005: 169). Of significant concern is that these sentiments are no longer being echoed by conservative, right-wing political parties and organizations only. They are also being legitimized by more liberal, humanitarian-focused groups such as the U.N. and liberal-minded academics (Ibrahim 2005).

Immigrants who do not fit into the predefined mould of what constitutes a "good immigrant" will increasingly become the target of the new security-focused state. It is no surprise that hate crimes have risen dramatically since 9/11 (Statistics Canada 2004) and that many people of colour speak of experiencing racial profiling on a daily basis at the hands of various law enforcement agents (Bahdi 2003). The public acceptance of racist treatment towards people of colour is evident in the way in which the Canadian mainstream media described Muslims during the June 2006 arrest of seventeen Muslim men in Canada. The *Globe and Mail's* (2006) front-page story noted, "Parked directly outside his ... office was a large, gray, cube-shaped truck and, on the ground nearby, he recognized one of the two brown-skinned young men who had taken possession of the next door rented unit." As Robert Fisk points out, "What is 'brown-skinned' supposed to mean — if it is not just a revolting attempt to isolate Muslims as the 'Other' in Canada's highly multicultural society?" (Fisk 2006). Backed into a corner, Muslim groups and organizations have no choice but to join this process of "Othering" by distancing themselves from the men arrested and attempting to calm an increasingly hostile public through reinforcing the idea of peace as the centrepiece of their religion (*Globe and Mail* 2006). Good Muslims, they argue, are not violent and do not engage in terrorist activities. Within all these discussions, it is

> Immigrants who do not fit into the predefined mould of what constitutes a "good immigrant" will increasingly become the target of the new security-focused state.

clear that in a climate of fear, suspicion, and hostility produced by the association between Muslims and terrorist activities, homogeneity becomes the default security blanket, now made all the more possible by the new immigration Act.

A close look at the enforcement provisions of the IRPA shows that the process of blaming and punishing immigrants allows for a "suitable enemy" to blame for the problems of society (Christie 1986). Few strategies are as effective as processes of criminalization for reinforcing an ideology of "us" and "them," with the immigrant usually understood as non-white, poor, and/or female, occupying the status of the outsider (Bannerji 2000). The racialized, gendered, and class nature of this marking ensures that in the construction and definition of who is Canadian, access to this identity is far from equal. Casting immigrants into the role of the "other" has been beneficial in suppressing public fears and insecurities about immigrants "terrorizing" Canadians, taking jobs away from Canadians, and overtaxing the welfare system.

> Few strategies are as effective as processes of criminalization for reinforcing an ideology of "us" and "them," with the immigrant, usually understood as non-white, poor, and/or female, occupying the status of the outsider.

As immigration authorities seek to reclaim their ability to secure Canada's borders, and to argue that the integrity of the immigration system has not been compromised by "illegal" migrants, an increase in the degree of punishment to offenders allows governments to demonstrate their power through the use of force. Such has been the case in the European Union, where resolutions and legislation were brought in to counter a broad range of terrorist activities (these include not just terrorist organizations, but also anti-globalization protests, animal rights activism, and youth subcultures), resulting in the use of deportation and detention without trial against foreign nationals suspected of posing a security risk (Fekete 2004: 6).

Keeping Canada White

Historically, immigration control linked the decline of the nation with the sexual excesses and mental and moral degeneration of Aboriginal peoples and people of colour (Valverde 1991: 105). Racist ideas determined which groups of people would be regarded as having more character, and thus be considered more "civilized." People of British descent were viewed as morally superior for their ability to self-regulate and exercise self-control (Valverde 1991: 105). Importantly, this position was not contested, but rather taken for granted by moral reformers at the turn of the century in Canada (Valverde 1991: 106). The historical studies on immigration of Barbara Roberts (1988) and Donald Avery (1995) confirm the presence of these beliefs. The Canadian government sought to attract the most desirable immigrants, which it had identified — not surprisingly — as white, British, English-speaking, and Protestant. As Strange and Loo (1997: 117) note, "Determining who could become or remain Canadian was one more way to shape the moral character of the nation." Immigrants identified as "low quality" or morally degenerate would find themselves subjected to various forms of regulation, with deportation being the most drastic measure imposed. Here, gendered and racialized ideologies shaped the circumstances that would be defined as undesirable. For men, unemployment or left-wing affiliation were sufficient to warrant deportation, while for women, having children out of wedlock, carrying a disease like VD or tuberculosis, or appearing to court more than one man would bring them to the attention of immigration officials (Strange and Loo 1997: 119). In terms of racial exclusions, simply being non-white was sufficient to be classified as undesirable. The exclusion of Black and Chinese people from Canada was made on the belief that they posed a moral threat that could not be overcome by any means, and therefore special measures needed to be taken to ensure that they did not corrupt the moral integrity of the nation (Bashi 2004; Strange and Loo 1997). Examples of measures taken included the *Chinese Immigration Act, 1923*, which excluded anyone of Chinese descent from immigrating to Canada, prohibiting the employment of white women by Asian employers, and preventing Chinese people from forming families in Canada (Strange and Loo 1997: 120–21).

An overarching feature of immigration policies in Canada, both historically and at present, is to build a nation of people who fulfill the highest moral standards. As Strange and Loo (1997: 145) observe, ideals of purity, industry, piety, and self-discipline were regarded as essential features of Canadianness. Few would argue that these standards continue to characterize and shape present-day immigration policies, often to the detriment of non-white immigrants seeking to come to Canada. Vukov (2003) points out how contemporary public articulations about desirable and undesirable immigrants in both the news media and governmental policy with respect to sexuality and security issues reinforce the long-standing fears that sexually deviant immigrants and criminals continue to threaten the process of replenishing and sustaining a secure population base. Likewise, Angel-Ajani (2003: 435) argues that this climate of anti-immigrant rhetoric relies on the dual discourses of criminalization and cultural difference. Within this climate of insecurity, a wide range of screening practices have been enacted to ensure that people belonging to designated groups are properly filtered out. The construction of Middle Eastern, West Asian, and Muslim peoples as security threats to the nation since September 11, and the introduction of new policy measures to secure our border, underscore the ways in which definitions of undesirable immigrants are highly racialized (Vukov 2003: 345).

The narrative that emerges from the IRPA supports this vision of Canada, with the good immigrant reaffirming Canada's essential goodness and "the bad immigrant forcing otherwise generous people into taking stern disciplinary measures" (Razack 1999: 174). A critical component of this ongoing story is that "good" is equated with whiteness and with being Canadian, while "bad" is associated with being an immigrant, an outsider to the nation. Thobani's (2000) study of the Immigration Policy Review in 1994 highlights this most clearly. She found that throughout the public consultation process, Canadians expressed concerns that their national values were being eroded and degraded by immigrants who did not share these values (Thobani 2000: 44). While Canadians saw themselves as respectful, honest, and hard-working, immigrants were consistently represented as criminal, disease-ridden, and lazy. Thobani notes that by placing immigrant values in the context of social and cultural diversity, definitions of immigrants and Canadians are reproduced in racialized terms. Audrey Kobayashi (1995: 71) sums up the situation in asserting that immigration law is a central site for articulating how Canada imagines itself:

Immigration law is in Canada one of the most significant cultural arenas, a contested territory wherein people's relations with one another and with the places they designate as home are expressed. To aid them in that expression, people have faith in the law; it establishes a moral landscape and it codifies our myths about ourselves. It is our recourse to defining ourselves and others, as well as a means of systematically reproducing our imagined reality.

These comments highlight why the harsh treatment of immigrants, particularly immigrants of colour, is so uncontroversial. For to question how immigration practices are carried out within Canada would not just be a challenge to the fairness of the system, it would also call into question how Canada envisions itself. Such a challenge would be neither lightly accepted nor welcomed.

Scapegoating Immigrants

As the boundaries between insider and outsider become more ambivalent and converge with nostalgia for a bygone period of immigration, immigrants of colour are the ones classified and defined as inauthentic, "illegal," or outsiders. Anti-racists allege that racial identity remains a key marker of those who are not perceived as belonging, as "legitimate" immigrants of the nation. Even though Canada moved away from blatant forms of discrimination in its immigration policies in the 1960s and 1970s, racism and patriarchy continued to define spatial and/or social margins in portrayals of the dominant vision of the nation (Simmons 1998; Kobayashi 1995).

> Even though Canada moved away from blatant forms of discrimination in its immigration policies in the 1960s and 1970s, racism and patriarchy continued to define spatial and/or social margins in portrayals of the dominant vision of the nation.

The racialization of immigration, which focuses on the process of constructing racial identities and meanings, enables ideas about "race" to proliferate. Now, cultural differences, rather than racial inferiority, become the distinguishing markers between us and them. Avtar Brah (1996: 165) writes that this form of racism is "a racism that combined a disavowal of biological superiority or inferiority with a focus on 'a way of life,' of cultural difference as the 'natural' basis for feelings of antagonism towards outsiders." This tendency has made it possible, for example, for recurring themes to continue to characterize immigration debates — themes alleging that too much racial diversity will lead to conflict, that immigrants have large families that expect to be supported by the welfare state, that immigrants are criminals with no respect for the law, or that immigrant workers take jobs away because they are willing to work for low wages (Hintjens 1992). In Canada and other Western nations, immigrants are now required to speak the official languages as proof of their adequate assimilation into mainstream culture (Fekete 2004: 22). As Thobani (2000: 293) observes, such demands elevate Europeanness/whiteness over other cultures and ethnicities, and clearly redefine the national Canadian identity as being "white" while seemingly appearing to be race-neutral.

The lack of public outcry over the treatment of immigrants in the new legislation suggests that the public's imagination has been captured in such a way that immigration is understood as a sign of Canada's decline. While Canada cannot do without immigrants, those who are admitted are expected to adhere to Canadian values and adopt a "Canadian" way of life. Non-compliance is not an option, because the failure to assimilate has become a sign of being someone who is a potential contributor to uprisings and terrorist activities. While Canada has always been distrustful of racialized immigrants, IRPA highlights how we need to find a "suitable enemy" for whom we can blame all our failures and insecurities. Recent amendments to the IRPA suggests that the emphasis on security and enforcement shows no signs of abating. Russo points out that since Harper's conservative government took over, they have accelerated the evolution of laws and policies linking law and order and security issues with immigration reform (Russo 2008).

Racialized immigrants have been, and continue to be, the scapegoat containers for a variety of economic and cultural insecurities (Beisel 1994). One consequence of this is that any benefits that immigrants provide to host societies like Canada are drowned out by the discourse of exclusion (*Toronto Star* 2006a). Yet it would be a mistake to believe that immigrants and those working within the immigrant community are unwittingly accepting the recent immigration reforms that construct refugees and asylum seekers as illegitimate and fraudulent. Although the Conservative government has capitalized on the hardened public attitudes to bring forward an immigration reform agenda that marks only the most resourceful immigrants as "desirable," there remains a substantial number of Canadians who refuse to accept this portrayal of immigrants and refugees. The backlash against the Fraser Institute's recent report that immigrants are a drain on Canada highlights this growing tide of resistance. An op-ed in the *Vancouver Sun* captures the ideological background to the Conservative government's position:

> Indeed, the arguments sound suspiciously like those of the old Reform Party, which gave gloomy voice to utilitarian assumptions about acceptable skill sets and wealth required of prospective immigrants....
>
> The notion that the most recent arrivals are paying insufficient tax and drawing excessive benefits remains one of the persistent memes in Canadian society. And it is almost always based on selective statistical evidence while ignoring the unassailable fact that of the 34 million people in Canada, 33 million are either immigrants or the descendants of immigrants who helped to build a national economy which ranks in the top eight globally. (*Vancouver Sun* 2011)

As the current government seeks to implement more punitive reforms, immigration advocacy groups have been developing a strong grassroots movement to challenge these reforms. Although largely hidden from public view, two recent gains made by immigration activists suggest that resistance to the Conservative government immigration agenda has not been in vain. First, activists worked tirelessly to unite opposition parties to defeat Bill C-49 at the second reading in the House of Commons (*Vancouver Sun* 2010). Had the Conservative government gone ahead with the vote, it would certainly have been unsuccessful. Second, significant reforms demanded by opposition parties were made to the *Balanced*

Refugee Reform Act prior to its implementation (*Embassy* 2011). Key amendments included changing the timelines for scheduling interviews and hearings to allow immigrants more time to prepare their cases, and revoking the denial of appeal to refugee claimants based on nationality (*Embassy* 2011). These victories suggest that there is a diverse range of views of immigrants and refugees, and many immigration advocacy groups continue to campaign and educate Canadians about the realities of migration. In addition, with the increasing support of the international community such as Human Rights Watch[11] and Amnesty International, current immigration and refugee reforms will be even more carefully scrutinized to ensure that Canada does not violate it's obligations to the global community. Audrey Macklin and Sean Rehaag sum it up:

> About 30,000 asylum seekers arrive in Canada each year. In the fall, shortly after the arrival of around 500 Tamils on a boat in British Columbia, some 30,000 Burmese refugees fled into neighbouring Thailand — over a period of 48 hours. Let's get some perspective. (*Toronto Star* 2010d)

Although it is an uphill battle, particularly in light of the Conservative majority win in the last federal election, the path towards an inclusive and anti-racist immigration system in Canada continues to be fought on many different levels with numerous campaigns that call on the government to take a humanitarian approach to immigrants and refugees. A recent decision by the Federal Court of Appeal which ruled that Ottawa cannot refuse an immigration application by an individual who is too poor to pay the $550 processing fee (*Toronto Star* 2011) is one of the many small victories that will shape how Canada treats its newcomers in the twenty-first century.

Glossary of Key Terms

Criminalize: Turning an activity into a criminal offence by making it illegal.

Deportation: The act of expelling a non-citizen from a country, usually on the grounds of illegal status or for having committed a crime.

Discrimination: The unjust or prejudicial treatment of different categories of people or things.

Immigrant: A person who comes to live permanently in a foreign country.

Protected person: A person who has been granted refugee protection by the government of Canada.

Refugee: A person in flight who seeks to escape conditions or personal circumstances found to be intolerable.

Smuggling: Consensual transactions where the transporter and the transportee agree to circumvent immigration control for mutually advantageous reasons.

Trafficking: The recruitment, transportation, transfer, harbouring, or receipt of persons, by means of the threat or use of force or other forms of coercion.

Questions for Discussion

1. Do you think immigration control is possible without engaging in racist or discriminatory behaviour?

2. Should multiculturalism be abandoned for the sake of national security? Can and should these issues be prioritized?

3. How can we create a more inclusive society in light of the culture of fear of the "other" that now exists?

4. Should refugees who arrive in Canada via irregular means (e.g., on a boat with others) be treated differently than refugees who arrive through regular channels (e.g., on a plane)?

Websites of Interest

Citizenship and Immigration Canada <cic.gc.ca/english/index.html>
Canada Border Services Agency <cbsa-asfc.gc.ca/menu-e.html>
Canadian Heritage <pch.gc.ca/index_e.cfm>
No One Is Illegal Vancouver
Status Campaign <ocasi.org/STATUS/index.asp>
Noborder network <noborder.org/news_index.php>
Canadian Council for Refugees <web.net/~ccr/fronteng.htm>
Stop Racial Profiling <stopracialprofiling.ca/news.html>

Notes

This chapter is an updated version of Wendy Chan, "Illegal Immigrants and Bill C-11: The Criminalization of Race," in Law Commission of Canada (ed.), *What Is a Crime?* Vancouver: UBC Press: 2002.

1. With the point system, immigrants would be assessed on the basis of age, education, language skills and economic characteristics and be assigned points for each of these categories. Applicants who had a sufficient number of points would be eligible for entry (Boyd and Vickers 2000).

2. For more details about the investor's program, see Citizenship and Immigration Canada website <cic.gc.ca/english/business/invest-1.html>.

3. See Citizenship and Immigration Canada (CIC) website for information about the program <cic.gc.ca/english/pub/caregiver/index.html>.

4. Critics of this program have pointed out how many women are exploited and ill-treated by their employers. See Martinez, Hanley, and Cheung 2004; and Langevin and Belleau 2000.

5. A Convention refugee is anyone who holds a well-founded fear of persecution based on one or more of five grounds as defined in the *U.N. Convention Relating to the Status of Refugees*: reasons of race, religion, nationality, membership in a particular social group, or political opinion. See Galloway 1997.

6. According to its website <maytree.com>, "The Maytree Foundation is a Canadian charitable

foundation established in 1982. Maytree believes that there are three fundamental issues that threaten political and social stability: wealth disparities between and within nations; mass migration of people because of war, oppression and environmental disasters, and the degradation of the environment."

7. The public reaction to the Chinese migrants was generally one of hostility; they tended to be regarded as "bogus" refugees. Many of them were detained and eventually deported back to China. See briefs by Coalition for a Just Immigration and Refugee Policy 2001; NAWL 2001; the Getting Landed Project 2002; African Canadian Legal Clinic 2001; UNHCR 2001.

8. Supporters of the migrants argued the government had overreacted in this situation, while critics contended that the government needed to take harsher measures.

9. This view of the 1975 *Immigration Act* has been challenged by critical immigration scholars who contend that, while the Act did not directly discriminate against particular racial and ethnic groups, the outcome of the point system nonetheless resulted in differential access to immigration. See Thobani 2000; Jakubowski 1997.

10. Racialization "refers to the historical emergence of the idea of 'race' and to its subsequent reproduction and application" (Miles 1989: 76). This suggests that the criminalization of certain racialized groups within the Canadian context can be understood, first, in light of the ways in which white, majority groups have been constructed as race-less, and, second, within the context of historical relations between First Nations peoples, early settlers, and recent immigrants and migrants.

11. Human Rights Watch, 2011, "Open Letter to Canada's Prime Minister Stephen Harper and Federal Party Leaders on Human Rights Priorities," May 9. <hrw.org/en/news/2011/05/09/open-letter-canada-s-prime-minister-stephen-harper-and-federal-party-leaders-human-r>.

References

Abu-Laban, Sharon, and Susan A. McDaniel. 1997. "Aging, Women and Beauty Standards." In Nancy Mandel (ed.), *Feminist Issues: Race, Class and Sexuality*. Second edition. Toronto: Prentice-Hall.

Abu-Laban, Yasmin. 1998. "Welcome/Stay Out: The Contradiction of Canadian Integration and Immigration Policies at the Millennium." *Canadian Ethnic Studies* 30.

Abu-Laban, Yasmin, and C. Gabriel. 2002. *Selling Diversity*. Peterborough: Broadview Press.

African Canadian Legal Clinic. 2001. "Brief to the Legislative Review Secretariat." <aclc.net/submissions/immigration_refugee_policy.html>

Amnesty International. 2010. "Refugee Rights Must Be Protected in Anti-Smuggling Legislation." <amnesty.ca/iwriteforjustice/take_action.php?actionid=540&type=Internal>.

Angel-Ajani, A. 2003. "A Question of Dangerous Races?" *Punishment and Society* 5.

Avery, D. 1995. *Reluctant Host: Canada's Response to Immigrant Workers 1896–1994*. Toronto: McClelland and Stewart.

Bahdi, R. 2003. "No Exit: Racial Profiling and Canada's War Against Terrorism." *Osgoode Hall Law Journal* 41.

Bannerji, Himani. 2000. "The Paradox of Diversity: The Construction of a Multicultural Canada and 'Women of Colour.'" *Women's Studies International Forum* 23.

Bashi, V. 2004. "Globalized Anti-Blackness: Transnationalizing Western Immigration Law, Policy and Practice." *Ethnic and Racial Studies* 27.

Beisel, D. 1994. "Looking for Enemies, 1990–1994." *Journal of Psychohistory* 22, 1.

Bhabha, J. 2005. "Trafficking, Smuggling and Human Rights." *Migration Information Source* March.

Brah, A. 1996. *Cartographies of Diaspora: Contesting Identities*. New York: Routledge.

Buchignani, N., and D. Indra. 1999. "Vanishing Acts: Illegal Immigration in Canada as a Sometimes Social Issue." In D. Haines and K. Rosenblum (eds.), *Illegal Immigration in America*. Westport, CT: Greenwood Press.

Canadian Press. 2001. "U.N. Rights Report Criticizes Canada for Treating Migrants Like Criminals." April 12.

CBC *Online*. 1999a. "Officials Recommend Migrants Remain in Custody." September 2. <cbc.ca/story/canada/national/1999/09/02/migrants990902.html>.

____. 1999b. "Department Seeks More Teeth to Detain Migrants." September 23. <cbc.ca/story/canada/national/1999/09/23/migrant990923.html>.

____. 1999c. "Chinese Migrants Denied Due Process, Critics Charge." November 5. <cbc.ca/story/canada/national/1999/11/05/migrants991105.html>.

CBSA (Canadian Border Services Agency). 2010. "CBSA Detentions and Removals Programs: Evaluation Study." <cbsa-asfc.gc.ca/agency-agence/reports-rapports/ae-ve/2010/dr-rd-eng.html>.

CCR (Canadian Council for Refugees). 2000. "A Hundred Years of Immigration to Canada 1900–1999: A Chronology Focusing on Refugees and Discrimination." <ccrweb.ca/history.html>.

____. 2001. "Bill C-11 Brief." <ccrweb.ca/files/C11submissionmay2010.pdf>.

____. 2010a. "C-47-Key Concerns." <ccrweb.ca/en/c49-key-concerns>.

____. 2010b. "Some Comments on Bill C-49." <ccrweb.ca/en/comment-c49>.

____. 2010c. "Refugee Reform: Weighing the Proposals." <ccrweb.ca/en/refugee-reform>.

Christie, N. 1986. "Suitable Enemies." In H. Bianchi and R. van Swaaningen (eds.), *Abolitionism: Towards a Non-Repressive Approach to Crime*. Amsterdam: Free University Press.

CIC (Citizenship and Immigration Canada). 2001a. *Facts and Figures 2000: Immigration Overview*. Ottawa: Minister of Public Works and Government Services.

____. 2001b. "Bill C-11 — Immigration and Refugee Protection Act: Overview." At <cic.gc.ca/english/irpa/c11-overview.html>

____. 2010a. "Ministers Toews and Kenney discuss Preventing Human Smugglers from Abusing Canada's Immigration System Act." At <cic.gc.ca/english/department/media/releases/2010/2010-10-22.asp>

____. 2010b. *Canada Facts and Figures 2009: Immigrant Overview-Permanent and Temporary Residents*. Ottawa: CIC Research and Evaluation Branch.

Coalition for a Just Immigration and Refugee Policy. 2001 "Position Paper on Bill C-11." Toronto.

Creese, G. 1992. "The Politics of Refugees in Canada." In V. Satzewich (ed.), *Deconstructing A Nation*. Halifax: Fernwood Publishing.

Crepeau, F., and E. Jimenez. 2004. "Foreigners and the Right to Justice in the Aftermath of 9/11." *International Journal of Law and Psychiatry* 27.

Crepeau, F., and D. Nakache. 2006. "Controlling Irregular Migration in Canada." IRPP *Choices* 12, 1.

Davergne, C. 2004. "Sovereignty, Migration and the Rule of Law in Global Times." *Modern Law Review* 67.

Dent, J. 2002. "No Right of Appeal: Bill C-11, Criminality, and the Human Rights of Permanent Residents Facing Deportation." *Queen's Law Journal* 27.

DFAIT (Department of Foreign Affairs and International Trade). 2004. "Canada's Actions against Terrorism since September 11." <dfait-maeci.gc.ca/anti-terrorism/canadaactions-en.asp>.

Economic Council of Canada. 1991. *New Faces in the Crowd: Economic and Social Impacts of Immigration*. Ottawa: Economic Council of Canada, Study No. 22-171.

Embassy. 2011. "It's Not Too Late to Change Course on Immigration, Refugees." May 4.

Fekete, L. 2004. "Anti-Muslim Racism and the European Security State." *Race and Class* 46.

Fisk, R. 2006. "Has Racism Invaded Canada?" <counterpunch.org/fisk06122006.html>.

Frideres, James. 1996. "Canada's Changing Immigration Policy: Implications for Asian Immigrants." *Asian and Pacific Migration Journal* 5.

Galloway, D. 1997. *Immigration Law*. Concord, ON: Irwin.

Garcia y Griego, M. 1994. "Canada: Flexibility and Control in Immigration and Refugee Policy." In W. Cornelius, P. Martin, and J. Hollifield (eds.), *Controlling Immigration: A Global Perspective*. Stanford: Stanford University Press.

Getting Landed Project. 2002. "Protecting the Unprotected: Submission to the House of Commons Standing Committee on Citizenship and Immigration" <cpj.ca/getting_landed>.

Global Detention Project. 2009. "Canada Detention Profile." <globaldetentionproject.org/countries/americas/canada/introduction.html>.

Globe and Mail. 2006. "Terrorism Cases Strikingly Similar." June 10.

Haigh, R., and J. Smith 1998. "Return of the Chancellor's Foot? Discretion in Permanent Resident Deportation Appeals under the *Immigration Act*." *Osgoode Hall Law Journal* 36.

Hassan-Gordon, T. 1996. "Canada's Immigration Policy — Detention and Deportation of Non-Europeans." <hartford-hwp.com/archives/44/032.html>.

Hintjens, H.M. 1992. "Immigration and Citizenship Debates: Reflections on Ten Common Themes." *International Migration* 30.

Ibrahim, M. 2005. "The Securitization of Migration: A Racial Discourse." *International Migration* 43.

Jakubowski, L. 1997. *Immigration and the Legalization of Racism*. Halifax: Fernwood Publishing.

Kelley, N., and M. Trebilcock. 1998. *The Making of the Mosaic: A History of Canadian Immigration Policy*. Toronto: University of Toronto Press.

Kobayashi, A. 1995. "Challenging the National Dream: Gender Persecution and Canadian Immigration Law." In P. Fitzpatrick (ed.), *Nationalism, Racism and the Rule of Law*. Aldershot: Dartmouth.

Langevin, L., and M. Belleau. 2000. "Trafficking in Women in Canada: A Critical Analysis of the Legal Framework Governing Immigrant Live-in Caregivers and Mail-Order Brides." Ottawa: Status of Women Canada. <swc-cfc.gc.ca/pubs/pubspr/066231252X /index_e.html>.

Li, P. 2001. "The Racial Subtext in Canada's Immigration Discourse." *Journal of International Migration and Integration* 2, 1.

____. 2003. *Destination Canada*. Don Mills: Oxford University Press.

Marchi, S. 1995. "Speech: Tougher Tools For Deporting Criminals." *Canadian Speeches* 9 (August/September).

Matas, D. 1989. *Closing the Doors: The Failure of Refugee Protection*. Toronto: Summerhill.

Maytree Foundation. 2001. "Brief to the Senate Committee on Social Affairs, Science and Technology regarding Bill C-11, Immigration and Refugee Protection Act." Toronto, October. <maytree.com/Publications&Resources/Publications /SenateBriefBillC11.htm>.

Miles, Robert. 1989. *Racism*. London: Routledge.

Morrison, J., and B. Crosland. 2001. "The Trafficking and Smuggling of Refugees: The End Game of European Asylum Policy?" *Independent Expert Report/unhcr Working Paper* 38. <unhcr.org/cgi-bin/texis/vtx/doclist?page=research&id=3bbc18ed5>.

NAWL (National Association of Women and the Law). 2001. "Brief on the Proposed Immigration and Refugee Protection Act (Bill C-11)." <nawl.ca/ns/en/publications.html>.

____. 2006. "Update: Immigration and Refugee Protection Act and Women." <nawl.ca/ns/en/is-irl.html#update>.

National Post. 2011. "Immigrants Cost $23B a Year: Fraser Institute Report." May 17.

Noorani, A., and C. Wright. 1995. "They Believed the Hype: The Liberals Were Elected as 'the Friend of the Immigrant': A Year Later, They're Fanning the Flames of Crime Hysteria with their New Pals, the Tabloids and Preston Manning." *This Magazine* 28 (December/January).

Oxman-Martinez, J. Hanley, and L. Cheung. 2004. "Another Look at the Live-in Caregivers Program." Metropolis Research Report No. 24. <im.metropolis.net/research-policy/research_content/doc/oxman-marinez%20LCP.pdf>.

Palmer, D. 1996. "Determinants of Canadian Attitudes Toward Immigration: More than Just Racism?" *Canadian Journal of Behavioural Science* 28.

Public Safety and Emergency Preparedness Canada. 2004. "Securing Canada: Laying the Groundwork for Canada's First National Security Policy." <psepc-sppcc.gc.ca/national_security/publications_e.asp>.

Razack, S. 1999. "Law and the Policing of Bodies of Colour in the 1990s." *Canadian Journal of Law and Society* 14.

Roach, K. 2005. "Canada's Response to Terrorism." In V. Ramraj, M. Hor, and K. Roach (eds.), *Global Anti-terrorism Law and Policy*. Oxford: Cambridge University Press.

Roberts, B. 1998. *Whence They Came: Deportation From Canada, 1900–1935*. Ottawa: University of Ottawa.

Robinson, W.G. 1983. "Illegal Migrants in Canada: A Report to the Honourable Lloyd Axworthy, Minister of Employment and Immigration." Ottawa: Employment and Immigration Canada.

Rudner, M. 2002. "The Globalization of Terrorism: Canada's Intelligence Response to the Post-September 11 Threat Environment." *Canadian Issues* 24 (September).

Russo, Robert. 2008. "Security, Securitization and Human Capital: The New Wave of Canadian Immigration Laws." *World Academy of Science, Engineering and Technology* 44.

Simmons, A. 1998. "Globalization and Backlash Racism in the 1990s: The Case of Asian Immigration to Canada." In E. Lacquian, A. Lacquian, and T. McGee (eds.), *The Silent Debate: Asian Immigration and Racism in Canada*. Vancouver: Institute of Asian Research.

Standing Committee on Citizenship and Immigration. 2001. *Hands Across the Border: Working Together at Our Shared Border and Abroad to Ensure Safety, Security and Efficiency*. Ottawa: Public Works.

StarPhoenix [Saskatoon]. 2010. "Wrong to Punish Refugees Forced to Use Smugglers." November 25.

Statistics Canada. 2004. "Pilot Survey of Hate Crime." June 1. <statcan.gc.ca/daily-quotidien/040601/dq040601a-eng.htm>.

Strange, C., and T. Loo. 1997. *Making Good: Law and Moral Regulation in Canada, 1867–1939*. Toronto: University of Toronto Press.

Teitelbaum, M., and J. Winter. 1998. *A Question of Numbers: High Migration, Low Fertility and the Politics Of National Identity*. New York: Hill and Wang.

Thobani, S. 2000. "Closing Ranks: Racism and Sexism in Canada's Immigration Policy." *Race and Class* 42, 35.

Toronto Star. 2006a. "Letter To Editor: 'Afraid Every Morning I Wake Up.'" May 28.

____. 2006b. "Editorial: Our New Pioneers." March 30.

____. 2010a. "Anger Greets Asylum-Seekers." August 16.

____. 2010b. "We Need Immigrants as Boomers Retire." August 26.

____. 2010c. "New Refugee Legislation Misses the Mark." October 28.

____. 2010d. "Playing Politics with Refugees." December 3.

____. 2011. "Justice Tempered with Compassion." May 17.

UNHCR (United Nations High Commissioner for Refugees). 2001. "Comments on Bill C-11: Submission to the House of Commons Standing Committee on Citizenship and Immigration."

Ottawa, ON, March. <web.ca/ccr/c11hcr.PDF>.

Valverde, Mariana. 1991. *The Age of Soap, Light and Water: Moral Reform in English Canada, 1885–1925.* Toronto: McClelland & Stewart.

Vancouver Province. 2010. "Migrants' Journey Treacherous." August 16.

Vancouver Sun. 2010. "Kenney Vows to Take Refugee Bill to a Vote." December 2.

____. 2011. "Opinion: The Big Picture Shows Immigrants Are a Good Bet." May 30.

Vukov, T. 2003. "Imagining Communities Through Immigration Policies." *International Journal of Cultural Studies* 6.

9

Fat Phobia and the Politics of Gender

Marianne Parsons

YOU SHOULD KNOW THIS

- 90–95 percent of participants in all weight loss programs failed to attain and sustain weight loss beyond two to five years.
- Formerly fat women say that, rather than regain their weight, they would deliberately choose to be blind, deaf, or have a limb amputated.
- More than a quarter of college students believe that becoming fat is the worst thing that could happen to a person.
- One study found that more than two-thirds of doctors surveyed thought that fat patients were morally weak while another study found that nearly a quarter of nurses said that obese patients "repulsed them."
- "51 percent of black girls claim total body satisfaction, as compared to 31 percent of white girls and 30 percent of Hispanic girls," according to a survey conducted by *Teen People* in August of 2005.
- Alarmingly, a survey of married couples revealed that 11 percent would abort a child known in advance to be genetically predisposed to obesity.
- Fewer than 26,000 Americans die each year from weighing too much, a number that is even smaller than those who are estimated to die from being "underweight."

Sources: Hesse-Biber 2007; LeBesco 2004; Lyons 2009; Oliver 2006; Poulton 1996.

YEARS AGO I ATTENDED AN INTERACTIVE ART EXHIBIT focusing on female embodiment. Assembled in a circle in the middle of the room were casts of the frontal view of women's bodies; each cast facing several large mirrors that were placed in the middle of the circle. Attached to the top of each cast was a set of ear phones linking me to the recorded voice of the woman whose body was being represented. The back of each cast was left open to allow participants to — metaphorically — "step into" the body of each woman. I could see the reflection of the casted body of each woman in the mirrors and hear each woman's voice as I made my way around the circle, imagining an embodiment that was similar yet different from mine. What struck me the most was the consistency in the self-appraisals of their bodies; bodies that were viewed — by themselves and others — as being not quite good enough or never good enough.

We live in a time of intense focus on the body. The body is increasingly being viewed as something that individuals are in control of — a work in progress that needs to be sculpted — a "project" intimately connected to our "self-identity" (Shilling 2003). The body is the first frame of reference in our interactions with others, impacting greatly on our perceptions of people. We think we know something about their relationships to their own bodies — "body regimes" — and from that "knowledge" can gain insight into their social habits (Shilling 2003). Within this social context certain bodily forms have currency, that is, are viewed as having "value." Bodies existing outside of this limited sphere are significantly less valued or not valued at all (Shilling, 2003). Fat bodies exist in this latter space; a space where various forms of prejudice and discrimination are commonplace occurrences in the lives of fat people (Gard 2011; Kirkland 2008; Oliver 2006; Millman,1980).

> Westerners, in particular, live in a social environment where the condemnation of fat people is not only acceptable but openly embraced.

Socially constructed as a medical condition and pathological state that requires "fixing," fatness has become the focus of broad-based efforts to politicize the societal "problems" associated with weight gain and weight retention. The current rhetoric surrounding the "obesity epidemic" — referred to as the "terror within" by U.S Surgeon General Koop — has served to reinforce and justify anti-fat sentiments and related social practices that have existed in North American society since the late nineteenth century (Levy-Navarro 2009). Westerners, in particular, live in a social environment where the condemnation of fat people is not only acceptable but openly embraced (Gard 2011). For example, in response to a column published in the *Globe and Mail* titled "Would Employers Be Right to Discriminate on the Basis of Fatness?" Frank McGillicuddy writes a letter to the editor titled, "Right to Discriminate," espousing the view that fat people deserve to be discriminated against, based on their body size and presumed "character" flaws associated with fatness. In its entirety:

> Fat people do not have the same right to non-discrimination that women and visible minorities do. Obese people (apart from the single-digit percentage of them that have legitimate glandular disorders) *choose their condition through an array of bad decisions* of both passive and active nature. Basically, they either ingest too much of the wrong food, or they do not expend enough calories on a daily basis, or both. True, childhood and cultural eating habits may have some role to play initially, but we do not excuse other substance abusers for environmental factors. In any case, *overweight individuals can hardly deny that they have a problem, and if they are aware beings they show tremendous lack of discipline.* Therefore, those who waste the opportunity to effect change in their lifestyles, so as to improve their quality of life, can *hardly complain if they are discriminated against* during the hiring or evaluation process — they are *displaying character traits* that may be detrimental to their success in a given position. Rejection due to obesity may *shock some of these people out of their complacent lethargy and cause them to face their challenge*, or it may give them the impetus to consider other avenues for which their skill-set may be more suited. The majority of overweight people can change themselves, so *to blithely accept them in their present distorted state* does them and our society a great disservice. (McGillicuddy 1991: A16, my emphasis)

Fat-phobic attitudes such as these serve to fuel the flames of stigmatization, prejudicial views, and discriminatory social practices that impact fat people in their everyday lives. Those who harbour fat-phobic attitudes "are likely to also express negative beliefs about racial minorities and poor people and to display authoritarian personality traits" (Kirkland

2008: 105). Given that fatness is considered to be a "voluntary" condition under the control of the individual — a position that McGillicuddy clearly articulates — fat people who fail in their attempts to lose weight or sustain weight loss are regarded with suspicion and disdain, and their bodies viewed as "revolting" (LeBesco 2004). Visual media is a key culprit in the proliferation of fat-phobic images and discourse. "Reality" TV shows, for example, depict fat contestants engaging in extreme dieting and exercise regimes under "boot camp" type conditions. Such tactics are painful reminders of the second-class status fat people occupy in a thin-oriented social landscape. In these ways, FAT (or fatness — see Glossary) is a social issue.

Women, in particular, are targeted as subjects of these types of weight loss strategies and related beautification regimes. For example, makeover shows chronicle the transformative progression from *plainness* to "a greatly improved state of *good looks and well-being*" (McRobbie 2009: 124, my emphasis). In the relentless pursuit of idealized images of the body, the worldwide proliferation of commercialized images relies heavily on the consumption of female bodies. Women's bodies are on display in virtually every space that our technological world inhabits and are constantly being measured and scrutinized against a standard that few can achieve — "absolute flawlessness" (Kilbourne 2010). The media obsession in the pursuit of perfect female bodies — bodies that adhere to socially constructed notions of feminine beauty through rigorous participation in various body work practices— has impacted our perceptions of attractiveness, particularly for girls and women, who are at the centre of the "beauty cult" (Hesse-Biber 2007; Shilling, 2003; Silverman 2010).

The open ridiculing of women's bodies within mainstream media is a testament to the pervasiveness of this ideal and a form of misogyny. Take, for example, the pictures of female movie stars in bathing suits that grace the covers of tabloid magazines with headlines that speak to bodily "flaws" — weight gain, cellulite, wrinkled skin, and so on. Women are constantly reminded that their bodies don't measure up, a preoccupation that garners billions of dollars for the cosmetic and weight loss industries every year (Hesse-Biber 2007). The global surveys conducted by the Dove "Campaign for Real Beauty" reveal the depth of women's body insecurities:

> The 2005 survey of 3,300 women aged 15 to 64 in ten countries reveals depressing evidence about women's body image and the "appearance anxiety" created by beauty ideals. *Only one in ten thousand women reported being happy about the way they looked* .... And the white bias of globalised beauty ideals was clear from some of the responses by women from Asia, South America and the Middle East. A desire to change one's hair, eye colour and shape, or skin colour was mentioned more frequently by women living in these regions. (Redfern and Aune 2010: 20–21, my emphasis)

The "white bias" reflects the fact that the fashion and beauty industry has been dominated by white women since its early beginnings, in particular fair-skinned, blonde-haired, blue-eyed women. These images have provided fertile ground for the social construction of idealized white feminine beauty. Women from racialized groups are relative newcomers to the commercial sphere of modelling and advertising and are often portrayed in ways that reinforce racist notions of the "Other"; for example, mainstream women's "glamour" magazines are replete with images of Black female models dressed in animal print designs placed against the backdrop of a safari-type setting (Kilbourne 2010). The movie industry is a key culprit in the fabrication of stereotypical images and story lines that reinforce racist, classist, and sexist viewpoints and practices (hooks 1995). Given the absoluteness of the Eurocentric body ideal for women — thinness being a key criterion — women whose bodies exist outside of this narrowly defined ideal are viewed as not having met the standard for female beauty. Within this cultural context, being female and fat becomes an act of "transgression" (LeBesco 2004; Stukator 2001).

A fat woman, by virtue of being fat, has "let herself go" (Hartley 2001). This view is not surprising given that "Women… are literally terrified of getting fat. In survey after survey, being fat is listed as a primary fear" (Hartley 2001: 64). The fear and hatred of fat — fat phobia — emerges from the construction of the fat body as "Other." The bodies of fat women are located at the far ends of the body/sexual spectrums; bodies that are simultaneously hypersexualized and desexualized (Hartley 2001), simultaneously highly visible and invisible. Fat women are hypersexualized as "fat(ness) exaggerate(s) the outward sexuality of the female body; breasts and hips become fuller and more prominent," at the same time desexualized as fatness in women is viewed as being "unfeminine" (Hartley 2001: 68). Kirsty Alley, as characterized in the "reality" TV show *My Big Fat Life*, embraces both a hypersexualized image — the middle-aged female "cougaroo" — and the desexualized identity of the fat woman whose body is now significantly less valued: fat and ageing. Her only possible redemption would be permanent weight loss, as fatness represents a state of abnormality requiring change (read: fat woman as "Other"). In a misogynist patriarchal culture a woman is her body by virtue of being bodily defined. In these ways FAT is a women's issue.

Fatness and Thinness as Body Ideals

FAT — more specifically fatness — has a history. There were times and places where fatness was embraced, celebrated, viewed as being aesthetically pleasing, and sexy. This remains the case in countries like Niger where mothers actively encourage their daughters to gain weight as means to make them more beautiful, more "sexually attractive" (Popenoe 2005). Fatness for women is valued in this cultural context as it is a sign that the family has the economic resources to feed their daughters. When food is scarce fatness is embraced; when food is plentiful thinness becomes the prevailing body ideal. "Since food abundance has been relatively rare historically, it is not surprising that… around 80 percent of human societies on record have had a preference for plumper women" (Popenoe 2005: 17). Plumpness is related to fertility; women whose bodies stored calories well were more likely to be successful childbearers, a process vital to the continuation of that particular society. Not surprising, fat women are the focus of cave paintings and various other ancient art forms. Archaeologists have uncovered sculpted clay

> Around 80 percent of human societies on record have had a preference for plumper women.

female figures of ample bodily dimensions; carvings that date back at least fifteen thousand years ago (Klein 2001). The most well known among them is Venus of Willendorf:

> She's about the fattest woman one could imagine. Two enormous mountains for breasts, perfectly rounded, plumped-up mounds, tower over a taut belly... her hips curve into an endless ass.... At the focus of all these sweeping hills of flesh is a fat and beautifully fashioned vulva. In the center of it all is a navel, vast and dark and deep. (Klein 2001: 21)

Klein suggests the possibility that these "goddesses of love" were considered to be archetypes of female attractiveness — "object(s) of erotic and sensual pleasure" (23). Fat women — beautiful and sexy — how could this possibly be the case? His view runs contrary to the argument put forth by some archaeologists who claim that the primary function of these ancient carvings was to symbolize fertility, to "foster conception and protect pregnancy" (Klein 2001: 21). This may well be the case. However, the conflation of fatness with fertility precludes the viewing of these female figures — and the women whose bodies they represent — as sexual in and of themselves. Researchers studying these ancient goddess symbols too often bring with them current cultural views regarding the meanings associated with fatness for women. Venus de Milo, for example, would be considered "fat" in contemporary Western society (Klein 2001). The women depicted in many of the paintings of seventeenth century artist Sir Peter Paul Rubens — fleshy round women — would also be viewed as fat by today's standards (Oliver 2006).

The politics of fatness and thinness for women are historically and culturally bound. At various points in time either body ideal has been valued and highly eroticized as the female beauty ideal. Body insecurities arise when the body that you have deviates from the culturally accepted norm. Hanan Al-Shaykh reveals her own body insecurities growing up as a thin child and thin adolescent in Morocco in the mid twentieth century:

> I used to envy the ripe, round cheeks of the other girls, and their chubby arms and legs. I was jealous of the fattest girl in our class, with her many chins, thick forearms, and huge bottom that shook at the tiniest movement.... I was jealous, jealous and turned inward, convincing myself that I was different. (Al-Shaykh 1994: 197)

Bathing with other women in the public baths in Morocco — as a child and later as an adult — are poignant reminders of her feelings about her thinness, a body perceived by others as being a "barren wasteland." Her attempts to increase her size through weight gain were unsuccessful and she remained thin into adulthood. While studying in Egypt, she was pursued by a male student who gave her the following advice:

> You're pretty. I love you. If only you weren't so skinny. Try and put on a bit of weight. You'd be a really beautiful woman. I'll tell you how to make me fall in love with you. If you do as I say you'll become like a big ripe peach. (Al-Shaykh 1994: 202)

Al-Shaykh makes the observation that "his girlfriend didn't care when she saw him pursuing me because she was sure he couldn't fall in love with a woman whose arms and legs were practically nonexistent" (Al-Shaykh 1994: 202).

During these years there were times when she experienced feelings of sadness and anxiety about her body, viewing her body as not measuring up to the feminine beauty standards of her culture. The ushering in of the thin beauty ideal in the 1960s was embraced by Al-Shaykh; finally, a beauty ideal that she could relate to. Eventually, she moved to Europe where she discovered a cultural context that allowed her to embrace the body that she had. Feeling good about her body in this social space, she was brave enough to wear a bikini for the first time, unashamed to reveal her slender physique.

Phobic views toward thinness in a culture where beauty is associated with fatness for women, can be just as oppressive as fat phobia in the current era. There are women who, like Al-Shaykh, have a propensity to be very thin, finding it difficult to gain weight. In the same ways that fatness is judged as being a "voluntary" condition under the control of individual, so too is thinness within cultural contexts where fatness is valued (Popenoe 2005). The point here is simply this: regardless of the body type that a particular women has, the cultural context has a profound impact on her relationship to her body. Cultural body ideals play on women's insecurities surrounding their bodies and perceived bodily "flaws"; this is the foundation upon which the cosmetic and weight loss industries have built their fortunes (Hesse-Biber 2007).

Fatness and Thinness in the North American Context

Over the last century female beauty ideals within North American culture have radically shifted toward a slender physique (Fraser 2009). Discussions surrounding this trend began to emerge in the United States, beginning in the 1880s and continuing into the 1920s. Fraser argues that the cultural acceptance of the slender beauty ideal during this time period relates to three key social changes: 1) the medicalization of fat as unhealthy; 2) growth of an industrial economy which led to greater access to food for much of the population; and 3) the need for clear class distinctions.

In the late nineteenth century "heaviness" for women — previously considered to be attractive and associated with health and vitality — began to be questioned on the grounds of the "health risks" associated with fatness (Fraser 2009). The discourse surrounding the social construction of fatness as a medical problem laid the foundation for the emerging view of slenderness as the new beauty ideal for women. Woods Hutchinson, a professor of medicine, argued against the new slender ideal and made a concerted effort to ensure that his view was widely known through his various writings on this topic. "Adipose," he wrote, "while often pictured as a veritable Frankenstein, born of and breeding disease, sure to ride its possessor to death sooner or later, is really a most harmless, healthful, innocent tissue" (Hutchinson 1894, cited in Fraser 2009: 11). "Hutchinson reassured his *Cosmopolitan* readers that fat was not only benign, but also attractive, and that if a poll of beautiful women were taken in the city, there would be at least three times as many plump ones as slender ones" (Fraser 2009: 11). Hutchinson's criticism of the view of fat as unhealthy and unattractive extended to include the world of fashion. In 1926 he made the following remarks in the *Saturday Evening Post*:

> In this present onslaught upon one of the most peaceful, useful, and law abiding of all our tissues... fashion has apparently the backing of *grave physicians*, of *food reformers* and *physical trainers*, and even of great *insurance companies*, all chanting in unison the new commandment of fashion: "Thou shalt be thin!" (Hutchinson 1926, cited in Fraser 2009: 11, my emphasis)

The emerging discourse surrounding the pathologization of fat reinforced the view of fat as "unhealthy" and expanded the discourse to include statements about the psychological state and personal habits of fat people. In this regard, fat came to be viewed as representing "an outward and visible sign of an inward spiritual disgrace, of laziness, [and] of self-indulgence" (Hutchinson 1926, cited in Fraser 2009: 12). Hutchinson criticized physicians for encouraging weight loss in young girls and women. His warning surrounding this "new" attitude toward eating and body size rings true today: "The longed-for slender and boyish figure is becoming a menace... not only to the present, *but also for future generations*" (Hutchinson 1926, cited in Fraser 2009: 12, my emphasis).

> The longed-for slender and boyish figure is becoming a menace... not only to the present, but also for future generations.

Despite Hutchinson's criticisms of the thin ideal, this new discourse on dieting and thinness had already taken hold in the medical profession. Nineteenth-century medical personnel and experts from various disciplines (anthropology, in particular) used a variety techniques for measuring the body in their efforts to define "normalcy" — for example, anthropometry — often reflecting racist, sexist, and ableist views (Anderson 1996). By the late nineteenth century, the human body could be measured against a perceived norm, information routinely used by actuaries representing the interests of insurance companies. The initial formulation of the current body-mass index (BMI) began earlier, in the 1830s, by the Belgian astronomer Adolphe Quetelet whose pioneering work formed the foundation for the creation of the notion of "ideal" weight (Oliver 2006). By charting the heights and weights of "French and Scottish army conscripts," he arrived at a distribution we now know as the bell curve or normal curve, and developed a formula defining "the weight of 'normal' conscripts" (Oliver 2006: 16–17):

> He happened to observe that the weight of "normal" conscripts (that is, those closest to the middle of the distribution) was proportional to their height squared; this general formula would later be used to determine BMI.... [He] reasoned that this must be what the ideal weight *should be*; anyone who deviated from this average could be considered to be either under- or over-weight. This pseudoscientific conception of an "ideal" weight thus provided the first scientific notions of what overweight could be. (Oliver 2006: 17, emphasis in original)

The basis of Quetelet's discovery was not put to use until a century later as a means to predict death rates for insurance companies. Oliver makes it clear, however, that the "BMI was never intended to be a gauge of someone's health" (Oliver 19). Fatness and thinness thus became problematized; today's focus falls squarely on fatness as the culprit. The medical terms "overweight," "obese," and "morbidly obese" became central to defining populations as medically fat.

As the nineteenth century came to a close, continued industrialization and urbanization led to greater access to food for much of the general population, which meant that a great number of people had the means to become plump (Oliver 2006). Fatness, previously viewed as being "a sign of prestige," was now viewed as a sign of moral weakness, while thinness came to represent control over the body, in particular control over bodily appetites (Oliver 2006). Thinness became associated with artists and members of the intelligentsia. The poet Lord Byron embarked on an extreme regime of dieting as a means to emulate the look of being "fashionably ill." His contemporaries, poet John Keats and author Emily Bronte, actually became emaciated as a result of contracting tuberculosis. The wealthy viewed the contracting of tuberculosis and becoming thin as "signs that one possessed a delicate, intellectual, and superior nature" (Fraser 2009: 12). Thinness became associated with class distinction and moral virtue. In the words of Benjamin Franklin, "eat for Necessity, not Pleasure, for *Lust knows not where Necessity ends*" (Fraser 2009: 13, my emphasis). Lustfulness, in this case referring to eating, is often paired with sexual craving and indulgence. (Think of a typical "night on the town" where enjoying food with a lover often precedes sexual activity).

The dawn of the twentieth century witnessed the continued development of the "thinner, freer, more modern body" (Fraser 2009: 13). Keeping track of caloric intake and weight became a focus of medical practice, where only a few decades prior (1880s) physicians were advising patients to increase their weight (Fraser 2009). Doctors eagerly participated in prescribing "weight loss" remedies to their patients for a fee. Thinness and the modern body were now analogous: advertisers were quick to take advantage of the emerging consumerism, "learn(ing) early to offer women an *unattainable dream of thinness* and beauty to sell more products" (Fraser 2009: 13, my emphasis).

Within the last one hundred years, the only time that being curvaceous — "well-padded," "pleasantly plump" — was embraced as a pleasing aesthetic for women in Western culture was during the 1940s and 1950s; a time when domesticity for women was at an all time high and fertility rates soared, giving birth to the baby boom. The movie stars during this era — Marilyn Monroe and Jane Mansfield, for example — would be considered far too fat to hone their craft in today's movie industry, where female movie stars wear dress sizes as small as size zero, or even double zero. We now live in a culture where the double-digit dress sizes 12 and 14 are considered to be larger sizes for women; "larger size" is interpreted as meaning larger than the "normal" (acceptable size) for women. The readers of FHM (*For Him Magazine*) beg to differ:

> Men's magazine FHM recently conducted an online survey asking whether its readers found a size 8, size 12 or size 14 model most attractive. The survey drew 60,000 responses — four-fifths said they were more attracted to the size 12 or size 14 models. (Silverman 2010: 159)

Judging women's bodies in this manner is highly problematic as it reinforces the sexual objectification of women. That said, the rift between the current cultural definition of thinness for women and the results of this online survey point to the strength of social constructions of femininity that require female bodies to be contained. Girls and women are inundated with the cultural message that containment — bodily and socially — is essential to the social construction of the "feminine self."

Thinness and Patriarchy

> Standards require that the ideal feminine body be small. A woman is taught early to contain herself, to keep her arms and legs close to her body and take up as little space as possible. This model of femininity suggests that real women are thin, nearly invisible.... Not surprisingly, those women who claim more than their share of territory are regarded with suspicion. (Hartley 2001: 61)

Men, on the other hand, have the freedom to occupy more space in the social realm, "to take up as much space as they can get away with" (Hartley 2001: 62). Oppressive notions surrounding fatness for women — women taking up space — become realized in the expectation that women's bodies conform to standards deemed acceptable within patriarchy. "The male gaze, characterized... as a 'patriarchal psychic tapeworm,' serves as a continual reminder that the female body must be smaller than man's to be acceptable" (Hartley 2001: 67). The widespread acceptance of a thin body ideal for females feeds body preoccupation and body criticism among girls and women. This "self-hatred" is an embodiment of patriarchal views that seek to contain women and their collective bodies, both physically and metaphorically (Hartley 2001). The vast array of bodily practices designed to reshape the female body underscore the cultural assumption that the female body is "fundamentally flawed," in need of fixing (Hartley 2001). Females internalize this cultural message very early in the socialization process (Silverman 2010), fully understanding that a great part of their worth is tied to their attractiveness, in particular their body (Dyhouse 2010). In the words of a young college woman:

> My body is the most important thing. It's like that's all I ever had because that's all everyone ever said about me. My mother would say that I am smart and stuff, but really they focused on my looks. And even my doctor enjoys my looks. He used to make me walk across the room to check my spine and he'd comment on how cute I walked, that I wiggled. Why comment on it at all? (Hesse-Biber 2007: 33)

Good question. The sexual objectification of young women is so commonplace that incidents like this rarely even register on the radar as being outrageous acts of male professional/sexual privilege — a condition that is indicative of the pervasiveness of broad-based forms of patriarchal power. Females are well aware that being thin and attractive gives a woman access to power, however fleeting and short-lived that power might be. Women are under constant pressure to emulate, or at least make an "effort" to emulate, the prevailing feminine body ideal through rigorous participation in various body regimes (food restriction being central to this process). The existence of fat phobia and fat oppression are poignant and constant reminders to girls and women that their value decreases as their weight increases (Harding and Kirby 2009; Silverman, 2010). The current

> The current widespread acceptance of fat reduction strategies designed to reshape the female body is a continuation of misogynist containment practices.

widespread acceptance of fat reduction strategies designed to reshape the female body is a continuation of misogynist containment practices, leaving little room for fat women to embrace their bodies as they are, without modification or weight loss. The construction of the obesity epidemic parallels the current obsession with thinness and the accompanying fat-phobic discourse wherein fatness is reviled and thinness embraced.

The Construction of the Obesity Epidemic

"Most North Americans alive today have no memory of a time when thinness was *not* a national obsession, and thus have no choice but to regard the artificial as normal" (Poulton 1996: 17). This observation is even more salient now, sixteen years later, given that issues surrounding the obesity "epidemic" have been centre stage in mainstream discourse for the past ten years. A cursory review of the top issues in the press in any given week reveals that we are living in a time where stories (relayed as "facts") surrounding the bodies, social habits, health statuses, and lifestyles of fat people are the focus of public discussion. Fatness has become the concern of many, constructed as an all encompassing "social ill," and a virtual plague on society (Gard 2011; Oliver 2006).

Within the decade spanning 1994–2004, reporting of the obesity epidemic in "news media stories" increased from thirty-three stories in 1994 to almost 700 by 2004 in the United States (Oliver 2006: 36). The beginning of the new millennium was the turning point in the intensification of media focus on the obesity "epidemic."

> Nearly all the major newspapers starting running headlines. Newsmagazines, such as *Newsweek, Time,* and *U.S. News and World Report* ran cover stories. ABC, CBS, NBC, and other television news networks aired special features. The word was spreading — obesity was a deadly disease of apocalyptic proportions (Oliver 2006: 37).

Between 1999 and 2000 the number of news stories increased from fewer than fifty to 107. This number "doubled again" in 2002 and by 2004 had reached the remarkable level of almost 700 stories. Like Oliver, Gard (2011) questions the sensationalistic news reporting on the obesity epidemic as he remains unconvinced that an epidemic of such proportions actually exists. For example, in the press obesity experts have compared the obesity "epidemic" to global warming:

> It is not clear what obesity experts who make this claim know about global warming… even the most gloomy climate scientists accept that predictions about the planet's future climate are subject to a wide margin of error. What, then, are

obesity scientists actually saying when they compare obesity to global warming (Gard 2011: 20)

Gard goes on to note other sensationalistic statements made by the press who have compared the obesity epidemic to a SARS outbreak, and have alarmed citizens that our world is virtually being "engulfed" by this "pandemic" (2011: 20). At the forefront of this rhetoric is the fat-phobic view that fatness represents a pathological state of being, that being fat is necessarily "unhealthy," and that fat people are undesirable in the broadest sense of the term.

In *Fat Politics*, J. Eric Oliver (2006) debunks many of the myths surrounding the obesity epidemic, questioning the very foundation of the "evidence" put forth by claims makers in the business of promoting the notion of fatness as a disease and the existence of an epidemic surrounding fatness. Oliver does not question the fact that Americans are, in fact, fatter than they were in the 1960s, a trend that began to be noticed in the 1980s. He does argue that the "facts" surrounding obesity — its causes, its effect on health, and its categorization as a "disease" — need to be problematized. For example, the original research study that claimed to establish the legitimacy of the existence of an obesity epidemic, and fatness as necessarily unhealthy, relayed research findings to the general public based on data that Oliver argues were very misleading. These data were published in a report contained within the highly respected *Journal of the American Medical Association*. The calculation of death rates associated with obesity was central to their argument that obesity had become more widespread and therefore a public health concern. Oliver challenges the validity of these claims on the basis of the research methodology employed:

> Researchers did not calculate the 400,000 deaths by checking to see if the weight of each person was a factor in his or her death. Rather, they *estimated* a figure by comparing the death rates of thin and heavy people using data that were nearly thirty years old.... Moreover, they also made a number of errors in their basic calculations. (2006: 3)

The U.S. Congress spearheaded an inquiry to investigate these issues and changes were made to the report. The rush to establish obesity as a major health concern of epidemic proportions was, at least in part, economically motivated:

> It is difficult to find *any* major figure in the field of obesity research or past president of the North American Association for the Study of Obesity who does not have some type of financial tie to a pharmaceutical company or weight loss company. (Oliver 2006: 30)

The ultimate irony is that, if the majority of fat people took the advice of health experts and lost significant amounts of weight, many of these researchers would be out of business, at least temporarily. The continued use of the BMI (body-mass index) as the standard measure for obesity and health is highly problematic as it does a poor job of measuring either (Oliver 2006). In fact, the BMI has been used as a political tool to artificially inflate the actual number of "overweight" and "obese" people (Oliver 2006; Monaghan et al. 2010). The U.S. National Institute of Health lowered the BMI in 1998 resulting in "over 30 million Americans suddenly becoming overweight without actually gaining any weight" (Monaghan et al. 2010: 50). A BMI within the range of 25 to 29 became defined as "overweight"; 30 or above as "obese" (Oliver 2006: 22).

However, these standardized notions of fatness are all relative depending on the group of people we are looking at. The notion of "overweight" among female supermodels or movie stars would most likely be considered "thin" for the majority of women (Oliver 2006), and many male athletes would be considered "obese" by the standards set by BMI. Within this context of standardized weight estimates Michael Jordan would be considered "overweight" and Arnold Schwarzenegger "obese" (Oliver 2006).

The establishing and tracking of the obesity epidemic is an enterprise of vast proportions. Monaghan et al. employ the term obesity epidemic entrepreneurs (and entrepreneurship) to refer to those "varied actors, interests, practices and manner of constructing medicalized fatness as a social issue or crisis" (2010: 38). These entrepreneurs include: 1) "Creators" (those involved in establishing the existence of the "obesity epidemic" through "scientific discourses"); 2) "Amplifiers/Moralizers" (the media involvement in the sensationalization of obesity); 3) "Legitimators" (government bodies legitimizing the epidemic and formulating policy); 4) "Supporters" (those who mobilize efforts regarding the dissemination of information and informing the public; 5) "Enforcers/Administrators" (professionals in the field of weight loss who reinforce the view of fatness as "pathological" and place blame on the individual); and 6) "The Entrepreneurial Self" (the neoliberal view of "self-regulation" regarding care of the body, weight loss as the "moral" responsibility of the individual) (Monaghan et al. 2010: 47–63). These categories overlap and intersect at various points; it is beyond the scope of this chapter to discuss these issues in detail. However, it is useful to contemplate the vastness of the effort that has been exerted to establish fat as a primary concern on the public health agenda; an effort that pays off in the end. "For America's public health establishment, an obesity epidemic is worth billions" (Oliver 2006: 6).

Within the context of an already body-obsessed, diet-crazed, fat-hating culture, the obesity epidemic fits neatly into the dominant neoliberal ideological framework: once the spark was ignited vis-à-vis the media the obsession with fat became all consuming (Oliver 2006). Yet another layer of discourse that serves to oppress fat people by reinforcing fat-phobic attitudes and behaviours had been added to the existing cultural attitudes. This is not surprising as we live in a time where the responsibility for health and related health "problems" is placed squarely on the shoulders of individuals (Monaghan et al. 2010; Raphael 2010).

This view of fatness as a sign of deviance has a long history, dating back to the historical construction, within Christian religious thought, of fat people as morally weak (Oliver 2006). Oliver traces fat phobia to its historical roots within Puritanism and the rise of "monopolist capitalism." As stated previously, fatness came under suspicion in the late nineteenth century both aesthetically — as the body ideal began to shift to a thinner physique — and medically, in that fat became associated with disease and mortality. The development of fat-phobic attitudes at this time were reflective of Christian beliefs espoused during the Middle Ages, predicated on notions of the "sins of the flesh" — lust, gluttony, greed, sloth, wrath, envy, and pride. Primary among them was/is gluttony:

> Overeating, like many sins of the flesh, was considered immoral because it was associated with animal impulses and indicated a weakness of reason and self-restraint. Gluttony was also dangerous because *it was thought to foster other sins of the flesh* .... Gluttony was the medieval equivalent of a *"gateway drug"* that would lead to other vices. A *lustful, passionate body* could only be tamed through a discipline of regimented activity and religious practice. (Oliver 2006: 64, my emphasis)

> Gluttony was the medieval equivalent of a "gateway drug" that would lead to other vices.

In this regard, Oliver (2006) argues that the fat body came to be viewed as being antithetical to religious teachings of self-control and the denial of carnal (bodily) pleasures. Self- sacrifice and hard work — the cornerstone of Protestantism and capitalist enterprise — was applied also the body, more specifically to the need to control bodily appetites. The medicalization of fat played a major role in further entrenching fat phobia, in particular the view of the fat body as "abnormal," as "Other." Medical terms like "underweight," "overweight," "obese," and "morbidly obese" are so entrenched in our thinking patterns about body size and what constitutes fatness that we forget that these terms have been constructed within institutional frameworks, by particular groups of people. Medical personnel, actuaries, researchers of various stripes, and weight loss consultants, all of whom have vested interests in promoting ideas surrounding the pathology of fat and fatness, collude with the notion that the "obesity epidemic" is of catastrophic proportions (Oliver 2006).

Weight Loss Regimes

In the West the weight loss industry is a central organizing force in the lives of fat people, in particular fat women. This can mean participation in the counting of calories, weighing of food, keeping track of "points" — or some combination thereof — weighing oneself on a regular basis, and "working out" on machines that can give you readouts of your vital statistics and calculate the number of calories burned while exercising. These and various other methods associated with weight reduction, weight maintenance, or muscle building make people mindful of energy ingested and energy expended. However, the long term success of such strategies as measured by sustained weight loss is highly questionable, bordering on mythical, given that the overwhelming majority of people gain back all that they have lost, including additional pounds (Harding and Kirby 2009).

The recidivism rates are high among women — and it is mostly women — who participate in organized weight loss strategies, like attending various diet groups, such as Weight Watchers. Ruth Mortimer (2010), in her editorial piece titled "Weight Watchers Has No Plans to Slim Down," argues that the weight reduction strategy recently developed by this company, namely the ProPoints Plan (since revitalized and re-named PointsPlus) is a good marketing strategy. The ProPoints Plan is being touted as something new, which is "complicated," as followers must learn the various rules and techniques required to be successful. The marketers point out, "If the food plan was easy enough to follow without any guidance, why would someone need Weight Watchers?" (14). By changing to this "new" plan, this company is able to increase their revenue through "a healthy merchandise business that includes a ProPoints calculator and various other paraphernalia" (Mortimer 2010: 14). In the U.S., weight loss is a major industry, with Americans "spending a startling $50 billion a year" in the pursuit of thinness (Hesse-Biber 2007: 75).

Investing in a membership at Weight Watchers can be expensive, with an initial membership fee of $25.00 and $15.95 if you pay on a per-week basis (weekly fee paid even if you skip a week). If you add to this the various paraphernalia needed to stay on the plan, it becomes a costly venture, particularly given that the highest numbers of fat people are found among the poor (Oliver 2006; LeBesco 2004) and that women are more likely than men to be employed in lower paying jobs (for example, part-time work) (Raphael 2010). Even if weight loss strategies such as this did work, many women could not afford it. We look to "lifestyle choices" to explain disease and death; however, issues surrounding poverty and living conditions have a much stronger influence on health outcomes (Raphael 2010). The conditions of poverty are stress inducing — low pay, insecure employment, poor working conditions, inadequate housing, food insecurity — are common experiences among the poor. Under these conditions, Raphael argues that eating a "carbohydrate-dense" diet can be viewed "as a coping response to difficult life circumstances" (Raphael 2010: 37).

Carbohydrate-dense foods are cheap and high in calories. They are, therefore, the foods of choice for poor people, whose resulting fatness is blamed on their lax and neglectful food choices rather than being seen as the result of social conditions that limit their choices around food and physical activity, both of which are costly. During the winter months in Canada, a head of broccoli can cost as much as $3.99. A dozen hot dogs and a loaf of white bread can be purchased for the same price (or less) and can feed three children their lunch for several days! Mothers — especially mothers who are poor, mothers who work for pay, and mothers from racialized groups — are often held responsible for their children's weights ("mother blame") (Boero 2009). This neoliberal stance of individual responsibility for "healthy lifestyle choices" further punishes the poor by blaming them for their situation rather than recognizing the health outcomes precipitated by structured inequality (Raphael 2010). "Images like fat poor Mexican American women going into Wal-Mart, shows that they are the new target for an old process by which elites maintain their feelings of superiority" (Kirkland 2008: 143).

Exercise is also an expensive proposition. Supportive footwear is necessary for a fat person to be able to walk longer distances: such footwear can cost upwards of $150. Becoming thin is an investment that few can afford especially those who are both fat and poor. The media takes full advantage of this individualistic approach to weight loss by developing programming focusing on the sensationalism associated with both weight gain and weight loss. Of particular concern is the practice of using fat people as contestants on TV shows that applaud dramatic weight loss through extreme measures.

Extreme weight loss and exercise fanaticism (as witnessed in the TV show *The Biggest Loser*, for example) places fat contestants in conditions where their bodies are made "vulnerable" and are viewed as spectacles — a strategy that serves to reinforce fat-phobic attitudes (Winter 2004). Their vulnerability deepens as they are required to engage in self-confessionals, openly discussing their relationship to their bodies and often "deriding themselves and their bodies for being weak, ugly, and unhealthy" (Winter 2004: 17). Internalized fat phobia breeds shame and self-hatred: confessing that shame and demonstrating a yearning to change oneself to "fit" the prevailing body ideal is a fundamental requirement of these types of shows. Winter makes the observation that contestants tend to be "chosen for their good looks, and their curves in form-fitting tank tops and shorts" (2004: 17). In fact, the winner of *The Biggest Loser* (May 2011) was Olivia Ward (recipient of $250,000 for her efforts). Her sister Hannah came in second place. Both women are facially attractive, curvy women. This is vitally important for the dramatic "after" scene as they jump through their giant sized "before" photos — like butterflies emerging from their chrysalis — complete with head-to-toe makeovers, leaving behind their stigmatized identities as fat women.

Fat phobia and Fat Oppression in Everyday Life

> Fat women are ... not valuable because they are in violation of so many of the rules. A fat woman is visible, and takes up space. A fat woman stands out. She occupies personal territory in ways that violate the rules for the sexual politics of body movement.... She has clearly fed herself.... Thus, for women to not break the rules ... *women must fear fat, and hate it in themselves.* (Brown 1989, cited in Hartley 2001: 66; my emphasis)

Fat women are highly visible by virtue of their size and body proportions, most people stare at the fat woman when she enters a public space in the same way that stigmatized people from other groups (persons with disabilities, for example) are held in public fascination.

For women to not break the rules... *women must fear fat, and hate it in themselves.*

At the same time, fat women are incredibly invisible. For example, fat women are rarely the central character in fictional literature (Frater 2009) or chosen to play the leading role in a romantic play or film (Jester 2009). When they do play a key role in a television series, they are often portrayed in stereotypical ways. The character Penelope Garcia (in the TV series *Criminal Minds*), for example, epitomizes a particular genre of the stereotypical image of the single "overweight" woman — nurturing, kind of quirky, dressed in unconventional clothing, and, for much of the series, not dating. She is also incredibly bright and integral to cracking the case. The character Mimi Bobeck (in the TV series *The Drew Carey Show*) is the absolute epitome of a caricature of the stereotypical fat woman. The power Mimi wields through her various antics is undermined by her physical presence (clown-like attire and heavy make-up) and intense persona as an "over-the-top," somewhat deranged, hypersexualized fat woman. Within this particular genre "the fat woman is made into a spectacle for our amusement. While the laughter she evokes may or may not be bound to her wit, a narrative gag, or prank, it invariably pertains to her physical body" (Stukator 2001: 200).

Oppressive views and accompanying social practices become successful at the point at which members of the oppressed group have internalized their own oppression in the form of self-hatred (hooks 1992). Racism, sexism, homophobia, ableism, and ageism, to name a few, embody this process; a process of this magnitude takes time, beginning in early childhood. Girls as young as three years old "worry about being fat"; children fear fat because they are well aware of the fact that fatness is viewed as being a "bad" thing (Silverman 2010: 10). Given that personality characteristics and self-identities are formed in childhood and adolescence, these early experiences of fat phobia can negatively impact a person for the rest of their lives. You would be hard pressed to find a household where weight loss strategies, exercise regimes, and "healthy lifestyle" practices (for most, a euphemism for dieting, exercise, and weight loss) were never mentioned (Harding and Kirby 2009). Even if you did find such a household, it would have to be one where there was virtually no contact, or very limited contact, with the outside world through technological means. While such communities do exist, the vast majority of children in western societies grow up listening to fat-phobic attitudes from parents, relatives, older siblings, friends, and various media sources (Silverman 2010). Disney and Nickelodeon children's programming, for example, reinforces fat-phobic views within a gendered context by drawing on mainstream "beauty ideals" of whiteness and thinness for females; a portrayal that negatively impacts young female viewers who compare themselves to these idealized characters. Thin "beautiful" characters are presented in a positive light and heteronormative gender scripts are central themes — heteronormativity referring to the mainstream cultural imperative that heterosexuality is "natural," "normal," and "desirable." For example, dating a boy is often presented as something girls must aspire to do (Temple and Liebler 2010).

Parents and teachers reinforce these gender-based heteronormative fat-phobic views through various means. Young girls and adolescent females are particularly vulnerable to being scrutinized and criticized with regard to their body size. For her book, *Good Girls Don't Get Fat*, Robyn Silverman interviews girls, aged nine to fourteen, focusing on a variety of issues relating to weight, bullying, and the culture of thinness. In the following section I draw on the experiences of three of the girls she interviewed: "Kit," "Shay," and "Fiona." Kit recalls her experience of fat phobia at the age of eleven when seeking help from a teacher for bullying. She had written down her thoughts and experiences in a diary she titled *High School Musical* and felt that she was prepared to have the talk. During lunch break she spoke with her teacher in private:

> I finally go up the courage to tell him that some of the kids were calling me "Big Fat Kit Kat" — you know, in that painful singsong way…. Do you know what he said? "Well, if you lost some weight, people wouldn't make fun of you anymore, would they?" It was devastating. I threw out my diary when I got home. (Silverman 2010: 125)

Fat youth who encounter fat oppression in the form of being teased or bullied often suffer from "symptoms of depression, loneliness, general anxiety, and social physique anxiety" (Weinstock and Krehbiel (2009: 122). Teachers' effectiveness at stopping teasing and bullying relies, at least in part, on co-operation from the students themselves. Shay, aged fifteen, states:

> Teachers are so stupid. They think that an hour assembly on bullying will make us nice and a weeklong program on kindness will make us kind. It's such a joke. Kids are signing the "kindness pledge" with one hand and texting about how stupid it is with the other. (Silverman 2010: 126)

In their research examining the teasing and bullying of fat youth, Weinstock and Krehbiel (2009) reveal the commonplace occurrence of this form of peer victimization: fat youth being key targets for schoolyard teasing and bullying. Drawing on research studies comparing the teasing and bullying of overweight and non-overweight children, Weinstock and Krehbiel (2009) reveal that those classified as overweight were teased significantly more often and suffer social ostracism in a variety of ways. As a result of this peer victimization fat children are more likely to feel lonely, have poor self-perception, suffer from depression and anxiety about their appearance and miss school more frequently, "especially on days with gym class" (Weinstock and Krehbiel 2009: 122). Fat adolescents experience teasing at an alarming rate (63 percent and 58 percent for females and males, respectively); for females, the percentages increase when family members are the source of teasing (28.6 percent compared to 16.1 percent for males) and dramatically so when peers are the source (63 percent for females compared to 24.7 percent for males) (Weinstock and Krehbiel 2009). Clearly, the teasing and bullying of fat youth is a gendered issue, the primary targets being females. In fact, girls often engage in negative self-talk about their bodies, metaphorically dissecting them and noting each and every "flaw" (Silverman 2010). Silverman (2010) refers to this negative internal dialogue as "the bully within": the internalized anti-fat message that exists among the girls in her study. Some of these girls used a variety of painful weight loss strategies — "pain for pounds" — to remind themselves not to eat. These strategies include hitting oneself in the stomach (the pain results in diminished appetite), snapping a rubber wrist band as a reminder not to eat (leaving painful welts), piercing the tongue (which makes eating painful), and the list goes on (Silverman 2010). Adolescent girls are highly influenced by their peer group regarding "weight control"; that is, both "overweight girls" and "underweight girls" are more likely to engage in practices leading to weight reduction if other girls in their weight range are engaging in such behaviours (Mueller et al. 2010).

Weight-related teasing among adolescents and internalized fat phobia reflect the larger societal attitude — learned in the home and through the media (Silverman 2010) — that fat people are fair targets for various forms of abuse and discriminatory social practices, just because they are fat (Kirkland 2008). Parents often espouse fat-phobic views and embrace oppressive, shaming practices through the monitoring of their daugh-

> Parents often espouse fat-phobic views and embrace oppressive, shaming practices through the monitoring of their daughters' body sizes and weights.

ters' body sizes and weights. This is particularly problematic when shaming occurs in a public setting. Fiona recalls such an incident:

> We were at a barbeque when I was about thirteen and everyone was asked if they wanted another burger. When they looked at me my Mom chimed in, "She doesn't need another burger." When I told her I was still a little hungry and that I really hadn't eaten that much, she pulled up my shirt and slapped me on my belly and said, "Oh, yes you have." (Silverman 2010: 44)

Families like Fiona's, who embrace the "thin ideal," are particularly critical and vocal in their appraisals of their daughters' weights (Silverman 2010; Hesse-Biber 2007: Nichter 2000). Girls growing up in these families are more likely to develop eating disorders and harbour negative views of their bodies (Silverman 2010).

Among African-American girls there is a tendency to view fatness less critically, since they draw on different criteria in their appraisals of themselves than that used by white girls (Hesse-Biber 2007; Nichter 2000). African-American girls describe the "ideal black girl" as "smart, friendly, not conceited, easy to talk to, fun to be with, (having) a good sense of humor... [and] well-groomed" (Nichter 2000: 165), and less likely to think of beauty in terms of being a particular weight. Having a sense of "style" that speaks to who you are is highly praised and encouraged by family members and friends (Nitcher 2000). The majority of African-American girls in Nitcher's study (64 percent) said that being "a little overweight" was better for health than being "a little underweight." This coincides with the view espoused by African-American women who are less likely than white women to associate fatness with being "unhealthy."

That is not to say that African American women are free from the effects of fat-phobic attitudes and related social practices (Wilson 2009), or free from concerns regarding body image, in particular the desire to lose weight (Blue and Berkel 2010; Willemsen and Hoek 2006; Nitcher 2000). This is especially the case for middle-class African-American women, who may be more likely to internalize and adopt the "dominant" perspective that "thin is everything" (Nitcher 2000: 17). Oprah Winfrey's very public struggle with her body weight is a testament to the pervasiveness of this ideal among the Hollywood elite. Nonetheless, resistance is possible and a necessary step in the process of social change, especially for girls who will someday be women and bear the full mantle of mainstream constructions of femininity and body containment practices.

"Kiss my Assets": Resisting Fat phobia

In her chapter titled "Kiss my Assets: The Secrets of Girls Who Thrive at Every Size," Silverman emphasizes the role that SPARK (support, passion, action, reason, and knowledge) can play in the lives of girls:

> Our children must have... an interest, talent, skill, asset or dream (academic, relational, athletic, artistic or intellectual) that excites them and enables them to

discover their true passions, along with encouragement from trusted adults to nurture it. (2010: 175)

> Embracing fat as a legitimate and acceptable form of embodiment can be a starting point for the liberation of the body.

Being in touch with how you feel, understanding what your needs are, and communicating that to others are first steps in moving forward and embracing a "belief system" that encourages a more positive self-image (Silverman 2010). To push this even further, resisting the dominant anti-fat message by embracing fat as a legitimate and acceptable form of embodiment can be a starting point for the liberation of the body. As articulated by Marilyn Wann (1998: 28–29) for her blog *FAT!SO? Manifesto #6*:

> Practice saying the word fat until it feels the same as short, tall, thin, young, or old.... Use the word fat with your parents, with your partner. Let friends in on your secret. Say, "By the way, I'm fat." You're not overweight, not plump, not bloated. You're fat! Combine the word fat with other words in new and unusual ways: sexy fat, fat and fabulous, fat pride. Use fat in a sentence: "You're looking good. Are you getting fat?" "I met a handsome fat man the other day." "Gee, I wish I could be fat like her." Try out these radical phrases on people you meet and watch their stunned reactions.

Yes, "watch their stunned reactions" indeed! Fat phobia is about women taking up space, it is about being "unruly," it is about any form of embodiment or any form of expression that seeks to disrupt conventional boundaries. It is about most women believing that their worth is inextricably tied to their bodies. Contrary to General Koop's conceptualization of the obesity epidemic as the "terror within," it is in fact women's relationships to their bodies, in particular their fear of fatness, that is the real "terror within."

Glossary of Key Terms

Anthropometry: A field of study examining the size and shape of various aspects of the human body. For example, historically used to differentiate between groups of people based on perceived notions of "race" (the size and shape of human skulls were measured to "identify" people as belonging to certain "races"). Such practices were highly problematic as they reinforced racist ideologies and practices.

Body regimes: The multitude of body practices (e.g., dieting, exercise, for example) that seeks to change/shape the body in attempts to conform to normative cultural standards of embodiment (Shilling 2003).

Body work: The everyday rituals of caring for the body; for example, bathing, styling our hair, removing bodily hair, applying make-up, and so on (Shilling 2003).

Discourse: How things are talked about and understood in everyday human interactions including oral/written form, formal and informal conversation.

FAT: That measures of "fatness" are socially constructed dependent upon culturally and historically defined notions of body size; the naming and embracing of fatness as a legitimate form of embodiment; and the notion that FAT can be used as a political tool for social change.

Fat phobia: The fear and hatred of fat, fatness, and fat people.

Heteronormative: The mainstream ideological perspective that heterosexual relations are deemed to be "natural," "normal," and "desirable."

Misogyny: The hatred of women.

Patriarchy: A system of male supremacy whereby men dominate the social, political, and economic structures of society.

Social construction: A theoretical perspective in the social sciences that views human experiences as being created though social interaction with others.

Questions for Discussion

1. How difficult do you think it would be to not talk about your body (its weight/proportions, amount/type of food eaten, or perceived "flaws") for a twenty-four-hour period?

2. In what ways is negative talk about food (food as "evil/sinful") reflective of a fat-phobic view?

3. In what ways is the "policing" of women's bodies (sizes and weights) a central aspect of body containment practices and fat phobia?

4. What thoughts enter your mind when you see a fat person in public?

5. Have you ever been attracted to a fat person but worried about what others might think?

Websites of Interest

Fat Chicks Rule <fatchicksrule.blogs.com/fat_chicks_rule/>
National Association to Advance Fat Acceptance <naafaonline.com/dev2/>
Big Fat Deal
Fat fu
Association for Size Diversity and Health

References

Anderson, Karen. (1996). *Sociology: A Critical Introduction.* Toronto: Nelson Canada.
Al-Shaykh, Hanan. 1995."Inside a Moroccan Bath." In Patricia Foster (ed.), *Minding the Body: Women Writers on Body and Soul.* New York: Double Day.
Blue, Erika, and LaVerne A. Berkel. 2010. "Feminist Identity Attitudes, Negative Affect, and Eating Pathology in African American College Women." *Journal of Black Psychology* 36, 4.
Boero, Natalie. 2009. "Fat Kids, Working Moms, and the 'Epidemic of Obesity.'" In Esther Rothblum

and Sondra Soloway (eds.), *The Fat Studies Reader*. New York: New York University Press.

Dyhouse, Carol. 2010. *Glamour: Women, History, and Feminism*. London: Zed Books

Fraser, Laura. 2009. "The Inner Corset: A Brief History of Fat in the United States." In Esther Rothblum and Sondra Solovay (eds.), *The Fat Studies Reader*. New York: New York University Press.

Frater, Lara. 2009. "Fat Heroines in Chick-Lit: Gateway to Acceptance in the Mainstream?" In Esther Rothblum and Sondra Solovay (eds.), *The Fat Studies Reader*. New York: New York University Press.

Gard, Michael. 2011. *The End of the Obesity Epidemic*. New York: Routledge

Harding, Kate, and Marianne Kirby. 2009. *Lessons From the Fat-O-Sphere: Quit Dieting and Declare a Truce with Your Body*. New York: Penguin Group.

Hartley, Cecilia. 2001. "Letting Ourselves Go: Making Room for the Fat Body in Feminist Scholarship." In Jana E. Braziel and Kathleen LeBesco (eds.), *Bodies Out of Bounds*. Berkeley: University of California Press.

Hesse-Biber, Sharlene. 2007. *The Cult of Thinness*. Oxford: Oxford University Press.

hooks, bell. 1992. *Black Looks: Race and Representation*. Boston: South End Press

____. 1995. "Beyond a Politics of Shape: White Supremacy and the Black Female Body." *Z Magazine* September.

Jester, Julia Grace. 2009. "Placing Fat Women on Center Stage." In Esther Rothblum and Sondra Soloway (eds.), *The Fat Studies Reader*. New York: New York University Press.

Kilbourne, Jean. 2010. *Killing Us Softly 4*. Sut Jhally (Video Director) and Jeremy Earp (Production Director). Produced by Media Education Foundation.

Kirkland, Anna. 2008. *Fat Rights: Dilemmas of Difference and Personhood*. New York: New York University Press.

Klein, Richard. 2001. "Fat Beauty." In Jana E. Braziel and Kathleen LeBesco (eds.), *Bodies Out of Bounds*. Berkeley: University of California Press.

LeBesco, Kathleen. 2004. *Revolting Bodies: The Struggle to Redefine Fat Identity*. Amherst and Boston: University of Massachusetts Press.

Levy-Navarro. 2009. "Fattening Queer Theory." In Esther Rothblum and Sondra Solovay (eds.), *The Fat Studies Reader*. New York: New York University Press.

Lyons, Pat. 2009. "Prescription for Harm: Diet Industry Influence, Public Health Policy, and the 'Obesity Epidemic'." In Esther Rothblum and Sondra Solovay (eds.), *The Fat Studies Reader*. New York: New York University Press.

McGillicuddy, Frank. 1991. "The Right to Discriminate." [Letter to the Editor.] *Globe and Mail*, September 11: A16.

McRobbie, Angela. 2009. *The Aftermath of Feminism: Gender, Culture and Social Change*. London: Sage Publication.

Millman, Marcia. 1980. *Such a Pretty Face*. New York: W.W. Norton.

Monaghan, Lee F., R. Hollands, and G. Pritchard. 2010. "Obesity Epidemic Entrepreneurs: Types, Practices and Interests." *Body and Society* 16, 2. <bod.sagepub.com>.

Mortimer, Ruth. 2010. "Weight Watchers Has No Plans to Slim Down." *Marketing Week*, November 18. <marketingweek.co.uk>.

Mueller, Anna S, Jennifer Pearson, Chandra Muller, Kenneth Frank, and Alyn Turner. 2010. "Sizing up Peers: Adolescent Girls' Weight Control and Social Comparison in the School Context." *Journal of Health and Social Behavior* 51, 1.

Nichter, Mimi. 2000. *Fat Talk: What Girls and Their Parents Say About Dieting*. Cambridge, MA: Harvard University Press.

Oliver, Eric. 2006. *Fat Politics: The Real Story Behind America's Obesity Epidemic.* Oxford: Oxford University Press.

Popenoe, Rebecca. 2005. "Ideal." In Don Kulick and Anne Meneley (eds.), *Fat: The Anthropology of an Obsession.* New York: Penguin Group.

Poulton, Terry. 1996. *No Fat Chicks: How Women Are Brainwashed to Hate Their Bodies and Spend Their Money.* Toronto: Key Porter Books.

Raphael, Dennis. 2010. *About Canada: Health and Illness.* Halifax and Winnipeg: Fernwood Publishing.

Redfern, Catherine, and Kristin Aune. 2010. *Reclaiming the F Word: The New Feminist Movement.* London: Zed Books.

Shilling, Chris. 2003. *The Body and Social Theory.* London: Sage Publications.

Silverman, Robyn. 2010. *Good Girls Don't Get Fat: How Weight Obsession Is Messing Up Our Girls and How We Can Help Them Thrive Despite It.* Don Mills, ON: Stonesong Press.

Stukator, Angela. 2001. "It's Not Over Until the Fat Lady Sings": Comedy, The Carnivalesque, and Body Politics. In Jana Evans and Kathleen LeBesco (eds.), *Bodies Out of Bounds: Fatness and Transgression.* Berkeley: University of California Press.

Temple, Northrup, and Carol M. Liebler. 2010. "The Good, the Bad, and the Beautiful: Beauty Ideals on Disney and Nickelodeon Channels." *Journal of Children and Media* 43, 3.

Wann, Marilyn. (1998). *FAT!SO?: Because you DON'T have to APOLOGIZE for your SIZE!* Berkeley: Ten Speed Press.

Weinstock, Jacqueline, and Michelle Krehbiel. 2009. "Fat Youth as Common Targets for Bullying." In Esther Rothblum and Sondra Soloway(eds.), *The Fat Studies Reader.* New York: New York University Press.

Willemsen, Ellen M.C., and Hans W. Hoek. 2006. "Sociocultural Factors in the Development of Anorexia Nervosa in a Black Woman." *International Journal of Eating Disorders* 39, 4.

Wilson, Bianca, D.M. 2009. "Widening the Dialogue to Narrow the Gap in Health Disparities: Approaches to Fat Black Lesbian and Bisexual Women's Health Promotion." In Esther Rothblum and Sondra Soloway (eds.), *The Fat Studies Reader.* New York: New York University Press.

Winter, Amy. 2004. "The Biggest Losers and the Lies They Feed Us." *Off Our Backs* November–December.

10

Resisting Conformity
Women Talk About Their Tattoos

Jessica Antony

YOU SHOULD KNOW THIS

- Tattooing, as defined by Health Canada, is the art of depositing pigment 1-2mm into the skin, creating a design. A tattoo gun, which is used for this practice, involves a cluster of small needles that vibrate hundreds of times per minute, puncturing the skin to deposit the ink.
- In the mid to late 1990s, tattooing was listed as one of the top growing businesses in the U.S.
- In a 2000 study of teens aged twelve to nineteen, 29 percent had a tattoo or were planning on getting a tattoo.
- According to the CBC's survey of Canadian prisons in 2004, 47 percent of males and 53 percent of females were tattooed.

Sources: CBC 2004; Kosut 2006: 1036; Health Canada 2001.

HISTORICALLY, TATTOOS HAVE HAD A NEGATIVE IMAGE (Hawkes et al. 2004: 593). Tattooed bodies were thought to be monstrous — as examples of bodily excess, as sex objects or hypersexual beings, or as primitive, threatening, or circus-like spectacles. Tattoos were associated with undesirable class location and sexual behaviour — a "destructive decoration that flouts the possibility of untainted flesh" (Braunberger 2000: 1). Situated within a racist ideology, tattooing and body art were interpreted not as "the rational choice of an enlightened individual, but constitute[d] instead a primitive response more usually associated with the uncivilized behaviour of savages" (Widdicombe and Wooffitt 1995: 139). Lower class, marginalized people embodied the notion of tattooing — the sailor, military man, biker, gang member, or prisoner — and were seen as deviant and counter cultural.

Today, however, what was once a practice reserved for the so-called "seedy underbelly" of society has become, in the eyes of some, just an appropriated marketing tool. In the last few years, the 7-Eleven convenience store chain has started selling an energy drink, called "Inked," to their young customers who are either tattooed or "those who want to think of themselves as the tattoo type" (Associated Press/CBS News 2007). The drink's can features tribal-style designs, while the promotional posters include the outstretched, tattooed arm of a white male. This new marketing strategy, said 7-Eleven's manager of non-carbonated beverages, was created to sell a drink "that appealed to men and women, and the tattoo culture has really become popular with both genders." Tattooing can be used to sell products to the young or those who, according to 7-Eleven, "think and act young" (Associated Press 2007). Other corporations are jumping on this marketing bandwagon as well, offering, for example, four free tires to anyone who has Dunlop's flying "D" logo tattooed on their body (MSNBC 2007). It would seem that tattooing's dubious past has all but disappeared.

The Western history of tattooing, however, has posed a conundrum for contemporary North American capitalist culture: in order to create a tattoo market by commodifying tattoos in the pursuit of profit, a distance from this history had to be established. While tattoos were once a form of deviance, they are now much more embedded in mainstream culture — they are made normal through reality television shows, such as *LA Ink* and *Miami Ink*; through increasingly tattooed professional athletes and musicians, such as Allen Iverson, Mike Tyson, and John Mayer; or even simply through the proliferation of tattoo shops and parlours throughout North America. In order to enable their capitalist commodification, tattoos and body art required a social acceptability — especially for the middle-class consumer.

One way in which social acceptability has been accomplished is through appropriating Eastern culture (DeMello 1995, 2000) — a culture in which tattoos have had considerable significance and mark a rite of passage in the achievement of personal growth. This new generation of tattooing is one that has been defined both by rejecting the traditional working-class meanings and history associated with the practice and by appropriating and creating new meanings, a new history, and a new discourse surrounding tattooing practices. The focus of this new generation is on the tattoo as a means of personal and spiritual growth and the creation of individuality (DeMello 2000) — a set of meanings that differ significantly from the working-class meanings traditionally associated with tattooing, such as masculinity and patriotism. Furthermore, the creation of an entirely new history focuses on the roots of tattooing in Japanese and Polynesian cultures, rejecting the association of tattooing with the low-class and marginalized individuals that originally introduced the practice to Western society. As well, this new discourse surrounding tattooing borrows from the self-help discourse of the 1970s and 1980s, as tattoo enthusiasts now locate tattooing as an identity-altering practice.

Nevertheless, the remnants of Western history have not been completely erased. There is still the association of tattoos as a sign of difference and resistance. In this regard, the mainstream acceptability and popularity of tattoos have proved problematic for women who want to use tattooing as a means of expressing their identities. The tattoo is particularly strange as it represents at once permanence and change. While in the physical it is permanent (tattoos are very difficult, almost impossible to remove from the skin), the meanings surrounding tattoos change over time. The problem for women, then, becomes two-fold: within our capitalist and patriarchal society, how do tattooed women negotiate the tension between tattoos as a sign of conformity (to mainstream consumer culture) and one of resistance or reinvention (as a challenge to patriarchal gender roles)? Given the increasingly commodified nature of tattooing in mainstream Western culture, are women's tattoos merely a reflection of that consumerist culture? Or, are women's tattoos a flouting of gender roles and resistance to a pa-

> The problem for women, then, becomes two-fold: within our capitalist and patriarchal society, how do tattooed women negotiate the tension between tattoos as a sign of conformity (to mainstream consumer culture) and one of resistance or reinvention (as a challenge to patriarchal gender roles)?

triarchal culture that pushes women to act and carry themselves in certain, oppressive ways? Are so-called "feminine" tattoos — butterflies and flowers, for example — considered not subversive enough to be seen as a resistance of patriarchy?

I am interested in addressing these questions not only as a fan of tattoos, but also as a tattooed woman myself. I acquired my first tattoo at the age of eighteen while on a trip to Australia, shortly after I graduated from high school. Since then I have become a collector, adding ten more tattoos to my body — the tenth being a piece, still in progress, that will cover my entire right arm. I became interested in the questions surrounding the problem of tattoos for women as I experienced some of these negotiations myself — feeling unfeminine with such large, prominent tattoos, or thinking about my own tattoos as a commodity in comparison to those whose skin has not been inked.

In order to explore the social and individual meaning of women's tattoos, I spoke with eighteen tattooed women. These women told me the stories of their tattoos: why they got them, how they decided on them, and how they feel about them. These "tattoo narratives" (cf. DeMello 2000) serve as a means of making connections between each tattoo project and a broader historical context, ultimately reconciling for these women the tension between conformity and resistance.

Authenticity, a key theme in my analysis and the women's stories, has a number of meanings. It is used to refer to the desire, expressed by the women I spoke with, to create a legitimate, original self-identity through their tattoo projects; a sincere, long-term commitment to a tattoo; and the sense of uniqueness that comes from being marked as different. The women acknowledged the nuances of authenticity not overtly, but through the ways in which they explained and understood tattooing. DeMello argues that, in appropriating the Eastern history of tattooing, contemporary North American tattoo enthusiasts have created a new tattoo "text." This new tattoo text, in presenting tattoos as a symbol of individuality, allows for tattoos to become a part of the mainstream — it allows for them to be culturally commodified.

Cultural commodification, or the repackaging of once low-class cultural symbols into products for the consumption of the mainstream, is what bell hooks describes as "eating the Other" (hooks 1992). She argues that, through cultural commodification, the media inundate us with "messages of difference" that your sense of self-identity can be found in the Other or, in the case of tattoos, in a practice that was once reserved for the marginalized. The Other then becomes a product, commodified for the mainstream, as the media tell us that "the 'real fun' is to be had by bringing to the surface all those 'nasty' unconscious fantasies and longings about contact with the Other" (hooks 1992: 21) that are entrenched in Western culture.

Commodification is an integral process in capitalism. As Karl Marx and Friedrich Engels (1998) argued long ago, in capitalism there is an incessant, relentless search by capitalists for new markets, for constantly pushing the market into areas of human life that have not been turned into products to buy, sell, and consume. As they put it in *The Communist Manifesto*, over 160 years ago:

> The bourgeoisie, wherever it has got the upper hand... has left no other nexus between man and man [sic] than naked self-interest, than callous "cash payment."

It has drowned out the most heavenly ecstasies of religious fervour, of chivalrous enthusiasm, of philistine sentimentalism, in the icy water of egotistical calculation. It has resolved personal worth into exchange value, and in place of the numberless indefeasible chartered freedoms, has set up that single, unconscionable freedom — Free Trade. (Marx and Engels 1998: 3)

There are no bounds to the desire to turn everything into products for sale. We see this in the attempts in Canada to make health and health care not a right of human beings but a privilege of those able to pay for it (see Pat Armstrong in this book on the privatization of health care; also see Sally Miller on the commodification of the right to eat). This desire to turn everything into a product takes many forms, ranging from the socialization of labour, to privatization and corporatization (see Marxists.org n.d.). As we will see, even self-identity is fair game in the push for commodification.

Commodification can indeed be found all around us, whether we're conscious of it or not. One example is evident in the drive to turn drinkable water into a product to be bought and sold. Maude Barlow, in her book *Blue Gold: The Global Water Crisis and the Commodification of the World's Water Supply* (2001), argues that as the global demand for drinkable water increases beyond sustainable levels, governments around the world are pushing to privatize water as a means of controlling its distribution. This will turn what is a basic human need — water to drink, grow crops and feed livestock — into a product that only those with the money to buy it can afford. She argues that turning water into a commodity to be bought and sold is a fundamental problem: "Instead of allowing this vital resource to become a commodity sold to the highest bidder, we believe that access to clean water for basic needs is a fundamental human right" (Barlow 2001: 4).

Another example of commodification can be found all over Canada and the Western world. Che Guevera, an Argentinean revolutionary who is most famous for leading the Cuban Revolution with Fidel Castro in the late 1950s, was a Marxist who fought against the economic injustices in Latin America and the capitalist dictators that did nothing to alleviate their people's poverty. He fought specifically against the capitalist system of commodification — that is, the fruits of impoverished people's labour being exploited by those from wealthy countries. Now, we find T-shirts, mugs, hats, posters, and calendars emblazoned with Che's image, mass-produced — often by the labour of marginalized or impoverished people who are not paid a fair wage — and sold to the mainstream as an image of so-called rebellion, rebellion devoid of Che's original meaning. Elizabeth Hurley, a British movie star, was photographed a few years ago holding a Louis Vuitton handbag embroidered with an image of Che. Alexander Boldizar summed up this example of commodification quite succinctly:

Fans would point out that he was a Marxist fundamentally opposed to the fetishization of commodities. Detractors would mention that at La Cabana he executed several thousand of exactly the sort of people who'd be most likely to shell out several thousand for a handbag. Lawyers would point out that Korda [the photographer of the famous Che image] was never paid for the intellectual property rights of the photograph. And even those who are neither fans, nor detractors, nor lawyers, who simply admire his picture as a countercultural symbol, must get a bit of cognitive dissonance when that symbol is on the most bourgeois of bags. (2008)

In short, the image of a man who spent his life fighting the commodification of labour has now been commodified. This example points to the deep underlying dynamic of the commodification imperative: empty the meaning from anything and everything human and humane; reduce all to the essence of capitalism — things, people, emotions, and rights are only meaningful as products to be bought and sold as the basis for profit-making. Yet, is this process complete and all encompassing? Does everyone go along with the commodification imperative?

> The commodification imperative — reduce all to the essence of capitalism: things, people, emotions, and rights are to be only meaningful as products to be bought and sold as the basis for profit-making.

This new text, then, that is created when the practice of tattooing is appropriated from Eastern cultures is important in making sense of the ways in which the women I spoke with understand their tattoos. But to see this tattoo process as only commodification falls short because it does not recognize the constant shifting in the specific meaning of and narratives surrounding tattoos, political or otherwise. The ways in which we talk about tattoos has changed (as analysts like DeMello argue). I agree it has and must in order for tattoos to reach the place in mainstream culture where we see them today. However, I want to take the argument one step further in suggesting that, though tattoo discourse has changed as tattoos have become commodified, tattoo wearers — particularly women — are not merely marking themselves with a product devoid of any meaning except that of a popular commodity. That is, tattoos are not simply a commodification meant to represent a sense of false individuality — they are more complex than that, and they can represent genuine cultural connections made by women as they undertake their tattoo projects. More generally speaking, the sense of individuality and authenticity that tattoos represent for some women constitute one of the ways in which women negotiate conformity and resistance in a patriarchal, capitalist culture. In this sense, then, cultural commodification is nuanced and, in the case of tattoos as a form of self-identification, the struggle for self-identity is indeed one of the ways in which women confront and resist the ongoing capitalist effort to turn everything into a commodity, including permanent body modifications. Tattoos and tattooing are, then, a window on this process of commodification and the resistance to it in patriarchal capitalism.

However, in order to understand the contemporary problem of the tattooed woman — the negotiation between resistance and conformity — it is important to examine the historical context within which modern-day tattooing, and thus, tattooed women, is situated.

Historical Context

Tattooing reaches back thousands of years and can be found in nearly all parts of the world at some time (Caplan 2000: xi). Going back to colonial times, Westerners have had contact with cultures that revered tattooing. These practices eventually found their way into Canadian and U.S. culture.

North American (colonial) tattooing is rooted in the sea voyages of early European travellers of the late eighteenth and early nineteenth centuries. Explorers to the South Pacific came into contact with the tattooed Other in Polynesia, Micronesia, and Melanesia. While Europeans had experienced tattooing as early as the 1600s, it was James Cook who first documented the "pervasiveness of 'tattooing' (a derivation of the Tahitian term *ta-tu* or *tatau*) among South Pacific cultures" (Atkinson 2003: 31).

European explorers' exposure to tattooed tribal natives had a profound effect — the explorers considered the tattooed natives to be savage and weird and saw tattooing as a frightening foreign ritual. Native peoples were captured and transported back to Europe with the explorers as "living evidence of primitivism in the New World" (Atkinson 2003: 31). Sold and paraded through European museums and sideshows, these individuals — women especially — were seen by Europeans as the "radical self-expression, physical vanity, and exuberant sexuality they had denied themselves … in the service of their restrictive deity" (Atkinson 2003: 31). Many Natives were baptized and given new, Christian names in an attempt to liberate them "from their 'spiritual and physical slavery'" (Oettermann 2000: 195). Many European sailors returned home decorated with tattoos, exposing the upper and middle classes of European society to the practice, and arguably "reaffirming [their] understanding of their own cultural advancement and progress, as the outwardly uncontrolled libidinal bodies of 'backward' tribal cultures of the world articulated a brutality long overcome in Western cultures" (Atkinson 2003: 31).

The practice among South Pacific Islanders changed too as a result of colonizers' visits. Tattoo designs soon came to include images such as ships, flags, guns, cannons, and even portraits of European royalty. Their meanings shifted, as well. For example, Hawaiian tattoos were once thought to protect the person from harm, but after the introduction of guns and other weapons the significance of protective tattooing dwindled away. The Maori of New Zealand have traditionally tattooed their faces as a sign of status and lineage; however, after European explorers and colonizers began trading goods for the tattooed heads they found so fascinating, the Maori stopped tattooing their faces in fear of being decapitated (Govenar 2000: 213; Atkinson 2003: 32).

During this period, Europeans saw tattooing as both fascinating and deplorable — a paradox of sorts — and interpreted the tattooed body as a source of exotic entertainment. Sailors tattooed their bodies as both a keepsake of their overseas adventures and as a form of excitement, setting themselves apart from the majority in European society. With more and more sailors coming home with cultural inscriptions permanently marked on their bodies, tattooing started to creep into mainstream European culture and eventually (colonial) North American culture (Atkinson 2003: 33). In 1876 at the Centennial Exposition in Philadelphia, some of the first tattooed native people were put on display for the enjoyment and wonder of the audience. Even as members of the Navy were coming home adorned with tattoos, the majority of European and North American society had little to no knowledge of the practice.

Taking their cue from the success of tattooed sideshow performers, tattooed Navy servicemen coming back from overseas started to exhibit themselves in travelling circuses and sideshows. Part of the attraction, however, was the notion of a savage native from a foreign land covered in frightening markings. As the Navy men were obviously of European heritage, they concocted elaborate back-stories to accompany their exhibitions. Many would claim to have been captured by savages and tattooed against their will, thus perpetuating the notion of tattooing as the frightening ritual of an "uncivilized Other" (Atkinson 2003).

The designs that were popular largely consisted of patriotic symbols, religious imagery, and erotic illustrations of women. These designs, Alan Govenar (2000: 217) argues, constituted a "folk art form" generated by word of mouth and imitation. This folk art provides, to some extent, insight into the cultural context of the time, as tattoo artists were necessarily aware of the demands of their audience. The social coercion that the designs adhered to promoted not only conformity, but tradition, thus serving as a visual representation of important symbols of the day. Primarily patriotic and religious, these designs communicated loyalty, devotion, and (oddly enough) conservative morals (Govenar 2000).

By the end of the 1930s tattoo exhibits were becoming less exciting and exotic as more and more people were becoming tattooed and exposed to tattoos. Tattooed performers then had to develop more elaborate back-stories to entice their audiences — such as the "abducted farmer's daughter," who was tattooed against her will — and women, in particular, found it necessary to dress more provocatively in order to maintain the interest of the audience (Govenar 2000: 225). As tattoos became more common, sideshow audiences turned to the circus for entertainment. To attract audiences, women took centre stage as tattooed attractions — women who were often the wives and girlfriends of tattooists or were simply lured into the profession with the promise of fame and fortune (Atkinson 2003: 35). The show then became somewhat pornographic, as women would take the stage and strip before the crowd, displaying their tattooed bodies. These shows became some of the most popular midway attractions through to the 1940s.

The introduction of tattoos into the carnival and sideshow exhibitions ultimately served as a means of exploring desires and emotions that were socially repressed at the time in a controlled way. Tattoos were seen as a form of deviance and tattooed bodies were considered savage and frightening. The sideshows provided the means for "North Americans to experience subversive pleasures with and tortures of the flesh without sacrificing commonly held cultural understandings of corporeal respectability" (Atkinson 2003: 36); that is, North Americans were able to enjoy these pleasures from a distance, without subjecting their own bodies to the taboo of marking the skin, which was seen as lacking respectability. This era firmly established the association between tattooing and social deviance, a particularly important connection to note as this association has carried through to the present. Returning home after the Second World War, servicemen found that their symbolically patriotic tattoos now held a great deal of negative social value. The significance and patriotism once associated with tattooing started to diminish, and by 1946 new recruits were no longer interested in becoming tattooed. Tattoos were even restricted in the military in the 1950s — if they limited the effectiveness of a man's ability to work (due to infection, for example), he would be prosecuted. In the context of the increasingly urban, family-centred nature of North American culture in the 1950s, tattoos were once again associated with disrepute and deviance. Societal values shifted toward material comfort and middle-class conformity, and tattoos were strongly identified with lower-class, criminal individuals and groups. Once a symbol of group expression and national pride, tattoos were now interpreted as a widespread sign of criminality (Govenar 2000).

Radical Shifts: Contemporary Commodification

The political upheaval of the 1960s and 1970s brought with it a great many cultural shifts, including the popular conception of tattooing. Women, in particular, began to question and fight normative notions of femininity and gender roles, resurrecting tattoos as a means of redefining themselves as women. Margot Mifflin explains:

> [Women] began casting off their bras as they had their corsets a half-century earlier, tattoos were rescued from ignominy and resurrected in the counterculture by women who were rethinking womanhood. The arrival of the Pill in 1961 had given women a new sexual freedom; a little over a decade later legalized abortion secured their reproductive rights. Not surprisingly, the breast became a popular spot for tattoos—it was here that many women inscribed symbols of their newfound sexual independence. (1997: 56)

With the swell of popularity — especially among women — in tattooing, the middle classes began to become involved in the historically marginalized practice. Cultural icons such as musicians and actors started to embrace the practice, thus enticing young, middle-class individuals to follow suit. While the popularity of the practice was already entrenched among the marginalized classes, the 1960s and 1970s saw an increase in its popularity among more privileged classes, thus introducing tattooing to the mainstream and drawing widespread attention to the practice. The designs that had held up since the early 1900s, however, were no longer of interest to young people. Not able to identify with the extremely patriotic imagery, they demanded more customized, personal images, which opened up the art to the appropriation of designs from other cultures. Tattoo artists as a whole also became a more educated, artistic group in keeping with the demand for more complicated, personalized designs. Young tattoo artists began to see tattooing as a representation of identity, "treating the body as less and less of a canvas to be filled with tattoos and more as an integral part of the self, the young middle-class insurgence into the tattoo artist profession redefined many of the old ideologies held strongly in the trade" (Atkinson 2003: 45). Artists experimented with different styles and shops moved from the urban ghetto to the youth centres of the city.

The 1970s and 1980s saw more people than ever before embrace tattooing as a form of self-expression. Michael Atkinson explains this process:

> Influenced by political movements that shook conservative understandings of the body to the ground, interpretations of tattoos were more varied and subject to contextual construction. As women and more "respectable" social classes participated in tattooing it transformed into a practice of political identity construction. (2003: 46)

By the 1990s tattoos had become mainstream phenomena, with scores of tattoo shops cropping up in many major North American cities. In the present context, therefore, artists must now be able to adapt to new styles, designs, and needs of their customer base. New methods of communication, and thus, marketing, have brought a whole new dimension to the tattoo industry, with tattoo magazines, websites, message boards, and online communities developing and flourishing, bringing artists and enthusiasts alike together "into an information-rich community of social actors" (Atkinson 2003: 48). As people are now able to learn more about the process of tattooing via online resources, as well as communicate with tattoo enthusiasts around the world, more and more people are being drawn into the practice as both tattoo artists and tattooees.

As tattooing becomes more and more a mainstream phenomenon, the ability to decipher a tattooed body's authentic membership in a particular counter culture, while once quite apparent, now becomes not so easily done. Tattoos have become commodified — a trend, an immediate mark of individuality that can be bought and sold. Nevertheless, tattoos still serve as a means of communication. *What* they communicate, however, is indeed more difficult to determine.

Appropriation or Connection?

A typical non-critical commodification analysis argues that tattoos have become a false representation of self-identity — one that has been appropriated from the lower classes and is lacking any real political meaning. Margo DeMello (2000), for example, makes just such an argument by examining the role of class hierarchy in the tattoo community, coupled with the re-inscription of the culture with the influx of middle-class wearers and artists in the so-called new generation of tattooing.

DeMello begins her investigation by outlining the history of Western tattooing and examines the state of the practice after World War Two, as technological, artistic, and social changes were affecting the practice. The introduction of academically trained tattoo artists, the use of tattooing as a counter-cultural symbol, and the appropriation of exotic designs and images (as opposed to traditional, old-school Americana designs) created a shift in the culture, which DeMello refers to as the "Tattoo Renaissance." As a result of this cultural transformation, tattooing began to appeal to a more middle-class clientele. Within the new tattoo generation, there is the distinction between "high" and "low" tattooing practices, which have been perpetuated and maintained within the tattoo culture through media interpretations, academic approaches, and publications produced from within the community. Media accounts in particular — both those produced within and outside the tattoo community — have had a significant effect on the polarization of the tattoo culture. Mainstream media have focused on the increased popularity of tattooing among more conventional individuals, ultimately softening the public image of the practice and making it easier to digest. Tattoo publications produced within the community have focused on fine art tattooing (or "high" tattooing), moving away from the biker and sailor image traditionally associated with tattooing (or "low" tattooing). These two main sources of information dissemination have redefined the tattoo community.

The reappropriation of what was considered a low-class art form is similar to the appro-priation of 1940s Hollywood glamour in gay camp: camp being the "re-creation of surplus value from forgotten forms of labour… by liberating the objects and discourses of the past from disdain and neglect" (DeMello 1995: 11). In this sense, camp involves the resurrection of objects and discourses of the past that are generally seen as negative and are forgotten — they are discourses that are taboo and lack respectability and are generally ignored by mainstream society. They are resurrected and reimagined for the dominant class's purposes. The problem being, however, that these forms are not forgotten but are actually still used by those so-called low-class people. DeMello argues that while the middle-class appropria-tion of tattooing may seem liberatory, it is in fact an illustration of how "characteristics of social difference are appropriated within our culture to provide the trappings of individual difference" (Williamson, cited in DeMello 1995: 11). The cultural appropriation of many traditions, then, is based on a pre-existing text through which new cultural symbols can be created; however, the middle-class appropriation of tattooing is different in that middle-class tattoo wearers do not possess the lower-class text (such as a similar socio-economic status) — thus that previous text is ignored and the new, middle-class text is created. Put another way, the appropriation of tattoos results in tattoos' origins and history in the practices of the low-class and marginalized (bikers, sailors, punks) being erased as middle-class tattoo wearers have no connection to or use for that history.

Perpetuating this new tattoo cultural text is the separation of low-class from middle-class (or biker and fine art) tattoos. The separation of the two allows middle-class tattoo wearers to reject and separate themselves from a tradition historically seen as negative but still maintain the symbolic individuality. The distinction, DeMello argues, is upheld not for aesthetic reasons, but for political and social ones. Since the prior text has been rejected, and with it the prior history of tattoos (including their association with bikers, prisoners, sailors, and prostitutes), a new history must be developed — one based on a "mythical, primitive past" (DeMello 1995: 13). This new, fictionalized past legitimizes a tradition historically seen as negative. It is through middle-class tattoo magazines (like *TattooTime*) that this past is perpetuated and introduced into the public discourse. *TattooTime*'s first edition (*The New Tribalism*), as well as Re/Search's *Modern Primitives,* represents this desire to return to a primitive past and to naturalize the practice of tattooing.

So has tattooing's negative past been effectively eliminated? DeMello argues that it has not, the evidence being tattoo culture's increasing presence in the mainstream, especially given tattooing's shady roots, through both mainstream and alternative media publications. She argues that, if anything, this presence illustrates "the power of the media to effect, if not real social change… at least symbolic transformations" (DeMello 1995: 14).

While the cultural appropriation of Eastern tattooing history is important in understand-ing the context in which the contemporary tattoo industry resides, I found that the women I spoke with used the stories or narratives about their tattoos as a means, not of appropriating something, but rather of connecting them *with* something: a history, a cultural belonging, or a sense of identity. Tattoos have necessarily become commodified and bereft of meaning, partly in using the narratives from Eastern culture, in order for them to be made acceptable to the mainstream and middle-class. The women I spoke with, however, recognized their tattoos' commodified nature and were able to find meaning through connecting their tattoos with their sense of identity. Thus, these links are not understood as cultural appropriation, but rather cultural *connection*. In these terms, we can see the nuances of appropriation and the complexity of the ways in which it permeates contemporary tattooing practices. Moreover, the ways in which the women used tattoo narratives to make connections and to give meaning is representative of the struggle and tension that they face as tattooed women and the ways they reconcile these challenges. It is in hearing these narratives that we can see how, like cultural narratives generally, they are changing and shifting over time, from one historical era to another. That is, tattoos can be seen and interpreted as a fad or a commodity by some, but their meanings to tattoo wearers are nuanced and shifting. For the wearers, tattoos have meaning beyond their appropriation by mainstream culture as a meaningless product to be bought and sold.

The Fluidity of Tattoo Discourse

As the meanings of tattoos change so too does the language we use to discuss them. How do we understand them? How do we think about them? Analyses not critical of the commodification process often say that the mainstream media, academic publications, and tattoo artist/enthusiast publications are responsible for shaping the way that the tattoo community is presented and understood and thus the way people, both tattooed and not, talk about tattoos.

The mainstream media have portrayed tattooing and the tattoo culture in the past as something to fear (tattoos are for deviants, tattoos are dangerous, and so forth). Media coverage now focuses on the increasing popularity of tattoos. Explaining what tattooing *used* to be and who *used* to get tattooed illustrates the practice's seedy roots and association with nefarious characters and then focusing on the new generation of tattooed people — the middle-class, educated people — effectively silences those groups of people (such as bikers and prisoners) who were traditionally associated with the practice. By selecting those who are interviewed, the mainstream media choose who is allowed to talk and who is given a voice. Academic representations of the practice are similar in that they highlight the distinctions between middle- and low-class tattoo users and fail to recognize the possibility of the media's role in creating this distinction in the first place. Also in line with mainstream media's presentation of the practice is academia's failure to elaborate on low-class tattooing, such as the distinctions between the tattoo use of bikers, sailors, and prisoners, for example. This is dismissed in favour of a focus on the popular use of artistic tattooing.

Those who are given a voice all seem to say the same thing and use the same discourse to talk about their tattoos. Borrowing from the self-help discourse of the 1970s and 1980s, these new-generation tattooed individuals discuss how tattoos have given them a sense of individuality, aided in their personal growth, or heightened their spirituality. These motivations for becoming tattooed can be easily contrasted with the reasons people (such as bikers) *used* to give for getting tattoos: they were drunk, they wanted to prove their masculinity, or they had no real reason at all. Mainstream media representations are made to be easily accessible and understandable to even non-tattooed readers:

> By first focusing their articles around a select group of middle-class individuals, most of whom have relatively small, inoffensive tattoos; by second, denying all of those who do not fit into this category the right to be represented, except as the absent unit of comparison; and third, by centering the discussion around ideas which are very popular outside of the tattoo community, the journalists are able to make the world of tattooing a safe and understandable place. (DeMello 1995: 6)

While tattoos may be seen as counter-cultural, the contemporary discourse around them is not: combining popular self-help and personal growth discourse with middle-class, educated tattooers and tattooed people, contemporary representations of tattooing feature it as a safe and accessible phenomenon.

The new discourse surrounding tattooing borrows from the self-help discourse of the 1970s and 1980s, as tattoo enthusiasts see tattooing as an identity-altering practice. The self-help movement is:

> Pop-psychology and self-awareness that developed in the 1970s and continues today. Self-help describes a movement whose adherents use psychotherapy, twelve-step programs, and other psychological techniques to become happier and to eliminate negative behaviours or attitudes such as codependency, depression, and eating disorders, or to achieve loving relationships with others. (DeMello 2000: 144)

This movement appealed to "therapeutic sensibilities" (Lasch, cited in DeMello 2000: 144) and an increasing interest in mental and emotional health and the power that is "ascribed to the individual will in achieving this" (144). Additionally, the new age movement, which began around the same time, saw middle-class individuals experimenting with Eastern religions and "consciousness-transforming techniques" (144), borrowing practices like Buddhism, tarot, Wicca, and meditation. Within this social climate, tattoos came to be interpreted as a transformative practice, a way of getting in touch with one's spiritual essence. Many popular tattoo images and designs are derived from this new age philosophy, such as zodiac signs, yin yang, or Sanskrit and Japanese writing. With modern Western society seen as repressive, alienating, and lacking ritual, non-Western symbols and practices were adopted as they were thought to be more meaningful than those found in Western culture. It is through narratives derived from the self-help and new age movements that people developed meaning for their tattoos. DeMello argues that these meanings are especially important "within a middle class context that traditionally has not viewed tattoos in a positive light," and that they "form the basis of the individual's personal understanding of his/her tattoo" (149).

Judy, thirty-two, has one tattoo and explained that while she is proud of it, and sees it as a symbol of her strength and independence as a woman; most people are shocked to find out that she has one:

> I think sometimes it surprises people when they find out that I have a tattoo. Like, I have a fairly recent new group of friends that I've been hanging out with. I happened to mention that I had a tattoo and all of the girls were very shocked. I know this group of friends happens to be middle class to upper middle class. I think they don't really see

a white, middle-class girl getting a tattoo. Those are the people that are a little more shocked and don't see it blending with my personality.

Judy's friends seem to understand tattooing as a practice that derives its meaning from the marginalized classes.

Thus, three main narratives have shaped the new generation of tattooing — its redefinition and reinscription — and are used to describe tattoos by this new generation of tattooed individuals: individuality, spirituality, and personal growth. These themes, DeMello argues, have shaped both the nature of the tattoo community and the meaning of the tattoo. The increasing middle-class participation in tattooing has resulted in a transformation of the tattoo culture itself.

In her research, DeMello found that while both men and women favoured narratives of individuality, spirituality, and personal growth, women alone also explained their tattoos in terms of control, healing and empowerment. Women were more apt to interpret their tattoos as a means of reclaiming their bodies — women's bodies are, as many scholars (see Butler 1999 and Grosz 1994, for example) have argued, the site "for the inscription of power and the primary site of resistance to that power" (173); thus women may interpret their tattoos as a means of marking their bodies in an effort to negate the marks of oppression and patriarchy they feel on their bodies. While the most common narratives, DeMello argues, have been popularized by the middle class and are thus more popular among the middle class, the themes of empowerment common among tattooed women do not fall within such definitive class boundaries. Lower-class women, she notes, have had much more experience using their bodies as a site of resistance (through, for example, clothing and hairstyles) and, similarly, have been getting tattooed for much longer than middle-class women have. Despite this, however, DeMello argues that heavily tattooed women of both classes "can be said to control and subvert the ever-present 'male gaze' by forcing men (and women) to look at their bodies in a manner that exerts control" (173). DeMello even connects this sense of control and empowerment to the tattooed ladies of the 1920s and 1930s circuses and sideshows — in important ways, these women were independent and decided to make a living for themselves. While women today do not get tattooed to earn a living, it can be argued that tattoos on women serve as a sign of independence.

These anti-patriarchal discourses have, indeed, been influenced by dominant middle-class liberatory discourses, and the women (myself included) who see their tattoos as a means of securing an empowering identity connect with and infuse their own tattoo narratives with references to opposing the male gaze. Nevertheless, tattoo narratives, like any discourse, are constantly changing. They are used to "re-create," both for the teller and the listener, the complex justifications for the tattoos — justifications that are constantly changing. As tattooing becomes mainstream, however, many tattooed people's claims that their tattoos are deeply meaningful and spiritual come into question, which, according to DeMello, suggests a class backlash: "The very same middle-class tattooists who were at the forefront of the renaissance now look nostalgically back to the old days of blue-collar values" (191). While Judy may not necessarily subscribe to the "blue-collar values" of earlier tattoo wearers, she recognizes and notes the ways in which the mainstreaming of tattoos has left many, as some would argue, devoid of meaning:

> When I see women with flowers and Chinese characters, they don't know what they're saying. They're White like me and they have Chinese chicken-guy-cue on the back of their neck or on their foot. That really irritates me. They're trying to be cool. They're trying to be something and that's not the way to do it. I don't feel tattooing is the way to make you free and strong and independent. It might be a symbol of that for some people but, just looking at other women, it really depends on the individual tattoo.

Judy interprets the preponderance of tattooing as having a negative effect on the practice as a whole, with symbols and designs permeating the industry and effectively lessening the power of some individual tattoos. The increasing popularity of tattoos creates a whitewashing effect: in order to stand out, one will have to wear increasingly more visible and subversive tattoos. Sara echoed this sentiment:

> It's become such an everyday thing that it really takes something quite extraordinary for me to be like, "Wow, that's cool." Like, if I see a woman who has a whole back piece or something insane, that's rad... Women who aren't tattooed, I look at them and I'm like, "Wow, you're pure."

Sara's comment illustrates the changing discourse around tattooing. While at one time a tattoo can be seen as shocking — to Judy's friends, for example — in another context, tattoos become an "everyday thing" and it is instead those *without* tattoos that become shocking.

While the research on tattoo discourse is indeed helpful in understanding the ways in which the women I spoke with tell their tattoos, much of it falls short in that there is the argument, or often just the assumption, that contemporary tattooing has lost its message or become meaningless outside of the capitalist culture of commodification and consumerism. It is here that I suggest that we need to turn back again to the fluidity of tattoo discourse (as with all discourse) rather than to glorify the easy-to-read tattoos of the days of sailors and bikers. While it has been argued that the traditional, working-class tattoo was characterized as "lacking in sophistication and significance and is worn by people who put very little thought into their tattoos" (DeMello 2000: 193), a number of tattoo artists today are arguing that classic Western tattooing did, in fact, have a simple, recognizable message that has been lost in contemporary fine art tattoo imagery, tattoo trends, and tattoo magazines. DeMello notes:

> The traditional American tattoo — with its easy-to-read imagery that reflected the old-fashioned values of God, mother, and country — is being displaced in favor of the contemporary tattoo, with its often unrecognizable imagery and exotic content. The contemporary tattoo is high fashion, but at the same time alienates those whose tattoos are no longer favored. (2000: 193)

These traditional tattoos are able to tell a story all by themselves while contemporary tattoos often require the wearer to construct a narrative in order to explain them. Given the discussions I had with the tattooed women, I maintain that contemporary tattoos hold

> It is through adapting their tattoo narrative to the historical, social, and cultural context of the moment that contemporary tattoos remain meaningful.

just as much meaning as did the traditional designs. It is through adapting their tattoo narrative to the historical, social, and cultural context of the moment that contemporary tattoos remain meaningful to tattoo wearers through the wearer's lifespan. While traditional designs may have seemed simplistic in their message, I believe that the overarching association with deviance was perhaps the most overt message they delivered. The story they are able to tell all by themselves is one that we have come to understand through a changing discourse. Just as an eagle meant something in the early part of the century, a Chinese character or a flower means something today. After all, not all tattoo wearers construct elaborate stories to connect their tattoos to a larger history. As with Sara, for example, some women find meaning not in the specific tattoo but in its resultant marking, that is, in the experience of being marked as tattooed.

Five Tattooed Women

Karen is a thirty-eight-year-old Mohawk mother of two. She teaches Aboriginal History of Canada and works as a student advisor. She got her first tattoo, a unicorn on her arm, when she was sixteen, and since then has collected five more tattoos, the majority of which hold personal family and cultural significance for her. At nineteen, she had a dragon tattooed on her hip, "just for fun… because dragons are cool," and a small frog and mushroom on her shoulder that she told me she would likely get covered up in the future. Years later she had the unicorn covered with a large tribal piece on her left arm and shoulder that is based on tribal designs from around the world, which is "intended to represent the concept of all [her] relations." On her right arm she has a wolf that was done in honour of her grandfather, who is a member of the wolf clan. On her right leg is a turtle surrounded by Celtic knot work, which she explained is in honour of her parents: "Because my father's turtle clan, because my grandmother's turtle clan, it's matrilineal, and my mom's British so I have the Celtic knot work." Most recently, she's had the confederacy wampum belt tattooed across her back. She had been intending to get this particular tattoo for the past ten years, but the time wasn't right until recently, when she completed her master's degree. "And then when I start my PhD, I'm going to get my status card tattooed on my ass," she said.

When Karen started getting tattooed as a young girl, however, tattooing wasn't the mainstream practice that it is today. "I'm old enough to remember when it was an act of rebellion, not conformity, and that's exactly what it was. I left home at a very young age, so I was a street kid, and it was part of that culture," she said. When I asked her what made her choose her first design, a unicorn, Karen told me about her experience getting that tattoo:

> I was at a big house party at a flop house, because I mean we were all street kids, and there was some guy who had just gotten out of Stoney [Mountain Penitentiary] with his little homemade jail gun and was like, "Hey anybody want a tattoo?" And that was pretty much what he knew how to draw, one of the things he knew how to do. So [I said] "Okay." So that's kind of how I got that one. But, I mean, it's covered up now.

Karen describes her tattoos as an expression of her identity, of her self. For her, tattoos represent both her "ethnic and cultural identity as well as [her] spiritual beliefs." "Your body's a temple," Karen continued. "You've only got it once, you might as well paint the walls, right?" In addition to representing her cultural and spiritual identity, her tattoo projects have all been thought out and planned in consultation with her artist to balance both her body and the art. "All of my tattoos have been thought out," Karen said, "I mean, there's a reason behind them all. They either mark a point in my life or they have some sort of meaning. It's never just sort of 'Oh that looks cool, put it here,' which so many tattoos today are."

Sara is twenty-six years old and a recent graduate from a community college communications program. She has three tattoos, the first of which, a line drawing of a woman that would eventually become a part of Salvador Dali's painting "The Burning Giraffe," was a gift from her parents for her twenty-first birthday. Six months after her first tattoo, she had a piece done on her calf — a collection of images from one of her favourite books, Clive Barker's *The Thief of Always*, that represent key ideas that the book portrays. "It's a tree with a tree house in it and its got a kite and the tree house has a ladder doing down and then there's a fish coming up on the bottom; it's all just different parts from the book," said Sara. A short while later, Sara had three large peonies, her favorite flower, tattooed on her right arm.

Unlike many women that I talked to, Sara doesn't associate any deep, personal significance with her tattoos: "I didn't get them because I had gone through some horrible trauma, and I didn't get them because I wanted to make a particular statement." Sara explained to me that she got her tattoos for aesthetic reasons — "because I like them" — rather than to cover a particular body part or relay a particular message to others through her choice of design. Sara explained that she does not immediately identify as a "tattooed person" and chooses not to show them off. What is important to her, however, is that her tattoos are unique, not easily defined and not something you would see on either the wall of a tattoo shop or the arm of another tattoo enthusiast. She takes pride in her tattoos, even though, as she explained, some think of them as "weird."

Kendra e-mailed her responses to my questions, as she is currently living and teaching English in Thailand. A twenty-three-year-old, Kendra had the Chinese characters for "true love" tattooed on her left calf seven years ago, at seventeen. She chose this design because, as she explained, true love is something she believes in and aspires to. After spending some time in Paris, France, the "city of romance," ideas of love were floating around in her head: "True love represented the hope I had (and still have) for the future. I decided on Chinese because my best friend is Chinese Canadian and I always thought the language looked beautiful." Kendra's tattoo makes her feel special and hopeful, and it serves as a reminder for her never to "settle." She sees her tattoo as a legacy, a means of self-expression, "like holding the answers to a secret."

Kendra told me that once she was tattooed, she felt older, if at times a bit "cliché" given the popularity of Chinese characters as a tattoo design. At one time shy about her body, Kendra started wearing clothing in an attempt to show off her tattoo, and is now really happy with her choice of location, as it is a place on her body that won't change as she ages: "At least it won't get saggy and gross like if it was on my boob or my tummy."

Kendra was initially worried about the pain and the ability to cover the tattoo, as once she is finished with her time in Thailand she will be working as a teacher in Manitoba, where there are strict guidelines concerning the visibility of body modifications. She explains, "When I was in university and student teaching I heard a principal say he would 'never hire anyone with a visible tattoo.' Funny thing was the grade 1, 2, 5, and 6 teachers all had tattoos. Guess they never told him. I stuck to wearing pants."

Katie is a twenty-eight-year-old graduate student of theology. She has two tattoos, both of which were completed within the last year and a half: one is a simple, open concept line drawing of a dove on her left shoulder; the other is a large "vine with Greek text as the trunk" starting at her foot and ending about five inches above her knee. The text is "Koine Greek, which is what the New Testament was written in, and it's a Bible passage, and it translates into 'Lord I believe help my unbelief.'" Raised Mennonite and having worked as a youth pastor for four years, Katie's faith has been and still is a large part of her identity. As well, the image of peace that she has tattooed on her left shoulder is something she feels constitutes her self. While Katie is proud of her faith, she told me that people react to her differently once they find out that her leg piece holds religious connotations:

> That's probably one thing that makes me uncomfortable with my leg piece, is when people ask what the text means, all of a sudden they find out that I'm a person of faith, and they react to me differently. I don't want people to feel like I'm trying to evangelize to them because I've got this, it's my faith and it's my faith struggle and my faith journey. That's why I got it. It had nothing to do about wanting the world to know.

Despite some of the negative reactions to her tattoos that she gets from people, Katie finds the fun in it as well: "In the back of my mind I have a couple of joking translations that I would give people because who the hell's going to understand Greek? Like, if I'm out at a bar and some person is like, 'Hey what's that mean?' [I'll say] 'Look but don't touch' or 'It's all Greek to you.'"

Once she had the piece on her leg done, Katie realized she was "that girl with the huge-ass tattoo on her leg." But she doesn't mind the attention. Alternative culture has always appealed to her, so she felt that it made sense for her to have such a visible tattoo. While being so visibly tattooed noticeably changes the interactions she has with people, Katie isn't ashamed of her artwork, but rather sees her body now as more of a potential canvas for future projects.

Lynda is fifty-four years old and has two sons, aged thirteen and twenty-nine. She got her first tattoo for her fiftieth birthday, and her eldest son went along and got one too. The tattoo, a small purple lily on her chest just under her collarbone, symbolizes a number of things for Lynda: lilies are a symbol of rebirth, which correlates to her entering a new stage in her life and celebrating moving forward; she chose purple as it is one of the highest energy centres for chakras; and purple is also a colour associated with royalty, as she explained that "anyone who knows me knows that I kind of like to be the Queen of Everything." Lynda had also given considerable thought to the placement of her tattoo. It was located on a part of her body that wouldn't change much over time and could be easily covered, and because the location was easily visible to her, the tattoo acts as a reminder that this is a good stage in her life. She researched tattoo studios in Winnipeg with her eldest son, who had already been tattooed and was quite encouraging of her decision to be tattooed, for about two to three years before she had it done. Lynda first spoke with an artist at one studio with whom she did not feel comfortable before finally finding a place that felt right.

Lynda explained to me that fifteen years ago she thought of tattooing as a strange practice, but now she finds happiness in having this pretty piece of art permanently on her skin. While she told me that she has always had issues with her body image, Lynda said that her tattoo has changed how she sees herself. "Finally having something that is quite pretty that I chose leaves me more open to accepting [my body] because it's the part of me that's always going to be beautiful," she said. Being tattooed later in life has made an impact on her self-identity as well:

> I think it did make a difference because reaching your 50s is a difficult age, I think as women we all have those goddess archetypes in us and I know my Aphrodite had been submerged for many years and it was like a coming out, and I mean, it's very simple, it's just a little tattoo, but it really is quite powerful.

Additionally, because her generation has not subscribed to tattooing in the same way that younger generations have embraced it, she enjoys the "shock impact" when people see that she is tattooed. Working with a number of people who are younger than her, she said, "I'm the age of their mothers and their mothers aren't getting tattooed, so that obviously sort of switches things around for them, and somehow this tattoo takes a few years off, makes me more contemporary maybe?" In this regard, she has fun with her tattoo — keeping it covered most of the time at work, as it is still something that is personal for her, but showing it off in particular settings or when the topic comes up in conversation. "People don't know what to do with it sometimes, so I just have fun with it, it's just fun!"

These women use tattoo narratives to make connections to a number of things: for Karen, her tattoos connect her to her cultural heritage and to a past in which tattooing was considered an overt form of rebellion; for Sara, tattoos serve as a means of marking her as different; Kendra's tattoo connects her to culturally important notions like friendship and love; for Katie, her tattoo is a connection and reminder to her struggles with her faith; and for Lynda, her tattoo connects her with a sense of identity. However, the connections made are done so in the context of a capitalist and patriarchal culture.

Tattoos Commodified

While these five women all have different reasons for being tattooed, and approach tattooing in different ways, they share the fact that they have become a part of a culture that is growing like wildfire. Tattooing has moved from the sphere of the rebellious and into the mainstream over the past few decades, helped in part by its use in advertising campaigns (7-Eleven's "Inked" energy drink, for example) or television programming, such as *Miami Ink* and *LA Ink*. Tattoos have saturated our culture to the point where they no longer garner the immediate shock and attention that they did many years ago. In some important ways, tattoos have become normalized.

This normalization of tattooing was not lost on the women I interviewed. During our conversations many of the women said they regard tattoos in much the same way they do any other element of fashion. As Breccan, twenty-seven, told me: "It's like permanently wearing a very flashy skirt or something." Katie said that she doesn't particularly feel a bond with other tattooed women, as it has become such a popular form of body modification, "it would be the same as walking down the street and seeing someone dressed in the same style that you dress." Karen associates her tattoos with fashion as well, in the sense that they are an extension of her personality, "like wearing fancy shoes or a really nice dress or something like that, except it's permanent."

Some of the women I spoke with commented that today there are so many people with tattoos, piercings, and other body modifications that it is those who are "pure" — those who are without any modifications — that may be the true rebels. That is, they see tattoos as having become "trendy." Sara noted that as tattoos have become so much a part of our culture now, when you see someone who doesn't have a tattoo, "they're almost prevailing more, and they're almost like the anti- or counter-culture now."

So, knowing and given this (commodified) context in which the practice of tattooing is presently situated, is that all there is to the story? Do women simply see tattoos as fashion or do they see them more as a struggle to incorporate resistance, to invest their tattoos with some political context and meaning? The women I spoke with understand that tattoos have become commodified, rendered "normal" and fashionable, but how do they negotiate this? Given the context in which tattooing has become normalized, what, in spite of this process, makes them different? There are a number of ways in which the women I interviewed negotiate this tension between the conformity associated with tattooing, given its mainstream popularity in Western culture, and their efforts to resist that commodification in the endeavour to construct an authentic sense of self.

Reconciling Trendiness/Maintaining Authenticity

> I don't think I would relate to somebody who had a massive tribal tattoo on their arm just for the sake of getting one. I think that's, I think that's part of the big issue is just, like, getting one just to say you have one. (Amber, twenty-one, five tattoos)

As I mentioned at the outset, authenticity is a theme and term that is used in a variety of ways. For the women, authenticity can be an expression of long-term commitment, uniqueness, and individuality, as well as a partial reaction to trendiness and fashionability, as Amber alludes to in the quote above. In speaking with each woman, I came to understand how she defined authenticity — overtly or otherwise — and her desire to make connections that are constantly shifting, or to locate herself in a larger historical context. The nuances of what it means to be authentic and how one can connect in a legitimate way through her tattoos ultimately highlighted for me that appropriation is complex and certainly not a linear process. The nuances represented by the women's understandings of their tattoos also put DeMello's argument in a new and more complicated light.

The women I spoke with have agency — they aren't, like all of us, empty vessels into which mainstream (and shifting) culture is simply poured. While they are aware that tattooing has become a trend, they are constantly both reconstructing and relocating themselves within this process of mainstreaming, of trendiness. Reconciling the desire to express themselves on their own terms and the desire to be regarded as authentic is not an easy task. Karlie, a twenty-two-year-old insurance claims adjuster with three tattoos, reflected this point:

> Well, I think there's a lot of people who, you know, critique tattoos, think that every tattoo has to be very personal, have huge deep meanings, and it can't be like, funny or whatever. But as much as I do agree with them in some sense, that your tattoos should mean something, they don't always have to be serious. That's just me. I plan on getting some ridiculous tattoos, but other people would look at those and be like "Well why the hell did you get that? That's absolutely ridiculous." But, I don't know, I think some people take it a little bit too seriously, and sometimes I'm completely guilty of that. Even though I'm getting them, I'm judging people for them. But a lot of people just take it really seriously and they don't always need to. But on the flip side, some people don't take it seriously enough and get little fluffy unicorns on their lower back.

Karlie's comments illustrate the complexity of issues that tattooed women are faced with in their decision to get tattooed. Rejecting the need for a personal story to contextualize a tattoo design, which in its mainstream popularity has become a sign of *in*authenticity to some tattooed women, can lead to the opposite: choosing a tattoo design that is devoid of meaning, which Karlie suggests is similarly inauthentic. The women I spoke with have recognized this difficult binary; yet, they have found ways in which to work around it and justify for themselves the legitimacy of their tatto projects.

Karen, thirty-eight, has tattoos that are all strongly connected to her family and spiritual identity. Although, when she started getting tattooed in the late 1980s and early 1990s, tattooing was a means of rebellion for her:

> Well, I guess there was always a push [for me] to be unique and different. I was never mainstream. You know, I was never one with the crowd and it was just one way of making myself distinct and making myself unique, right? I don't fit in and that's totally cool. So it's just another way of expressing that, really.

Karen has also witnessed the change in the industry itself, along with the public perception of tattooing:

> Back in the day it was illegal, right? We just did it out the kitchen, right? I mean, like, I'm old enough to remember when getting tattoos were an act of rebellion as opposed to conformity. Which is really what all mine are, um, and, I mean, back in my day people would cross the street to avoid you if you had piercings and tattoos and looked like a punk rocker, with purple hair, right? And they did, people would look at me like "Holy shit, you're a freak." Now people don't even blink twice, it's become mainstream. So yeah, some of my earliest tattoos were work done in the kitchen, with home made guns and things like that, the jail house style, because, I mean, you really didn't have much of a choice back in the 80s.

Despite the development of the industry into a mainstream practice, Karen locates herself as someone who remains committed to tattooing's rebellious roots. She doesn't see herself as subscribing to trends. Rather, given her own lengthy history with the practice, tattooing constitutes for her an act of rebellion *and* a means of adornment — no matter how much more difficult it may be to define tattooing as rebellious in today's culture.

For Sara, the uniqueness of her tattoos serves as means of separating herself from the mainstream. She explained, "I never felt the need to be like, 'Oh I think I'm so boring-looking that I need to go do this or that,' because I think everybody fits in their own niche. But I think my tattoos just sort of set me apart a little bit more." When she made the decision to get tattooed, Sara knew she wanted to get something that was a little different: "I didn't want to just go down and pick out from all the artist flash…. I didn't want to get something that everybody else would have." In this way, Sara locates herself outside of the trendiness and the mainstream because her tattoo projects are not easily defined and not something typically found on the walls of a tattoo studio. She explains her "unusual" tattoos:

> I guess you have to kind of really look at it and sort of figure out and discern what everything is…. So, I think that they make a statement that I've chosen to do something to myself to sort of differentiate myself from the masses. But in the same breath, I don't want it to seem like I felt that I was some ordinary plain Jane to begin with.

Despite her tattoos setting her apart from the mainstream, Sara recognizes that the practice is still very much "an everyday thing," but she doesn't get wrapped up in the popularity and hype of the practice: "People make a much bigger deal out of it than I ever made out of getting them, and, like, honestly sometimes I forget I have them." This suggests that, while her tattoos serve as a connection to a counter-cultural practice that is seen as somewhat deviant, Sara has chosen to reject the claims to celebrated, definitive individuality that has propelled the practice into the mainstream to begin with. It is clear that, in these terms, authenticity is a complex phenomenon.

Additionally, the women find their own meaning and context within the practice by connecting it with events in their lives, honouring their family members, or honouring their faith. For Lynda, the decision to become tattooed wasn't one that was tied up in her subscription to a new trend. In fact, she admitted that in the past she found the practice strange. Instead, she sees tattooing as a permanent way to celebrate herself — as a rite of passage in turning fifty. She explained, "Well a lily is a symbol of rebirth, and I was very excited about getting it to symbolize entering a new stage in my life, becoming a crone, that whole moving forward celebration." She also expressed her understanding of tattooing as a new art form for women to explore:

> I think mostly men had owned the art, or the realm, and I think it's our new art form. Maybe we've pushed the limits more, because I don't think anyone's really encouraged us, women, to get tattooed. But I think it could have to do with it being a safe way for women to express themselves, because you can do it but not be in somebody's face about it. You don't have to talk about it, it's just a statement.

Katie sees her tattoos as a part of her identity. Her faith is a large part of her identity, and her tattoos reflect that. For her, tattooing is not about participating in a trend, but rather is about her struggle with her own faith: her leg piece reads, "Lord I believe help my unbelief." In her words:

> That's the story of my faith. I've spent a lot of years not believing and a lot of years believing but still being uncomfortable with believing. I've been a minister, I was a youth pastor for four years, full time. It was really hard. I mean this, it comes from the book of Mark, and I'm not really one of those people to sit around and quote Bible passages, but this one just stuck with me because it takes faith to say "Lord I believe help my unbelief." It really leaves room for questions and doubts and insecurities about it and all that kind of stuff.

It is also evident that the women are not all getting tattooed for the same reason; they have very different, and often very personal, reasons for getting a tattoo. What is similar among the women, however, is the personal narrative that each constructs by way of explaining her tattoos. These narratives, like other cultural discourses, are expressed in similar, learned terms. Kendra, for example, attaches a great deal of personal meaning to her calf tattoo — the notion of "true love" is something that holds a lot of significance for her in her life. She explains:

> True love is something that I believe in. True love meaning the ultimate love — something that is real, romantic, unique, extraordinary, beautiful, passionate, and life long. I got the tattoo when I was quite young and I saw true love in everything. I was really hopeful about love despite never having been in a relationship at that point. I saw relationships in movies, on television, in magazines, and in school. The concept of true love was always floating around in my head. What sealed the deal was when Pacey on Dawson's Creek named his boat 'True Love' in an episode. I could see true love everywhere and knew that it had a strong meaning for me. I wanted something as special as that in my life, I believed in it.

This idea of love is one that is learned through dominant discourse — television shows, for example — and Kendra's tattoo, as it connects her to the idea of true love, suggests an expression of emotional value. Tattoos, in this regard, can connect us with learned cultural values. For Kendra, being tattooed was a way of expressing her desire for true love and having a tattoo feels like "a legacy." Her tattoo provides her with a message of hope:

> Sometimes women settle, and I wanted my tattoo to remind me to never settle. I have seen love fall apart and I have seen people fool themselves into thinking they are in love. True love is the ultimate experience in love and something that I hope to experience in my life. I think I am on my way. In fact, I know I am.

While Kendra acknowledges the "cliché" of having Chinese characters tattooed on her, she maintains her claim to authenticity — her justification for the originality of her tattoo — as she was the first of her friends, and the first of many of her classmates, to be tattooed:

> It made me feel special to have something with so much personal meaning in it. I also felt a little cliché at times. Chinese characters aren't exactly unique. I got a lot of attention for being the first kid in my class to have a tattoo. Soon after, two of my friends got one.

They both got lower back tattoos and both regretted their decisions afterwards. They didn't spend a lot of time thinking about their designs. One decided in two weeks, the other in one week. But as for me, I was really proud of my tattoo and thought it was special. It made me feel special and hopeful to have the message on me.

In this way, authenticity can take on several meanings — in Kendra's case, being the first of her classmates and friends to be tattooed lent her tattoo (which she acknowledged as "cliché") a sense of legitimacy in its originality. The meaning of her tattoo has shifted, as she implied, as the design she chose has become quite popular — at once new and original, the symbol of the Chinese character is familiar. For Kendra, the meaning of her tattoo remains a permanent reminder of her hope for true love being a part of her life. In this regard, tattoos are somewhat paradoxical, as they are about permanence, but at the same time their meanings shift and change.

In the same way that the reasons for getting tattooed vary from woman to woman, the importance placed on tattoo projects by the women shifts over time, suggesting that significance is a fluid concept. Jenn, a twenty-eight-year-old legal assistant who sports a large tribal back piece in addition to a group tattoo that she had done with her sisters, explained to me that tattooing has become less of a priority as she's grown older:

> Yes, the years I was getting my back done, it seemed like the most important thing to do. But now with a mortgage and trying to start a family it's not really something I think about. I mean, it's there and it's part of me but it's not something I think about every day — it doesn't define me anymore.

Interestingly, some of the women reject the need to attach personal significance to their tattoos, thereby resisting the self-help discourse that locates tattooing as a means of personal growth. For instance, Sara was aware that some women were motivated to get tattooed as a way of coping with difficult life experiences: "I think it's great, you know, if somebody who's had some horrible trauma done to them and then they need, this is something that they need to do to heal themselves, then right on." But this was not Sara's motivation. April, twenty-seven, who has a chrysanthemum tattooed on the side of her torso made this point more directly:

> I don't personally think that everyone does it to make a statement, because, like mine, a lot of people ask me if there's any meaning behind it, and I'm like "No not really".... It shouldn't have to mean anything. If you want there to be a meaning behind it, look up the actual meaning of it, like the phoenix rising out of the fire, or the particular type of flower. Like, there's always going to be a meaning behind something. If it's personal, for personal taste, then that's your meaning. Like, the meaning is who you are and why you have it on you.

"Well I'll just find a meaning for tattoos after I get them. Meanings of tattoos will always change too."

Similarly, Ryse, a twenty-one-year-old woman with five tattoos, told me that her notion of meaning is not static, but rather always changing: "Well I'll just find a meaning for tattoos after I get them. Meanings of tattoos will always change too."

Commodification or Resistance?

With the new generation of tattoo enthusiasts comes a new text through which tattooing is understood — a new history, focusing on the Japanese or Polynesian roots of tattooing, effectively distances middle-class tattoo wearers from Western tattooing's low-class, marginalized roots. In order to market tattooing as a safe, acceptable commodity by which to mark your individuality or identity, capitalist culture has framed the practice in terms of its ability to aid in personal growth, as a rite of passage, or marker of strength similar to the uses of tattooing among tribal cultures.

DeMello's theory helps to make sense of the ways in which tattoo discourse has changed over the years and the nuanced and often complex ways in which tattooing is interpreted and perceived by contemporary enthusiasts. Indeed, the women I spoke with echoed the complexity of issues that arise with the decision to become tattooed and the motivations for becoming tattooed. The ways in which these women understand and talk about the meanings of their tattoos, necessarily shaped and informed by the discourse of tattooing that permeates the current social climate, reflect DeMello's argument. Personal significance and authenticity play large roles in the ways in which these women construct their tattoo projects, and the fluidity of meaning and authenticity then necessarily affects the ways in which tattoos are perceived and discussed. Their construction of tattoo narratives to tell the story of their tattoos were ways that these women could make connections with, rather than, as DeMello argues, appropriate, a larger history.

> Their construction of tattoo narratives to tell the story of their tattoos were ways that these women could make connections with, rather than appropriate, a larger history.

Additionally, it is in the message relayed by the women where the argument accepting commodification is countered. Rather than see contemporary fine art tattoos as unrecognizable and exotic, the women find meaning in their tattoos through their adaptation to the changing nature of tattoo discourse. It is through their tattoo narratives that their tattoos resist conformity and remain authentic — be that original, legitimate, or sincere, long-term commitments to the culture of tattooing — *despite* its commodification. This would suggest, more broadly speaking, that the commodification of cultural artifacts does not necessarily strip them of their political content. While cultural commodification, or "eating the Other," is a mechanism in consumerist capitalism by which the culture of marginalized people can be and is appropriated and repackaged to be sold to the mainstream — what would appear to be the process of stripping those aspects of their meaningful, non-consumption, non-market content — the political content does not, it seems, disappear entirely. While capitalist culture often neglects human rights and human-ness in the interests of marketing goods that are seen as having no meaning other than profit, rendering them devoid of real human meaning, it would appear the commodification of tattoos is not complete. It is true that tattoos have now become a means of selling products: blockbuster films often use tattoos

> While capitalist culture often neglects human-ness in the interests of profit... commodification is not complete.

as a way to distinguish rebellious or edgy characters, more and more popular musicians of all genres are tattooed, and ad campaigns use tattoos to sell anything from energy drinks to credit cards (see Kosut 2006). They have gone from being a sign of deviance to a form of body modification that is acceptable by the mainstream. The difference, however, is that the tattoo is one product that cannot be bought without being intimately linked to its actual production. As Mary Kosut notes:

> As a tattooed person, you are the witness, participant, and life-long bearer of a unique production process; a process in which the producer and consumer unite in complicated exchange that is simultaneously ritualistic, economic/consumeristic, and individualistic. (2006: 1041)

Along with the actual process of getting a tattoo, the women I spoke with were able to find meaning, meaning that often shifted over time and adapted to their lives and identities, while recognizing the commodified and gendered nature of their tattoos. People want and need meaning in their lives, meaning deeper than fashion and consumersim — that is what underlies the narratives the women attached to their tattoos. Oppressive institutions like capitalism and patriarchy can be and are resisted on a number of levels. In the case of tattooing, the women I spoke with were able to access aspects of tattooing's past — despite its commodification — to find meaning and value.

Glossary of Key Terms

Appropriation: Appropriation refers to the ways in which cultural practices, often those of marginalized classes or peoples, are claimed by dominant society and re-purposed for their own use. An example would be the ways in which Eastern tattooing practices were claimed and re-purposed by Western society in an attempt to legitimate tattooing for mainstream society.

Authenticity: Authenticity refers to the desire to create a legitimate, original self-identity through tattoo projects in the face of the commodified and gendered nature of tattoos; a sincere, long-term commitment to a tattoo; and the sense of uniqueness that comes from being marked as different.

Commodification: Commodification is the inherent process in capitalism to extend the market into ever more areas of human life, rendering all things, including humans themselves, meaningful only as products to buy, sell, and consume as a means to making profit.

Cultural commodification: bell hooks, for example, refers to cultural commodification as "eating the Other." Cultural commodification is the practice in capitalism within which a particular cultural aspect, often of a marginalized group, is appropriated, stripped it of its original meaning, and repackaged for the consumption of mainstream society.

Identity: Identity refers to a person's sense of self, those aspects that distinguish a person from those around him or her.

Old school tattoos/tattoo designs: Images made popular with the introduction of tattooing to Western culture by sailors are referred to as old school tattoos/tattoo designs. These images — such as flags, ships, knives, snakes, panthers, roses and erotic images of women and mermaids — invoked patriotism and masculinity.

Other: Othering refers to the way in which those not a part of the dominant class, race, or gender are (mis)represented and (mis)treated by mainstream society. Marginalized classes are seen as different and inferior and treated as such. Othering is an expression of power by the dominant over the marginalized.

Questions for Discussion

1. What are some cultural artifacts, other than tattooing, that have been appropriated by Western society?

2. What kinds of problems can arise when subcultures are commodified? What benefits are there?

3. What are your own impressions of the practice of tattooing? What do you think of someone when you see that they are tattooed?

4. Were you surprised at all by the ways in which the women talked about their own tattoos?

5. How does the way in which the women in this chapter interpret their own tattoos and resist conformity reflect on the ways in which everyday people can resist capitalism and patriarchy?

Websites of Interest

Tattoo Artist Magazine
Sailor Jerry Tattoos <sailorjerry.com/tattoos/>
Body Modification Ezine
Margot Mifflin

References

Associated Press/CBS News. 2007. "Tattoos Lose Their Cool: Want a Blasting Berry Tattoo with That Fruit Roll-Up?" December 4. <cbsnews.com/stories/2007/12/04/entertainment/main3573970.shtml>.

Atkinson, M. 2002. "Pretty in Ink: Conformity, Resistance, and Negotiation in Women's Tattooing." *Sex Roles* 47.

Barlow, Maude. 2001. *Blue Gold: The Global Water Crisis and the Commodification of the World's Water Supply*. Revised edition. Ottawa: Council of Canadians. <canadians.org/water/publications/Blue_Gold.html>.

Boldizar, Alexandar. 2008. "Handbags of the Apocalypse." *Asian Contemporary Arts and Culture*. <cartsmag.com/articles/detail.php?Title=Handbags%20of%20the%20Apocalypse&ID_Comment=29>.

Braunberger, C. 2000. "Revolting Bodies: The Monster Beauty of Tattooed Women." NWSA *Journal* 12, 2.

Butler, Judith. 1999. *Gender Trouble: Feminism and the Subversion of Identity*. New York: Routledge.

Caplan, J. 2000. "Introduction." In J. Caplan (ed.), *Written on the Body: The Tattoo in European and American History*. London, UK: Reaktion Books.

CBC. 2004. "Body Art: The Story Behind Tattooing and Piercing in Canada." CBC *News Indepth* <cbc. ca/news/background/tattoo/>.

DeMello, M. 1995. "Not Just For Bikers Anymore: Popular Representations of American Tattooing." *Journal of Popular Culture* 29, 3.

_____. 2000. *Bodies of Inscription: A Cultural History of the Modern*, Durham & London: Duke University Press.

Govenar, A. 2000. "The Changing Image of Tattooing in American Culture, 1846–1966." In J. Caplan (ed.), *Written on the Body: The Tattoo in European and American History*. London, UK: Reaktion Books.

Grosz, Elizabeth. 1994. *Volatile Bodies: Toward a Corporeal Feminism*. Indiana: Indiana University Press.

Hawkes, D., C.Y. Senn, and C. Thorn. 2004. "Factors That Influence Attitudes Toward Women with Tattoos." *Sex Roles* 50.

Health Canada. 2001. "Special Report on Youth, Piercing, Tattooing and Hepatitis C: Trendscan Findings." < phac-aspc.gc.ca/hepc/pubs/youthpt-jeunessept/>.

hooks, bell. 1992. *Black Looks: Race and Representation*. Cambridge, MA: South End Press.

Kosut, M. 2006. "An Ironic Fad: The Commodification and Consumption of Tattoos." *Journal of Popular Culture* 39, 6.

Marx, Karl, and Friedrich Engels. *The Communist Manifesto*. Halifax: Fernwood Publishing.

Marxists.org. n.d. "Encyclopedia of Marxism: Commodification." <marxists.org/glossary/terms/c/o. htm#commodification>.

Mifflin, M. 2001. *Bodies of Subversion: A Secret History of Women and Tattoo*. New York: Juno Books.

MSNBC. 2007. "Tattoo Ads Turn People into 'Walking Billboards.'" November 26. <msnbc.msn. com/id/21979076/ns/business-us_business/t/tattoo-ads-turn-people-walking-billboards/#. Tr7WmPFZQZc>.

Oetterman, S. 2000. "On Display: Tattooed Entertainers in America and Germany." In J. Caplan (ed.), *Written on the Body: The Tattoo in European and American History*. London, UK: Reaktion Books.

Torgovnick, M. 1991. *Gone Primitive: Savage Intellects, Modern Lives*. Chicago: University of Chicago Press.

Widdicombe, S., and R. Wooffitt. 1995. *The Language of Youth Subcultures: Social Identity in Action*. New York: Prentice Hall.

11

It Begins With Food
Food as Inspiration and Imperative for Social Change

Sally Miller

YOU SHOULD KNOW THIS

- One billion people in the world are hungry, while one billion are now obese.
- In Canada, farmers receive the same prices, not adjusted for inflation, that they received in the 1970s.
- Around 15 percent of Canadians live with food insecurity (not knowing if they will have enough food to eat).
- 17 percent of people accessing food banks in Canada have jobs; 38 percent of them are children.
- Between 1993 and 2006, around 150,000 farmers in India have committed suicide by drinking the pesticides that drove them into debt.
- In 2007, the Food and Agriculture Association (a well-known international food security organization) reported that there was enough food harvested that year to feed the world 1.5 times over.
- There are more prisoners in the U.S. now than full-time farmers.
- Over the last twenty-five years, 100 percent of Canadian farmers' net income came from farm support programs, off-farm income and loans.
- In B.C. alone, it is estimated that emissions from the consumed food totals six million tonnes of carbon dioxide equivalent.

Sources: Holt-Gimenez and Patel 2009; Food Banks Canada 2010; Lee et al. 2010; NFU 2010; Qualman and Tait 2004; Rideout et al. 2007.

IN ALL SOCIAL ACTION, FROM BUYING LUNCH TO MARCHING in a rally, we shape, explore, and take moral positions that define our actions. This cultural process occurs through the narratives we tell about our experience, the understanding we create and work out together in dialogue with other cultural actors. Nowhere is this more dramatic and urgent than in our words about food. Food, along with shelter, is essential to our survival, but is also the stage for us to discuss and work out our relations with others, from our favourite childhood meals to the choice of snack between classes.

Food is an idiom for social expression, most recently as a vivid stage for the concentration of power and wealth in the hands of a few. The food system has become the focus of intensive corporate concentration, economic power, and the systematic dismantling of community and democratic ownership over food and agriculture. Like all works of culture, this has proceeded through the stories we tell about it — from the corporations that claim their seed will feed the world to the thousands of activists working together to save local and peasant agricultures. As cultural actors and activists, we choose which stories to highlight and act upon. How did we come to shape and consent to a world in which so many people are hungry and have lost access to land to feed themselves? How do we shape and confirm new ways for eating, distributing, and growing food? This chapter explores the current state of the food system, the ways in which it is failing people everywhere, including in Canada, and the movements for resistance and change that can take us beyond the current food crisis.

The Complexities of Food

Food has been the flashpoint of resistance and the tinder for the fire of change around the world for many decades. Food and agriculture are also the site of an unprecedented concentration of power. This has spectacular conjunctions of our inhumanity towards others with the systematic dismantling of democracy and equity structures, and the development of economic mechanisms devoted to profit and the consolidation of power. This tragic conjunction of circumstances is rapidly draining the earth of resources and resilience. One billion of us go to bed hungry; one billion of us are obese — as profits shift unevenly towards the powerful, so too do the calories.

There is enough to feed the world, and has been for many decades; the Food and Agriculture Organization calculates that in 2007 there was one-and-a-half times the food needed to feed everyone sufficiently (Holt-Gimenez and Patel 2009: 7). The problem is not with yield, but with distribution and poverty. These are issues of power, not crop failure. More recently, rampant speculation with food commodities and the growing competition between grain for food and grain for fuel have exacerbated the situation. However, as Davis (2002) has pointed out, famine and starvation are a result of human systems responding to climate variation. As wealth becomes concentrated in the hands of a few people and transnational corporations (TNCs) like Cargill, Dupont, and McDonald's, the number of have-nots increases. Those with sufficient money can buy whatever food they want, including exotic items like coffee that has been squeezed through the gut of an Indonesian civet, blowfish sushi that contains a neurotoxin that may stimulate your senses or kill you, gourmet chocolates with rare salts and organic ingredients, deep sea fish that have never seen the light of day before. Those without money starve or suffer from chronic malnutrition and food insecurity leading to death.

The Moral Economies of Food

A food system based on conventional economic principles assumes that price is determined in a negotiation between supply and demand, which will always leave some people out; for widgets this is fine, you can have too many widgets, but for food, if you are one of the unlucky ones who can't afford the price, you go hungry. In the parlance of neoclassical economics, this group is called those "not willing to pay," as if it is our own choice to go hungry or watch our children starve. This fantasy removes the need for compassion from food economics. It is key to the shift that has had to take place in the cultures of food, and that must be reinforced over and over again by the way corporations and governments talk about food.

We all have a great deal to say about food; opinions, knowledge, exclamations, and concerns burble out of us like fast-running water in a brook. The dynamic cultures of food, which bring us together, link us to previous generations, comfort us, and cause us anxiety, also determine the place of food in resistance and social change. Most people are diffident about discussing economic issues — our wages, or the difficulties we have making car payments. In North America, poverty is con-

> Talking about food gives us a way to change our economies of food.

sidered an individual shame. Systemic concerns are nebulous in our stories about poverty. The latter tend to focus on individual effort and failure. We are more ready to discuss food issues — even those struggling with food insecurity can talk about their favourite meals, the best places to get deals, their food memories from childhood. Talking about food gives us a way to change our economies of food.

Food and Resistance

Resistance to the global food system is greatly facilitated by the fact that food plays such an important role in our social expression. Food provides a means of expression, reflection, and rumination over the supreme moment of capitalism that we have reached. The choice of food to address a global breakdown in economic and social equity is not neutral; food and agriculture hold central and defining positions in movements for alternatives (Patel and McMichael 2009; see also Goodman and Watts 1997: 7). Since the key to understanding and changing our world can be found in the narratives we use to assert, confirm, and create our version of the world and our experience in it, food and narratives about it represent an ideal starting point to think about a better world.

The reasons why food provides an ideal starting point for social change are complex: they include the relation of food and agriculture to a culture's identity as well as to the imperatives of survival. Holt-Gimenez and Patel link this, as many others do, to identity (2009: 182): "control over one's food is essential to control over oneself." Manning writes (2004: 163), "Food tells a people's collective story in the same way that the molecules we eat assemble the body." Food can be a powerful force for change, but change in action, culture, and behaviour necessarily is ignited from and invites changes in the stories we tell about ourselves.

The Power of Narrative

Narratives, whether of food, war, or fairies, are not created equal. To change the identities and lives we create through food, we must address the uneven distribution of power, status, and wealth, which have ensured that some stories are more heard, believed, and acted on than others. Just as we are not making objective decisions in the false plenty of a supermarket, we are also facing a panoply of narratives of unequal rhetorical and political power. The failure to persuade or to become dominant is rarely intimately connected to truthfulness; it has more to do with the culture and power embodied and embedded in the story. Statistical reports of hunger (over three million in Canada, 12 percent of the U.S. population living with food insecurity, 982 million hungry people in the world) seem more apt to be taken seriously than dramatic and enraged pleas. The register of numbers and science-derived facts has a higher status than tones of anger and outrage.

How we recognize or define truth ensures that we have a cultural standard for narrative: reports told with anger and passion have less chance of persuasion, at least among the powerful, than ones told without emotion. But shouldn't we be angry about so many hungry people on our doorsteps? Perhaps we should be more concerned about people who seem unmoved by the atrocities in the food system — is it really possible to speak without emotion about the 150,000 farmers in India that have committed suicide since 1993 by drinking the pesticides that drove them into debt (Holt-Gimenez and Patel 2009: 32)? To be able to talk about these things without rage seems a little pathological. The credibility of a tale is also influenced by the teller's class and political status (often measured and reflected in precisely the scientific vocabulary and accent of one's speech): the higher the class position of the speaker the greater the credibility of their tale.

The unequal power of narratives, rhetoric and speakers creates a sense of inevitability or naturalness about narratives that are, after all, only one more way of looking at the world. This can become very dangerous, as we abide by, and shape our decisions around a narrative that has become the commonly believed context, and therefore no longer questionable. For instance, the failure of neoclassical economic solutions has become resoundingly clear. The international organizations like the World Bank, World Trade Organization (WTO), and International Monetary Fund (IMF) have recommended and enforced patterns of structural adjustment for developing countries. These prescriptions require countries to reduce their social safety nets and introduce survival necessities like food, water and land to the commodity market in order to receive the loans they need. These requirements have led to increasing hunger, lack of social protections for people who fall ill or lose their jobs, and nightmare scenarios, such as the situation in Bolivia when the privatization by Bechtel Corporation of the public water led to riots. Protesters were murdered in the streets as they demanded access to water to live.

The globally powerful offer solutions that are more of the same: strengthen the global institutions that oversee agriculture (like the WTO) and create even freer markets and more reduced safety nets in developing countries. This persistence in the face of unavoidable evidence is the result, not of science that is constantly available for re-evaluation, but of a deeply held religious and cultural faith.

The Globalization of Food

The question of Canada's miserable failure as a wealthy country to address the needs of many residents cannot be understood outside the context of the globalization of food. Like many other countries, Canada has been negatively affected by the increasing profit-taking of transnational corporations (TNCs). Some TNCs now rival sovereign nations in the size of their "economies." In Canada and abroad, global policies have enforced and supported the goals and purposes of these TNCs.

> The question of Canada's miserable failure as a wealthy country to address the needs of many residents cannot be understood outside the context of the globalization of food.

Canada and TNCs

The first global announcement of the international determination to eliminate hunger was made in 1948, when the *Universal Declaration of Human Rights* was declared and signed by Canada (Rideout et al. 2007: 566–67).

Since that time, hunger has continued to increase, but the pronouncements and promises about eliminating hunger have become fainter and more modest. Although international agreements have confirmed the right to food, the U.S. has consistently refused to sign them and has in fact lobbied against these treaties. Since the first promises were made, subsistence farming and social supports have been systematically dismantled around the world.

The WTO and other international organizations have been instrumental in making this dismal situation a reality. Power is distributed unevenly at these international bargaining tables, with powerful factions like the U.S. and E.U. driving decisions and policies. This has enabled the U.S. and E.U. to use the power of international institutions to protect their agricultural subsidies (which create artificial pricing structures). Farmers in the global north, protected by taxpayer-funded subsidies that the WTO has agreed to ignore, can undercut local food pricing in developing countries. At the same time, international trade organizations, corporations, and governments have prevented developing countries from either establishing their own subsidies or from protecting their markets from export dumping from farmers in the north. In addition, the powerful elites in these institutions are not neutral, objective observers, but are often the same people who rotate positions and directorships between the agro-TNCs who benefit and the institutions that regulate. For instance, Michael Taylor, appointed to the Food and Drug Administration, was Vice President for Public Policy at Monsanto from 1998 to 2001 (Kenfield 2009). As Mattera (2004) reports in USDA Inc., Ann Veneman, secretary of the USDA from 2001 to 2005, had been on the board of Calgene (which later became part of Monsanto).

While the trade organizations create food regimes sympathetic to the global north, international finance institutions offer struggling countries appealing loans to recreate the industrial agriculture that dominates in the north. The debt load has been willingly taken on in Canada and in the global south. "To earn a net income dollar today, farmers must borrow and risk seven times as much debt as they did in the 1970s, and three times as much as in the '80s" (NFU 2010: 19). The debt comes with promises of higher yields and a solution to stagnant food prices in Canada and to the need for cash in the south and north. It often comes with strings attached: in Canada, loss of farmer power over agriculture; in the south, loss of national social safety nets and public goods like water and food.

In Canada, the result has not been prosperity but grinding debt, loss of autonomy, and eventually forced sales of land. "Canadian farmers' net income from the markets (with farm support payments subtracted out) has totaled less than zero. Due to a grinding farm crisis, over the past twenty-five years, 100 percent of farm families' net income has come from farm support programs, off-farm jobs, and loans" (NFU 2010: 6).

The package offered to farmers to change their way of farming and eating was marketed first in the global south under the terms of the Green Revolution; similar packages were developed for the north. Industrial farming models brought farmers designer seeds that had shown higher yields in tests back in the laboratory, and chemical inputs that would increase production. What was not mentioned at first was that the inputs and new hybrid seeds would starve the land of natural nutrients; that monocropping of these cash crops would lead to rapid soil erosion and degradation; that the new regime required expensive levels of irrigation only available to wealthy farmers; and that the mountain of debt the farmers would find themselves under once they started on the treadmill of feeding their soil chemically would be one from which they might never emerge. For instance, in India many farmers moved from a mix of high-yielding indigenous seeds to a focus on wheat and rice, losing a diversity of crops for food as well as fodder for animals (Shiva 2000: 45). In Canada, diverse farm regimes have been replaced by acres of corn or soybeans for export. In addition, the higher concentration of meat in global diets means that more than two-thirds of all arable land is currently put to use for livestock (both pasture and for animal feed crops) (Weis 2007: 40).

As hunger encroached in lands where it had previously been managed through farming of diverse crops for local consumption rather than for export, the winners of the global trade game (the U.S. and the E.U.) invented a new form of compassion in the form of food aid. The need for food in the south coincided with surpluses of wheat and other commodities in the north. Farmers and governments needed to find new markets for this surplus product.

The Politics of Famine

Famine often occurs in a context of plenty. As Davis (2002) reports, famines occur despite the presence of local storehouses bulging with grain, or even a busy export market that removes grain from the country even as the country's people starve. The problem is distribution and power, not lack of food (Patel 2009). Famine is not so much a matter of an unbalanced numerical formula (the amount of grain needed for a certain number of people) as it is a complex and tragic result of political decisions, social dislocations (from war and colonization) and the systematic relocation of smallholder farmers to the urban labour pool to make way for industrial agriculture or mass irrigation projects.

> Famine often occurs in a context of plenty.

In addition, the imposition of cheap food from the north puts the final nail in the coffin of local agriculture, as local farmers are unable to compete with the cheap northern food. In 1987, as Holt-Gimenez and Patel report (2009: 38), Haiti's rice was largely supplied by local growers. The U.S.-backed regime that took power after 1986 instituted neoliberal reforms to open Haiti's markets to imports. Today, most of the rice consumed in Haiti is imported, and the FAO listed Haiti as one of the twenty-two countries at greatest risk of hunger due to rising food prices. Food aid, often a response to the hunger crisis that results from this type of regime, is not a long-term practical response to hunger, as it destroys the ability of local systems to resolve current or future crises and makes them dependent on cheap food imports. Food aid is simply a management technique for surpluses from large farms in the global north, where surpluses were produced that needed to find a market. Studies have also shown that these imports are an inefficient response to hunger. Much of the aid never reaches the hungry: it is absorbed by markets and more powerful actors before it reaches regions that need it (Holt-Gimenez and Patel 2009; Pottier 1999; Pretty 1995). Notably, Canada has recently untied food aid from Canadian production, under pressure from Oxfam Canada, the Canadian Foodgrains Bank, and other organizations, thus potentially redirecting some food aid to those who actually need it (Bailey 2011: 39).

In the last decade this flawed system of so-called food aid has reached a point of cataclysm, as exporting countries have reduced or banned exports to protect their own agriculture, just as hunger has risen in southern countries that no longer have the land, knowledge, or tools to produce their own food. Meanwhile, for those who have the money to buy food (many Canadians for instance), diet-related illnesses like obesity, diabetes, and heart attacks are reaching epidemic proportions. We have finally reached the peculiar and desperate situation where the same percentage of the world population is suffering from obesity as suffers from hunger (Holt-Gimenez and Patel 2009: 3).

Canada and the Global System

This unhappy history is by no means confined to relations between north and south. Although Canada tends to identify itself as a global economy winner, the truth is disturbing and complicated. Uneasily included at the tables of the dominant powers, Canada has more in common with developing countries. Like southern countries, Canada has lost its agriculture, land, and control over its food system to systematic dumping by subsidized foreign agri-food corporations and is subject to structural adjustment pressures and liberalization of national markets that are more familiar in our tales from the south (Qualman and Wiebe 2002). NAFTA, which was hailed by many as a historic trade agreement, also exposed our markets to greater levels of imports from the U.S., where many crops are heavily subsidized.

> Although Canada tends to identify itself as a global economy winner, the truth is disturbing and complicated. Uneasily included at the tables of the dominant powers, Canada has more in common with developing countries.

Canada boasts extensive fertile farmland and food resources, yet imports a great deal of its food from the U.S. and elsewhere (almost half including all food products). According to the Nova Scotia Federation of Agriculture, in 2001, 97 percent of the fruit in Canada was imported (NSFA, Statistics Canada Food Consumption in Canada Cat. No. 32–229. Appendix C). The Nova Scotia Federation of Agriculture estimates that only 8.4 percent of the food on Nova Scotia tables is grown locally, down from 15 percent fifteen years ago (NSFA 2011). This import trade leaves Canadian eaters at the mercy of international food price fluctuations, and Canadian farmers at the mercy of prices set by associations for subsidized commodities (wheat, corn, soy, etc.). In addition, the National Farmers Union (2010) reports that foreign corporations have begun to set up Canadian subsidiaries in order to purchase Canadian farmland, now considered a lucrative investment by financial speculators.

The bare story of the global food crisis has been recapitulated in many important popular and scholarly works. It is hard to avoid a feeling of hopelessness or mounting ineffectual anger when contemplating this history. Although it is important to recognize the depth of misery and despair the current food regimes have created, the story risks missing key points that indicate ongoing resistance and hope for a better world. For instance, where does one place agency in this history? Are the international institutions maliciously and knowingly dismantling people's livelihoods, or is there an insidious and agentless force obedient to the imperatives of power and profit? Are the peasant farmers, Canadian smallholders, and single mothers who pay rent before they buy food in Toronto passive victims of inexorable forces and/or evil corporations/CEOs? Or are they at all times inventive, responsive, and resistant to their loss of power, resources, and solutions?

It is not even accurate to say that agri-food industries are "winners" in the sense of someone who got there first on their own merits. The agri-industrial complex depends for its success on tax breaks, taxpayer funded subsidies, free sinks (also known as the environment) for waste, subsidized oil, systemic racism, expropriation of indigenous land, and exploited imported and resident labour (Holt-Gimenez and Patel 2009: 85). Canada is still one of the wealthiest nations in the world, particularly judged by the standards of GNP and GDP. Perhaps it is more accurate to say that all these stories are true at different times, and in different contexts. As Gramsci has eloquently expressed it, social change (Forgacs 2000: 244–45) is like an orchestra rehearsing, a cacophony of different tunes and voices necessary to create a powerful musical pattern in the performance. The struggle over food is a struggle over different ways of telling the tale, knowing the world, and choosing to act.

Canada's Food System

Let us review the effects of the globalization of food in Canada, and tease apart the stories for change that arise in this contested landscape. In Canada, considered "one of the wealthiest countries in the world," a grim reality mars the quality of our communal life. In 2000/1, the Community Health Survey reported that "14.7 percent of Canadians aged twelve and older experienced food insecurity" (Rideout et al. 2007: 568). In March of 2010, the number of Canadians accessing food banks reached a record high: 867,948, a 9 percent increase over the same period in 2009 (Food Banks Canada 2010: 2). Almost half of food bank users are children (Weimer 2009: 5). These are the stories that do not often make the front page.

Canada's Farm Crisis

At the same time, we are losing our local food producers. The number of farmers in Canada has steadily dropped for years. In fifteen years between 1991 and 2006, over 60,000 farmers exited the profession (Statistics Canada 2011). As Desmarais (2007: 64) points out, "realized net farm incomes in 2006 were worse than the levels that farmers had experienced in the 1930s." The National Farmers' Union cites Statistics Canada figures that show that "over the past twenty-five years, 100 percent of farm families' net income has come from farm support programs, off-farm jobs, and loans" (NFU 2010: 6).

Our farmland is also disappearing, sold off to housing speculators and developers and most recently to foreign investors. As the NFU reports in *Losing Our Grip*, Canadian land is up for grabs; transnational finance corporations now rhapsodize about Canadian land as an excellent investment opportunity. Of course, we should wonder to ourselves, if it is considered so valuable for overseas investors, why are we so ready to sell it off? Or is it not so much readiness as that Canada is in the malign grip of the same pincers that captured land in Brazil for soybeans and now agri-fuels? Farmers may not want to leave the land, but between overwhelming debt loads, food prices that haven't changed since the 1970s, and the tantalizing prize of immediate cash for land, who would not be "willing to sell"? The National Farmers' Union reports that, in Canada "to earn a net income dollar today, farmers must borrow and risk seven times as much debt as they did in the 1970s, and three times as much as in the '80s" (2010: 19). Qualman and Tait (2004) write, "On a per-farm basis, adjusted for inflation, farmers' net income over the past decade has been lower than at any time since the 1930s. To stay on the land, most families must now rely on off-farm jobs." It should be no surprise that, given an opportunity, farmers in this situation are ready to sell their land. While we continue to elect governments that facilitate this crisis,[1] it seems unfair to expect farmers to care more about feeding us than we do.

Agricultural Policy in Canada

Unfortunately, governments are not innocent or passive in this project. In fact, Canadian governments have loosened the ownership regulations to facilitate the fire sale of Canadian land (NFU 2010: 14). As far back as 1969, there were recommendations from the federal government to reduce the number of Canadian farmers by 50–65 percent (Qualman and Tait 2004: 6). This goal is rapidly being achieved in Canada, and worldwide. The strategy was based on a belief that fewer and larger farms would lead to greater efficiencies, but recent research has been able to show higher yields and more efficient use of land from small-holder farms (Pretty 1995).

Although we read about consolidation and concentration in the U.S. agri-industrial complex, it is easy to forget that Canada has also done a stellar job at consolidation and oligopoly control by a few, perhaps exceeding achievements in the U.S. Qualman and Tait write, "In Canada, each link of the agri-food chain is dominated by fewer than ten (and often as few as two) multibillion-dollar transnationals. The single exception is the farm link, where nearly a billion of the world's farmers operate in an intensely competitive sector" (2004: 19). With Metro's recent purchase of A&P, four large companies dominate Canadian grocery retail from coast to coast, with 68 percent of the market share (Sparling, Quadri, and van Duren 2005: 2). One of these conglomerates is Safeway, a U.S. company. Large agri-food TNCs also prioritize vertical integration, which means that they own and operate not just retail stores, but processing facilities, storage warehouses, and distribution infrastructure — every aspect of food in fact except the high-risk agricultural sector. This is particularly true in livestock production; large TNCs like Tyson Foods own the input, processing, and distribution facilities and dictate feed and pharmaceutical regimes while leaving the risk of raising the animals to the farmers (Weis 2007: 79).

Like our sisters and brothers in the south, we may soon lose the wherewithal to grow our own food, and will be completely at the mercy of the price choices and export flow determined by the U.S. Canadian farmers will be tenants on their own land, if they stay in farming at all, "a situation," reports the NFU, "that would look familiar and comforting to a thirteenth century lord" (2010: 23). As Weis points out, the Canadian situation is inextricably entwined with the global food system, international corporations, and global finance. He notes that "an increasingly global lens is needed to understand the problems facing farmers in most parts of the world" (2007: 177).

As Rideout et al. write (2007: 567–68), a system that is concerned with the consolidation of profit and power into the hands of a few transnational corporations is indifferent to nutritional, social, and environmental health. Consumers, who are on the receiving end of an unhealthy food system, express in their bodies the toxicity of neoliberal agricultural economics. In addition to high profile food-related illnesses (e. coli outbreaks, poisoned water sources), diet-related illnesses that stem from an unhealthy food system are all on the rise — obesity, diabetes, heart-related illnesses, etc. Alongside hunger, approximately one in three Toronto children (aged two to eleven) is either overweight or obese. Toronto Public Health's report (2010) states that, "According to a 2010 report from Statistics Canada, children as a group are 'taller, heavier, fatter and weaker than in 1981,' which may lead to accelerated 'non-communicable disease development, increased health care costs, and loss of future productivity."

In a system that provides food to those who can pay for it (despite so far empty declarations of the right to food in Canada, except perhaps in Quebec) (Rideout et al. 2007: 571), hunger is a demon that will continue to infect the society. For example, about 9 percent (379,100) of households in Ontario are food insecure, rising to about 11 percent of households with children (Health Canada 2007). As well, adults with the lowest household incomes, at 29 percent, experience food insufficiency at more than double the provincial average (Cancer Care Ontario 2005: 17).

Like a flint that creates sparks, food is a touchstone for society's ills; hunger is exacerbated by many other ills (Scharf, Levkoe, and Saul 2010). Many working poor rely on food banks for food, as low-income wages are insufficient for shelter and food, and people living in poverty will necessarily pay rent before buying food. Supermarkets increase stress for urban poor by locating where people are able to pay for food; food deserts (where there are no food stores) and higher prices have both been identified in low-income neighbourhoods (Larson and Gilliland 2008). The dismantling of local food infrastructure in Ontario has included the loss of local food processing, distribution, and storage and transportation options for small to medium scale farmers (Carter-Whitney and Miller 2010). There are fewer jobs in the food sectors, and many farmers have been forced out of business. Lee et al. point out that, incredibly enough, the 100-mile diet may be dependent on labour from workers traveling 3000 miles, as farm-workers are increasingly replaced by migrant labour (2010: 7).

The agri-food system also creates long-term effects in environmental degradation as well as the social costs of poor health and job loss. Holt-Gimenez and Patel (2009: 3) summarize the global situation: "A financial cornucopia producing over $6 trillion a year in wealth, industrial agri-food is tragically one of the planet's major drivers of global poverty and environmental destruction." Monocropping, the single crop focus used throughout Canada, and now imported in industrial agriculture systems to the global south, creates a perfect scenario for soil erosion. The need for straight crop rows, accessible to large-scale mechanized planters and harvesters, creates long gullies that are ideal for draining water and soil from farmers' land.

There are also more subtle losses from the triumphal progress of the agri-industrial complex. Farmers have lost more than soil, jobs, and livelihood, they have also lost the knowledge to farm sustainably (Desmarais 2007: 44). As Shiva (1993) points out, farmers have been systematically removed from the place of innovation in agriculture, and have had to cede the important role of problem-solving and innovation to crop scientists, seed and technology providers, and other non-farming technicians. In many sectors the farmers are in the position of serfs on their own land, following recipes (for feeding regimes) and prescriptions (for hormones and low levels of antibiotics). In these factory farms, methods are dictated by the corporations who represent the farmers' only market option. The corporations may own everything on the farm except the land itself. In a few short decades essential information has been lost about saving seed, building soil immunity, ecosystem resilience, etc. As Shiva has pointed out (1993), the change of strategies of thought is not innocent; it serves to utterly separate the course of humanity from nature, and makes our misuse of environmental resources reasonable and inevitable. In addition, the agri-food complex transfers power from peasants and farmers to an elite pool of scientists and marketers who work for the agro-TNCs, and are answerable, not to communities, but to the corporate CEO and shareholders.

Resistance: Beyond Victors and Victims

As resistance to the global food system rises, we begin to hear a story beyond victors and victims. Aside from the story of immiseration in Canada's rural lands and urban highrises, there are other stories that are not told often enough. These are the stories of resistance: those who have been disenfranchised, dislocated, and left behind by the triumphal sweep of neoliberal economics have never taken it lying down (Patel 2009: 107; Pottier 199: 109); they have resisted from the beginning, from the first moment that the *Agreement on Agriculture* looked like a made-for-the-U.S. solution to global agriculture, to the food riots in Egypt — the culmination of decades of inequality and social injustice — that toppled an unpopular dictator.

While we are familiar with the story that a few large corporations hold all the power in the food system, we are less familiar with the story of how the power was transferred — who colluded in that transfer, which communities stood against it, what bureaucracies, coercions and duplicitous tactics brought us to where we are (see Friedmann for important analysis of this history).

The problem with ahistorical descriptions is that, if we don't know how we got here, we don't know how to get back out. For instance, it has become natural to see food as private property and to assume food must come from land that is privately owned. Yet not very long ago, poor people got a great deal of food and fuel from common land, and shared communal management of irrigation, grazing rights, firewood harvest rights, etc. (Patel 2009). As Patel (2010: 7) points out, "Private property requires society to approve of it being taken out of common hands. Property is, in other words, social — there's nothing natural about the way some people are allowed to exclude others from land, for instance" (2010: 7). As well, the determination of what should be submitted to market exchanges is a social decision; we have agreed that food should be bought and sold as a commodity for profit, available to those who can afford it. However, as the numerous movements and commitments to the right to food indicate, we are also able to think about it differently, and argue that none of our neighbours or fellow planetary denizens should be hungry (Madeley 2002: 2).

Power and Story: How Telling Makes It So

Our attitudes to food and agriculture, our beliefs that we enshrine in policies, trade agreements, and law, are a matter of cultural identity (Hart, in Goodman and Watts 1997: 62). Weis writes,

> From seasonal cultivation routines to harvest to preparation to mealtime, food has long been a central part of cultural identities, and a major aspect of the escalating power of agro-TNCs lies in their extraordinary ability to sever both the material and conceptual links between farmers and consumers and replace these with opaque webs of sourcing, processing, distributing, retailing and branding while… managing to naturalize this. (2007: 186)

> Our attitudes to food and agriculture, our beliefs that we enshrine in policies, trade agreements, and law, are a matter of cultural identity.

This severance and substitution has not succeeded completely: a trace has been left in our culture that tells a story of compassion and care for others (everyone has a right to food), of the commons and sharing, and of important alternatives that have begun to collaborate to create an international resistance and an alternative food identity for us all (Bello 2004: 27).

In the negotiation of what we believe, whom we trust, who has the last word (in other words, culture), power, and status have a determining effect on which stories get told. The stories told by the powerful assume an artificial inevitability; as the U.K.'s Prime Minister Margaret Thatcher was wont to say as she dismantled and privatized England's public systems, "there is no alternative." If we restore an analysis of power to the equation, we see, for instance, that there is nothing free about the "free market"; the success of transnational corporations depends very much on their power to set trade rules to suit their own profit goals, and to mobilize taxpayer money to subsidize their activities — through price subsidies and less visible subsidies that include public funds for environmental clean-up, waste disposal, public health investments, transportation system funding, etc. (Holt-Gimenez and Patel 2009: 2). Corporate success would not have happened without the public goods paid for by us to keep their system running.

Stories of Resistance and Protest

The work to undo the social, economic, and environmental mess of global capitalism is a narrative task; to begin to hear and tell alternative stories. It includes an essential recognition that capitalism itself is not monolithic — it should not take a global financial meltdown to recognize that capitalism takes different forms and breaks down in different ways depending on the cultural context (Hart, in Goodman and Watts 1997: 56).[2] The first step to thinking alternatives is to whisk the curtain aside to see the wizard, and to realize that the stories of the powerful can be changed.

> The work to undo the social, economic, and environmental mess of global capitalism is a narrative task; to begin to hear and tell alternative stories. It includes an essential recognition that capitalism itself is not monolithic.

just as they have changed our stories beyond recognition. Whatmore (in Goodman and Watts 1997: 289) writes that globalization is "a socially contested rather than logical process in which many spaces of resistance, alterity, and possibility become analytically discernible and politically meaningful."

For instance, the mass protests at the global trade talks in Seattle, Quebec, Doha, and Cancun featured food and agriculture as prominent issues that mobilized scores of different groups, from southern peasant organizations to youth activists in the north (Weis 2007). The stories of the protests were not conveyed to us in a disinterested fashion however; the focus is on eruptions of violence, on costumed agitators, on broken storefront windows. These versions eliminate the stories of thousands of peaceful protestors, the peasant groups and food security organizations, the children marching with parents, the network of support and planning that ensured that the protestors had backup and legal support in case the police turned violent.

Food "riots"[3] erupted around the world in response to food price rises in 2008 and in 2010 (Lee et al. 2010: 12; Holt-Gimenez and Patel 2009). According to Hendrix (2009: 2), food protests have taken place recently in over thirty countries. They were a trigger point in Egypt's recent democracy movement that toppled Mubarak's regime; they are significant in protests around the world. Patel (2009: 132–33) reminds us that it is inaccurate to say these actions were "fueled by nothing more than mute or inarticulate pangs of hunger"; they "were also an expression of deeper anger at the politics surrounding food that had resulted in high prices and low incomes" (also see Patel and McMichael 2009).

Resistance Is Multiple

Although the mass protests have been a powerful statement, as Halweil and Nierenberger (2010: 6) of the Worldwatch Institute write, "there is no single solution. In fact, it is the one-size-fits-all approach that has been so crippling." Mass movements to change food regimes are only one part of resistance; most actors engage in more than one form of protest, combining protest, policy advocacy, and alternative practice as a way of creating new communities of food. Many local non-governmental organizations (NGOs) fight to reduce poverty, recognizing that lack of access to food is often a

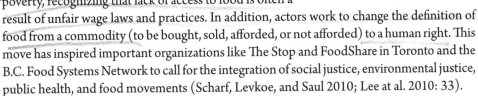

> Mass movements to change food regimes are only one part of resistance; most actors engage in more than one form of protest, combining protest, policy advocacy, and alternative practice as a way of creating new communities of food.

result of unfair wage laws and practices. In addition, actors work to change the definition of food from a commodity (to be bought, sold, afforded, or not afforded) to a human right. This move has inspired important organizations like The Stop and FoodShare in Toronto and the B.C. Food Systems Network to call for the integration of social justice, environmental justice, public health, and food movements (Scharf, Levkoe, and Saul 2010; Lee at al. 2010: 33).

Alternative Food Systems

Numerous alternative practices have appeared and captured the imaginations and loyalty of Canadians. These tend to be erected somewhere between the advocacy organizations and the market economy. For instance, the African Food Basket farms a significant garden area to provide culturally familiar foods for some of Toronto's ethnic populations, and supports the development of community gardens for key food-insecure groups in Toronto. Many of these initiatives derive from rethinking land use: community gardens on public lands, or sometimes vacant or contested land, as in the case of the recently bulldozed South Central Farm in Los Angeles. In another model, guerrilla gardening lays claim to unused urban spaces through the "guerilla" planting of seeds.

In Canada, the recent "Carrot City" exhibition mobilized activists, architects, and planners to rethink the use of urban space for food, creating designs for intensive farming, vertical farming, and mixed use to revivify neighbourhoods. Urban farming is no mere pipe dream; much of Havana's food is grown within the city limits (Funes et al. 2003). Other innovations that have been launched recently include various programs to link urban gardeners with people with backyards they are willing to share, providing some of the harvest in exchange for the gardening work. One enterprising urban farmer in Toronto, Erica Lemieux, is now farming a quarter-acre across eight backyards around the city and selling her produce at the Sorauren Farmers' Market (Porter 2011). As Patricia Allen (2008: 159) has pointed out, many urban agriculture initiatives in the global north are disproportionately accessed and championed by the privileged; those living in poverty may not be able to afford the time to work in exchange for food when they more urgently need cash for rent money or fuel to get to their jobs. Several farmers' markets in Toronto are piloting a market vouchers program for low-income people in order to address this problem.

Alternatives: Food Relocalization Movements

Calls to relocalize food (Bello 2004; Halweil and Nieremberger 2010), which focus on growing, distributing, and eating more local food, encapsulate some of the possibilities for a reframed food system. These approaches advocate changes in scale, ownership, and relationships from one end of the supply chain to the other. The local food movement has captured activist and media imaginations but must be interrogated rigorously. At this point, the results of relocalization are often only available to the privileged, who can afford to pay more for food and who have a choice in their food (those who rely on drop-in centres and food banks cannot prioritize local food, as they have little choice in what they eat). Technically, relocalization is not impossible; various studies have explored the positive effects on the local economy of shifting even a few imported foods to local sources (Xuereb 2005; Stopes 2002; Swenson 2009). Lee et al. (2010: 6) write that "if B.C. could shift just 1.5 percent of its overall consumption per year to local sources, the province would supply 80 percent of its food needs by 2030." The advantages are also unquestionable, as they point out: "One U.S. study estimated that if all food was localized, the reduction in emissions would be roughly equivalent to households shifting their diet one day per week from red meat and dairy to a vegetable-based diet" (28). Relocalization also provides important benefits through new jobs and manufacturing opportunities.

Alternatives: New Land Use Practices

More substantial changes to land use and access to food may come from the land trust movement and programs for Greenbelt protection near urban centres, or protected land for farming such as B.C.'s Agricultural Land Reserve (ALR). These programs seek to formally register lands as protected for agricultural or conservation purposes. The ALR is managed by the province and has almost five million acres that are designated as priority areas for agricultural use, with other uses restricted and controlled.[4] In effect, by pricing the land in terms of value by use (including environmental goods) rather than market value, such initiatives contest the submission of land to the free market. Elsewhere in the world, serious land reform movements are underway. For instance, the Brazilian MST (Landless Workers Movement) has reclaimed large tracts of unused land from absentee landowners (Wright and Wolford 2003).

Power in Alternative Food Movements

In food movements and actions, it is important to continue to raise the questions of power: who is acting for change, and who has access to the alternatives (Patel and McMichael 2009: 10). Holt-Gimenez and Patel argue that the recent global food crisis has mobilized the world's poor and marginalized as they were hardest hit by the increase in food prices (2009: 159). Likewise, Patel points out that women are disproportionately affected by the globalization of food (Patel 2009; also Pottier 1999). The collaboration between democracy movements and food actions is crucial to the achievement of a more just and equitable food system. We are told that to effect change we must vote with our food dollar, but does this mean we should abandon all our fellow humans who can't afford to pay — who can't, in short, afford the kind of food dollar democracy they are offered? Real democracy rises above the impoverished rhetoric of choice offered only to those who can pay (Bello 2004: 10), replacing mere voting with true economic democracy.

Food Policy for Change

New institutions like food charters (that declare the universal right to food), food policy councils that seek to enforce it through collaboration among diverse actors, and municipalities that formalize the right to food in government programs are at the forefront of the movement to restore real democracy to the food system. Belo Horizonte in Brazil became a global leader for food change by embedding the human right to food in actual government programs (Rocha 2000). These were designed to fulfill the promise of the right to food, which has remained an empty promise in places like Canada (see also Ecuador's new Food Sovereignty Law [Holt-Gimenez and Patel 2009: 180]). Organizations like FoodShare in Toronto have looked to Belo Horizonte's municipal policies for inspiration in their own work. Manitoba was the first to have a province-wide food charter stating the right to food.[5] Toronto also passed a municipal food charter, in 2001.

Initiatives that establish new principles for food systems — equity, the right to food, democracy — must also consider the structure of power they inaugurate in their innovation. This consideration can enable actors to resist co-optation as their success grows. The co-operative form, as well as the radical forms, of participatory democracy (as in the case of the MST; see Wright and Wolford 2003: 35) have been at the forefront of significant movements for change in food and agriculture. In Cuba, co-operatives have been essential alternatives to state or private ownership, providing a measure of control to actors that has some advantages over a state-run system. In Argentina and Venezuela, economic catastrophe has led to the rapid rise of worker co-ops, as labour takes charge of the means of production to create an economy that works for all people rather than just a few. In Canada, important farmers' co-ops like GayLea, OntarBio, and the Canadian Wheat Board (no longer a co-op) have helped dairy and grain farmers stay in business and command fair prices for their goods through co-ordinated efforts. Co-operatives change the relation of people to alternatives. While community gardens may reinforce a charity model (people grow food there which they donate to food banks or provide to poor people), a co-operatively owned project like the multi-stakeholder West End Food Co-op in Toronto restores power to the actors, including workers, consumers, producers, and community food agencies. In these projects, all stakeholders may participate in decision making, equipment purchase, and long-term planning, as well as growing and eating.

A democratic culture of food provisioning is no minor change; we are unused to, and largely untrained in, participatory democracy (Rebick 2000; Miller 2008). Real democracy requires much more than stating your opinion; it means listening to others, considering the good of all, considering your interests and position carefully to reach consensus through argument, negotiation, and consultation. It will take many years to learn or relearn this, just as it will take years to recover lost agricultural skills for sustainable farming.

Alternatives that Reframe the Food System

Many local food movements, as well as peasant movements around the world, view the solutions and alternatives as dependent on a reorganization of every aspect of the food system, from our relations to land, to distribution, to ownership of food infrastructure and

> Many local food movements, as well as peasant movements around the world, view the solutions and alternatives as dependent on a reorganization of every aspect of the food system, from our relations to land, to distribution, to ownership of food infrastructure and access.

access. As Holt-Gimenez and Patel (2009: 98) point out, "ending hunger will require restructuring the ways we produce, process, distribute and consume our food." It will also require new ways of being with each other; as Patel (2009: 22) writes: "seeing fellow human beings as mere co-consumers blinds us to the deeper connections between us, and distorts our political choices…. There's no space to renegotiate so that everyone gets to eat, no way to become a co-producer."

Ontario is in a crisis around local food infrastructure, which has been dismantled over the years as foreign options and labour became more financially appealing for global capitalists. The last tender fruit processing plant closed in 2006. A government program pays farmers to uproot and destroy their fruit trees, to replace them with something more economically viable (though what that would be in the current agricultural climate is unclear — condominiums, perhaps). In a recent study of policies and strategies to restore local food infrastructure in Ontario (Carter-Whitney and Miller 2010; see also Atamenenko n.d.), over forty farmers and stakeholders were interviewed. Respondents recognized a catastrophic lack of options for value-added processing in Ontario, and recommended solutions that reframe the food chain from farming to processing to storage, distribution and marketing.

Food Sovereignty Movements

Food sovereignty movements have taken the story of a better world to a new level. They integrate the various types of resistance into alternatives that are insistently democratic and rely on principles of social justice and well-distributed power. Holt-Gimenez and Patel (2009: 86) write, "food sovereignty proposes that people, rather than corporate monopolies, make the decisions regarding our food." La Vía Campesina is a new and powerful international peasant organization that seeks to create food sovereignty alternatives in which, as Desmarais (2007: 33) writes, "agriculture is farmer-driven and based on peasant production. It uses local resources and is geared to domestic markets. Agriculture not only plays an important social function but is also economically viable and ecologically sustainable." Patel (2009: 119) reports that La Vía Campesina now boasts 150 million members in sixty-nine countries. La Vía Campesina's member organizations are diverse and place specific; the international organization has been created out of a careful scheme of participation and representation that builds on a grassroots democracy. In Canada, the National Farmers Union is a key participant in La Vía Campesina's work.

One key point in La Vía Campesina's work is that the membership is restricted to peasants (Desmarais 2007). Across international borders, the members are therefore in an equal place of power (or disempowerment) in relation to the world food economy. Well-meaning NGOs, which do not have their biological survival at stake, are welcome to participate as allies but do not have access to membership. Members are from north and south, and include members of the various landless movements in the south, as well as Canada's National Farmers Union, and the U.S.-based Coalition of Immokalee Workers (CIW). CIW is a coalition of agricultural workers that includes the tomato workers in Florida who have forced major chains like Taco Bell and McDonald's to increase the tomato pickers' pay by one penny per pound. They have also advocated and fought against the modern-day slavery that exists for many of these workers, which includes forced confinement, inhuman working hours and workplace practices, and wages that force workers into debt to sustain their families. In case the slavery comparison seems outrageous, it is important to note that the CIW cited the same laws used during the abolition of slavery to free the Immokalee workers now (Desmarais 2007; Holt-Gimenez and Patel 2009: 172).

Rewriting the Narratives of the Global Food Economy: Agroecology

The narratives in these new movements for social change carry significant new principles that profoundly challenge the global economies of food. In addition to formalizing the sharing and transfer of power in strong democratic structures, La Vía Campesina and its members are reinventing ideas of property ownership and entitlement, and reinventing the philosophies of interactions with the land in agricultural systems. The latter is captured under the rubric of agroecology and, together with the reinvention of the meaning of property, creates and embeds in cultures new ways of being with the land.

Agroecology is not simply a return to traditional farming methods, although it may incorporate centuries-old techniques and varieties (Holt Gimenez and Patel 2009: 110). As an agricultural practice, it recognizes the power and sustainability of techniques and varieties that are innovations based on immediate contexts, climates, and local demands and possibilities. It is a way of thinking in tune with an agricultural ecosystem that tests and solves problems where they arise, in the context of local pests and beneficials, climatic benefits and challenges, and the realities of locally financed and managed farming. As Madeley writes, "small biodiverse farms, growing a number of crops in the same field, are proving to be the new agriculture that is more likely to grow the food that is needed by this and future generations" (Madeley 2002: 41).

For instance, in agroecology, drought would not be lifted out of the particularity of place, as it is by the agro-TNCs who create designer seeds and mass irrigation projects to combat it. In a sustainable farm, unlike industrial agriculture that addresses problems with single-seed or technology solutions, the farmer will plant a mix of crops and varieties (polycultures), ensuring harvest and sustainable yield from at least one of the varieties. The rotation in drought-prone areas will include a drought-resistant variety that may not yield as well, but in drought years that variety will ensure a crop for the farmer (see Pretty's *Regenerative Agriculture* [1995] for many more examples). The examples of place-specific solutions in sustainable agriculture are a marvel of ingenuity and innovation. For instance, Featherstone Estate Winery in Ontario uses cover crops to control weeds between the vines, sheep to reduce the grape leaves and increase the fruit's exposure to light, and a Harris hawk to control the incursions of birds.

As Holt-Gimenez and Patel point out, agroecology is not just crop insurance for those who cannot afford a policy; it has actually been proven to provide yields and efficiency that are the equal of industrial agriculture results (2009: 103). They report that a University of Michigan study shows that sustainable agriculture could even produce more kilocalories per person per day than industrial agriculture (2009: 107). Agroecology also mirrors other sustainable systems in solving multiple problems through one elegant solution (such as a team of sheep that both provide fertilizer and help to trim the grapevines). Sustainable agriculture protects and restores the environment rather than degrading it and making it necessary to replace lost nutrients each year with chemical inputs. The multiplicity of varieties, crops, and strategies is supported by direct markets like farmers' markets and community supported agriculture programs, both thriving market strategies in Canada.

Agroecology, unlike organic farming, is more than agricultural techniques. As practised and championed by small farmers and peasant organizations like the landless movements and La Vía Campesina, it includes an analysis and reframing of power among agricultural actors which sets it apart from other solutions (Desmarais 2007). Wright and Wolford point out that agroecology addresses a relocalization of the entire supply chain from land to plate: "An agro-ecological approach would be based on serving local markets with a diversity of high-value products and capturing most of the value by eliminating middlemen through farmers' markets and on-farm processing" (2003: 294). An agriculture focused on feeding farm families and providing local communities with food, rather than cash crops or biofuels, creates a vision of permanence and interdependence quite different from the imaginings of industrial agricultural and world trade organizations. For instance, Foodlink Waterloo Region promotes a regional food cluster that includes farmers, the Elmira co-operative produce auction, a new local food distributor, a new farmer-owned processing facility, restaurants and a large university (the University of Guelph). The new markets benefit from increased awareness through local food branding and outreach from Foodlink and others.

New Relations to Land Through Agroecology

The agricultural thinking of agroecology changes the relations between farmers and land. An industrial agriculturalist could farm anywhere — from Zambia to Missouri, the techniques are the same: add the necessary nutrients, arrange for consistent irrigation, and use high-yield hybrid varieties in a monocrop planting. For an agroecologist, their solutions, seed varieties, techniques, and innovations are based on place-specific assessments and interventions; the farmers' future becomes intimately tied to the particular land they farm, and they are more attentive to things like soil degradation, soil strength and immunity, and erosion. The soil is perceived as their wealth (Wright and Wolford 2003: 288). As Weis (2007: 92) points out, the ownership and use relations to land in alternative agricultural practices are also place- and culture-specific, ranging from "from redistribution into small private holdings, to reformist land tenure restructuring, to massive nationalization and collectivization schemes."

Agroecology also changes the relations between farmers, as well as between farmers and communities. Most agroecology movements embed participatory democracy as well as farmer-to-farmer education in their initiatives. Farmer Field Schools have been ignited around the world; farmers are sharing information, exchanging knowledge and providing key networks of support in their quest to reinvent agriculture. FarmStart in Ontario is an excellent example of this peer mentoring: new farmers get access to land on a joint farm, and can share tips and ideas as well as access expert input. The new peasant organizations are adamant and radical in their approach to democracy, inaugurating participatory practices that move well beyond voting. In the Brazilian MST for instance, peasants occupy unused land to reclaim it from absentee landholders. They farm in the face of the imminent threat of violent eviction by private security or the military. Yet they maintain an insistence on participatory democracy, with carefully designed councils and rotating representation to manage and operate the land and community, and ongoing education in the encampment, both between farmers and within the community (Wright and Wolford 2003; Patel 2007: 207). The change in decision making and power distribution is as important as the right to food and sustainable agriculture (Hines 2000: 31; Holt-Gimenez and Patel 2009: 98).

In Canada, there are many indications that we are rethinking our relationship to land, from guerrilla gardeners who plant gardens in unused urban spaces, to the reclaiming of public lands in parks and elsewhere to grow food in community gardens. Likewise, the Greenbelt in Ontario and B.C.'s Agricultural Land Reserve protect key agricultural lands and in some ways remove them from the conventional land market. FarmStart in Ontario has worked hard to achieve and protect land access for new farmers (including newcomers who want to farm).

Agroecology movements and peasant movements have restored, revived, and enriched the relations between people and land, while incidentally creating alternatives to the principle that makes land a vehicle for private ownership for profit. These solutions build on existing ideas and wisdom. As Patel (2009: 107) writes, "there are always practices, ideas and experiences that persist, and offer tools with which we might begin to think of new ways of valuing beyond profit-driven markets." They also improvise and innovate in response to new challenges. Weis cites land reform as the key to these new ways, both in the north and south: "Ultimately, the work of building more localized, socially just and ecologically rational food economies hinges on challenging the grossly inequitable property rights that the global enclosures have wrought and working to reconfigure uneven landscapes" (2007: 182). Of the movements for resistance reviewed here, agroecology movements may be the most powerful. They have the potential to create a new way of living on our planet that will not destroy it by our use and presence.

The vivacity and strength of the agroecological and peasant movements confront and belie the attempts by global trade organizations and industrial agriculture proponents (from seed companies to the northern governments) to claim inevitability for the trajectory they propose for all agricultural systems (see Weis 2007: 162 on inevitability; also Hines 2000: 62). In the face of the tapestry of agroecology solutions (Pretty 1995), the agro-industrial solutions seem pale and insubstantial. Rather than addressing many problems at once and instituting creative solutions that achieve the maximum level of results for all problems, agri-food sees one problem at a time, and discounts or ignores secondary effects.

A classic example is the determination of agro-TNCs (Patel 2007) to foist a genetically engineered rice on developing country farmers. Systematic destruction of local agriculture has eliminated access to vegetables that provided sufficient vitamin A in traditional diets. The new rice provides much needed vitamin A through genetic manipulation of the seed's DNA, a process that has been proven to be uncertain at best, particularly when it is at large in complex ecosystems. Unfortunately, people would have to consume almost fifty bowls of this rice per day to get enough vitamin A to meet their nutritional needs (Patel 2007: 137).

New Ways of Thinking, New Ways of Eating

The battle for agriculture that can feed the world and not destroy the planet is a battle between different ways of thinking and the cultural negotiation of meaning that defines our moral structure and our relations with each other, the planet, and other species. As Weis and Patel have pointed out, once we have descended the slippery slope of industrial agriculture and accepted its sheen of inevitability, it is hard to go back. We are set the urgent task of learning new ways of thinking (Weis 2007: 30; Patel 2009: 173). The beliefs that accompany the move to industrial agriculture have left us adrift with few resources and tools to rebuild a sustainable world.

Yet as calcified as the agro-industrial complex seems to be, it has engendered resistance and alternatives across the world, in the peasants movements described above, and in local movements to reclaim land and sustainability through urban agriculture, land trusts, farmer co-ops, etc. Desmarais (2007: 24) writes, "The brutal force of globalization contributed to the emergence of a great variety of new social actors. It also led to new structures of collective action among traditional social actors, including peasant organizations." These movements are not merely angry reactions to social injustice and disempowerment; instead they reframe the moral principles and ethics of action. They eschew the celebration of individual needs and the search for power and profit accumulation in favour of shared interests, community interdependences, economic democracy, and the shared management of common resources for interlocking and integrated needs. They seek to establish what Shiva calls "living economies" (2005).

Coalitions and the Power to Change

A key strategy in sustainable agriculture and similar movements is to reunite interests that have been systematically separated (Patel 2009; Pretty 1995; Lee at al. 2010: 32). Some jurisdictions have begun to address this, particularly in the realm of public health and the social determinants of health. These actors recognize that personal health cannot be separated from a healthy food system, healthy and resil-

> A key strategy in sustainable agriculture and similar movements is to reunite interests that have been systematically separated.

ient communities, and a web of strong community relations and supports (see Toronto's *Cultivating Food Connections* Report [2010] for an excellent example of recommendations for integrated food and health solutions). Likewise in global movements for change, the demands and interests have begun to converge in important ways. Holt-Gimenez and Patel (2009: 164) write, "The socioeconomic realities and political strategies of these actors and organizations are diverse, and have sometimes led to tensions and work at cross-purposes. However, with the food and financial crises, their demands are converging, and point to a powerful consensus."

Polanyi argued that markets have been severed from cultural and social contexts and need to be re-embedded to work and nourish people and cultures (see Patel 2009: 189). As Patel (2009: 190) remarks, "We need the imagination to reclaim both democracy and the economy — we need to understand the basic flaw in imagining the two could be separated. This means telling ourselves different stories to replace the fantasies about the free market." Markets, whether global and profit-oriented or local and community-oriented, are productions of cultures and cultural actors which are replete with a certain moral outlook and define a cultural identity that may be savoury or unsavoury. We have been led by narratives of partial truths or outright lies to believe that an agriculture that eliminates farmers and their knowledge, consolidates power and profits, and requires scarcity (i.e., hunger) to survive, is the only possible historical path ("inevitability") and certainly the only one that can "feed the world" and address climate change and other environmental crises. We have continued to believe these narratives long after their ability to convince should have expired in the face of rising global temperatures and immiseration among farmers and consumers around the world. It is time to lay aside these old stories that no longer offer us acceptable precepts for action or living and to begin to tell new ways of ownership, being, and identity. As one peasant organization in India pledges, "I shall adopt the broader meaning of common ownership… instead of thinking in terms of I should get more than others, I aspire that other[s] should not get less than me" (quoted in Shiva 2005: 69). The exercise of power can be measured not by how much one can get for oneself, but in one's ability to ensure, in concert with others, that everyone has enough.

Glossary of Key Terms

Agri-food complex (agri-food industrial complex): Large-scale agriculture focused on commodity markets rather than food production. It is characterized by consolidation and centralization of power in very large corporations, and vertical integration (in which agri-food corporations own every sector of the supply chain from production to processing and distribution to retail/consumption).

Agroecology: "The application of ecological concepts and principles to the design and management of sustainable agricultural ecosystems" (Altieri 2009). "A farming philosophy that farms *with* nature, developing and maintaining soil fertility, producing a wide range of crops, and matching the farming to the needs, climate, geography, biodiversity and aspirations of a particular place and community" (Patel 2007: 306, emphasis added).

Food security: From the World Food Summit Plan of Action: "Food security exists when all people, at all times, have physical and economic access to sufficient, safe and nutritious food to meet their dietary needs and food preferences for an active and healthy life" (FAO 1996).

Food sovereignty: "The people's democratic control of the food system, the right of all people to healthy, culturally appropriate food produced through ecologically sound and sustainable methods, and their right to define their own food and agriculture systems" (La Vía Campesina 2010).

Neoclassical economics: Neoclassical economics (expressed politically in neoliberalism) is the theory of economics that promotes the removal of social supports and safety nets to "liberalize" or "free" markets. It theorizes that greater efficiencies are achieved when market actors are allowed free reign to consolidate market power. It emphasizes the private sector as the main actor in national economies. It is argued that this approach will result in the greatest good for all.

Relocalization (of food): The movement to reduce the long-distance transportation of food and to have food grown, produced, processed, and consumed in the same region.

Transnational corporations (TNC): Corporate entities that operate in more than one country and across borders. They are able to move operations where labour and other costs of operating (like environmental penalties for pollution, or the cost of raw materials) are low. Many of them have economies that are larger than sovereign nations.

"Willingness to Pay" theory: A key concept from neoclassical economics that hypothesizes that price is identified in a free market by exchanges between supply and demand, with a balance reached where sellers are willing to sell and buyers are willing to buy. It is applied to all commodities, including land and food, and results in scarcity of the necessities of life for those who cannot afford to pay. Willingness to Pay is countered by the "right to food," and more recently, the "right to grow food," philosophies that argue that everyone has the right to the basic necessities of life.

Questions for Discussion

1. Why is food an important trigger for social change movements?

2. How do the following change the way people relate to food, to land, and to each other: community gardens, food co-ops, Brazil's Landless Workers Movement?

3. What are ways to change the food system that will ensure lasting change?

4. What are the reasons that Canada is not necessarily a winner in the global food system?

Websites of Interest

Food and Agriculture Organization of the United Nations <fao.org>
La Vía Campesina <viacampesina.org>
Organic Consumers Association
Canadian Centre for Policy Alternatives

Notes

1. As Lester Brown (2011) reports in *World on the Edge*, farmers have begun to sell their irrigation water, as they make more selling water to municipalities than they do raising crops.
2. For an important and ground-breaking consideration of this problem, see J.K. Gibson Graham (1996), *The End of Capitalism (As We Knew It)*.
3. Note the choice of word in most reports — "riot" seems so much more violent than "protest." "Demonstration" is even more modest, though the term seems to eliminate much hope of change, as if protest were a display in a shop window.
4. See the Agricultural Land Reserve website at <alc.gov.bc.ca/alr/Establishing_the_ALR.htm> for more information on this important initiative.
5. See Food Matters Manitoba at <foodmattersmanitoba.ca/> for more on this important initiative.

References

Allen, Patricia. 2008. "Mining for Justice in the Food System: Perceptions, Practices and Possibilities." *Agriculture and Human Values* 25.

Atamenenko, Alex. n.d. *Food for Thought: Towards a Canadian Food Strategy*. Special Report. New Democratic Party of Canada.

Bailey, Robert. 2011. *Growing a Better Future: Food Justice in a Resource Constrained World*. Oxfam. <oxfam.org/grow>.

Bello, Walden. 2004. *Deglobalization: Ideas for a New World Economy*. Halifax, NS: Fernwood.

Brown, Lester R. 2011. *World on the Edge: How to Prevent Economic and Environmental* Collapse. New York: W.W. Norton.

Cancer Care Ontario. 2005. "Volume 2, Supplement 2: Ontario's Food Security and Cancer Prevention." *Insight on Cancer: News and Information on Nutrition and Cancer Prevention.* Toronto: Canadian Cancer Society (Ontario Division).

Carter-Whitney, Maureen, and S. Miller. 2010. "Nurturing Fruit and Vegetable Processing in Ontario." Metcalf Food Solutions Papers. Toronto: Metcalf Foundation.

Davis, Mike. 2002. *Late Victorian Holocausts: El Nino Famines and the Making of the Third World.* New York: Verso.

Desmarais, Annette Aurelie. 2007. *La Vía Campesina: Globalization and the Power of Peasants.* Halifax: Fernwood Publishing.

FAO (Food and Agriculture Organization of the United Nations). 1996. "Rome Declaration on World Food Security." World Food Summit, November 13–17. <fao.org/docrep/003/w3613e/w3613e00.HTM>.

_____. 2010. *The State of Food Insecurity in the World: Addressing Food Insecurity in Protracted Crises.* Rome: FAO. Developed with World Food Programme.

Food Banks Canada. 2010. *Hunger Count 2010: A Comprehensive Report on Hunger and Food Bank Use in Canada, and Recommendations for Change.* <antipovertyministry.ca/media/HungerCount2010_web.pdf>.

Forgacs, David (ed.). 2000. *An Antonio Gramsci Reader: Selected Writings 1916–1935.* New York: Schocken Books.

Friedmann, Harriet. 1993. "After Midas' Feast: Alternative Food Regimes for the Future." In P. Allen (ed.), *Food for the Future: Conditions and Contradictions of Sustainability.* New York: John Wiley.

_____. 1993a. "The Political Economy of Food: A Global Crisis." *New Left Review* 197, January–February: 29–55.

_____. 2007. "Scaling Up: Bringing Public Institutions and Food Corporations into the Project for a Local, Sustainable Food System in Ontario." *Agriculture and Human Values* 24: 389–98.

Funes, F., L. Garcia, M. Bourque, N. Perez, and P. Rosset. 2003. *Sustainable Agriculture and Resistance: Transforming Food Production in Cuba.* Oakland: Food First Books.

Gibson-Graham, J.K. 1996. *The End of Capitalism (As We Knew It): A Feminist Critique of Political Economy.* Malden, MA: Blackwell Publishers.

Goodman, D., and M. Watts. 1997. *Globalising Food: Agrarian Questions and Global Restructuring.* New York: Routledge.

Halweil, Brian, and Danielle Nierenberger. 2010. "Charting a New Path to Eliminating Hunger." *State of the World 2011: Innovations that Nourish the Planet.* Washington DC: Worldwatch Institute.

Hamilton, Blair. 2005. *Agricultural Land Trusts: Preserving Small Farm Heritage.* June. Canadian Centre for Policy Alternatives-MB. <policyalternatives.ca/sites/default/files/uploads/publications/Manitoba_Pubs/2005/Agricultural_Land_Trusts.pdf>.

Health Canada. 2007. "Income-Related Household Food Security in Canada." *Canadian Community Health Survey, Cycle 2.2, Nutrition (2004).* Publication No. 4696. Ottawa: Health Canada.

Hendrix, Cullen, Stephan Haggard, and Beatriz Magaloni. 2009. "Grievance and Opportunity: Food Prices, Political Regime and Protest." Paper prepared for presentation at the International Studies Association convention, New York, February 15–18.

Hines, Colin. 2000. *Localization: A Global Manifesto.* London: Earthscan Publications Ltd.

Holt-Gimenez, Eric, and R. Patel, with A. Shattuck. 2009. *Food Rebellions! Crisis and the Hunger for Justice.* Cape Town, Africa: Pambazuka Press.

Kenfield, Isabella. 2009. "The Return of Michael Taylor: Monsanto's Man in the Obama Administration." *Counterpunch* August 14–16. <organicconsumers.org/articles/article_18866.cfm>.

La Vía Campesina. 2010. "Statement from the People's Movement Assembly on Food Sovereignty." <viacampesina.org/en/index.php?option=com_content& view=article&id=934:statement-from-the-peoples-movement-assembly-on-food-sovereignty&catid=21:food-sovereignty-and-trade&Itemid=38>.

Larsen, Kristian, and J. Gilliland. 2008. "Mapping the Evolution of 'Food Deserts' in a Canadian City: Supermarket Accessibility in London, Ontario, 1961–2005." *International Journal of Health Geographics* 7, 16.

Lee, Marc, Herb Barbolet, Tegan Adams, and Matt Thomson. 2010. *Every Bite Counts: Climate Justice and B.C.'s Food System.* November. Canadian Centre for Policy Alternatives.

Lynch, Derek. 2009. "Environmental Impacts of Organic Agriculture: A Canadian Perspective." *Canadian Journal of Plant Science* 89, 4 (July). <cielap.org/pdf/Lynch_EGSOA_CJPS.Final.SSV2_doc.pdf>.

Madeley, John. 2002. *Food for All: The Need for a New Agriculture.* Halifax, NS: Fernwood Publishing.

Manning, Richard. 2004. *Against the Grain.* New York: North Point Press.

Mattera, Philip 2004. "How Agribusiness Has Hijacked Regulatory Policy at the U.S. Department of Agriculture." Corporate research project of Good Jobs First. Washington DC: USDA Inc. <scribd.com/doc/73696926/USDA-INC-By-Philip-Mattera>.

Miller, Sally 2008. *Edible Action: Food Activism and Alternative Economics.* Halifax/Winnipeg: Fernwood Publishing.

NFU (National Farmers Union Canada). 2010. "Losing Our Grip: How a Corporate Farmland Buy-up, Rising Farm Debt, and Agribusiness Financing of Inputs Threaten Family Farms and Food Sovereignty." A report by Canada's National Farmers Union. June 7. <nfu.ca/briefs.html#briefs>.

NSFA (Nova Scotia Federation of Agriculture). 2011. "Reduced Food Miles Brings Benefits." <nsfa-fane.ca/programs_and_projects/Food_Miles>.

Patel, Raj. 2007. *Stuffed and Starved: Markets, Power and the Hidden Battle for the World Food System.* Toronto: Harper Collins.

____. 2009. *The Value of Nothing.* New York: Picador.

Patel, Raj, and Philip McMichael. 2009. "A Political Economy of the Food Riot." *Review* xxxii, 1.

Porter, Catherine. 2011. "Backyard Farming in the GTA." *Toronto Star.* April 6. <thestar.com/news/article/970270--porter-backyard-farming-in-the-gta>.

Pottier, Johan. 1999. *Anthropology of Food: The Social Dynamics of Food Security.* Malden, MA: Blackwell Publishers.

Pretty, Jules N. 1995. *Regenerating Agriculture: Policies and Practice for Sustainability and Self-Reliance.* Washington, DC: Joseph Henry Press.

Qualman, Darrin, and Fred Tait. 2004. *The Farm Crisis, Bigger Farms and the Myths of 'Competition' and 'Efficiency.'* Ottawa: Canadian Council for Policy Alternatives. October.

Qualman, D., and N. Wiebe. 2002. *The Structural Adjustment of Canadian Agriculture.* Ottawa: Canadian Centre for Policy Alternatives. November.

Rebick, Judy. 2000. *Imagine Democracy.* Toronto: Stoddart Publishing.

Rideout, Karen, Graham Riches, Aleck Ostry, Don Buckingham, and Rod MacRae. 2007. "Bringing the Right to Food Home to Canada: Challenges and Possibilities for Achieving Food Security." *Public Health Nutrition.* <journals.cambridge.org/article_S1368980007246622>.

Rocha, Cecilia. 2000. "An Integrated Program for Urban Food Security: The Case of Belo Horizonte, Brazil." Unpublished paper.

Scharf, Kathryn, Charles Levkoe, and Nick Saul. 2010. *In Every Community a Place for Food: The Role of the Community Food Centre in Building a Local, Sustainable, and Just Food System.* Metcalf Food Solutions Papers. Toronto: Metcalf Foundation.

Shiva, Vandana 2005. *Earth Democracy: Justice, Sustainability and Peace.* Boston: South End Press.

____. 1993. *Monocultures of the Mind.* London: Zed Books.

Sinclair, Scott, and J. Grieshaber-Otto. 2009. *Threatened Harvest: Protecting Canada's World-Class Grain System.* Ottawa: Canadian Centre for Policy Alternatives. March. <policyalternatives.ca/publications/reports/threatened-harvest>.

Sparling, David, Terry Quadri, and Erna van Duren. 2005. *Consolidation in the Canadian Agri-Food Sector and the Impact on Farm Incomes.* Ottawa: Canadian Agri-Food Policy Institute. June. Draft Discussion Document. <capi-icpa.ca/archives/pdfs/PapID11_DSparling.pdf>.

Statistics Canada. 2011. *Census Of Agriculture: Section 6, Characteristics of Farm Operators, Canada and Provinces: Census Years 1991 to 2006.* <statcan.gc.ca/pub/95-632-x/2007000/t/4185586-eng.htm>.

Stopes, Christopher, Charles Couzens, Mark Redman, and Sarah Watson. 2002. "Local food: The Case for Re-localising Northern Ireland's Food Economy." Belfast, NI: Friends of the Earth.

Swenson, Dave. 2009. *Investigating the Potential Economic Impacts of Local Foods for Southeast Iowa.* Ames, IA: Leopold Center for Sustainable Agriculture, Iowa State University.

Toronto Public Health 2010. *Cultivating Food Connections: Toward a Healthy and Sustainable Food System for Toronto.* Toronto: City of Toronto. May.

Weimer, Candace. 2009. *Bridging the Gap from Poverty to Independence: What Is the Role of Canadian Food Banks?* Regina: Canadian Council for Policy Alternatives. February 26. <policyalternatives.ca/publications/reports/bridging-gap-poverty-independence>.

Weis, Tony. 2007. *The Global Food Economy: The Battle for the Future of Farming.* Halifax, NS: Fernwood Publishing.

Wright, Angus, and W. Wolford. 2003. *To Inherit the Earth: The Landless Movement and the Struggle for a New Brazil.* Oakland: Food First Books.

Xuereb, Marc. 2005. *Food Miles: Environmental Implications of Food Imports to Waterloo Region.* Waterloo, ON: Region of Waterloo Public Health.

12

Energy, Climate Change, and the Politics of Sustainability

Debra Davidson and Mike Gismondi

YOU SHOULD KNOW THIS

- Tar sands production has grown four-fold since 1990, exceeding 1.3 million barrels per day (MBD) in 2008; forecast to reach 3.3 MBD by 2015.
- To recover one barrel of bitumen by in situ extraction, 1000 cubic feet of natural gas are required, compared to 250 cubic feet for extraction by open-pit mining.
- Tar sands production emits roughly three times the volume of greenhouse gases per barrel than conventional oil, not including emissions from upgrading, refining, and transport.
- Greenhouse gases resulting from the high energy requirements in tar sands extraction and processing currently represent 5 percent of Canada's emissions at thirty megatonnes (MTs) but are projected to increase to 300 MTs by 2050. Total emissions for all of Canada in 2008 were 734 megatonnes.
- Scientists predict a four to five degree warming in the Athabasca region by mid-century, which will likely increase evaporation above any increases in precipitation, resulting in projected declines in seasonal flow in the Athabasca River, north of Fort McMurray, of up to 50 percent.
- According to the Canadian Association of Petroleum Producers, oil sands operations use approximately 176 million cubic metres of water per year, 160 million of which are drawn from the Athabasca River.
- Surface mining of bitumen to date has created a 530 square kilometer open pit in northeast Alberta.
- Contaminated wastewater is deposited in tailings ponds, which now cover 130 square kilometres. That's 840 billion litres or 330,000 Olympic swimming pools.
- Among the nastier of outputs that end up in the water as a result of tar sands activities are polycyclic aromatic hydrocarbons (PAHs), mercury, and napthenic acids. PAHs include a number of compounds, many of which are suspected or known carcinogens, and increasing concentrations have been found in the Athabasca River downstream from extraction operations.
- Air emissions also affect water quality, when deposited onto the snow pack (Kelly et al. 2010). Substantial particulates have been found in the snow pack within a fifty km radius of upgrading plants — an estimated 11,400 metric tons during four months of snowfall. If snowmelt is released as a pulse, this would amount to a major oil spill annually.

Sources: Alberta Chamber of Resources 2004; Alberta Environment 2009a, 2009b, 2009d; CAPP n.d.; Environment Canada n.d.; Greenpeace 2010; Schindler 2005; Suzuki 2011; Timoney and Lee 2009.

FOR THE LAST FEW DECADES, MOST CANADIANS have assumed that Canadian environmental issues are addressed by government regulators, corporations, and publics who are ably assisted by scientific expertise. An alternative view insists that political power defines who has an opportunity to influence environmental governance, and which issues get attention. Political elites seek to contain public concerns and dominate the meaning and practice of sustainability in Canada, while neighbourhood groups, environmental and NGO organizations, and their scientific advocates seek to challenge the legitimacy of the politically powerful.

Over the last decade, the issues of energy security and climate change have moved to the main stage in this struggle over sustainability in Canada, and thus we devote our attention in this chapter to these tandem political issues. Declining reserves of conventional fossil fuels, in the absence of considerable reductions in consumption, pose a significant threat to virtually all standards of living, as energy supply affects everything from recreational pursuits to the provision of food. In tandem with this trend is the ever-growing volume of greenhouse gases in the atmosphere bringing us closer each day to the brink of runaway climate change.

> This project is clearly one of the most significant industrial manipulations of the environment in the modern era, associated with the age-old trade-off of short-term, concentrated economic gains for long-term, irreversible ecological impacts, but at a scale that is arguably unprecedented.

Front and centre on that stage, but illustrating environmental degradation and sustainability issues generally, is the Alberta tar sands, now recognized as the second largest oil reserve in the world after Saudi Arabia (EIA 2009). This project is simultaneously the most significant industrial manipulation of the environment in the modern era, as well as the age-old trade-off of short-term, concentrated economic gains for long-term, irreversible ecological impacts, but at a scale that is arguably unprecedented. Encouraged by technological advances, high oil prices, aggressive provincial marketing, and extensive private investment, the Alberta reserve has become the largest industrial operation in the world (Nikiforuk 2008). Tar sands production has grown four-fold since 1990, exceeding 1.3 million barrels per day (MBD) in 2010, and is forecast to reach 3.3 mbd by 2015 (CAPP n.d.). Over U.S.$125 billion in investment is planned for the next decade, with most major oil companies holding stakes (Clarke 2008: 83). The politics of tar sands development cannot be considered a regional phenomenon, however. As with many other projects with political implications, it is increasingly defined by a global system of flows — of capital, power, information, and environmental impact. Energy development in the Athabasca oil sands is formally under the jurisdiction of the Canadian federalist system, and yet informally subject to supranational and global flows of markets, geopolitics, and public opinion. The state and corporate beneficiaries of tar sands development must thus direct their legitimation efforts toward multiple audiences, and respond to a political context that is continually in flux.

Critics note that the extraction and processing of the tar comes with a tremendous environmental cost that is quite possibly unparalleled in the energy industry. International attention has been focused on the greenhouse gases resulting from the high energy requirements in the extraction process[1]: representing 5 percent of Canada's emissions at 30 megatonnes (MTs) but projected to reach 300 MTs by 2050 (Alberta Environment 2009a).[2] Tar sands production emits roughly three times the volume of greenhouse gases per barrel than conventional oil, not including emissions from upgrading, refining, and transport (Paehlke 2008; Shiell and Loney 2007). Closer to home, a myriad of other environmental concerns loom. Most of the bitumen to date has been extracted via surface mining, creating a 530 square kilometre

> Tar sands production emits roughly three times the volume of greenhouse gases per barrel than conventional oil, not including emissions from upgrading, refining, and transport.

open pit (Alberta Environment 2009b). Contaminated wastewater is deposited in tailings ponds, which now cover 130 square kilometres (Alberta Environment 2009d). A smaller but growing proportion of the tar is extracted through an in situ process consisting of injecting steam underground to make deeper deposits viscous enough to be pumped to the surface, disturbing a smaller but by no means insignificant area of land, while also requiring substantially higher energy input (Alberta Chamber of Resources 2004). The extraction process is water-intensive, consuming two to five barrels of water for every barrel of bitumen mined, and half a barrel in the in situ process (Alberta Environment 2009c). In situ extraction will inevitably surpass surface mining in the next decades since the vast majority of the resource can only be extracted in this manner (Sinclair 2011).

Other impacts travel along paths forged by the biosphere's natural trajectories, including water withdrawals from a major regional watershed that serves as an important ecological corridor between the Canadian Rockies and the Arctic, and the production of several air pollutants, particularly sulphuric compounds, which follow patterns of air flow to reach endpoints near and far. The resource must be transported long distances to urban centres to the south and east, requiring extensive pipelines that have their own environmental footprint, flowing south and east along a continuously expanding network of specialized pipelines that deliver 75 percent of the synthetic crude to U.S. consumers.

Adding to these environmental costs are growing concerns about energy security, or, more accurately, Canada's lack of it. The proportionality clause of the North American Free Trade Agreement (NAFTA), signed in 1993, requires Canada (and Alberta) to continue to export "the same proportion of oil and gas as in the past three years, even if Canadians run short" (Laxer 2006, 2011).

> Adding to these environmental costs are growing concerns about energy security, or, more accurately, Canada's lack of it.

Recognizing the ecological, ethical, and political contradictions of the Alberta tar sands, some concerned citizens and scientists have expressed what Amsler (2009: 116) describes as "a sense of incredulity that people would not act to avert the possibility of unprecedented environmental and social catastrophe." In a recent issue of *Nature* (23 September 2009), climate and ecosystem scientists urge us to recognize that there are "planetary boundaries that must not be transgressed" to prevent "human activities from causing unacceptable environmental change." They point out that thresholds for ecological changes are non-linear, and tipping points may be surprising. Beck (2009) and others view such uncertain conditions as opportunistic circumstances, anticipating a collective social reaction with the capacity to motivate intentional choices and take up alternative actions. Similarly, Homer-Dixon (2007) has argued that the rapid climate warming might spur human creativity and innovation and accelerate carbon descent, what Homer-Dixon coined as the "upside of down." Such confidence in the prospect of a co-operative response, however, needs to be tempered by a critical evaluation of the ability of the politically

> Before social change occurs, the legitimacy of prevailing institutions must be challenged, and current contentions over the legitimacy of the tar sands may well be a harbinger of our ability to address the challenges posed by energy and climate change.

powerful to sustain certain disruptive processes. Before social change occurs, the legitimacy of prevailing institutions must be challenged, and current contentions over the legitimacy of the tar sands may well be a harbinger of our ability to address the challenges posed by energy and climate change.

Flows of Petrochemicals; Flows of Power

The tar sands project is immersed in a global network of flows, beginning with flows of capital, and capital's eternal bed partner, politics. The penetration of the tar sands in the global economy is readily marked by the list of country origins of current investors, including among others Korea, China, Britain, France, Norway, Japan, and, of course, the United States. Decisions regarding the export of tar sands products are also constrained by the dictates of several international trade agreements, most explicitly NAFTA (Laxer 2011).

In contrast to the southerly flow of fossil fuels (and the power and wealth it facilitates), the ancient route of the Athabasca River, from which water is extracted and into which waste leaks, conveniently flows north, into remote regions inhabited predominantly by Aboriginal peoples — away from the powerful and toward the powerless. The Athabasca River is the main artery of the Arctic drainage area, as well as being one of the world's largest rivers. The tar sands exemplify patterns of directionality and flow in our current era of "Liquid Modernity." That is, the tar sands highlight the extent to which our society is, despite claims that it rests on a non-material knowledge and information economy, still very much based on solidly material goods like oil; we have by no means "dematerialized." To the contrary, the juxtaposition of material and immaterial flows is vivid, charting dynamic shifts in power and consequence. Such shifts are by their nature unpredictable, simultaneously creating conditions for the rapid emergence of large-scale hazard and opportunities for transformation.

> The tar sands exemplify patterns of directionality and flow in our current era of "Liquid Modernity" that highlight the extent to which we have by no means "dematerialized."

The speed and volume of capital's global circulation is matched by that of information, encompassing both words and images describing the tar sands, which have entered global circulation in the millions of gigabytes. The theatres that citizens have come to rely upon for democratic deliberation have evolved as well, both in form and audience. The discourses emanating from traditional, localized theatres, such as the political speech, public hearing or worksite protest, are quickly digitized for immediate global consumption, encouraging disseminators to direct their message to an ever-growing audience. These forums are joined by an exponentially growing number of very specialized web-based discussion boards, media sources, blogs, and chat rooms.

The very attention accorded to the tar sands today has arisen in large part in response to the contributions from this project to another global process: climate change. Perspectives regarding the global significance of the contribution of greenhouse gas emissions from the Athabasca tar sands vary tremendously, with proponents attempting to minimize and opponents attempting to maximize its relativity to other sources. This numbers game is only political banter, however: the deeper significance of the tar sands' contribution to global warming is representational — our commitment to this form of development represents a development trajectory that ensures exacerbation, not mitigation, of climate change, associated as it is with an ever-increasing ratio of emissions per barrel as we necessarily probe deeper into the bitumen reserve.

Spaces Between the Flows

Petrochemical products circulate the globe in large quantities, yet all such resources must come from somewhere, and go to somewhere. The spatial separation between frontier developments — such as the Athabasca tar sands — and population centres has historically tempered public reaction to the land-based impacts of such developments. This is certainly the case in Canada, in which the national population is heavily concentrated in urban centres within a few hundred kilometres of the U.S. border, while most such developments take place much further north. The very spatial extent of the country has nourished an "unlimited frontier" imaginary among Canadians well into the twenty-first century — tempering concern for land disruption. At the same time, those natural resources come from so far away that they effectively become de-linked from a particular place, thereby relieving consumers of responsibility for production's impacts (Princen, Maniates, and Conca 2002). Bitumen is itself quite literally attached to this remote place, expressing a stubborn resistance to being removed. The only feasible means of transporting (and consuming) bitumen is in the form of a liquid, which it most certainly is not, in its original form. The necessity of converting it into a liquid for the purposes of export is directly associated with the level of water and energy inputs required, and the environmental disruption generated. Even the sand's contribution to global climate change cannot be disembedded from place — the very intensity of emissions being determined by the physical properties of the resource itself and by its distance to markets.

In addition, resources that are fixed in space are subject to tenure, and the institutions with political jurisdiction over those spaces have a disproportionate degree of power to dictate the pace and character of development trajectories. While many social-scientific treatments of development focus on nation-states, doing so would be inappropriate in the current context. With a federalist political structure in which a tremendous amount of jurisdiction over land and environmental concerns remains at the provincial level, the Province of Alberta enjoys a tremendous amount of political weight that stretches beyond its jurisdictional authority: as one commentator put it, "the province [Alberta] can control its own destiny more than any other because, in the years to come, Canada will need Alberta far more than Alberta will need the rest of Canada" (Maich 2005). While such political power has without question been enabled by the geographic location of the resource itself, it has not been simply bestowed upon the Province directly, since the power embodied in the resource does not emanate from its mere existence, but rather in its potential for commodification.

To this end, the Province of Alberta has been actively — even aggressively — encouraging tar sands development for nearly a century. Without significant levels of state endorsement and fiscal subsidization the tar sands would not likely have been developed, nor would such development be able to persist (Gillmor 2005). Since the first premier took office in 1905, provincial government administrations have prioritized the development of the tar deposits by engaging in close relations with industry, supporting research, and providing fiscal incentives to investors. The Province was a primary sponsor of the research necessary to generate the technological developments that enabled tar sands development (Chastko 2004). The energy industry contributed an average of 42 percent of provincial GDP, 31 percent of provincial employment, and 32 percent of government revenues over from 1971–2004 (Mansell and Schlenker 1995). This rent comes in exchange for substantial (albeit many would argue inadequate) state subsidization of development, including decades of research prior to and since commercialization, all manner of physical infrastructure needed to traverse the extensive spaces between sites of production and consumption, exclusion of a substantial land base from other forms of development, and the social service demands of a boom economy.

The power of the Albertan state to influence the development of the tar sands is mirrored by the potential political power of Alberta's citizens relative to citizens elsewhere. This is the case in part because Alberta's citizens formally wield the greatest power to remove the legitimacy of the Albertan state, in the voting booth. Secondarily, however, the relative distance between the tar sands and the vast majority of members of global civil society minimizes the visceral and experiential reaction among members of that non-local citizenry that might engender mobilization, rendering local citizens the more likely source of sustained opposition. Albertans, however, have not engaged in substantive levels of organized opposition to date. Rather, voters have expressed consistent support for the Progressive Conservatives — the provincial party that has been the most outspoken advocate for tar sands development, acting according to neoliberal ideological guidelines. The Progressive Conservatives actually gained seats during the most recent election, at a time when tar sands development was at its most acrimonious.

The low potential for local opposition to the tar sands is reflected in other trends as well. According to recent polling efforts, it is not clear that, even were Alberta the site of a particularly strong civil society, such strengths would be applied to mobilization against the tar sands. A poll of Albertans conducted by Probe Research in 2006 found that 41 percent of respondents held somewhat positive and 37 percent very positive views about development of Alberta's oil sands.[3] The most cited reason for support was the perceived economic benefits. Other survey questions suggest some sources of grievance, however: 63 percent disagreed that Alberta was receiving maximum revenue from the oil sands, 87 percent agreed that companies could do more to protect the environment, and 50 percent felt the pace of development was too fast.

Guided by Voices: Interpreting Future Trajectories

Travelling along these discursive channels are messages of support, critique, and resistance that transpire into ebbs and flows in legitimacy — of the tar sands as an industrial project, of the state and corporate entities that are its proponents, of the ideologies invoked — and by extension the potential for social transformation through and beyond this historical nexus of energy and climate crisis. While we are cautious about future prospects for transformation, the tar sands are unquestionably jarring to the imaginaries that have served to endorse

industrialization, and thus can and have motivated questioning and mobilization. Those environmental hazards
that often capture the imagination of risk scholars include
that class of dangers that tend toward the nano-scopic:
the unseen, undetected, parts-per-billion elements, the
very inconceivability of which strikes fear. But the gar-

> The tar sands are unquestionably jarring to the imaginaries that have served to endorse industrialization and thus can and have motivated questioning and mobilization.

gantuan is no less inconceivable, and thus the incomprehensibility of the scale of disruption
associated with the tar sands itself has an analogous shock value.

The tar sands project most certainly still enjoys the support of powerful interests hailing
from multiple origins, but there are some indications that the hegemony once enjoyed by
these parties is on shaky ground. The unprecedented level of discussion of the tar sands in
sessions of the Provincial Legislative Assembly in recent years provides one ready indicator,
suggesting that while state endorsement of tar sands development did not pose a legitimacy
threat historically, this political landscape has changed. While scholars often highlight the
obstacles to social movements whose task it is to challenge the existing social order, observers should not discount the increasing effort required among those in power to maintain
their position of dominance in complex global polities, when such dominance depends far
more on the delicate contours of discursive legitimacy rather than the blunter forms of coercion relied upon in days gone by. The provincial state's pursuit of tar sands development
has become a contested terrain precisely because local decisions have global implications.
In this instance, tar sands development has deleterious effects on the global environment,
but at the same time, the resource in question is essential and global supplies are declining.
Exporters of raw materials are sensitive to their legitimacy in the global marketplace, vulnerable to reputational threats, consumer boycotts, and investor hesitancy. The Albertan state
faces distinct audiences — foreign investors, a cosmopolitan global civil society, importing
states, and global consumers — from all of whom they must seek legitimacy.[4]

Voices of the Converted

While Alberta has been endorsing tar sands development for at least fifty years, the level of
attention this development has been given by elected officials recently is unprecedented.
This can be seen as a moment of dislocation, during which discursive regularities or routines
must be modified, and actors must mobilize new discourses and connect the previously
unconnected in order to defend (or acquire) legitimacy (cf. Howarth 2000; Hajer and
Versteeg 2005). Fortunately for the proponents of many development projects, the direct
indications of environmental degradation are often obscure and open to an extraordinary
degree of interpretive flexibility, such that interpretations themselves can determine political
outcomes (Freudenburg, Gramling, and Davidson 2008).

Tar sands development presents a stark contrast to any vision of sustainability that could
reasonably be invoked, but, in an effort to maintain legitimacy, it is presented as just that by
proponents — initially as clean energy and now as "ethical oil." Proponents invoke deep-
seated cultural ideals of individualism and identity: this is *our* resource, and we will develop
it *our* way, just as we always have. At the same time, Progressive Conservative Party members

have engaged in a symbolic metamorphosis, transforming a natural resource industry into a New Age, information- and technology-based one. Tar sands development is posed simply as the only reasonable option, necessary for security, economy, and society alike. The PC Party has so far been able to tread this precarious terrain by couching tar sands development in the context of master frames that resonate with multiple audiences, including sustainable development, the threat of terrorism, and "peak oil." They have done so by taking three primary legitimacy claims posed by concerned citizens, and turning them on their head.

Legitimacy Threat 1: Failure to Protect Environmental Well-Being

The growing alarm regarding the environmental impacts associated with tar sands development have raised the spectre of a crisis of state legitimacy. International "Dirty Oil" boycotting campaigns have brought environmental sustainability, however reluctantly, to the centre of the PC Party's political discourse. PC Party members have countered opponents with reference to environmental stewardship, ascription to technological optimism, and the selective use of numbers and metaphors to diminish the perceived extent of environmental impact. Elected officials have taken every opportunity to expound on the province's record of reductions in the intensity of greenhouse gas emissions (per economic output) while avoiding completely admissions of the substantive increases in total emissions as economic growth ensues:

> Alberta's oil sands account for just 4 percent of Canada's greenhouse gas emissions, and less than one tenth of 1 percent of all global greenhouse gases. Nevertheless, oil sands projects have reduced their carbon dioxide emissions intensity by up to 45 percent since 1990, and we're working to reduce it even further. (Alberta Premier Stelmach, World Heavy Oil Congress, Edmonton, Alberta, March 10, 2008)

> A lot of Canadian experts see carbon capture and storage as the most practical and promising way for Canada to reduce greenhouse gas emissions safely and effectively…. We have a chance to be a real leader here … just as Alberta has always been a leader on climate change. (Stelmach, Calgary Chamber of Commerce Luncheon, Calgary, Alberta, January 30, 2008)

Here Premier Stelmach offers complementary messages to two different in-groups: business and technical leaders of the oil industry, and the Calgary Chamber of Commerce. His messages of carbon intensity emissions reduction and carbon capture go hand-in-hand to counter international criticism of the tar sands' contributions to global climate change. Both speeches assign to government and industry the positive qualities of leadership and innovation, handily disqualifying critics. The Premier's use of seemingly impressive figures on emissions intensity reductions are embellished with promises of continued improvements, while the apparent authority of "Canadian experts" is called upon to enhance confidence in an altogether questionable technological enterprise — carbon sequestration, or the capture of carbon emissions for storage underground. This allusion to the "can-do" Albertan attitude is brought forth in multiple encounters by PC Party members, dissuading skeptics and re-creating climate change villains into champions. These are not semantic games. The use of euphemisms like "intensity reductions" has been roundly criticized by global media as transparent spin-doctoring of such proportions as to pose a "reputational threat" to big oil itself (Phillips 2008). Despite such international critique, this discourse coincided with the announcement by the Premier of the

> This allusion to the "can-do" Albertan attitude is brought forth in multiple encounters by PC Party members, dissuading skeptics and re-creating climate change villains into champions.

commitment of $2 billion in taxpayers' money to support research and development into carbon sequestration. Rather than denying the reality of environmental impact, PC Party members emphasize the tremendous social benefits that would be compromised by stricter environmental regulation:

> Make no mistake — Alberta's climate change plan is a real response to a real problem. It recognizes Alberta's role as a global energy supplier. And it will deliver real reductions, in a realistic timeframe… without sacrificing growth or quality of life. (Stelmach. Calgary Chamber of Commerce Luncheon, Calgary, Alberta, January 30, 2008)

Finally, in a spectacular reframing feat, environmental costs would be borne were we to actually stop development, since tar sands development generates revenues that support environmental sustainability:

> A growing economy… pays for the infrastructure to support public transit — which in turn reduces personal vehicle use. And it helps fund the research that will provide *long-term* solutions to the environmental issues we face. (Stelmach, Canadian Urban Transit Association Annual Conference, Edmonton, Alberta, May 28, 2008)

> Shutting the door to Alberta oil would mean opening the door to offshore suppliers who don't place as high a premium on the environment. (Stelmach, Sixth Annual TD Securities Oil Sands Forum, Calgary, Alberta, July 9, 2008)

With the implication that the real environmental culprits are individual car drivers, the state is relieved of the need to address emissions from the tar sands. Narrative techniques like these increase the legitimacy or "jurisdictional authority" of proponents and delegitimize naysayers (Luhmann 1989). Saving the environment will kill the economy, so politicians become the "real heroes."

Legitimacy Threat 2: Failure to Ensure Economic Well-Being

Several concerns have been raised by members of opposition parties, civil society organizations, and community residents, regarding the effects of the energy boom on the long-term well-being of the provincial economy. These include overinvestment in a volatile resource industry, distortion of the provincial labour market (many businesses outside of the tar sands, particularly those dependent upon skilled trades workers, are unable to pay competitive wages during booms [Alberta Federation of Labour 2003, 2007, 2009]), and demands on public subsidies to support development combined with low royalties. The royalties captured from tar sands production have been consistently lower than those captured by the governments of Norway and Alaska, for example (Taylor et al. 2004). Some have argued for transitioning the provincial economy in anticipation of eventual resource depletion. PC Party members counter these threats to legitimacy with the authority of neoliberal ideology: it would be imprudent to intervene, because markets are most efficient when left to their own devices. The state's responsibility is not to control development but to ensure that market forces prevail unfettered; to manage the impacts of development, and explicitly not its pace:

> I want to make one thing very clear. There has been talk by the federal Liberals — and others — of a moratorium on development of Alberta's oil sands. My government does not believe in interfering in the free marketplace. You cannot just step in and lower the boom on development and growth — in the oil sands or elsewhere. If that were to happen, the economic consequences for Alberta, and for the economy of Canada, would be devastating. (Stelmach, Rotary Club of Calgary Valentine's Luncheon Address, Calgary, February 13, 2007)

Although it may not be obvious to the outsider, this Valentine's Day speech raises the spectre of federal interference in Alberta, a hot button trope that invokes memories of the National Energy Program, which was blamed by many for the significant economic hardship in Alberta in the 1980s. To reinforce this message, PC Party members have emphasized in multiple venues that the real threat would be to actually fail to develop the tar sands:

> When someone comes to me and suggests to me that I could be tremendously reducing the amount of greenhouse gases... that are emitted in this province by simply restricting or limiting or ending any further expansion of oil and gas in the oil sands in particular, that's true.... But, clearly, there would be consequences of that, and the consequences, I would suggest to you, would be rather dramatic. Instead, it's the responsibility of the government to consider what the consequences are, to consider both sides of any issue before carrying forward. (Renner, Legislative Assembly, Monday, November 5, 2007)

Minister Renner's claim to "consider both sides" of the issue paints critics as one-sided, biased, and irresponsible. The PC Party's discourses reject moratorium and transition talk in favour of riding the wild waves of the current boom (Daub 2010), reversing citizen concerns and depicting a slowdown as the real looming financial catastrophe:

> You're saying shut it down. I could not disagree more with that because I want people to be able to feed their families. (Boutilier, Minister of Environment, Legislative Assembly, June 14, 2007)

> In order to fully understand the share that Albertans have received from this re-source, we need to take into consideration the fact that this industry has generated literally thousands and thousands of jobs for Albertans, very high-paying jobs. It has allowed us to expand our post-secondary education institutions. It's allowed us to expand our health care and medical facilities. It has allowed the province of Alberta to grow some 60,000 to 80,000 souls a year in the last number of years. It has made Alberta a very vibrant industrial community for all Albertans. (Knight, Legislative Assembly, November 5, 2007)

Boutilier's image of environmentalists taking food off the plates of hungry families appeals to Alberta's large working class; this is an age-old diversionary tactic that scapegoats the environmentally concerned, while drawing attention away from discussion of the probable link between his government's neoliberal economic planning and the systemic vulnerability of resource-reliant communities. Likewise, Energy Minister Knights' jobs-versus-environment framing device employs a growth paradigm

> The AFL condemns the temporary foreign worker program as racist.

that resonates well with listeners, without mention that a large proportion of jobs are filled by temporary foreign workers. The AFL condemns the temporary-foreign-worker program as racist, and used by government to please employers and facilitate a cheap, flexible workforce with fewer rights than ordinary Canadians, and with little promise of permanent residency or immigration (AFL 2009b). Many critics, including the labour movement, also point out that the regional economy has been heavily distorted by wage inflation (AFL 2003, 2009a).

Legitimacy Threat 3: Challenges to Security

The theme of security, in the traditional sense of maintaining internal order and eliminating military threats, emerges in response to concerns regarding social disorder in Fort McMurray, and in terms of the potential for tar sands infrastructure to be targets of terrorism. PC Party members counter these concerns with assurances of safety, and go farther to frame tar sands development as necessary to North American continental security:

> I don't know how it makes more sense to ship oil across the world from the Middle East than to use a friendly, stable, continental supplier like Alberta. (Stelmach, Calgary Chamber of Commerce Luncheon, Calgary, Alberta, January 30, 2008)

The parameters of this security storyline have been expanded, enabling proponents not only to counter security concerns raised by opponents, but also to draw on a broader discursive context in which both terrorism and "peak oil" have become prominent. The Premier placed particular emphasis on this two-pronged narrative in speeches to audiences in the United States:

> If the last few years have taught us anything, it's that real energy security requires secure, reliable, affordable energy. That's what Alberta offers — and it's right here in North America within a politically stable, U.S.-friendly, and business-oriented jurisdiction. Alberta is positioned to play a vital role in U.S. energy security. That's a

role we want to play. Alberta is second only to Saudi Arabia in global oil reserves...
[and] the only non-OPEC oil producer with the potential to substantially increase
energy production in the short-term. Those two facts put Alberta at the epicenter of
a new world order in energy. (Stelmach, Alberta Enterprise Group Energy Forum,
Washington, D.C., January 16, 2008)

The Premier paid tribute to energy security in several speeches to Albertan audiences
as well, often describing Alberta as "the key to *continental* energy security" (e.g., Global
Petroleum Conference, Calgary, June 10, 2008, emphasis added), suggesting that our ability
to serve such an honourable role is essential to Alberta's future.

Depictions of Alberta as a stable, U.S.-friendly caretaker of one of the world's last remaining deposits of oil draw on reminiscences of previous oil shortages, and the anxiety
of consumers and politicians about the threat of terrorism. Environmental degradation,
by contrast, appears an acceptable price to pay. Simultaneously, continentalism sidelines
concerns about the lack of domestic autonomy in energy policy, as dictated by the NAFTA
proportionality clause, which amounts to a one-way transfer of energy resources to the United
States, thereby enhancing Canada's energy *insecurity*.

> Grandiose claims regarding the size of the reserve do not account for the very high energy inputs required to bring this resource to market.

Reflecting the close alignment between the discourse
adopted by the PC Party and Alberta's industry leaders,
this storyline is also employed by the Alberta Enterprise
Group, a business advocacy organization and an outspoken proponent of the oil sands. Among other things,
this narrative enables proponents to cite global supply and demand as the only legitimate
determinants of the pace of development:

> World energy demands may see the doubling or tripling of oil sands production.
> (Johnson, Legislative Assembly, March 14, 2007)

> I think it is patently naive to think that Alberta is just going to curtail their produc-
> tion in oil. We have over 80 percent of North America's oil reserves right here in
> our province. (Oberle, Legislative Assembly, April 11, 2007)

These statements introduce anonymous and inanimate causal forces driving the expansion of development, justifying government's relinquishment of control over the pace
of development, and limiting its responsibility (and success) for the challenging task of
managing the problematic consequences of development.

> When deliverability can no longer rise to meet growing demand owing to geological, geopolitical and declining net energy issues, we have the beginning of a civilization-defining moment.

The narrative implores listeners to consider that, although we
didn't ask for this burden, we will assume responsibility for it
with the determination and leadership that is Alberta's legacy.
In exchange, the motivations of concerned citizens are subtly
redefined, characterized in broad brushstrokes as naïve at best,
anti-Albertan at worst. Finally, grandiose claims regarding the
size of the reserve do not account for the very high energy

Net Energy and Energy Return on Investment (EROI)

Net Energy refers to the amount of energy available after all of the energy required to extract, transport, refine, and consume it is accounted for. The decline in conventional fuels and increasing reliance on non-conventional fuels represents a significant moment because we are approaching an energy return on investment that marks a "Net Energy Cliff." As depicted in the graph below, the "Cliff" is that point at which the ratio of the energy gained (*dark gray*) to the energy used (*light gray*) decreases exponentially.

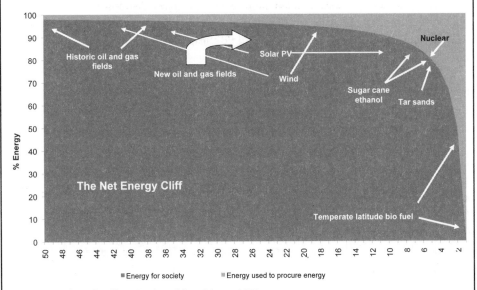

Source: Murphy and Hall 2010, adapted from Mearns 2008.

Early EROI estimates account only for energy used at the site of production. Recent analyses assess the Energy Return on Investment *at the point of use,* which includes the energy to find, produce, refine, and transport to point of use. As remaining deposits available to be exploited decline in quality, the effort it takes to transform those deposits into a usable energy form increases. Energy analysts have gone one step further, to include the energy required to *use* the energy, which encompasses all those energy costs consumed in the manufacture of automobiles and the maintenance of our transportation infrastructure, so-called *infrastructure metabolism.* According to assessments of this extended EROI, once a traditional EROI of 3:1 is reached, investments in development become questionable (the estimated EROI for the tar sands is between 4:1 and 3:1 (Murphy and Hall 2010).

According to Hughes (2010: 73):

> We're not running out of hydrocarbons yet. What we are running out of is cheap, easily extractible hydrocarbons. This is *not* a resource problem, it's *a rate of supply problem* or *deliverability* problem. When deliverability can no longer rise to meet growing demand owing to geological, geopolitical and declining net energy issues, we have the beginning of a civilization-defining moment.

inputs required to bring this resource to market — an input that today primarily consists of natural gas, which, as critics rightfully argue, is a clean-burning but declining resource used for home heating throughout Canada.

Contours of Resistance

A significant role played by social movements is their introduction of new interpretive frames in the public sphere (Benford and Snow 2000). Framing processes are designed to challenge accepted truths, and yet must be able to mobilize an expanded support network and thus must resonate with sympathizers (Klandermans 1984). This is no easy task, suggesting a need for acute awareness of the cultural and political climate within which organizations function (Benford and Snow 2000).

Certainly environmental movement organizations can and have played an important role in tar sands politics. Can this network of social movement organizations stop the tar sands, and perhaps move beyond this goal to generate a transition away from oil-dependence? We are skeptical; however, we tend to agree with Gamson (1975: 28) that "success is an elusive idea." Even if these organizations cannot stop the tar sands, or foster a transition directly, they can nonetheless play a critical indirect role, by introducing new ideas and a degree of skepticism into the public sphere (Giugni 1998). As such, we can identify clues in the collective action frames employed.

There are three tiers of organizational activity in tar sands politics. First are the well-established regional environmental groups that have been critiquing the tar sands for well over a decade, some of which have found themselves in the precarious position of depending on funding from the very corporations they criticize. These organizations, like the Pembina Institute and the Environmental Law Centre, have provided valuable counter-information for local debates, but, by and large, have adopted "consensus-building" tactics, designed to ensure a seat at the table, rather than turning the tables (Pellow 1999). This tactic demands a form of collaborative frame-making that must be sufficiently challenging to resonate with the views of movement sympathizers, and at the same time compatible with the prerogatives of state and industry elites. Regional organizations make clear that their agenda does not include shutting down the tar sands; rather, they tend to call for more scientific and technological investments, and compliance with existing laws. As a politically conservative state dependent on resource staples, Alberta is in many ways a hostile political arena for an environmental organization, and thus this strategy makes a lot of sense. Organizational leadership also undoubtedly is aware of the reluctance of many Albertans to bring to a halt what is perceived to be the economic mainstay of the province.

We have also seen a newly emergent cohort of international movement organizations, including the giants like Greenpeace, Natural Resources Defense Council, the Polaris Institute, and so on, which have developed specific tar sands campaigns. Newer, more targeted groups have emerged as well, like Tarsands Watch and Oil Sands Truth. These organizations have played a notable role in bringing international awareness to the tar sands, and as such they have had a tremendous influence over the framing of non-local discourses. In particular, they have successfully introduced the powerful "Dirty Oil" frame into popular discourse, replete with negative symbolic connotations of its tainted identity, bringing to mind analogies to "dirty money," "blood diamonds," and the like. Well-established international environmental organizations have been focused primarily on reducing the tar sands' greenhouse gas emissions and their implication for Canada's compliance with the Kyoto Protocol (although compliance became a moot point when Prime Minister Harper withdrew Canada from the Protocol), while for the emergent targeted groups, like Corporate Ethics International's rethinkalberta.com campaign, the call for action is to stop the tar sands, by promoting divestment via consumer and tourism boycotting and direct pressure on investors. These frames do make some strategic sense — the most plausible means of pressuring Canada to comply with an international accord intended to address a global environmental problem is via international publics, particularly if those publics can induce their own state governments to join them. But then the likelihood of successfully stopping tar sands production is slim, considering the very large and diverse set of investors and consumers who would need to be convinced in order to completely close the international marketplace to Alberta bitumen.

Key to shifting international opinion has been a series of interventions by individuals and groups whose bodies of photographic work have trumped the images offered by corporate and state endorsers. Because of the circulating capacity of the Internet, they have provided a global flow of stills and videos illustrating the scale of industrial operations and its ecological impacts. The images circulate at different scales and among different publics: they include Don van Hout's personal canoe journey down the Athabasca River in 2007; Louis Helbig's aerial photography "Beautiful Destruction" shot from his own airplane as he flew over "restricted airspace" above tar sands operations; *National Geographic*'s special issue on Fort McMurray (2009); and the disturbing industrial landscape photography of Edward Burtynsky and his world-renowned study of *The End of Oil*. These and many other photographic and moving images have been repurposed, recirculated, and sutured into critical oppositional discourses. If an image says more than a thousand words, and we think they do, then the tar sands tale has been told to hundreds of millions of people, who, drawn to them like highway accidents, may just be recognizing in those images a common future and basis for global citizenship.

Non-local resistance continues to grow, with a prominent role increasingly being played by retailers like Lush and Vogue Magazine. Creative campaigns by Greenpeace and others designed to deter vacationing in Alberta have raised the ire of the Alberta government.[5] Over the last two years, popular books like Andrew Nikiforuk's book *Tar Sands: Dirty Oil* (2008) and documentaries such as *Dirty Oil* (2009) by Babelgum, have received critical acclaim and viewer fanfare alike.

Regional-level concern has maintained a persistent cadence too, led by the Pembina Institute, whose critical analyses expose well-documented economic, climatic, and ecological impacts of the tar sands (Pembina 2010). Most recently the Parkland Institute released a scathing report on energy royalties in Alberta (Boychuk 2010), offering convincing evidence that not only are royalty and tax rates set well below international industry standards, but the provincial government has also not even diligently collected from energy companies according to the current regime. Unfortunately this report received barely a nod in the regional press.

The fact that an industrial enterprise on a remote frontier has gained international stature, inspiring direct actions all over the globe, is nothing short of remarkable. But the very selection of certain frames diverts attention away from others, and those others may be quite significant to instigating a post-oil transition to a low carbon economy. Most notably, these activist frames do not resonate with the frames that have been embraced by that population we consider to be of greatest interest — concerned Albertan citizens.

In Alberta, a number of small, loosely organized local grassroots groups have begun to spring up, like the Keepers of the Athabasca, and the Friends of the Peace River. The positions taken by both non-Aboriginal and Aboriginal people in these networks of local organizations have been far more critical than those of the established organizations, but then their support base is also much smaller. Moreover, the frames employed by grassroots organizations are in much closer alignment with several concerned but unaffiliated citizens who have used public forums to call for a moratorium on development and pose direct challenges to state legitimacy.

Citizens in the Tar Sands

Some residents of Alberta live near projects, both existing and proposed. According to provincial legislation, these people have special "directly affected" status. There are many more residents who live beyond the boundaries of official designations of affect, but who take issue with those boundaries. Then there are the silent ones, thousands of workers who either by virtue of their tenuous employment, foreign status, fear of reprisal, or simple lack of personal investment in a place not called home, are notably disengaged in public discourse on the tar sands. Including those who are indirectly employed in the energy industry, this group includes some one in six Albertans. In many ways these conditions are not unique to tar sands development, but rather are endemic to contemporary natural resource industries. The pace and scale of development in modern staples economies means that producing areas will never have a sufficiently large resident skilled workforce and won't have the time to train one. So these industries become dependent on a mobile workforce, and that mobile workforce becomes dependent on perpetual relocation.

The Alberta Federation of Labour recognizes the benefits from tar sands jobs, but is critical of the impact of inflation on workers inside and outside the industry, the increase in foreign workers, and the export of value-added industries. The Canadian Communications, Energy and Paperworkers Union (CEP) membership (over 150,000) is anticipating how they might adapt to more stringent environmental regulations. They have rejected simple (zero sum) arguments that environmental controls mean job losses, and they are exploring a new concept of "just transition":

> an approach to public policy that seeks to minimize the impact of environmental policies on workers in affected industries (e.g., through retraining programs, preferential placement opportunities, development, or diversification assistance in affected regions). (Daub, 2010: 116)

Calgarians, living in the finance and management capital of the energy industry, woke up to Greenpeace one sunny morning in 2010 with a message hanging from the Calgary Tower highlighting the cozy relationship between the tar sands industry and the federal and provincial governments. Reprinted with permission of Greenpeace.

Involving workers from the oil sands industry in the discussion of the pace of development is crucial for moving beyond the boom mentality that "fed a sense of needing to take advantage of the tar sands while it lasted," to a more progressive "desire to... create stable dependable economic futures." The CEP's framing of work and climate change as social justice issues includes moral conceptions of environmental sustainability and the socially just distribution and prevention of risks (Daub: 2010: 133, and 116, 124, 125).

Original Inhabitants

Aboriginal peoples have been among the most alarmed by tar sands development, for good reason: they make up a high proportion of downstream and directly affected residents, and they rely to a much higher degree than the rest of us on the services provided by their local watershed for their livelihood. The First Nations, Métis, and non-registered Aboriginal peoples of the Athabasca region are understandably tired of the efforts needed to counter the repeated infringements on their rights by state-endorsed industrial development. In February 2008, Treaties 6, 7, and 8 signed off on a common resolution calling for a stop to new oil sands approvals until a comprehensive watershed management plan approved by their Treaty communities could be implemented (AEN 2008). Storylines offered by members of Aboriginal groups certainly resonate with those of other local citizens, but are also extended to the impacts on their livelihood:

> The Métis want to be certain that... they can exist and thrive as a people in Wood Buffalo.... Every day the land is left scarred and without reclamation efforts is a real day lost in our people's use of the lands. It adversely impacts both us and the flora and fauna. (Metis Consultation Sessions, Oil Sands Consultations, Fort McMurray, March 26, 2007)

The rights enjoyed by First Nations and Métis include the right to "consultation" regarding proposed activity on traditional territories, giving them what at least on paper constitutes influence above and beyond that enjoyed by non-Aboriginals. Unlike most European descendants, the cultural beliefs of most Aboriginal groups espouse responsibility for future generations, and this responsibility often motivates political engagement. For some, allegiance to both the state and non-Aboriginal citizenry is tenuous given that their ancestry predates the formation of these institutions.

Those critical voices that do emerge are worth listening to carefully (Taylor et al. 20009). Albertans are in a key position to influence the fate of this local enterprise with global reach — they are the ones with the formal, constitutionally ordained power to withdraw the legitimacy of the provincial state. While global "Others" can apply pressure, they can't vote the current leadership out of office. However, those testifying at the Oil Sands Consultations, supporting grassroots protest organizations, writing letters to the editor, and so on, represent that body of thoughtful individuals in Alberta willing to support change: they can play an important leadership role in the province.

> Those critical voices that do emerge are worth listening to carefully.

The Conflict Intensifies

The success of a movement is in many respects measured by the emergence of counter-movement activity (Meyer and Staggenborg 1996). Pro-tar sands forces have spent millions to promote this enterprise over the decades, much of it taxpayers' money. More recently, state and industry proponents have invested new resources specifically to counter-movement activities, directed at international audiences, while at the same time forging defence alliances with Albertans. In August 2010, the Alberta Government announced an advertising campaign "aimed at improving the image of the oil sands industry,"[6] launched shortly after Greenpeace's unfurling of a banner on the CN Tower in Calgary, the business centre of Canada's oil industry. Industry defenders have been quick to counter consumer boycott campaigns with boycotts of their own, as Alberta Enterprise Group (AEG) did in August 2010, calling on Albertans and Canadians to boycott Gap and Levi-Strauss. The Government of Alberta's recent *Just the Facts* and *Oilsands 101* website campaigns[7] claim to "correct" the misinformation planted by protestors, by presenting positive image galleries and video clips featuring industry employees, and images of tailings ponds that look more like picnic areas than waste ponds. Likewise, a ramped up "Get the Real Story" Internet media campaign has been led by the Canadian Association of Petroleum Producers.[8] Deep-well drilling and "clean hydro-carbon" futures have been hailed as the green future of the industry.

These promotional campaigns have been joined by a series of pro-industry books[9] that provide more extensive justification for tar sands development. This suite of books displays an evolution of framing tactics in response to growing opposition.

Unlike earlier tropes that characterized tar sands development in terms of free markets and technological optimism, contemporary counter-frames are more nuanced, framing the tar sands as not exactly clean, but less dirty than alternatives; as a problematic or challenging, but necessary, development in an energy-hungry world; and as a means of transition to a new energy age.

In December 2010, the *National Post* declared that the fight over image was heating up, with state interests finally stepping up to the plate.[10] Extensive media coverage of a recent publication in the *Proceedings of the National Academy of Sciences* (Kelly et al. 2010), which provided evidence that directly challenged state and corporate claims of "naturally occurring" toxins in the river, raised the bar another notch. This time the federal and provincial states both responded, with parallel independent reviews of the adequacy of environmental monitoring. The federal review resulted in findings that could hardly have been more incriminating. The newly formed Canadian Oilsands Advisory Panel concluded that current environmental monitoring activities lacked leadership, were unco-ordinated, the findings not readily incorporated into management, and not focused on the probable impacts of emerging activities like in-situ drilling. The panel also felt compelled to note in their report that "our site visits had an indelible impact. It is hard to forget the sheer extent of landscape disruption" (Dowdeswell et al. 2010: 32). Then, in January 2011, David Suzuki, Canada's best known naturalist, presented a two-hour special called "Tipping Point — Alberta's Oil Sands," in which the work of Kelly et al. was featured (Suzuki 2011).

In all these struggles, we can observe a distinct discourse being expressed by unaffiliated citizens, one that expresses responsibility for a global citizenry, and has held the state accountable for their impacts on global "Others." This discourse, despite the lack of co-ordination, appears remarkably congruent. The strong themes among citizens testifying at the Oil Sands Consultations include:

1. Moratorium on new projects until sufficient planning and safeguards are in place, including attention to cumulative environmental impacts.
2. This is our resource, and we're not getting our fair share; the benefits accrue to the few and the costs to the many.
3. The rapid pace of development is out of control; we don't buy the belief that the economy will automatically "fix" things: we need planning.
4. There is no validity to claims of no negative environmental impacts; those impacts aren't even being adequately assessed.
5. The state's interest in hearing citizens' concerns is not genuine, as evidenced by continued rapid development.
6. Our global reputation is being tarnished.
7. We have a responsibility for the global impacts of our actions.
8. Concerns for downstream Aboriginal peoples and northerners should come before profits.

Here are just a handful of representative examples of citizens engaged in a re-articulation of citizenship:

> I speak as a citizen of Calgary and of Alberta, but also as a citizen of Canada and of the Earth which is, after all, our only home.... Ultimately, the issue that we face in considering the future of the oil sands in Athabasca is not economic or political, or even social. It is a moral and ethical question that strikes right at the heart of who we are. (Oil Sands Consultations, Calgary, April 24, 2007)

> Having visited communities in Alberta in the heart of the Tar/Oil Sands, and the sites themselves, I am embarrassed and disappointed that the province, and our country, is allowing such unchecked booms and busts, such short-sighted long-term devastation to go on. It is time for leaders to wake up and take notice that the world is watching, and Alberta development policies are behaving like a drunken teenager, disrespectful of his family, which in this case are Canada and the globe. (Oil Sands Consultations, Written submission, April 23, 2007)

> The public, the private sector and government must consider the ethical and moral responsibility for protecting the environment, as well as promoting the economic and social development of the Alberta oil sands. (Oil Sands Consultations, Fort McMurray, September 27, 2006)

Although environmental non-government organization (ENGO) representatives did not tap into this citizenship frame to a great extent, there were some notable contributions:

I think we've got a responsibility to our own people, and to the rest of the world frankly, given the privileges that we enjoy, to show some leadership in dealing with what is probably the greatest threat facing human kind of the twenty-first century: the global climate crisis. (Oil Sands Consultations, Fort McMurray, September 28, 2006)

A Tipping Point?

We have traced the discursive paths of support and resistance in current energy politics, in which the Athabasca tar sands are centre stage. None of this activity has had any obvious effect on the pace of development as of yet; investment has ramped up again, the Alberta Government Oil Secretariat has unveiled plans for a new infrastructure and even a new resource city 200 kilometres north of Fort McMurray to house workers and families, and the Athabasca landscape continues to be dug, drilled, paved, and pipelined at an ever-growing pace.

On the other hand, just as climatic processes can reach a tipping point, demarcating an irreversible system shift, so too can social processes, as evidenced by the mass civil protests currently taking place in the Middle East. While we cannot forecast the outcome of conflicts over tar sands production, we can forecast that the culmina-

> Just as climatic processes can reach a tipping point, demarcating an irreversible system shift, so too can social processes.

tion of information that provides blatant contradictory evidence to the claims of sustainability and social progress offered by tar sands proponents will continue to provide sources of validity to the resistance and challenges to the legitimacy of this industrial enterprise and its proponents. The outcome of this conflict is worth watching closely, as it offers a harbinger of society's future relationship with energy. A collective movement to stop the tar sands will send a resounding signal to the global political elite that the costs of such developments of non-conventional fossil fuels will not be borne quiescently and that the time has come to consider alternative development paths.

Glossary of Key Terms

Carbon sequestration: The removal of carbon from the atmosphere for storage in carbon sinks through a variety of processes.

Civil society: The sum total of voluntary, civic, and other social organizations that exist in a given polity for the purposes of promoting social interest.

Climate change: Any change in average global temperature and precipitation attributed to natural or human causes.

Discourse/framing: Both concepts are part of the process of meaning-making. How language, keywords and phrases, buzzwords and labels, or the framing and rationalizations of tar sands developments by language, can direct or influence people's attitudes, thoughts, and actions in society. The focus is at a level greater than the word elements themselves, rather on the power effects caused by "ways of speaking" and how these envelop discussions, or direct thinking down certain pathways and not others, or even erase major differences of fact and opinion.

Ecological justice: A concept referring to the ethical unacceptability of inequitable distributions of ecological degradation throughout the populace.

Greenhouse gas emissions intensity: The ratio of greenhouse gas emissions to economic development, which can be measured in a variety of units, including gross domestic product, or number of commodities produced (e.g., barrels of oil).

Legitimacy: Popular consent that a governing regime, policy, or practice is valid.

Net energy/energy return on investment: The amount of energy remaining for use after all the energy requirements of bringing a particular energy resource to market have been accounted for.

Petro-state: A nation-state with a high degree of economic dependency on the export of fossil fuels.

Public sphere: Consists of those areas, both physical and virtual, in which individuals have the ability to come together and discuss issues of common interest.

Rent: Payments received for the use of land and natural resources.

Social contract: In democratic systems, refers to the contract between states and citizens, such that citizens agree to provide consent and taxes to a ruling body in exchange for the protection by the state of an agreed-upon set of rights.

Tar sands/oil sands: The technical term for the resource commonly referred to as tar sands or oil sands is bitumen, a thick, tar-like substance that, in some deposits, such as the Athabasca, occurs within bodies of sand.

Questions for Discussion

1. Defenders of the oil sands industry argue that we can become more efficient in our use of water and technology to sequester carbon and turn it into "clean energy" through human innovation. Others have shown that increases in efficiency have in the past only encouraged further production expansion (Bunker and Ciccantell 2005), what some call "the curse of energy efficiency" (Foster, Clark, and York 2010). Provide historical examples that might be used to support each claim and discuss.

2. Images of the destruction as a result of the tar sands are widely used to promote social awareness and change. While the image of Earth as a Blue Planet spoke of "our home," images of the tar sands speak of "our future," one in which humans are complicit in ecological and social destruction resulting from the exploitation of the last remaining oil on the planet. To what extent might satellite and other images of destruction support arguments for social and political change? Can we build a politics around them? What else might be needed?

3. Let's begin with the ends rather than the means: the foundational premise that to maintain livability for humans on the planet and maintain eco-social resilience, energy consumption would need to be reduced drastically: let's say by 90 percent by the end of next century. Describe the kind of transitions that you believe would be required to move towards a post-carbon society.

Websites of Interest

Louis Helbig <beautifuldestruction.ca/> and <beautifuldestruction.ca/stockcontactshee.html>

National Geographic Oil Sands Images (Photos by Peter Essick) <ngm.nationalgeographic.com/2009/03/canadian-oil-sands/essick-photography>

Peter Essick Aurora Photos <auroraphotos.com/SwishSearch?Keywords=essick+mcmurray&submit=Go!>

Oilsands Truth <oilsandstruth.org>

Pembina Institute

Petropolis Greenpeace Film

Greenpeace Canada Tar Sands Campaign <greenpeace.org/canada/en/campaigns/tarsands/Photos/>

The Nature of Things: Tipping Point — Alberta's Oil Sands <cbc.ca/video/#/Shows/The_Nature_of_Things/1242300217/ID=1769597772>

Notes

Debra Davidson and Mike Gismondi have just completed a full-length analysis of the tar sands in *Challenging Legitimacy at the Precipice of Energy Calamity*.

1. To recover one barrel of bitumen by in situ extraction, 1000 cubic feet of natural gas are required, compared to 250 cubic feet for extraction by open-pit mining (Alberta Chamber of Resources 2004).

2. Total emissions for all of Canada in 2008 were 734 megatonnes (Environment Canada n.d.).

3. Reported at <tarsandswatch.org/overwhelming-majority-albertans-support-pause-new-oil-sands-approvals>.

4. To trace these discursive paths, we conducted an analysis of the transcripts of sessions of the Provincial Legislative Assembly (*Hansards*), Premier's speeches, the Public Oil Sands Consultations held in 2006–7, and various corporate publications. In the following section, we present a brief synopsis of the findings of this research. A more detailed presentation of this study can be found in our book, *Challenging Legitimacy at the Precipice of Energy Calamity* (Springer Press 2011).

5. See, for example, <cbc.ca/canada/calgary/story/2010/08/09/calgary-rethink-alberta-oilsands-tourism-poll-brit-us.html#ixzz0xRMzjIPd>.

6. <cbc.ca/canada/edmonton/story/2010/08/05/calgary-alberta-oilsands-ad-campaign-winnipeg.html>.

7. <energy.alberta.ca/OilSands/1710.asp>.

8. <capp.ca/Pages/default.aspx#D7MQCUKeT0Gb>.

9. *Ethical Oil* (Levant 2010), *Black Bonanza* (Sweeny 2010), and *The Impending World Energy Mess* (Hirsch, Bedzek, and Wendling 2010).

10. <fullcomment.nationalpost.com/2010/12/02/kevin-libin-emerging-oil-sands-ad-battle-getting-personal>.

References

AEN (Alberta Environmental Network). 2008. "Momentum Builds for Canada's Boreal Forest." <aenweb.ca/node/2018#2>.

AFL (Alberta Federation of Labour). 2003. "Running to Stand Still: How Alberta Government Policy Has Led to Wage Stagnation During a Time of Prosperity." <afl.org/index.php/View-document/16-Running-to-Stand-Still.html>.

____. 2007. "Anatomy of a Boom." <//programming.afl.org/index.php?option=com_content&id=826:anatomy-of-a-boom-2007&view=article&Itemid=154>.

____. 2009a. "Lost Down the Pipeline: In These Difficult Economic Times, Is the Alberta Government Doing Enough to Keep Value-Added Oil-Sands Jobs in Canada?" April. <afl.org/index.php/Download-document/116-Lost-Down-the-Pipeline-April-2009.html>.

____. 2009b. "Entrenching Exploitation: Second Report of AFL Temporary Foreign Worker Advocate." April 1. <afl.org/index.php/Reports/entrenching-exploitation-second-rept-of-afl-temporary-foreign-worker-advocate.html>.

Alberta Chamber of Resources. 2004. <acr-alberta.com/FEATUREARTICLES/ArticleArchives/AlbertasNaturalResources/tabid/143/Default.aspx>.

Alberta Energy. "Alberta's Energy Future." <energy.alberta.ca/Org/pdfs/AB_ProvincialEnergyStrategy.pdf>.

____. n.d. "Oil Sands." <energy.alberta.ca/OilSands/1710.asp>.

Alberta Energy Resource Conservation Board. 2008. "Alberta's Energy Reserves 2007 and Supply-Demand Outlook 2008–2017." <ercb.ca/docs/products/STs/st98-2009.pdf>.

Alberta Environment. 2009a. "Alberta's Oil Sands and Greenhouse Gases" [online]. <environment.alberta.ca/2588.html>.

____. 2009b. "Reclaiming Alberta's Oilsands" [online]. <environment.alberta.ca/02012.html>.

____. 2009c. "Frequently Asked Questions — Oil Sands" [online]. <environment.gov.ab.ca/info/faqs/faq5-oil_sands.asp>.

____. 2009d. "Tailings Facts" [online]. <environment.alberta.ca/2595.html>.

____. 2009e. "Greenhouse Gas Emissions Intensity" [online]. <gov.ab.ca/env/soe/climate_indica-tors/15_ghg.html#Links>.

Alberta, Treasury Board Oil Sands Secretariat. 2009. *Responsible Actions: A Plan for Alberta's Oil Sands.* Feb. Edmonton: Alberta.

Amsler, S. 2009. "Embracing the Politics of Ambiguity: Toward a Normative Theory of 'Sustainability.'" *Capitalism, Nature, Socialism* 20, 2.

Babelgum. 2009. *Dirty Oil.* Director: Leslie Iwerks. <babelgum.com/dirtyoil>.

Beck, U. 2009. *World at Risk.* Cambridge, UK: Polity Press.

Bellamy Foster, J., B. Clark, and R. York. 2010. "Capitalism and the Curse of Energy Efficiency: The Return of the Jevons Paradox." *Monthly Review* 62, 6.

Benford, R.D., and D.A. Snow. 2000. "Framing Processes and Social Movements: An Overview and Assessment." *Annual Review of Sociology* 26.

Boychuk, R. 2010 *Generosity for Energy Sector, Tough Times for Everyone Else.* Edmonton: Parkland Institute.

Bunker, S.G., and P.S. Ciccantell. 2005. *Globalization and the Race for Resources.* Baltimore: Johns Hopkins University.

CAPP (Canadian Association of Petroleum Producers). n.d. "Homepage." <capp.ca/Pages/default.aspx#D7MQCUKeT0Gb>.

____. 2004. *Developing Alberta's Oil Sands: From Karl Clark to Kyoto.* Calgary: University of Calgary.

____. 2009. "Crude Oil: Forecasts, Markets, and Pipeline Expansions." <capp.ca/GetDoc. aspx?DocId=152951>.

____. 2010. "Water — What We're Doing." <canadasoilsands.ca/en/what-were-doing/water.aspx>.

____. 2010. *Environmental Challenges and Progress in Canada's Oil Sands.* <capp.ca/getdoc. aspx?DocID=135721>.

Clarke, T. 2008. *Tar Sands Showdown: Canada and the New Politics of Oil in an Age of Climate Change.* Toronto: Lorimer.

Daub, S. 2010. "Negotiating Sustainability: Climate Change Framing in the Communications, Energy and Paper Workers Union." *Symbolic Interaction* 33, 1.

Davidson, D.J., and N.A. MacKendrick. 2004. "All Dressed Up and Nowhere to Go: The Discourse of Ecological Modernization in Alberta, Canada." *Canadian Review of Sociology and Anthropology* 41, 1.

Dowdeswell, L., P. Dillon, S. Ghoshal, A. Miall, J. Rasmussen, and J.P. Smol. 2010. "A Foundation for the Future: Building an Environmental Monitoring System for the Oil Sands." Minister of Environment, Government of Canada. <ec.gc.ca/pollution/default.asp?lang=En&n=E9ABC93B-1#s3b>.

EIA (Energy Information Administration). 2009. "Independent Statistics & Analysis: Canada." <eia. doe.gov/countries/country-data.cfm?fips=CA>.

Environment Canada. n.d. "Measuring Sustainability: Canadian Environmental Sustainability Indicators." <ec.gc.ca/indicateurs-indicators>.

____. 2008. *Canada's Greenhouse Gas Emissions: Understanding the Trends, 1990–2006.* <ec.gc.ca/ pdb/ghg/inventory_report/2008_trends/trends_eng.cfm#toc_3>.

Freidel, T. 2008. "(Not so) Crude Text and Images: Staging NATIVE in 'Big Oil' Advertising." *Visual Studies* 23, 3.

Freudenburg, W.R. 2005. "Privileged Access, Privileged Accounts: Toward a Socially Structured Theory of Resources and Discourses." *Social Forces* 84, 1.

____. 2006. "Environmental Degradation, Disproportionality, and the Double Diversion: Reaching Out, Reaching Ahead, and Reaching Beyond." *Rural Sociology* 71, 1.

Freudenburg, W.R., and M. Alario. 2007. "Weapons of Mass Distraction: Magicianship, Misdirection, and the Dark Side of Legitimation." *Sociological Forum* 22, 2.

Freudenburg, W.R., R. Gramling, and D.J. Davidson. 2008. "Scientific Uncertainty Argumentation Methods (SCAMS): Science and the Politics of Doubt." *Sociological Inquiry* 78, 1.

Gamson, W. 1975. *The Strategy of Social Protest.* Homewood, IL: Dorsey.

Gillmor, D. 2005. "Shifting Sands." *The Walrus.* April. <walrusmagazine.com/articles/2005.04-alberta-tar-sands/>.

Giugni, M.G. 1998. "Was it worth the effort? The Outcomes and Consequences of Social Movements." *Annual Review of Sociology* 98.

Greenpeace 2010. "Full Page Ad Targets Oilsands Tailings Ponds." <communities.canada.com/ calgaryherald/blogs/insidealberta/archive/2010/05/13/full-page-greenpeace-ad-targets-oilsands.aspx>.

Hajer, M., and W. Versteeg. 2005. "A Decade of Discourse Analysis of Environmental Politics: Achievements, Challenges, Perspectives." *Journal of Environmental Policy & Planning* 7, 3.

Harrison, L. 2010. "Alberta Invests $25 Million into Clean Energy Research." *Daily Oil Bulletin*, April 16.

Hirsch, R., R. Bedzek, and R. Wendling. 2010. *The Impending World Energy Mess: What It Is and What It Means to You!* Burlington, ON: Apogee Prime.

Hodgkins, A. 2010. "Educating for Democratic Citizenship in an Oil Dependent Economy." Conference presentation, Unwrap the Research, Fort McMurray. <uofaweb.ualberta.ca/crsc/pdfs/Unwrap_-_Educating_for_Democratic_Citizenship_in_an_Oil-dependant_Economy.pdf>.

Homer-Dixon, T. 2007. *The Upside of Down: Catastrophe, Creativity, and the Renewal of Civilization.* Toronto: Vintage Canada.

Howarth, D. 2000. *Discourse.* Buckingham, UK: Open University.

Hughes, David. 2010. "The Energy Issue: A More Urgent Problem than Climate Change?" In T. Homer-Dixon (ed.), *Carbon Shift: How Peak Oil and the Climate Crisis Will Change Canada.* Toronto: Vintage Canada.

Keith, D. 2010. "Dangerous Abundance." In T. Homer-Dixon (ed.), *Carbon Shift: How Peak Oil and the Climate Crisis Will Change Canada.* Toronto: Vintage Canada.

Kelly, A., D. Schindler, P. Hodson, J. Short, R. Radmonovitch, and C. Nielsen. 2010. "Oil Sands Development Contributes Elements Toxic at Low Concentrations to the Athabasca River and Its Tributaries." *Proceedings of the National Academy of Sciences* 107 (37): 16178–83. <pnas.org/content/107/37/16178.short>.

Kelly, G. 2009. *The Oil Sands: Canada's Path to Clean Energy?* Cochrane, AB: Kingsley.

Klandermans, B. 1984. "Mobilization and Participation: Social-Psychological Expansions of Resource Mobilization Theory." *Annual Sociological Review* 49.

Laxer, G. 2011. *Freezing in the Dark: Energy Security for Canadians.* Toronto: University of Toronto Press.

Laxer, G., and Parkland Institute. 2006. "Written Submission, Oil Sands Consultations, Sept 25."

Levant, E. 2010. *Ethical Oil: The Case for Canada's Oil Sands.* Toronto: McClelland and Stewart.

Libin, K. 2010. "Emerging Oilsands Ad Battle Getting Personal." *National Post,* 2 December. <fullcomment.nationalpost.com/2010/12/02/kevin-libin-emerging-oil-sands-ad-battle-getting-personal/>.

Luhmann, N., 1989. *Legitimation durch Verfahren.* Frankfurt am Main: Suhrkamp.

Maich, S. 2005. "Alberta Is About to Get Wildly Rich and Powerful. What Does That Mean for Canada?" *Macleans,* June 13. <macleans.ca/business/companies/article.jsp?content=20050613_107308_107308>.

Mansell, R., and R. Schlenker. 1995. "The Provincial Distribution of Federal Fiscal Balances." *Canadian Association of Business Economics.* <cabe.ca/jmv1/index.php?option=com_docman&task=doc_download&gid=124&Itemid=38>.

Marsden, W. 2007. *Stupid to the Last drop: How Alberta Is Bringing Environmental Armageddon to Canada (and Doesn't Seem to Care).* Toronto: Random House.

McCullum, Hugh. 2006. *Fuelling Fortress America: A Report on the Athabasca Tar Sands and U.S. Demands for Canada's Energy.* Edmonton: Parkland Institute.

Mearns, E., 2008. "The Global Energy Crises and Its Role in the Pending Collapse of the Global Economy." Royal Society of Chemists, Aberdeen, Scotland. <europe.theoildrum.com/node/4712>.

Meyer, D.S., and S. Staggenborg. 1996. "Movements, Counter Movements, and the Structure of Political Opportunity." *American Journal of Sociology* 101, 6.

Murphy, D.J., and C.A.S. Hall. 2010. "Year in Review — EROI or Energy Return on (Energy) Invested." *Annals of the New York Academy of Sciences* 1185.

Nature. 2009. "Earth's Boundaries?" Editorial, *Planetary Boundaries.* 23 September.

Nikiforuk, A. 2008. *Tar Sands: Dirty Oil and the Future of a Continent.* Vancouver: Greystone.

Paehlke, Robert C. 2008. *Some Like It Cold: The Politics of Climate Change in Canada.* Toronto: Between the Lines.

Pasqualetti, M. 2009. "The Alberta Oil Sands from Both Sides of the Border." *Geographical Review* 99, 2 (April).

Patels, W. 2010. "Let's Boycott All Greenies (and California)." *Global Post*, July 15. <globalpost.com/webblog/canada/lets-boycott-all-greenies-and-california>.

Pellow, D.N. 1999. "Framing Emergent Environmental Movement Tactics: Mobilizing Consensus, Demobilizing Conflict." *Sociological Forum* 14, 4.

Pembina Institute. 2010. <pembina.org/>.

Phillips, S., 2008. "Head in the Sands." *Alberta Views* December.

Pratt, L. 1976. *The Tar Sands: Syncrude and the Politics of Oil.* Edmonton: Hurtig Publishers.

Princen, T., M.F. Maniates, and K. Conca. 2002. *Confronting Consumption.* Cambridge, MA: MIT.

Raynolds, Marlo, Matthew McCulloch, and Rich Wong. 2006. *Carbon Neutral by 2020: A Leadership Opportunity in Canada's Oil Sands (Full Report).* October 23. Drayton Valley, AB: Pembina Institute for Alternative Development.

Raynolds, Marlo, and Dan Woynillowicz. 2008. *A Checklist for Alberta's Climate Change Plan: What to Look for in a Comprehensive Action Plan for Alberta.* Drayton Valley, AB: Pembina Institute for Alternative Development.

Schindler, D. 2005. "Climate and Water Issues in the Athabasca River Basin." *Aurora Online.* <aurora.icaap.org/index.php/aurora/article/view/4/4>.

Schneider, Richard R., and Simon Dyer. 2006. *Death by a Thousand Cuts: The Impacts of in situ Oil Sands Development on Alberta's Boreal Forest.* Drayton Valley, AB: Pembina Institute and Edmonton, AB: Canadian Parks and Wilderness Society.

Shelley, T. 2005. *Oil: Politics, Poverty and the Planet.* Halifax, NS: Fernwood.

Shiell, Leslie, and Suzanne Loney. 2007. "Global Warming Damages and Canada's Oil Sands." *Canadian Public Policy* 33, 4.

Sinclair, Peter. 2011. *Energy in Canada.* Don Mills, ON: Oxford Canada.

Suzuki, D. 2011. "Tipping Point — Alberta's Oil Sands." January 27. <cbc.ca/video/#/Shows/The_Nature_of_Things/1242300217/ID=1769597772>.

Sweeny, A. 2010. *Black Bonanza: Canada's Oil Sands and the Race to Secure North America's Energy Future.* Mississauga, ON: Wiley.

Taylor, A., T. Freidel, and L. Edge. 2009. *Pathways for First Nation and Métis Youth in the Oil Sands.* Canadian Policy Research Networks Report.

Taylor, A., C. Severson-Baker, M. Winfield, D. Woynillowicz and M. Griffiths. 2004. "When the Government Is the Landlord: Economic Rent, Non-Renewable Permanent Funds, and Environmental Impacts Related to Oil and Gas Developments in Canada." Pembina Institute. <pubs.pembina.org/reports/GovtisLLMainAug17.pdf>.

Timoney, K.P., and P. Lee. 2009. "Does the Alberta Tar Sands Industry Pollute? The Scientific Evidence." *The Open Conservation Biology Journal* 3.

Urry, John. 2010. "Consuming the Planet to Excess." *Theory, Culture & Society* 27, 2–3.

Weaver, Andrew. 2008. *Keeping Our Cool: Canada in A Warming World.* Toronto: Penguin.

13

Social Media and Social Justice Activism

Leslie Regan Shade and Normand Landry

YOU SHOULD KNOW THIS

- Canadians spend more time on the Internet than those in other countries, with the average Canadian online for forty-two hours per month.
- In May 2011 Twitter had 200 million registered users who posted an average of 140 million tweets per day. Seventy per cent of Twitter traffic comes from outside the U.S. The highest use of Twitter was May 1, 2011, right before President Obama's announcement of Osama Bin Laden's death. Twitter posts of 140 characters were at their highest at 5,106 per second, and slowed down to 5,008 tweets after his announcement.
- Some of the major social media corporations based in Silicon Valley are highly interconnected via lucrative social and economic networks. Five start-up companies who emerged in the last five years (Facebook, Zynga, Groupon, Twitter, and LinkedIn) are estimated to be worth more than U.S.$71 billion.
- While Google, Microsoft, and Yahoo Corporations have signed on to the code of ethics protecting freedom of speech and privacy for citizens in restrictive or repressive countries, social media companies Facebook and Twitter have yet to sign on to the Global Network Initiative.
- According to Ron Deibert, Director of the Citizen Lab at the University of Toronto, and Rafal Rohozinski, CEO of the SecDev Group in Ottawa, a heightened cyber military-industrial complex is now estimated to be worth between U.S.$80 billion and U.S.$150 billion annually. Authoritarian regimes are some of the largest consumers of these technological systems, which are highly complicit in shutting down opposition voices and surveilling enemies.

Sources: Bradshaw 2011; Deibert and Rohozinski 2011; Kopytoff 2011; Perreaux 2010; Rusli 2011.

IN DECEMBER 2010, A TWENTY-SIX-YEAR-OLD UNEMPLOYED Tunisian university graduate named Mohamed Bouazizi set himself on fire in protest after the fruits he was selling in the town of Sidi Bouzid were confiscated by government officials who alleged he was operating his stand without a licence. Three weeks later he died in hospital, sparking massive street revolts by Tunisian citizens frustrated by government corruption and widespread unemployment. Tunisia's repressive government intervened, imposing curfews, closing schools and universities, arresting citizens, and violently setting the police on to the thousands of citizens who had taken to the street. Tunisia was infamous for its authoritarian media and Internet system, decried by the International Federation of Journalists (IFJ) and its affiliate, the Syndicat national des journalistes tunisiens (SNJT), in their campaign for journalistic independence.

Initially Western mainstream media ignored the Tunisian protests, partly because of a lack of official information from the government, but citizens, using various social media,

were able to spread timely information about the protests to the world, and mobilize Tunisian citizens and
the Tunisian diaspora, including a large community in
Montreal. Information was disseminated via Facebook
(even after the government deleted pages critical of the
government), WikiLeaks, the Tunisian blog *Nawaat*, which posted amateur videos online,
proxy servers that could bypass government monitoring, and Twitter — which was also able
to more easily circumvent government censorship (Al Jazeera English 2011). After twenty-
three years of autocratic rule, President Ben Ali fled the country, which is now undergoing
a shift in governance that Tunisians hope will usher in a reign of democratic transparency.

> Technologies can embody power,
> and technological design can
> conceal vested interests and goals,
> values and worldviews.

Many Western commentators dubbed the actions in Tunisia "The Twitter Revolution,"
celebrating the use of social media for mobilizing Tunisians and toppling the Ben Ali government. But others were more cautious, attributing the actions of Tunisians to "decades of
frustration, not in reaction to a WikiLeaks cable, a denial-of-service attack, or a Facebook
update" (Zuckerman 2011). Jillian York, also hesitant to ascribe power to networked technologies, remarked that "I am glad that Tunisians were able to utilize social media to bring
attention to their plight. But I will not dishonor the memory of Mohamed Bouazizi — or
the sixty-five others that died on the streets for their cause — by dubbing this anything but
a human revolution" (York 2011).

There is considerable debate over the power and influence of social media in political
discourse and for activism. Technologies can embody power, and technological design can
conceal vested interests and goals, values and worldviews; policy, politics, and technology
are thus intrinsically and inherently linked. Vested interests can run the political gamut,
from social media companies that are unabashedly corporatist and oriented towards market
profitability, often to the detriment of citizen's privacy rights (Facebook), to those that are
communitarian in spirit, allowing users to own their own information and control their
privacy (Diaspora*). Facebook exemplifies the dramatic reconfiguration of personal privacy
online, with CEO Mark Zuckerberg's evangelical belief in "radical transparency'" — the company's credo that creating more open and transparent identities creates a healthier society
(Kirkpatrick 2010). Diaspora*, the "open-source" social network site with its origins in the
"free culture movement," now in beta mode (under development), is championed as the
"anti-Facebook" for its principles of user control (Nussbaum 2010).

While the use of social media as a vehicle to spark democratic reform in the Arab region
has been widely discussed (several weeks after the Tunisian uproar, Egyptians took to the
streets demanding reform under Hosni Mubarak's leadership; in response the government
ordered all telecommunications providers to shut down, thus "taking the country's citizens
and institutions off the digital map" [El Akkad 2011]),
the use of social media for Canadian activism has not
been as fraught. It is, however, contested terrain.

Social media for activism is contested because
corporate-owned social media sites such as Facebook
dictate the terms of the users' participation in their plat-

> Social media for activism is
> contested because corporate-
> owned social media sites such as
> Facebook dictate the terms of the
> users' participation.

forms, related to privacy, intellectual property, and freedom of speech. These terms can be contrary and even antithetical to the public interest. Privacy is one such terrain, wherein users' personal data can be tracked, targeted, mined, and then sold to third-party companies, who in turn use this information to selectively target the same surveilled users with personalized ads for products. This "commodification" of users on social media is skillfully adopted from the marketing sector, and is a practice that has grown in stature and stealth as companies increasingly seek to develop and deepen new and more lucrative revenue streams.

Social media for activism is also contested because as social justice activists increasingly use social media for human rights activities, their activities may go against the corporate-owned terms of service. For instance, Facebook, Flickr, and YouTube require that users use their real names to create a profile, but human rights activists who are fearful of reprisal and punishment by authoritarian regimes and have signed up using pseudonyms have found their content removed because they violated the community norms of the sites (Preston 2011a; Preston 2011b). Social media companies must grapple with these tensions if their platforms are to be used as an effective tool for social justice.

In this chapter, several controversial Canadian case studies of social media activism are examined: the Toronto G20 protests in the summer of 2010, where social media tools proliferated, reporting news, organizational tactics, and accounts of police brutality; the Robert Dziekanski case, where a citizen journalist videoed a situation in which the RCMP mercilessly tasered a Polish immigrant in the Vancouver International Airport; and the use of social media by homeless activists to document their lives and advocate for recognition. The chapter will also reflect upon whether social media are an effective tool for social justice activism, or if they have contributed towards a culture of complacent couch potato politics, or "slacktivism."

What Are the Social Media?

Social media refer to a range of Internet technologies that allow for participative communicative practices; they are tools that empower users to contribute to developing, collaborating, customizing, rating, and distributing Internet content. Also commonly referred to as "Web 2.0" technologies, user practices are called "user-created content–UCC," or "user-generated content (UGC)." In 2007 the Organisation for Economic Co-operation and Development (OECD) released a study on the social, economic, and policy implications of the "participative web." Characteristics of UCC include content made publicly available over the Internet, reflecting some creative component, whether original or adapted. Implicit for UCC is that content is created outside of professional, paid labour, with no industry or institutional affiliation and little to no financial remuneration — hence UCC is "pro-am" labour (referring to the blurriness between professional and amateur labour).

Predicated on access to good "broadband" connections and often, but not always, comprised of younger users, the motivations for those producing UCC can be many: creative and fun expression, establishing and extending communities of interest, seeking fame and notoriety, or civic participation. Models for recompense include voluntary contributions, charging viewers for services, selling goods and services to the community, establishing advertising-based models, and licensing of content and technologies to third parties. The social impacts of UCC are multifarious: a promise of increased democratization of media production, a valorization of amateurs, a potential for increased participation, collaboration and sharing, and the facilitation of open platforms for political debate. But alongside these many opportunities are challenges, in particular, privacy ("identity theft," — a disregard for the protection of personal information, "third-party marketing"); copyright (determining what can be considered "fair dealing" with regard to the ownership of content); informational integrity (protecting against illegal and inappropriate content, promoting and preserving freedom of expression); and security and safety.

The most popular social media include social network sites, blogs/microblogs, wikis, and video-sharing sites. Intrinsic to these technologies are their facility for users to upload their own content, reconfigure, remix, and comment on content; and for activist purposes, mediated mobilization, which fosters collaboration and participation. Such mobilization, writes Leah Lievrouw (2011), "is not merely the collection and allocation of resources (people, time, funding, technology, space), it also creates a sense of belonging, solidarity, and collective identity among participants that is expressed through their collaborative activities" (174).

Social Network Sites

Social network sites link together individuals, associations, or groups sharing common interests, shared histories, backgrounds and affiliations, kinship, similar tastes, or ideas. Users can post personal or institutional status, update profiles, and publish information, news, pictures, links, or videos. Information provided by users can either be made publicly available or restricted to areas the user deems "private." With more than 500 million users, Facebook.com, for example, claims supremacy as the world's most popular social network website. Flickr.com currently remains the biggest photo sharing social network platform.

Blogs

Blogs are relatively simple websites that can be operated, modified, and updated by users without the need of extensive programming or technical skills. They are typically interactive in the sense that they frequently call for comments and participation from readers. They contain text, picture, sound, and video files and archive past events and activities. While previously generally associated with personal journals and websites, blogs have been professionalized and are now used by corporations, journalists, free lancers, political entrepreneurs, and analysts for publicity, advertising, and branding activities. Wordpress.com and Blogger.com are among the biggest pre-hosted blog services currently available.

Microblogs

Microblogs are registered accounts hosted by a particular social network site linking together individuals, groups, and communities. Microblog accounts allow users to publish in real-time small and concise posts made of short sentences and hypertexts — links to other websites. These posts are accessible through the social network site, smartphones, and in some countries, by short message service (SMS). With more than 175 million registered users, Twitter is the definitive goliath of the microblogosphere.

Wikis

Wikis are collaborative websites that can be updated and edited by their users. Content is provided and monitored by users: web pages are created, published, edited, and revised by a community of users willingly participating and investing time in a commons knowledge project. Wikis often rely on "open-source software" and are often associated with non-profit endeavours, projects, and activities. The multilingual, web-based online encyclopaedia Wikipedia might just be the most successful, widespread, and well-known wiki available on the web.

Video-Sharing Sites

Video-sharing sites provide a forum for viewing videos — amateur and professional — on the Internet and increasingly on mobile phones. By far the most popular video-sharing site is YouTube, owned by the giant Google. In 2010 the daily viewing of videos on YouTube reached two billion (Stross 2010). While they will not reveal the size of its video library, the company estimates that twenty hours of video are uploaded to the site every minute, with the average user spending fifteen minutes a day on the site (Helft 2009).

Social Media and Activism: A Primer

Technologies are designed, produced, and distributed with an understanding of who its potential users are and their imagined interactions. Some of these uses are sanctioned, desired, and anticipated by the technological designers and manufacturers; others are restricted, forbidden, and opposed with rigour by either the proprietor of the technology or public authorities. Users can surprise technological entrepreneurs by developing innovative, original, and unforeseen ways to interact and mobilize technology, but often these unintended uses are harshly resisted and suppressed by the owners of these technologies, often in the guise of morality, national security, or public order.

Social media, the latest and (for the time being) the hippest infant of communication technologies, is currently at the forefront of a global struggle to shape the many ways that citizens are appropriating and using technologies to expand their boundaries of freedom. Many of these social media, some of which were mythically developed with much passion and pluck in the San Francisco Bay Area garages by university students, are now intrinsically enveloped within the capitalist structures of commerce and entertainment, and worth billions of dollars in revenue. And in many instances, the blurring between these powerful platform producers and distributors and the users and their content can be vexing, particularly as content is increasingly monetized, terms of service for use is cavalier towards personal privacy (favouring third party marketing) and user content is the intellectual property of the corporate owners.

> Social media is at the forefront of a global struggle to shape how citizens are appropriating and using technologies to expand their boundaries of freedom.

History tells us that citizens and activists are quick to discover and exploit the unexplored potential of communication technology (Curran 2002; Shaw 2005; Jong, Shaw and Stammers 2005; Raley 2009). The subversion of technological consumer products by activists relies on a refusal to be constrained by prescribed uses and a desire to both build on technological opportunities and bypass technological constraints. The open-source movement is the perfect example of this. Reacting against the closed proprietary nature of most commercial software, open-source activists refuse the lockdown imposed by major corporations on software and instead develop their own competitive tools and applications. The Apache HTTP server, the web browser Firefox, the GNU/Linux operating system, and the content management system Drupal are commonly used open-source tools. Users also commonly "jailbreak" mobile devices such as the iPhone in order to install third party applications that are not under the sole ownership and control of the parent company — in this case the Apple Corporation. Hackers, pirates, programmers, and file-sharers are also keen to write and share software that meets their needs, goals, and desires without bending to the requirements of copyright holders.

Corporations are keen to impose lockdowns on the technological products they manufacture in order to limit and control the uses that can be made of them by their users. Apple, who exercises close control over the software applications that can be run on its products, lost a major battle in July 2010 when U.S. regulators declared that jailbreaking an iPhone was legal in the country, stating that there was "no basis for copyright law to assist Apple in protecting its restrictive business model" (Kravets 2010). Nonetheless, twenty-one-year-old hacker George Francis Hotz (also known as GeoHot), famous for being allegedly the first person to have jailbreaked an iPhone, was sued early in 2011 by Sony Corporation after providing the Playstation 3 (PS3) game console's master key and divulging the steps to jailbreak the popular device. Sony and Hotz reached a settlement a few months after the start of the proceedings. According to the hacker, the issue behind the case was "the freedom to use the device that you paid for in any ways you see fit" (Hammad 2011). These examples are indicative of an emerging larger power struggle between users and intellectual property holders around the control and regulation of their access and use, and whether users can be punished for unsanctioned applications.

Consumer products such as the personal computer, the "smart" mobile phone, the iPod, and the video camera have become, in the hands of activists, tools of subversion and resistance. They are instruments of political information, ideological affirmation and debate, publicity, co-ordination, knowledge sharing, and political action. The stories told through these devices are ones of passion and despair, of hope and change, of anger and injustice. A global network of friends, allies, and supporters now fits in one's pocket. Examples of this are numerous. Cameras found on mobile phones can be used by activists to hold public authorities responsible for their actions, to record abuses and human rights violations (especially those that occur during public demonstrations), and to rectify, correct, or challenge information provided by the mainstream media. The case of the Tunisian revolution is illustrative of this use. Other global examples include Amnesty International U.K.'s "Break the Silence" campaign, which distributes pocket radios to allow the Burmese to bypass state censorship and to educate and inform the population about their human rights.[1] WITNESS provides training, support, and video cameras to activists and local groups in many countries so they can record abuses and exactions.[2] The social and political uses of these technological devices derive from the creativity and the tactical choice made by activists.

Social media has come to play a central role in the spontaneous co-ordination of upscale protests and demonstrations. Since the 1999 anti-globalization protests in Seattle, which effectively shut down a World Trade Organization (WTO) meeting, protesters have increasingly relied on a decentralized, nebulous, hard-to-shutdown communication architecture used for co-ordination, intelligence and publication (Karatzogianni 2006). The explosion of social media over the first decade of the twenty-first century has played an important part in the building of movements and protest activities. These media exemplify the potential that communication technology holds for social resistance and mobilization.

Social media build communities of interest: they link together individuals who share similar interests in issues and people. They are community-driven and community-fuelled technologically mediated social spaces that expand, reassert, and reinforce often weak social ties. As such, they are highly relevant tools of social mobilization. They contribute to the organization of movements, protest activities, and information distribution on a contagion model. They help to get the word out in ways previously unthinkable. Like a virus, politically charged information passes around people who meet online, sometimes infecting them and spreading among networks, mutating in new strains, scattering in unsuspected hubs and locations. This has major impact for recruitment activities.

> Like a virus, politically charged information passes around people who meet online, sometimes infecting them and spreading among networks.

For one, social media contribute to the establishment of relevant distribution channels among various publics, activists, and sympathizers. These channels are then able to constitute the backbone of networks constituted by dormant agents, adherents, and potential supporters to be called upon when needed (Carty 2011). Secondly, social media and protest activities are linked by a process of activation. Previously established networks of friends, allies, and colleagues are activated in precise, often punctual, settings: a demonstration, an online protest, a boycott. And thirdly, immediacy — another essential attribute of social media — has a major impact in the recruitment process preceding protest activities. "Flash-mobs" (or smart-mobs), spontaneous demonstrations, and public protests can be organized in a matter of hours, making them unpredictable and harder to monitor or to anticipate by public authorities.

Communication technologies have come to be seen both as tools and as a mode for organizing protest and dissent. As a tool for organization, communication technology has been used for movement building, as well as for tactical interventions; as a mode of organization, it refocuses contentious politics — and social mobilization — around the production and distribution of alternative cultural codes, narratives, and symbols. Social media provide the platforms to ease and facilitate such processes and are thus used to deploy, construct, and organize epistemic communities of shared identity and meaning.

Bennett (2003) argued years ago that new communication tools change the very conduct of contentious politics. Communication technology does not merely reduce the costs or increase the efficiencies of social mobilization, but, rather, "*the nature of social transactions, themselves, is changing* due to the capacity of distributed communication networks to ease personal engagement with others" (Bennett 2003: 149, emphasis in original). The Internet and social media have fostered the widespread adoption of the SPIN organizational model among activist communities; social mobilization now has to be seen as segmented, polycentric, integrated, and networked.[3]

The tactical relevance of social media for activism is considerable. Best practices guides on how to use social media for social marketing and social change are proliferating (see Kanter and Fine 2010; Aaker, Smith, and Adler 2010). Tactical Tech, an international NGO linking progressive social activism with digital communication technology, trains people to see and use social media in order to mobilize, witness and record testimonies and events, visualize communications and messages, amplify personal stories, add humour to (sometime tragic or grim) communications, manage contacts, use complex data, deploy the collective intelligence of the communities, allow feedback and questions, and investigate and expose abuses. They have produced a video documentary highlighting "10 Tactics to Turn Information Into Action" using social media and have produced tool-kits on using mobile phones for development, understanding the security and privacy concerns for human rights activism, and visualizing information for advocacy.[4]

This tactical relevance of social media, however, is not confined to online activities and community-building activities. It is also found in the increasing influence of "swarming" as a confrontational doctrine applied by activists of the information age during protests and demonstrations. Swarming, which relies on "the deployment of myriad, small, dispersed, networked manoeuvre units," is defined as "a deliberately structured, co-ordinated, strategic way to strike from all directions, by means of a sustainable pulsing of force and/or fire, close-in as well as from stand-off positions" (Arquilla and Ronfeldt 2000: vii). As a tactical doctrine, swarming is used both by the military and protesters to overflow adversaries' defenses and co-ordinate action.

Swarming is especially relevant for hackers and pirates, who build "botnets" — networks of thousands of personal computers infested by malicious software called "zombie computers" — literally swarming (or flooding) targeted websites, addresses, or portals with hundreds of thousands of requests per second. The result is a "distributed denial-of-service attack" (DDOS). Michael Calce, a fifteen-year-old Montreal youth better known as Mafiaboy, attracted global media attention early in 2000 by launching a series of DDOS attacks against major global corporations such as Amazon.com, Yahoo!, Ebay, CNN.com and Dell, Inc. These attacks panicked both public authorities and the corporate world and revealed the vulnerability of vital commercial computer architectures to hackers and pirates. Calce was hunted down by the FBI and the RCMP and quickly arrested. He later repented and published his story (Calce with Silverman 2008).

A fascinating and unique botnet experiment took place in December 2010 when a nebulous group called Anonymous harnessed the power of social media to conduct a DDOS attack against firms which collaborated with public authorities in their attempt to cut off international whistleblower organization WikiLeaks from its financial revenue sources. Using Twitter, Facebook, online handbills, and other social portals, Anonymous called for the voluntary insertion of personal computers in botnets targeting firms considered corporate accomplices of state censorship. PayPal, Visa, and MasterCard were notably targeted.

The venture, called Operation Payback, was meant to launch a global "cyberwar" against censorship. Operation Payback was unique because it relied on social media's power and the keen co-operation of those who are usually the unwilling accomplices of hackers and pirates (Duncan 2010).

Microblogging further plays an increasingly important co-ordinating and informative role on the ground during public protests. Live, unfiltered feeds seeded by activists inform public demonstrators of the dangers lying ahead, the rapid shifting of adversaries' forces, the identities of those arrested (or human-rights abusers), and of the locations where the arrests are taking place. Social media participates in the establishment of an enlarged sensory system relying on the constant communication of small, simple units able to ensure global co-ordination and efficiency without a centralized architecture. It has come to play a considerable role in producing real-time, citizen-oriented coverage of protests, social uprisings, and political contestation.

Social media matter for activists at organizational, tactical, and political levels. However, activists must also be cognizant of the politics of these corporately owned social media platforms and their insinuation into users' everyday activities. This is especially so when it comes to the privacy rights of users amid the surreptitious surveillance possibilities wrought by digital technologies.

Surveilling Dissent

Concerns over privacy and surveillance from networked communication technologies are real and serious. Yet the massive adoption of social media by consumers has also led, to a certain degree, to a reversal, and a turnaround, about surveillance issues. The activities of public authorities, state agents, and even (to a lesser degree) powerful individuals are more and more challenged by recordings produced and distributed on social media websites by private, often anonymous citizens. These recordings frequently challenge police assertions of facts and their denial of reckless brutality; they provide recordings and testimonies of human rights abuses, violations of basic civil and social rights, wrongdoings, lies, propaganda, and political flip-flops. They are meant to shame power by exposing the truth, but also to request justice — either in the face of public opinion or before a court of justice. No longer can public authorities discard witnesses or activist narratives as unreliable and erroneous: the public and authorities alike are called — or forced — to bear witness. The use of social media during the 2010 G20 Summit in Toronto and the Robert Dziekanski case in 2007 illustrate well the power of citizen-created social media to challenge official discourses — and to call for accountability in the judicial system.

Toronto G-20

In June 2010 Toronto was the host city for the fourth meeting of the G20 international heads of state, an annual meeting for the discussion of global economic trade and co-operation. Anticipating co-ordinated and extensive protests (the planned march of over 25,000 people), the Integrated Security Unit (the RCMP, Toronto Police Service, the Ontario Provincial Police, and the Canadian Forces) was established to manage a security apparatus. Notoriously, a fence was erected in the downtown corridor to contain citizens so they would not breach the protected governmental zone. Its cost — a staggering $5.5 million (Wallace 2010) — outraged many, as did the "$2-million fake lake, a boat that won't float, and a $23-million media centre that the media won't use" (Taber 2010). The combined costs for the pre-summit in the Muskoka "cottage country" and Toronto came to $857 million (CBC News 2010b).

Social media were widely used by journalists and activists before and during the summit. The Toronto Police Service (2010) also published a guide to social media, with links to their official updates on Twitter and Facebook. Twitter was widely used as a real-time communicative platform by activists for organizing, mobilizing, strategizing, and updating street tactics for sanctioned marches and spontaneous moves. It was also used by all the mainstream media to provide synchronous updates and live blogging of text and photographs by reporters and guest bloggers (*Globe and Mail, National Post, Toronto Star*, and CBC were particularly active), and of course by alternative media (*The Dominion, Rabble,* The Real News Network, and the Alternative Media Centre). "Anybody who had a smart phone using Twitter had a real-time intelligence feed of everything that was going on' says Internet strategist Jesse Hirsh, who describes the experience that night as 'transcendent'" (Zerbisias 2010).

Journalist Steve Paiken of TVO tweeted live his witnessing of police roundups, intimidation, and violence from police of peaceful protesters at the base of Spadina Avenue:

> here come the cops again. weapons drawn.
> ppl sitting again. middle of esplanade
> police in full riot gear moving closer.
> ppl still sitting in middle of street crowd surrounded.
> cops on both sides now don't mind saying it… this is scary.
> one dumb person on either side & this could get dangerous.
> suddenly 20 cops is now 100 can't tell what kin[d] of weapons are being pointed.
> can't be live rounds, can it?
> new riot squad now here. why? this is peaceful. (quoted from Silverman 2010)

His eyewitness account was widely re-tweeted and at one time rumours spread that he had been arrested. On his blog he condemned police actions, writing: "I have reported from war zones in Bosnia, Croatia, Serbia, Lebanon, and Israel. But last night's confrontation between peaceful demonstrators and riot squad police was the scariest situation I've ever been in, in almost thirty years of reporting" (Paiken 2010).

Alongside the security perimeter that was visibly evident, was a less discernible, but covertly omnipresent surveillance perimeter. Almost $1.2 million (Paperny 2010) was spent on seventy-seven CCTV security cameras that covered the downtown core, with police stating that they would only be used for the event and would be taken down "when there's no longer an issue of security" (Yang 2010). It was later revealed that post-summit the Toronto Police purchased fifty-two of the cameras. The Surveillance Club TO photo-documented the cameras, creating a Flickr stream of images during and after the event.

Critiquing their supposed security efficacy amid an abuse of law enforcement power and abrogation of the *Canadian Charter of Rights and Freedoms* with respect to warrantless searches, arrest of peaceful citizens, and snatch-and-grab arrests, Milberry commented: "In this context of police violence, abuse of power and apparent lawlessness, the function of CCTV cameras, as part of the G20 security apparatus, shifted from that of crime prevention and public safety. It became, instead, forensic, with cameras upheld as investigative tools after the fact" (2010).

Indeed, the Canadian Civil Liberties Association (CCLA) condemned the arrest of over 1,000 people and the violation of the civil and constitutional rights of many citizens that were participating in a legitimate protest. They called for an independent public inquiry to ascertain the scope of police actions and the infringement of rights under the *Charter of Rights and Freedoms* and the *Public Works Protection Act*. The CCLA stressed the importance of the right of peaceful assembly and the right to be heard for all citizens, arguing that:

> Freedom of peaceful assembly is as important as the right to vote in a democracy. It should be treated with the same respect. Democracy is governance for the people by the people and politicians are expected to hear, consult, and engage with the people in between elections to govern effectively. But access to politicians is unequally distributed: rich people have their lobbyists and poor people have their feet. Marching in favour of or against a proposed policy is often the only way to be heard for people whose op-ed will not be published in the Toronto Star and whom the Minister will not meet at a cocktail party or a fundraising event. (CCLA 2010)

Over 5,000 amateur videos and mainstream media coverage documenting the march, police actions, eye-witness accounts, and testimonials were posted on YouTube. "Officer Bubbles," as an over-zealous police officer has come to be known, was the object of intense mockery and teasing on social media websites and blogs when a video of him threatening to arrest for assault a young female protester blowing soap bubbles in his direction went viral. The video footage was a hot topic in the North American media, including the right-wing Fox News, and several animations spoofing the incident circulated on YouTube (Gillis 2010). "Bubbles," whose real name is Constable Adam Josephs, filed a $1.2 million lawsuit against YouTube, alleging that the animations, which show a policeman physically similar to Josephs arresting an array of people, including Santa Claus and President Barack Obama, subjected him to ridicule and threats against his family. Said his attorney, "This level of ridicule goes beyond what is reasonable…. The reason we brought the lawsuit is that people have the right to protect themselves against this kind of harassment" (CBC News October 2010a). The lawsuit also requested that YouTube reveal the identity of the animator.

Six months after the summit, access to information documents obtained by the *Globe and Mail* revealed that the government was monitoring the online websites, Internet chats and feeds, and Twitter communications of activist organizers, individuals, unions, and universities leading up to the June meeting (Chase 2011). Such surveillance is an everyday and even mundane component of security regimes, which consists of a global surveillance apparatus linking together international organizations and countries in interconnected circuits of communication, often without adequate public oversight.

Let Me Show You a Bunch of Liars: The Dziekanski Case

The Robert Dziekanski case is a heart-rending case study of how communication technology can support challenges made to official discourses and assertions of fact and illustrates poignantly the role played by social media in building international protest and opposition. It is a demonstration that technological consumer devices can, if and when used for social justice, hold public authorities accountable for their egregious actions.

> Technological consumer devices can, if and when used for social justice, hold public authorities accountable for their egregious actions.

On October 14, 2007, Robert Dziekanski died tragically at the Vancouver International Airport after being stunned multiple times with a conducted energy weapon (or Taser gun, manufactured by Taser International) by a Royal Canadian Mounted Police officer. Dziekanski, a forty-year-old Polish immigrant, was found, confused and agitated, by police officers who were responding to 911 calls made by people who witnessed his condition and behaviour.

Dziekanski was tasered within twenty-five seconds of the police officers' arrival on site and was shocked four more times after being aggressively taken to the ground (CBC News 2007b). He was declared dead when medical help arrived on site. Police officers justified the prompt use of such force as a requirement of self-defence and protective action in face of an unpredictable, agitated, and combative man. The officer who used the conducted energy weapon on Dziekanski testified in a later investigation that the victim was approaching the four police officers "in a combative stance" and that he believed Dziekanski had the intention to attack them with a stapler he had grabbed (CBC News 2009). This assertion of facts did not hold for long.

Paul Pritchard, then a twenty-three-year-old eyewitness traveller, was standing nearby and captured Dziekanski's Taser death on digital camera. Pritchard was disturbed by what he saw and filmed; it appeared to him that the police officers resorted to the use of their weapons prematurely. At the request of the police, Pritchard handed over the video recording on the understanding that it would be returned to him within forty-eight hours. He was later told that he would not get the footage back — his camera was returned to him with a new memory stick, the RCMP keeping his for the investigation. The police argued that public release of the video could "compromise the investigation" (CBC 2007a).

Fearing a police cover-up, Pritchard engaged an attorney, held a press conference, and went to court to get the recording back. The RCMP eventually complied and returned the footage. Pritchard took the recording to the media, where it became national and international news. The footage quickly found its way online on numerous blogs, YouTube, citizens' news and social networks websites. It sparked international citizen outage and infuriated the Polish government. Dziekanski's death led to numerous investigations and became a matter of political concern both in British Columbia and the rest of the country.

The final inquiry report on the death of Robert Dziekanski was released on June 18,

2010. It severely blamed the police officers for their use of conducted energy weapons and for deliberately misrepresenting their actions to investigators. These misrepresentations, the commissioner of the report wrote, were "deliberate" and were "made for the purpose of justifying their actions" (Braidwood Commission 2010). The report further denounced the "RCMP's regrettable media response" to Dziekanski's death and its refusal to correct factually inaccurate information. According to the Braidwood inquiry's final report,

> The inaccuracies include the following: that Mr. Dziekanski was combative and violent, that chairs were flying, that violence was escalating, that the conducted energy weapon was deployed against him only twice, and that he continued to be combative, kicking and screaming after being handcuffed. Based on what the investigation subsequently determined, these descriptions were inaccurate and without question they portrayed Mr. Dziekanski's behaviours as more threatening and dangerous than we now know them to have been. (Braidwood 2010: 260)

On April 1, 2010, Dziekanski's mother received a public apology from the RCMP and announced that she accepted an out-of-court settlement with the RCMP, the Vancouver Airport Authority, and the Canadian Border Services Agency.

Pritchard's video footage played a great part in publicly exposing these inaccuracies. Two years after the horrific incident in the Vancouver airport, he was awarded the first-ever Citizen Journalism Award from Canadian Journalists for Free Expression (CJFE), who hailed him for having "the courage to bear witness and do the right thing" (CJFE 2009).

Giving Voices to the Streets: Homeless Nation

The mainstream attractiveness of social media relies on three interrelated elements: their flexibility (people can interact with them in various ways in order to achieve numerous and often quite personal goals), their networking power (their relevance and importance grow with the number of its users or contributors), and — perhaps foremost — their ease of use. Blogs, wikis, and social networking tools and websites are made to be as simple to use as possible. Their very nature is to provide considerable publishing power to non-expert users. As such, they can become powerful tools to be used by those who have much to say but cannot have their stories told in mainstream media; by marginalized communities who face issues of enduring poverty, exclusion, and criminalization; and by individuals and groups who are systemically excluded from telling their very own stories. The stories told through these media are often ones of passion and despair, of hope and change, of anger and injustice; they express the social histories of their makers.

Homeless Nation, a Canadian multimedia web portal "by and for the homeless," provides just that. Launched in 2003 by documentary filmmaker Daniel Cross, the portal is part of a larger project aimed at providing homeless communities with the tools and training to tell their stories, reconnect with friends and families, and exchange information. It is a place where marginalized communities can publish videos, sounds, pictures, and text and break the circle of isolation and solitude. Homeless Nation outreach workers connect with the homeless on the streets, at community events, at shelters and at protests; "we meet Canada's homeless individuals where they are, and collaborate to add as many voices to the chorus as we can." Volunteers work to place donated computers into drop-in centres and shelters for access by the homeless, and they provide computer and Internet training for the homeless so they can create and share their stories. The website further describes Homeless Nation as "a place for people to share their experiences and to learn about others... a place to look for lost friends... a place to connect to resources in Canada where one can find shelter, food, health care, harm reduction, and legal assistance."[5]

Homeless Nation is part of a larger category of "citizens' media," a set of media productions bringing what Clemencia Rodriguez (2004) calls a "metamorphic transformation of alternative media participants (or community media, or participatory media, or radical media, or alternative media) into active citizens." Rodriguez argues:

> Citizens' media is a concept that accounts for the processes of empowerment, conscientisation [a process of "consciousness raising"], and fragmentation of power that result when men, women, and youth gain access to and re-claim their own media. As they use media to re-constitute their own cultural codes to name the world in their own terms, citizens' media participants disrupt power relationships, exercise their own agency, and re-constitute their own lives, futures, and cultures. (n.p.)

The flexibility, networking power, and ease of use of social media can provide marginalized communities with the tools to contest social codes and legitimized identities that often criminalize or victimize them, and also to empower individual and groups to transform their very lives by providing a positive and rewarding learning and communication experience. Homeless Nation is one example among many other progressive initiatives built on social media technology. Another vibrant example is Mapping Memories: Experiences of Refugee Youth, an initiative from Concordia University and the Montreal refugee community, where youth were trained in creative media-making to tell their own stories about their refugee experiences.[6]

Am I Talking to Myself? Critiques of Online Activism

Social activism is, at its core, a communicative phenomenon. It is built upon and organizes change through communication processes: ideas, values, and information need to be shared; supporters and adherents have to be recruited; antagonistic arguments and discourses need to be discarded and replied to. The role of technology and of the regulatory framework under which it operates are consequently central to the very life and dynamics of collective mobilization. As Jong, Shaw, and Stammers argue: "It should be obvious that we cannot understand activism without seeing how it communicates politically, or contemporary media without looking at how activists are both using and transforming political communication" (2005: 2).

Yet some argue that online activism — the use of digital communication technology in general, and of social media in particular to foster social change — is of limited potential at best, or a mere illusion at worst. Online activism, such sceptics say, might just be "slacktiv-

> Online activism... might just be "slacktivism" — lazy and lousy activism that makes people feel good about themselves but does not provide any real challenge to the power holders one aims to influence.

ism" — lazy and lousy activism that makes people feel good about themselves but does not provide any real challenge to the power-holders one aims to influence. In one example, facing an unprecedented level of unpopularity, Quebec's Prime Minister Jean Charest was confronted early in 2011 by an online petition signed by nearly 250,000 people requesting his resignation. Launched a few months before as a citizen initiative, the petition found support among provincial opposition parties and was hosted on the National Assembly website. While the numbers of signatories was impressive, Quebec's civil society and political class failed to build on the momentum and to provide any meaningful political action that would have more that a symbolic and ephemeral impact.

Malcolm Gladwell, a New Yorker columnist, is one sceptic. He argues that the use of social media by activists ought to be considered as "a small change" (2010). Quoting the work of social movement expert Doug McAdam, Gladwell argues that high-risk activism is very much a "strong-tie" thing — something social media, which relies on the reinforcements and maintenance of weak social ties, can never claim to build. "Social networks," he writes, "are effective at increasing participation — by lessening the level of motivation that participation requires." When protest activities require high levels of motivation — when there is high personal involvement, risk, or danger — social media become incapable of providing the fundamental strategic and motivational requirements of efficient social action. The very architectural principle of social media — the network — is further judged incompatible with significant social activism, which requires hierarchical decision-making structures.

Gladwell's comments echo those of activist and academic Angela Davis, who rose to prominence during the American struggles for civil rights and African American freedom:

> Organizing is not synonymous with mobilizing. Now that many of us have access to new technologies of communication like the Internet and cell phones, we need to give serious thought to how they might best be used. The Internet is an incredible tool but it may also encourage us to think that we can produce instantaneous movements, movements modeled after fast food delivery. (Davis 2005: 129–30)

Evgeny Morozov, a visiting scholar at Stanford University and a former fellow of the Open Society Institute, is another critic. His assessment of net activism, *The Net Delusion* (2011), was published on the eve of the Tunisian unrest, and his critique about the hype of social media in fomenting popular protest in repressive regimes generated much debate in the media and in online forums.

Morozov offers a trenchant analysis of cyber-utopianism, "the idea that the Internet favors the oppressed rather than the oppressor" (2011: xiii) and blames it on the "starry-eyed digital fervor of the 1990s" (2011: xiii) led by what he claims are former hippies now ensconced in elite universities intent on resurrecting the democratic impulses of the 1960s. Morozov also blames the "Google Doctrine," "the enthusiastic belief in the liberating power of technology accompanied by the irresistible urge to enlist Silicon Valley start-ups in the global fight for freedom" (2011: xiii). He further argues that the prevalence of "Internet-centrism" has seeped into discourses on democratic reform, thus obscuring a consideration of other contextual factors that can foster such reforms.

He warns of the dangers of repressive regimes surveilling the new spaces of social media dissent more assiduously than they do anti-government gatherings in public spaces, and is wary of the American dominance of social media infrastructures, themselves also potentially part of a larger military-industrial-security and surveillance regime. These technologies are not inherently apolitical, Morozov comments, and are instead ensconced in regimes of power operating under an often libertarian mantra of "Internet freedom." This tension has been highlighted in more recent events, discussed earlier in this chapter, wherein human rights activists in China and the Middle East have found their effective use of social media compromised by arduous terms of service exercised by American corporate social media platform companies.

Will the revolution be tweeted? Of course it will — as it will be broadcasted, blogged, painted, danced, and screened. Social media, as all media appropriated by activists (whether they are referred to as citizens' media, alternative media, radical media, or community media, see Rodríguez 2001; Downing 2001; Couldry and Curran 2003) are fundamental tools used by activists deeply immersed in cultural struggles — struggles where the meaning, importance, and articulation of a society's values and

> Will the revolution be tweeted? Of course it will — as it will be broadcasted, blogged, painted, danced, and screened.

beliefs are waged. As Keane argues "a healthy democratic regime is one in which various types of public spheres are thriving, with no single one of them actually enjoying monopoly in public disputes about the distribution of power" (2004: 376).

Movement-controlled media are fundamental tools of political information, ideological affirmation and debate, publicity, co-ordination, knowledge-sharing, internal cohesion and identity reinforcement, planning, and political action. They can provide challenges to what Thompson (1995) defines as the "symbolic power" of authorities, referring to the "capacity to intervene in the course of events, to influence the actions of others and indeed to create events, by means of production and diffusion of symbolic forms" (Thompson 1995: 17). They are at the centre of a "delivery system for consciousness raising, political education, and training" (Barney 2004: 126). They matter.

It Is a Contested Terrain

Mainstream social media sites are not natural allies of activists. Social media are comprised of software products owned by capitalistic interests and invested in the reproduction of capitalistic relationships. They are deeply inserted in the global political economy of com-munication that marginalizes — and often criminalizes — those who resist the social, economic, and political order that nurtured their development.

These media are further selling a very precise product: their users' private data and information. Facebook especially has been heavily criticized for its infringement of its users' privacy rights. An investigation into Facebook's privacy policies was conducted by the Privacy Commissioner of Canada in 2009, following a complaint instigated by University of Ottawa students and the Canadian Internet Policy and Public Interest Clinic. The Privacy Commissioner was, among other things, concerned with the sharing of personal information with third-party developers publishing games and quizzes on the social networking site, the confusing distinction between deactivation and deletion of accounts, the privacy of non-users invited to join the site, and the management of accounts of deceased users (Office of the Privacy Commissioner of Canada 2009). Facing significant political and legal pressure, Facebook agreed in August 2009 to proceed with the establishment of new privacy safe-guards. Concern about adherence to the Commission's recommendations, however, remains. Facebook CEO and founder, Mark Zuckerberg argued in 2010 that privacy is no longer "a social norm," sparking international debates about user's privacy rights (*Telegraph* 2010). Facebook has further repeatedly outraged privacy groups and civil liberties organizations over the last few years by introducing privacy settings that diminish privacy while increasing the level of personal information available online to third-party marketers.

Facebook is also a tool for surveillance and monitoring owned and used by capitalist interests. This, in itself, is a matter of concern for both activist communities and ordinary citizens. Mainstream social media derive considerable — actually monumental — rev-

> Facebook is a tool for surveillance and monitoring owned and used by capitalist interests. This is a matter of concern for both activist communities and ordinary citizens.

enues from the selling of users' personal information to the actual customer of the social media — marketers, advertising companies, corporations, and third-party companies. How they do it, following which guidelines, and with what degree of transparency and accountability is a matter of deep democratic concern. Facebook's half a billion users' habits and activities are tracked, monitored, stored, and sold. This company has never intended to promote or support progressive social movements. It is a formidable and highly attractive profit-oriented entry point into the personal lives of its users throughout the world — who are reconfigured as consumers rather than citizens (Sarikakis 2010).

Nevertheless, like any other technological consumer product, these very features of mainstream social media can be used in subversive ways by dedicated activists. It is a matter of creativity, imagination, and resistance — attributes that have much more to do with ingenuity than with technology. And, despite painstaking and deliberate care, technology, with the assistance of diverse social actors, often detours from its original "intentionality" track. "Technology leads a double life," wrote the late York University professor David Noble, "one which conforms to the intentions of designers and interests of power and another which contradicts them — proceeding behind the backs of their architects to reveal unintended consequences and unanticipated possibilities" (Noble 1984: 324–25). The highly creative and imaginative uses of Twitter and Facebook made by activists and concerned citizens in the recent uprisings in the Arab world is a striking example of this double use.

Those who refuse to be monitored and confined are called to develop their own social media tools (wikis, blogs, social networking sites).[7] And while these won't have the same outreach appeal as the tools garnering huge financial support from initial public offerings and venture capitalists, they ought to be considered as micro-social media, aimed at reinforcing social ties between activists, and highly relevant for social organization and information-sharing. Indymedia, built in 1999 from the rioting streets of Seattle, might be the most famous movement-oriented, citizen-operated network of wikis publishing news and information. (See Lievrouw 2011 for an overview of its origins and pioneering uses of participatory journalism through its open publishing platform.)

The spread of new, high quality and affordable communication technologies among citizens and activist communities also ought to be understood as providing a greater opportunity for the ordinary citizen to produce and distribute meaning, information, and values and beliefs that can be highly critical of the official discourses of economic and political power holders. Over the last few years, social media have been seized by activists as an entry point to impact the mediasphere — either by generating significant online traffic on precise content or through providing mainstream media with stories, pictures, sound bites, and recordings that enrich the needs of these resource-strapped media organizations.

Furthermore, in a world where control over the production and distribution of information flows is an essential attribute of power, the confinement of individuals and groups to positions of passive receptivity is equated with subordination (Melucci 1996: 180). Escaping from a status of mere media consumer is a qualitative shift from being the mere object of communication to becoming the communicative subject itself. This transformation has deep political ramifications. Speaking out is always political; it represents a refusal of noiselessness, submission, passivity, and conformity. Because social media can provide the platforms to ease and facilitate such processes, they are thus used to deploy, construct, and organize epistemic communities of shared identity and meaning.

In the end, the relevance of social media for activism relies on what it provides to its users: an access gate to open publication, admission to a fully customizable and near-infinite series of networks, efficient distribution channels for content and information, and a collaborative space for meeting and exchanging with others. All of these can hardly be discarded as irrelevant. Yet critics of online activism are right about this: social media is a tool, not an end in itself. There is nothing inherently emancipatory about it. Social media will not create the revolution. But as many recent events demonstrate, social media have become an integral component in contemporary social and political struggles, as those who struggle harness these participatory tools to tell their stories about social justice in creative, passionate, and imaginative ways.

Glossary of Key Terms

Botnet: A network frequently made of thousands of personal computers infested by malicious software and placed under control of an individual referred to as a "bot herder." Botnets are used by bot herders to launch denial-of-service attacks.

Broadband: High-speed telecommunication connectivity. Broadband connections provide greater speed than analog connections to users accessing the Internet and telecommunication services. Broadband connectivity consumes a higher amount of bandwidth and requires a technological architecture able to deliver it.

Commodification: Taking objects or often non-commercial products and services and transforming them into entities valued for their marketable function and use in exchange processes.

Cyberwar: The strategic use of digital technology and computer communications by states or politically active groups in order to infiltrate designated targets or to disrupt communications, destroy property, or cause damage to their adversaries.

Denial-of-service attack (DDOS): An operation that overflows a server with requests with the goal of interrupting, disrupting, or stopping activities taking place on targeted websites. DDOS occur when botnets are activated by a "bot herder."

Fair dealing: A strategy that aims at providing space for fair critique, private study, and public information on material protected by intellectual property law. Fair dealing, which requires acknowledgement of the author or creator of the protected material, is a limited exception to the exclusivity of intellectual property.

Flash-mobs: Spontaneous, short-lived public events reuniting groups of people in the same location. Flash-mobs are frequently organized through the use of digital communications devices and social media technology. Though varying in scale, purposes, and shape, flash-mobs rely in essence on a disruption of ordinariness and predictability.

Free culture movement: A social movement promoting the creation and distribution of content on the Internet. It advocates for copyright reform that is least restrictive and that permits the free sharing of culture under various conditions such as under Creative Commons licences.

Hackers: Individuals who use their knowledge and computer skills to break into and infiltrate digital devices and networks. Hackers have different motivations and ethics. Fame, profit, political purposes, curiosity, and personal satisfaction are among the most common incentives to hacking.

Identity theft: Assuming someone else's identity in order to access their private and personal accounts, access valuable information, or steal the financial resources of the victim.

Libertarian: An individual whose political philosophy emphasizes an individualistic conception of liberty, freedom, and responsibility. Libertarians typically show hostility towards state regulation, involvement or participation in private or public life.

Open-source software: Software that allows users to access, modify, and reprogram their source code in order to improve or personalize them to their needs and interests. As with closed-source software (such as Windows), open-source software (such as Linux) are protected by license agreements providing rules and regulation of uses and distribution.

Pirates: Individuals or groups who illegally modify, share, or distribute privately owned information, content, or data. File-sharing and website hacking are often associated with piracy by both public authorities and representative of intellectual property rights organizations.

Slacktivism: Public demonstrations of support in regard to a particular social issue or cause that requires little or no direct commitment, participation, or involvement from supporters. Slacktivism is depicted by critics as useless or personal public relations activities.

Social media: Internet technologies that allow for participative communication practices. Social media are tools that empower users to contribute to developing, collaborating, customizing, rating, and distributing Internet content. Their design aims at facilitating the constitution of networks among users.

Swarming: Offensive strategy and military doctrine aimed at overrunning the adversary's defences through co-ordinated attacks coming from numerous directions and locations simultaneously.

Third-party marketing: The use of social media, Internet technology and websites by companies and entrepreneurs to interact with, gather information from, and obtain feedback from targeted customers, groups, and individuals.

WikiLeaks: A non-profit organization whose primary activity rests in the online publication of classified, leaked, and secret information. Officially launched in 2007 as a project of the Sunshine Press, WikiLeaks relies mostly on anonymous sources and whistleblowers for obtaining sensitive information. The organization is currently headed by controversial public figure Julian Assange.

Questions for Discussion

1. Are social media a tool of control, monitoring, and surveillance, or an opportunity for progressive social mobilization?

2. Is online activism "slacktivism?"

3. What uses can be made of social media by progressive activists?

4. Which specificities of social media make it relevant for social justice activism?

5. What do the Robert Dziekanski and the "Officer Bubbles" cases reveal about the political dimension of information communications technology (ICT) in general, and of social media technology in particular?

6. Why do organizations such as Homeless Nation believe that it is important that marginalized communities be given access to communication technology?

Websites of Interest

Electronic Frontier Foundation — Social Network Monitoring <eff.org/foia/social-network-monitoring>

Independent Media Center <indymedia.org/en/index.shtml>

International Free and Open Source Science Foundation

OpenMedia.ca <openmedia.ca>

Privacy International

Rabble.ca: Social Justice Resources <rabble.ca/podcasts/channel/social-justice>

Surveillance Studies Centre — Queen's University

Tactical Technology Collective

WITNESS

World Association for Christian Communication

Notes

1. See <amnesty.org.uk/news_details.asp?NewsID=18827>.
2. See <witness.org>.
3. Segmentation invokes the porous boundaries between groups and organizations sharing resources and co-ordinating action. Polycentrism refers to the multiple hubs and centres around which a movement is organized. Integration refers to ideological frameworks uniting activists, where inclusiveness has come to be fostered by new communication technologies. Finally, networks of activists are found in various settings; they are active in multiple groups and hold various commitments and identities. See Bennett 2003: 22.
4. See the Tactical Tech website <tacticaltech.org/>.
5. Homeless Nation <homelessnation.org/>.
6. Mapping Memories <storytelling.concordia.ca/refugeeyouth/>.
7. New York University students are currently developing an open-source, privacy-responsible social network alternative to Facebook, called Diaspora*. See <wired.com/epicenter/2010/05/nyu-students-aim-to-invent-facebook-again-weve-got-your-back/>. For a brief critical account of Facebook, see <wired.com/epicenter/2010/05/facebook-rogue/>.

References

Aaker, Jennifer Lynn, and Andy Smith, with Carlye Adler. 2010. *The Dragonfly Effect: Quick, Effective Ways to Use Social Media to Drive Social Change*. San Francisco: Jossey-Bass.

Al Jazeera English. 2011. "Social Media's Role in the Tunisian Uprising." January 15. <youtube.com/watch?v=UoRspCp5Xn0>.

Arquilla, John, and David Ronfeldt. 2000. *Swarming and the Future of Conflicts*. Santa Monica: RAND Corporation.

Barney, Darin David. 2004. *The Network Society*. Cambridge; Malden, MA: Polity.

Bennett, W.L. 2003. "Communicating Global Activism: Strengths and Vulnerabilities of Networked Politics." *Information, Communication & Society* 6, 2.

Bradshaw, Tim. 2011. "Bin Laden Death Sees Twitter Traffic Soar." *Financial Times*, May 3. <ft.com/cms/s/0/44a50716-757e-11e0849200144feabdc0,dwp_uuid=f39ffd26-4bb2-11da997b0000779e2340.html#axzz1LQxUGNXr>.

Braidwood Commission on the Death of Robert Dziekanski. 2010. *Why? The Robert Dziekanski*

Tragedy. British-Columbia, May 10. <braidwoodinquiry.ca/report/>.

Calce, Michael, with Craig Silverman. 2008. *Mafiaboy: How I Cracked the Internet and Why It's Still Broken*. Toronto: Penguin Group.

Carty, Victoria. 2011. *Wired and Mobilizing: Social Movements, New Technology, and Electoral Politics*. New York; London: Routledge.

CBC News. 2007a. "Police Say They Won't Return Witness's Video of Airport Taser Incident." October 3. <cbc.ca/canada/british-columbia/story/2007/10/30/bc-taservideo.html>.

____. 2007b. "Taser Video Shows RCMP Shocked Immigrant Within 25 Seconds of Their Arrival." November 15 <cbc.ca/canada/british-columbia/story/2007/11/14/bc-taservideo.html#ixzz1Aq5WY9Sn>.

____. 2009. "Dziekanski Jolted Again after Falling to Floor, Mountie Testifies." March 2. <cbc.ca/canada/british-columbia/story/2009/03/02/bc-taser-inquiry-millington.html>.

____. 2010a. "Toronto's 'Officer Bubbles' Sues YouTube." October 16. <cbc.ca/canada/toronto/story/2010/10/16/toronto-g20-cop.html>.

____. 2010b. "G8-G20 Costs Top 857-Million." November 5. <cbc.ca/canada/toronto/story/2010/11/05/g20-costs-tabled.html>.

CCLA (Canadian Civil Liberties Association). 2010. "Looking Back, Moving Forward: Two Months After the G20." August <ccla.org/our-work/focus-areas/g8-and-g20/two-months-after-the-g20/>.

Chase, Steven. 2011. "From YouTube to Twitter, Ottawa Heard It All During the G-20." *Globe and Mail*, January 11. <theglobeandmail.com/news/politics/from-youtube-to-twitter-ottawa-heard-it-all-during-the-g20/article1866449/>.

CJFE (Canadian Journalists for Free Expression). 2009. "CJFE Honours Paul Pritchard with the First CJFE Citizen Journalism Award." Press release. <cjfe.org/node/289>.

Couldry, Nick, and James Curran (eds.). 2003. *Contesting Media Power: Alternative Media in a Networked World*. Lanham, MD: Rowman & Littlefield.

Curran, James. 2002. Media and Power. London; New York: Routledge.

Davis, Angela Y. 2005. *Abolition Democracy: Beyond Empire, Prisons and Torture*. New York: Seven Stories Press.

Deibert, Ron, and Rafal Rohozinski. 2011. "The New Cyber Military-Industrial Complex." *Globe and Mail*, March 28. <theglobeandmail.com/news/opinions/opinion/the-new-cyber-military-industrial-complex/article1957159/>.

Downing, John. 2001. *Radical Media: Rebellious Communication and Social Movements*. Thousand Oaks, CA: Sage Publications.

Duncan, Geoff. 2010. "WikiLeaks Supporters Using Volunteer and Zombie Botnets." DigitalTrends. <digitaltrends.com/computing/wikileaks-supporters-using-volunteer-and-zombie-botnets/>.

El Akkad, Omar. 2011. "In a Span of Minutes, a Country Goes Off-line." *Globe and Mail*, January 29: A16.

Freeston, Jesse (producer). 2010. "Bursting Officer Bubbles. Toronto: The Real News." <youtube.com/watch?v=GP_LB_ZhcTA&feature=youtube_gdata_player>.

Gillis, Wendy. 2010. "Toronto's 'Officer Bubbles' Gains Web Notoriety." *Toronto Star*. <thestar.com/news/gta/torontog20summit/article/836982--toronto-s-officer-bubbles-gains-web-notoriety>.

Gladwell, Malcolm. 2010. "Small Change: Why the Revolution Will Not Be Tweeted." *The New Yorker*, October 4. <newyorker.com/reporting/2010/10/04/101004fa_fact_gladwell?currentPage=all>.

Hammad. 2011. "Geohot's Next Project: Jailbreak iPhone 5 & Sony Ericsson Xperia Play" [Video].

<itechmax.com/2011/02/26/geohots-next-project-jailbreak-iphone-5-sony-ericsson-xperia-play-video/>.

Helft, Miguel. 2009. "YouTube's Quest to Suggest More, So Users Search Less." New York Times, December 30. <nytimes.com/2009/12/31/technology/Internet/31tube.html?ref=youtube>.

Jong, Wilma de, Martin Shaw, and Neil Stammers. 2005. *Global Activism, Global Media.* London; Ann Arbor, MI: Pluto Press.

Kanter, Beth, and Allison H. Fine. 2010. *The Networked Nonprofit: Connecting with Social Media to Drive Change.* Hoboken, NJ: John Wiley & Sons.

Karatzogianni, Athina. 2006. *The Politics of Cyberconflict.* London; New York : Routledge.

Keane, John. 2004. "The Structural Transformations of the Public Sphere." In Frank Webster et al. (eds.), *The Information Society Reader.* London; New York: Routledge.

Kirkpatrick, David. 2010. *The Facebook Effect: The Inside Story of the Company That Is Connecting the World.* New York, NY: Simon & Schuster.

Kopytoff, Verne G. 2011. "Sites Like Twitter Absent from Free Speech Pact." *New York Times,* March 6. <nytimes.com/2011/03/07/technology /07rights.html?_r=1&ref=facebookinc>.

Kravets, David. 2010. "U.S. Declares iPhone Jailbreaking Legal, Over Apple's Objections." *Wired,* July 26. <wired.com/threatlevel/2010/07/feds-ok-iphone-jailbreaking/>.

Lievrouw, Leah A. 2011. *Alternative and Activist New Media.* Malden, MA: Polity Press.

Melucci, Alberto. 1996. *Challenging Codes: Collective Action in the Information Age.* Cambridge; New York: Cambridge University Press.

Milberry, Kate. 2010. "No Surprise! G20 Cams *Not* Down." <geeksandglobaljustice.com/>.

Morozov, Evgeny. 2011. *The Net Delusion: The Dark Side of Internet Freedom.* New York, NY: Public Affairs.

Noble, David F. 1984. *Forces of Production: A Social History of Industrial Automation.* New York, NY: Knopf.

Nussbaum, Emily. 2010. "Defacebook." *New York Magazine,* September 26. <nymag.com/news/features/establishments/68512/>.

OECD (Organisation for Economic Co-operation and Development). 2007. "OECD Study on the Participative Web and User-Created Content: Web 2.0, Wikis, and Social Networking." <213.253.134.43/oecd/pdfs/browseit/9307031E.PDF>.

Office of the Privacy Commissioner of Canada. 2009. "Facebook Agrees to Address Privacy Commissioner's Concerns." Press release. <priv.gc.ca/media/nr-c/2009/nr-c_090827_e.cfm, August 27>.

Paiken, Steve. 2010. "An Awful Night for Democracy in Toronto." June 27. <tvo.org/cfmx/tvoorg/theagenda/index.cfm?page_id=3&action=blog&subaction=viewpost&blog_id=43&post_id=12960>.

Paperny, Anna Mehler. 2010. "Cameras, Sound Cannons Among G20 Equipment Police Aim to Keep." *Globe and Mail,* November 15. <theglobeandmail.com/news/national/toronto/cameras-sound-cannons-among-g20-equipment-toronto-police-aim-to-keep/article1800269/>.

Perreaux, Les. 2010. "We're Gaga Over the Internet, But Why?" *Globe and Mail,* December 29: A17.

Preston, Jennifer. 2011a. "Facebook Officials Keep Quiet on Its Role in the Revolts." *New York Times,* February 14. <nytimes.com/2011/02/15/business/media/15facebook.html>.

____. 2011b. "Ethical Quandary for Social Sites." *New York Times,* March 27. <nytimes.com/2011/03/28/business/media/28social.html?ref=facebookinc>.

Raley, Rita. 2009. *Tactical Media.* Minneapolis: University of Minnesota Press.

Rodríguez, Clemencia. 2001. *Fissures in the Mediascape: An International Study of Citizens' Media.* Cresskill, NJ: Hampton Press.

____. 2004. *The Renaissance of Citizens Media.* Media Development 2. <waccglobal.org/en/20042-citizenship-identity-media/506-The-renaissance-of-citizens-media.html>.

Rusli, Evelyn M. 2011. "The Money Network." *New York Times,* April 7. <dealbook.nytimes.com/2011/04/07/the-money-network/?ref=facebookinc>.

Sarikakis, Katherine. 2010. "The Precarious Citizen: Control and Value in the Digital Age." Nordicom Review 31. <nordicom.gu.se/common/publ_pdf/320_11%20sarikakis.pdf>.

Shaw, Martin. 2005. "Peace Activism and Western Wars: Social Movements in Mass-Mediated Global Politics." In Wilma de Jong et al. (eds.), *Global Activism, Global Media.* London; Ann Arbor, MI: Pluto Press.

Silverman, Craig. 2010. "Steve Paiken Tweets From the G20 Sidelines." June 27. <toronto.openfile.ca/blog/topics/g20/2010/steve-paikin-tweets-g20-frontlines>.

Stross, Randall. 2010. "YouTube Wants You to Sit and Stay Awhile." New York Times, May 29. <nytimes.com/2010/05/30/business/30digi.html?ref=youtube>.

Surveillance Club TO's Flickr Stream. <flickr.com/photos/51260381@N05/>.

Taber, Jane. 2010. "Tories Pilloried for Fake Lake at G8/G20 Media Centre." *Globe and Mail,* June 7. <theglobeandmail.com/news/politics/ottawa-notebook/tories-pilloried-for-fake-lake-at-g8g20-media-centre/article1595348/>.

Telegraph. 2010. "Facebook's Mark Zuckerberg Says Privacy Is No Longer a 'Social Norm.'" January 11. <telegraph.co.uk/technology/facebook/6966628/Facebooks-Mark-Zuckerberg-says-privacy-is-no-longer-a-social-norm.html>.

Thompson, John. 1995. *The Media and Modernity.* Cambridge, UK: Polity.

Toronto Police Service. 2010. "A Social Media Guide to G20 Summit." June 27. <torontopolice.on.ca/modules.php?op=modload&name=News&file=article&sid=4829>.

Wallace, Kenyon. 2010. "G20: Toronto's Controversial Security Fence Cost 5.5M." National Post, June 10. <news.nationalpost.com/2010/06/10/g20-torontos-controversial-security-fence-cost-5-5-million/>.

Yang, Jennifer. 2010. "Toronto Streets Get More Surveillance Cameras for G20." Toronto Star, May 14. <thestar.com/news/gta/article/809633--toronto-streets-get-more-surveillance-cameras-for-g20>.

York, Jillian C. 2011. "Not Twitter, Not Wikileaks: A Human Revolution." January 14. <jilliancyork.com/2011/01/14/not-twitter-not-wikileaks-a-human-revolution/>.

Zerbisias, Antonia. 2010. "Coverage of the G20 Proved Twitter's News Edge." Toronto Star, July 11. <thestar.com/news/insight/article/834367--coverage-of-the-g20-proved-twitter-s-news-edge>.

Zuckerman, E. 2011. "The First Twitter Revolution? Not So Fast." Foreign Policy, January 14. <foreignpolicy.com/articles/2011/01/14/the_first_twitter_revolution?page=0,1>.

14

Privatization Is Not a Cure
Health Care 'Reform' in Canada

Pat Armstrong

YOU SHOULD KNOW THIS

- Four out of five paid health-care workers are women, as are four of five of those providing unpaid personal care on a daily basis.
- A majority of medical school and pharmacy graduates today are women.
- Nearly half of the women in health services are not usually counted as health-care workers in official statistics.
- 83 percent of those coming to Canada under the Live-In Caregiver Program are women from the Philippines.
- The fastest growing occupation in health services is personal care provider.
- There are fewer registered nurses today relative to the size of the population than there were twenty years ago.
- Twice as many women as men are prescribed antidepressants.
- Drug expenditures take up more and more of our health-care dollars, second only to hospitals in 2009.
- While, in 2008–2009, Caesareans were the way nearly a quarter of the women in Newfoundland and Labrador gave birth, this was the case for only 14 percent of the women in Manitoba.

Sources: Spencer et al. 2010: 26; CIHI 2010, 2009a, 2009b; Olivieri 2009: xi.

HEALTH CARE IS UNDOUBTEDLY AN ISSUE FOR all Canadians. An overwhelming majority of Canadians identify health-care reform as their primary concern, and in poll after poll Medicare shows up as Canada's most popular social program. But health is also, in great part, a women's issue (Armstrong and Deadman 2008; Grant et al. 2004). Women are particularly concerned about health-care reforms, and this is because they not only account for the majority of those who use the system but also provide 80 percent of the services that make up the health-care system; and with women providing most of the care, what happens to women as care providers has an impact on all Canadians. Any analysis of health-care reform then has to pay particular attention to women.

As one study put it, "Ask a Canadian what distinguishes Canada from the United States and likely as not she will take out her health insurance card" (Myles and Pierson 1997: 13, quoted in O'Connor, Orloff, and Shaver 1999: 5). Health care has provided a clear example of a universal program that has worked to reduce inequalities in access to care. As Julia O'Connor, Ann Shola Orloff, and Sheila Shaver (1999: 5–6) put it, "No Canadian woman will go without pre-natal care, nor will she face harsh trade-offs between welfare with health coverage for her children and paid work with no benefits — as is so common for poor, and many working class, American women." Public health care has also provided women with decent paid work while relieving some of the pressure to provide unpaid care at home. At the same time, however, welfare states have reinforced women's responsibility for care and taken over only some of the caring work. Indeed, the "social organization of caring structures women's opportunities and can impose significant costs and consequences" (Baines, Evans, and Neysmith 1998: 4), including risks to their own health. Those particularly subject to physical strain as a result of such unpaid carework are older women who live with those for whom they provide care and who are unable to pay for support or quit their paid work (Duxbury, Higgins, and Shroeder 2009: 79).

Today, fundamental transformations in Canada's public system are undermining both women's access to care and women's work in care, and in public debates very little attention is being paid to the impact of these changes on women. These transformations are mainly about forms of privatization, if we understand privatization in social as well as economic terms. Privatization of health care refers to several different policy initiatives that limit the role of the public sector and define health care as a private responsibility. The initiatives include shifting the burden of payment to individuals; opening health-service delivery to for-profit providers; moving care from public institutions to community-based organizations and private households; transferring care work from public-sector health-care workers to unpaid caregivers; and adopting the management strategies of private-sector businesses, applying market rules to health-service delivery, and treating health care as a market good. Although there are those who openly promote privatization as a cure to what they define as a crisis, a great deal of this privatization is done by stealth and is absent from public debate.

These multiple forms of privatization have both different and combined consequences for access to care and the kind of care that Canadians receive. Some, such as the move to adopt business practices within the public system, are difficult to see. Others, such as the sale of hospitals to for-profit firms or public-private partnerships, are more obvious, although the consequences of such policies may be less clear. The gendered consequences of these different forms of privatization are negative, not only for women, but also for men and the country as a whole. In spite of the complexity of reforms and the difficulty of seeing these processes until their impact is felt, women and men have been resisting these reforms in multiple ways.

Making a Welfare State: Health Care Canadian-Style

What started in a single Prairie province a few years after the Second World War had become, by the end of the 1960s, a national health insurance system that demonstrated to Canadians how a public system could work (Armstrong and Armstrong 2010). The social-democratic government in Saskatchewan introduced first a government insurance scheme to pay for hospital care and then a similar plan to pay for necessary medical care provided by doctors. Although health care is primarily a provincial responsibility, the federal government was able to promote public payment on a national scale by offering to fund half the costs of all medically necessary hospital and doctor care. The promise was contingent on provinces conforming to what have come to be called the five principles of the *Canada Health Act*:

universality, accessibility, comprehensiveness, portability, and public administration. The Act clearly states that citizens have the right to care based on medical rather than financial need. The impulse was both democratic and financial, and it derived from pressure not only from workers' organizations and women's community groups but also from some provincial and local governments.

When public hospital insurance was introduced, most hospitals were owned by either charitable organizations or local governments. When public medical insurance was introduced, most doctors were in private practice charging fee-for-service. The public health plan did little to change these arrangements, in part because the power of those offering the services was firmly entrenched. Although the Royal Commission that led to the establishment of the national insurance scheme recommended that the plan be extended to home and long-term care, dental services, and drugs, the federal government focused on doctors and hospitals and thus limited the five principles to these services. For-profit insurance companies — companies that had held only a minority of the market — were left covering extras such as private rooms and dental care. They were prohibited from covering services paid for under the public plan.

Like the National Health Service (NHS) in Britain, the plan covers specific services rather than specific groups of people. But unlike the NHS, in Canada the services are not all publicly provided, patients are free to visit any doctor or hospital they choose, and when services are part of the public plan there is no option of paying for those services privately. The *Canada Health Act* prohibits user fees, or what in other countries are often called co-payments or deductibles.

From the beginning, then, Canada's public-health system was a mixture of the private and public. For doctors the system is one of public payment for private practice, and for hospitals it is often public payment for private, albeit non-profit, provision. Yet insurance companies were prevented from entering the public field, and doctors had to opt in fully to the public plan and negotiate fees with their provincial authorities. There is considerable provincial variation, given that there are multiple ways of conforming to the Act's five principles. The variation is even greater when it comes to services, such as home care and long-term care, which are not clearly protected under the *Canada Health Act*.

With its private provision, the Canadian system is not "socialist" in any ordinary sense of that term. Still, the concept of universality, or "everybody in, nobody out," does promote the idea of collective responsibility and shared risk. Accessibility, or the provision of services on equal terms and conditions without financial or other obstacles, means services for all according to need rather than ability to pay. Comprehensiveness, despite in practice being the weakest of the five principles, at least makes possible democratic debate and planning over the allocation and integration of health-care resources. Portability has the effect of eliminating concern over basic health-care coverage on the part of labour force workers and those dependent on them, because it means that the coverage is organized by province, not by employer. The public administration of each province's single-payer scheme prevents private insurers from enriching and empowering themselves in this huge potential market. In practice, this principle also demonstrates that the public sector can be efficient and effective, as multiple government investigations have shown (Commission on the Future of Health Care in Canada 2002).

Developing Care for Women

National health insurance has had a particularly profound impact on women. The enormous expansion of hospital services has resulted in a significantly increased demand for health-care labour. While men have traditionally dominated the medical profession, women fill eight out of ten jobs in paid care (CIHI 2007). In the early years of the public system, the wages and conditions of work reflected the limited power of this traditional women's work. Since then a number of factors have contributed to the growing strength of the health-care labour force. Struggles inside and outside the sector have gained women the right to remain employed after they marry and after they become pregnant. The portability provision is particularly important for women, whose paid employment is more likely than men's to be precarious (Armstrong and Laxer 2006; Vosko, Macdonald and Campbell 2009). Greater access to publicly funded health services means that fewer women are tied to the home by the need to provide care for family members. Women have come together in large workplaces, and they have been able to remain at or return to the same work after their children reach school age, which means they have been able to organize effectively in unions and professional organizations (Armstrong and Armstrong 2009; Armstrong and Silas 2009). Their struggles have been aided by the state's inability to "run away" (a tendency common among for-profit firms), by the state's international commitments to human rights, by labour shortages, by booming economies, and by pressure on the state to act like a model employer. Although some legislation, such as that concerning equal pay for work of equal value, applies only to the public sector in many provinces, at least health care as provided under the *Canada Health Act* is defined as public sector. Labour legislation has also made it easier to organize in this sector, as has the impact of the women's movement.

The health sector has been important as well in providing more equal opportunities for women. It has offered decent jobs to women of colour and women who are recent immigrants. Indeed, women from visible minority groups and immigrant populations are better represented here than in any other sector. This partly reflects immigration rules that give preference to those who can fill jobs with high demand, and partly the ideas about what work immigrants can do. But it also reflects the employment equity programs in place in the public sector. Those programs represent a victory for women's groups as well as the workings of a liberal welfare state philosophy. There has also been a trend towards more equal distribution within medicine. When women successfully broke the enrollment quota system that privileged men in medical schools, they rushed in large numbers into medical training. Although women still constitute a minority of practising physicians and surgeons, they now form a majority of medical graduates (CIHI 2009c: 34).

None of this is to suggest that things have been perfect and perfectly harmonious in women's health-care work. Sharp differences among recognized skills and in conditions remain within what is a hierarchically organized, gendered, and racially segregated service. Many registered nurses define themselves as professionals rather than workers. As a result they have failed to join the labour centrals in several provinces precisely because they have not seen themselves as unionists. Many of the immigrants who do find health-care work are not in jobs that match their credentials, and people of colour and immigrants remain clustered at the bottom of the pyramid (Das Gupta 2009). Several unions are involved in the sector — and even in specific workplaces, often representing workers employed in the same kind of job. Hospital workers have fared better than those employed in other health services, and more of these other workers are still without union protection. Such divisions among women can limit their strength, leaving them vulnerable to neoliberal strategies. Nevertheless, health care provides jobs for 13 percent of the country's employed women, at significantly higher pay than offered for most women's work, and with better conditions than those found in much of the private sector (Armstrong and Laxer 2006; Statistics Canada 2005a).

In addition to being the overwhelming majority of health-care providers, women also make up the majority of health-care recipients, primarily because of their role in reproduction, the medicalization of their bodies, and their greater longevity. In areas such as long-term care, they account for as much as 80 percent of the clientele (Banerjee 2009). The national health insurance plan has made care much more accessible for women, both because care services have been greatly expanded and because no charges are applied to care defined as medically necessary. The absence of charges means that women, who form the majority of the poor, are no longer denied care on the basis of ability to pay and no longer have to face means tests to receive care. Equally important, the system has reduced the differences in the quality of care that women receive. Everyone, in theory at least, is serviced by the same providers and at the same facilities. As a result, the quality is more uniform across classes, races, and genders.

> In addition to being the overwhelming majority of health-care providers, women also make up the majority of health-care recipients.

This is not to say that all differences have disappeared or that the care we have is necessarily appropriate. Aboriginal peoples, for example, are still quite poorly served by the system (Dion-Stout, Kipling, and Stout 2001). The federal funding, combined with the principles that the provinces must respect to secure this funding, has helped to reduce differences among provinces, but many regional differences remain. Rural women and Northern women frequently have difficulty getting care, especially from specialists (Sutherns, McPhedran, and Haworth-Brockman 2004). Language barriers often limit women's access to care, as does a lack of cultural sensitivity in the design and delivery of many services.

Male medical dominance has been a powerful motivator for the women's health movement. The dominance has been reinforced by a public system that, as Canadian medical historian Malcolm Taylor (1987) put it, gave the doctors a blank cheque. Indeed, funding concentrated on hospitals and physicians has contributed to the overmedicalization of many women's ills. By introducing hospital and then physician insurance, on conditions favourable to the doctors, governments reinforced the medical model of illness. The sources of illness were increasingly viewed as being exclusively biological, and the practice of medicine was defined in strictly scientific terms. The body was regarded in engineering terms as a collection of parts to be fixed or cured, and the authority of the physician was strengthened (Armstrong and Armstrong 2010: ch. 2). Still, unlike fields, such as dental care, which were not covered by the *Canada Health Act*, universal access to hospital and physician services undoubtedly improved with public funding, reducing the class differences among women.

In short, in Gosta Esping-Andersen's sense of the term, Canada "decommodified" hospital and medical services by making them public and did so in ways that had many benefits for women, mitigating to some extent the impact of class in both care work and care access (Esping-Andersen 1990). At the same time, from the perspectives of households and especially of the women within them, the public-health system "commodified" these services by providing them as part of the paid, public-sector economy. This public provision meant not only support for care work done in the home but also less state intrusion into households and women's personal lives. It also meant less decommodified care work in the home. Current developments in Canada can be understood only when analysis includes these varied, and contradictory, forms.

From the Welfare State to the Managerial State: Building for Sale

At the federal level, new notions of public management have held sway for more than a decade. Like many other states, the Canadian federal state set about reinventing government (Osborne and Gaebler 1993) along market-oriented lines. As Prime Minister Jean Chrétien (quoted in Thomas 1996: 46) put it in the mid-1990s, the country needed "smarter and more affordable government," which meant, among other things, privatization and downloading. The federal government of the 1990s established a new model for itself as employer, shifting to for-profit strategies and contracted services. In health care the federal government did not have many services to privatize, and it faced an electorate committed to public care. Still, it took steps that contributed significantly to what has been called "privatization by stealth" (Battle 1998) — a kind of privatization that is often difficult to see or identify, and thus more difficult to debate and resist.

The process began when the government altered its funding support by offering provinces room to tax as a substitute for some of the cash previously provided to them for health care. Next, the amount of the remaining cash transfers was reduced, and then not only reduced further but also combined with education and welfare support into a lump sum payment called the Canada Health and Social Transfer (later called the Canada Social Transfer). As a result, it is no longer very easy to tell how much the federal government contributes to health care, although the provinces often try to make this calculation for political reasons. It has thus become much more difficult for the federal government to use funding as means of enforcing the five principles of the *Canada Health Act*, even if it can be assumed that it wants to do so. More recently, the federal government significantly increased funding and suggested that this new money go to several areas, including home care and wait times. Each jurisdiction is to report on progress but no enforcement mechanisms were attached and no efforts have been made to use old ones.

At the provincial and territorial level, where the main constitutional responsibility for health care rests, governments also began to take steps that had the effect of privatizing health care. Services in all the forms identified by Paul Starr (1990) — activities, assets, costs, and control — are being privatized, shifted to the for-profit sector. What Starr leaves out, however, is the transfer of the responsibility for both cost and care onto individuals in ways that have a profound impact on women — the same decommodification that Esping-Andersen left out of his analysis. He also left out the impact on women, an impact that changes to some extent based on how we understand privatization and its forms.

Privatizing Costs

Under the *Canada Health Act* of 1984, provinces are required to provide universal coverage for all medically necessary hospital and physicians' services. "Extra-billing" for these services is prohibited. However, there is no such prohibition against fees in other areas such as long-term care, drugs taken outside hospitals, and home care. Few jurisdictions cover what are often called complementary and alternative therapies under their provincial plans.

In response to federal government reductions in federal cash transfers for health care, education, and social services, provinces and territories introduced major cuts in health spending and new means of increasing revenues. They cut back services or increased various forms of private payment such as user fees, deductibles, and co-payments in areas not covered by the Act. In some cases, provinces delisted certain health services, such as eye check-ups, by removing them from coverage under the public health insurance system. In other cases, they failed to cover new therapies. Most provinces redefined hospital care to exclude many people and shorten stays for others. They also moved people from hospitals into long-term care facilities and home care, where fees could be charged.

This shift to private payment is obvious when we look at health expenditures. During the 1990s, the amount that governments spent per person on health care went down although it has increased somewhat in recent years. Between 1988 and 2008, expenditure on private health insurance almost tripled and out-of-pocket expenditures increased from $277.50 to $750.50 per person (CIHI 2010: Section 3). Some 30 percent of that money was coming from private sources, representing a significant increase in the private share over the last decade even though there was a slight decline as public spending increased in the last couple of years (CIHI 2010, Section 3). Canadians are now paying more for private health expenditures, including prescription drugs, eye care, dental care, home care, long-term care, and non-physicians' services. Some of this is paid for by private insurance, while the rest comes directly out of pocket.

Much of the increase in expenditures can be attributed to drug costs. In 1975 drugs accounted for just over 8 percent of health expenditures. By 2008 drugs accounted for 16 percent (CIHI 2010: Section 3). Canadians now spend more on drugs than on doctors. This is partly a result of the move out of hospitals, where drug costs are covered. Several jurisdictions have public drug plans, but user fees have been added and increased, and many Canadians have no coverage at all (Gagnon with Hébert 2010). Equally important, Canada's decision to give drug manufacturers twenty

> Much of the increase in expenditures can be attributed to drug costs. In 1975 drugs accounted for just over 8 percent of health expenditures. By 2008 drugs accounted for 16 percent. Canadians now spend more on drugs than on doctors.

years' patent protection has contributed to rising prices just as more and more care is drug dependent (Lexchin 2001).

Some of the increase in private costs results from new definitions of services. Hospitals have been redefined to include only the most acute care. This redefinition is particularly important in determining not only who stays in a hospital but also whether patients pay fees when they do stay there. Under the Ontario regulations, a charge to the patient for accommodation is allowed if, in the opinion of the attending physician, the patient requires chronic care and is more or less permanently resident in the institution (Ontario, *Health Insurance Act*, Regulations 552: section 10(1)). The Ontario *Public Hospitals Act* further requires municipalities to pay a daily rate for indigent people admitted to hospitals who are declared by the attending physician "not to require continued medical and skilled nursing care in a hospital but only [require] custodial care." The Act allows hospitals to refuse admission to "any person who merely requires custodial care" (Ontario, *Public Hospitals Act*: sections 21, 22). Through this mechanism, the province can get around the federal legislation requiring coverage for all hospital care. Medicare covers medications and supplies used by hospital patients, but when patients are discharged from the hospital or receive treatment at home, they often have to purchase these same medications and supplies. This condition represents a transfer of costs from the public sector to private health expenditures. Once they make this shift to other services, patients can be charged fees as well.

Both women and men are hurt by these government cutbacks and rising private expenditures, although women bear more of the burden because they visit physicians more than men and use hospitals more when they are in their twenties and thirties (CIHI 2010: Section 5). Moreover, women and men do not have the same financial resources to cope with these changes. Women, on average, earn less than men, have lower incomes, and are more likely to live in poverty. Poverty is particularly the case in old age, and with women living longer than men, there are many more poor old women. Women are also less likely than men to have supplementary health insurance coverage through paid employment (Jenkins 2007). Immigrant women and women of colour, who are disproportionately concentrated in precarious employment, are more unlikely than other women to have such coverage (Armstrong and Laxer 2006; Vosko 2000). As a result, women face greater financial barriers when health-care costs are privatized.

This form of privatization means that women must pay a higher proportion of their smaller incomes on care and that more of them go without food or electricity so that they can pay for care (Bernier and Dallaire 1997: 143). It also means that more women go without necessary care. A Quebec study found that, with added fees, the use of medication dropped among seniors and welfare recipients, the majority of whom are women: "The decline in use of essential drugs had negative effects on the health of the most vulnerable groups and increased their use of health services" (Bernier and Dallaire 1997: 143).

Private payment schemes limit access to those who can afford to pay, further disadvantaging women. As a result, differences in access are emerging among women

> Private payment schemes limit access to those who can afford to pay, further disadvantaging women.

as well as between women and men. There is, however, at least one bright spot. Several provinces have moved in recent years to license and fund midwives. In addition, a growing body of literature demonstrates that health-care costs are not out of control and that public care is the only sustainable option (Evans 2010).

Privatization Through Deinstitutionalization

During the 1990s one of the cornerstones of health-care reform was the shift from institutional to home- and community-based care. In the process, more responsibility for care was shifted out of the public system and access to care was reduced. Hospitals have been a primary focus of health reform for several reasons. First, they comprise the single largest item in provincial/territorial health-care budgets (CIHI 2010; Section 2). Labour costs account for most of the spending on institutions. Although the female-dominated workforce once did much of the labour as unpaid trainees or as very low-paid employees, the unionization of almost all the women employed in hospitals significantly improved both pay and conditions of work (Perspectives on Labour and Income 2005). Not surprisingly, then, various governments bent on reducing costs looked to hospitals and their labour force.

Second, hospitals are explicitly covered by the *Canada Health Act*. Setting out the conditions for federal funding, the Act lists a wide range of services, tests, technologies, drugs, and care work that is to be provided without fees within hospitals. As long as patients stay in the hospital, they are not individually responsible for the cost of necessary care. Private insurance is prohibited for insured care, but private insurers may cover costs not paid by the public insurance scheme. In order to lower the level of public expenditures, reformers have thus sought to limit admission to and reduce the time spent in hospital. They have also developed much more stringent definitions of hospitals and of the necessary care provided within them.

The third reason for the focus on hospitals is that new technologies, drugs, and techniques have created conditions for the transformation of hospital care. Some of this new technology, such as magnetic resonance imaging, is expensive to purchase and operate, increasing costs and making it beyond the reach of many hospitals. Some aspects, such as microscopic surgery, make it possible to reduce recovery time. Some, such as portable dialysis machines, mean that services previously provided in-hospital can be transferred to the home. Combined with the pressure to cut overall public expenditure, these new approaches have contributed to shortened patient stays and the move to day surgery and out-patient services.

Fourth, hospitals appear to the reformers to be quite similar to large, private-sector corporations. Strategies developed for large corporations therefore seem to offer appropriate models for hospital reform, especially when such models seem to increase efficiency and effectiveness defined in monetary terms.[1] The imitation of corporate strategies is evident in the centralization of hospital services through amalgamation, and so too are the limitations. Although Barbara Markham and Jonathan Lomas (1995: 24–35) argue there is no empirical evidence to demonstrate economic efficiency, quality, or human resource gains with multi-hospitals, and some evidence to suggest that costs will increase, flexibility and responsiveness to individual patients' needs will decline, and relationships with employees will deteriorate, governments have continued to move in this direction.

Hospital reform is not simply driven by costs and corporate models, though. It is also guided by various assumptions and critiques of the system. The title of a report prepared for the federal/provincial/territorial deputy ministers of health summed up a central theme: "When Less Is Better" (Health Services Utilization Task Force 1994). It is a theme echoed in the Ontario deputy ministers' report, which argues that hospitals tend often to be dangerous and uncomfortable places that should be avoided as much as possible in the interests of health. This approach fits well with the moves to shorten patient stays, deinstitutionalize, downsize, and bring care closer to home. It also fits well with feminist critiques of an illness system focused on treatment and the medicalization of life processes such as birthing. Feminists, too, have often supported a move to community and home, resisting the medicalization associated with hospital stays and the medical control they implied. Women's groups, government planners, and various research organizations maintain that much of the care provided is ineffective in promoting health. Indeed, feminist critiques have been used to justify moves that are implemented in ways that contradict the objectives that feminists were seeking in the move away from the medicalization of care.

Increasingly, reformers have also been arguing that we cannot afford the demands created by an aging population and that we need to move more responsibility for care to the individual. Undoubtedly the seniors population is increasing and the majority of the elderly are women. In 2005, those over age sixty-five made up 13 percent of the population, compared to 10 percent in 1981. While there were almost equal numbers of women and men in the sixty-five to sixty-nine age group, women accounted for almost 75 percent of those aged ninety or over (Statistics Canada 2006: 13). Yet only 7 percent of those over sixty-five live in institutions (Statistics Canada 2006: 191) and only 7 percent of those living in private homes need assistance with daily living (Gilmour and Park 2005). In other words, 86 percent are not dependent on others for care. Indeed, those aged sixty-five to seventy-four were more likely to provide help than receive it (Statistics Canada 2006: 4.3.6). Equally important, the available research indicates that the rising costs related to the growing number of senior women are at least as much a result of medicalization as they are of ill health (Chappell 1992: 171–75). As Morris L. Barer, Robert Evans, and Clyde Hertzman (1995: 218) explained years ago regarding aging in British Columbia, "The common rhetoric which portrays the health-care system as struggling to respond to the overwhelming 'needs' created by demographic changes (and therefore obviously requiring more resources) serves to divert attention away from the real question: Why are elderly people getting so much more health care?" The question is even more relevant today. Given that most of the elderly are women, the additional question is why are senior women receiving so much medical treatment and what does it have to do with being a woman, or a woman from a particular group?

> Increasingly, reformers have also been arguing that we cannot afford the demands created by an aging population and that we need to move more responsibility for care to the individual.

In sum, hospitals have been targeted not only because they provide expensive, guaranteed public services. They have also been a focus of concern because they seem to be the most amenable to new strategies taken from the private sector and because they have been criticized by a wide range of groups, including those taking women's perspectives. Hospital restructuring reflects all these influences.

In redefining hospitals as being restricted to the most acute care, governments have moved more complex care to long-term care facilities that once primarily housed the frail elderly. Some mental-health facilities have also been closed, and the most complex cases have also been sent to long-term care facilities. Some care has been shifted to community organizations. Many patients have been sent home, where less care is provided under public services and more care is an individual responsibility.

The shift out of institutions has important consequences for women. For one thing the shift reduces their access to care. Fewer services are available, and services for women in particular may be defined out of public care. Some hospital closures have been resisted on the grounds that they would reduce women's access to services, for example, especially given that women are more likely than men to reply on public transport.

In the case of Pembroke Civic Hospital in Ontario, a *Canadian Charter of Rights and Freedoms* challenge argued that the closure of the hospital would leave only a Catholic hospital to serve the area and, as a consequence, would restrict access to health services involving sexuality and reproduction, particularly abortion. The court rejected this argument. The judge maintained that one physician gave evidence that he had never experienced interference in carrying out his medical responsibilities related to sexuality and that abortion had not been provided in either hospital for the last fourteen years. On the basis of this evidence, the judge concluded that the "closure of the Civic will have no impact on the current access of Pembroke residents to abortions services" and that other claims "around reproductive health issues" were "generally unsubstantiated" (*Pembroke Civic Hospital and Lowe v. Health Services Restructuring Commission* 1997: 11). Women's groups did not have the resources to appeal the decision. The Catholic hospital is now the only hospital servicing the community.

In Toronto, Wellesley Hospital launched a court appeal against the order closing it down and transferring services to St. Michael's Hospital. Located in the city core, Wellesley had served many of the most marginalized women in the community and had also been one of the pioneers in de-emphasizing the medical model in normal births and in welcoming midwives with admitting privileges. The Charter challenge to its closure argued that the rights of patients, particularly homosexuals and women seeking birth control, would be violated because those patients would have to obtain treatment at a Catholic hospital. The hospital was not successful in the challenge, and the services were transferred. St. Michael's "moved swiftly to halt all abortions and vasectomies and restrict other birth control procedures at the former Wellesley hospital site" (Daly 1998: A1).

Protests were somewhat more successful in the case of Women's College Hospital in Toronto. The Health Services Restructuring Commission ordered Women's College closed and the services transferred to the Sunnybrook Health Sciences Centre, a hospital originally established to serve war veterans and located in the northeast area of the city. The Friends of Women's College, a group representing providers and patients, fought a long battle to defend the hospital's control of its services. According to the hospital's submission to the Commission, the concerns related to three main areas: "the loss of governance and its likely impact on a dedicated focus on women's health; the need for experienced leadership in province-wide initiatives, namely the Women's Health Council; and the preservation of academic women's health programming in the downtown core" (Women's College Hospital 1997: 1). The long battle was, to some extent at least, resolved by a private member's bill that kept Women's College's downtown site open as an ambulatory centre, with its own governing board. Even when services are maintained in amalgamated sites, however, women still have to travel further for care, and much of their care is submerged into other priorities. In 2006 the Ontario government announced it would once more make Women's College an independent institution and would renew the downtown site for ambulatory care. It was a victory for those who had long struggled to create a care place for women, albeit one that limits the extent of the services they can provide. Sunnybrook will handle medicalized maternity care, for example.

Significantly, when the Commission charged with reforms ordered the Pembroke General Hospital to develop a plan to ensure representation on the governing board, it included the "cultural, linguistic, religious and socio-economic makeup of the community," but not gender. To a large extent, women's concerns have been at best ignored.

The shift to an intensified emphasis on acute cases also means a decline in care within institutions. Even if women are successful in entering care facilities for services, they find fewer people available to provide the care. Moreover, there has been little effort to accommodate the new care needs in long-term facilities either through training or through an increase in the number of providers (Armstrong, Boscoe, and Clow et al. 2009; Arsmtrong, Banerjee, Szebehely et al. 2009). Ontario went even further, removing the requirement that there be a minimum of 2.2 hours of care and at least one registered nurse at work at all times in these facilities (Armstrong, Jansen, Connell and Jones 2003). And there has been even less effort made to ensure training and enough providers for care in the home or community. Shorter hospital stays have also reduced the amount of time available for patient education. Yet this is even more important when patients are sent home "quicker and sicker" to look after themselves.

These reforms have a particularly sharp impact on women, given that women form the overwhelming majority of those in care facilities and the majority of those needing care at home. Moreover, research suggests that women who need home care get less public care than do their male counterparts (Morris 2001). Care in the home is also not necessarily a switch to a safe haven, as feminists have long made clear. Violence and isolation are obvious problems. Less obvious are the problems of making homes healthy places for work and care. The disposal of hazardous waste is just one example. Another is the danger involved in lifting and moving sick people without help.

The shift out of institutions also brings job loss and a deterioration in the jobs that remain. As one study found, "Between 1994 and 1996, 85 percent of Canadian hospitals reduced their workforce by more than 10 per cent" (Wagner and Rondeau 2000: iv), and new jobs in community care did not make up for job loss in the in-

> These reforms have a particularly sharp impact on women, given that women form the overwhelming majority of those in care facilities and the majority of those needing care at home.

Figure 14.1 Days Lost per Year due to Disability, Women and Men, Health Care and Social Assistance Industry, 1987, 2009.

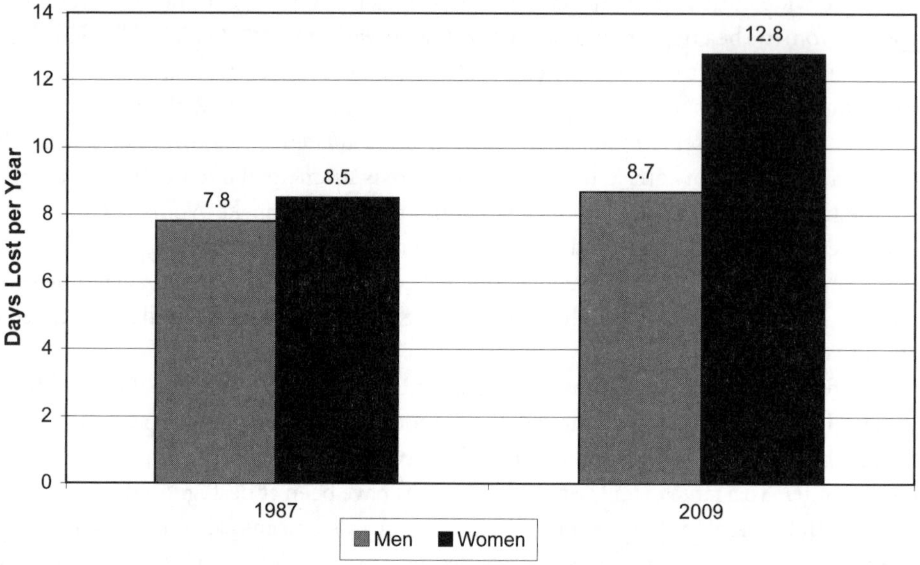

Source: *Chart created by Kate Laxer, based on* CANSIM *data, Statistics Canada, "Women Working in Health Care, Statistical Profiles."*

stitutional sector (Kazanjian 2000: 6). Not surprisingly, with job reduction has come lower employee satisfaction and conflict among those who remain, which, again, means women. The workers feel responsible and are held responsible for care under deteriorating conditions, in part at least because they are women (Armstrong et al. 2000). The consequences of these managerial strategies are obvious in the high rates of illness and injury, especially among nurses and those in assisting occupations (see Figure 14.1). "There are high burnout rates, feelings of job insecurity especially among less experienced nurses, and work-family conflict," the CIHI (2001: 87) pointed out more than a decade ago, and the trend continues.

Hospitals also pay better wages, and thus the shift of care to other facilities means lower incomes as well. With new money, new evidence, and new pressure from nurses, some rehiring has taken place. At the same time, those doing the cooking, cleaning, laundry, and dietary and clerical work in care have seen their jobs deteriorate further (Armstrong, Armstrong, and Scott-Dixon 2005; Cohen and Cohen 2004).

Privatization Through For-Profit Delivery

Reductions in government services allow for-profit firms to fill the gaps. Canada now has for-profit laboratories, for-profit cataract surgery, for-profit dialysis, for-profit cancer care, and for-profit home care (Mehra 2007). All of these services have been justified as compensating for inadequacies in the system — inadequacies created by government cutbacks.

Some of these procedures and services are covered under the public health insurance system, but others must be paid for privately. In some circumstances, the facilities have charged patients additional fees, over and above the fees covered by Medicare, even though these charges are a violation of the *Canada Health Act* prohibition of extra-billing. The Alberta government introduced legislation that would allow private, for-profit hospitals to offer services and receive payment under Medicare, while Quebec has simply allowed the practice to happen.

In some provinces, private for-profit nursing homes and private for-profit home-care companies are involved in the delivery of health services. Private, for-profit companies have also received contracts to provide various non-medical services in health-care facilities. Management, cleaning, kitchen and maintenance services, and purchasing and facilities management have all been contracted out, increasingly to multinational corporations that have little to do with care. Indeed, these services have been redefined as hotel services, contradicting both what we know about the road back to good health and the way in which these workers define themselves (Armstrong, Armstrong, and Scott-Dixon 2008; Cohen and Cohen 2004). Managers often make the decision to contract out certain services based on the assumption that private companies are more efficient and can provide the same services at reduced costs. However, substantial evidence suggests that for-profit services are often of poorer quality, more costly, and subsidized by lowering workers' wages (Canadian Union of Public Employees 2006).

The shift to long-term care and home care is also increasingly a shift to for-profit delivery (McGregor and Ronald 2011). The public purse often pays for at least part of the care costs in long-term facilities, but giant international corporations provide more and more of this care. Home-care programs that include nursing, homemaking, meal preparation, personal care, and other services are, in some places, delivered by the public health-care system. In other places, private, for-profit home-care companies have contracts with the government to provide these services. Here too privatization is justified as being more efficient and effective, but there is little evidence to support this claim.

In Manitoba, for example, after some home-care delivery was offered to a major U.S. corporation, "The privatization of parts of the home care system was abandoned after it was found that none of the private corporations who bid on the contract could deliver the volume of services at or

> Privatization is justified as being more efficient and effective, but there is little evidence to support this claim.

below the expenditure level provided by the public system" (Willson and Howard 2001: 228).

In addition to contracting out services, encouraging private companies to fill the gaps, and shifting more care to areas already privatized, governments have promoted public-private partnerships. Operating in these partnerships means operating like the private sector. Many of the processes formerly open to public scrutiny become confidential business processes. There is no evidence that this secrecy leads to improved services, lower costs, or even less government debt (Canadian Union of Public Employees 2001).

This shift to private care has consequences for women much like those resulting from privatizing costs and responsibility. Their access to care is reduced as costs rise and differences among women in both access and employment increase. When services are contracted out to private companies, these businesses often attempt to protect their profit margins by employing non-unionized workers at lower rates of pay. Women working as nursing home aides, hospital cleaners, and food service workers have seen their work privatized and their wages drop along with their job security (Cohen and Cohen 2004). Meanwhile, as more of the funding goes to for-profit organizations that claim the need for confidentiality and as more of the services are contracted to foreign firms, women find it more difficult to influence how public money is spent on care.

Privatization Through Management

Along with a shift to for-profit delivery has come the adoption of for-profit methods in managing health-care reform. It has become increasingly difficult to distinguish public-sector employment from employment in the for-profit sector as governments emphasize market strategies and business practices.

Indeed, from the 1990s, hospital reform was defined primarily as a management issue. Some hospitals have hired managerial consultants to manage or to advise on management, while others have purchased software and other aids from the private sector to provide the basis for new managerial approaches. What they have in common is a reliance on people trained mainly as managers rather than as providers (Armstrong and Armstrong 2010: ch. 4). And these managers are often trained for management in the private sector and use techniques developed in that sector (Armstrong et al. 1997). For example, in his book on how to manage hospitals in the 1990s, the then president of St. Joseph's Hospital in London, Ontario, explained that the management techniques he was promoting had been tried in Motorola, Xerox, and Federal Express but were untried in health care (Hassen 1993). The authors of *Reinventing Hospitals* describe how "the Mississauga hospital adopted the model of change that has taken the business world by storm by successfully transforming several large corporations: reengineering" (Cybulski et al. 1997: 9).

These new managers have fundamentally reorganized hospital work. Hierarchies have been flattened, leading to a significant decrease in management positions held by registered nurses, one of the few areas with a high proportion of female managers (Baumgart 1997; McGillis Hall and Doran 2001). Some providers initially supported this move, assuming that there would be more participation in decision making, but experience has led to concerns that flattened hierarchies do the reverse. The Ontario Nursing Task Force noted that, as a result, "The ability of nurses to be fully integrated into the decision-making process on matters that affect health-care consumers has been diminished." It recommended opportunities to participate in a meaningful way at all levels of the organization (Ontario 1999). Similarly, the mainly female non-nursing staff has also found that the promise of participation was never fulfilled. Instead, the choices of these other hospital staff members were increasingly restricted by the new processes that replaced the old hierarchies dominated by nursing and medical staff (Armstrong et al. 1997; Armstrong, Armstrong, and Scott-Dixon 2008).

This lack of choice is linked to new management systems designed to measure, redistribute, and regulate work within the hospital in the same ways introduced at Motorola or other private-sector workplaces. As in the case of flattened hierarchies, many health-care workers initially welcomed the introduction of patient classification schemes, clinical care

pathways, and other workload and work process measures (Choiniere 1993). These measurement techniques seemed to offer the possibilities of greater independence, relief from
tasks inappropriate to training, and demonstrating the actual work done each day. Instead,
they have tended to result in increased workloads, reduced individual control over work, and
both deskilling and multi-tasking (Armstrong et al. 1994, 1997). In the name of reducing
costs and maximizing efficiency, health-care administrators have raised patient/staff ratios,
reorganized health services, shifted personnel, reassigned duties to less skilled workers,
and increased the use of casual workers. Cost-cutting measures are changing the pace and
organization of work. These changes have often been introduced without consultation with
front-line health-care workers. During the 1990s, nurses and other workers in the health-
care system repeatedly raised concerns over understaffing, heavier workloads, and increased
levels of stress and injury in the workplace.

One study of the period 1994 to 1996 found an increase in nursing services per patient
combined with a decrease in support services, although the data are based on "a crude es-
timate" that assumes all patients receive and need the same hours of care (O'Brien-Pallas,
Baumann, and Lochhass-Gerlach 1998: 41). The report cautions that these figures were
prepared before the largest decline in nursing personnel and they fail to take into account
the medical and nursing complexity of patients, the impact of fewer nurse managers, and
the casualization of labour. By the end of the 1990s, according to the Canadian Institute for
Health Information (2002: 87), "only 52 per cent of nurses had full-time jobs and casual
employment was more common here than in any other sector." While the proportion of
nurses working full-time has increased in recent years, there are still a significant number
working part-time. Furthermore, "There are high burnout rates, feelings of job insecurity
especially among less experienced nurses, and work-family conflicts." A 2006 study concludes
that a key to what is now defined as a nursing shortage is "reasonable workloads, supportive
management, flexible work schedules, safe environments, and opportunities to perform to
the full scope of their practice" (Priest 2006: 2). In other words, although the data suggest
adequate nursing levels, a more detailed analysis reveals problems for both patients and
providers. What the data do make clear is that support staff, who are disproportionately
immigrant and visible minority women, have lost jobs and those remaining do more with
less (Armstrong, Armstrong, and Scott-Dixon 2008).

There have been a variety of responses to the new managerial practices. Some groups
have sought to refine the measurement tools, trying to make those aspects of care work
that are central to women's concerns both visible and valued. Others have argued that the
measures have built-in values that cannot be eliminated by adding more variables, and that
alternative methods are required, ones that take the professional judgement of providers
into account. There are important debates taking place about the significance of credentials
and of scope of practice rules relating to various professions. These debates often pit women
against women with, for example, RNs and licensed practical nurses (LPNs) disagreeing about
who can do what. The new management theories tend to reject limitations on who can do
what, proposing to divide work into easily learned tasks that can be assigned to those with
the least training. The Nursing Task Force supported higher credentials for nurses, and

women's groups have supported the transfer of certain practices from physicians to midwives and nurse practitioners.

This increased emphasis on measuring patient outcomes and identifying the most efficient treatments could help to reduce unnecessary procedures and improve care. However, the methods used to measure patient outcomes and define effective treatments seldom include the kinds of care and support that women providers define as being important to health and well-being. The focus is usually on tasks, costs, waste, discharge, and the short term. The care involved in the work is hard to measure and quality is difficult to see, especially over a limited period. Many of the skills, and much of the effort, are invisible not only because they are difficult to measure but also because they are associated with women's natural abilities.

At the same time as business practices have been applied to public work, market strategies have been applied to the system. The most obvious example is home care in Ontario. The government now requires that home-care services be commissioned under a managed competition model. While the traditional non-profit provider organizations are allowed to enter the competition, the competitive process encourages them to operate like for-profit ones. Moreover, the bidding process creates enormous job insecurity, even among those employers willing to hire full-time. Meanwhile, governments are removing, or limiting, regulations such as employment and pay equity, in the name of market efficiency.

As the public sector becomes more like the private sector, the gains that women made as employees in the public sector are disappearing. Their commodified care work is no longer very easy to distinguish from work in other sectors. Women struggle to make up the care deficit created by these strategies, and this struggle has increasingly obvious consequences for their health. It is also obvious in care for the patients, who are increasingly expected to take responsibility for their own health (Armstrong et al. 2001).

Privatization Through Home Care

Increasingly, health-care reforms are sending more care, and more complex care, home. Cost-cutting strategies, combined with new developments in medical techniques, mean that people are sent home from institutions quicker and sicker — or they are not sent into institutions at all. It is now possible to give oxygen and intravenous injections at home, as well as to provide a host of other treatments that could once only be carried out in a hospital. And it is cheaper for the public system, at least in the short term, to have care provided at home. It is cheaper because when people are sent home for care, both the care work and the care costs are shifted away from the public system (Grant et al. 2004).

In addition, more people have chronic diseases, and new diseases, such as HIV/AIDS, have appeared. People with severe disabilities are living longer. Most of them live at home, and many need considerable care. With women forming the majority of the elderly as well as a significant proportion of younger people with health problems, they are more likely than their male counterparts to have their care needs unmet. The public system has not moved to increase services in response to these changing demands, and instead has left more care in household or community hands.

336

Care in the home is women's work. In addition to providing almost all (80 percent) of the paid home care, women also provide a significant proportion of the unpaid, daily personal care for the elderly and those of all ages with long-term disabilities or short-term illnesses. "While equal proportions of men and women were caregivers, women were more likely to be primary caregivers (31 percent) than were men (20 percent)" (Lilly et al. 2010: 4). When men were primary caregivers, they provided fewer hours of care, an average of eleven hours a week compared to sixteen for women (Lilly et al. 2010: 5). And unlike the men who were primary caregivers, these women said there were no substitutes available to do the work. Moreover, women make up a majority of the volunteers in the community who do personal care work. Home-care programs are based on the assumption

> Shifting care from institutions to private households thus primarily transfers care work from paid female health-care workers to unpaid female caregivers.

that caregiving is a family responsibility and that women are available to take on caregiving roles. Access to home-care services is often limited to those who have exhausted the caregiving capacity of family members. Shifting care from institutions to private households thus primarily transfers care work from paid female health-care workers to unpaid female caregivers. The very process reinforces women's responsibility for such work.

Women are more likely than men to provide personal care and offer emotional support. Men's contribution is more likely to be concentrated in care management, household maintenance, shopping, and transportation. In other words, women are more likely to provide the care that is required daily, care that has little if any flexibility based on time, while men provide care that can be more easily planned and organized around paid work. Men are more likely than women to get paid help when they provide care, based on the twin assumptions that men must do their paid jobs and that men lack the skills necessary for the work. Yet women provide, and are expected to provide, unpaid care even when they have jobs in the labour market; and many of them do not have the skills required to provide the complicated care work now done at home (Morris 2001; Armstrong et al. 2001).

Although women are much more likely than men to be "conscripted" into unpaid care, there are differences among women in terms of the care they provide and the choices they have about providing care. In the kinds and amounts of care women provide, income, education, and geographical location matter at least as much as cultural traditions do. The poorer a women is, the fewer choices she has. The more rural her location, the more hours of care she provides. Caregivers in immigrant and visible minority communities often face racism and language and cultural barriers in their search for support. Aboriginal women are frequently disadvantaged and poorly served. Lesbians and gay caregivers also experience discrimination in their efforts to provide care. Mothers of children with disabilities do most of the primary caregiving in their households, clearly indicating that care work is not equally distributed (Clow and Kemp 2012).

Women are also paid to provide a range of services in the home. Nurses, therapists, homemakers, and care aides are most likely to be women. Many are immigrants. It is not uncommon for these women to have obtained medical or nursing education in their countries of origin, education that is not recognized in Canada. As a result, they bring an impressive range of skills to their job, but those skills are not acknowledged in their job titles or pay. Moreover, research indicates that their conditions of work are deteriorating (Aronson, Denton, and Zeytinoglu 2004)

There is nothing new about women doing the bulk of paid and unpaid caregiving. What is new is the kind of care provided at home, the number of people cared for at home, and the small number of people in households available to give care. Also new is the much greater participation of women in the paid labour force. Most women are now doing paid work, and taking employment for the same reasons that men do. Only a minority of them have the possibility of staying home full-time. As a result fewer people are left in the home to provide care, and even fewer who have the skills required to provide the kind of care being sent home. Birth rates have declined, and even though children tend to remain dependent on their parents much longer than in the past, most offspring live away from the family home once they reach adulthood. Although rising housing costs and policies such as immigration rules that require families to support dependants are contributing to a small growth in families sharing households, most homes house no more than three or four people, and many have only one occupant.

Significantly, though, the care being sent home is not care being sent back home. The kinds of complicated care now provided at home were never provided there in the past. Thus households in general, and women in particular, are facing new care demands. Health-care reforms mean more and different work at home for women (Armstrong and Kits 2001). This work, too, can be dangerous to women's health. Home can provide supportive environments for giving and receiving care, a place where people can be surrounded by their familiar things and retain some control over their lives. Much depends on the nature of their health-care needs, on the nature of their households, and on the nature of supports available.

For paid providers, working in a home can mean independence and variety in their work. But it can also mean isolation, working without the kind of equipment or support that makes work safe, and continually facing unfamiliar conditions that make care difficult to provide. It can mean facing the risk of violence or other abuse. Health and safety standards are more difficult to establish or apply in the home. In addition, working in a home means dealing with the often conflicting demands of family and friends. Those who provide care in the home are usually paid less than their counterparts who work in hospitals or long-term care facilities. They are less likely to be protected by a union, or to have benefits packages. Fewer have formal training. Many of them work on a casual basis and have to travel long distances between homes without being paid during that time. The increasing emphasis on cost-cutting means that these care providers have less time for each visit and less control over their work (Aronson, Denton and Zeytinoglu 2004).

Unpaid providers often gain considerable satisfaction from providing care at home, but they face many of the same adverse conditions as paid providers. They have the additional stress of juggling other household demands and, frequently, of providing intimate care for family members. Daughters, for example, do not often find it easy to change their father's diapers, and their father may reject this care as well. Even fewer of them have training for the job, and care demands may create conflicts with both paid providers and other unpaid ones. Perhaps most importantly, because there is no or little public support available, unpaid caregivers usually have no control over when, for how long, and whether they provide care.

Those receiving care can experience a loss of control if supports are denied, or if the care provided fails to reflect their culture and individual needs. Both paid and unpaid providers may invade their privacy, and hospital equipment squeezed into their home may not only make it unfamiliar but also dangerous. The danger can be increased by the difficulty of maintaining a clean environment, and of getting access to food that is suitable for the ill or disabled person, or by problems with the disposal of medical waste and by isolation. Moreover, cost-cutting strategies can mean that those needing care seldom have the same caregiver over time and instead face a parade of changing individuals, each of whom is a stranger with a somewhat different way of providing care.

The focus in health-care reforms has been on financial costs. The advocates assume that home care reduces public costs, primarily because much of the care cost and care work is shifted to the individuals and households and because providers who are paid from the public purse are paid less than those in facilities. Surprisingly little research has been done to test this assumption, especially research that looks at long-term private and public costs.

Research has, however, been done that shows the costs are especially high for women if we consider both financial and health costs. For women, unpaid caregiving can mean career interruption, time lost from work, income decline, and a shift to part-time work or even job loss. These costs are felt far into the future in terms of low or no pensions and a loss of social contacts and satisfaction from paid work. But many of the costs are more difficult to measure or see.

The physical demands of care, especially combined with little training or supports and time pressures, can lead to exhaustion and frequent injury, as well as headaches, chronic diseases, and a greater vulnerability to illness. According to one Canadian study, those particularly subject to physical strain are older women who live with those for whom they provide care and who are unable to pay for support or quit their paid work (Duxbury, Higgins, and Shroeder 2009: 79). Emotional strain was highest for women with little money, without children and for those who were providing care for elderly dependents (2009: 80). With the work characterized as high-demand and low-job-control (2009: 81), it is not surprising that women's health suffers when they provide unpaid care, and so does their paid work. Conflicts often arise with paid caregivers, and among the unpaid ones, frequently disrupting support networks. Female unpaid caregivers report feeling guilt: about being healthy, about not understanding the illness, about not making the right choice for those receiving care, about feeling trapped (Blakley and Jaffe 1999). The guilt is compounded by their role as confidante and decision maker, and by cultural and other pressures that assume that women who care about someone must care for them. They suffer from depression and stress. The pressures are particularly acute for those unable to afford private support services or get public ones because of eligibility rules or their geographical location.

> The costs are especially high for women if we consider both financial and health costs. For women, unpaid caregiving can mean career interruption, time lost from work, income decline, and a shift to part-time work or even job loss.

Those receiving care face obvious and less obvious costs as well. Drugs and equipment provided in facilities are seldom paid for by public home-care services. Renovations are often required, as well as special supplies. Public home-care services and eligibility criteria vary considerably from jurisdiction to jurisdiction, but most charge some fees for at least some of the services they provide. Recipients too frequently feel guilt, both about using the public system and about depending on the daughters, mothers and spouses, or, less frequently, sons and friends. Moreover, care by untrained providers or restricted hours of paid services can mean that they receive less than adequate care. The consequence can be deterioration in health that leads to a long-term care facility, and thus greater public costs. Caregiving and care receiving also have benefits and rewards; but these rewards and benefits are hard to realize in the absence of support, relief, and choice about giving or receiving care.

In addition, more care work and care costs sent home necessarily mean greater inequality among those who give and receive care, because those with money are better able to pay for care. Home care is not clearly covered by the *Canada Health Act* principles that require universal access, and thus it is possible to introduce means tests, user fees, and eligibility requirements that also contribute to inequality. Privatization through home care carries enormous costs for women in terms of time, health, and control. It also increases differences among women in terms of both choice and care.

Privatization Does Not Solve Health-care Problems

Canada has never had a fully developed public health-care system. Public services have been concentrated in doctor and hospital care, with other services covered to varying degrees in the different provincial/territorial jurisdictions. Still, the public system has provided Canadians in general and women in particular with decent paid employment and better, more equal access to care, even as it continued to reinforce their responsibilities for other aspects of care work.

Privatization is changing all of this. Some care costs, care work, and care responsibility have been privatized. At the same time more care delivery has been shifted to the for-profit sector, and the public sector that remains now operates more like a business. Inequalities in access to care and in the nature of care work have increased, and this is especially the case for women. The shift has not proved to either decrease costs through increased efficiency or improve the quality of care as promised. At the same time, all care providers face deteriorating conditions for work, and care recipients face deteriorating conditions for care. Given that most of those giving and receiving care are women, women are losing the most ground in this privatization process, and some women are losing much more than other women.

Women have been resisting these incursions into public care. Paid providers have gone on strike to defend care as well as their own working conditions. Nurses' strikes across the country have helped to limit the introduction of business practices, and some unions, such as the Hospital Employees Union in British Columbia, have

> Women have been resisting these incursions into public care. Paid providers have gone on strike to defend care as well as their own working conditions. Unpaid providers are becoming increasingly vocal and organized.

sought to limit privatization of delivery through their contract negotiations. Unpaid providers are becoming increasingly vocal and organized. Patients have been demanding access to care. Many know that the private payment alternative would be a mistake for Canada, and the overwhelming majority oppose privatization.

As the evidence of privatization by stealth becomes increasingly clear, women are becoming increasingly evident in their protests. The kind of public care they envisage can be seen in the 2001 Charlottetown Declaration on the Right to Care, which begins by stating: "Canadian society has a collective responsibility to ensure universal entitlement to public care throughout life without discrimination as to gender, ability, age, physical location, sexual orientation, socioeconomic and family status or ethno-cultural origin. The right to care is a fundamental human right."[2] The Declaration ends by making it clear that "these rights to care must be viewed through a lens that recognizes the importance of gender analysis, diversity, interdependence between paid and unpaid care, and linkages among social, medical and economic programs" (National Women and Health Care Reform Group n.d.)

Glossary of Key Terms

Canada Health Act: Federal legislation setting out the five principles that provincial/territorial governments must follow if they are to receive federal funding for health care: accessible, universal, comprehensive, portable, and publicly administered.

Care deficit: These days most of the emphasis is on financial deficits; that is, on money. The term "care deficits" refers to the failure to provide the conditions for the provision of adequate care and is intended to emphasize not only its importance but also that this failure results in other kinds of costs.

Commodification: The process of a good or service becoming part of the market and exchanged for money.

Decommodification: The process of a good or service that was once exchanged for money being provided without financial transfers.

Delisting: The process of removing some services or procedures from coverage under the public health system.

Privatization: The process of moving from a public to a private system. Privatization can happen within the public system as well as outside it. It can involve a range of tangible and visible changes, such as the sale of a hospital or the granting of a contract to a for-profit firm. It can also involve intangible and less visible changes, such as the shifting of responsibility for health to the individual in terms of the dominant ideology.

Privatization by stealth: The process of shifting care to the for-profit sector or household in ways that are difficult for the public to see or prevent.

Questions for Discussion

1. Are some forms of privatization beneficial in terms of equal access to services?

2. What does it mean for women as a group and for different groups of women if there are fees for health-care services?

3. Can we organize health-care work in the same way that we organize car production? If not, why not?

4. How can privatization be made more visible?

5. What should the role of care providers be in developing and administering health-care delivery? Should different kinds of providers play different roles?

6. Should unpaid care providers be trained, tested, and regulated?

7. Are ancillary workers in health care health-care workers? What are the implications, for the organization of work, of how we define this work?

Websites of Interest

Canadian Women's Health Network <cwhn.ca>
Canadian Centre for Policy Alternatives <policyalternatives.ca>
Canadian Health Coalition <chc.ca>
Canadian Institute for Health Information <cihi.ca>
Canadian Health Services Research Foundation <chsrf.ca>
Romanow Commission on the Future of Health Care in Canada <healthcommission.ca>
World Health Organization <who.int/topics/womens_health/en/>

Notes

In exploring the various forms of privatization and their consequences for women, this chapter draws heavily on research brought together in *Exposing Privatization: Women and Health Care Reform in Canada* (Armstrong et al. 2001). Women and Health Care Reform, a group drawn from the Centres of Excellence for Women's Health, commissioned the articles in that collection, which detail how reforms are played out in different ways within provincial jurisdictions and what this means for women in different locations. The themes are drawn out here; the specifics can be found in that text. The original version of this paper was presented at the Third International Congress on Women's Work and Health, June 2–5, 2002, Stockholm, Sweden.

1. See, for example, Hassen 1993. For the contrary view, see Henry Mintzberg 1989, especially ch. 10. Mintzberg observed that we now have the cult of measurable efficiency in health care. "We're starting to find out what we lost, but it took years to find out. They knew what they were saving instantly" (quoted in Swift 1999: 19).

2. The National Coordinating Group on Health Care Reform and Women (Now Women and Health Care Reform) website <cewh-cesf.ca/healthreform> shows the declaration from the National Think Tank on Gender and Unpaid Caregiving held in Charlottetown, November 8–10, 2001. This declaration was signed by forty-six of the fifty-five participants.

References

Armstrong, Pat. 1997. "The Promise and the Price: New Work Organizations in Ontario Hospitals." In Pat Armstrong et al. (eds.), *Medical Alert: New Work Organizations in Health Care*. Toronto: Garamond.

Armstrong, Pat, Carol Amaratunga, Jacqueline Bernier, Karen Grant, Ann Pederson, and Kay Willson. 2001. *Exposing Privatization: Women and Health Care Reform in Canada*. Toronto: Garamond.

Armstrong, Pat, and Hugh Armstrong. 2009. "Contradictions at Work: Struggles for Control in Canadian Health Care." In Leo Panitch and Colin Leys (eds.), *Morbid Symptoms: Health under Capitalism*. Pontypool Wales: Merlin Press and New York: Monthly Review Press.

_____. 2010 *Wasting Away. The Undermining of Canadian Health Care* Toronto: Oxford University Press.

Armstrong, Pat, Hugh Armstrong, Ivy Lynn Bourgeault, Jacqueline Choiniere, and Eric Mykhalovsky. 2000. *Heal Thyself. Managing Health Care Reform*. Toronto: Garamond.

Armstrong, Pat, Hugh Armstrong, Jacqueline Choiniere, Eric Mykhalovsky, and Jerry P. White. 1997. *Medical Alert: New Work Organizations in Health Care*. Toronto: Garamond Press.

Armstrong, Pat, Hugh Armstrong, and Krista Scott-Dixon. 2008. *Critical to Care: The Invisible Women in Health Services*. Toronto: University of Toronto Press.

Armstrong, Pat, Albert Banerjee, Marta Szebehely, Hugh Armstrong, Tamara Daly, and Stirling Lafrance. 2009. *They Deserve Better: The Long-Term care Experience in Canada and Scandinavia*. Ottawa: Canadian Centre for Policy Alternatives.

Armstrong, Pat, Madeline Boscoe, Barbara Clow, Kraen Grant, Margaret-Haworth Brockman, Beth Jackson, Ann Pederson, Morgan Seeley and Jane Springer (eds.). 2009. *A Place to Call Home: Long-Term Care in Canada*. Halifax, NS: Fernwood.

Armstrong, Pat, Jacqueline Choiniere, Gina Feldberg, and Jerry White. 1994. *Take Care: Warning Signals for Canada's Health System*. Toronto: Garamond.

Armstrong, Pat, and Jennifer Deadman (eds.). 2008. *Women's Health Intersections of Policy, Research, and Practice*. Toronto: Women's Press.

Armstrong, Pat, Irene Jansen, Erin Connell, and Mavis Jones. 2003. "Assessing the Impact of Restructuring and Work Reorganization in Long Term Care." In Penny Van Esterik (ed.), *Head, Heart and Hands: Partnerships for Women's Health in Canadian Environments*. Volume 1. Toronto: National Network on Environments and Women's Health.

Armstrong, Pat, and Olga Kits. 2001. *One Hundred Years of Caregiving*. Ottawa: Law Commission of Canada, unpublished.

Armstrong, Pat, and Kate Laxer. 2006. "Mapping Precariousness in the Canadian Health Industry: Privatization, Ancillary Work and Women's Health." In Leah Vosko (ed.), *Precarious Employment: Understanding Labour Market Insecurity in Canada*. Montreal: McGill-Queen's University Press.

Armstrong, Pat, and Linda Silas. 2009. "Taking Power: Making Change and Nurses' Unions in Canada." In Marjorie McIntyre and Carol McDonald (eds.), *Realities of Canadian Nursing: Professional, Practice, and Power Issues*. Third edition. Philadelphia: Lippincott, Williams & Wilkins.

Aronson, Jane, Margaret Denton, and Isik Zeytinoglu. 2004. "Homecare in Ontario: Deteriorating Working Conditions and Dwindling Community Capacity." *Canadian Public Policy XXX*. 1. <economics.ca/cgi/jab?journal=cpp&view=v30n1/CPPv30n1p111.pdf>.

Banerjee, Albert. 2009. "Long-Term Care in Canada: An Overview." In Pat Armstrong et al. *A Place to Call Home: Long-Term Care in Canada*. Halifax, NS: Fernwood.

Baines, Carol T., Patricia M. Evans, and Sheila M. Neysmith. 1998. "Women's Caring: Work Expanding, State Contracting." In Carol T. Baines, Patricia M. Evans, and Sheila M. Neysmith (eds.), *Women's Caring: Feminist Perspectives on Social Welfare*. Toronto: Oxford University Press.

Barer, Morris L., Robert Evans, and Clyde Hertzman. 1995. "Avalanche or Glacier? Health Care and the Demographic Rhetoric." *Canadian Journal on Aging* 14.

Battle, Ken. 1998. "Transformation: Canadian Social Policy Since 1985." *Social Policy and Administration* 32, 4.

Baumgart, Alice. 1997. "Hospital Reform and Nursing Labour Market Trends Across Canada." *Medical Care* 35, 10 (supplement).

Bernier, Jocelyne, and Marlène Dallaire. 1997. "What Price Have Women Paid for Health Care Reform? The Situation in Quebec." In Pat Armstrong et al. (eds.), *Medical Alert: New Work Organizations in Health Care*. Toronto: Garamond.

Blakley, Bonnie, and JoAnn Jaffe. 1999. "Coping as a Rural Caregiver: The Impact of Health Care Reforms on Rural Women Informal Caregivers." <cewh-cesf.ca/PDF/pwhce/coping-rural-caregiver.pdf>.

CIHI (Canadian Institute for Health Information). 2001. *National Health Expenditure Trends 1975–2001*. Ottawa: Canadian Institute for Health Information.

____. 2002. *Canada's Health Care Providers*. Ottawa: Canadian Institute for Health Information.

____. 2007. *Canada's Health Care Providers, 2007*. Ottawa: Canadian Institute for Health Information.

____. 2009a. *Regulated Nurses: Canadian Trends, 2005 to 2009*. <secure.cihi.ca/cihiweb/products/nursing_report_2005-2009_en.pdf>.

____. 2009b. *Drug Expenditures in Canada 1985–2009*. <secure.cihi.ca/cihiweb/products/NHEX_Trends_Report_2010_final_ENG_web.pdf>.

____. 2009c. *Supply, Distribution and Migration of Physicians*. <secure.cihi.ca/estore/productFamily.htm?pf=PFC1382&locale=en&lang=EN&mediatype=0>.

____. 2010. *National Health Expenditures Trends 1975–2010* Ottawa: CIHI. <secure.cihi.ca/cihiweb/products/NHEX_Trends_Report_2010_final_FR_web.pdf>.

____. 2010. "Health Care in Canada 2010: Evidence of Progress, But Care Not Always Appropriate." <cihi.ca/CIHI-ext-portal/internet/en/Document/health+system+performance/indicators/performance/RELEASE_16DEC10>.

CUPE (Canadian Union of Public Employees). 2001. "On Public Private Partnerships for Health Care." *The CUPE Facts* November.

____. 2006. *Developments in Privatization of Public Services* <cupe.ca/privatization/Developments_in_priv>.

Chappell, Nina. 1992. *Social Support and Aging*. Toronto: Butterworths.

Choiniere, Jacqueline A. 1993. "A Case Study Examination of Nurses and Patient Information Technology." In Pat Armstrong, Jacqueline Choiniere, and Elaine Day (eds.), *Vital Signs: Nursing in Transition*. Toronto: Garamond.

Cohen, Marjorie Griffin, and Marcy Cohen. 2004. *A Return to Wage Discrimination: Pay Equity Losses Through Privatization in Health Care*. Vancouver: Canadian Centre for Policy Alternatives.

Commission on the Future of Health Care in Canada: The Romanow Commission. 2002. "Building on Values: The Future of Health Care in Canada." <hc-sc.gc.ca/hcs-sss/com/fed/ro adamanow/index-eng.php>.

Clow, Barbara, and Kristi Kemp. 2012. "Caring at Home in Canada." In Pat Armstrong et al. (eds.), *Thinking Women and Health Care Reform*. Toronto: Women's Press

Cybulski, Nancy, Jo-Anne Marr, Isabel Milton, and Dalton Truthwaite. 1997. *Reinventing Hospitals: On Target for the 21st Century*. Toronto: McLeod.

Daly, Rita. 1998. "Abortions Banned in Wellesley Takeover." *Toronto Star,* April 10: A1.

Das Gupta. 2009. *Real Nurses and Others*. Black Point, NS: Fernwood.

Dion-Stout, Madeleine, Gregory D. Kipling, and Roberta Stout. 2001. *Aboriginal Women's Health: Synthesis Project.* Final report. <cewh-cesf.ca/PDF/cross_cex/synthesisEN.pdf>.

Duxbury, Linda, Christopher Higgins, and Bonnie Shroeder. 2009 *Balancing Paid Work and Caregiver Responsibilities: A Closer Look at Family Caregivers in Canada.* Ottawa: Human Resources and Skills Development Canada. <cprn.org/documents/51061_EN.pdf>.

Esping-Andersen, Gosta. 1990. *The Three Worlds of Welfare Capitalism.* New Jersey: Princeton University Press.

Evans, Robert. 2010 *Sustainability of Health Care. Myths and Facts.* medicare.ca/main/the-facts/9-sustainability-of-health-care/langswitch_lang/en

Gagnon, Marc-André with Guillaume Hébert. 2010 *The Economic Case for Universal Pharmacare* Ottawa: Canadian Centre for Policy Alternatives.

Gilmour, H. and J. Park (2005) Dependency, Chronic Conditions, ad pain in Seniors Health reports Supplement, Vol. 16. <statcan.gc.ca/pub/82-003-s/2005000/pdf/9087-eng.pd>.

Grant, Karen, Carol Amaratunga, Pat Armstrong, Madeline Bosco, Ann Pederson and Kay Willson (eds.). 2004. *Caring For/Caring About: Women, Home Care and Unpaid Caregiving.* Aurora, ON: Garamond.

Hassen, Philip. 1993. *Rx for Hospitals: New Hope for Medicare in the Nineties.* Toronto: Stoddart.

Health Services Utilization Task Force. 1994. *When Less Is Better: Using Canada's Hospitals Efficiently.* Ottawa: Health Services Utilization Task Force.

Jenkins, Alison. 2007. *Women and Private Health Insurance. A Review of the Issues* <cwhn.ca/fr/node/39385>.

Kazanjian, Arminée. 2000. *Nursing Workforce Study, Volume V: Changes in the Nursing Workforce and Policy Implications.* Vancouver: Health Human Resources Unit, Centre for Health Services and Policy Research, University of British Columbia.

Lexchin, Joel. 2001. "Pharmaceuticals: Policies and Politics." In Pat Armstrong, Hugh Armstrong, and David Coburn (eds.), *Unhealthy Times: Political Economy Perspectives on Health and Care in Canada.* Toronto: Oxford University Press.

Lilly, Meredith, Audrey Laporte, and Peter C. Coyt. 2010. "Do They Care Too Much to Work? The Influence of Caregiving Intensity on the Labour Force Participation of Unpaid Caregivers in Canada." *Journal of Health Economics* 29, 6.

Markham, Barbara, and Jonathon Lomas. 1995. "A Review of the Multi-Hospital Arrangements Literature: Benefits, Disadvantages and Lessons for Implementation." *Health Care Management Forum* 8, 3.

McGillis Hall, Linda, and Diane Irvin Doran. 2001. *A Study of the Impact of Nursing Staff: Mix Models and Organizational Change Strategies on Patient, System and Nurse Outcomes.* Ottawa: Canadian Health Services Research Foundation.

McGregor, Margaret, and Lisa Ronald. 2011. *Residential Long-Term Care for Canadian Seniors Nonprofit, For-Profit or Does it Matter?* Montreal: Institute for Research on Public Policy.

Mehra, Natalie 2007 *Private Clinics Report: First Do No Harm: Lessons from Ontario's Experience with For-Profit Diagnostic and Hospital Clinics.* Toronto. <web.net/ohc/first%20do%20no%20harm.pdf>.

Mintzberg, Henry. 1989. *Mintzberg on Management.* New York: Free Press.

Morris, Marika. 2001. *Gender-Sensitive Home and Community Care and Caregiving Research: A Synthesis Paper.* Ottawa: Women's Health Bureau, Health Canada.

National Women and Health Care Reform Group. n.d. "The Charlottetown Declaration on the Right To Care." <womenandhealthcarereform.ca/publications/charlottetownen.pdf>.

O'Brien-Pallas, Linda, Andrea Baumann, and Jacquelyn Lochhass-Gerlach. 1998. "Health Human

Resources: A Preliminary Analysis of Nursing Personnel in Ontario." Toronto: Nursing Effectiveness, Utilization and Outcomes Research Unit.

O'Connor, Julia S., Ann Shola Orloff, and Sheila Shaver. 1999. *States, Markets, Families: Gender, Liberalism and Social Policy in Australia, Canada, Great Britain and the United States.* Cambridge: Cambridge University Press.

Olivieri, Nancy. 2009. "Foreword." In Anne Rochon Ford and Diane Saibil (eds.), *The Push to Prescribe Women and Canadian Drug Policy.* Toronto: Women's Press.

Ontario. 1999. "Good Nursing, Good Health: An Investment in the 21st Century." Report of the Nursing Task Force. Toronto: Ontario Ministry of Health.

Osborne, David, and Ted Gaebler. 1993. *Reinventing Government: How the Entrepreneurial Spirit Is Transforming the Public Sector.* New York: Penguin.

Pembroke Civic Hospital and Lowe v. Health Services Restructuring Commission. 1997. Ontario Divisional Court, 394/97. June 25.

Perspectives on Labour and Income. 2005. "Unionization." *Perspectives on Labour and Income* 17, 3 (Autumn).

Priest, Alicia. 2006. *What's Ailing Nurses? A Discussion of the Major Issues Affecting Nursing Human Resources in Canada.* Ottawa: Canadian Health Services Research Foundation.

Spencer, Sarah, Susan Martin, Ivy lynn Bourgeault, and Eamon O'Shea. 2010. *The Role of Migrant Care Workers in Aging Societies: Report on Research Findings in the United Kingdom, Ireland, Canada and the United States* Geneva: International Organization for Migration.

Starr, Paul. 1990. "The New Life of the Liberal State: Privatization and the Restructuring of State-Society Relations." In John Waterbury and Ezra Suleiman (eds.), *Public Enterprise and Privatization.* Boulder, CO: Westview.

Statistics Canada. 2005a. "Child Care." *The Daily* February 7.

____. 2006. *A Portrait of Seniors in Canada.* <statcan.gc.ca/pub/89-519-x/89-519-x2006001-eng.pdf>.

Sutherns, Rebecca, Marilou McPhedran, and Margaret Haworth-Brockman. 2004. *Rural, Remote and Northern Women's Health: Policy and Research Directions.* Winnipeg: Prairie Centre of Excellence for Women's Health. <pwhce.ca/pdf/rr/Rrn_Summary_CompleteE.pdf>.

Swift, Jamie. 1999. "Saving the Corporate Soul." *Canadian Forum* June.

Taylor, Malcolm. 1987. *Health Insurance and Canadian Public Policy.* Montreal: McGill-Queen's University Press.

Thomas. Paul G. 1996. "Visions Versus Resources in the Federal Review." In Amelita Armit and Jacques Bourgault (eds.), *Hard Choices or No Choices: Assessing Program Review.* Toronto: Institute of Public Administration of Canada.

Leah Vosko. 2000. *Temporary Work: The Gendered Rise of a Precarious Employment Relationship.* Toronto: University of Toronto Press.

Vosko, Leah, Martha Macdonald, and Iain Campbell. 2009. *Gender and the Contours of Precarious Employment.* London: Routledge.

Willson, Kay, and Jennifer Howard. 2001. "Missing Links: The Effects of Health Care Privatization on Women in Manitoba and Saskatchewan." In Pat Armstrong et al. (eds.), *Exposing Privatization: Women and Health Care Reform.* Toronto, ON: Garamond Press.

Wagner, Terry H., and Kent V. Rondeau. 2000. "Reducing the Workforce: Examining its Consequences in Health Care Organizations." *Leadership in Health Services* 13.

Women's College Hospital. 1997. "Maintaining Women's Health Values in the Context of Change." May 9. Submission to the Health Services Restructuring Commission. Available at <cewh-cesf. ca/healthreform>.

15

Private Interests at Public Expense
Transforming Higher Education in Canada

Claire Polster

YOU SHOULD KNOW THIS

- In 1998, government operating grants provided 81.4 percent of university operating revenues and student tuition provided 13.9 percent. By 2008, government grants provided 57.5 percent of operating revenues, and tuition provided 34.7 percent.
- At the beginning of the 1990s, average undergraduate tuition fees in Canada were $1,464. By 2009, tuition fees had risen more than three-fold to $4,917.
- In 2009, average graduate tuition fees for international students surpassed $15,500. At some universities, students pay up to $26,000 a year in tuition fees and a staggering $40,000 a year for professional programs such as medicine and law.
- After graduate and professional fees were deregulated in Ontario, the participation rates of low-income families at the University of Western Ontario were cut in half.
- Whereas in 1999, only 15.5 percent of Canadian university professors were non-permanent, by 2005, this proportion had doubled to 31.7 percent.
- An analysis of cancer drug studies found that those funded by the pharmaceutical industry were nearly eight times less likely to reach unfavourable conclusions than were similar studies funded by non-profit organizations.
- For less than a fifth of the cost, Peter Munk helped establish a school of global studies at the University of Toronto that bears his name and directs $66 million of public money toward an institution that is subject to the Munk family's approval and required to report to a board appointed by Munk "to discuss the programs, activities, and initiatives of the School in greater detail."

Sources: CAUT 2009a; CFS 2009a, 2009b, 2005; Lin 2006; Washburn 2005: 84; McQuaig and Brooks 2010.

WITH THE EXCEPTION, PERHAPS, OF HEALTH CARE, there are few things that Canadians value more than public education. Our education system has traditionally been successful in enabling students simultaneously to develop their individual personalities and potential, to prepare to make a living, and to become thoughtful citizens who help to shape the nature and future of their society, and it has done this with an impressive degree of efficiency and equity (Robertson 2005: 6). While Canadians' commitment to education has remained at historically high levels (see, for example, Livingstone and Hart 2010), the nature of our public system has been quietly and gradually changing in recent years. Rather than being publicly supported for public purposes, education is becoming privatized, both in the sense that it is increasingly seen and treated as an individual rather than a social

> Education is increasingly seen and treated as an individual rather than a social responsibility and shaped by and oriented to market values and practices.

responsibility and in the sense that it is progressively shaped by, and oriented to, market values and practices rather than public or collective ones.

This privatization of Canadian education is visible at all levels of the system. It is reflected in the frequent knocks on our doors by youngsters selling chocolates or collecting empty bottles to help purchase the "extras" — and, increasingly, the basics — that their schools can no longer afford due to cuts in public funding. It is manifested in the ubiquitous advertising on school walls, bathroom stalls, and vending machines, and in the many kinds of deals and arrangements (such as the Wal-Mart adopt-a-school and Campbell's labels programs) forged between cash-strapped schools and wealthy corporations seeking invaluable publicity and opportunities to grow their customer bases. Privatization is also evident in our schools' adoption of a growing number of principles and practices that predominate in the private sector. These range from the centralization of administrative control and the contracting out of janitorial, food, and other services to the growing use of standardized testing and other performance measures, and even the establishment by some school districts of private businesses as a means of generating additional funds (Froese-Germain et al. 2006, British Columbia Teacher's Federation 2006).

It is at the level of the university, however, where the privatization process is most clear and advanced. As numerous analysts have observed, a university education in Canada is increasingly regarded and treated as a private rather than public good, much less as a citizenship right (Turk 2000b). As well, our universities are progressively seeing themselves as, and operating as and/or with, businesses in the research, teaching, and other work that they do.

This chapter focuses on the nature and implications of the ongoing privatization of Canada's universities. It does this in order to highlight some of the main ways in which public education in our country is being transformed and to address what this means for our citizens and our nation. My main argument is that we can and should resist the privatization of our universities in particular and of our public education system more generally. For although this process may provide benefits to some individuals and corporations, it does not serve the majority interest. Indeed, it may ultimately undermine even the interests of its advocates.

"Traditional" or mainstream analyses frequently assert that the privatization of Canadian higher education is a natural or inevitable development that is sweeping across public institutions and cannot be stopped. Alternatively, or at the same time, these analyses maintain that privatization is a beneficial development that should not be stopped.[1] Proponents of privatization argue that running our universities more as businesses increases their overall efficiency and effectiveness, which in turn serves the interests of those who work and learn within them as well as the taxpayers who fund them. They also argue that aligning universities' research and other operations more closely with the needs of the private sector enhances national economic competitiveness and thereby helps sustain our citizenry's high quality of life.

By contrast, I argue that privatization is neither natural nor inevitable: it is produced by people and can therefore be altered — even reversed — by them. Indeed, resisting privatization is not simply possible, but desirable. In a variety of ways, privatization transforms the internal operations of our universities in ways that compromise the interests of many of those who work and learn within them. Further, given that this process leads universities to prioritize private needs and interests at the expense of those of the general public, it not only fails to enhance our collective well-being, but also harms it.

Privatizing Higher Education in Canada

In its simplest form, the term "privatization" describes the process through which a resource or service is moved out of the public or collective sphere and into the private sphere, generally through sale. Thus, for example, in the 1980s and 1990s, the federal and provincial governments of Canada privatized many firms that had been state-owned and run — including de Havilland Aircraft, Teleglobe Canada, Canadair, CN Hotels, Air Canada, Petro-Canada, the Potash Corporation of Saskatchewan, and B.C. Ferries — selling them to private interests, sometimes at rock-bottom prices (Padova 2005). In the case of Canadian education in general, and higher education more particularly, however, privatization is not this straightforward. Rather than being a matter of selling off education (or otherwise transferring it) to private corporations, the relationship is much more complex: our universities are increasingly influenced by and oriented to the needs of the private sector (as well as some wealthy individuals), all the while being funded largely by the public.[2] In other words, rather than being subject to an outright sale to the private sector, the uses and benefits of university resources are being progressively ceded to private interests at the public's expense.

The term privatization also applies to a second, related development within Canadian universities: the progressive cultivation and normalization of an individualistic, self-serving ethic as opposed to a collective, public ethic. As our universities become more market-driven, those who work and learn within them are encouraged and/or compelled to place their private interests over and above collective interests — which include the interests of their peers, of their academic departments or faculties, and even of the broader community that the university is charged to serve.

Taken together, these two general trends and the myriad dynamics that bring them into being are changing what Canadian universities do and what they fundamentally are. From public-serving institutions that meet a wide variety of social needs in a plurality of ways, our universities are becoming private-serving institutions in which people increasingly orient themselves towards their own needs and interests and those of well-resourced organizations and individuals. This transformation not only jeopardizes the real and perceived value of our institutions of higher learning, but also poses significant threats to the well-being of many if not all Canadians, both now and in the future.

> From public-serving institutions that meet a wide variety of social needs in a plurality of ways, our universities are becoming private-serving institutions in which people orient themselves towards their own needs and interests and towards those of well-resourced organizations and individuals.

Two additional points regarding this chapter's approach to privatization are worth noting. First, it is not possible, particularly within this limited space, to provide a complete account of the process through which our universities are being transformed from public-serving into private-serving institutions. As such, the following discussion focuses on only selected aspects of this transformation occurring within three areas or functions of the university (namely academic research, governance, and teaching) and on only some of the interactions between them.

Second, the primary analytic tool this article uses to track the transformation of Canadian higher education is that of social relations. Social relations refer to those ongoing courses or patterns of human activity through which people produce a given feature of the social world — in this case, the university — in its particular form (Smith 1987; Campbell and Gregor 2002). In this analysis, I explore how the social relations of Canadian higher education are being reorganized or reconfigured so that the university changes from a publicly oriented institution into an institution that progressively works for, with, and as a business, and so that those within the university become more attuned to private interests (either of their own or of wealthy individuals and groups) as opposed to the public interest. One way of conceptualizing this analysis is to see it as tracking the reconstruction of the various pathways through which key players in higher education (including university administrators, academics, students, and various communities outside of the university) are brought into contact with one another. As old pathways are dismantled and as key players are brought together (or kept apart) for new purposes and/or in new ways, both their own roles and the role of the university as a whole begin to shift in a new direction.

University Research

A useful entry point into the privatization of Canada's universities is to examine the transformation of their knowledge production — or research — function. Prior to the 1980s relatively little research collaboration occurred between Canadian academics and members of the private sector. While some academics did various forms of research and other work (such as consulting) for corporations, such alliances were relatively few in number and kind, and they were held in relatively low priority, if not esteem, in most universities (Naimark 2004: 54–55). For the most part, university research tended to be conducted by academics and with academics in response to emerging problems and dynamics within their fields of inquiry and often in the service of the broader community. The privatization and commercialization of university research were rare.[3] Rather, research results tended to be widely disseminated and/or freely shared both within the academic community and beyond (Tudiver 1999: 11).

Since the 1980s, due to a number of factors, including government cuts to university operating budgets and concerns about Canada's competitiveness in the global, knowledge-based economy, research alliances between academics and the private sector have been strongly promoted, supported, and rewarded on most if not all Canadian university campuses, becoming in the process a widespread phenomenon. These alliances take on a great diversity of forms, ranging from small-scale research contracts to collaborative research centres, institutes, and networks, technology transfer offices, and "innovation" or "smart" parks, etc.[4] While the kinds of university/industry research alliances are varied, they generally involve corporate partners footing a portion of the bill for some academic research. In exchange for this funding, the partner may shape the topic of the research and some of the conditions under which it proceeds. It is increasingly common for the research partner to also acquire intellectual property rights to some or all of the research results.

In a variety of ways, these research partnerships with industry collectively and cumulatively help transform our universities from public-serving into private-serving institutions. First, they alter both the process through which research decisions are made and the kinds of research done in the university. As opposed to being shaped by the professional judgments and choices of autonomous academics, research decisions are increasingly made by well-resourced parties external to the university. Further, rather than being directed at serving the public interest, these research projects are designed to meet the partners' particular interests, which may or may not also serve, and may even conflict with, the collective good (such as when technological innovations cause job loss or environmental harm). More than simply allowing corporate sponsors to command disproportionate shares of academics' time, energies, and talents in the short term, and to do so at a small fraction of their real costs, such alliances also help skew the general scientific research agenda towards industry needs and interests in the long term. As the research needs of other social groups (particularly those who cannot afford to sponsor academic research) are neglected in favour of the needs of paying clients, academics' capacities and willingness to meet those other needs may decline and/or fail to get passed on to the next generation of Canadian researchers. Indeed, this trend is already appearing in some fields. In biology, for example, the shift towards the lucrative field of molecular biology is eroding other approaches, such as organismic approaches to biology, which can offer citizens less costly and more environmentally friendly solutions to various problems such as pest control (Press and Washburn 2000: 50).

As well as changing the kinds of research that our universities do, alliances with industry are transforming how academic research is done. Whereas university research has traditionally been an open, collaborative, and collective activity, these partnerships are helping to convert it into a more closed and competitive business-like affair. For example, academics working with or for industry partners are routinely obliged to sign secrecy agreements, prohibiting them from discussing, much less sharing, their research with colleagues until, and sometimes even after, the associated intellectual property rights have been secured. According to an important 1997 survey by Harvard researcher David Blumenthal, 58 percent of companies that sponsor academic research require researchers to delay the release of results for six months or more (Bollier 2002: 142). Subsequent studies confirm that this practice continues (see, for example, Blumenthal et al. 2006). Academics involved in partnerships with industry may also be compelled to work with very short time lines and with an eye to profitability as opposed to being free to pursue all the promising research avenues that emerge. In addition to their effects on the particular professors involved in research alliances with corporations, these market-driven norms and practices spill over into the broader academic enterprise. In a variety of ways, they further erode the collective nature of academic science as well as the many social benefits that flow from that work (including less costly, more efficient, and higher quality knowledge production) (Atkinson-Grosjean 2006: 23–28).

Finally, research alliances with business transform the ways in which, and conditions under which, academic research is accessed and used. Instead of a public good that is shared freely with all researchers and others who can use it, the research produced in these alliances is increasingly becoming the private property of research partners. If and when research

> Instead of a public good that is shared freely, academic research is increasingly becoming the private property of university research sponsors.

results are made available to other academics or members of the public, it is more often through some kind of commercial transaction, such as paying a licensing fee or direct purchase. Needless to say, the privatization and commercialization of academic research render it far less accessible to most academics and citizens, who must now pay for previously free knowledge, often at the very high prices that stem from monopoly conditions. This was the case, for example, with the discovery by researchers at the University of Utah of an important human gene responsible for breast cancer. Rather than making this discovery freely available to other scientists, the Utah researchers patented it and granted monopoly rights to Myriad Genetics Inc., which hoarded the gene and restricted other scientists from using it (Washburn 2005: xi). This form of privatization also serves to transform university administrators' and academics' perceptions of their own interests and how they respond to those interests.

In recent years, spurred on by the efforts of federal and provincial governments, as well as their growing entrepreneurial expertise gained from involvement with the private sector, university administrators have come to realize that they not only need to serve the research needs of paying clients, but are also in a position to exploit the fruits of academic research on their own. As a result, they have pursued a range of entrepreneurial activities based on their academics' research, which include establishing commercial development offices, selling ringside seats to leading-edge research, setting up spin-off companies, licensing valuable intellectual property, and the like. Such initiatives are not small-scale ventures that are peripheral to the activities of universities. Rather, they are complex undertakings that are consuming more and more of the available money, effort, time, and other resources of a university (see, for example, Read 2003; Lacroix 2010). Administrators' growing involvement in entrepreneurial activities further entrenches private-sector values and practices within our public universities. It also leads universities to prioritize their own interests over and above those of the general public. Indeed, one might argue that it is producing a reversal in the relationship between our universities and the broader community. For instead of using public funds to serve public purposes, our universities are using increasing shares of public funds to finance private ventures aimed at enriching themselves.

The university's greater involvement in entrepreneurial activities also has an impact on individual academics, transforming their professional interests and either enticing or compelling them to prioritize those new interests. For example, as universities share the spoils of business initiatives with those researchers who produce profitable knowledge, some academics have an unprecedented opportunity to become rich from their research. This gives them greater incentive to pursue lucrative research questions and areas, which are not always the most scientifically valuable or socially useful ones. A classic example of this is the growing attention, within the medical field, to the relatively minor but highly profitable "life-style" concerns of wealthy people, such as erectile dysfunction, and the marked inattention to the more widespread and serious diseases of the poor, such as malaria and tuberculosis (Mahood 2005). Moreover, "many of the new drugs coming to market are really 'me-too' drugs: inevitably more expensive than their predecessors (which have come off patent) but no more efficacious and often more dangerous" (Schafer 2008: 67).

The growing importance of corporate partnerships and commercialization to universities is leading administrators to reward academics involved in these activities in a number of other ways, both formal (such as through the tenure and promotion process) and informal (by according them greater institutional prestige and influence). This reward system encourages faculty (especially newer and untenured faculty) to become involved in privately oriented research activities instead of publicly oriented projects. Indeed, academics who refrain from allying with private partners, and particularly from privatizing their research results, are not only forgoing the benefits that accrue to those who are involved in these activities, but may also be compromising their advancement and perhaps even their position within the university. It is also not uncommon for faculty who criticize the university's involvement in business ventures as a conflict of interest or a betrayal of its public-service mission to face various forms of sanction within the institution, ranging from mild disapproval to harassment and even job loss (for discussion of three disturbing cases, see Woodhouse 2009 and Healy 2008 [where he recounts how his job offer was revoked after he publicly questioned the safety of a drug produced by one of the university's corporate sponsors]). In actively supporting the public's interest, then, academics may end up jeopardizing their private interests. This problem makes it progressively difficult for academics to sustain a public serving ethic.

In general, many of these changes interact with and reinforce one another to strengthen the ties that pull the university away from a public-serving orientation and towards a private-serving role. For instance, the university's involvement in partnerships with industry facilitates and promotes involvement in business ventures of its own, which, in turn, promotes and facilitates even more partnership with industry.

University Governance

From the post–Second World War period up until the late 1970s, universities were run as collegial and democratic institutions (sometimes more in theory than in practice). At all levels of the university, academic decisions were made collectively, by professors, through established collegial structures and processes, such as those of academic senates and faculty councils. While administrators, who were relatively few in number, had substantial power in the institution, they tended to see themselves as, and to act as, leaders of the collegium. They saw their job as facilitating and supporting academics' work and protecting the university's autonomy from undue outside influences on the part of government and others. Particularly in response to their activism in the 1960s, students were also afforded considerable opportunity to have significant input into academic affairs (such as through designated seats on departmental, faculty, and university-wide committees). Further, while only a small number of people from outside the university were able to directly participate in academic governance (such as through university senates and boards of governors), the university's relatively autonomous and democratic nature resulted in a high degree of responsiveness to a variety of social constituencies and of accountability to the wider community (Newson and Buchbinder 1988: ch. 3; Cameron 1991: ch. 7; Tudiver 1999: ch. 4).

Beginning with cutbacks in government funding for universities in the 1970s, and continuing with corporate research alliances and universities' involvement in knowledge businesses of their own, the nature of Canadian university governance began to change. These (and other) developments led to a significant increase in the size of academic administrations, and especially of research administrations. They also led to a substantial change in the nature and practice of administration. Rather than being leaders of collegial and democratic universities, administrators began to see themselves as, and to act as, the managers of these increasingly complex organizations and of those who work and learn within them.[5] As a result they attempted to centralize as much power as possible and to adopt a range of the values and practices that predominate in the business world, thereby rendering the universities more like private-sector institutions and more amenable to the desires and demands of the private sector (Newson 1992).

One of the ways that university administrators are centralizing power is by progressively bypassing collegial bodies and making more decisions either on their own or through hand-picked advisory committees. Such actions are often legitimized by the need to capture fleeting commercial and other opportunities which may be lost if decision making gets "bogged down in democracy." Administrators are also centralizing power by replacing long-standing collegial processes with various "consultative" exercises (frequently conducted online), which offer a more limited — and malleable — form of academic participation. Another approach is to define more and more issues as being purely administrative and thus not within the purview of the broader collegium. This has been done, for example, in the context of deals that afford campus monopolies to providers of various products, from soft drinks to software, which have significant impacts on the general campus environment.

Perhaps most troubling is the growing amount of secrecy pervading university operations. Instead of being open to academic (and public) scrutiny and deliberation, more and more research and other agreements (including monopoly sales agreements) between university administrators and external partners are being made and kept under the cloak of secrecy. This practice, which is frequently justified by the need to protect partners' proprietary information, very clearly sacrifices academic tradition and community interests to the desires and demands of particular individuals and corporations (Newson and Polster 2008: 129).

> More and more research and other agreements between university administrators and external partners are being made and kept under the cloak of secrecy.

University administrators are changing university operations in other ways that render them more like corporations. One significant aspect of this transformation is the adoption of private-sector practices, such as the use of performance indicators of various kinds, which serve to reduce professors' autonomy and increase managerial scrutiny and control (Bruneau and Savage 2002). A more general feature in decision making related to a growing number of university issues, is the progressive displacement of academic considerations by economic criteria, ranging from who is hired and rewarded, and how resources are allocated to various academic units, to what research areas are and are not prioritized. This shift was starkly reflected in a recent hiring of a dean: a participant in the process stated that "as long as he brings in $20 million, the rest doesn't matter" (Polster 2007). Another subtle but equally powerful change is the importing into universities of corporate language in which presidents are "CEOs," faculty members and staff are "human resources," and students are "clients" (Turk 2000a: 6). More than merely new forms of address, such terms imply and help to institutionalize very different kinds of roles for, and relationships between, those who work and learn in the university.

The university is not simply being run more as a business. To an unprecedented degree, it is also being run by members of the private sector and other wealthy individuals. The phenomenon of private sponsors gaining greater say over what academic research is done and how it is done appears not only in the context of isolated research projects, but also in the context of larger units and institutions on campus, such as university/industry research centres, networks, and institutes, over which corporate partners or wealthy benefactors command considerable authority. Thus, for example, for less than one fifth of its cost, Peter Munk helped establish a school of global studies at the University of Toronto. The school not only bears his name and directs $66 million of public funds to a project of his choosing, but is also subject to the Munk family's approval and required to report to a board appointed by Munk "to discuss the programs, activities, and initiatives of the School in greater detail" (McQuaig and Brooks 2010).

Increasingly, private sponsors are being granted extraordinary say over other academic matters as well. It is not uncommon for them to be given an indirect or direct hand in curricular and hiring decisions, and even voting positions on university committees, in exchange for donations in cash or in kind. Such was the case when medical students at the University of Toronto were provided a book on managing pain, which was funded and copyrighted by the maker of the prescription pain killer OxyContin, by a non-faculty lecturer with financial ties to the drug company (Ubelacker 2010), and when the mere loan of some high-end equipment gave Sony Classical Production a seat on the curriculum committee of McGill University's Faculty of Music (Shaker 1999: 3). This change in academic governance is facilitated by, and reinforces in turn, the other changes in university administration. For instance, as members of the collegium and the general public are progressively excluded from university decision-making processes, it becomes more difficult to challenge both the particular actions and the broader cultural transformation of the university that render it more open to corporate influence and control.

As is the case with academic research, changes in the social relations of academic governance also serve to alter the interests of those within the university and to encourage them to prioritize their personal well-being over the common good. For example, these changes are reducing the payoff that academics get from participating in university governance, given that important decisions are less frequently being made within established collegial bodies and that university service is progressively less valued and rewarded (particularly in relation to activities that generate income for the institution). As a result, many professors are opting to minimize if not abandon their university service work in favour of their research and teaching work, which may be more personally and professionally rewarding (Newson and Polster 2008: 140–41). While this retreat from collegialism may serve academics' immediate individual interests, it undermines the collective interest and ultimately the public interest — because among other factors, it reduces, in the short run, the efficacy of those academics who remain committed to preserving our universities as democratic institutions and, in the long run, the number of academics who are familiar with and committed to this vision.[6]

The changing social relations of academic governance are also leading some faculty and others, such as lower-level administrators, to alter the ways in which they participate in the process, so that rather than seeing themselves as members of a collective pursuing common goals, they act more as individuals pursuing their private goals. For instance, as university planning decisions are increasingly being made outside of collegial bodies, academics, department heads, and/or deans are far less able to collectively negotiate positions and policies that serve the majority interest. As such, many of them are attempting to informally influence planning processes — if and when the planning has a direct effect on them — as individuals (or small groups) advocating only for their particular needs. This is especially clear in decisions about which areas the universities and/or faculties will target as "strategic priorities." Rather than insisting that such decisions be made collectively in order to serve the general interests of the institution or faculty, more and more members of the academy are working "behind the scenes" to ensure that their own areas get prioritized, regardless of the effect that this may have elsewhere on their institutions and colleagues (Polster 2007). This strategy leads others to follow suit, if only to ensure that their interests are not compromised. Thus the collective well-being is progressively subordinated to individuals' well-being, and academic solidarity and power vis-à-vis increasingly managerial senior administrations are further fragmented and diminished.

Ongoing changes in university governance and academic research interact in various ways that further promote and reinforce privatization. For example, the centralization of power by academic administrators facilitates the establishment of university/industry research alliances and the commercialization of academic research. In turn, the latter encourage — indeed, compel — administrators to run universities more as businesses by curbing collegialism, transparency, and other long-standing academic traditions and values (Newson 2005: 10). These changes also contribute to and, in turn, are reinforced by changes in the social relations of Canadian university teaching.

University Teaching

Teaching was at the heart of the postwar university. While professors were expected to contribute to knowledge production and academic governance, their first priority, based on a common understanding, was teaching students (Pocklington and Tupper 2002: 11). As a result, most university courses were taught by full-time faculty members. Relatively small class sizes promoted a high degree of interaction between professors and students, and among students themselves. By the 1960s, with the dramatic expansion of Canada's university system, higher education had progressively come to be seen as a citizenship right, rather than a privilege of the rich. Tuition and other fees were kept low and student grants and loans were made widely available to ensure that higher education was affordable and accessible to all qualified Canadians (Axelrod 1982; Rounce 1999).

Beginning in the 1970s, and continuing on a relatively consistent basis since, governments have been reducing the funding provided to universities for operating costs, which include teaching costs (see, for example, CAUT 1999, 2009b).[7] For example, as noted in "Things You Should Know," government funding dropped from 81.4 percent to 57.5 percent in ten years, from 1998 to 2008. At the same time, and in part to make up for cuts in government support, universities have entered into a variety of private initiatives that are, nonetheless, frequently very costly to the institution. To participate in corporate research alliances, for example, universities need to spend significant funds developing proposals, attracting partners, building labs, and purchasing equipment. They also need to support a growing cadre of administrators and other specialists (including high-priced lawyers) to help broker and negotiate complex agreements, monitor them, and resolve inevitable conflicts. To cope with the rising costs in a context of diminished operating revenues, university administrators have adopted a number of strategies related to university teaching. These strategies serve to further privatize Canadian higher education and erode its public-serving nature.

One strategy is to substantially reduce teaching costs. Thus, across most, if not all, Canadian campuses, class sizes have swelled, library holdings have diminished, classroom and other facilities have deteriorated, and courses and programs have been slashed, particularly in the humanities and arts.[8] Universities have also upped their use of part-time and graduate student instructors,[9] who are paid far less than full-time faculty and receive far fewer benefits and opportunities for professional development (Turk 2008; CFS 2010a). These kinds of arrangements both stem from and contribute to the growing influence of private-sector approaches within the university, leading in particular to the displacement of academic values by economic criteria or bottom-line thinking.

> Class sizes have swelled, library holdings have diminished, classroom and other facilities have deteriorated, and courses and programs have been slashed, particularly in the humanities and arts.

In addition to reducing the resources invested in teaching, university administrators have opted to increase tuition and other student fees. According to the Canadian Federation of Students (CFS 2009a), in the space of less than twenty years, average undergraduate tuition fees more than tripled, going from $1,464 in the early 1990s to $4,917 in 2009.[10] This option privatizes higher education in the sense that it becomes more of an individual and less of a social or collective responsibility; universities become increasingly inaccessible to growing numbers of Canadians. The option also privatizes education in the sense that many students have to work longer hours to finance their schooling and thus have less time to socialize or get involved in other campus activities (CFS 2010a). Their own university education, as well as that of their peers, becomes an increasingly isolated or private rather than communal experience — a kind of privatization exacerbated for, and by, the growing numbers of students who are taking some, or all, of their courses online.

As they have developed their entrepreneurial acumen and expertise, administrators have come to regard university teaching not simply as a cost that needs to be managed, but also as an untapped money-making opportunity. They are thus becoming involved in a variety of lucrative teaching ventures, ranging from providing exclusive "boutique" programs (such as executive M.B.A. degrees that run in the tens of thousands of dollars per year), to developing and/or delivering courses for private companies, to hosting foreign programs on Canadian campuses for a cut of the profits (see, for example, Day 2006). To capitalize on the huge commercial opportunities opening up in the international education market, they have expanded the profitable courses and programs offered to foreign students (both through distance education and various partnership agreements with foreign institutions such as Navitas, a private company that recruits international students and provides their first year of instruction on Canadian campuses (Pearson 2010), and more aggressively recruited foreign students, who pay increasingly exorbitant, differentiated fees. According to the CFS (2009b), "In fall 2009, average graduate tuition fees for international students surpassed $15,500, more than triple the already high fees paid by Canadian citizens. At some universities, students pay up to $26,000 a year in tuition fees and a staggering $40,000 a year for professional programs such as medicine and law."

These kinds of initiatives serve to further erode the quality of education provided to the general student body, as they divert university resources and efforts towards more valued "clients," whether they are the students who pay substantially higher fees for their education or the private partners whose education ventures make money for the university. They also further erode both public values, such as equity in, and access to, higher education, and public-serving practices, such as providing openness and accountability in university affairs.[11]

At the same time that our universities are becoming more businesslike in relation to the education they provide, they are also becoming more businesslike in relation to the students they serve. This shift is manifested in the growing amounts of time and resources universities are investing in branding, advertising, and other marketing activities aimed at attracting greater numbers (and different kinds) of students. It is reflected in the greater use of technology and standardized procedures and protocols to manage student affairs. It is also apparent in the widespread use of teaching evaluations, student exit surveys, and other instruments to assess and improve "customer service" and satisfaction (Woodhouse 2009). These and other such measures divert precious resources away from the practice of teaching and towards the corporate services that promote and manage teaching, further eroding public education. They also reflect, and help entrench, a different relationship between the university and its students: as opposed to participating members of an educational community, students are seen and treated more and more as isolated consumers who purchase various services from the institution.

The changing relations of university teaching also transform the interests of those within the academy and encourage them to place their private well-being over and above that of the collective. In the case of students, reduced opportunities to work together to meaningfully shape university education are leading them to act on, and for, their individual interests. Thus, for example, rather than allying with their peers to improve the quality of education for all, high-achieving students — for whom universities are competing — are entering into more frequent and aggressive negotiations with academic institutions to secure the best possible terms and conditions for their education only (Alphonso 2006a; Reich 2001: 203–04). More generally, as students are progressively treated as customers, many of them are orienting to their education as customers, expecting teaching practices and decisions — particularly those surrounding grades — to please them. This trend is evident in the growing number of accounts of students challenging evaluations of their work and even demanding A's for their courses "because they paid for them" (Alphonso 2006b: A3; Newson 2005: 35–36). In a context in which administratively imposed performance indicators, such as standardized student evaluation forms, play a greater role in academics' performance reviews, some faculty members (particularly part-time and untenured faculty) find themselves pressured to prioritize their own interests over students' interests by tailoring their teaching expectations and standards to conform with their customers' demands (Woodhouse 2009: ch. 5). In so doing, these faculty members also compromise the interests of colleagues who opt to resist this pressure, as well as compromising the interests of the public, which is harmed in a variety of ways by the reduction in the quality of higher education.

Power

In general, the ongoing privatization of higher education — and all education — in Canada serves to entrench and intensify inequality within our society. It does this, in part, by shifting resources and power upwards, concentrating them in the hands of those who already have resources and power. For example, as tuition fees (and especially fees for professional and elite programs) escalate, privileged youth and adults are comprising a growing share of the university student population. According to the CFS, "the participation of students from families with incomes above $100,000 is 80.9 percent, while participation drops to 58.5 percent for those from families below $25,000" (CFS 2009a: 5).

> The ongoing privatization of education serves to entrench and intensify inequality within our society.

These students are also more able to take better advantage of their educational opportunities than are their less affluent peers. Similarly, as universities become more involved in research partnerships and business ventures of various kinds, the institution's research resources and results are progressively being made available to those who can afford to pay for them, to the detriment of those who cannot.

In addition to greater access to the university's resources, wealthy citizens and corporations are gaining greater control over the direction of the institution as a whole. As administrators run universities more and more like corporations, they are closing down the spaces for members of the academic community and the broader community to have input into university affairs. At the same time they are either offering or acceding to expanded opportunities for members of the private sector and other well-resourced individuals to shape academic decisions and decision-making processes. Not only does privatization thus undermine the redistributive function of public higher education (its ability to level inequalities by transferring resources from the wealthy to the poor), but it also serves to reverse that function. Rather than the rich subsidizing the educational and research needs of people with more limited financial resources, the general public is increasingly subsidizing the rich, paying the lion's share of the costs of the university's teaching and research resources — which people in general are progressively less able to use and over which they are losing control.[12]

The upwards shift of university resources serves to entrench and intensify inequalities in our society in a multiplicity of ways. As fewer disadvantaged students — and, increasingly, middle-class students — are able or willing to shoulder the huge financial burdens of higher education, the relative advantages of the wealthy stand to increase.[13] This advantage takes hold especially in the global, knowledge-based economy in which higher education plays a pivotal role in individuals' (and in the collective's) prosperity and quality of life. Further, as corporations and some individuals gain greater access to university research resources and results, they are able to sustain and expand their advantages in relation both to their competitors and to consumers. For instance, companies that obtain broad patents on important academic discoveries can stifle competition, pre-empt the development of alternative products and processes, and charge high monopoly prices for their products (Washburn 2005). The upwards shift of control over the university further reinforces inequalities in our society, as it provides well-resourced parties with "an inside track" into university policy and decision making, a position they can use to privilege, and perpetuate, both their particular interests and their collective, class interests. Given that transparency and accountability in university affairs are being reduced at the same time, wealthy individuals and corporations are able to advance their agendas with an unprecedented lack of scrutiny and a high degree of impunity.

Privatization does not simply further privilege the privileged. It simultaneously harms the majority of our citizens, and particularly disadvantaged citizens, by diminishing various resources that enable them not only to resist increasingly unequal power relations in our society but also to otherwise enhance the quality of their lives. For instance, as our universities become more fully influenced by and oriented to corporate needs, the knowledge produced becomes progressively instrumental and narrow, and thus less critical and diverse. This tendency limits the opportunities for those within the university and for the population at large to question and critique the status quo. It also deprives both those inside and outside universities of the knowledge necessary to transform their world in ways that more closely conform to their needs and interests. Thus, for example, as universities have become more involved in research and entrepreneurial ventures with agribusiness and pharmaceutical companies, it has become more difficult — both scientifically and politically — for those within all parts of the institution (and thus for those outside of it) to question and challenge the assumptions and implications of genetic engineering and the curative approach to health. The suppression in 2003 by the University of Manitoba of a graduate student's film on genetically modified crops, which portrayed Monsanto — a powerful multinational corporation with strong research and other links to the university — in a negative light provides a powerful illustration of this difficulty (see Sanders 2005; chapter 14 here; for additional examples, see Schafer 2005; Washburn 2005). So too does Healy's chilling account of the harassment — at the hands of corporations, university administrators, and academic colleagues — experienced by researchers, including himself, who have been openly critical of the pharmaceutical industry (Healy 2008). At the same time, universities are developing and disseminating relatively

> As our universities become more influenced by and oriented to corporate needs, the knowledge produced becomes progressively instrumental and narrow, and thus less critical and diverse.

little alternative knowledge, such as knowledge of organic farming or of holistic approaches to illness prevention, that citizens can draw upon — even were they so inclined — to better serve their own needs and enhance the collective well-being.

The privatization of higher education also erodes important skills that enable citizens to achieve greater equality and advance the public interest. For instance, when Canada's universities were run more openly and communally, they served as important training grounds for democracy. Many civic leaders cut their political teeth on university politics, and many more citizens developed a sense of their right to become actively involved in public institutions as well as the skills and savvy to do so effectively during their university years (for a Canadian example, see Pitsula 2006: ch. 12, 13; the movie *Berkeley in the Sixties* provides a vivid U.S. example). As universities progressively limit the opportunities for students and others to participate in academic affairs, and instead compel and entice them to engage with the institution as isolated consumers or employees, they rob people of important opportunities to acquire and hone democratic sensibilities and capacities that are key to achieving positive change within both the institution and the broader society. (For an interesting exploration of this issue, see Brule 2004.)

Perhaps most troubling is that privatization undermines, both within the university and outside of it, various values and commitments that inspire and reinforce efforts to promote social equality and justice, such as a concern for the common good. The university deals a serious blow to the common good in and through its involvement in the privatization and commercialization of knowledge, which not only leads it to make withdrawals from our common stock of knowledge without depositing much in return, but also makes it more difficult for others to replenish our rapidly diminishing pool of free knowledge (our "knowledge commons") (Washburn 2005; Bollier 2002; Shulman 1999). To an alarming degree, growing numbers of university administrators and academics are even betraying the common good by knowingly jeopardizing citizens' well-being in the pursuit of profit — a trend that has become all too evident through the growing number of scandals and lawsuits in which universities have become embroiled. (For a thorough and chilling account of many of these, including the wrongful death of Jesse Gelsinger in the United States and the sagas of doctors Nancy Olivieri and David Healy, who were penalized for putting the interests of patients above those of university corporate partners in Canada, see Washburn 2005).[14]

Our universities are failing to nurture the common good in a host of other ways. Academic administrators and others are restricting the opportunities for members of the university community to raise and defend the public interest in the context of institutional decision and policy making. They are also reducing the resources and rewards provided to those involved in communally oriented programs and projects in the university, and suppressing and penalizing various forms of resistance to privatization that students and staff undertake in defence of the collective good. At the same time, many people in universities are promoting greater individualism and competitiveness in a myriad of ways, such as when they bestow honours and privileges on academics who privately profit from their research, and when they encourage — and even help train — graduate and some undergraduate students to do the same.

Perhaps the greatest threat to the common good is the progressive normalization of the corporate perspective within the university. The more that this perspective is taken for granted and passed on by those who work and learn in the institution, the more the pursuit of private interests is placed above question — and is even redefined as the primary means of achieving the common good.

> The more that the corporate perspective is taken for granted, the more the pursuit of private interests is placed above question — and is even redefined as the primary means of achieving the common good.

While the privatization of higher education serves the interests of the privileged at the expense of the majority of citizens, it also fundamentally undermines the interests of the privileged, in a number of ways. Although wealthy students are getting more education, and superior education, relative to others, the overall quality of their educational experience is declining not only through the growing homogeneity, isolation, and competitiveness within the student body, but also because of the university's progressive orientation to education as a business and to students as an income source. Similarly, while particular corporations may derive immediate benefits from research alliances, privatization harms the longer term interests of the corporate sector as a whole. It erodes many of the features of academic research — such as its open and collaborative nature and the ability to engage in the curiosity-driven inquiries that are more frequently the source of significant scientific breakthroughs — that enhance the quality of research as well as its actual and potential economic contributions (Polster 1994: ch. 7; Atkinson-Grosjean 2006: 23–28; Healy 2008; Schafer 2008). More generally, as the privatization of the university helps to enrich privileged individuals and organizations, it simultaneously impoverishes (and imperils) the larger social and natural contexts that they inhabit. Although wealth and power can insulate the privileged from some of the harmful effects of this result, ultimately the only way of dealing with these problems is through collective solutions — but then, privatization impedes the development of such solutions in various ways, both directly and indirectly.

Although the university, as an institution, seems to benefit from privatization in that it gains new capacities to generate funds as well as new allies and support (particularly from within the corporate sector), it too may be seriously harmed by this process. As our universities fundamentally change what they are and what they do, and as more citizens come to understand what this means for their personal and collective well-being, public support for these institutions is likely to wane. Given that the public is still the major funder and supporter of the university, this diminishing support bodes ill for the future of the institution. A lack of public support will render the university far more vulnerable to the needs and demands of wealthy individuals and corporations, whose ability not simply to influence, but also to exploit, the university will increase in proportion to the public's abandonment of the institution.

While its implications are thus very serious and troubling, we need to remember that the privatization of higher education in Canada is an ongoing process, not a completed one. The university is indeed becoming more privately oriented in all of its aspects and activities; however, there are still many places and individuals within the academy that remain dedicated to serving and promoting the public interest. There is also a growing number of opportunities, arising both within and outside of the university, to generate and mobilize resistance to the privatization of higher education.

Resistance

In spite of (or perhaps because of) the isolating and disempowering effects of privatization, various groups around the country have taken a number of steps to expose, and oppose, it in recent years. One of the most active of these groups is Canadian students. Through their local, regional, and national organizations, many students have launched actions to resist specific impacts of privatization and the more general process itself. These actions include campaigns to oppose tuition hikes and monopoly deals between universities and corporations (most notably those involving Coke and Pepsi), as well as efforts, such as the Corporate Free Campus project[15] at the University of Toronto, to educate students and others about the general nature and implications of the privatization of Canadian higher education (CCPA 2005: ch. 1).

> Various groups around the country have taken steps to expose, and oppose, privatization in recent years. One of the most active of these groups is Canadian students.

Many faculty have also resisted privatization. Both individually and collectively (such as through the collective bargaining process and in the context of faculty strikes), they have opposed various developments, including the growing use of performance measures, increases in class sizes, and the greater emphasis on income-generating activities, that erode the quality of their own working lives and of the education, research, and other forms of service they can offer to the public. In addition to working within their own organizations, students and faculty have collaborated with one another and with various public-interest groups to raise awareness about privatization and to mount opposition to initiatives that entrench and advance it. Campaigns were waged, for example, against a 1991 bid to establish a private International Space University on the York University campus[16] (Saunders 1992), a 2004 plan to redevelop the old Varsity Stadium site at the University of Toronto (Salterrae 2004), a plan to establish a privately funded college on the campus of Simon Fraser University (McCuaig 2006), and various proposals in 2010 at the University of Toronto (including a plan to close the respected Centre for Comparative Literature) that were perceived to threaten the humanities at that institution (Pitas 2010).The York University and Varsity Stadium projects were defeated due to collective action, as were various plans for the humanities at the University of Toronto. Beyond their direct and immediate impacts, efforts such as these help to build alliances and solidarity as well as valuable knowledge and experience that can inspire and strengthen future efforts to oppose privatization. Thus, whether they win or lose particular struggles, those involved in these forms of resistance make an important contribution to preserving public higher education in our country.

While these forms of opposition are extremely important, other approaches could also be adopted to enhance resistance. Rather than simply reacting to various initiatives and practices that promote privatization, opponents of the process might proactively establish alternative initiatives and practices that model the kind of public-serving university they hope to preserve and revitalize. One example would be to establish equivalents of the Dutch science shops on Canadian campuses. Science shops are university institutions that make academic resources and expertise available to local citizens groups in order to resolve various problems or serve other needs. They address a broad spectrum of issues ranging from investigating and helping to remedy various kinds of environmental contamination in local neighbourhoods to conducting feasibility studies and helping to produce detailed plans for local development projects (scienceshops.org). Two key principles of science shops are that the groups involved do not pay for the research done for them and any results that emerge from research projects are kept in the public domain. The presence on our campuses of such institutions could challenge, and interrupt, many of the assumptions and practices associated with privatization, such as the desirability of commercializing academic knowledge and the privileging of the research needs of paying clients. Equally, if not more importantly, science shops could help sustain and rejuvenate a progressive and public-serving vision for the university. They could also help to create conditions to realize this vision, by revitalizing or instilling a public service ethic in both academics and students, and by encouraging all citizens (especially those with little power) to see and treat the university as a collective resource that they are entitled to use and that should, and can, be responsive and accountable to them.

Another approach to strengthening resistance is to organize a number of broad and co-ordinated national campaigns, each of which highlights one selected aspect of the privatization process. This approach allows opponents of privatization to concentrate their resources all at once and on the same issue, rather than diffusing them on a multiplicity of isolated actions across the country. The best candidates for these campaigns are those aspects of the university's privatization that are most deeply intertwined with other aspects (because pulling on these threads is likely to cause other issues to unravel as well). They are also those aspects of privatization that speak to deeply held and widely shared values and concerns and are thus able to interest and mobilize a large cross-section of the Canadian population.

One such issue around which a national campaign could be built is the privatization and commercialization of academic research. The university's involvement in intellectual property connects with a number of other aspects of privatization, including the skewing of academic research towards industrial needs and interests, greater secrecy and managerialism in the university, rising tuition fees, and the university's growing involvement in various conflicts of interest and scandals. Because this issue is so deeply enmeshed in the privatization process, it cannot be easily dismissed, nor can it be resolved through simple or technical measures (such as guidelines or regulations) that would leave privatization essentially intact. A second advantage of building a campaign around this issue is that it touches on widespread and deeply felt concerns within our society and could thus help mobilize and unite a broad coalition of support. Within the university, it could help bring together students who are suffering from intolerable debt loads, academics whose access to increasingly expensive research materials is being reduced, and members of departments and faculties that are being penalized for their inability or unwillingness to engage in private knowledge production. It could also bring together a wide range of groups outside the university — people who have more general concerns about the privatization of the commons of knowledge, including farmers, health professionals, Aboriginal people, artists, and even a growing number of corporate leaders and entrepreneurs (Shulman 1999; Bollier 2002). A campaign like this would not only stand a good chance of succeeding, but also enhance the chances of success of subsequent campaigns against the privatization of higher education.[17] At the same time such campaigns could help strengthen efforts to oppose privatization at other levels of the education system and perhaps within other valued public institutions, such as the Canadian health-care system.

Opponents of privatization might also focus more of their efforts on outside developments that are contributing to changes within the university. Much of the impetus for the privatization of the university has come from government, particularly the federal government. Beginning in the mid-1970s and intensifying since then, the federal government's conception of the university has shifted from a resource for social development to an instrument of economic competitiveness (Polster 1994: ch. 2; Atkinson-Grosjean 2006). This shift has led politicians to reduce the basic operating funds that they provide to universities and to directly and indirectly encourage the schools to ally with the corporate sector and become involved in entrepreneurial initiatives of their own. To a large extent, this shift in the government's conception and treatment of the university has stemmed from a shift in the nature of government itself. Rather than producing university policy in-house, the government has progressively been ceding responsibility for higher education policy making to unelected and unaccountable advisory bodies, such as the Canadian Science, Technology and Innovation Council, which are dominated by corporate and academic executives and those who are supportive of their interests. Not surprisingly, these groups have used the opportunity to advance and institutionalize visions and policies for the university that serve their particular needs rather than those of the broader society (Polster 1994; Atkinson-Grosjean 2006. Also see reports of Canada's former National Advisory Board on Science and Technology and Advisory Council on Science and Technology, as well as those of the Science, Technology and Innovation Council).[18]

As part of the effort to resist the privatization of the university, citizens might, then, also resist the privatization of government. They might work to ensure that those elected by the public (along with other public servants) produce policy for the public, and that they do so in a way that is transparent, accountable, and responsive to a broad range of social interests and needs. This strategy could go a long way towards undercutting many of the conditions that sustain privatization in the university and elsewhere. In so doing, it would reduce and ease the work that opponents of privatization have to do and further enhance the effectiveness of their resistance.

Glossary of Key Terms

Academic collegialism: Refers to the values and practices in and through which academics collectively govern the university. Examples of key collegial structures include university senates and faculty councils.

Commercialization: The process through which a product is introduced into the marketplace. The commercialization of academic research means that knowledge produced in whole or in part with public funds is not made freely available to the public, but is accessible only to those who are able and willing to pay for it.

Dutch science shops: Bodies on many university campuses that provide research services, often free of charge, to help local groups address issues of concern such as environmental contamination and community economic development.

Intellectual property rights: IPRs legally establish monopoly protection for creative works such as writing (copyright), inventions (patents), and identifiers (trademarks). IPRs effectively extract ideas and other forms of knowledge from the knowledge commons or the public domain, that is, that pool of freely available knowledge to which we may all contribute and from which we may all draw.

Privatization: Most simply, privatization involves the transfer of assets or services from the government to the private sector. It can also involve the incorporation into public bodies of values and practices that predominate in the private sector as well as the production of a range of partnerships between public and private bodies.

Social relations: Ongoing courses of human activity in and through which aspects of society (such as higher education) are given their particular shape and form. As social relations change, old options and possibilities for social action may be closed down, while others are opened up.

Questions for Discussion

1. What impact has rising tuition had on your own experience at university and on the experience of your peers?

2. How are students involved in shaping policy at your university? How has this changed from the past, and how might the situation be improved in the future?

3. What kinds of university/industry alliances exist at your institution, and what kinds of business ventures is your university involved in? How do these affect the teaching and research at your university?

4. What other forms of privatization are visible at your university (for example, corporate advertising on campus)? What are their impacts on the general university environment?

5. What actions have been taken by people at your university to draw attention to the issue of privatization? What further actions could be taken?

6. How do you feel about making university free for all qualified students? Why?

7. Some people argue that all knowledge produced in public universities should remain in the public domain (freely accessible to all). What is your position on this and why?

8. Proponents of university/industry alliances argue that promoting economic competitiveness is the highest form of public service that the university can provide. What is your response to this assertion?

9. In what ways is privatization at other levels of the education system similar to and different from privatization at the level of the university? What are the main benefits and harms of privatization at these other levels of the system?

Websites of Interest

Canadian Association of University Teachers <caut.ca>

Canadian Centre for Policy Alternatives — The Education Project <policyalternatives.ca/projects/ education-project>

Canadian Federation of Students <cfs-fcee.ca>

British Columbia Teachers Federation <bctf.ca>

Forum on Privatization and the Public Domain <forumonpublicdomain.ca>

Living Knowledge <scienceshops.ca>

Notes

1. These analyses can be found in government reports on higher education, such as those produced in the context of the national innovation strategy. See <innovationstrategy.gc.ca>.
2. Although an increase in private and for-profit higher education has occurred in Canada in recent years (CFS n.d.), the vast majority of Canada's universities are still public.
3. The privatization and commercialization of academic research involve converting the knowledge produced in the university (which is always either fully or partially publicly funded) into private, intellectual property and exploiting that property to generate profit.
4. There is no central list that includes all of these research partnerships in Canada, much less tracks their growth over time. However, several agencies, such as Industry Canada and the national research granting councils, do discuss (and, in some cases, track the growth of) some of these alliances in documents such as annual reports. Various analysts of higher education have also addressed the growth of these alliances in more general terms. For one example, see Tudiver 1999: ch. 3.
5. This trend has been exacerbated as growing numbers of non-academics have been hired as university administrators.
6. In abandoning university governance, academics also undermine their longer term private interests. For as managerial and private power becomes progressively less contested and contestable, academics become increasingly subject to others' priorities and demands in all aspects of their work, including their research and teaching work.

7. The dynamics of higher education funding in Canada are complex, but it is important to note that at the same time that the federal government has been reducing support for university operating costs — in absolute or relative terms — it has also, especially in recent years, been dramatically increasing the support provided to universities for academic research, and particularly for industrially oriented and partnership research — which in turn has contributed to certain aspects and consequences of privatization.

8. Comprehensive data on the impacts of reduced investment in university education are difficult to find: however, several partial accounts may be found in the Canadian Centre for Policy Alternatives' "Missing Pieces" series and in other publications of that organization. Howard Woodhouse offers a particularly shocking account in the context of his discussion of the University of Saskatchewan. He notes that at the same time that the university contributed $7.3 million to the Canadian Light Source (which is used to commercialize research at the university) "130 faculty positions had been lost, staff drastically reduced, library holdings slashed, and buildings were literally falling down" (Woodhouse 2003).

9. Data on part-time instructors in Canada are limited. However, in 2000, a Statistics Canada study noted that from 1992/93 to 1997/98 the number of full-time faculty in Canada decreased by 9.6 percent whereas the numbers of part-time faculty increased in almost all provinces. For example, in Western Canada, the number of part-time faculty rose by 13.5 percent and a significant 43.7 percent in full-time teaching equivalence (Statistics Canada 2000). Further, whereas in 1999, only 15.5 percent of university professors were non-permanent, by 2005, this proportion had doubled to 31.7 percent (Lin 2006).

10. The increases have been even more dramatic in professional programs. According to the Canadian Association of University Teachers (CAUT 2003: 1), "Medical fees, adjusted for inflation, climbed 320 percent between 1990 and 2003. Tuition for law school rose 217 percent while dental programs charged students an incredible 400 percent more in 2003 than in 1990."

11. Universities generate funds in many other ways, including exclusive marketing deals and allowing companies to advertise on campus. While these forms of privatization do not generally have an impact on course content, they do affect the broader lessons that students learn, both indirectly and directly, such as when criticism of their university's corporate sponsors is discouraged if not penalized on campus (Newson and Polster 2008: 144).

12. The careful reader might question this comment, given that wealthy students and research sponsors are themselves paying a larger share of the costs of the education and research resources to which they are gaining access. While this is true, it is also true that the bulk of the costs of these resources is still paid by the general public in the form of direct and indirect government support to universities. For example, although the proportion of university operating costs paid by students increased from 13.9 percent to 34.7 percent from 1988 to 2008, the share of these costs paid by the public remained consistently higher, at 81.4 percent and 57.5 percent respectively (CAUT 2009a). Many right-wing authors have used the "reverse subsidy" argument to support calls for greater privatization in higher education and elsewhere. ("Why should the poor continue to pay for resources that the rich disproportionately take advantage of?") However, an equally feasible, more just, and ultimately more productive solution would be to reverse privatization and to increase public access to public resources, such as by dramatically reducing, and eventually eliminating, university tuition fees.

13. Privatization also intensifies other inequalities, such as those of gender, race, and dis/ability. For example, given that women tend to earn substantially less than men, even with equivalent education credentials (Statistics Canada 2010), they are less able, and may become less willing,

to assume the heavy burdens associated with higher education. For an excellent discussion of the impacts of privatization on racialized groups see CFS 2010b.

14. Beyond the specific harms incurred by the particular individuals involved, cases such as these more fundamentally undermine the common good in that they erode the actual and perceived reliability and trustworthiness of our academic institutions. This development threatens to leave our society without a disinterested source of expertise to which we can turn for assessments or advice on important social, economic, and political questions and thus poses serious risks to our individual and collective well-being both now and in the future.

15. According to a Canadian Centre for Policy Alternatives (2005: 19) report, "The Anti-Corporate Rule Action Group of OPIRG Toronto began the Corporate-Free Campus project in 1998 to expose, challenge, and build alternatives to corporate connections at U. of T. As part of the project, tours of campus examine corporate involvement within particular buildings, and the campus was put 'under construction' to work toward corporate-free zones."

16. The bid to establish the International Space University (ISU) on the York University campus was submitted, in secret, by the Centre of Excellence on Space and Terrestrial Science, which was located on the York campus and to which a large number of York faculty were cross-appointed. After the bid was leaked to the public, members of the university community and of a wide variety of public interest groups organized to oppose the project, for a number of reasons: the institution would be a private university — a first for Canada at the time; it would charge $25,000 in tuition fees; it would be parasitic on York student programs, library, and computer facilities; it would divert a substantial amount of government money from the public higher education system (the provincial and federal governments committed millions of public dollars to the ISU); and it would in various ways support and strengthen the U.S. military-industrial complex. After a broad-based and creative campaign by opponents of the bid, the ISU chose to locate elsewhere. For more details on the bid and the campaign, see Saunders 1992.

17. Broad and co-ordinated national campaigns could be organized around a number of other issues, such as the erosion of democratic control over the university and the mismanagement of public resources that stems from increasingly intense competition both within and between universities. In addition to establishing science shops, many other proactive initiatives could be pursued, such as creating free universities in our cities (Woodhouse 2009) and integrating universities into local and regional community economic development projects (Polster 2000).

18. Student organizations and others have addressed some of these issues, particularly cuts in government transfers to universities; but other more fundamental transformations in higher education policy and policy making also need to be addressed.

References

Alphonso, Caroline. 2006a. "In Academia, the Early Bird Gets to Learn." *Globe and Mail*, January 27: A3.

____. 2006b. "Among Brazen Undergrads, A is for Aggressive." *Globe and Mail*, May 1: A3.

Atkinson-Grosjean, Janet. 2006. *Public Science, Private Interests: Culture and Commerce in Canada's Networks of Centres of Excellence*. Toronto: University of Toronto Press.

Axelrod, Paul. 1982. *Scholars and Dollars: Politics, Economics, and the Universities of Ontario 1945–1980*. Toronto: University of Toronto Press.

Blumenthal, David, Eric Campbell, Manjusha Gokhale, Recai Yucel, Brian Clarridge, Stephen Hilgartner, and Neil Holtzman. 2006. "Data Withholding in Genetics and Other Life Sciences: Prevalence and Predictors." *Academic Medicine* 81, 2.

Bollier, David. 2002. *Silent Theft: The Private Plunder of Our Common Wealth*. New York: Routledge.

British Columbia Teacher's Federation. 2006. "Annual Report on Privatization and Commercialization of Education." <bctf.ca/uploadedfiles/Education/Privatization/2007>.

Brule, Elizabeth. 2004. "Going to Market: Neo-Liberalism and the Social Construction of the University Student as Autonomous Consumer." In Marilee Reimer (ed.), *Inside Corporate U: Women in the Academy Speak Out*. Toronto: Sumach Press.

Bruneau, William, and Donald Savage. 2002. *Counting Out the Scholars: The Case Against Performance Indicators in Higher Education*. Toronto: James Lorimer.

Cameron, David. 1991. *More than an Academic Question: Universities, Government and Public Policy in Canada*. Halifax: Institute for Research on Public Policy.

Campbell, Marie, and Frances Gregor. 2002. *Mapping Social Relations: A Primer in Doing Institutional Ethnography*. Aurora, ON: Garamond Press.

Canadian Association of University Teachers (CAUT). 1999. "Not in the Public Interest — University Finance in Canada 1972–1998." *CAUT Education Review* 1, 3.

CAUT. 2003. "University Tuition Fees in Canada, 2003." *CAUT Education Review* 5, 1.

____. 2005. "Paying the Price: The Case For Lowering Tuition Fees in Canada." *CAUT Education Review* 7, 1.

____. 2009a. "Average Annual Cost of University Tuition ($2009)." Publications and Research, Quick Facts. <caut.ca/pages.asp?page=517>.

____. 2009b. "University Finances 2007–2008." *CAUT Education Review* 11, 1.

CCPA (Canadian Centre for Policy Alternatives). 2005. *Challenging McWorld II*. Ottawa: CCPA.

CFS (Canadian Federation of Students). 2005. "Tuition Fees in Canada: A Pan-Canadian Perspective on Educational User Fees." *CFS Fact Sheet* 11, 1.

____. 2009a. *Tuition Fees in Canada*. Ottawa: CFS. <cfs-fcee.ca/html/english/ research/factsheets/CFS-Fact%20Sheet-Tuition%20Fees.pdf>.

____. 2009b. *Tuition Fees for International Undergraduate Students*. Ottawa: CFS. <cfs-fcee.ca/html/english/research/factsheets/CFS-Fact%20Sheet-Int%20Undergrad%20Tuition %20Fees.pdf>.

____. 2010a. *Public Education for the Public Good*. Ottawa: CFS. <cfs-fcee.ca/downloads/CFS-2010-PublicEducation.pdf>.

____. 2010b. "The Racialised Impact of Tuition Fees." Ottawa: CFS. <cfsontario.ca/mysql/CFS-Racialised-Impact-of-Tuition-Fees.pdf>.

____. n.d. "Campaigns and Lobbying: Private Universities and Colleges." <cfs-fcee.ca/html/english/campaigns/private.php>.

Day, Terence. 2006. "Private For-Profit College to Open at SFU." <universityaffairs.ca/private-for-profit-college-to-open-at-sfu.aspx>.

Froese-Germain, Bernie, Colleen Hawkey, Alec Larose, Patricia McAdie, and Erika Shaker. 2006. *Commercialism in Canadian Schools: Who's Calling the Shots?* Ottawa: Canadian Centre for Policy Alternatives.

Healy, David. 2008. "Academic Stalking and Brand Fascism." In James Turk (ed.), *The Corporate Campus: Commercialization and the Dangers to Canada's Colleges and Universities*. Toronto: Lorimer.

Lacroix, Anik. 2010. *Survey of Intellectual Property Commercialization in the Higher Education Sector*. Ottawa: Statistics Canada.

Lin, Jane. 2006. "The Teaching Profession Trends From 1999–2005." *Education Matters* 3, 4.

Livingstone, David, and Doug Hart. 2010. *The 17th OISE Survey: Public Attitudes Toward Education in Ontario 2009*. Toronto: OISE/UT.

Mahood, Sally. 2005. "Privatized Knowledge and the Pharmaceutical Industry." Paper presented at

Free Knowledge: Creating a Knowledge Commons in Saskatchewan Conference. University of Regina, Regina, Saskatchewan, November 17–18.

McCuaig, Amanda. 2006. "Campus Fiasco: Campus Community Opposed to IBT Agreement." *The Peak* 22 (5) February 6.

McQuaig, Linda, and Neil Brooks. 2010. *The Trouble with Billionaires.* Toronto: Viking Canada. (Excerpt reprinted at <thestar.com/printarticle/859721>).

Naimark, Arnold. 2004. "Universities and Industry in Canada: An Evolving Relationship." In Paul Axelrod (ed.), *Knowledge Matters: Essays in Honour of Bernard J. Shapiro.* Montreal and Kingston: McGill-Queen's University Press.

Newson, Janice. 1992. "The Decline of Faculty Influence: Confronting the Effects of the Corporate Agenda." In William Carroll et al. (eds.), *Fragile Truths: 25 Years of Sociology and Anthropology in Canada.* Ottawa: Carleton University Press.

____. 2005. "The University on the Ground: Reflections on Canadian Experience." Paper presented at CEDESP Conference on the Impact of Research on Public Policy on Higher Education, Rincon, Puerto Rico, June 2–3. <gobierno.pr/NR/rdonlyres/447D7354-F1EC-4315-8F47-50281A2BA19F/0/Newson.pdf>.

Newson, Janice, and Howard Buchbinder. 1988. *The University Means Business.* Toronto: Garamond.

Newson, Janice, and Claire Polster. 2008. "Reclaiming Our Centre: Toward a Robust Defence of Academic Autonomy." In Adrienne Chan and Donald Fisher (eds.), *The Exchange University: Corporatization of Academic Culture.* Vancouver: UBC Press.

Padova, Allison. 2005. *Federal Commercialization in Canada.* Ottawa: Library of Parliament, Parliamentary information and Research Service, Economics Division.

Pearson, Matthew. 2010. "Foreign Student Plan Stirs Carleton Debate: First-Year of University Program Would Be Privately Run." *Ottawa Citizen* October 8.

Pitas, Jeannine. 2010. "How Comparative Literature Was Saved at U of T: The Role of Student Activism." <rabble.ca/blogs/bolggers/campus-notes/2010/how-comparative-literature-was-saved-u-t-role-student-activism>.

Pitsula, James. 2006. *As One Who Serves.* Montreal and Kingston: McGill-Queen's University Press.

Pocklington, Tom, and Allan Tupper. 2002. *No Place to Learn: Why Universities Aren't Working.* Vancouver: UBC Press.

Polster, Claire. 1994. "Compromising Positions: The Federal Government and the Reorganization of the Social Relations of Canadian Academic Research." Unpublished doctoral dissertation. Toronto: York University.

____. 2000. "Shifting Gears: Rethinking Academics' Response to the Corporatization of the University." *Journal of Curriculum Theorizing* 16, 2.

____. 2007. The Nature and Implications of the Growing Importance of Research Grants to Canadian Universities and Academics." *Higher Education* 53.

Press, Eyal, and Jennifer Washburn. 2000. "The Kept University." *Atlantic Monthly* 285, 3.

Read, Cathy. 2003. *Survey of Intellectual Property Commercialization in the Higher Education Sector, 2003.* Ottawa: Statistics Canada, Science, Innovation and Electronic Information Division.

Reich, Robert. 2001. *The Future of Success.* New York: Alfred A. Knopf.

Robertson, Heather-jane. 2005. "The Many Faces of Privatization." Paper presented at the BCTF Public Education Not for Sale II Conference. Vancouver, BC. (February 18).

Rounce, Andrea. 1999. "Student Loan Programs in Saskatchewan, Alberta and at the Federal Level: An Examination Using the Neo-Institutionalist Approach." Unpublished masters thesis. Regina: University of Regina.

Salterrae. 2004. "Varsity Centre Crumbles: University Yields to Pressure, Tears Down Stadium Before It's even Built." October 4. <salterrae.ca/archive/2--4/3/article1.php>.

Sanders, Jim. 2005. "Monsanto, Lawyers, Lies and Videotape: Seeds of Censorship Sown at University of Manitoba." *Canadian Dimension Magazine.* <canadiandimension.com/articles /2005/08/30/55/>.

Saunders, Doug. 1992. "Space Academy Inc: Bidding for Canada's University on the Final Frontier." *Our Schools, Our Selves* 4, 1.

Schafer, Arthur. 2005. "Who're Ya Gonna Call? Not the Corporate University." *Canadian Dimension* 39, 5.

____. 2008. "The University as Corporate Handmaiden: Who're Ya Gonna Trust?" In James Turk (ed.), *Universities at Risk: How Politics, Special Interests and Corporatization Threaten Academic Integrity.* Toronto: James Lorimer.

Shaker, Erika. 1999. "The Privatization of Post-Secondary Institutions." *Education Limited* 1, 4.

Shulman, Seth. 1999. *Owning the Future.* Boston: Houghton Mifflin Company.

Smith, Dorothy E. 1987. *The Everyday World as Problematic: A Feminist Sociology.* Toronto: University of Toronto Press.

Statistics Canada. 2000. "Part-time University Faculty." *The Daily* August 29. <statscan.ca/Daily/ English/000830/d000830c.htm>.

____. 2010. "Women in Canada: Economic Well-Being." *The Daily* December 16. <statcan.gc.ca/ daily-quotidien/101216/dq/101216c-eng.htm>.

Tudiver, Neil. 1999. *Universities For Sale: Resisting Corporate Control over Higher Education.* Toronto: Lorimer.

Turk, James. 2000a. "What Commercialization Means for Education." In James Turk (ed.), *The Corporate Campus: Commercialization and the Dangers to Canada's Colleges and Universities.* Toronto: Lorimer.

____. 2000b. *The Corporate Campus: Commercialization and the Dangers to Canada's Colleges and Universities.* Toronto: Lorimer.

____. 2008. "Restructuring Academic Work." In James Turk (ed.), *Universities at Risk: How Politics, Special Interests and Corporatization Threaten Academic Integrity.* Toronto: James Lorimer.

Ubelacker, Sheryl. 2010. "Course Revised Over Complaint about Drug-Company Influence." *Globe and Mail* December 24: A6.

Washburn, Jennifer. 2005. *University Inc.: The Corporate Corruption of Higher Education.* New York: Basic Books.

Woodhouse, Howard. 2003. "Commercializing Research at the University of Saskatchewan." *Saskatchewan Notes* 2, 8.

____. 2009. *Selling Out: Academic Freedom and the Corporate Market.* Montreal: McGill-Queen's University Press.

16

Crime as a Social Problem
From Definition to Reality

Les Samuelson

YOU SHOULD KNOW THIS

- In Canada the top 1 percent earned almost a third of all income growth during the decade from 1997 to 2007 — more than any other generation of rich Canadians.
- In 2005 while not admitting any wrongdoing, CIBC paid $2.4 billion to settle a lawsuit in which CIBC was accused of helping Enron to hide its financial dealings.
- Under the new March 31, 2004, Bill C-45 "Westray Bill" Criminal Code amendment to impose serious penalties for workplace injuries or death, only one conviction to date, out of four charges, has occurred.
- The number of Aboriginal women serving federal prison time has jumped 90 percent since 2001.
- The healing lodge at Maple Creek, Saskatchewan, for federally sentenced Aboriginal women, opened in October 1995. It is an important "holistic" step towards changing dismal judicial and social realities for Aboriginal women.

Sources: *Toronto Sun* 2010; Hagan and Linden 2009; CCOHS 2011; Postmedia 2011; Winterdyk 2006.

IN *THE RICH GET RICHER AND THE POOR GET PRISON* (2010), Reiman and Leighton critically evaluate the implicit ideology of the criminal justice system, noting that any such system conveys a subtle yet powerful message in support of established institutions. It does this, they say, primarily by concentrating on individual wrongdoers, diverting our attention away from our institutions, away from considering whether our institutions themselves are wrong, unjust, or indeed "criminal" (Reiman and Leighton 2010: 179). Reiman and Leighton focus upon the "evils of the social order" that accrue from major inequalities of economic power in society — that is, they look at how working-class individuals are prosecuted differently than upper-class people or corporations for causing physical or economic harms.

However, as critical criminological analyses have repeatedly emphasized, our society is also characterized by massive inequalities of power based upon class, race, and gender. Thus, a range of these analyses focus on how legal practices reinforce class-based inequalities, the patriarchal subjugation of women and post-colonial social injustice for Aboriginal peoples. These inequalities generate differences of involvement and treatment within our criminal justice system, from the definition of crime to the responses of criminal justice personnel to offenders and victims. Certain individuals and groups are not born more "criminal" than any others, but the life conditions they may face vary greatly. Thus, for critical criminologists, a central "justice" concern is with how underlying social inequalities and processes operate to bring marginalized/oppressed people into the criminal justice system, while privileged individuals — if dealt with at all — tend to be treated leniently.

Class

There is no question that massive inequalities of wealth in Canada have been growing in the last two decades:

> Canada's richest people have amassed a record share of the nation's economic growth, according to a study by the Canadian Centre for Policy Alternatives. The top 1 percent earned almost a third of all income growth during the decade from 1997 to 2007, according to the study, which examines the wealth of Canada's richest citizens since the Second World War.
>
> "That's a bigger piece of the action than any other generation of rich Canadians has taken," said Armine Yalnizyan, CCPA's senior economist and author of the report. "The last time Canada's elite held so much of the nation's income in their hands was in the 1920s." Even then their incomes didn't soar as fast as they are today. (*Toronto Sun* 2010)

The class-biased nature of law has two basic dimensions. One dimension involves acts that are either defined in legislation as crime or are controlled through regulatory law. The second dimension involves the justice system's differential processing of working-class and professional-class individuals and corporations for "criminal acts."

Critical criminologists hold that a relatively small group of individuals control much of the wealth and political power in our society. While not necessarily acting in unison, this elite is able to influence the political-legal process so that both criminal and regulatory law does not treat seriously the social, economic, and physical harms inflicted upon society by corporations. By contrast, the crimes committed by working-class people, which are frequently a result of their life circumstances, are prosecuted more severely under the law; incarceration is often the end product.

Put simply and bluntly: "Corporate actors regularly and repeatedly violate ... standards of moral and legal behaviour, do much more physical and economic harm than any other violators of these standards, and continue to be treated as upright members of our society, giving meaning to Clarence Darrow's aphorism that most people classified as criminals are 'persons with predatory instincts without sufficient capital to form a corporation'" (Glasbeek (2002: 118).

On the one hand, the Canadian state has failed to define as "crime" much corporate behaviour that has economic and physical costs, to individuals, society, and the environment, far exceeding the costs of street crime (Gordon and Coneybeer 1995; Snider 1994). Corporate crime, or "suite crime," is defined as "crime" committed by a corporate official in the pursuit of organizational goals, usually profit. Some of these acts are illegal under either criminal or civil law; yet many such acts that are economically and physically harmful to society are not. This criterion is ostensibly the core element in the prohibitions and punishments of the Canadian Criminal Code.

The costs to society of actual corporate crime far exceed those of street crime. Colin Goff (2011) tackles this issue via a related, but not identical, concept, white-collar crime — crimes of fraud and injury that are carried out during the course of a (seemingly) legitimate occupation. Gomme (2007: 304–06) notes that business crime that is known and makes its way into official records represents only the tip of the iceberg. Still, the annual Canadian losses due to embezzlement, computer crime, commercial fraud, unnecessary auto repairs, unneeded home improvements, price fixing, illegal corporate mergers, false advertising, and other business crimes are staggering. The accounting firm Ernst and Young estimates the costs of white-collar crime in Canada at $20 billion (Gomme 2007: 306). "The federal government estimates that in 1998, economic crimes such as securities and telemarketing fraud [alone] cost Canadians $5 billion" (Goff 2011: 125). Using early 1990s U.S. data, Laureen Snider (1994: 276) puts the issue into focus: "all the street crime in the U.S. in a given year is estimated to cost around $4 billion, much less than 5% of the average take from corporate crime."

Consider the Enron $63 billion investors fraud orchestrated by CEO Kenneth Lay. Enron started as a profitable pipeline company delivering natural gas. But CEO Hay and his senior executives wanted much greater, and quick profits (Hagan and Linden 2009: 514–15). To keep the company growing, Enron executives began to use illegal financial measures to make it appear that profits were continuing to increase. The "culture of greed" at Enron (Hagan and Linden 2009: 514) was enormous and had help from many of Wall Street's big "respectable" players:

> Executives were not content with the millions of dollars they had taken from the company. As the illegal schemes began to unravel and the company began to slide into bankruptcy, Enron paid $681 million to 140 top executives, including $67 million to CEO Kenneth Lay, who continued to encourage employees and members of the public to buy Enron stock even as he and his executives stripped the company of much of its remaining capital.…
>
> While Enron executives must take most of the blame for the company's demise, they had help from the managers of other large corporations. The Arthur Andersen accounting firm, one of the world's largest, allowed Enron's many lapses of legal and ethical standards to slip by its auditors in order to help it obtain lucrative consulting contracts with Enron. Many of Wall Street's largest banks and brokerage firms collaborated with Enron in order to profit from stock commissions, consulting contracts, and interest from loans. (Hagan 2009: 515)

Enron apparently got help from one of Canada's biggest banks, CIBC. "While *not admitting any wrong doing*, in 2005 CIBC paid *$2.4 billion* to settle a lawsuit in which CIBC was accused of helping Enron to hide its financial dealings" (Hagan and Linden 2009: 515, emphasis added).

Too often such corporate greed is dismissed as entirely economic and thus less a problem than street crime that is violent. Yet, as Gomme (2007: 306) notes:

> This is a grave misperception — business crime is frequently violent. The volume of assaults and murders in Canada pales in comparison with the number of inju-

ries, debilitating and life-threatening diseases, and deaths attributable to business enterprises and professions engaging in unsafe practices, marketing dangerous products, violating workplace safety regulations, and polluting the air, the water, and the land. Death in the workplace ranks third, after heart disease and cancer, as a major killer of Canadians.

Schmalleger (2007: 42) calculated a ratio of 2:1 workers killed by jobs versus murder for the U.S. in 2004. This is likely true in Canada. Even these figures likely underestimate the seriousness of corporate violence. Beirne and Messerchmidt (2006: 204) conclude: "We are actually safer in the street than indoors; the evidence presented here suggests that we are safer almost anywhere than in the workplace."

Is all this physical violence and injury just accidental? It is estimated that 40 percent of industrial "accidents" are a result of working conditions that are both unsafe and prohibited under existing law. About 25 percent, while not illegal, are dangerous nonetheless (Gomme 2007: 306). Yet, these violations and harms are not pursued with the same vigour as street crime injuries.

To classify these industrial deaths as "accidents," as is generally the case, completely obscures the context within which they occur. The 1982 *Ocean Ranger* oil-rig tragedy, which cost eighty-four lives, puts the case more clearly. According to the conclusions of the official investigation itself, "Intervention could have offset design flaws and overcome lax shipping classifications, inadequate seaworthy standards and poor marine training of staff and prevented the disaster" (quoted in McMullan and Smith 1997: 62). I grew up in St. John's, the supply depot for this rig. Local people working on the rig had nicknamed the rig the "Ocean Danger" because of its poor safety standards and operation.

In 1992 the Westray mine explosion in Nova Scotia, one of Canada's worst, claimed twenty-six lives and was also no accident. "Initial investigations suggest the existence of careless management, unsafe working conditions that included explosively high levels of methane and coal dust, outdated equipment and a remarkably lax and inept regulations and enforcement system" (McMullan and Smith 1997: 62). Glasbeek (2002: 121) notes that, by the time of the explosion at the Westray mine, a staggering record of fifty-two breaches of the health and safety standards had been compiled. With fifty-two non-criminal charges under the *Occupational Health and Safety Act*, thirty-four were stayed by Crown prosecutors, who expressed fears they might interfere with criminal prosecutions. Subsequent to a final Supreme Court of Canada March 2007 decision, prosecution against two mine managers charged with twenty-six accounts of manslaughter and criminal negligence causing death was abandoned. They decided not to pursue the charges because there was not enough evidence to secure convictions.

Importantly, on March 31, 2004, Bill C-45, also known as the "Westray Bill," amended the Criminal Code to establish new legal duties and imposed serious penalties for workplace injuries or death. A Canadian Centre for Occupational Health and Safety (CCOHS 2011) report notes that to date there has only been four charges laid, with one conviction, one dropped, and two still before the courts.

Even when convicted of similar misbehaviour, the well-to-do are often treated more leniently by the criminal justice system. Consider these two cases of fraud. In June 2001 a medical practitioner convicted of fraud for overbilling the publicly funded health-care system by just under a million dollars — money used to take luxury trips to Germany, Italy, California, and New Zealand and stay in five-star hotels with his partner — was sentenced to a conditional sentence of two years, to be served, not in jail, but in the community. The medical disciplinary board added to the sentence by suspending his ability to bill the health-care system for a short length of time. The "harshly dealt-with" practitioner appealed the medical disciplinary board's decision. Next, consider the case of college student Kimberly Rogers. She was convicted of welfare fraud for collecting it and student loans to help finance four years of community college:

> Kimberly Rogers had died alone and eight months pregnant, in her sweltering apartment in Sudbury, Ontario, while under house arrest for welfare fraud. What many do not realize is that the policies and conditions that set the stage for this tragedy are still in place and in some respects have actually worsened.
>
> Kimberly Rogers was charged with welfare fraud after collecting both social assistance and students loans to help cover the costs of attending four years of community college. She was convicted in April 2001 and the penalty was six months under house arrest (with the right to be allowed out of her hot apartment three hours per week); a requirement to repay more than $13 thousand dollars in benefits; eighteen months probation and loss of the right to have part of her student loan forgiven.
>
> At the time of Roger's conviction, Ontario Works regulations specified that anyone convicted of welfare fraud would be automatically suspended from receiving benefits for three months. This stipulation has since been made tougher. Anyone convicted of welfare fraud in the province of Ontario will be banned for life from ever being able to collect social assistance. (Keck 2002)

After her May 2001 launch of the first Ontario citizen *Charter of Rights and Freedoms* challenge to Ontario's Welfare (Ontario Works Benefits) laws:

> Rogers' benefits were reinstated for the interim, but this was not the end of her problems. Even with Ontario Works benefits, she was unable to support herself and her unborn child. After a deduction of 10 percent (towards repayment to Ontario Works) Rogers received $468 per month. With $450 going towards paying the rent. Rogers was left with $18 to cover all other necessities…. "I ran out of food this weekend. I am unable to sleep and I cry all the time (Kimberly Rogers, affidavit to court May 2001). Tragically, while still under house arrest, Kimberly Rogers died just weeks after the Ontario Superior Court of Justice released its exceptional decision. (Keck 2002)

Glasbeek (2002: 123) notes: "A study of welfare fraud documented that 80% of all persons convicted of welfare fraud of this type were given jail sentences. In contrast, another study shows that "prison" is imposed in 4 percent of all tax evasion cases, even though the amount stolen vastly exceeds that stolen by welfare abusers. Unemployment benefit frauds reveal the same pattern: the rate of incarceration is twice that by tax evaders." Corporations, even government "corporations," and the privileged can apparently kill, maim and rob with relative impunity while the poor get prison — or worse, in the case of Kimberly Rogers. This is one form of the class bias of criminal law.

Another form lies in the fact that corporate harmfulness is often not even defined as criminal. Most often, costly and harmful corporate behaviour, when classified as illegal, falls within regulatory law rather than the Criminal Code, where most street crime is placed. This distinction is often made on the basis of legal notions of culpability, which were established to prosecute individual offenders for street crime but not corporations or corporate officials for industry-related killings. In Canada prior to 1941, corporations were immune to any criminal liability because they were deemed to have no minds of their own (McMullan 1992: 80). There was little progress in this area until the late 1970s and early 1980s when cases heard before the Supreme Court of Canada began to fit corporate offenders into an individualist model of liability, evidence, procedure, and sanction (McMullan 1992: 80).

But there is dispute and confusion over whether the *Canadian Charter of Rights and Freedoms* under sections 7 and 1(d) is meant to enforce relatively rigid *mens rea* (guilty mind) requirements for the prosecution of corporate offenders. In Canada, the Crown must prove "blameworthiness" to get a Criminal Code conviction. It refers to "the guilty mind, the wrongful intention" — a necessary element in establishing criminal conduct (Verdun-Jones 2007: 66).

McMullan (1992: 80–81) also states that in the Irwin Toy Ltd. case the Supreme Court of Canada ruled that a corporation's economic rights were not protected by section 7 of the Charter, as are the "life, liberty or security of the person." While the matter is still up in the air, Canadian judicial history suggests that Canadian courts have not been inclined to extend the scope of corporate criminal proceedings to include the illegal acts or omissions of a corporation's agents or employees. In addition to the problem of *mens rea*, corporations have been almost exclusively prosecuted for regulatory violations — such as those governing health and safety — and not for the consequences of those violations (Reasons, Ross, and Patterson 1986; McMullan 1992). For example, a company would be fined for not installing safety bolts in a construction crane, but not prosecuted for the death of several workers who were below the crane when it collapsed. Corporations have frequent and vociferous input into the regulations governing them, generally under the guise of being enlisted to co-operate in creating "workable laws." The result is a lax system of regulation.

Corporations are often able to avoid prosecution for illegal activity, but when they are prosecuted, the penalty is usually an inconsequential fine levied against the corporation, and the ruling does not usually single out individual corporate decision makers legally or publicly. Even when the court does name individual corporate offenders, the penalties, both legal and social, are usually only nominal.

Snider (2002) notes that the 1999 investigation of insider stock trading in Canada was carried out by a newspaper, not the securities commission. "Some (corporate) insiders were making fortunes ... (but) until this was publicized, neither the Ontario Securities commission nor the Toronto Stock Exchange had taken any... action" (Snider 2002: 224). Unfortunately, even with much public fanfare about tightening regulations around corporate governance and stock trading, the Canadian government "crackdown" on corporate misbehaviour has followed the lead of the U.S. *Sarbanes-Oxley Act* — the main concern is not with the losses suffered by "the proverbial average citizen" but with the threat to the markets that these misdemeanours pose (*National Post* 2002; see also Neu and Green 2005: ch. 11).

These conditions reflect a major class bias in the application of criminal and regulatory law. It should not be hard to understand why, in the 1970s, 90 percent of the seventy largest U.S. corporations were habitual offenders, with an average of fourteen convictions per corporation (Edwin Sutherland 1977; see also Clinard and Yeager 1980). John Hagan (1992: 465) reports that more than half of Canada's largest corporations have been recidivists, with an average of 3.2 decisions against them.

Perhaps we need corporate "three strikes and you're out" legislation. The federal Conservative government is "getting tough" on street crime with its 2011 omnibus crime bill, with mandatory sentences, no consideration for time served while waiting for trial and so on. Forthcoming are tough amendments to the Criminal Code and sentencing practices.

The lenient attitude towards corporate crime and white-collar criminals might be hardening. Opinion polls reveal that popular thinking and sentiment are in favour of tougher laws, regulations, and sanctions regarding corporate misconduct. In some instances judicial decisions have emphasized corporate responsibility for harmful acts. For example, the operations manager of a waterfront oil recycling company was jailed for ninety days when he admitted that the company, knowingly and fraudulently, spilled hazardous chemical waste into the Toronto harbour (Gomme, 2007: 327). Finally, there have been proposals to break down both the individual and organizational inducements to corporate crime and the traditional defences for it, through the creation of a culture that does not tolerate corporate crime. The proposed solutions include: "shaming and positive repentance, new legal tools and controls, corporate accountability and restructuring, new forms of penalty and criminal sanctioning, and the application of countervailing force against corporate crime" (McMullan 1992: 118).

In the mid 1990s, it appeared that, at least in some respects, the rich won't always get richer while the poor get prison. Snider (1994: 278) stated, "Pro-regulatory pressure groups (for example, environmental activities, 'green' politicians trying to eliminate chemicals from farmers' fields, unionists working to secure stronger health and safety laws in the workplace, and feminists working to control the pharmaceutical industry) are absolutely central to the regulatory process." A few years later, Snider (2002: 231) was much more pessimistic about what she termed the "corporate counter-revolution," whereby corporate marauding is receiving very little attention and political-legal action:

> Government obligation to help the marginalized and desperate has disappeared, but its obligation to punish the powerless has been reinforced .... By decriminalizing and deregulating profitable corporate acts that were once seen as corporate crime, and by downsizing regulatory agencies and cutting regulatory staff, governments

at all levels have been quick to shed their historic responsibility to protect citizens from corporate excess, fraud, and abuse of power.

A recent event in Canada highlights these concerns. In the "wake" of the Gomery inquiry, Paul Coffin, a Montreal ad executive, pleaded guilty to defrauding Canadian taxpayers of $1.5 million in the Quebec sponsorship scandal. The Crown asked for a thirty-four-month federal prison term. The judge, in line with Coffin's views, ordered a speaking tour to lecture business students on "ethics." This was part of his two years less a day conditional sentence with no jail time (*National Post* 2005). The Crown later appealed Coffin's sentence, and he was eventually sentenced to eighteen months in prison.

> By decriminalizing and deregulating profitable corporate acts... governments at all levels have been quick to shed their historic responsibility to protect citizens from corporate excess, fraud, and abuse of power.

Race

In white settler societies, Aboriginal peoples and people of colour are overrepresented in their criminal justice systems. Canada, Australia, and the United States all have similar experiences (Samuelson 1995). This is not some accident of history, or the result of a pathology of "lawlessness" among non-white people. The overrepresentation of Aboriginal people in the Canadian justice system is but one legacy of the destruction and dislocation of Aboriginal peoples that took place under European colonialism.

> In white settler societies, Aboriginal peoples and people of colour are overrepresented in their criminal justice systems. Canada, Australia, and the United States all have similar experiences.

The European colonial political and economic subjugation of territories around the world has been rapidly diminishing. However, it is largely the white colonial population of European origin — and not the original inhabitants of these relatively new nations — who are enjoying freedom from colonialism and its concomitant exploitation and oppression. Essentially, Aboriginal peoples are still treated as a colonial population, and Canada has been no exception in this practice. After all, Canada has kept a good number of its "Indians" in concentration camps, known as reserves, for over 150 years and has regulated their behaviour in all aspects of their lives. Getting this colonialist fact recognized and changed in our ostensibly post-colonialist era is apparently much harder to do in Canada than in the international arena.

Mary Ellen Turpel/Aki-kwe (1992) notes that Canada and Canadians like to think of itself and themselves as strong supporters of international rights, ready to contribute troops under the United Nations banner, if need be, to places like Bosnia, Kuwait, Afghanistan, and Iraq; but not so when the subject of First Nations rights is raised in international political circles. For example, as director of the Canadian Institute for Human Rights and Democratic Development, Ed Broadbent remarked in the early 1990s that he would be in a particularly difficult position when he raised questions about human rights abuses in other countries because "These countries will be saying to me: what about Aboriginal rights in Canada?" Canada, Turpel (1992: 80) points out,

> has been found in violation of international human rights standards on two separate occasions by the United Nations Human Rights Committee because of its treatment of Aboriginal peoples. In 1990 the Canadian government sent 1,500 armed troops to the Gulf War in Kuwait. But it also sent over 3,000 troops to Mohawk lands in Eastern Canada after armed Mohawks blocked a gravel road to protest the expansion of a golf course by the neighbouring non-Aboriginal town of Oka. (Waldram 1994: 53)

> Canada... has been found in violation of international human rights standards, by the U.N. Human Rights Committee for its treatment of Aboriginal People.

Not much changed into the 2000s. The United Nations Fifth Review of compliance with the International Covenant on Civil and Political Rights, in 2005, cited Canada as drawing severe criticism from the United Nations Human Rights Committee (FAFIA/AFAI website). The Committee was particularly concerned about Canada's treatment of women prisoners, many of whom are Aboriginal. The U.N. committee directed Canada to fully implement the recommendations of the Canadian Human Rights Commission and to report back to them in one year. The U.N. is losing patience with Canada's long-standing abuses of the rights of Aboriginal women. In particular, the Human Rights Committee emphasized the need to remove male staff from direct contact with women prisoners, to limit the use of segregation, and to establish immediately an independent external redress and adjudication body for federally sentenced prisoners.

As Tim Hartnagel (2009: 152–53) notes, the overrepresentation of Aboriginal people in the justice system holds for nearly all categories of offenders, all types of institutions, and all regions of the country — a trend that has remained in place since such information became available. Julian Roberts and Ronald Melchers (2003: 211), compared provincial custodial sentenced admissions for Aboriginal and non-Aboriginal offenders between 1978 — the first year, they say, when national statistics, including the ethnicity of offender, were published — and 2001.[1] During this period Parliament and the Supreme Court tried to address the problem. Parliament, in 1996, passed section 718.2(e) of the Criminal Code, giving special consideration to the circumstances of Aboriginal offenders. The Supreme Court, in 1999, upheld those new provisions in *R. v. Gladue*, affirming its remedial purpose in attempting to reduce the high rate of Aboriginal incarceration. Unfortunately, little progress has been made. Indeed, Hartnagel (2009: 153) presents similar, but slightly updated data. He shows that in Saskatchewan, the province with by far the highest overincareration, by 2003–04, Aboriginals moved up to 80 percent of those admitted to adult correctional facilities. And, as shown in Table 15-1, by 2007–08, overincarceration of Aboriginal people continues unabated.

The cautionary views of the *Alberta Justice on Trial* report are supported by a much more recent statement by Curt Griffiths (2004: 188). Despite efforts over the past two decades to

Table 16.1 Aboriginal Sentences Admissions to Custody, 1978–78, 2000–01, 2007–08

Province/Territory	Aboriginal admissions to custody, 1978–79	Aboriginal admissions to custody, 2000–01	Aboriginal admissions to custody, 2007–08
Saskatchewan	61%	76%	81%
Yukon	51%	72%	76%
Manitoba	50%	64%	69%
Alberta	26%	39%	35%
British Columbia	15%	20%	21%
Ontario	9%	9%	9%
Nova Scotia	-	7%	7%
Newfoundland and Labrador	3%	7%	21%
Quebec	1%	2%	2%
Prince Edward Island	3%	1%	1%
Provincial/territorial total	16%	19%	18%

Sources: Roberts and Melcher 2003; Canadian Centre for Justice Statistics 2009.

address the specific needs of Aboriginal peoples and to reduce their overrepresentation in the justice system, Curt Griffiths (2004: 188) notes that their incarceration rates not only remain high, but also that "it is predicted that the number of Aboriginal inmates will *double* in the coming years" (emphasis added).

On October 17, 2006, Stephen Harper's Conservative government introduced its "three strikes legislation" in the House of Commons. Under this law, third-time violent/ sexual offenders would automatically be categorized as "dangerous offenders" and be liable to indefinite prison sentences. The Crown would not have to prove the case; the onus would be on the accused to prove otherwise. Many observers thought that this bill would hit Aboriginal offenders the hardest, leaving them with "no hope" (*Star Phoenix* 2006). The news was appropriately juxtaposed with a report from Canada's correctional investigator released just a day earlier. Correctional investigator Howard Sapers called the treatment of Aboriginal Peoples in the federal justice system a "national disgrace." Overall the federal inmate population went down 12.5 percent between 1996 and 2004; during the same period our national crime rate in general also went down. But during the same period the number of First Nations people in federal institutions increased by 21.7 percent, a 34 percent difference between non-Aboriginal and Aboriginal inmates. The numbers of Aboriginal women in prison increased by "a staggering 74.2 percent." (Canada 1996).

The *StarPhoenix* (2006) article ended by noting, with some conscience and historical clarity: "It is a world where a population that the Canadian government institutionalized and traumatized through the residential school system would be further disadvantaged." Ironically, the article notes, it was a non-Native man born in Ontario, Peter Whitmore, who came to be the "poster boy" for the new legislation. Whitmore's act of abducting and sexually assaulting two children is undoubtedly a heinous offence, but it is the Aboriginal offender who seemed likely to pay the most individually and collectively if Bill C-27, the "three-strikes" legislation were to go through.

While women in general constitute a pronounced minority in the justice system, Aboriginal women are the most disproportionately represented group in both provincial and federal institutions. The best estimates tell us that, although Aboriginal women made up 3 percent of the population of women in Canada, in 2001–02 they accounted for between 20 and 23 percent of female provincial and territorial inmates, and 16 to 20 percent of federal female inmates. Aboriginal males made up 8 percent of provincial and territorial inmates and 14 percent of federal inmates (Statistics Canada 2001: 11; Winterdyk 2006: 395).

This overrepresentation has been growing in the past decade. It is also predicted to go higher in the federal prisons with the Harper-Conservative "build-and-fill" prison agenda. Michelle Mann, an Ottawa-based lawyer and expert on Aboriginal justice (Postmedia 2011), predicts more Aboriginal people will be jailed:

> Aboriginal women now make up about a third of all federally incarcerated women, despite representing only three per cent of the population. The number of Aboriginal women serving federal time has jumped 90 per cent since 2001. There are about 500 women in total serving sentences of two years or more in Canada.

Aboriginal women are treated far from leniently by the justice system. "They make up some 50 percent of women classified as maximum-security prisoners, yet about 58 percent of them are charged with minor assaults and only 13 percent are charged with serious assaults" (Winterdyk 2006: 395).

To fully understand Aboriginal women's overinvolvement in the justice system, and their (discriminatory) high-risk classifications, we must consider the kinds of lives that they often experience. Consider the following "life profile" of a federally sentenced Aboriginal woman:

> She may leave home because she experienced violence (whether she was abused or she witnessed abuse) and her home life has become unbearable. Or she may live under very rigid conditions that she leaves because she wants to become independent. Or she may be lured away by friends who have a life of drugs, alcohol and partying. She may work the streets because she needs money to live on and she does not have the education, skills and training to get a job. She may be subjected to racism, stereotyping and discrimination because of her race and colour. However, her experience on the streets becomes violent as she continues to experience sexual, emotional, and physical abuse. She is likely to become involved in an abusive relationship. There are usually children born from this relationship and the social, emotional and economic struggle continues. The cycle of an unhealthy family continues. (Griffiths 2004: 187–88)

To make matters worse, when they are incarcerated Aboriginal women face additional factors that impede healing. As Satzewich and Wotherspoon (1993: 198) pointed out in the early 1990s, these factors include "severely inadequate prison facilities and programs, cultural and gender-biased assessment standards, failure to acknowledge and treat the realities of Aboriginal women's abusive life histories, and unsympathetic prison regimes." Unfortunately, over a decade later, not much had changed in that regard. According to the findings of the Elizabeth Fry Society, many Aboriginal women continue to experience abusive lives, often plagued with substance abuse (Winterdyk 2006: 396). Aboriginal women are regularly denied services for women and access to specific programs designed for Aboriginal offenders: essentially, Aboriginal female offenders continue to be marginalized. The Healing Lodge for federally sentenced Aboriginal women in Maple Creek, Saskatchewan, is an important example of an attempt by Corrections Canada and Aboriginal peoples to change these dismal judicial and social realities.

Why does this overincarceration exist in the first place? The statistics themselves don't really provide an answer to this question; in fact, they could be taken to indicate that there are factors (or in the new corrections language, "risks") within Aboriginal people themselves that propel them towards illegal and anti-social behaviour. A critical analysis, however, would offer another explanation: that the conditions are the result of prejudice and discrimination among Canadians generally and criminal justice personnel in particular.

The overinvolvement of Aboriginal peoples in crime and with the justice system, and the resistance of Aboriginal peoples to that experience, take place within the political, social, and economic context of ongoing colonialism. An overinvolvement in crime is but one of the social problems generated by the relatively "passive genocide" perpetrated against Aboriginal peoples, largely under the rhetoric and guise of "assimilation." The Royal Commission on Aboriginal Peoples (1996: 5–7) argued that Aboriginal overinvolvement indicates the existence of "social" rather than "criminal" problems. The most central social problems are the ones that society creates for Aboriginals — not those created by any individual criminal pathology. Put simply, the problem is racism.

The frequent public perception of Aboriginal people as "drunks," "lazy," and "criminal" has long confused symptoms with the underlying causes (Hylton 1982: 125). Confusing symptom with cause is convenient, because it allows for a one-way street of criminal justice policies and programs that address the "problem of crime" without seriously challenging the status quo of the Canadian political economy. Like most systems of domination, this condition depends on the development, by people in power, of strong ideologies and typifications that justify their control over subject populations. This was certainly true historically in Canada, and unfortunately it has now re-emerged in modern form. A 1997 poll of Canadians confirmed a general backlash of attitudes towards "Indian," Inuit, and Métis people. Almost half of Canadians believe Aboriginals have an equal or better standard of living than the average citizen. Some 40 percent believe that Aboriginals "have only themselves to blame for their problems" (*Star Phoenix* 1997).

A 2003 poll shows a similar negative picture: nearly two-thirds of Saskatchewan people, and 42 percent of Canadians, indicated that they were in favour of doing away with Aboriginal treaty rights. On the issue of Aboriginal land claims, the poll found that half of all Canadians believed "fewer or none" of the hundreds of such claims or deals were valid. In response to this poll, Nancy Pine, a spokesperson the National Assembly of First Nations, concluded that there is significant body of opinion that is out of sync with the constitutional reality of this country: "Treaty rights, land rights and even self-government have been constitutionalized since 1987 and have been repeatedly upheld by the courts" (*Star Phoenix* 2003).

Geoffrey York's (1990) book, *The Dispossessed,* provides a telling picture of the treatment of Aboriginal peoples. He reports on a study of capital murder cases from 1926 to 1957, which found that the risk of execution for an anglo-Canadian who killed a white person was 21 percent, whereas an "Indian" who killed a white person in the same circumstances had a 96 percent risk of execution. Research discovered memos from Indian Affairs bureaucrats recommending that "Indian" offenders be executed because Aboriginal peoples needed "special deterrence" (York 1990: 157). Into the late 1980s, differential charging of Aboriginal people by police for relatively minor public-order offences was widespread. Research done in Regina, for example, "found that 30 percent of the Indians arrested for drunkenness were charged and sent to court. By contrast only 11 percent of non-Natives were charged and sent to court" (York 1990: 149). The Aboriginal Justice Inquiry of Manitoba (AJI) concurred, stating that overpolicing must be blamed on persisting stereotypical racist attitudes and actions directed against Aboriginal people (AJI 1991: 595).

The problem of racism in policing has become an important dimension of the concern about the relatively high number of killings by police of Blacks and Aboriginals in questionable circumstances (Forcese 1992). Scott Wortley (2002) and Carl James (2002) have taken up this concern in their research; James (2002:303) notes:

> the discourse of the media around police shootings has "demonized and criminalized Blacks and exonerated white police officers." This discourse contributes to the "acceptance" of shootings by police "as justifiable homicide," acts that are "mainly engendered by Blacks themselves" and as such are "mainly a Black problem." This discourse ... is part of the social and legal banishment of Black people. This is evident not only in the media's racist images of Blacks (including those in leadership positions, whom the media discredit), but also in the "absence and negation of their concerns and issues," withholding of their "democratic rights and entitlement," and their physical removal from the society through incarceration and deportations. All of these practices have become so normalized within institutions and in society generally that they operate in ways that make the general public believe that Black victims are indeed responsible for their own deaths.

Commissions have been struck to evaluate this problem, but the poor record of implementation of Aboriginal justice initiatives does not bode well for eliminating racist views among police and putting curbs on police practice. For example, there was a huge outcry within the Aboriginal community over the shooting by police of Dudley George, an Aboriginal man, at the 1995 Ipperwash protest, and the subsequent initial finding of no guilt for the police. The 2006 inquiry into the Ipperwash incident found the shooting of Dudley George, an unarmed peaceful protester, was unjustified. A concern of the inquiry, apart from racist police action, was: Did the police receive a provincial "political directive" to direct them to "deal" with the incident?

Unfortunately, but notably, the city of Saskatoon had consistently appeared in Amnesty International's annual list of human rights abuses. The organization's 2001 report described in detail what have come to be known as "Starlight Tours," among other allegations of "patterns of police abuse against First Nation men in Saskatoon" (*StarPhoenix* 2001).

> Darrel Night says he was driven by police in January 2000 to a field near the Queen Elizabeth power plant and abandoned in freezing conditions. It's also suspected the same thing happened to Aboriginal men Rodney Naistus and Lawrence Wegner, whose bodies were found in the area on Jan. 29 and Feb. 3. Neither of the men were wearing jackets. (*Star Phoenix* 2001: A1)

The Crown subsequently laid charges against two Saskatoon police officers, who were both fifteen-year veterans, in the Night case. They were charged with unlawful confinement and assault, and were convicted and sentenced to eight months' jail time — but they did four months. The 1990 similar freezing death of Neil Stonechild resulted in yet another inquiry. After fourteen years of police-judicial inaction, the 2004 Report of the Commission of Inquiry Into Matters Relating to the Death of Neil Stonechild (Saskatchewan 2004) was released. A witness, Jason Roy, stated that he saw Stonechild in the back of a police car on the night in question. He was shouting, Roy testified, "They gonna kill me." While the two constables involved denied the charges, the inquiry concluded, based on the police's own records, that they did have Neil Stonechild in their custody the night he died. Both officers were fired by police chief Sabo two weeks after the report's release.

Discussion of more appropriate criminal and social justice programs, which would be reflective of both the past and present cultural and structural conditions of Aboriginal peoples, began to receive attention in the mid-1970s (Ekstedt and Griffiths 1988), but exploded in the 1990s. Various reports emphasize the need for Aboriginal self-determination, the resolution of land claims, and the reconstruction of a viable modern Aboriginal society within Canada as the most fundamental "justice" concerns. Piecemeal reforms that are not part of this larger initiative, however well-meaning they may be, achieve little substantial success. Unfortunately, the lack of implementation of Aboriginal commission recommendations from the mid-1970s (Ekstedt and Griffiths 1988) has continued in recent years. The Royal Commission on Aboriginal Peoples (RCAP 1993, 1996) justice reports noted that some modest reforms had occurred. However, most of the recommendations made in the recent justice inquiries had not been addressed, especially proposals that required substantial restructuring and transfer of control to Aboriginal peoples. Post-colonial justice is in important respects being rationed out to Aboriginal peoples.

The RCAP (1996: 82–128) final justice report laid out seven basic areas of Aboriginal justice initiatives:

1. *Aboriginal policing.* Until the early 1970s policing services to Aboriginal communities were largely carried out by the RCMP. The early 1970s saw the beginning of Band policing, which was expanded substantially in 1978 in Quebec (Amerindian Police Council) and Manitoba (Dakota Ojibway Tribal Council). In 1992 the federal government announced a policy of transferring all on-reserve policing to Bands by about the year 2000. By August 2007 the federal and provincial governments had funded 162 tripartite (federal-provincial-band) Aboriginal policing agreements throughout Canada. This was for 614 federally recognized "Indian" bands (Canada, 2007) .

2. *Indigenization.* This initiative attempts to make the system less alienating without substantially changing the structure and control of the criminal justice system, and/or Aboriginal overinvolvement, at least directly. It is a favoured government response. There are three main venues: Aboriginal justices of the peace and judges; Aboriginal court workers; and cultural awareness programs/training for justice personnel.

3. *Indian Act "provisions" for on-reserve justice initiatives.* Sections of the *Indian Act* (s.81, s.83) provide for Band bylaws, but are restricted by the requirement of Minister of Indian Affairs approval. Section 107 of the *Indian Act* is utilized to replace the "Indian agent" with on-reserve courts. This practice is especially active in Mohawk communities at Kahnawaké and Akwesasne.

4. *Diversion programs and related activities.* These are alternatives for justice system processing. Guilt/innocence is generally replaced by an admission of "responsibility." Diversion is one option to jail. With diversion there is no criminal record. Diversion has been active at different times across the country from Nova Scotia (at Shubenacadie) to Toronto (Aboriginal Legal Services of Toronto) and the Yukon (Kwanlin Dun Justice Project, Whitehorse).

5. *Elders panels and sentencing circles.* In elders panels, elders or community leaders sit with the judge and advise on sentencing openly or privately. In sentencing circles, accused, victim, family, and community members sit in the circle to discuss the case/sentence; the judge has the final say.

6. *Young offender initiatives.* The *Young Offenders Act* of 1982, contrary to popular myth, was very punitive in terms of incarceration for youth, especially Aboriginal youth. The 2002 *Youth Criminal Justice Act* was intended to be much more punitive than its predecessor (Alvi 2008). Canada is looking to possibly emulate New Zealand family group conferencing, which is based on Maori restorative justice and resulted in a 50 percent decline in youth custody, and a 90 percent police satisfaction rate.

7. *Aboriginal initiatives in prison.* This initiative focuses on holistic healing. Increasingly, Aboriginal prisoners maintain their right to participation in spiritual and healing ceremonies. In response, 1992 legislation by Parliament obligates Correctional Services Canada (CSC) to provide programs designed to meet Aboriginal offender needs. Changing the old CSC is very difficult, but in the 1990s a new holistic healing facility opened near Edmonton for federally sentenced Aboriginal men; this is in addition to Maple Creek for federally sentenced Aboriginal women (see LaPrairie 1996).

Justice system reforms can be notable and lead to a greater empowering of Aboriginal peoples, but some stark life facts for Aboriginal people still exist. And, by contrast to the recommendations of Aboriginal justice inquiries, the current government crime strategy is to build and fill more prisons. The Harper federal government has been working obtusely, often with misinformation and in denial of academic and community protests, to "fill more prisons." Representing virtually every major religious group in Canada, the Canadian Church Council on Justice and Corrections sent a letter to Prime Minister Stephen Harper (CCJC 2011):

> December 17, 2010
>
> Dear Mr. Prime Minister
>
> The Church Council on Justice and Corrections (CCJC) is most concerned that in this time of financial cuts to important services you and the government of Canada are prepared to significantly increase investment in the building of new prisons.... Increasing levels of incarceration of marginalized people is counter-productive and undermines human dignity in our society. By contrast, well-supervised probation or release, bail options, reporting centres, practical assistance, supportive housing, programs that promote accountability, respect and reparation: these measures have all been well-established, but they are underfunded. Their outcomes have proven to be the same or better in terms of re-offence rates, at a fraction of the cost with much less human damage....
>
> Sincerely, The Church Council on Justice and Corrections

Gender

Historically, criminology, even critical criminology, almost entirely ignored women. For example, Taylor, Walton, and Young's 1973 groundbreaking book, *The New Criminology,* did not contain one word about women (Gregory 1986). An analysis of Canadian criminal justice (Griffiths and Verdun-Jones 1994) devotes only about seven out of 660 pages to discussing women and justice. Still, gender has emerged as a rapidly growing component of criminology and socio-legal studies (see Chesney-Lind and Bloom 1997; Dobash and Dobash 1995; Comack and Balfour 2004).

> Historically, criminology, even critical criminology, almost entirely ignored women

Within criminology, analyses of women and crime tend to be grounded in a mainstream criminological concern with the causes of crime. This approach usually emphasizes the generally low rate of female involvement in crime relative to men (Hagan 1985; Hartnagel 2009). For example, in 1995, women accounted for only 12.2 percent of all adults charged with violent crimes in Canada; even their property crime involvement rate — about 23 percent of all offenders — still indicated a reasonably large gender gap (Statistics Canada 1996). By 2002 the number of women charged with violent crime had increased to 16 percent, while property crime remained at 23 percent (Hartnagel 2004: 128).

The increases in female criminality in recent decades have caused a great stir. From 1968 to 2000 the rate for all Criminal Code offences increased by 43 percent for males and 184 percent for females (Hartnagel 2004). As early as the mid-1970s, Canada was said to be witnessing the rise of the "new female criminal," apparently a result of the encroachment of liberated women on a traditional male preserve (Adler 1975). Social roles for women were said to be changing, with women achieving greater equality of involvement not only in society generally, but also in the crime. This has been dubbed the "converging role thesis." But, even in the context of these large rate increases, 2005 statistics show that females made up only a little over 18 percent of all persons accused for violations against the person and just over 24 percent for total violations against property (Juristat 20(1): Table 1). Hartnagel (2000) states that 77 percent of the increase from 1968 to 1996 in women charged with Criminal Code offences was for non-violent crime. From 1968 to 2000 the proportion of all women charged for violent crime increased from 10 percent to 26 percent (Hartnagel 2004: 130). Increases in female violent crime, and female gangs, are receiving considerable media and academic analysis, but, into the late 2000s, "the highest rates for women charged continue to be for less serious thefts of property" (Hartnagel 2009: 147).

Many years ago, Holly Johnson and Karen Rodgers (1993: 98) noted that women's involvement in crime

> is consistent with their traditional roles as consumers, and increasingly, as low income, semi-skilled, sole support providers for their families. In keeping with the rapid increase in female-headed households and the stresses associated with poverty, greater numbers of women are being charged with shoplifting, cheque forging and welfare fraud.

Comack (2004: 174) reiterates this view. Comack's (1996a, 1996b, 2002) analyses of women in conflict with the law have found very similar relationships between the everyday conflicts and dilemmas of women and their troubles with the law.

While role convergence and a less "chivalrous" or "paternalistic" (see Chunn and Gavigan 1995) judicial system cannot totally be ruled out as factors in women's involvement in crime, a more fruitful explanation would lie elsewhere. Continuing extensive female job ghettoization, the feminization of poverty (Johnson and Rodgers 1993; Broad 2000: ch. 2, 3; for the United States, see Gimenez 1991), and the development of a youth consumer market frequently directed at teenage females (Greenberg 1977) are more basic to the understanding of female patterns and rates of involvement in crime.

Thus, it is not surprising that most women serving sentences in federal and provincial territorial corrections are from marginalized backgrounds: "Their past and current situations are likely to include poverty, histories of abuse, long term drug and alcohol dependency, responsibilities for primary care of children, limited educational attainment, and few opportunities to obtain adequately paid work" (Griffiths 2004: 187). Sadly, virtually every critical observer concurs that prison still only teaches women at best to "do their time," medicated if necessary. More likely, prisons only add another bitter layer to their life experiences and do not deal with their underlying problems and issues (Boritch 2002). Reincarceration is thus too often a reality, and a push to move them up the "high-risk" carceral scale of inmate classification, usually with added debilitation not rehabilitation.

The justice system's treatment of women who have been the victims of crime has also been the object of considerable critical scrutiny in the past three decades. The main areas of concern have been the system's biases, injustices, and ineffectiveness in dealing with women who have been the victims of domestic violence and sexual assault (Comack 2004).

Domestic Violence

Domestic violence, almost always against women, occurs in a large number of Canadian families. The early research estimated, for example, that at least 10 percent of women in Canada were battered by their partners each year (MacLeod 1980). Unlike street crime, where victim and offender are overconcentrated in the lower socio-economic level of society, this violence is spread across all social classes. Ruth Mann (2003: 41) notes that, overall in Canada in 1991, 87 percent of 27,000 domestic assault charges were laid against men. That same year, 77 percent of eighty-eight homicides involving an opposite-sex spousal or dating partner resulted in the death of a woman. The Violence Against Women Survey found that 25 percent of Canadian women over the age of sixteen had experienced violence from a current or postmarital partner (Comack 1996b: 155). Moreover, in 1995 a woman was six times more likely to be killed by a spouse than by a stranger (Statistics Canada 1996).

Past police policy in Canada frequently emphasized minimal intervention on the part of police. A 1983 study by Burris and Jaffe found that police laid assault charges in only 3 percent of all family violence cases, even though 20 percent of the victims were advised to seek medical treatment and 60 percent were told to lay their own charges. In the early 1980s criminal justice and especially police policy in this area underwent a significant change (Burris and Jaffe 1983). In 1981, the police force in London (Ontario), one of the first in Canada to make change, instituted a policy encouraging officers to lay assault charges in cases of domestic violence. Officers were told that they did not have to witness the assault — they only needed to have reasonable and probable grounds to believe that an assault had occurred (for example, injury serious enough for them to advise a woman to seek medical attention). This was followed by a similar initiative in Manitoba. The changes in police practice in Manitoba not only led to a dramatic increase in charges laid but also to equally dramatic increases in convictions for spousal abuse and in the development of treatment programs for batterers; and to a change in the attitudes of Crown prosecutors to abuse cases (see Ursel 1998).

The problem of the victims' reluctance to press charges is frequently cited as a reason for police non-intervention in domestic violence. Under the new Ontario policy, the number of private informations — where the victims had to press charges themselves — dropped substantially, from forty-six to thirteen. This change was all the more important, given that police-laid charges were more likely to go to criminal court and end in guilty verdicts than were charges pressed through family courts, and the police charges took only about three-quarters of the time to reach their final disposition (Burris and Jaffe 1983). Feminists had philosophical problems with this in that it was tantamount to taking power out of the woman's hands to decide her own future and handing power over to the state.

In line with this initiative — and the data from the controversial 1981–82 Minneapolis policing experiment, which found a recidivism rate of 19 percent for arrested abusers compared to a rate of 35 percent for cases dealt with by mediation only (Currie and MacLean 1992) — in 1983 a national directive (so-called "zero tolerance" for domestic abuse) encouraged police to lay charges in wife-battering cases.[2] Canada was the first country to adopt such a nationwide directive. As Comack (1992) notes, police training was upgraded to stress sensitive intervention in wife assault cases, and several provinces — such as Manitoba — have established specialized courts to deal with domestic violence (Ursel 1998; Prairie Research Associates 1994).

The end product of these initiatives is that the courts began to deal with increasing numbers of abusive men. Comack (1996b: 156) states, "In the province of Manitoba alone, for example, the number of individuals (approximately 96 percent of whom were men) charged with spousal assault increased from 1136 in 1983 to 2779 in 1990." Moreover, in the early years at least, the number of transition houses providing shelter for battered women more than tripled, from eighty-five in 1982 to 264 in 1987 (MacLeod 1987). Intervention services aimed at alleviating or eliminating domestic violence against women expanded, as did battered women's shelter system, through the 1990s. From April 1, 1999 to March 31, 2000, 57,200 women and children were admitted to 448 shelters (Mann 2003: 41).

Much criticism and controversy exist over the "success" of zero-tolerance initiatives. There are serious concerns about how the focus on violence against women can feed into a reactionary law-and-order lobby (Currie 1990; Currie, MacLean, and Milovanovic 1992; MacLeod 1987). Interwoven here is the concern that this "institutionalization" of women's issues fails to deal with the unequal distribution of societal resources and power. Currie, MacLean, and Milovanovic (1992: 29) frame the problem well: "Within a discourse that concerns legal rights, police protection, and criminal justice, this issue is transformed into a technical matter that can be safely met within the current system without any significant changes in relations of power [between men and women]" (see Comack and Balfour (2004) for a similar and recent critique of zero tolerance).

> Much criticism and controversy exist over the "success" of zero-tolerance initiatives.

However, as Jane Ursel (1998) argues in her discussion of the experiences of the battered women's movement and the Winnipeg Family Violence Court, the positive dimensions of state-sponsored approaches to domestic violence must be recognized: "Not all actors and agencies in the field will share the analysis of patriarchy common to the founders of the battered women's movement" (Ursel 1991: 285; see also Rock 1986: 218). Nonetheless, she does find an element of encouragement: "It has been demonstrated that, as a result of state involvement, the number of services for wife abuse victims increased" (Ursel 1991: 283). Still, Comack (1996b: 158) directs us to the continued importance of radical transformation in our society, when she writes of the Montreal massacre at the École Polytéchnique:

While the murder of fourteen women in Montreal has understandably received the attention and publicity it deserves, it is also noteworthy that the violence that women encounter at the hands of men has become "routine." In August 1990 alone, eleven women in Montreal were killed by their male partners, many of them estranged. Yet, two of every three women going to a shelter in Montreal are turned away because of lack of space.

Sexual Assault

Not surprisingly, patterns of, and responses to, sexual assault mirror those regarding domestic violence. Research in the 1980s estimated that one in four Canadian women would be sexually assaulted, yet what is most noteworthy is that only 38 percent of an estimated 17,300 sexual assaults, overwhelmingly against females, were reported to police. While a third of the victims of sexual assault cited fear of revenge by the offender, 43 percent cited the attitude of the police or courts as the reason for not reporting the incident (Canada, Solicitor General 1985). As Comack (1996b: 157) notes, an important distinction must be made between law as legislation and law as practice. Sexually assaulted women generally have long been more afraid of the additional suffering and humiliation that the justice system was likely to inflict on them than they are of reprisals by the offender. The conviction of only a small fraction of rapists has done little to reassure victims of sexual assault (Snider 1991: 252).

Efforts have been made in Canada to reduce the trauma visited upon sexually assaulted women. A 1983 reform to the Criminal Code abolished the legal charge of rape, as well as the separate charges of indecent assault on a male and indecent assault on a female. Contrary to much public concern and fear over girls being sexually molested, before 1983 the maximum penalty for indecent assault on a female was only half that for indecent assault on a male (five versus ten years). In a male-dominated criminal justice system, it was apparently much less deviant for offenders (generally males) to sexually molest girls than boys.

In place of the rape law, the federal government created three levels of sexual assault. The intent was to reduce the stigma of rape (and, hence, increase reporting by victims) and to emphasize, as many academics and feminists had strenuously contended, that rape was primarily a violent act of male domination in sexual form. The old rape prohibition was, moreover, primarily a paternalistic form of social control against females, not protective legislation, because it reinforced the idea of women as the property of men (husbands, for example, were immune from criminal sanction under the old law). Not surprisingly, the charge of rape was not even in the "Offences Against the Person" section of the pre-1983 Criminal Code. Rape was in section four of the Canadian Code under "Sexual Offences, Public Morals and Disorderly Conduct."

The procedural law governing the examination of persons alleging sexual assault and the rules of evidence in such cases have also been changed.[3] Before 1983 the testimony of the victim alleging rape had to be corroborated by other evidence. If not, the judge had to instruct the jury on the danger of convicting the accused based upon uncorroborated testimony (Brannigan 1984: 27–28). However, the judge did not have to issue any such warning in criminal trials generally — for example, if the victim was identifying an individual who had stolen her purse. As well, government abolished the "doctrine of recent complaint," which implied that if a woman reported an offence at the first reasonable opportunity, she was supposedly more "trustworthy" or "believable" in her claim than if she waited until later. The law also formally limited the extent to which the victim can be questioned about her previous sexual activity in a sexual assault trial — the so-called "rape shield provision" (Task Force on the Status of Women 1985: 109–13).

Still, much skepticism remained over the extent to which these changes would produce any significant increase in the reporting of sexual assault by females, or would alter the judicial stereotyping and traumatization of sexually assaulted women. As Marni Allison (1991: 2) notes, "changing the content of law does not ensure that implementation of the changes will reflect the objectives of the legislature." This scepticism was apparently warranted. In August 1991 the Supreme Court of Canada, in a 7–2 decision, struck down the "rape shield provision." The Court ruled that it could deny the accused the right to a fair trial, as enshrined in sections 7 and 11(d) of the Charter. In 1992 the Canadian Parliament quickly responded with new legislation, Bill C-49, which amended the Criminal Code to clarify when "No means No" and to restrict the obtaining and admissibility of evidence on the victim's sexual conduct.

Several analysts argued that Bill C-127 (the 1983 rape law change) offered little hope that rape would diminish (Boyle 1984: Heald 1985; Snider 1985; Ruebsaat 1985; Hinch 1988). Although the new legislation attempted to address some of the inequities in the original law, the present law — especially in relation to its application — remains decidedly sexist and unjust.

This view received substantial support in the Department of Justice's 1990 evaluation of the 1983 sexual assault legislative changes. The study noted that the most substantial change came from the victims. From 1982 to 1990 the number of women coming forward to report a sexual assault climbed from 12,848 to 32,861. As for other areas of the criminal justice system, the report concluded: "It is apparent that the situation has not changed since the introduction of the new legislation. In particular, unfounded rates, rates of cases cleared by charge, and conviction rates have remained more or less constant" (Canada, Department of Justice 1990: 55). A more recent study echoes this conclusion (Schissel 1996: 126)

By 1999 little had changed: 78 percent of sexual assaults were not reported to police, almost half of the respondents did not report sexual assault to police because they were reluctant to get the police involved (Gomme 2007: 190), because they believed the police would not help them, and/or because they feared retaliation. By 2004 and 2009, the Canada General Social Survey showed that only about 8 percent of sexual assaults reported to the survey were reported to police. Sadly, in 2003 fully 98 percent of 23,000 sexual assaults known to police are coded by police as "basic" or level 1 (Canadian Centre for Justice Statistics). In 2005 (Hartnagel 2009: 118) of the 23,303 total sexual assaults recorded by police only 567 — or 2.4 percent were recorded as beyond "basic" level 1. These data hardly show much confidence, primarily by women, in the "justice" system for victims of sexual assault.

Importantly, Comack (2009: 203) notes that legal case decisions in the mid-1990s, such as that in the Bishop O'Connor residential-school case of rape and sexual assault, allowed the accused's defence attorney access to otherwise confidential victim treatment and counselling records. She notes, "Women who were sexually assaulted had to decide whether they would seek counseling or initiate criminal prosecution of their assailant." A highly controversial February 25, 2011, judicial statement at sentencing in a sexual assault (rape) case is but a continuation of similar "blame-the-victim" statements made in sexual violence cases (CBC News 2011):

> [Judge] Dewar said "sex was in the air" when he spared a man jail time by handing him a two-year conditional sentence last week instead, and allowed him to remain free in the community.
>
> During the sentencing, Dewar also commented on the way the women dressed and her actions the night she was forced to have sex by a man in the woods along a dark highway outside Thompson.
>
> The judge pointed out the victim and her friend were dressed in tube tops, no bras, and high heels and noted they were wearing plenty of make up.
>
> Dewar called the man a "clumsy Don Juan" who may have misunderstood what the victim wanted.
>
> The victim who left the attack covered in bruises stated: "I don't think what he said was right. We were young and we were dressed classy. For him to say that the way we looked was basically asking for it is wrong and makes me angry." As a female protester said to the CBC news: "I don't get dressed, you know, for a night out on the town in hopes to get raped."

Women in Prison

Shelagh Berzins and Lorraine Cooper (1982: 401) note that a "historical review of the treatment of the federal female offender in Canada reveals a mixture of neglect, outright barbarism and well-meaning paternalism"; a pattern that seems to be continuing to the present (see Boritch 2002; Carey 1996). Female offenders have been contradictorily portrayed as "poor and unfortunate" women in need of protection and as "scheming temptresses who are lazy and worthless" (Cooper 1993: 33). Many feminists challenge the "well-meaning," "in need of protection" dimension; at most, it masks the social control and subjugation of women (Currie 1986). Put succinctly and accurately, "Prison, as a microcosm of society, reflects all those inequalities which discriminate against women, be their source historical, social or administrative convenience" (Ekstedt and Griffiths (1988: 337).

Imprisoned women have expressed feelings of frustration, pain, anger, anxiety, and grief. Kathleen Kendall (1993: 4) notes that women "stressed that their incarceration stripped them of control over their own lives including their schedules, activities and space," a situation reminiscent of many women's experiences of abuse prior to incarceration. In the face of all this, the correctional staff and the parole board still expect women to take self-determined action in "mak-

> Women stress that their incarceration stripped them of control over their own lives including their schedules, activities and space — a situation reminiscent of many women's experiences of abuse prior to incarceration.

ing responsible choices" to become "law-abiding citizens." As Kendall (1993) points out, "Women are caught in a paradox between what they are allowed to do and what they are told or expected to do."

The key institution for incarcerated women in Canada was the Federal Prison for Women (P4W) in Kingston, Ontario. P4W opened its doors in 1934, just across the road from the Kingston Penitentiary for Men, which had previously housed federally sentenced women. All federally sentenced women from across Canada were then to be gathered into a central-ized institution, basically modelled after federal male penitentiaries. The management of P4W continued to be the responsibility of the male penitentiary warden. P4W had no gun towers, but, neither did it have outside windows, recreation grounds within the enclosure, provision for outdoor exercise of any kind, or educational facilities for the female prisoners (Cooper 1987: 13).

Federal penitentiaries for men were spread across the country, but with the exception of federally sentenced women doing time in provincial institutions (through a federal-provincial agreement), until recently only the Kingston facility existed for women. The Correctional Service of Canada (CSC) saw the use of one centralized federal facility for the relatively small number of women as being the most cost-effective system. Within this one facility, all feder-ally sentenced women were housed as maximum-security prisoners, which also provided a justification for limiting the quantity and quality of programs.

It is thus not surprising that virtually every major commission investigating Canada's penal system, from the 1938 Archambault Report onward, severely criticized conditions at P4W and generally recommended its closure. They tended to conclude that the relatively small number of female prisoners should be housed in their home provinces. Indeed, be-tween 1968 and the late 1980s no fewer than thirteen government studies, investigations, and private-sector reports had reiterated this basic conclusion (Cooper 1987). The recal-citrance of the Canadian justice system to change is indicated by the 1979 firing of Berzins and Cooper, whose task was to improve services and programs at P4W. The two women produced a review of the programs at P4W, noting major deficiencies compared to those available to federally incarcerated men. Their report did not meet with the approval of the Commissioner of Corrections, although it did become public by accident.

In 1981, the group Women for Justice, distressed by the lack of change that had ac-companied report after report, finally achieved a Human Rights of Canada Commission decision. The commission ruled that the CSC discriminated against female prisoners at P4W.

A high suicide rate, especially for Aboriginal women, who were often incarcerated far from home, and the suicide of Sandra Sayer connected P4W to systemic discrimination. Sayer, a twenty-four-year-old Saulteaux, was found hanging from the bars of her cell less than two months before her expected release date — which was not an unusual incident at P4W. In early February 1991 a group of female prisoners had barricaded themselves in the prison recreation room to protest the fourth Aboriginal inmate suicide in sixteen months. The prison's response was to quell the protest by use of an assault team, dogs, and tear gas (*StarPhoenix* 1991a: A15). Rather than specialized psychiatric facilities for traumatized female inmates, the prison had segregation facilities where the inmates were confined to Spartan, locked cells twenty-three hours a day. They lost the comforts of their home cells — the family photographs on walls, the television, the books — at a critical time. They were stripped of their clothing and left wearing paper gowns (*StarPhoenix* 1991b: D1).

All of this belies the characterization of imprisoned women as "high needs, low risk" (Task Force on Federally Sentenced Women 1990). The Task Force established five funda-mental principles for women in prisons:

1. empowering women (programs to raise self-esteem);
2. providing more meaningful choices in programs and community facilities (wider range of options);
3. treating women with respect and dignity (to enhance self-respect);
4. providing a physically and emotionally supportive environment; and
5. sharing responsibility for the women's welfare (co-operation by government, correc-tional, and voluntary organizations and members).

The plan called for regional facilities, a healing lodge, and a community release strategy. Moreover, each of these facilities was to differ from traditional "male-oriented" corrections.

After the publication of the Task Force report, the announcement was finally made that P4W would be closed, and that five new regional facilities and a "healing centre" for Aboriginal women at Maple Creek, Saskatchewan, would be built. But change would not come easily at P4W. In April 1994 the male Institutional Emergency Response Team (IERT) from Kingston Penitentiary was sent to P4W to "quell a violent incident." The public release of the horrific, brutal institutional response to an inmate-staff confrontation, which was videotaped, resulted in a 1996 Commission of Inquiry (the Arbour Inquiry). The final report was critical of the substantial abuse of these inmates and the violation of numerous CSC formal procedures (Canada 1996). For example: "Mace was used to subdue three of the inmates.... Although Correctional Service policy contains elaborate provisions with respect to decontamination following the use of mace, in this case, decontamination was limited to pouring some glasses of water over the inmates' eyes" (Canada 1996: 31). The report concluded, "nearly every step that was taken in response to this incident was at odds with the intent of the new [*Creating Choices*] initiatives" (Canada 1996: 24). More specifically:

> [the Arbour Inquiry] documented the violations of the rule of law, policy, and institutional regulations in a number of areas, including the use of segregation, the use of force by the IERT, and the manner in which the women had been strip-searched and subjected to body cavity searches. Serious concerns were raised as to whether the CSC was capable of implementing the necessary reforms to ensure that the rules of law and justice were adhered to without outside intervention and monitoring. The Arbour report also contained 14 primary recommendations relat-ing to cross-gender staffing in correctional institutions for women, the use of force and of IERTs, the operation of segregation units, the needs of Aboriginal women in

correctional institutions, ways of ensuring accountability and adherence to the rule of law among correctional personnel, and procedures of handling inmate complaints and grievances. (Griffiths 2004: 182)

Changing Society, Not Fighting Crime

To move beyond piecemeal and partial socio-legal reforms in the area of gender and social justice, for example, we need to develop a more comprehensive theoretical, analytical, and policy-based socialist-feminist critique of our society. As Dawn Currie (1986: 237) said many years ago:

> What is necessary is a distinctly "feminist" criminology which can explain crime in general while studying women in particular. The goal of such an investigation should be not only to understand the involvement of women in officially recorded crime, but to understand the oppression of women, without this becoming a tool of oppression itself.

Thus, we need a dynamic and integrated analysis of the interrelationships between patriarchy, capitalist society, and state control of women (Brooks 2002; Comack and Balfour (2004). Critical criminologists have come to see locating racism in such an analysis as an integral part of this project as well. Still, is it likely that the unequal definition of crime and involvement and treatment of women and marginalized individuals in the justice system will be significantly reduced in the near future?

Just possibly, success will come through initiatives seeking to reduce the overuse of incarceration for relatively petty offences, changes in sexual assault laws and court procedures, and justice system programs better suited to the needs of Aboriginal and female offenders. Yet these kinds of initiatives will only partially confront the status quo in Canadian society. To reduce the prevailing inequities we need to focus on the society's structural and cultural conditions and its distribution of power — the elements that are at the centre of the problem. At this level basic changes are difficult to achieve, because they confront the underlying, socially entrenched inequalities of life conditions and power relations. As Jeffrey Reiman (2007) states, in order for a real "society" to exist there must be two-way-street social justice.

Harry Glasbeek (2002: 283) puts this very well at the end of his book *Wealth by Stealth*:

> As C. Douglas Lummis argued in *Radical Democracy*, to be a democrat is not an abstraction. It is a state of being: "Democracy is a world that joins *Demos* — the people with *Krakia* — power…. It describes an ideal, not a method for achieving it…. It is a historical project… as people take it up as such and struggle for it."
>
> These proposals take up what we have learned in the previous pages about the enemy of this historical project, and they are intended to help fuel the spirit of would-be democrats as they engage in their struggles to bring together *people* and

power, break down the corporate shield, and lay the groundwork for a humanizing transformation of our polity.

Only if we recover, and enrich our political lives as democratic citizens, will we be able to be effective participants in local and worldwide movements to tackle the enormous human problems we face.

Glossary of Key Terms

Charter of Rights and Freedoms, sections 7 and 1(d): Prior to 1941, corporations were immune to any criminal liability because *mens rea*, "guilty mind," could not corporately exist. Section 7 and section 1(d) of the Charter have been used to argue against this rigid *mens rea* requirement in prosecution of corporate crime.

Corporate crime/suite crime: Harmful economic, human, and environmental acts committed by corporate officials in the pursuit of organizational goals, usually profit, and generally unpunished by the state.

Critical criminology: Grounded in the Marxist concepts of social class conflict and praxis, this theory sees crime and criminal justice as reflecting and reproducing the inequalities in society. As well, it is an advocacy perspective in that the point of critical analysis is not just to study society, but to eliminate unjust social acts and inequalities.

Domestic violence: Usually violence against women by their partners. The Violence Against Women Survey found that 25 percent of women over sixteen years of age experience violence from a current or postmarital partner.

European colonialism: The takeover by white settlers of land belonging to Aboriginal peoples, resulting in their near-genocidal destruction, both physically and culturally.

Ipperwash Inquiry: Ontario's 2006 inquiry into the Ontario Provincial Police sniper, September 1995, shooting of Dudley George, a peaceful protester.

Overrepresentation of Aboriginal people: In Western Canada, since the Second World War, Aboriginal Peoples have been incarcerated both provincially and federally far in excess of their percentage of general population.

Political economy: A form of analysis that links political and economic power. An influential study of political economy contends that wealth and political power are concentrated in the hands of a few individuals and corporations, giving them substantial political, legal, and economic control over our ostensibly democratic society.

Postcolonial justice: An alternative system of justice for Aboriginals that includes Aboriginal self-determination and resolution of land claims in conjunction with traditional healing and harmony restoration.

Prison for Women (P4W): A federal prison that opened in 1934 to house federally sentenced women. Conditions were very harsh, paternalistic, and far inferior to prisons for men. Inmate despair and suicide were thus a major problem. The prison was closed in July 2000.

Questions for Discussion

1. Critically evaluate the truth of the statement that "criminal law and the justice system protect us from serious economic and physical harm."

2. To what extent does the Canadian justice system treat upper-class individuals more favourably than lower-class people? Is Canada a "haven" for corporate crime?

3. Was it fair to sentence Paul Coffin to lecture business students on ethics, for having committed a $1.5-million-dollar fraud? Should he be sentenced to jail time given that the Crown appealed the sentence?

4. Explain the nature of the overinvolvement of Aboriginal peoples in the justice system, and outline any signs of positive change in this area.

5. Are women treated better by the justice system than men are? Explain.

6. How likely is it that inequalities of involvement and treatment in the justice system based upon class, ethnicity, and gender will disappear in the near future? Will "law and order" criminal justice policies be a help or a hindrance to this project?

Websites of Interest

Aboriginal Peoples in Canada <statcan.ca/english/freepub/85F0033MIE /85F0033MIE01001. pdf>
Royal Commission on Aboriginal Peoples <ainc-inac.gc.ca/ch/rcap/index_e.html>
TR Young's Redfeather Institute <tryoung.com/lectures/049te>
National Clearinghouse on Family Violence <hc-sc.gc.ca/hppb/familyviolence/>

Notes

1. Getting exact data on the actual percentage of Aboriginal individuals in the justice system is difficult, in part because racial background, based on self-identification, is not always included in justice system records.
2. See Currie and MacLean (1992) for a critique of the Minneapolis research.
3. One of the most criticized cases has been the well-known ruling in *Pappajohn v. the Queen* (1980). In this case, the controversial decision given in *Morgan* (1975) was upheld. In *Pappajohn* the Supreme Court of Canada held that an honest mistake of belief to consent was grounds for a defence to the charge of rape, whether there were reasonable grounds for a defence as permitted only in circumstances where there was evidence to support such a belief. This "honest-mistake-of-fact" defence was allowed in *Pappajohn*, even though, in the latter part of the alleged repeated raping, the victim was bound to the bedposts and gagged.

References

Aboriginal Justice Inquiry of Manitoba. 1991. *The Justice System and Aboriginal People*. Volume 1. Winnipeg: Queen's Printer.

Adler, F. 1975. *Sisters in Crime*. New York: McGraw.

Allison, Marni. 1991. "Judicious Judgements? Examining the Impact of Sexual Assault Legislation on Judicial Definitions of Sexual Violence." In Les Samuelson and Bernard Schissel (eds.), *Criminal Justice Sentencing Issues and Reform*. Toronto: Garamond.

Alvi, S. 2008. "A Criminal Justice History of Children and Youth in Canada: Taking Stock of the YCJA Era." In C. Brooks and B. Schissel (eds.), *Marginality and Condemnation*. Winnipeg and Black Point: Fernwood Publishing.

Beirne, Piers, and James Messerchmidt. 2006. *Criminology*. Los Angeles: Roxbury.

Berzins. L., and S. Cooper. 1982. "The Political Economy of Correctional Planning for Women: The Case of the Bankrupt Bureaucracy." *Canadian Journal of Criminology* 24.

Boritch, Helen. 2002. "Women in Prison in Canada." In Bernard Schissel and Carolyn Brooks (eds.), *Marginality and Condemnation: An Introduction to Critical Criminology*. Black Point, NS: Fernwood Publishing.

Boyle, Christine. 1984. *Sexual Assault*. Toronto: Carswell.

Brannigan, A. 1984. *Crimes, Courts and Corrections*. Toronto: Holt.

Broad, D. 2000. *Hollow Work, Hollow Society: Globalization and the Casual Labour Problem in Canada*. Black Point, NS: Fernwood Publishing.

Brooks, Carolyn. 2002. "New Directions in Critical Criminology." In Bernard Schissel and Carolyn Brooks (eds.), *Marginality and Condemnation: An Introduction to Critical Criminology*. Black Point, NS: Fernwood Publishing.

Burris, C., and P. Jaffe. 1983. "Wife Abuse as a Crime: The Impact of Police Laying Charges." *Canadian Journal of Criminology* 25.

Canada. 1996. "Office of the Correctional Investigator Backgrounder: Aboriginal Inmates: The Numbers Reveal a Critical Situation." Ottawa: The Correctional Investigator Canada.

_____. 2007. *International Comparison of Indigenous Policing Models*. Ottawa: Public Safety Canada.

Canada, Department of Justice. 1990. *Sexual Assault Legislation in Canada: An Evaluation-Overview*. Ottawa: Supply and Services.

Canada, Solicitor General. 1985. "Female Victims of Crime." Canadian Urban Victimization Survey. Ottawa: Supply and Services.

Canadian Centre for Justice Statistics. 2009. "The Incarceration of Aboriginal People in Adult Correctional Services." *Juristat* 85-002X. Ottawa: CCJS.

Carey, Carolyn. 1996. "Punishment and Control of Women in Prison: The Punishment of Privation." In Bernard Schissel and Linda Mahood (eds.), *Social Control in Canada: A Reader in the Social Construction of Deviance*. Toronto: Oxford University Press.

CBC News. 2011. "Judge's Sex-Assault Comments Spark Rally." February 25. <cbc.ca/news/canada/manitobastory/2011/25/mb-rally>.

CCJC (Church Council on Justice and Corrections). 2011. "Prison Facts: The Costs — A Letter to the Prime Minister." January 21. <ccjc.ca/2011/01/12/prison-facts-the-costs/>.

CCOHS (Canadian Centre for Occupational Health and Safety). 2011. "Bill C-45 — Overview." Ottawa: Canadian Centre for Occupational Health and Safety. <ccohs.ca/oshanswers/legisl/billc45.html>.

Chesney-Lind, M., and B. Bloom. 1997. "Feminist Criminology: Thinking About Women and Crime." In B. MacLean and D. Milovanovic (eds.), *Thinking Critically about Crime*. Vancouver: Collective.

Chunn, D., and S. Gavigan. 1995. "Women, Crime and Criminal Justice in Canada." In M. Jackson and C. Griffiths (eds.), *Canadian Criminology*. Toronto: Harcourt Brace.

Clinard, M., and P. Yeager. 1980. *Corporate Crime*. New York: Free Press.

Comack, Elizabeth. 1992. "Women and Crime." In R. Linden (ed.), *Criminology: A Canadian Perspective*. Second edition. Toronto: Harcourt Brace.

____. 1996a. *Women in Trouble: Connecting Women's Abuse Histories to Their Conflicts with the Law*. Halifax: Fernwood.

____. 1996b. "Women and Crime." In R. Linden (ed.), *Criminology: A Canadian Perspective*. Third edition. Toronto: Harcourt Brace.

____. 2004. "Feminism and Criminology." In Rick Linden (ed.), *Criminology: A Canadian Perspective*. Toronto: Thomson-Nelson.

____. 2009. "Women and Crime." In R. Linden (ed.), *Criminology: A Canadian Perspective*. Sixth edition. Toronto: Nelson.

Comack, Elizabeth, and Gillian Belfour. 2004. *The Power to Criminalize: Violence, Inequality and the Law*. Black Point, NS: Fernwood Publishing.

Cooper, Shelagh. 1987. "The Evolution of the Federal Women's Prison." In E. Adelberg and C. Currie (eds.), *In Conflict with the Law: Women and the Canadian Justice System*. Vancouver: Press Gang.

____. 1993. "The Evolution of the Federal Women's Prison." In Ellen Adelberg and Claudia Currie (eds.), *In Conflict with the Law: Women and the Canadian Justice System*. Vancouver: Press Gang Publishers.

Currie, Dawn. 1986. "Female Criminality: A Crisis in Feminist Theory." In B. MacLean (ed.), *The Political Economy of Crime*. Scarborough, ON: Prentice-Hall.

____. 1990. "Battered Women and the State: From a Failure of Theory to a Theory of Failure." *Journal of Human Justice* 1, 2.

Currie, Dawn, and B. MacLean (eds.). 1992. *The Administration of Justice*. Saskatoon: Social Research Unit, Department of Sociology, University of Saskatchewan.

Currie, Dawn, B. MacLean, and D. Milovanovic. 1992. "Three Traditions of Critical Justice Inquiry: Class, Gender, and Discourse." In D. Currie and B. MacLean (eds.), *Rethinking the Administration of Justice*. Halifax: Fernwood Publishing.

Dobash, Russell P., and R. Emerson Dobash. 1995. "Reflections on Findings from the Violence Against Women Survey." *Canadian Journal of Criminology* 37, 3.

Ekstedt, J., and C. Griffiths. 1988. *Corrections in Canada*. Toronto: Butterworths.

Forcese, D. 1992. *Policing Canadian Society*. Scarborough, ON: Prentice-Hall.

Geoff, C. 2011. *Criminal Justice in Canada*. Fifth edition. Toronto: Nelson

Greenberg, D. 1977. "Delinquency and the Age-Structure of Society." *Contemporary Crises* l.

Gimenez, Martha E. 1991. "The Feminisation of Poverty: Myth or Reality?" *Social Justice* 17, 3.

Glasbeek, Harry. 2002. *Wealth by Stealth: Corporate Crime, Corporate Law and the Perversion of Democracy*. Toronto: Between the Lines.

Gomme, Ian. 2007. *The Shadow Line: Deviance and Crime in Canada*. Toronto: Thomson-Nelson.

Gordon, R., and I. Coneybeer. 1995. "Corporate Crime." In M. Jackson and C. Griffiths (eds.), *Canadian Criminology*. Toronto: Harcourt Brace.

Gregory, J. 1986. "Sex, Class and Crime: Towards a Non-Sexist Criminology." In B. MacLean (ed.), *The Political Economy of Crime*. Scarborough, ON: Prentice.

Griffiths, Curt. 2004. *Canadian Corrections*. Toronto: Thomson-Nelson.

Griffiths, C., and S. Verdun-Jones. 1994. *Canadian Criminal Justice*. Second edition. Toronto: Harcourt Brace.

Hagan, J. 1985. *Modern Criminology.* Toronto: McGraw.

____. 1992. "White Collar and Corporate Crime." In R. Linden (ed.), *Criminology: A Canadian Perspective.* Second edition. Toronto: Harcourt Brace.

Hagan, J., and R. Linden. 2009 "Corporate and White Collar Crime." In R. Linden (ed.) *Criminology: A Canadian Perspective.* Sixth edition. Toronto: Nelson

Hartnagel, T. 2000. "Correlates of Criminal Behaviour." In R. Linden (ed.), *Criminology: A Canadian Perspective.* Fourth edition. Toronto: Harcourt Brace Canada.

____. 2004. "Correlates of Criminal Behaviour." In Rick Linden (ed.), *Criminology: A Canadian Perspective.* Toronto: Thomson-Nelson.

____. 2009. "Correlates of Criminal Behaviour." In R. Linden (ed.) *Criminology: A Canadian Perspective.* Sixth edition. Toronto: Nelson.

Heald, S. 1985. "Social Change and Legal Ideology: A Critique of the New Sexual Assault Legislation." *Canadian Criminology Forum* 7.

Hinch, R. 1988. "Inconsistencies and Contradictions in Canada's Sexual Assault Law." *Canadian Public Policy* 14, 3.

Hylton, J. 1982. "The Native Offender in Saskatchewan: Some Implications for Crime Prevention Programming." *Canadian Journal of Criminology* 24.

James, Carl. 2002. "'Armed and Dangerous!': Racializing Suspects, Suspecting Race." In Bernard Schissel and Carolyn Brooks (eds.), *Marginality and Condemnation: An Introduction to Critical Criminology.* Halifax: Fernwood Publishing.

Johnson, Holly. 1998. "Rethinking Survey Research on Violence against Women." In R.E. Dobash and R.P. Dobash (eds.), *Rethinking Violence Against Women.* Thousand Oaks, CA: Sage.

Keck, J. 2002 "Remembering Kimberly Roger." *Perception* 25, 314.

Kendall, Kathleen. 1993. "Creating Safe Places: Reclaiming Sacred Spaces." Paper prepared for the Seventh National Roundtable for Women in Prison Family Violence Programming in Jail and Prisons Workshop. Washington, DC.

LaPrairie, C. 1996. *Examining Aboriginal Corrections in Canada.* Ottawa: Supply and Services.

MacLeod, Linda. 1980. *Wife Battering in Canada: The Vicious Circle.* Ottawa: Canadian Advisory Council on the Status of Women.

____. 1987. *Battered But Not Beaten: Preventing Wife Battering in Canada.* Ottawa: Canadian Advisory Council on the Status of Women.

Mann, Ruth M. 2003. "Violence Against Women or Family Violence: The 'Problem' of Female Perpetration in Domestic Violence." In L. Samuelson and W. Antony (eds.), *Power and Resistance: Critical Thinking About Canadian Social Issues.* Third edition. Black Point, NS: Fernwood Publishing.

McMullan, J., and Stephen Smith. 1997. "Toxic Steel: State-Corporate Crime and the Contamination of the Environment." In John McMullan et al, *Crimes, Laws and Communities.* Halifax: Fernwood.

National Post. 2002. "Corporate Abuse Crackdown." October 11: 1.

____. 2005. "$1.5 M in AD Fraud, No Jail: Sponsorship Scandals' Coffin Sentenced to Speak on Ethics." September 20: 1.

Neu, Dean, and Duncan Green. 2005. *Truth or Profit: The Business Ethics of Public Accounting.* Black Point, NS: Fernwood Publishing.

Postmedia News. 2010. "Number of Aboriginal Women Behind Bars Will Rise: Report." January 2. <globalnews.ca/number+Aboriginal+women+behind+bars+will+ rise+report/story.html>.

Prairie Research Associates. 1994. *Manitoba Spouse Abuse Tracking Project Final Report Volume 1.* Winnipeg: Manitoba Research and Statistics Directorate.

Reasons, C., L. Ross, and C. Patterson. 1986. "Your Money or Your Life: Workers' Health in Canada." In S. Brickey and E. Comack (eds.), *The Social Basis of Law*. Toronto: Garamond.

Reiman, Jeffrey. 2007. *The Rich Get Richer and the Poor Get Prison*. Eighth edition. Boston: Pearson.

Reiman, J., and P. Leighton. 2010. *The Rich Get Richer and the Poor Get Poorer*. Boston: Allyn and Bacon.

Roberts, Julian, and Ronald Melchers. 2003. "The Incarceration of Aboriginal Offenders: Trends from 1978 to 2001." *Canadian Journal of Criminology and Criminal Justice* 45, 2.

Rock, Paul. 1986. *A View from the Shadows*. Oxford: Clarendon.

Royal Commission on Aboriginal Peoples (RCAP). 1993. "Aboriginal Peoples and the Justice System: Report of the National Roundtable on Aboriginal Justice Issues." Ottawa: Supply and Services.

____ 1996. *Bridging the Cultural Divide*. Ottawa: Supply and Services.

Ruebsaat, Gisela. 1985. *The New Sexual Assault Offences: Emerging Legal Issues*. Ottawa: Supply and Services.

Samuelson, L. 1995. "Canadian Aboriginal Justice Commissions and Australia's 'Anunga Rules: Barking Up the Wrong Tree.'" *Canadian Public Policy* 21, 2.

Saskatchewan. 2004. *Commission of Inquiry into Matters Relating to the Death of Neil Stonechild*. <justice.gov.sk.ca/stonechild/finalreport/default.shtml>.

Schissel, Bernard. 1996. "Law Reform and Social Change: A Time-Series Analysis of Sexual Assault in Canada." *Journal of Criminal Justice* 24, 2.

____. 2002. "Youth Crime, Youth Justice and the Politics of Marginalization." In Bernard Schissel and Carolyn Brooks (eds.), *Marginality and Condemnation: An Introduction to Critical Criminology*. Black Point, NS: Fernwood Publishing.

Schmalleger, Frank. 2007. *Criminal Justice Today*. Upper Saddle River, NJ: Pearson-Prentice Hall.

Snider, Laureen. 1985. "Legal Reform and the Law: The Dangers of Abolishing Rape." *International Journal of the Sociology of Law* 4.

____. 1991. "The Potential of the Criminal Justice System to Promote Feminism." In Elizabeth Comack and Steve Brickey (eds.), *The Social Basis of Law*. Second edition. Toronto: Garamond.

____. 1994. "The Regulatory Dance: Understanding Reform Processes in Corporate Crime." In R. Hinch (ed.), *Readings in Critical Criminology*. Scarborough, ON: Prentice.

____. 2002. "'But They're Not Real Criminals': Downsizing Corporate Crime." In Bernard Schissel and Carolyn Brooks (eds.), *Marginality and Condemnation: An Introduction to Critical Criminology*. Black Point, NS: Fernwood Publishing.

Statistics Canada. 1996. *Canadian Crime Statistics*. Ottawa: Statistics Canada.

____. 2001. *Aboriginal Peoples in Canada* (Catalogue No. 85 F0033M1E). Ottawa: Government of Canada.

____. 2009. "Female Offenders in Canada." *Juristat* 28, 1 (catalogue 85-002-X). <statcan.gc.ca/pub/85-002-x/2008001/article/10509-eng.htm>.

StarPhoenix, 1991a. "21 Female Prisoners Charged After Riot." February 13: A15.

____. 1991b. "Dying to Get Out of P4W." March 23: D1.

____. 1997. "Half of Canadians Polled Believe Natives Well-Off." June 21.

____. 2001. "Allegations of Police Abuse Put Saskatoon on Amnesty list." May 31: A1.

____. 2003. "Majority in Sask. Opposes Treaty Rights: Report." November 27: A1.

____. 2006. "Three-Strikes Bill Will Hit Natives." October 18: A10.

Sutherland, E.H. 1977. "Crimes of Corporations." In G. Geis and R. Meier (eds.), *White-Collar Crime: Offences in Business, Politics, and the Professions*. New York: Free.

Task Force on Federally Sentenced Women. 1990. *Creating Choices*. Ottawa: Correctional Service of Canada.

Task Force on the Status of Women. 1985. *A Feminist Review of Criminal Law.* Ottawa: Supply and Services.

Toronto Sun. 2010. "Canada's Richest Own a Third of Country's Wealth." December 1. <torontosun. com/money/2010/12/01/16388411.html>

Turpel, M. [Aki-Kwe]. 1992. "Further Travails of Canada's Human Rights Record: The Marshall Case." In J. Mannette (ed.), *Elusive Justice: Beyond the Marshall Inquiry.* Halifax: Fernwood Publishing.

Ursel, Jane. 1991. "Considering the Impact of the Battered Women's Movement on the State: The Example of Manitoba." In Elizabeth Comack and Steve Brickey (eds.), *The Social Basis of Law.* Toronto: Garamond.

____. 1998. "Eliminating Violence Against Women: Reform or Co-optation in State Institutions." In L. Samuelson (ed.), *Power and Resistance: Critical Thinking About Canadian Social Issues.* Second edition. Halifax: Fernwood Publishing.

Verdun-Jones, Simon. 2007. *Criminal Law in Canada.* Toronto: Thomson-Nelson.

Waldram, James B. 1994. "Canada's 'Indian Problem' and the Indian's Canada Problem." In L. Samuelson (ed.), *Power and Resistance: Critical Thinking about Canadian Social Issues.* Halifax: Fernwood Publishing.

Winterdyk, John. 2006. *Canadian Criminology.* Toronto: Pearson-Prentice Hall.

Wortley, Scot. 2002. "The Depictions of Race and Crime in the Toronto Print Media." In Bernard Schissel and Carolyn Brooks (eds.), *Marginality and Condemnation: An Introduction to Critical Criminology.* Black Point, NS: Fernwood Publishing.

Wotherspoon, Terry, and Vic Satzewich. 1993. *First Nations: Race, Class, and Gender Relations.* Scarborough, ON: Nelson.

York, Geoffrey. 1990. *The Dispossessed: Life and Death in Native Canada.* Toronto: Little.

Index